The Sociology of Health and Illness

Critical Perspectives

Second Edition

The Sociology of Health and Illness

Critical Perspectives

Second Edition

Edited by

Peter Conrad & Rochelle Kern

Brandeis University   *Columbia University*
School of Public Health

St. Martin's Press
New York

Acknowledgments

John B. McKinlay and Sonja J. McKinlay, "Medical Measures and the Decline of Mortality." Under the title "The Questionable Contribution of Medical Measures to the Decline of Mortality in the United States in the Twentieth Century," this article originally appeared in *Milbank Memorial Fund Quarterly/Health and Society,* Summer 1977, pp. 405–428. Reprinted by permission of the Milbank Memorial Fund and John B. McKinlay.

S. Leonard Syme and Lisa F. Berkman, "Social Class, Susceptibility, and Sickness." Reprinted by permission from *The American Journal of Epidemiology,* vol. 104, pp. 1–8, 1976.

Ingrid Waldron, "Why Do Women Live Longer Than Men?" Reprinted with permission from *Social Science and Medicine,* vol. 10. Copyright 1976, Pergamon Press, Ltd.

Victor R. Fuchs, "A Tale of Two States." Reprinted with permission of the author and Basic Books, Inc., from *Who Shall Live? Health Economics and Social Change.* © 1974.

Barbara Ellen Smith, "Black Lung: The Social Production of Disease." Reprinted with permission of the author and Baywood Publishing Company, Inc., from the *International Journal of Health Services,* vol. 11:3, 1981, pp. 343–359.

James S. House, "Occupational Stress and Coronary Heart Disease: A Review and Theoretical Integration." Reprinted and excerpted with permission of the American Sociological Association from *Journal of Health and Social Behavior,* vol. 15, March 1974, pp. 17–21.

Peter L. Schnall and Rochelle Kern, "Hypertension in American Society: An Introduction to Historical Materialist Epidemiology," was written for the first edition of this book, Copyright © 1981 by St. Martin's Press, Inc.

Anselm Strauss, "Chronic Illness." Published by permission of Transaction, Inc. from *Society,* vol. 10, no. 6. Copyright © 1973 by Transaction, Inc.

Jean Comaroff and Peter Maguire, "Ambiguity and the Search for Meaning: Childhood Leukaemia in the Modern Clinical Context." Reprinted with permission of Pergamon Press, Oxford, England, from *Social Science and Medicine* Vol. 15B (2), 1981, No. 315, pp. 115–123.

Joseph W. Schneider and Peter Conrad, "In the Closet with Illness: Epilepsy, Stigma Potential and Information Control." Reprinted by permission of the Society for Study of Social Problems and the authors.

Peter Conrad and Joseph W. Schneider, "Professionalization, Monopoly, and the Structure of Medical Practice." Reprinted with permission from Conrad, Peter, and Schneider, Joseph W.: Deviance and Medicalization, St. Louis, 1980, The C. V. Mosby Co.

Acknowledgments and copyrights continue at the back of the book beginning on page 499, which constitutes an extension of the copyright page.

Contents

Part Two / The Social Organization of Medical Care   123

Introduction

Creating and Maintaining the Dominance of Medicare   123

The Social Organization of Medical Workers and Services   172

Medical Industries   208

Financing Medical Care   232

Preface to Second Edition

In this revision of *The Sociology of Health and Illness: Critical Perspectives* we have maintained the overall framework of the first edition while adding several new sections, expanding some existing ones, and updating others. In all we include 16 new pieces here (three written especially for this volume) and retain 25 from the previous edition. The revision reflects changes in health care as well as trends in the sociology of health and illness.

Several of the changes in this edition are particularly noteworthy. The book now contains discussions of important new issues including the corporatization of medical care and the role of prevention. In addition, we have strengthened our coverage of the experience of illness, community initiatives, and comparative health policies. We continue to draw upon a variety of sources and reflect several critical perspectives. We hope that the continuity and the changes will make this book useful and challenging to both instructors and students.

We want to thank Irving Kenneth Zola and Catherine Kohler Riessman for their suggestions (not always heeded) for this revision. Thanks also to Shelley Daniels, Christine Sekerke, Lynn Schlesinger, and Vera Whisman for help with some of the inevitable details of revising this book.

Preface to First Edition

Medical sociology has grown very rapidly from a subspecialty taught occasionally in graduate departments to a major area of scholarly activity and student interest. Along with this growth we have witnessed a major shift of emphasis: Medical sociology has increasingly become the sociology of health and illness. For where sociologists once focused on the role of the physician, they are now examining the societal bases of health and illness. These developments reflect, in part, growing concern among both specialists and the public about a crisis in American health care—a crisis evident in the rapid development of chronic illness as our central medical and social problem, in the skyrocketing of medical costs, and in the "medicalization" of what were until recently considered social problems or life's natural contingencies. Although by some standards the present American medical system and profession may be considered among the best in the world, a health care crisis exists in such crucial areas as primary care, national distribution of medical services, and prevention of disease and illness.

In this volume we have sought to show students that both disease and medical care are related to the structure of society and that, accordingly, a sociology of medicine cannot exclude a sociology of health. For the readings collected here we draw on diverse sources. The articles are not only by sociologists but also by public health specialists, health activists, and social critics. We also include a number of original articles written especially for this book. Taken together, the readings place the relationship between society's institutions and its medical care system in a critical perspective. By "critical" we mean a perspective which assumes neither that the present organization of medicine is sacred or inviolable nor that any particular organization would solve all of the problems.

Following a General Introduction, the readings are arranged in four major sections. Section 1 examines "The Social Production of Disease and Illness"; Section 2 analyzes "The Social Organization of Medical Care"; Section 3 presents "Contemporary Critical Debates"; and Section 4, "Toward Alternatives in Health Care," suggests solutions. Introductions to each section set the readings in context and highlight the critical issues, focusing attention on both the structural and interactional aspects of the health care crisis. While the four sections are related and follow naturally from each other, they can be read or referred to in any order the instructor desires.

This book is the product of both excitement and frustration: our excitement about teaching in a field so enlivened by controversy and ferment; our frustration, term after term, in trying to make conveniently accessible to our own students a collection of materials that accurately conveyed the dynamic condition of the field. As we have worked to bring these materials together in a single volume we have been helped by many people who supported the project in various ways. Joseph Behar, Sandra Klein Danziger, Eliot Freidson, Kim Hopper, and Michael Radelet reacted favorably and helpfully to our early ideas about the book. John McKinlay, Peter Schnall, Irving Kenneth Zola, Nancy Zeman-Paul, and several anonymous reviewers read most of the manuscript and made valuable suggestions. Sharon Grosfeld and Linda Cushman cheerfully and capably completed the many clerical tasks necessary to prepare the manuscript. We thank Emily Berleth and Bob Woodbury of St. Martin's Press for their enthusiasm, help, and patience. Nina Schnall contributed in her own very special way; we thank you, Nina. Finally, we thank Libby and Peter, the doctors who share our lives, for their love and encouragement and for their visions of a better health care system.

The Sociology of
Health and Illness

Critical Perspectives

Second Edition

General Introduction

Three major themes underlie the organization of this book: that the conception of medical sociology must be broadened to encompass a sociology of health and illness; that medical care in the United States is presently in crisis; and that the solution of that crisis requires that our health care and medical systems be reexamined from a critical perspective.

Toward a Sociology of Health and Illness

The increase in "medical sociology" courses and the number of medical sociological journals now extant are but two indicators of rapid development in this field.[1] The knowledge base of medical sociology has expanded apace so that this discipline has moved in less than two decades from an esoteric subspecialty taught in a few graduate departments to a central concern of sociologists and sociology students. The causes of this growth are too many and too complex to be within the scope of this present work. However, a few of the major factors underlying this development may be noted.

The rise of chronic illness as a central medical and social problem has led physicians, health planners, and public health officials to look to sociology for help in understanding and dealing with this major health concern. In addition, the increase of governmental involvement in medical care has created research opportunities (and funding) for sociologists to study the organization and delivery of medical care. Sociologists have also become increasingly involved in medical education (as evidenced by the large number of sociologists currently on medical school faculties). Further, since the 1960s, the social and political struggles over health and medical care have become major social issues, thus drawing additional researchers and students to the field. Indeed, some sociologists have come to see the organization of medicine and the way medical services are delivered as social problems in themselves.

Traditionally, the sociological study of illness and medicine has been called, simply, medical sociology. Strauss (1957) differentiated between sociology "of" medicine and sociology "in" medicine. Sociology *of* medicine focuses on the study of medicine to illuminate some *sociological concern* (e.g., patient-practitioner relationships, the role of professions in society). Sociology *in* medicine, on the other hand, focuses primarily on *medical problems* (e.g., the sociological causes of disease and illness, reasons for delay in seeking medical aid, patient compliance or noncompliance with medical regimens). As one might expect, the conceptual dichotomy between these two approaches is more distinct than in actual sociological practice. Be that as it may, sociologists who have concentrated on a sociology of medicine have tended to focus on the profession of medicine and on doctors and to slight the social basis of health and illness. Today, for example, our understanding of the sociology of medical practice and the organization of medicine is much further developed than our understanding of the relationship between social structure and health and illness.

One purpose of this book is to help redress this imbalance. In it, we shift from a focus on the physician and the physician's work to a more general concern with how health and illness are dealt with in our society. This broadened conceptualization of the relationship between sociology and medicine encourages us to examine problems such as the social causation of illness, the economic basis of medical services, and the influence of medical industries, and to direct our primary attention to the social production of disease and illness and the social organization of the medical care system.

Both disease and medical care are related to the structure of society. The social organization of society influences to a significant degree the type and distribution of disease. It also shapes the organized response to disease and illness—the medical care system. To analyze either disease or medical care without investigating its connection with social structure and social interaction is to miss what is unique about the sociology of health and illness. To make the connection between social structure and health, we must investigate how social factors such as the political economy, the corporate structure, the distribution of resources, and the uses of political, economic, and social power influence health and illness and society's response to health and illness. To make the connection between social interaction and health we need to examine people's experiences, how "reality" is constructed, cultural variations within society, and face-to-face relationships. Social structure and interaction are, of course, interrelated, and it is central to the sociological task to make this linkage clear. Both health and the medical system should be analyzed as integral parts of society. In short, instead of a "medical sociology," in this book we posit and profess a *sociology of health and illness*.[2]

The Crisis in American Health Care

It should be noted at the outset that, by any standard, the American medical system and the American medical profession are among the best in the world. Our society invests a great amount of its social and economic resources in medical care; has some of the world's finest physicians, hospitals, and medical schools; is no longer plagued by deadly infectious diseases; and is in the forefront in developing medical and technological advances for the treatment of disease and illness.

This being said, however, it must also be noted that American health care is in a state of crisis. It has been judged to be so, not simply by a small group of social and political critics, but by concerned social scientists, thoughtful political leaders, leaders of labor and industry, and members of the medical profession itself. Although there is general agreement that a health-care crisis exists, there is, as one would expect, considerable disagreement as to the cause of this crisis and how the crisis should be dealt with.

What are some of the major elements and manifestations of this crisis as reflected in the concerns expressed by the contributors to this volume?

Medical costs have risen exponentially; in three decades the amount Americans spend annually on medical care increased from 4 percent to nearly 10 percent of the nation's gross national product. In 1980, the total cost was over $200 billion. Indeed, medical costs have become the leading cause of personal bankruptcy in the United States.

The increasing specialization of medicine has made *primary-care* medicine scarce. Less than one out of four doctors can be defined as primary-care physicians (general and family practitioners, and some pediatricians, internists, and obstetrician-gynecologists). In many rural and inner-city areas, the only primary care available is in hospital emergency rooms, where waits are long, treatment often impersonal, and continuity of care minimal (and the cost of service delivery very high).

Although it is difficult to measure the quality of health and medical care, a few standard measures are helpful. *Life expectancy*, the number of years a person can be expected to live, is at least a crude measure of a nation's health. According to United Nations data, the U.S. ranks nineteenth among nations in life expectancy for males and ninth for females. *Infant mortality*, generally taken to mean infant death in the first year, is one of our best indicators of health and medical care (particularly prenatal care). The U.S. ranks fifteenth in infant mortality, behind such countries as Sweden, Finland, Canada, Japan, the German Democratic Republic (East Germany), and the United Kingdom (United Nations Demographic Yearbook, 1974).

Our medical system is organized to deliver "medical care" (actually, "sick care") rather than "health care." Medical care is that part of the system "which deals with individuals who are sick or who think they may be sick." Health care is that part of the system "which deals with the promotion and protection of health, including environmental protection, the protection of the individual in the workplace, the prevention of accidents, [and] the provision of pure food and water. . . . " (Sidel and Sidel, 1983: xxi–xxii).

Very few of our resources are invested in "health care"—that is, in *prevention* of disease and illness. Yet, with the decrease in infectious disease and the subsequent increase in chronic disease, prevention is becoming ever more important to our nation's overall health and would probably prove more cost-effective than "medical care" (Department of Health, Education and Welfare, 1979).

There is little *public accountability* in medicine. Recent innovations such as Health Systems Agencies, regional organizations designed to coordinate medical services, and Professional Standards Review Organizations, boards mandated to review the quality of (mostly) hospital care, have had limited success in their efforts to control the quality and cost of medical care. (The recent incredible rise in malpractice suits may be seen not as an indication of an increase in poor medical practice but as an indication that such suits are about the only form of medical accountability presently available to the consumer.)

Another element of our crisis in health care is the *"medicalization"* of society. Many, perhaps far too many, of our social problems have been redefined as medical problems (e.g., alcoholism, drug addiction, child abuse, etc.). Many, again perhaps far too many, of life's normal and natural events have also come to be seen as "medical problems," regardless of pathology (e.g., birth, death, sexuality, etc.). It is by no means clear that such matters constitute appropriate medical problems per se. Indeed, there is evidence that the medicalization of social problems and life's natural events has now itself become a social problem (Zola, 1972).

Many other important elements and manifestations of our crisis in health care are described in the works contained in this volume, including the uneven distribution of disease and health care, the role of the physical environment in disease and illness, the monopolistic nature of the medical profession, the role of government in financing health care, sexism and racism in medical care, and the challenge of self-help groups. The particularities of America's health crisis aside, however, most of the contributors to this volume reflect the growing conviction that the social organization of medicine in the United States has been central to its perpetuation.

Critical Perspectives on Health and Illness

The third major theme of this book is that we must examine the relationship between our society's organization and institutions and its medical care system from a "critical perspective." What do we mean by a critical perspective?

A critical perspective is one that does not consider the present fundamental organization of medicine as sacred and inviolable. Nor does it assume that some other particular organization would necessarily be a panacea for all our health-care problems. A critical perspective accepts no "truth" or "fact" merely because it has hitherto been accepted as such. It examines what is, not as something given or static, but as something out of which change and growth can emerge. Moreover, any theoretical framework that claims to have all the answers to understanding health and illness is not a critical perspective. The social aspects of health and illness are too complex for a monolithic approach.

Further, a critical perspective assumes that a sociology of health and illness entails societal and personal values, and that these values must be considered and made explicit if illness and health-care problems are to be satisfactorily dealt with. Since any critical perspective is informed by values and assumptions, we would like to make ours explicit. (1) The problems and inequalities of health and medical care are connected to the particular historically located social arrangements and the cultural values of any society. (2) Health care should be oriented toward the prevention of disease and illness. (3) The priorities of any medical system should be based on the needs of the consumers and not the providers. A direct corollary of this is that the socially based inequalities of health and medical care must be eliminated. (4) Ultimately, society itself must be changed for health and medical care to improve.

Bringing critical perspectives to bear on the sociology of health and illness has informed the selection of articles contained in this volume. It has also informed editorial comments that introduce and bind together the book's various parts and subparts. Explicitly and implicitly, the goal of this work is toward the awareness that informed social change is a prerequisite for the elimination of socially based inequalities in health and medical care.

NOTES

1. Until 1960 only one journal, *Milbank Memorial Fund Quarterly* (now called *Health and Society*), was more or less devoted to medical sociological writings (although many articles on medicine and illness were published in other sociological journals). Today there are five more journals, all of which specifically focus on sociological work on health, illness, and medicine: *The Journal of Health and Social Behavior; Social Science and Medicine; International Journal of Health Services; Sociology of Health and Illness;* and a new annual volume, *Research in the Sociology of Health Care.* Such medical journals as *Medical Care* and *American Journal of Public Health* frequently publish medical sociological articles, as do various psychiatric journals.
2. Inasmuch as we define the sociology of health and illness in such a broad manner, it is not possible to cover adequately all the topics it encompasses in one volume. Although we attempt to touch on most important sociological aspects of health and illness, space limitations precluded presenting all potential topics. For instance, we do not include sections on professional socialization, the social organization of hospitals, and the utilization of services. Discussions of these are easily available in standard medical sociology textbooks. We have made a specific decision not to include materials on mental health and illness. While mental and physical health are not as separate as was once thought, the sociology of mental health comprises a separate literature and raises some different issues from the ones developed here.

REFERENCES

Sidel, Victor W., and Ruth Sidel. 1983. A Healthy State. rev. ed. New York: Pantheon Books.

Straus, Robert. 1957. "The nature and status of medical sociology." American Sociological Review 22 (April): 200–204.

U.S. Department of Health, Education and Welfare. 1979. Healthy People: The Surgeon General's Report on Health Promotion and Disease Prevention. Washington, D.C.: U.S. Government Printing Office.

Zola, Irving Kenneth. 1972. "Medicine as an institution of social control." Sociological Review 20:487–504.

Part One

The Social Production of Disease and Illness

Part One of this book is divided into four sections. While the overriding theme is "the social production of disease and illness," each section develops a particular aspect of the sociology of disease production. For the purposes of this book we define *disease* as the biophysiological phenomena which manifest themselves as changes in and malfunctions of the human body. *Illness,* on the other hand, is the experience of being sick or diseased. Accordingly, we can see disease as a physiological state and illness as a social psychological state presumably caused by the disease. Thus, pathologists and public health doctors deal with disease, patients experience illness, and, ideally, clinical physicians treat both. (cf. Cassell, 1979.) Furthermore, such a distinction is useful for dealing with the possibility of people feeling ill in the absence of disease or being "diseased" without experiencing illness. Obviously disease and illness are related, but separating them as concepts allows us to explore the objective level of disease and the subjective level of illness. The first three sections of Part One focus primarily on disease, the final one focuses on illness.

All the articles in Part One consider how disease and illness are socially produced. The so-called *medical model* focuses on organic pathology in individual patients, rarely taking societal factors into account. Clinical medicine locates disease as a problem in the individual body, and although this is clearly important and useful, it provides an incomplete and sometimes distorted picture. With the increased concern about chronic disease and its prevention (U.S. DHEW, 1979), the articles suggest that a shift in focus from the internal environment of individuals to the interaction between external environments in which people live and the internal environment of the human body will yield new insights into disease causation and prevention.

The Social Nature of Disease

When we look historically at the extent and patterns of disease in Western society we see enormous changes. In the early nineteenth century the infant mortality rate was very high, life expectancy was short (approximately forty years), and life-threatening epidemics were common. Infectious diseases, especially those of childhood, were often fatal. Even at the beginning of the twentieth century, the United States' annual death rate was 28 per 1000 population compared with 9 per 1000 today, with the cause of death usually pneumonia, influenza, tuberculosis, typhoid fever, and various forms of dysentery (Cassell, 1979: 72). But patterns of *morbidity* (disease rate) and *mortality* (death rate) have changed. Today we have "conquered" most infectious diseases; they are no longer feared and few people die from them. Chronic diseases such as heart disease, hypertension and stroke, and cancer are now the major causes of death in the United States (see Figure 3, p. 16).

Medicine is usually credited for the great victory over infectious diseases. After all, certain scientific discoveries (e.g., germ theory) and medical interventions (e.g., vaccinations and drugs) had been developed and used to combat infectious diseases and, so the logic goes, must have been responsible for reducing deaths from them. While this view may seem reasonable from a not too careful reading of medical history, it is contradicted by some important social scientific work.

René Dubos (1959) was one of the first to argue that it was social changes in the environment rather than medical interventions that led to the reduction of mortality by infectious diseases. He viewed the nineteenth-century Sanitary Movement's campaign for clean water, air, and proper sewage disposal as a particularly significant "public health" measure. Thomas McKeown (1971) showed that biomedical interventions were not the cause of the decline in mortality in England and Wales in the nineteenth century. This viewpoint has become known as the "limitations of modern medicine" argument (Powles, 1973) and is now well known in public health circles. The argument is essentially a simple one: Discoveries and interventions by *clinical medicine* were not the cause of the decline of mortality for various populations. Rather, it seems that social and environmental factors such as (1) sanitation, (2) improved housing and nutrition, and (3) a general rise in the standard of living were the most significant contributors. This does not mean that clinical medicine did not reduce people's sufferings or prevent or cure diseases in some people; we know it did. But social factors appear much more important than medical interventions in the "conquest" of infectious disease.

In the keynote article of this book, John B. McKinlay and Sonja M. McKinlay assess "Medical Measures and the Decline of Mortality." They offer empirical evidence to support the limitations of medicine argument and point to the social nature of disease. We must note that mortality rates, which are the data on which they base their analysis, only crudely measure "cure" and don't measure "care" at all. But it is important to understand that much of what is attributed to "medical intervention" seems not to be the result of clinical medicine per se (cf. Levine et al., 1983).

The limitations of medicine argument underlines the need for a broader, more comprehensive perspective to understanding disease and its treatment (see also Turshen, 1977); a perspective that focuses on the significance of social structure and change in disease causation and prevention.

REFERENCES

Cassell, Eric J. 1979. The Healer's Art. New York: Penguin Books.

Dubos, René. 1959. Mirage of Health. New York: Harper and Row.

Levine, Sol, Jacob J. Feldman, and Jack Elinson. 1983. "Does medical care do any good?" Pp. 394–404 in David Mechanic (ed.), Handbook of Health, Health Care, and the Health Professions. New York: Free Press.

McKeown, Thomas. 1971. "A historical appraisal of the medical task." Pp. 29–55 in G. McLachlan and T. McKeown (eds.), Medical History and Medical Care: A Symposium of Perspectives. New York: Oxford University Press.

Powles, John. 1973. "On the limitations of modern medicine." Science, Medicine and Man 1: 1–30.

Turshen, Meredeth. 1977. "The political ecology of diseases." The Review of Radical Political Economics 9 (Spring): 45–60.

U.S. Department of Health, Education and Welfare. 1979. Healthy People: The Surgeon General's Report on Health Promotion and Disease Prevention.

1

Medical Measures and the Decline of Mortality

John B. McKinlay and Sonja M. McKinlay

... by the time laboratory medicine came effectively into the picture the job had been carried far toward completion by the humanitarians and social reformers of the nineteenth century. Their doctrine that nature is holy and healthful was scientifically naive but proved highly effective in dealing with the most important health problems of their age. When the tide is receding from the beach it is easy to have the illusion that one can empty the ocean by removing water with a pail.
R. Dubos, Mirage of Health, *New York: Perennial Library, 1959, p. 23*

Introducing a Medical Heresy

The modern "heresy" that medical care (as it is traditionally conceived) is generally unrelated to improvements in the health of populations (as distinct from individuals) is still dismissed as unthinkable in much the same way as the so-called heresies of former times. And this is despite a long history of support in popular and scientific writings as well as from able minds in a variety of disciplines. History is replete with examples of how, understandably enough, self-interested individuals and groups denounced popular customs and beliefs which appeared to threaten their own domains of practice, thereby rendering them heresies (for example, physicians' denunciation of midwives as witches, during the Middle Ages). We also know that vast institutional resources have often been deployed to neutralize challenges to the assumptions upon which everyday organizational activities were founded and legitimated (for example, the Spanish Inquisition). And since it is usually difficult

for organizations themselves to directly combat threatening "heresies," we often find otherwise credible practitioners, perhaps unwittingly, serving the interests of organizations in this capacity. These historical responses may find a modern parallel in the way everyday practitioners of medicine, on their own altruistic or "scientific" grounds and still perhaps unwittingly, serve present-day institutions (hospital complexes, university medical centers, pharmaceutical houses, and insurance companies) by spearheading an assault on a most fundamental challenging heresy of our time: *that the introduction of specific medical measures and/or the expansion of medical services are generally not responsible for most of the modern decline in mortality.*

In different historical epochs and cultures, there appear to be characteristic ways of explaining the arrival and departure of natural viscissitudes. For salvation from some plague, it may be that the gods were appeased, good works rewarded, or some imbalance in nature corrected. And there always seems to be some person or group (witch doctors, priests, medicine men) able to persuade others, sometimes on the basis of acceptable evidence for most people at that time, that they have *the* explanation for the phenomenon in question and may even claim responsibility for it. They also seem to benefit most from common acceptance of the explanations they offer. It is not uncommon today for biotechnological knowledge and specific medical interventions to be invoked as *the major reason* for most of the modern (twentieth century) decline in mortality.[1] Responsibility for this decline is often claimed by, or ascribed to, the present-day major beneficiaries of this prevailing explanation. But both in terms of the history of knowledge and on the basis of data presented in this paper, one can reasonably wonder whether the supposedly more sophisticated explanations proffered in our own time (while seemingly distinguishable from those accepted in the past) are really all that different from those of other cultures and earlier times, or any more reliable. Is medicine, the physician, or the medical profession any more entitled to claim responsibility for the decline in mortality that obviously has occurred in this century than, say, some folk hero or aristocracy of priests sometime in the past?

Aims

Our general intention in this paper is to sustain the ongoing debate on the questionable contribution of specific medical measures and/or the expansion of medical services to the observable decline in mortality in the twentieth century. More specifically, the following three tasks are addressed: (a) selected studies are reviewed which illustrate that, far from being idiosyncratic and/or heretical, the issue addressed in this paper has a long history, is the subject of considerable attention elsewhere, attracts able minds from a variety of disciplines, and remains a timely issue for concern and research; (b) age- and sex-adjusted mortality rates (standardized to the population of 1900) for the United States, 1900–1973, are presented and then considered in relation to a number of specific and supposedly effective medical interventions (both chemo-therapeutic and prophylactic). So far as we know, this is the first time such data have been employed for this particular purpose in the United States, although reference will be made to a similar study for England and Wales; and (c) some policy implications are outlined.

Background to the Issue

The beginning of the serious debate on the questionable contribution of medical measures is commonly associated with the appearance, in

Britain, of Talbot Griffith's (1967) *Population Problems in the Age of Malthus*. After examining certain medical activities associated with the eighteenth century—particularly the growth of hospital, dispensary, and midwifery services, additions to knowledge of physiology and anatomy, and the introduction of smallpox inoculation—Griffith concluded that they made important contributions to the observable decline in mortality at that time. Since then, in Britain and more recently in the United States, this debate has continued, regularly engaging scholars from economic history, demography, epidemiology, statistics, and other disciplines. Habakkuk (1953), an economic historian, was probably the first to seriously challenge the prevailing view that the modern increase in population was due to a fall in the death rate attributable to medical interventions. His view was that this rise in population resulted from an increase in the birth rate, which, in turn, was associated with social, economic, and industrial changes in the eighteenth century.

McKeown, without doubt, has pursued the argument more consistently and with greater effect than any other researcher, and the reader is referred to his recent work for more detailed background information. Employing the data and techniques of historical demography, McKeown (a physician by training) has provided a detailed and convincing analysis of the major reasons for the decline of mortality in England and Wales during the eighteenth, nineteenth, and twentieth centuries (McKeown et al., 1955, 1962, 1975). For the eighteenth century, he concludes that the decline was largely attributable to improvements in the environment. His findings for the nineteenth century are summarized as follows:

> . . . the decline of mortality in the second half of the nineteenth century was due wholly to a reduction of deaths from infectious diseases; there was no evidence of a decline in other causes of death. Examination of the diseases which contributed to the decline suggested that the main influences were: (a) rising standards of living, of which the most significant feature was a better diet; (b) improvements in hygiene; and (c) a favorable trend in the relationship between some micro-organisms and the human host. *Therapy made no contributions, and*

*the effect of immunization was restricted to small-
pox which accounted for only about one-twentieth
of the reduction of the death rate.* (Emphasis added.
McKeown et al., 1975, p.391)

While McKeown's interpretation is based on the
experience of England and Wales, he has examined its credibility in the light of the very
different circumstances which existed in four
other European countries: Sweden, France, Ireland, and Hungary (McKeown et al., 1972). His
interpretation appears to withstand this cross-
examination. As for the twentieth century
(1901–1971 is the period actually considered),
McKeown argues that about three-quarters of
the decline was associated wth control of infectious diseases and the remainder with conditions
not attributable to microorganisms. He distinguishes the infections according to their modes of
transmission (air- water- or food-borne) and
isolates three types of influences which figure
during the period considered: medical measures
(specific therapies and immunization), reduced
exposure to infection, and improved nutrition.
His conclusion is that:

> The main influences on the decline in mortality
> were improved nutrition on air-borne infections,
> reduced exposure (from better hygiene) on water-
> and food-borne diseases and, less certainly, immu-
> nization and therapy on the large number of
> conditions included in the miscellaneous group.
> Since these three classes were responsible respec-
> tively for nearly half, one-sixth, and one-tenth of the
> fall in the death rate, it is probable that the
> advancement in nutrition was the major influence.
> (McKeown et al., 1975, p. 422)

More than twenty years of research by McKeown and his colleagues recently culminated in
two books—*The Modern Rise of Population*
(1976a) and *The Role of Medicine: Dream,
Mirage or Nemesis* (1976b)—in which he draws
together his many excellent contributions. That
the thesis he advances remains highly newsworthy is evidenced by recent editorial reaction in
The Times of London (1977).

No one in the United States has pursued this
thesis with the rigor and consistency which
characterize the work by McKeown and his
colleagues in Britain. Around 1930, there were

several limited discussions of the questionable
effect of medical measures on selected infectious
diseases like diphtheria (Lee, 1931; Wilson and
Miles, 1946; Bolduan, 1930) and pneumonia
(Pfizer and Co., 1953). In a presidential address
to the American Association of Immunologists in
1954 (frequently referred to by McKeown),
Magill (1955) marshalled an assortment of data
then available—some from England and Wales—
to cast doubt on the plausibility of existing
accounts of the decline in mortality for several
conditions. Probably the most influential work in
the United States is that of Dubos who, principally in *Mirage of Health* (1959), *Man Adapting*
(1965), and *Man, Medicine and Environment*
(1968), focused on the nonmedical reasons for
changes in the health of overall populations. In
another presidential address, this time to the
Infectious Diseases Society of America, Kass
(1971), again employing data from England and
Wales, argued that most of the decline in
mortality for most infectious conditions occurred
prior to the discovery of either "the cause" of the
disease or some purported "treatment" for it.
Before the same society and largely on the basis
of clinical experience with infectious diseases and
data from a single state (Massachusetts), Weinstein (1974), while conceding there are some
effective treatments which seem to yield a favorable outcome (e.g., for poliomyelitis, tuberculosis, and possibly smallpox), argued that despite
the presence of supposedly effective treatments
some conditions may have increased (e.g., suba-
cute bacterial endocarditis, streptococcal pharyn-
gitis, pneumococcal pneumonia, gonorrhea, and
syphilis) and also that mortality for yet other
conditions shows improvement in the absence of
any treatment (e.g., chickenpox). With the appearance of his book, *Who Shall Live?* (1974),
Fuchs, a health economist, contributed to the
resurgence of interest in the relative contribution
of medical care to the modern decline in mortality in the United States. He believes there has
been an unprecedented improvement in health in
the United States since about the middle of the
eighteenth century, associated primarily with a
rise in real income. While agreeing with much of
Fuchs' thesis, we will present evidence which
seriously questions his belief that "beginning in
the mid '30s, major therapeutic discoveries made

significant contributions independently of the rise in real income."

Although neither representative nor exhaustive, this brief and selective background should serve to introduce the analysis which follows. Our intention is to highlight the following: (a) the debate over the questionable contribution of medical measures to the modern decline of mortality has a long history and remains topical; (b) although sometimes popularly associated with dilettantes such as Ivan Illich (1976), the debate continues to preoccupy able scholars from a variety of disciplines and remains a matter of concern to the most learned societies; (c) although of emerging interest in the United States, the issue is already a matter of concern and considerable research elsewhere; (d) to the extent that the subject has been pursued in the United States, there has been a restrictive tendency to focus on a few selected diseases, or to employ only statewide data, or to apply evidence from England and Wales directly to the United States situation.

How Reliable are Mortality Statistics?

We have argued elsewhere that mortality statistics are inadequate and can be misleading as indicators of a nation's overall health status (McKinlay and McKinlay, forthcoming). Unfortunately, these are the only types of data which are readily accessible for the examination of time trends, simply because comparable morbidity and disability data have not been available. Apart from this overriding problem, several additional caveats in the use of mortality statistics are: (a) difficulties introduced by changes in the registration area in the United States in the early twentieth century; (b) that often no single disease, but a complex of conditions, may be responsible for death (Krueger, 1966); (c) that studies reveal considerable inaccuracies in recording the cause of death (Moriyama et al., 1958); (d) that there are changes over time in what it is fashionable to diagnose (for example, ischaemic heart disease and cerebrovascular disease); (e) that changes in disease classifications (Dunn and Shackley, 1945) make it difficult to compare some conditions over time and between countries (Reid and Rose,

1964); (f) that some conditions result in immediate death while others have an extended period of latency; and (g) that many conditions are severely debilitating and consume vast medical resources but are now generally non-fatal (e.g., arthritis and diabetes). Other obvious limitations could be added to this list.

However, it would be foolhardy indeed to dismiss all studies based on mortality measures simply because they are possibly beset *with known limitations*. Such data are preferable to those the limitations of which are either unknown or, if known, cannot be estimated. Because of an overawareness of potential inaccuracies, there is a timorous tendency to disregard or devalue studies based on mortality evidence, even though there are innumerable examples of their fruitful use as a basis for planning and informed social action (Alderson, 1976). Sir Austin Bradford Hill (1955) considers one of the most important features of Snow's work on cholera to be his adept use of mortality statistics. A more recent notable example is the study by Inman and Adelstein (1969) of the cirumstantial link between the excessive absorption of bronchodilators from pressurized aerosols and the epidemic rise in asthma mortality in children aged ten to fourteen years. Moreover, there is evidence that some of the known inaccuracies of mortality data tend to cancel each other out.[2] Consequently, while mortality statistics may be unreliable for use in individual cases, when pooled for a country and employed in population studies, they can reveal important trends and generate fruitful hypotheses. They have already resulted in informed social action (for example, the use of geographical distributions of mortality in the field of environmental pollution).

Whatever limitations and risks may be associated with the use of mortality statistics, they obviously apply equally to all studies which employ them—both those which attribute the decline in mortality to medical measures and those which argue the converse, or something else entirely. And, if such data constitute acceptable evidence in support of the presence of medicine, then it is not unreasonable, or illogical, to employ them in support of some opposing position. One difficulty is that, depending on the nature of the results, double standards of rigor seem to operate in the evaluation of different studies. Not surprisingly, those which challenge prevailing myths or beliefs are subject to the most stringent methodological and statistical scrutiny, while supportive studies, which frequently employ the flimsiest impressionistic data and inappropriate techniques of analysis, receive general and uncritical acceptance. Even if all possible "ideal" data were available (which they never will be) and if, after appropriate analysis, they happened to support the viewpoint of this paper, we are doubtful that medicine's protagonists would find our thesis any more acceptable.

The Modern Decline in Mortality

Despite the fact that mortality rates for certain conditions, for selected age and sex categories, continue to fluctuate, or even increase (U.S. Dept. HEW, 1964; Moriyama and Gustavus, 1972; Lilienfeld, 1976), there can be little doubt that a marked decline in overall mortality for the United States has occurred since about 1900 (the earliest point for which reliable national data are available).

Just how dramatic this decline has been in the United States is illustrated in Fig. 1 which shows age-adjusted mortality rates for males and females separately.[3] Both sexes experienced a marked decline in mortality since 1900. The female decline began to level off by about 1950, while 1960 witnessed the beginning of a slight increase for males. Figure 1 also reveals a slight but increasing divergence between male and female mortality since about 1920.

Figure 2 depicts the decline in the overall age-and sex-adjusted rate since the beginning of this century. Between 1900 and 1973, there was a 69.2 percent decrease in overall mortality. The average annual rate of decline from 1900 until 1950 was .22 per 1,000, after which it became an almost negligible decline of .04 per 1,000 annually. Of the total fall in the standardized death rate between 1900 and 1973, 92.3 percent occurred prior to 1950. Figure 2 also plots the decline in the standardized death rate *after* the total number of deaths in each age and sex category has been reduced by the number of deaths attributed to the

eleven major infectious conditions (typhoid, smallpox, scarlet fever, measles, whooping cough, diphtheria, influenza, tuberculosis, pneumonia, diseases of the digestive system, and poliomyelitis). It should be noted that, although this latter rate also shows a decline (at least until 1960), its slope is much more shallow than that for the overall standardized death rate. A major part of the decline in deaths from these causes since about 1900 may be attributed to the virtual disappearance of these infectious diseases.

An absurdity is reflected in the third broken line in Fig. 2 which also plots the increase in the proportion of Gross National Product expended annually for medical care. *It is evident that the beginning of the precipitate and still unrestrained rise in medical care expenditures began when nearly all (92 percent) of the modern decline in mortality this century had already occurred.*[4]

Figure 3 illustrates how the proportion of deaths contributed by the infectious and chronic conditions has changed in the United States since the beginning of the twentieth century. In 1900, about 40 percent of all deaths were accounted for by eleven major infectious diseases, 16 percent by three chronic conditions, 4 percent by accidents, and the remainder (37 percent) by all other causes. By 1973, only 6 percent of all deaths were due to these eleven infectious diseases, 58 percent to the same three chronic conditions, 9 percent to accidents, and 27 percent were contributed by other causes.[5]

Now to what phenomenon, or combination of events can we attribute this modern decline in overall mortality? Who (if anyone), or what group, can claim to have been instrumental in effecting this reduction? Can anything be gleaned from an analysis of mortality experience to date that will inform health care policy for the future?

It should be reiterated that a major concern of this paper is to determine the effect, if any, of specific medical measures (both chemotherapeutic and prophylactic) on the decline of mortality. It is clear from Figs. 2 and 3 that most of the observable decline is due to the rapid disappearance of some of the major infectious diseases. Since this is where most of the decline has occurred, it is logical to focus a study of the effect of medical measures on this category of condi-

Figure 1. *The Trend in Mortality for Males and Females Separately (Using Age-Adjusted Rates) for the United States, 1900–1973.* *

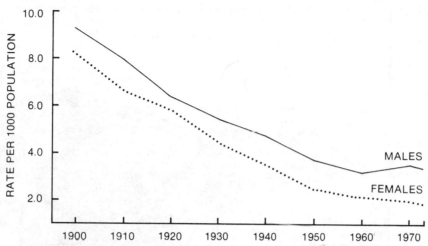

*For these and all other age- and sex-adjusted rates in this paper, the standard population is that of 1900.

Figure 2. *Age- and Sex-Adjusted Mortality Rates for the United States 1900–1973, Including and Excluding Eleven Major Infectious Diseases, Contrasted with the Proportion of the Gross National Product Expended on Medical Care.*

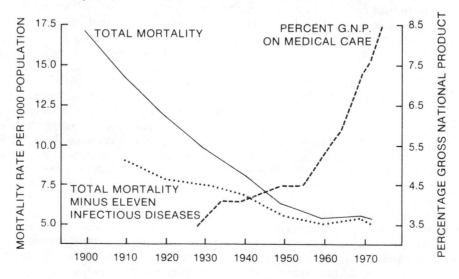

Figure 3. *Pictorial Representation of the Changing Contribution of Chronic and Infectious Conditions to Total Mortality (Age- and Sex-Adjusted), in the United States, 1900–1973.*

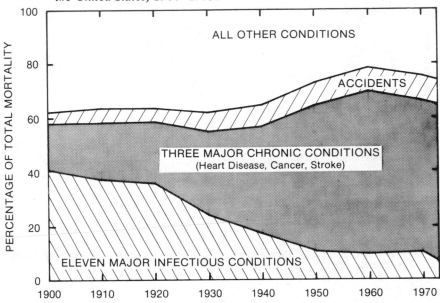

tions. Moreover, for these eleven conditions, there exist clearly identifiable medical interventions to which the decline in mortality has been popularly ascribed. No analogous interventions exist for the major chronic diseases such as heart disease, cancer, and stroke. Therefore, even where a decline in mortality from these chronic conditions may have occurred, this cannot be ascribed to any specific measure.

The Effect of Medical Measures on Ten Infectious Diseases Which Have Declined

Table 1 summarizes data on the effect of major medical interventions (both chemotherapeutic and prophylactic) on the decline in the age- and sex-adjusted death rates in the United States, 1900–1973, for ten of the eleven major infectious diseases listed above. Together, these diseases accounted for approximately 30 percent of all deaths at the turn of the century and nearly 40 percent of the total decline in the mortality rate since then. The ten diseases were selected on the following criteria: (a) some decline in the death

rate had occurred in the period 1900–1973; (b) significant decline in the death rate is commonly attributed to some specific medical measure for the disease; and (c) adequate data for the disease over the period 1900–1973 are available. The diseases of the digestive system were omitted primarily because of lack of clarity in diagnosis of specific diseases such as gastritis and enteritis.

Some additional points of explanation should be noted in relation to Table 1. First, the year of medical intervention coincides (as nearly as can be determined) with the first year of widespread or commercial use of the appropriate drug or vaccine.[6] This date does *not* necessarily coincide with the date the measure was either first discovered, or subject to clinical trial. Second, the decline in the death rate for smallpox was calculated using the death rate for 1902 as being the earliest year for which this statistic is readily available (U.S. Bureau of the Census, 1906). For the same reasons, the decline in the death rate from poliomyelitis was calculated from 1910. Third, the table shows the contribution of the decline in each disease to the total decline in mortality over the period 1900–1973 (column

Table 1. The Contribution of Medical Measures (Both Chemotherapeutic and Prophylactic) to the Fall in the Age- and Sex-Adjusted Death Rates (S.D.R.) of Ten Common Infectious Diseases, and to the Overall Decline in the S.D.R., for the United States, 1900–1973

Disease	Fall in S.D.R. per 1,000 Population, 1900–1973 (a)	Fall in S.D.R. as % of the Total Fall in S.D.R. $(b) = \dfrac{(a)}{12.14} \times 100\%$	Year of Medical Intervention (Either Chemotherapy or Prophylaxis)	Fall in S.D.R. per 1,000 Population After Year of Intervention (c)	Fall in S.D.R. After Intervention as % of Total Fall for the Disease $(d) = \dfrac{(c)}{(a)} \times 100\%$	Fall in S.D.R. After Intervention as % of Total Fall in S.D.R. for All Causes $(e) = \dfrac{(b)(c)}{(a)}\%$
Tuberculosis	2.00	16.48	Izoniazid/ Streptomycin, 1950	0.17	8.36	1.38
Scarlet Fever	0.10	0.84	Penicillin, 1946	0.00	1.75	0.01
Influenza	0.22	1.78	Vaccine, 1943	0.05	25.33	0.45
Pneumonia	1.42	11.74	Sulphonamide, 1935	0.24	17.19	2.02
Diphtheria	0.43	3.57	Toxoid, 1930	0.06	13.49	0.48
Whooping Cough	0.12	1.00	Vaccine, 1930	0.06	51.00	0.51
Measles	0.12	1.04	Vaccine, 1963	0.00	1.38	0.01
Smallpox	0.02	0.16	Vaccine, 1800	0.02	100.00	0.16
Typhoid	0.36	2.95	Chloramphenicol, 1948	0.00	0.29	0.01
Poliomyelitis	0.03	0.23	Vaccine, Salk/ Sabin, 1955	0.01	25.87	0.06

Table 2. Pair-Wise Correlation Matrix for 44 Countries, Between Four Measures of Health Status and Three Measures of Medical Care Input

Variable	Matrix of Coefficients							
	1	2	3a	3b	4a	4b	5	6
1. Infant Mortality Rate (1972)								
2. Crude Mortality Rate (1970–1972)	−0.14							
3.(a) Life Expectancy (Males) at 25 years	−0.14	−0.12						
3.(b) Life Expectancy (Females) at 25 years	−0.12	0.04	0.75					
4.(a) Life Expectancy (Males) at 55 Years	−0.01	0.10	0.74	0.93				
4.(b) Life Expectancy (Females) at 55 Years	−0.13	0.01	0.75	0.98	0.95			
5. Population per Hospital Bed (1971–1973)	0.64	−0.30	0.05	−0.02	0.17	0.0		
6. Population per Physician (1971–1973)	0.36	−0.30	0.11	0.04	0.16	0.07	0.70	
7. Per Capita Gross National Product: In $U.S. Equivalent (1972)	−0.66	0.26	0.16	0.18	0.07	0.22	−0.56	−0.46
Variable (by number)	1	2	3a	3b	4a	4b	5	6

SOURCES: 1. *United Nations Demographic Yearbook: 1974*, New York, United Nations Publications, 1975. (For the Crude and Infant Mortality Rates). 2. *World Health Statistics Annual: 1972*, Vol. 1, Geneva, World Health Organization, 1975, pp. 780–783. (For the Life Expectancy Figures). 3. *United Nations Statistical Yearbook, 1973 and 1975.* New York, United Nations Publications, 25th and 27th issues, 1974 and 1976. (For the Population bed/physician ratios). 4. *The World Bank Atlas.* Washington, D.C., World Bank, 1975. (For the per capita Gross National Product).

b). The overall decline during this period was 12.14 per 1,000 population (17.54 in 1900 to 5.39 in 1973). Fourth, in order to place the experience for each disease in some perspective, Table 1 also shows the contribution of the relative fall in mortality after the intervention to the overall fall in mortality since 1900 (column e). In other words, the figures in this last column represent the percentage of the total fall in mortality contributed by each disease after the date of medical intervention.

It is clear from column b that only reductions in mortality from tuberculosis and pneumonia contributed substantially to the decline in total mortality between 1900 and 1973 (16.5 percent and 11.7 percent, respectively). The remaining eight conditions *together* accounted for less than 12 percent of the total decline over this period. Disregarding smallpox (for which the only effective measure had been introduced about 1800), only influenza, whooping cough, and poliomyelitis show what could be considered substantial declines of 25 percent or more after the date of medical intervention. However, even under the somewhat unrealistic assumption of a constant (linear) rate of decline in the mortality rates, only whooping cough and poliomyelitis even approach the percentage which would have been expected. The remaining six conditions (tuberculosis, scarlet fever, pneumonia, diphtheria, measles, and typhoid) showed negligible declines in their mortality rates subsequent to the date of medical intervention. The seemingly quite large percentages for pneumonia and diphtheria (17.2 and 13.5, respectively) must of course be viewed in the context of relatively early interventions—1935 and 1930.

In order to examine more closely the relation of mortality trends for these diseases to the medical interventions, graphs are presented for each disease in Fig. 4. Clearly, for tuberculosis, typhoid, measles, and scarlet fever, the medical measures considered were introduced at the point when the death rate for each of these diseases was already negligible. Any change in the rates of decline which may have occurred subsequent to the interventions could only be minute. Of the remaining five diseases (excluding smallpox with its negligible contribution), it is only for poliomyelitis that the medical measure

appears to have produced any noticeable change in the trends. Given peaks in the death rate for 1930, 1950 (and possibly for 1910), a comparable peak could have been expected in 1970. Instead, the death rate dropped to the point of disappearance after 1950 and has remained negligible. The four other diseases (pneumonia, influenza, whooping cough, and diphtheria) exhibit relatively smooth mortality trends which are unaffected by the medical measures, even though these were introduced relatively early, when the death rates were still notable.

It may be useful at this point to briefly consider the common and dubious practice of projecting estimated mortality trends (Witte and Axnick, 1975). In order to show the beneficial (or even detrimental) effect of some medical measure, a line, estimated on a set of points observed prior to the introduction of the measure, is projected over the period subsequent to the point of intervention. Any resulting discrepancy between the projected line and the observed trend is then used as some kind of "evidence" of an effective or beneficial intervention. According to statistical theory on least squares estimation, an estimated line can serve as a useful predictor, but the prediction is only valid, and its error calculable, within the range of the points used to estimate the line. Moreover, those predicted values which lie at the extremes of the range are subject to much larger errors than those nearer the center. It is, therefore, probable that, even if the projected line was a reasonable estimate of the trend after the intervention (which, of course, it is not), the divergent observed trend is probably well within reasonable error limits of the estimated line (assuming the error could be calculated), as the error will be relatively large. In other words, this technique is of dubious value as no valid conclusions are possible from its application, and a relatively large prediction error cannot be estimated, which is required in order to objectively judge the extent of divergence of an observed trend.

With regard to the ten infectious diseases considered in this paper, when lines were fitted to the nine or ten points available over the entire period (1900–1973), four exhibited a reasonably good fit to a straight line (scarlet fever, measles, whooping cough, and poliomyelitis), while

Figure 4. *The Fall in the Standardized Death Rate (per 1,000 Population) for Nine Common Infectious Diseases in Relation to Specific Medical Measures, for the United States, 1900–1973.*

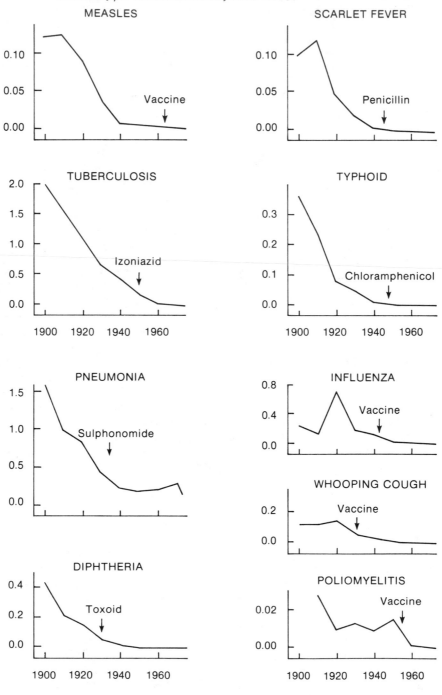

another four (typhoid, diphtheria, tuberculosis, and pneumonia) showed a very good quadratic fit (to a curved line). Of the remaining two diseases, smallpox showed a negligible decline, as it was already a minor cause of death in 1900 (only 0.1 percent), and influenza showed a poor fit because of the extremely high death rate in 1920. From Fig. 4 it is clear, however, that the rate of decline slowed in more recent years for most of the diseases considered—a trend which could be anticipated as rates approach zero.[7]

Now it is possible to argue that, given the few data points available, the fit is somewhat crude and may be insensitive to any changes subsequent to a point of intervention. However, this can be countered with the observation that, given the relatively low death rates for these diseases, any change would have to be extremely marked in order to be detected in the overall mortality experience. Certainly, from the evidence considered here, only poliomyelitis appears to have had a noticeably changed death rate subsequent to intervention. Even if it were assumed that this change was entirely due to the vaccines, then only about one percent of the decline following interventions for the diseases considered here (column d of Table 1) could be attributed to medical measures. Rather more conservatively, if we attribute some of the subsequent fall in the death rates for pneumonia, influenza, whooping cough, and diphtheria to medical measures, then perhaps 3.5 percent of the fall in the overall death rate can be explained through medical intervention in the major infectious diseases considered here. Indeed, given that it is precisely for these diseases that medicine claims most success in lowering mortality, 3.5 percent probably represents a reasonable upper-limit estimate of the total contribution of medical measures to the decline in mortality in the United States since 1900.

Conclusions

Without claiming they are definitive findings, and eschewing pretentions to an analysis as sophisticated as McKeown's for England and Wales, one can reasonably draw the following conclusions from the analysis presented in this paper:

In general, medical measures (both chemotherapeutic and prophylactic) appear to have contributed little to the overall decline in mortality in the United States since about 1900—having in many instances been introduced several decades after a marked decline had already set in and having no detectable influence in most instances. More specifically, with reference to those five conditions (influenza, pneumonia, diphtheria, whooping cough, and poliomyelitis) for which the decline in mortality appears substantial after the point of intervention—and on the unlikely assumption that all of this decline is attributable to the intervention—it is estimated that at most 3.5 percent of the total decline in mortality since 1900 could be ascribed to medical measures introduced for the diseases considered here.

These conclusions, in support of the thesis introduced earlier, suggest issues of the most strategic significance for researchers and health care legislators. Profound policy implications follow from either a confirmation or a rejection of the thesis. If one subscribes to the view that we are slowly but surely eliminating one disease after another because of medical interventions, then there may be little commitment to social change and even resistance to some reordering of priorities in medical expenditures. If a disease X is disappearing primarily because of the presence of a particular intervention or service Y, then clearly Y should be left intact, or, more preferably, be expanded. Its demonstrable contribution justifies its presence. But, if it can be shown convincingly, and on commonly accepted grounds, that the major part of the decline in mortality is unrelated to medical care activites, then some commitment to social change and a reordering of priorities may ensue. For, if the disappearance of X is largely unrelated to the presence of Y, or even occurs in the absence of Y, then clearly the expansion and even the continuance of Y can be reasonably questioned. Its demonstrable ineffectiveness justifies some reappraisal of its significance and the wisdom of expanding it in its existing form.

In this paper we have attempted to dispel the myth that medical measures and the presence of medical services were primarily responsible for the modern decline of mortality. The question now remains: if they were not primarily responsible for it, then how is it to be explained? An adequate answer to this further question would require a more substantial research effort than that reported here, but is likely to be along the lines suggested by McKeown which were referred to early in this paper. Hopefully, this paper will serve as a catalyst for such research, incorporating adequate data and appropriate methods of analysis, in an effort to arrive at a more viable alternative explanation.

NOTES

1. It is obviously important to distinguish between (a) advances in knowledge of the cause and natural course of some condition and (b) improvements in our ability to effectively treat some condition (that is, to alter its natural course). In many instances these two areas are disjoint and appear at different stages of development. There are, on the one hand, disease processes about which considerable knowledge has been accrued, yet this has not resulted (nor necessarily will) in the development of effective treatments. On the other hand, there are conditions for which demonstrably effective treatments have been devised in the absence of knowledge of the disease process and/or its causes.

2. Barker and Rose cite one study which compared the ante-mortem and autopsy diagnoses in 9,501 deaths which occurred in 75 different hospitals. Despite lack of a concurrence on *individual* cases, the *overall* frequency was very similar in diagnoses obtained on either an ante-mortem or post-mortem basis. As an example they note that clinical diagnoses of carcinoma of the rectum were confirmed at autopsy in only 67 percent of cases, but the incorrect clinical diagnoses were balanced by an almost identical number of lesions diagnosed for the first time at autopsy (Barker and Rose, 1976).

3. All age and sex adjustments were made by the "direct" method using the population of 1900 as the standard. For further information on this method of adjustment, see Hill (1971) and Shryock et al. (1971).

4. Rutstein (1967), although fervently espousing the traditional view that medical advances have been largely responsible for the decline in mortality, discussed this disjunction and termed it "The Paradox of Modern Medicine." More recently, and from a perspective that is generally consistent

with that advanced here, Powles (1973) noted the same phenomenon in England and Wales.

5. Deaths in the category of chronic respiratory diseases (chronic bronchitis, asthma, emphysema, and other chronic obstructive lung diseases) could not be included in the group of chronic conditions because of insurmountable difficulties inherent in the many changes in disease classification and in the tabulation of statistics.

6. In determining the dates of intervention we relied upon: (a) standard epidemiology and public health texts; (b) the recollections of authorities in the field of infectious diseases; and (c) recent publications on the same subject.

7. For this reason, a negative exponential model is sometimes used to fit a curved line to such data. This was not presented here as the number of points available was small and the difference between a simple quadratic and negative exponential fit was not, upon investigation, able to be detected.

REFERENCES

Alderson, M. 1976. *An Introduction to Epidemiology.* London: Macmillan Press. pp. 7–27.

Barker, D.J.P., and Rose, G. 1976. *Epidemiology in Medical Practice.* London: Churchill Livingstone, p. 6.

Bolduan, C.F. 1930. *How to Protect Children From Diphtheria.* New York: N.Y.C. Health Department.

Dubos, R. 1959. *Mirage of Health.* New York: Harper and Row.

Dubos, R. 1965. *Man Adapting.* New Haven, Connecticut: Yale University Press.

Dubos, R. 1968. *Man, Medicine and Environment.* London: Pall Mall Press.

Dunn, H.L., and Shackley, W. 1945. *Comparison of cause of death assignments by the 1929 and 1938 revisions of the International List: Deaths in the United States, 1940 Vital Statistics—Special Reports* 19:153–277, 1944, Washington, D.C.: U.S. Department of Commerce, Bureau of the Census.

Fuchs, V.R. 1974. *Who Shall Live?* New York: Basic Books, p. 54.

Griffith, T. 1967. *Population Problems in the Age of Malthus.* 2nd ed. London: Frank Cass.

Habakkuk, H.J. 1953. English Population in the Eighteenth Century. *Economic History Review,* 6.

Hill, A.B. 1971. *Principles of Medical Statistics.* 9th ed. London: Oxford University Press.

Hill, A.B. 1955. Snow—An Appreciation. *Proceedings of the Royal Society of Medicine* 48:1008–1012.

Illich, I. 1976. *Medical Nemesis.* New York: Pantheon Books.

Inman, W.H.W., and Adelstein, A.M. 1969. Rise and fall of asthma mortality in England and Wales, in relation to use of pressurized aerosols. *Lancet* 2:278–285.

Kass, E.H. 1971. Infectious diseases and social change. *The Journal of Infectious Diseases* 123 (1):110–114.

Krueger, D.E. 1966. New enumerators for old denominators—multiple causes of death. In *Epidemiological Approaches to the Study of Cancer and Other Chronic Diseases,* edited by W. Haenszel. National Cancer Printing Office, pp. 431–443.

Lee, W.W. 1931. Diphtheria Immunization in Philadelphia and New York City. *Journal of Preventive Medicine* (Baltimore) 5:211–220.

Lilienfeld, A.M. 1976. *Foundations of Epidemiology.* New York: Oxford University Press. pp. 51–111.

McKeown, T. 1976a. *The Modern Rise of Population.* London: Edward Arnold.

McKeown, T. 1976b. *The Role of Medicine: Dream, Mirage or Nemesis.* London: Nuffield Provincial Hospitals Trust.

McKeown, T.; Brown, R.G.; and Record, R.G. 1972. An interpretation of the modern rise of population in Europe. *Population Studies* 26:345–382.

McKeown, T., and Record, R.G. 1955. Medical evidence related to English population changes in the eighteenth century. *Population Studies* 9:119–141.

McKeown, T., and Record, R.G. 1962. Reasons for the decline in mortality in England and Wales during the nineteenth century. *Population Studies* 16:94–122.

McKeown, T.; Record, R.G.; and Turner, R.D. 1975. An interpretation of the decline of mortality in England and Wales during the twentieth century, *Population Studies* 29:391–422.

McKinlay, J.B., and McKinlay, S.M. *A refutation of the thesis that the health of the nation is improving.* Forthcoming.

Magill, T.P. 1955. The immunologist and the evil spirits. *Journal of Immunology* 74:1–8.

Moriyama, I.M.; Baum, W.S.; Haenszel, W.M.; and Mattison, B.F. 1958. Inquiry into diagnostic evidence supporting medical certifications of death. *American Journal of Public Health* 48:1376–1387.

Moriyama, I.M., and Gustavus, S.O. 1972. *Cohort Mortality and Survivorship: United States Death—Registration States, 1900–1968.* National Center for Health Statistics, Series 3, No. 16. Washington, D.C.: U.S. Government Printing Office.

Pfizer, C. and Company. 1953. *The Pneumonias, Management with Antibiotic Therapy.* Brooklyn.

Powles, J. 1973. On the limitations of modern medicine. *Science, Medicine and Man.* 1:2–3.

Reid, O.D., and Rose, G.A. 1964. Assessing the comparability of mortality statistics. *British Medical Journal* 2:1437–1439.

Rutstein, D. 1967. *The Coming Revolution in Medicine.* Cambridge, Massachusettes: MIT Press.

Shryock, H., et al. 1971. *The Methods and Materials of Demography.* Washington, D.C.: U.S. Government Printing Office.

The Times (London). 1977. The Doctors Dilemma: How to Cure Society of a Life Style That Makes People Sick. Friday, January 21.

U.S. Department of Health, Education and Welfare. 1964. *The Change in Mortality Trend in the United States.* National Center for Health Statistics, Series 3, No. 1. Washington, D.C.: U.S. Government Printing Office.

U.S. Bureau of the Census. 1906. *Mortality Statistics 1900–1904.* Washington, D.C.: Government Printing Office.

Weinstein, L. 1974. Infectious Disease: Retrospect and Reminiscence, *The Journal of Infectious Diseases.* 129 (4):480–492.

Wilson, G.S., and Miles, A.A. 1946. In Topley and Wilson's *Principles of Bacteriology and Immunity.* Baltimore: Williams and Wilkins.

Witte, J.J., and Axnick, N.W. 1975. The benefits from ten years of measles immunization in the United States. *Public Health Reports* 90 (3):205–207.

This paper reports part of a larger research project supported by a grant from the Milbank Memorial Fund (to Boston University) and the Carnegie Foundation (to the Radcliffe Institute). The authors would like to thank John Stoeckle, M.D. (Massachusetts General Hospital) and Louis Weinstein, M.D. (Peter Bent Brigham Hospital) for helpful discussions during earlier stages of the research.

Who Gets Sick? The Unequal Social Distribution of Disease

Disease is not distributed evenly throughout the population. Certain groups of people get sick more often, and some populations die at higher rates than others. The study of what groups of people get sick with what disease is called *epidemiology* and has been defined by one expert as ". . . the study of the distributions and determinants of states of health in human populations" (Susser, 1973: 1). By studying populations rather than individuals, epidemiologists seek to identify characteristics of groups of people or their environments which make them more or less vulnerable to disease (*morbidity*) or death (*mortality*).

A growing body of research has found significant associations between a range of social and cultural factors, and the risk for disease and death. The term *social epidemiology* has been adopted by some researchers to emphasize the importance of social variables in the patterning of disease. By focusing on the connections between social processes and the risk for disease, the study of social epidemiology provides the social scientist with an important opportunity to understand more fully the relationship between society and the individual. Among the historical predecessors of today's social epidemiology was the emergence in the nineteenth century of "social medicine" with a number of important studies in Western Europe. In England, Edwin Chadwick studied populations' death rates and identified relationships between disease and social problems—most notably poverty—laying an important foundation for the developing Public Health Movement (Chadwick, 1842, in Susser, 1973). Another early investigator in social medicine was Rudolf Virchow who was asked by the Prussian government to study the causes of a terrible typhus epidemic. His pioneering research identified connections between disease and a number of social factors, including the economy, conditions of work, and the organization of agriculture (Virchow, 1868, 1879, in Waitzkin, 1978).

The articles in this section examine selected associations between the distribution of disease and social variables, including social class, gender, and life style. These studies highlight the relevance of a social epidemiological perspective and point to several promising directions for future research.

In the United States one of the most striking and consistent patterns in the distribution of disease is its relationship to poverty. By and large, death and disease rates vary inversely with social class; that is, the poorer the population, the higher the risk for sickness and death (Kitagawa and Hauser, 1973; Kane et al., 1976). For example:

> Low income people in general have worse health than people with higher incomes. In 1976, about half of the population 45–64 years of age with family incomes of less than $5,000 were limited in their usual activity because of a chronic condition compared with about a sixth of the population with incomes of $15,000 or more.

Similarly people 45–64 years of age with low family incomes had more than three times as many bed-disability days per person as with people with higher incomes (19 days versus 6 days). (DHEW, 1978: ix.)

While it has been known for well over a century that poor people suffer from more disease than others, just how poverty influences health is not yet well understood. In their article, "Social Class, Susceptibility, and Sickness," S. Leonard Syme and Lisa F. Berkman explore the relationship between social class and sickness, reviewing the evidence of the influence of stress, living conditions, nutrition, and medical services on the patterns of death and disease among the poor. They particularly focus on how the living conditions of the lower class may compromise "disease defense systems" and engender greater vulnerability to disease.

Another interesting and consistent pattern is the difference between the distribution of disease and death in men and women. Women have higher illness rates than men, while men have higher death rates. (Such comparisons rely on "age adjusted" samples in order to eliminate the effects of age on gender differences.) There has been a great deal of disagreement about the explanation for these patterns, including debates over whether or not women actually do get sick more often than men or whether they are more likely to report symptoms or seek medical care (e.g., Nathanson, 1977; Verbrugge, 1979; Gove and Hughes, 1979). The growing feminist scholarship on women's health and the more recent epidemiological interest in studying patterns of physical disease in female populations have begun to clarify the debate. It now appears that women *do* in fact have higher rates of sickness than men *and* that they are more likely than men to report symptoms and utilize medical services (e.g., Nathanson, 1980; Wingard, 1982).

Ingrid Waldron's article asks "Why Do Women Live Longer Than Men?" and presents evidence of the importance of the social and psychological processes of gender socialization in our society. Waldron argues that there exists a complex interaction between gender related social-psychological characteristics and physical vulnerability to accidents and death that result in the differing patterns of disease between male and female populations. Her thesis leads her to predict that the continuing social and cultural changes in women's social roles will lead to a decrease in the ratio of male to female deaths. This prediction seems to be true: with women increasingly likely to be in the paid labor force, while continuing and even expanding their responsibility for the unpaid labor of housework and childcare, the historical health "advantage" of women seems to be disappearing (Verbrugge, 1982; Chavkin, 1984).

It is important to note that comparisons between male and female populations (*inter-gender* differences) may mask significant (*intra-gender*) patterns among women or among men. In fact, there is evidence that the distribution of disease and death within male and female populations is patterned by other social factors, and, importantly, that these patterns differ for men and women. Social class, race, age, marital status, presence and number of children in the home, and employment outside the home have all been found to be associated with rates of disease within male and female populations, accounting for at least some of the differences between the sexes (e.g., Nathanson, 1980; Haynes and Feinleib, 1980; Wingard, 1982).

In a fascinating little article, "A Tale of Two States," Victor R. Fuchs compares the health of the populations of two neighboring states: Nevada and Utah. While similar in many ways, these populations have very different patterns of death. Fuch argues that the explanation for this difference is to be found in the life styles of each of the populations and that these life style differences are the result of the cultural environments, values, and norms of each of the populations.

The findings of these articles and the developing social epidemiology to which they contribute challenge the traditional medical model by seeing social factors as part of the process of disease production. While not dismissing the possibility that some biological processes contribute to the risk for disease among some groups, the bulk of the evidence (including that presented by Waldron, as well as that discussed by Kern and Schnall in their article on hypertension) supports a view that much of the epidemiological significance of race, gender, and age results from the social and cultural consequences of being, for example, a black, a woman, or an old person.

The importance of social processes in disease production is also supported by the consistent findings of the significance of social networks (community and family ties) and stress, including the chronic stresses of jobs, family obligations, economic pressures, etc., as well as the stress produced by the relatively rare "stressful life events" (Dohrenwend and Dohrenwend, 1981). These stressful events are the more dramatic and unusual occurrences, such as divorce, job loss, or birth of a child, that produce major changes in people's lives. These researchers have found a consistent connection between these events and the individual's vulnerability to disease. Social networks and stress have been found to be associated with the development of physical diseases (e.g., coronary heart disease, hypertension) as well as psychological disorders (e.g., depression) (see for example, Berkman and Syme, 1979; Wheatley, 1981; Dohrenwend and Dohrenwend, 1981).

Clearly, there is a need for a new and broader conceptualization of disease production than the traditional medical model can provide. Attention must shift from the individual to the social and physical environments in which people live and work. The development of an adequate model of disease production must draw on the conceptual and research contributions of several disciplines not only to identify the social production of diseases, but to elaborate this process and provide important information on which to base effective primary intervention and prevention strategies.

REFERENCES

Berkman, Lisa F., and S. L. Syme. 1979. "Social networks, host resistance, and mortality: A nine-year follow-up study of Alameda County residents." American Journal of Epidemiology. 109:(July) 186–204

Brown, George, and T. Harris. 1978. Social Origins of Depression. London: Tavistock.

Chadwick, Edwin. 1842. Report on the Sanitary Condition of the Labouring Population of Great Britain. Reprinted 1965. Edinburgh: Edinburgh University Press.

Chavkin, Wendy, ed. 1984. Double Exposure, Women's Health Hazards on the Job and at Home. New York: Monthly Review Press.

Department of Health, Education, and Welfare. 1978. Health United States 1978. Public Health Service, Office of the Assistant Secretary for Health, National Center for Health Statistics, National Center for Health Statistics Research Center Building, 3700 East-West Highway, Hyattsville, MD 20782. DHEW Publication No. (PHS) 78-1232, December.

Dohrenwend, Barbara S., and Bruce P. Dohrenwend, eds. 1981. Stressful Life Events and Their Contexts. New York: Prodist.

Gove, Walter, and Michael Hughes. 1979. "Possible causes of the apparent sex differences in physical health: An empirical investigation." American Sociological Review. 44:126–146.

Haynes, Suzanne, and M. Feinleib. 1980. "Women, work and coronary heart disease: Prospective findings from the Framingham Heart Study." American Journal of Public Health. 70, 2 (February): 133–141.

Kane, Robert, J.M. Kasteler, and R.M. Gray, eds. 1976. The Health Gap, Medical Services and the Poor. New York: Springer.

Kitagawa, Evelyn M. and P.M. Hauser. 1973. Differential Mortality in the United States: A Study in Socioeconomic Epidemiology. Cambridge, MA: Harvard University Press.

Luft, Harold S., 1978. Poverty and Health, Economic Causes and Consequences of Health Problems. Cambridge, MA: J.B. Lippincott Co.

Nathanson, Constance. 1977. "Sex, illness and medical care: A review of data, theory and method." Social Science and Medicine. 11:13–25.

Nathanson, Constance. 1980. "Social roles and health status among women: The significance of employment." Social Science and Medicine. 14A: 463–471.

Susser, Mervyn. 1973. Causal Thinking in the Health Sciences, Concepts and Strategies in Epidemiology. New York: Oxford University Press.

Verbugge, Lois. 1979. "Marital status and health." Journal of Marriage and Family. (May): 267–285.

Verbrugge, Lois. 1982. "Sex differentials in health." U.S. Public Health Reports. 97, 5 (Sept–October): 417–437.

Virchow, Rudolf. 1958. Disease, Life and Man. Tr. Lelland J. Rather. Stanford: Stanford University Press.

Waitzkin, Howard. 1978. "A Marxist view of medical care." Annals of Internal Medicine. 89:264–278.

Wheatley, David, ed. 1981. Stress and the Heart. 2nd ed. New York: Raven Press.

Wingard, Deborah. 1982. "The sex differential in mortality rates." American Journal of Epidemiology. 115 (2): 105–216.

2

Social Class, Susceptibility, and Sickness

S. Leonard Syme and Lisa F. Berkman

Social class gradients of mortality and life expectancy have been observed for centuries, and a vast body of evidence has shown consistently that those in the lower classes have higher mortality, morbidity, and disability rates. While these patterns have been observed repeatedly, the explanations offered to account for them show no such consistency. The most frequent explanations have included poor housing, crowding, racial factors, low income, poor education and unemployment, all of which have been said to result in such outcomes as poor nutrition, poor medical care (either through non-availability or non-utilization of resources), strenuous conditions of employment in non-hygienic settings, and increased exposure to noxious agents. While these explanations account for some of the observed relationships, we have found them inadequate to explain the very large number of diseases associated with socioeconomic status. It seemed useful, therefore, to reexamine these associations in search of a more satisfactory hypothesis.

Obviously, this is an important issue. It is clear that new approaches must be explored emphasizing the primary prevention of disease in addition to those approaches that merely focus on treatment of the sick (1). It is clear also that such preventive approaches must involve community and environmental interventions rather than one-to-one preventive encounters (2). Therefore, we must understand more precisely those features of the environment that are etiologically related to disease so that interventions at this level can be more intelligently planned.

Of all the disease outcomes considered, it is evident that low socioeconomic status is most strikingly associated with high rates of infectious and parasitic diseases (3–7) as well as with higher infant mortality rates (8,9). However, in our review we found higher rates among lower class groups of a very much wider range of diseases and conditions for which obvious explanations were not as easily forthcoming. In a comprehensive review of over 30 studies, Antonovsky (10) concluded that those in the lower classes invariably have lower life expectancy and higher death rates from all causes of death, and that this higher rate has been observed since the 12th century when data on this question were first organized. While differences in infectious disease and infant mortality rates probably accounted for much of this difference between the classes in earlier years, current differences must primarily be attributable to mortality from non-infectious disease.

Kitagawa and Hauser (11) recently completed a massive nationwide study of mortality in the United States. Among men and women in the 25–64-year age group, mortality rates varied dramatically by level of education, income, and occupation, considered together or separately. For example, . . . white males at low education levels had age-adjusted mortality rates 64 per cent higher than men in higher education categories. For white women, those in lower education groups had an age-adjusted mortality rate 105 per cent higher. For non-white males, the differential was 31 per cent and, for non-white females, it was 70 per cent. These mortality differentials also were reflected in substantial differences in life expectancy, and . . . for most specific causes of death. . . . White males in the lowest education groups have higher age-adjusted mortality rates for every cause of death for which data are available. For white females, those in the lowest education group have an excess mortality rate for all causes except cancer of the breast and motor vehicle accidents.

These gradients of mortality among the social classes have been observed over the world by many investigators (12–18) and have not changed materially since 1900 (except that non-whites, especially higher status non-whites, have experienced a relatively more favorable improvement). This consistent finding in time and space is all the more remarkable since the concept of "social class" has been defined and measured in so many different ways by these investigators. That the same findings have been obtained in spite of such methodological differences lends strength to the validity of the observations; it suggests also that the concept is an imprecise term encompassing diverse elements of varying etiologic significance.

In addition to data on mortality, higher rates of morbidity also have been observed for a vast array of conditions among those in lower class groups (19–28). This is an important observation since it indicates that excess mortality rates among lower status groups are not merely attributable to a higher case fatality death rate in those groups but are accompanied also by a higher prevalence of morbidity. Of special interest in this regard are data on the various mental illnesses, a major cause of morbidity. As shown by many investigators (29–35), those in lower as compared to higher socioeconomic groups have higher rates of schizophrenia, are more depressed, more unhappy, more worried, more anxious, and are less hopeful about the future.

In summary, persons in lower class groups have higher morbidity and mortality rates of almost every disease or illness, and these differentials have not diminished over time. While particular hypotheses may be offered to explain the gradient for one or another of these specific diseases, the fact that so many diseases exhibit the same gradient leads to speculation that a more general explanation may be more appropriate than a series of disease-specific explanations.

In a study reported elsewhere (36), it was noted that although blacks had higher rates of hypertension than whites, blacks in the lower classes had higher rates of hypertension than blacks in the upper classes. An identical social class gradient for hypertension was noted among whites in the sample. In that report, it was concluded that hypertension was associated more with social class than with racial factors, and it was suggested that the greater prevalence of obesity in the lower class might be a possible explanation. The present review makes that earlier suggestion far less attractive since so many diseases and conditions appear to be of higher prevalence in the lower class groups. It seems clear that we must frame hypotheses of sufficient generality to account for this phenomenon.

One hypothesis that has been suggested is that persons in the lower classes either have less access to medical care resources or, if care is available, that they do not benefit from that availability. This possibility should be explored in more detail, but current evidence available does not suggest that differences in medical care resources will entirely explain social class gradients in disease. The hypertension project summarized above was conducted at the Kaiser Permanente facility in Oakland, California, which is a pre-paid health plan with medical facilities freely available to all study subjects. The data in this study showed that persons in lower status groups had utilized medical resources more frequently than those in higher status categories (37). To study the influence of medical care in explaining these differences in blood pressure levels, all persons in the Kaiser study who had ever been clinically diagnosed as hypertensive, or who had ever taken medicine for high blood pressure, were removed from consideration. Differences in blood pressure level between those in the highest and lowest social classes were diminished when hypertensives were removed from analysis, but those in the lowest class still had higher (normal) pressures. Thus, while differences in medical care may have accounted for some of the variation observed among the social class groups, substantial differences in blood pressures among these groups nevertheless remained. Similar findings have been reported from studies at the Health Insurance Plan of New York (38).

Lipworth and colleagues (39) also examined this issue in a study of cancer survival rates among various income groups in Boston. In that study, low-income persons had substantially less favorable one and three-year survival rates following treatment at identical tumor clinics and hospitals; these differences were not accounted for by differences in stage of cancer at diagnosis, by the age of patients, or by the specific kind of treatment patients received. It was concluded that patients from lower income areas simply did not fare as well following treatment for cancer. While it is still possible that lower class patients received less adequate medical care, the differences observed in survival rates did not seem attributable to the more obvious variations in quality of treatment. Other studies support this general conclusion but not enough data are available to assess clearly the role of medical care in explaining social class gradients in morbidity and mortality; it would seem, however, that the medical care hypothesis does not account for a major portion of these gradients.

Another possible explanation offered to explain these consistent differences is that persons in lower socioeconomic groups live in a more toxic, hazardous and non-hygienic environment resulting in a broad array of disease consequences. That these environments exert an influence on disease outcome is supported by research on crowding and rheumatic fever (5), poverty areas and health (40), and on air pollution and respiratory illnesses (41). While lower class groups certainly are exposed to a more physically noxious environment, physical factors alone are frequently unable to explain observed relationships between socioeconomic status and disease outcome. One example of this is provided by the report of Guerrin and Borgatta (16) showing that the proportion of people who are illiterate in a census tract is a more important indicator of tuberculosis occurrence than are either economic or racial variables. Similarly, the work of Booth (42) suggests that perceived crowding which is not highly correlated with objective measures of crowding may have adverse effects on individuals.

There can be little doubt that the highest morbidity and mortality rates observed in the lower social classes are in part due to inadequate medical care services as well as to the impact of a toxic and hazardous physical environment. There can be little doubt, also, that these factors do not entirely explain the discrepancy in rates between the classes. Thus, while enormous improvements have been made in environmental

quality and in medical care, the mortality rate gap between the classes has not diminished. It is true that mortality rates have been declining over the years, and it is probably true also that this benefit is attributable in large part to the enormous improvements that have been made in food and water purity, in sanitary engineering, in literacy and health education, and in medical and surgical knowledge. It is important to recognize, however, that these reductions in mortality rates have not eliminated the gap between the highest and the lowest social class groups; this gap remains very substantial and has apparently stabilized during the last 40 years. Thus, while improvements in the environment and in medical care clearly have been of value, other factors must be identified to account for this continuing differential in mortality rate and life expectancy.

The identification of these new factors might profitably be guided by the repeated observation of social class gradients in a wide range of disease distributions. That so many different kinds of diseases are more frequent in lower class groupings directs attention to generalized susceptibility to disease and to generalized compromises of disease defense systems. Thus, if something about life in the lower social classes increases vulnerability to illness in general, it would not be surprising to observe an increased prevalence of many different types of diseases and conditions among people in the lower classes.

While laboratory experiments on both humans and animals have established that certain "stressful events" have physiologic consequences, very little is known about the nature of these "stressful events" in non-laboratory settings. Thus, while we may conclude that "something" about the lower class environment is stressful, we know much less about what specifically constitutes that stress. Rather than attempting to identify *specific* risk factors for *specific* diseases in investigating this question, it may be more meaningful to identify those factors that affect *general* susceptibility to disease. The specification of such factors should rest on the identification of variables having a wide range of disease outcomes. One such risk factor may be life change associated with social and cultural mobility. Those experiencing this type of mobility have been observed to have higher rates of diseases and conditions such as coronary heart disease (43–46), lung cancer (47), difficulties of pregnancy (48, 49), sarcoidosis (50), and depression (30). Another risk factor may be certain life events; those experiencing what are commonly called stressful life events have been shown to have higher rates of a wide variety of diseases and conditions (51–57).

Generalized susceptibility to disease may be influenced not only by the impact of various forms of life change and life stress, but also by differences in the way people cope with such stress. Coping, in this sense, refers not to specific types of psychological responses but to the more generalized ways in which people deal with problems in their everyday life. It is evident that such coping styles are likely to be products of environmental situations and not independent of such factors. Several coping responses that have a wide range of disease outcomes have been described. Cigarette smoking is one such coping response that has been associated with virtually all causes of morbidity and mortality (58); obesity may be another coping style associated with a higher rate of many diseases and conditions (59,60); pattern A behavior is an example of a third coping response that has been shown to have relatively broad disease consequences (61). There is some evidence that persons in the lower classes experience more life changes (62) and that they tend to be more obese and to smoke more cigarettes (63,64).

To explain the differential in morbidity and mortality rates among the social classes, it is important to identify additional factors that affect susceptibility and have diverse disease consequences; it is also important to determine which of these factors are more prevalent in the lower classes. Thus, our understanding would be enhanced if it could be shown not only that those in the lower classes live in a more toxic physical environment with inadequate medical care, but also that they live in a social and psychological environment that increases their vulnerability to a whole series of diseases and conditions.

In this paper, we have emphasized the variegated disease consequences of low socioeconomic status. Any proposed explanations of this phenomenon should be capable of accounting for this general outcome. The proposal offered here

is that those in the lower classes consistently have higher rates of disease in part due to compromised disease defenses and increased general susceptibility. To explore this proposal further, systematic research is needed on four major problems:

(1) The more precise identification and description of subgroups within the lower socioeconomic classes that have either markedly higher or lower rates of disease: Included in what is commonly called the "lower class" are semiskilled working men with stable work and family situations, unemployed men with and without families, the rural and urban poor, hard core unemployed persons, and so on. The different disease experiences of these heterogeneous subgroups would permit a more precise understanding of the processes involved in disease etiology and would permit a more precise definition of social class groupings.

(2) The disentanglement of socio-environmental from physical-environmental variables: It is important to know whether high rates of illness and discontent in a poverty area, for example, are due to the poor physical circumstances of life in such an area, to the social consequences of life in such an area, or to the personal characteristics of individuals who come to live in the area.

(3) The clarification of "causes" and "effects": The implication in this paper has been that the lower class environment "leads to" poor health. Certainly, the reverse situation is equally likely. Many measures of social class position may be influenced by the experience of ill health itself. Further research is needed to clarify the relative importance of the "downward drift" hypothesis. One way of approaching such study is to use measures of class position that are relatively unaffected by illness experience. An example of one such measure is "educational achievement" as used by Kitagawa and Hauser (11). In this study, educational level was assumed to be relatively stable after age 20 and was felt to be a measure relatively unaffected by subsequent illness experience.

(4) The more comprehensive description of those psycho-social variables that may compromise bodily defense to disease and increase susceptibility to illness: The possible importance of life events, life changes, and various coping

behavior has been suggested but systematic research needs to be done to provide a more complete view of the factors involved in this process. Of particular interest would be research on the ways in which social and familial support networks (48,55) mediate between the impact of life events and stresses and disease outcomes.

The research that is needed should not be limited to the study of the specific risk factors as these affect specific diseases. Instead, the major focus of this research should be on those general features of lower class living environments that compromise bodily defense and thereby affect health and well-being in general. This research should go beyond the superficial description of demographic variables associated with illness and should attempt the identification of specific etiologic factors capable of accounting for the observed morbidity and mortality differences between the social classes.

The gap in mortality and life expectancy between the social classes has stabilized and may be increasing; the identification of those factors that render people vulnerable to disease will hopefully provide a basis for developing more meaningful prevention programs aimed toward narrowing the gap.

REFERENCES

1. Winkelstein W Jr, French FE: The role of ecology in the design of a health care system. Calif Med 113:7–12, 1970.
2. Marmot M, Winkelstein W Jr: Epidemiologic observations on intervention trials for prevention of coronary heart disease. Am J Epidemiol 101:177–181, 1975.
3. Tuberculosis and Socioeconomic Status. Stat Bull, January 1970.
4. Terris M: Relation of economic status to tuberculosis mortality by age and sex. Am J Public Health 38:1061–1071, 1948
5. Gordis L, Lilienfeld A, Rodriguez R: Studies in the epidemiology and preventability of rheumatic fever. II. Socioeconomic factors and the incidence of acute attacks. J Chronic Dis 21:655–666, 1969.
6. Influenza and Pneumonia Mortality in the U.S., Canada and Western Europe. Stat Bull, April 1972.
7. Court SDM: Epidemiology and natural history of respiratory infections in children. J Clin Pathol 21:31, 1968.
8. Chase HC (ed): A study of risks, medical care and infant mortality. Am J Public Health 63: supplement, 1973.
9. Lerner M: Social differences in physical health. In: Poverty and Health. Edited by J Kozsa, A Antonovsky, IK Zola. Cambridge, Harvard University Press, 1969, pp 69–112.
10. Antonovsky A: Social class, life expectancy and overall mortality. Milbank Mem Fund Q 45:31–73, 1967.
11. Kitagawa EM, Hauser PM: Differential Mortality in the United States. Cambridge, Harvard University Press, 1973.
12. Nagi MH, Stockwell EG: Socioeconomic differentials in mortality by cause of death. Health Serv Rep 88:449–465, 1973.
13. Ellis JM: Socio-economic differentials in mortality from chronic disease. In: Patients, Physicians and Illness. Edited by EG Jaco. Glencoe, Ill, The Free Press, 1958, pp 30–37.
14. Yeracaris J: Differential mortality, general and cause-specific in Buffalo, 1939–1941. J Am Stat Assoc 50:1235–1247, 1955.
15. Brown SM, Selvin S, Winkelstein W Jr: The association of economic status with the occurrence of lung cancer. Cancer 36:1903–1911, 1975.
16. Guerrin RF, Borgatta EF: Socio-economic and demographic correlates of tuberculosis incidence. Milbank Mem Fund Q 43:269–290, 1965.
17. Graham S: Socio-economic status, illness, and the use of medical services. Milbank Mem Fund Q 35:58–66, 1957.
18. Cohart EM: Socioeconomic distribution of stomach cancer in New Haven. Cancer 7:455–461, 1954.
19. Socioeconomic Differentials in Mortality. Stat Bull, June 1972.
20. Hart JT: Too little and too late. Data on occupational mortality, 1959–1963. Lancet 1:192–193, 1972.
21. Wan T: Social differentials in selected work-limiting chronic conditions. J Chronic Dis 25:365–374, 1972.
22. Hochstim JR, Athanasopoulos DA, Larkins JH: Poverty area under the microscope. Am J Public Health 58:1815–1827, 1968.
23. Burnight RG: Chronic morbidity and socioeconomic characteristics of older urban males. Milbank Mem Fund Q 43:311–322, 1965.
24. Elder R, Acheson RM: New Haven survey of joint diseases. XIV. Social class and behavior in re-

sponse to symptoms of osteoarthritis. Milbank Mem Fund Q 48:499–502, 1970.

25. Cobb S: The epidemiology of rheumatoid disease. *In:* The Frequency of Rheumatoid Disease. Edited by S Cobb. Cambridge, Harvard University Free Press, 1971, pp 42–62.

26. Graham S: Social factors in the relation to chronic illness. *In:* Handbook of Medical Sociology. Edited by HE Freeman, S Levine, LG Reeder. Englewood Cliffs, NJ, Prentice-Hall Inc, 1963, pp 65–98.

27. Wan T: Status stress and morbidity: A sociological investigation of selected categories of working-limiting conditions. J Chronic Dis 24:453–468, 1971.

28. Selected Health Characteristics by Occupation, U.S. July 1961–June 1963. National Health Center for Health Statistics, Series 10 21:1–16, 1965.

29. Abramson JH: Emotional disorder, status inconsistency and migration. Milbank Mem Fund Q 44:23–48, 1966.

30. Schwab JJ, Holzer CE III, Warheit GJ: Depression scores by race, sex, age, family income, education and socioeconomic status. (Personal communication, 1974).

31. Srole L, Langner T, Michael S, et al: Mental Health in the Metropolis: the Midtown Study. New York, McGraw Hill, 1962.

32. Jackson EF: Status consistency and symptoms of stress. Am Sociol Rev 27:469–480, 1962.

33. Hollingshead AB, Redlich FC: Social Class and Mental Illness. New York, John Wiley and Sons Inc. 1958.

34. Gurin G, Veroff J, Feld S: Americans View Their Mental Health. New York, Basic Books Inc. 1960.

35. Langner TS: Psychophysiological symptoms and the status of women in two Mexican communities. *In:* Approaches to Cross-cultural Psychiatry. Edited by AH Leighton, JM Murphy. Ithaca, Cornell University Press, 1965. pp 360–392.

36. Syme SL, Oakes T, Friedman G, et al: Social class and racial differences in blood pressure. Am J Public Health 64:619–620, 1974.

37. Oakes TW, Syme SL: Social factors in newly discovered elevated blood pressure. J Health Soc Behav 14:198–204, 1973.

38. Fink R, Shapiro S, Hyman MD, et al: Health status of poverty and non-poverty groups in multiphasic health testing. Presented at the Annual Meeting of the American Public Health Association, November 1972.

39. Lipworth L, Abelin T, Connelly RR: Socioeconomic factors in the prognosis of cancer patients. J Chronic Dis 23:105–116, 1970.

40. Hochstim JR: Health and ways of living. *In:* Social Surveys. The Commmunity as an Epidemiological Laboratory. Edited by I Kessler, M Levine. Baltimore, Johns Hopkins Press, 1970, pp 149–176.

41. Winkelstein W Jr, Kantor S, Davis EW, et al: The relationship of air pollution and economic status to total mortality and selected respiratory system mortality in men. I. Suspended particulates. Arch Environ Health 14:162–171, 1967.

42. Booth A: Preliminary Report: Urban Crowding Project. Canada, Ministry of State for Urban Affairs, August 1974 (mimeographed).

43. Syme SL, Hyman MM, Enterline PE: Some social and cultural factors associated with the occurrence of coronary heart disease. J Chronic Dis 17:277–289, 1964.

44. Tyroler HA, Cassel J: Health consequences of cultural change. II. The effect of urbanization on coronary heart mortality in rural residents. J Chronic Dis 17:167–177, 1964.

45. Nesser WB, Tyroler HA, Cassel JC: Social disorganization and stroke mortality in the black populations of North Carolina. Am J Epidemiol 93:166–175, 1971.

46. Shekelle RB, Osterfeld AM, Paul O: Social status and incidence of coronary heart disease. J Chronic Dis 22:381–394, 1969.

47. Haenszel W, Loveland DB, Sirken N: Lung-cancer mortality as related to residence and smoking histories. I. White males. J Natl Cancer Inst 28:947–1001, 1962.

48. Nuckolls KB, Cassel J, Kaplan BH: Psychosocial assets, life crisis, and the prognosis of pregnancy. Am J Epidemiol 95:431–441, 1972.

49. Gorusch RL, Key MK: Abnormalities of pregnancy as a function of anxiety and life stress. Psychosom Med 36:352–362, 1974.

50. Terris M, Chaves AD: An epidemiologic study of sarcoidosis. Am Rev Respir Dis 94:50–55, 1966.

51. Rahe RH, Gunderson EKE, Arthur RJ: Demographic and psychosocial factors in acute illness reporting. J Chronic Dis 23:245–255, 1970.

52. Wyler AR, Masuda M, Holmes TH: Magnitude of life events and seriousness of illness. Psychosom Med 33:115–122, 1971.

53. Rahe RH, Rubin RT, Gunderson EKE, et al: Psychological correlates of serum cholesterol in man: A longitudinal study. Psychosom Med 33:399–410, 1971.

54. Spilken AZ, Jacobs MA: Prediction of illness behavior from measures of life crisis, manifest distress and maladaptive coping. Psychosom Med 33:251–264, 1971.

55. Jacobs MA, Spilken AZ, Martin MA, et al: Life

stress and respiratory illness. Psychosom Med 32:233–242, 1970.

56. Kasl SV, Cobb S: Blood pressure changes in men undergoing job loss; A preliminary report. Psychosom Med 32:19–38, 1970.

57. Hinkle LE, Wolff HG: Ecological investigations of the relationship between illness, life experiences, and the social environment. Ann Intern Med 49:1373–1388, 1958.

58. US Dept of Health, Education, and Welfare: The Health Consequences of Smoking. National Communicable Disease Center, Publication No 74-8704, 1974.

59. US Public Health Service, Division of Chronic Diseases: Obesity and Health. A Source Book of Current Information for Professional Health Personnel. Publication No 1485. Washington DC, US GPO, 1966.

60. Build and Blood Pressure Study. Chicago, Society of Actuaries, Vol I and II, 1959.

61. Rosenman RH, Brand RH, Jenkins CD, et al: Coronary heart disease in the Western collaborative group study: Final follow-up experience of 8½ years. (Manuscript).

62. Dohrenwend BS (ed): Stressful Life Events: Their Nature and Effects. New York, Wiley-Interscience, 1974.

63. US Dept of Health, Education, and Welfare: Adult Use of Tobacco 1970, Publication No HSM-73-8727, 1973.

64. Khosla T, Lowe CR: Obesity and smoking habits by social class. J Prev Soc Med 26:249–256, 1972.

3

Why Do Women Live Longer Than Men?

Ingrid Waldron

Part I

The sex differential in mortality has increased strikingly over the past half century in the U.S. In 1920, the life expectancy for women was 56, only two years longer than that for men (1). By 1970, women's life expectancy was 75, almost eight years longer than men's (2). In 1920, male death rates were no more than 30 percent higher than female death rates at any age. By 1970, male death rates exceeded female death rates by as much as 180 percent for 15–24-year-olds and 110 percent for 55–64-year-olds.

Among young adults the excess of mortality for males is due primarily to accidents (3). At older ages, cardiovascular-renal diseases make the largest contribution to higher mortality among men. Rising male mortality for these causes of death and for lung cancer has been a major component of the increase in the sex differential in mortality (4). These trends were due in part to the sizeable increase in cigarette smoking by men during the first third of the twentieth century (5,6). Another substantial component of the increase in the sex differential in mortality has been the decline in maternal mortality and uterine cancer due to improvements in medical care. These data suggest that a wide variety of cultural factors, including automobile use, cigarette smoking and health care, contributes to the contemporary sex differential in mortality.

Further evidence of the importance of cultural factors is provided by international comparisons, which show that higher male death rates, although common, have not been universal. In many countries female death rates have exceeded male death rates at ages between one and forty and in some cases at older ages as well (7). Higher mortality among females has been observed most frequently in nonindustrial countries.

The sex differential in mortality also varies for different groups within the United States. For example the excess of male mortality is lowest among married adults, it is 10 percent greater among single and widowed adults, and it is 50 percent greater among divorced adults (data from 8). The excess of mortality for males who are not married is particularly large for causes like cirrhosis of the liver which are strongly influenced by behavior, and for diseases like tuberculosis in which health habits and care play an important role. Gove (9) has argued that the major reasons why the sex mortality differential is higher among males who are not married are that men do not adjust as well as women do to being unmarried, and that men derive greater advantages from being married, both in care received and in psychological well-being.

Genetic factors apparently also contribute to higher male mortality, although the evidence for this is not as strong as commonly has been believed. Males have higher mortality than females in many different species, and this has been cited as evidence for a genetic contribution to the higher mortality of men (10). However, although higher male mortality is widespread among insects, other Arthropoda and fishes (10), higher female mortality appears to be just as common as higher male mortality among our closer relatives, the birds and mammals (10–12). Among humans, higher female mortality is also common at certain ages, as described above. However, it is striking that, wherever statistics are available, males have had higher mortality during the first year of life (7). Males also have been found to have higher fetal mortality in most studies (13), although fetal mortality during late pregnancy is as high for females as for males in pairs of twins of opposite sex (14), in multiple births of triplets or more (15), and in a few geographical areas, for example Scotland (16). Male mortality is higher for many different causes of death (see Table 1). Several authors (10,17) have inferred from these observations that genetically determined metabolic differences may contribute to the higher mortality of males.

Another study which has been cited widely as evidence of the importance of genetic factors is Madigan's (18) comparison of life expectancy for Roman Catholic Sisters and Brothers in teaching Orders. Madigan found that the differential in life expectancy between Sisters and Brothers has been almost as large as the differential between women and men in the general population, even though the Sisters and Brothers had more similar adult roles. However, the higher mortality of the Brothers cannot be attributed solely to genetic causes, since the Brothers smoked and drank more than the Sisters and probably were socialized differently as children, and each of these differences would contribute to higher male mortality (as discussed in detail below).

This earlier work suggests that both cultural and genetic factors contribute to the longer life expectancy of women (19–21). Therefore, we have considered both cultural and genetic factors in our analysis of the specific causes of the sex differential in mortality in the contemporary U.S.

Our analysis is based on the identification of the causes of death which make a large contribution to the sex differential in mortality in United States. . . . For each of these causes of death we considered all the major factors believed to contribute to its etiology and selected for analysis those factors which appeared to be relevant to the sex difference in mortality.

Behavioral factors emerge as important determinants of the sex differential for . . . death. . . . The importance of behavioral factors is obvious in the case of accidents and suicide, and also for the respiratory diseases, which largely are due to smoking (22) as well as for cirrhosis of the liver, which is related to alcohol consumption (23). These causes of death with clear behavioral components are responsible for one-third of the excess of male mortality. Arteriosclerotic heart disease is responsible for an additional 40 percent of the excess deaths among males. The data presented in the next section suggest that men have higher death rates for arteriosclerotic heart disease in large part because they smoke cigarettes more and because they more often develop the aggressive, competitive Coronary Prone Behavior Pattern.

Table 1. Sex mortality ratios for all major causes of death, U.S., 1967*

Ratio of male to female death rates	Cause of death	Male death rate (Deaths/100,000 population)	Female death rate† (Deaths/100,000 population)
5.9	Malignant neoplasm of respiratory system, not specified as secondary	50.1	8.5
4.9	Other bronchopulmonic disease (71% emphysema)	24.4	5.0
2.8	Motor vehicle accidents	39.4	14.2
2.7	Suicide	15.7	5.8
2.4	Other accidents	41.1	17.4
2.0	Cirrhosis of liver	18.5	9.1
2.0	Arteriosclerotic heart disease, including coronary disease	357.0	175.6
1.8	Symptoms, senility and ill-defined conditions	14.9	8.3
1.7	Pneumonia, except of newborn	32.3	19.5
1.6	Other diseases of heart	17.9	11.1
1.6	Other diseases of circulatory system	18.2	11.1
1.5	Malignant neoplasm of digestive organs and peritoneum, not specified as secondary	53.0	36.2
1.4	All other diseases (residual)	32.4	22.4
1.4	Malignant neoplasm of other and unspecified sites	20.5	14.7
1.4	Birth injuries, postnatal asphyxia, and atelectasis	11.9	8.4
1.4	Certain diseases of early infancy	29.2	21.6
1.3	Other diseases peculiar to early infancy, and immaturity, unqualified	15.3	11.7
1.3	Nonrheumatic chronic endocarditis and other myocardial degeneration	26.8	20.5
1.2	General arteriosclerosis	17.2	14.8
1.2	Vascular lesions affecting central nervous system	96.3	83.3
1.0	Hypertensive heart disease	22.3	22.2
0.89	Malignant neoplasm of genital organs	17.9	20.1
0.89	Diabetes mellitus	14.9	16.8
0.008	Malignant neoplasm of breast	0.2	24.6
1.6	All causes	1081.7	657.0

The causes of death with the highest sex mortality ratios all have major behavioral components (calculated from data in ref. 98).

*All causes of death were included, except those responsible for less than 1% of the deaths (e.g. homicide).

†Female death rates have been age-adjusted to the male age distribution.

Arteriosclerotic Heart Disease

Death rates for arteriosclerotic heart disease, which is primarily coronary heart disease (CHD), are twice as high for men as for women. Cigarette smoking is associated with an elevation of CHD death rates ranging from 100 percent or more among middle-aged adults to 20 percent at the oldest ages (24). The elevated risk of CHD among smokers is probably due in part to the correlation between smoking and other risk factors (such as the Coronary Prone Behavior Pattern discussed below), but it is almost certainly also a direct consequence of the pharmacological effects of smoking (22). A rough quantitative estimate of the contribution of smoking habits to the sex differential in CHD death rates can be obtained by comparing the sex differential among nonsmokers to the sex differential for the general population. The contribution of cigarette smoking appears to be substantial, particularly for adults under age 65. Among middle-aged adults who have never smoked regularly, the CHD mortality for men exceeds that for women by 350 percent while for the total sample (including smokers) men's CHD mortality exceeds women's by 650 percent.

A variety of evidence suggests that another important cause of higher rates of coronary heart disease in men may be their involvement in paid jobs and in aggressive, competitive roles, in contrast to the greater orientation of women toward family and less competitive, more supportive roles. For example several studies have found that among men the risk of coronary heart disease is higher for those who have worked many hours overtime or who have held two jobs simultaneously (25). Also, in a projective test, men who subsequently developed CHD were more likely to locate their stories in a "socioprofessional" setting and not in a family or recreational setting (26).

A more specific formulation of the proposed hypothesis can be derived from studies of the "Coronary Prone Behavior Pattern." A person shows the Coronary Prone Behavior Pattern if he or she is work-orientated, ambitious, aggressive, competitive, hurried, impatient and preoccupied with deadlines (27). Large prospective studies have shown that men who display this Coronary Prone Behavior Pattern are twice as likely as other men to develop or die of coronary heart disease (27,28). Smaller retrospective studies (29–31) have also established that women who have coronary heart disease are more likely to display the Coronary Prone Behavior Pattern than controls.

Behavior pattern may make a larger contribution to the risk of coronary heart disease than does sex *per se* . . . for samples of men (32) and women (31) who have clear Coronary Prone Behavior Pattern (called Type A in these studies) or clear Type B (the opposite of Type A). These data must be interpreted with caution since the samples were small and were not obtained by systematic or even strictly comparable methods. Nevertheless, it is striking that Type B men had the same low prevalence of CHD as did Type B

women. This suggests that men who adopt a less competitive and rushed style of life are just as likely to avoid CHD as comparable women. At older ages, Type A men and women had the same high prevalence of CHD. The only category in which women had substantially lower rates of CHD was the younger Type A's, but even in this age range Type A women had more CHD than Type B men.

These data suggest the hypothesis that men have more coronary heart disease than women in part because the Type A or Coronary Prone Behavior Pattern is more prevalent among men. In a large sample of employed adults women were slightly less Type A than men (Shekelle, personal communication). Housewives may be even less Type A than employed women (31) and about half of adult women are housewives (33). Aggressiveness and competitiveness are two key components of the Coronary Prone Behavior Pattern. Maccoby and Jacklin, in their review of nearly 2000 studies of sex differences in behavior (34), conclude that, on the average, males are more aggressive and competitive than females.

Why do males develop more aggressiveness and competitiveness—more of the Coronary Prone Behavior Pattern—then females? Genetic factors make some contribution to the sex differences in aggressiveness (34), but the extent of aggressiveness among males varies enormously, depending on child-rearing and cultural conditions (35). Sex differences in competitiveness are fostered by parents and schools who push boys to achieve in the occupational world and girls to seek success in the family sphere (34,36–38). Occupational achievement apparently requires competitiveness, since in our society there are seldom as many jobs (particularly rewarding, high status jobs) as there are people who want and can do them (39,40). In the family sphere, on the other hand, warmth and love are believed to be much more appropriate and aggressive competitiveness much less appropriate than in the business world (37). Evidence that cultural pressures and expectations do have a substantial influence on the development of the Coronary Prone Behavior Pattern comes from the observation that this Behavior Pattern rarely develops in the social environment of many nonindustrial societies (27,35).

Thus, a variety of evidence suggests that cultural and socioeconomic pressures related to the role of men in our society push them to develop the Coronary Prone Behavior Pattern, and that this makes a major contribution to men's higher risk of coronary heart disease. Many aspects of this hypothesis need further testing; some of this testing has been started.

Although smoking and the Coronary Prone Behavior Pattern appear to be the most important behavioral factors contributing to the sex differential in arteriosclerotic heart disease, other behavioral differences also may play a role. For example women attend church more often than men do (41) and frequent church attenders of either sex have substantially lower death rates for arteriosclerotic heart disease, at least in one Protestant community studied (42). Extrapolating the risk differential nationally leads to a prediction that men's death rates for arteriosclerotic heart disease would be 7 percent higher than women's, based on sex differences in church attendance and exclusive of related differences in smoking.

Bengtsson and co-workers (30) reach conclusions similar to ours in their study of sex differences in coronary heart disease in 50–54 year-old Swedish women and men. They conclude that men's higher rates of CHD are related to their higher rates of smoking and drinking alcohol, higher aggression and achievement scores and greater self-reported stress. These authors believe that additional factors also contribute to the observed sex differences in CHD.

Further evidence for the substantial contribution of cultural factors to the sex differential in coronary heart disease is provided by the wide cross-cultural variation in the size of this differential. In some countries the sex differential is much smaller than in the U.S. (17,43). For example, in 1960 in Greece and Hungary, arteriosclerotic heart disease mortality was only 30 percent higher for males than for females (44). The age trend of the male excess also varies widely, with a peak at premenopausal ages in the U.S. and many European countries but a peak at postmenopausal ages in Japan and Colombia (data from [44]). On the other hand, men do have higher arteriosclerotic heart disease death rates in all countries studied, and this suggests

that genetic factors also contribute to the sex differential.

Sex Hormones and CHD

Most previous discussions of the sex differential in coronary heart disease have focused primary attention on the hypothesis that this sex differential is a result of the physiological effects of the sex hormones. The evidence for this hypothesis is suggestive, but it is ambiguous and inconsistent. Castration of men apparently does not reduce deaths due to cardiovascular disease (45), and castration of older men does not seem to reduce atherosclerosis (46). The data of Gertler and White (47) suggest that androgen levels of male coronary patients do not differ from androgen levels in a control group. Thus male hormones do not appear to increase the risk of coronary heart disease.

Do female hormones lower the risk of coronary heart disease? Several studies have found that oophorectomy of young women is associated with increased atherosclerosis and CHD (43,48–51) but other studies have not found a relationship (43,52,53).

. . . .

Women who use oral contraceptives have an increased risk of death due to myocardial infarction (55,56), cerebral thrombosis, deep vein thrombosis and pulmonary embolism (57,58). High doses of estrogen given to men produce increased rates of pulmonary embolism and thrombophlebitis (70) and cerebral thrombosis (54). We did not find data on the effects of male hormones on thrombosis.

. . . .

Respiratory Diseases and Smoking

For "malignant neoplasm of the respiratory system" (primarily lung cancer), men's death rates are six times higher than women's. For "other bronchiopulmonic diseases" (primarily emphysema), men's death rates are five times higher than women's. These mortality ratios are higher than for any other major cause of death (Table 1). Men have higher mortality for these diseases primarily because men smoke more and cigarette smoking is the major cause of both lung cancer and emphysema (6,22). If men and women who have never smoked regularly are compared, the sex mortality ratios for lung cancer and emphysema are drastically reduced. These data suggest that cigarette smoking is the primary cause of men's excess lung cancer and emphysema mortality.

Comparing those who have ever smoked cigarettes to nonsmokers of the same sex, lung cancer death rates are elevated ninefold for men, but only twofold for women. Similarly, emphysema death rates are elevated sevenfold among men smokers, but only fivefold for women smokers. The elevation of death rates is less for women smokers than for men in large part because women smokers inhale less, smoke fewer cigarettes and less of each cigarette and, in the past, women have begun smoking at older ages (22,24). In addition, industrial hazards aggravate the effects of cigarette smoking for many men (as discussed below).

The total pathological effect of smoking, particularly the elevation of coronary heart disease, lung cancer and emphysema, makes a major contribution to the sex differential in total death rates. For middle-aged adults who never have smoked regularly, men's mortality exceeds women's by only 30 percent compared to a male excess of 120 percent for the total sample. For older nonsmokers, men's mortality exceeds women's by 60–70 percent, compared to 100–150 percent for the total sample. Retherford (5) (in a similar analysis which was published while this manuscript was in the final stages of preparation) estimates that as much as half of the sex differential in life expectancy from the ages of 37 to 87 may be due to the effects of higher rates of cigarette smoking in men.

Why do more men than women smoke? Smoking by women was strongly discouraged by the social mores of the early twentieth century. The conventions of that period continue to influence the smoking patterns of people who were teenagers at that time, since relatively few people begin smoking cigarettes after age 20. As a consequence, the sex differential in cigarette smoking is largest for older people who were over 60 in 1970 and who thus were teenagers before 1930 (59). Many other social and motivational factors have been shown to influence cigarette smoking (60,61). Among these, the factor which probably contributes most to the sex differential in smoking is the strong component of rebelliousness which cigarette smoking has had for many teenagers. In general, girls tend to be less rebellious and more conforming to adult standards, probably in part because parents and teachers of schoolaged children allow boys more independence and expect girls to be more obedient (34,62–64). Girls' lesser rebelliousness is probably one reason why, until very recently, fewer teenage girls than boys have begun smoking.

Although cigarette smoking is the major cause of the higher rates of lung cancer in men, industrial carcinogens also make a substantial contribution. Men who work with asbestos have up to eight times higher a risk of (bronchogenic) lung cancer than other men (65). This elevated risk affects primarily cigarette smokers. Asbestos is widely used in construction and insulation materials, and about one man in 100 is now or has been exposed to asbestos dust at his work (66). Thus, asbestos may be responsible for one in 20 male lung cancer deaths in this country. Metallic dusts and fumes elevate lung cancer risk between 20 percent and 130 percent for various categories of metal workers (67). About one man in 30 works or has worked in such an occupation (68). Thus, metallic dusts and fumes may be responsible for one in 50 male lung cancer deaths. Taken together, the established and suspected industrial carcinogens appear to be a factor in roughly one out of every 10 male lung cancer deaths (67,69).

Part II

Accidents, Alcohol and Cirrhosis

Death rates for motor vehicle accidents are almost three times higher for males than for females. This is due in part to the fact that men drive more, but the major cause appears to be that men drive less safely. Male drivers are involved in 30 percent more accidents per mile driven, and 130 percent more fatal accidents per mile driven (71). These higher accident rates are correlated with driving habits that are less safe than those of women. For example among 917 drivers observed at an intersection in a large town and another intersection in a large city, 15 percent of the male drivers entered the intersection when the light was yellow or red compared to only 10 percent of the female drivers. Among the 283 drivers making a turn, 47 percent of the males and only 20 percent of the females failed to signal the turn (Naomi Sullam and Susan Johnston, unpublished observations). It is possible that men drive more at times when roads are crowded or under other hazardous conditions and this also may contribute to their higher accident rates.

For accidents other than motor vehicle accidents, death rates for females are less than half the rates for males. About half of the male excess is due to accidents "while at work." The rate of work accidents is higher for men because more men work and because their jobs are physically more hazardous (calculated from data in 70, 72). An additional third of the male excess is due to accidental drownings and accidents caused by firearms, which are five times as common among males (70).

It is evident from these statistics that men's higher accident fatalities are a result of behaviors which are encouraged in boys and men: driving, working at sometimes hazardous jobs, using guns, being adventurous and acting unafraid. The expectation that boys and men will be more adventurous and take more risks than girls and women is conveyed by the stories children read (36–39). In addition, males are expected to be brave, not to cry, and, as a result, males are generally less able to respond to a risky situation by admitting fear and backing out (34). Because of these attitudes males are more likely to be involved in fatal auto accidents, accidental drownings, etc.

Another cause of men's higher accidental death rates is their greater consumption of alcohol (73). Half of all fatal motor vehicle accidents involve drunken drivers. Other accidents and suicide also are associated with alcohol use. Most drinking drivers responsible for a fatal accident were alcoholics or at least had serious drinking problems (74). Men are particularly likely to be heavy drinkers, four times as likely as women (75). Since excessive alcohol consumption and the malnutrition which is a concomitant are major contributors to cirrhosis of the liver (23,76), it is not surprising that men's death rates for cirrhosis of the liver are twice as high as women's.

Cross-cultural comparisons show that sex differences in alcohol consumption are influenced by cultural factors (77). In one-third of nonindustrial societies studied, both sexes consume alcohol equally. Which of the cultural factors known to influence alcohol consumption might contribute to the sex differential in drinking in this country? One factor of possible importance is suggested by cross-cultural studies which show that heavy use of alcohol is correlated with greater socialization pressures to achieve and with lower tolerance of dependent behavior (77). As discussed in Part I, males in our society are under more pressure than females to achieve in careers and to be independent. Another factor which may contribute to sex differences is suggested by prospective studies in this country which show that disobedient, dishonest, impulsive adolescents are more likely to become alcoholics (78). These characteristics may be more common and more tolerated in males. Finally, attitudes toward alcohol are a major concomitant of heavy drinking (75), and more favorable attitudes are apparently fostered in males by the generally greater acceptance of drinking among men (75, 79).

Psychoactive drugs other than alcohol make a much smaller contribution to death rates, but their pattern of use confirms our description of men taking more risks and as therefore being more likely to have fatal accidents. At the turn of the century when opiates were widely available from legal sources and relatively safe to use, two-thirds of addicts were women. Now, when opiates are illegal and generally associated with a dangerous life style, more than 80 percent of the addicts are men (80). Today, more women use the relatively safe and socially acceptable mood-altering drugs (81). For example twice as many women as men use minor tranquilizers (82), drugs which do not appear to be associated with any notable elevation in risk of death (76). When men do use prescription psychoactive drugs, they are more likely to obtain them from non-medical sources (83).

Suicide

One cause of the higher suicide rates among men is the stress of competition for jobs. The suicide rates of men are more strongly correlated with unemployment rates than are the suicide rates of women (84, 85). During the recession phase of business cycles, men's suicide rates have risen an average of 9.5 percent per year, whereas women's suicide rates have risen only 2.9 percent per year (86). In addition, some occupations seem to be associated with higher suicide rates than the housewife role. Women physicians (87) and psychologists (88) have suicide rates about three times higher than women in general and as high as the suicide rates of men in their professions.

Although three times more men than women actually commit suicide, twice as many women as men attempt suicide without killing themselves (89). Suicidal men are particularly prone to use guns, with consequences which are often irreversible and fatal, whereas women are more likely to use poisons, which can be treated by the use of stomach pumps and antidotes (90). For every method, however, there are more male than female suicides, so some additional explanation must be sought for the preponderance of male suicides and female suicide attempts. The suicide attempt has been widely interpreted as a desperate, last ditch cry for help, rather than an actual attempt to end life (91). Women apparently are better able to use a suicide attempt as a cry for help, and it seems likely that this ability to some extent protects them from the need to actually kill themselves (92). In contrast, males "see themselves as strong, powerful, dominant, 'potent' " (34) and find it difficult to seek help; thus, they are more likely to use guns rather than poisons and to carry a suicidal act through to a fatal conclusion.

Cancer

Males have higher death rates for many additional causes of death. We will not analyze each

in detail, but will, in the next three sections, present some general observations.

The sex ratios for different types of cancer vary widely (Table 1). At one extreme, malignant neoplasms of the respiratory system are six times more common among men, primarily because men smoke cigarettes more (6). At the other extreme, deaths due to malignant neoplasms of the breast are 100 times more common among women. The normal stimulatory action of estrogens on breast growth seems to extend to stimulation of the development of breast cancers; removal of the ovaries before age 35 results in a decrease of over two-thirds in breast cancer rates at older ages (93).

. . . .

While no precise estimate can be made of the contribution of sex hormones and genetic differences to the sex differential in total cancer mortality, it is nevertheless clear that hormonal and other genetic differences make little if any net contribution to men's higher total cancer mortality. Even if, as an extreme assumption, the entire excess of digestive, peritoneal and "other" cancers among males were attributed to hormonal and other genetic factors, this excess is approximately balanced by the hormonally related excess of deaths due to breast and genital cancers among females (Table 1). Thus, there would be little sex differential in total cancer mortality were it not for men's excess of respiratory system cancers, and this excess is due primarily to greater cigarette smoking among men.

Sex Chromosome-Linked Conditions

Males generally have less resistance than females to infectious disease. . . .

Various . . . genetically determined biological differences apparently make only a small contribution to the sex differential in death rates. There are more than fifty pathological conditions which occur almost exclusively in males because they are caused by X-linked recessive mutations (94). Most of these pathologies are not common and the few common ones are rarely lethal.

Deaths due to all of these conditions constitute less than 2 percent of the excess of deaths experienced by males up to the end of the reproductive years (calculated from data in 94, 70). Deaths due to "deliveries and complications of pregnancy, childbirth, and the puerperium" are also now uncommon, equivalent to less than 1 percent of the sex differential in death rates (data from 70). Sex hormones have differential effects which result in numerous other physiological differences between the sexes, such as more fat deposition in women (95) and differences in liver enzymes (96, 97). However, these physiological differences have not been shown to make any substantial contribution to higher male death rates.

Health Care

A striking paradox in the study of sex differences in health is the fact that men have higher mortality but women have higher morbidity. Specifically, women report more symptoms, visit doctors more often and more often restrict their usual activities or spend a day in bed because of illness (19, 98–101). Several authors have proposed that this seeming paradox may be resolved by the following hypothesis. Men may tend to ignore minor somatic illnesses and not seek rest or medical help unless more serious illness develops; this failure to care for their health may contribute to their higher mortality (19, 101). This tendency on the part of men may be due in part to more stoic and self-reliant attitudes and in part to the pressures men feel not to miss work since they are usually the chief bread-winners for their families (102). An examination of the more detailed evidence available provides support for some, but not all aspects of this hypothesis.

When self-reported illness is compared with evaluations based on clinical examination, both men and women omit mention of many of the conditions found clinically. Men generally underestimate their illness more than women do (103–106). However, there is little sex difference in the extent of agreement between the specific conditions found clinically and the specific conditions reported by a respondent (103, 104).

For people who report having a symptom, there is little if any consistent sex difference in the proportion who go to see a doctor (99, 100, 107, 108). Women delay as long as men before seeking medical attention after the first symptoms of cancer (109, 110) or a myocardial infarction (111–113). However, women do visit doctors more on the average, corresponding to their higher rates of reporting symptoms (98–100). Women also make more use of preventive services than men do (19, 107, 114).

Most studies find no sex differences in the proportion of patients who comply with doctor's recommendations (115).

Such sex differences in health care as are observed do not seem to originate with experiences of early childhood. Under the age of about ten, boys have more illness than girls, more days of restricted activity, and slightly more doctor visits (19, 98, 99, 114). Studies of social attitudes have revealed no significant sex differences in estimation of which types of illness justify the adoption of the sick role (116, 117).

Thus, there seems to be no sex difference in the readiness to see a doctor once symptoms are perceived or in the willingness to comply with doctor's recommendations. On the other hand, women make greater use of preventive services, perceive more symptoms and apparently as a consequence visit doctors more often, and also more frequently reduce their activity because they feel poorly. In these ways women appear to take better care of their health, and this may contribute to their lower mortality.

Recent Trends

In recent years the ratio of male to female death rates has continued the steady upward trend which began around 1920 (4, 21). However, there is some evidence which suggests that a reversal of this trend may develop in the future. For the causes of death with the greatest excess of males deaths, the ratio of male to female death rates has fallen recently over much of the adult age span. From 1958 to 1967 (the span of use for the Seventh Revision of the International List of causes of death) the ratio of male to female death rates fell for motor vehicle accidents at all ages above 5, for suicide at ages 15–84, for malignant neoplasm of the respiratory system at ages 15–65, for emphysema at ages 25–74, for other accidents and arteriosclerotic heart disease at ages 15–54, and for cirrhosis of the liver at ages 45–74 (calculated from data in 70, 118). In most of these cases, the decline in the ratio of male to female death rates was due to a rise in female death rates.

These rising female death rates reflect a trend for more and more women to include in their life style various life-endangering habits which formerly have been more common among men. Probably the most important trend is the long-term rise in women's cigarette smoking (6), since this habit alone may be responsible for over a third of the sex differential in adult mortality. Another factor contributing to the relative rise of arteriosclerotic heart disease in women may be the increased time pressures (119) and role conflicts (120) that have resulted as an increasing proportion of women have taken jobs while still carrying primary responsibility for housework and care of children (121). Additional trends are indicated by the types of accidents for which females have shown the greatest rise relative to males, namely accidents involving firearms, drowning and aircraft (calculated from data in 70, 118). Finally, there has been an increase in the proportion of women who drink (79) which undoubtedly has contributed to the increase in women's death rates for cirrhosis of the liver, motor vehicle and other accidents.

Conclusions

Male mortality exceeds female mortality by 100 percent or more for seven major causes of death: coronary heart disease, lung cancer, emphysema, motor vehicle and other accidents, cirrhosis of the liver and suicide. Together these causes of death account for three-quarters of the sex differential in mortality in the contemporary U.S.

In the preceding sections we have analyzed the causes of higher male mortality for each of these causes of death. On the basis of these analyses we have made estimates of the proportion of the total sex differential in mortality which may be attributed to each of several major proximal causes. Very roughly, we estimate that one-third

of the difference between male and female death rates may be due to men's higher cigarette smoking (with the major contribution via increased coronary heart disease, lung cancer and emphysema); one-sixth may be due to a greater prevalence of the aggressive, competitive Coronary Prone Behavior Pattern among men (with the major contribution via increased coronary heart disease); one-twelfth may be due to men's higher alcohol consumption (with the major contribution via increased accidents and cirrhosis of the liver); and one-twentieth may be due to physical hazards related to employment (with the largest contributions via increased accidents and lung cancer). Other factors which probably contribute to higher male mortality have been discussed in previous sections and some of these may make as large a contribution as one or more of the factors listed above.

. . . .

Each of the factors which we have identified as a major contributor to mens's excess mortality involves a behavior which is more socially acceptable for males than for females, for example aggressive competitiveness, working at physically hazardous jobs, drinking alcohol and, especially in the early part of the century, smoking cigarettes. The sex differential in smoking and alcohol consumption seems also to be linked to underlying attitudes, such as rebelliousness and achievement striving, which are fostered to a greater extent in males.

Similar conclusions emerge from a brief examination of the minor causes of death, each of which is responsible for less than 1 percent of total deaths and is therefore excluded from our main analysis (data from 70). Male mortality exceeds female mortality by 100 percent or more for eight of these minor causes of death. Three of these eight have well-known behavioral components related to the male role (homicide, syphilis, and ulcers). Four are elevated in cigarette smokers and appear to increase as a result of cigarette smoking (bronchitis, buccal and pharyngeal cancers, urinary tract cancers and ulcers). Taken together, these minor causes of death account for an additional 6 percent of the excess of male mortality.

We conclude that sex differences in behavior are a more important cause of higher male mortality than are any inherent sex differences in physiology. Furthermore, although these sex differences in behavior may be due in part to genetic differences, cross-cultural and developmental studies clearly show that child-rearing practices and cultural factors strongly influence behavioral differences in both children and adults (34, 122, 123).

These results point to a hopeful and exciting conclusion: substantial reductions in men's excess mortality can be achieved by cultural and behavioral changes. Many possibilities can be imagined, ranging from changes in child-rearing practices and individual behavior to changes in institutions, laws and the physical environment. We will mention only a few examples with a demonstrated potential to reduce the behaviors which contribute to men's excess mortality or to reduce the lethal effects of these behaviors. In the last few years deaths due to motor vehicle accidents have been reduced by improved safety features of cars and by reductions in speed limits (124). Behavioral modification and group support techniques have been used in programs to help cigarette smokers stop smoking. Many programs have had a high relapse rate, with only a quarter or a third of enrollees not smoking at the end of a year (125). However, long-term success rates have been doubled by several improved methodologies developed recently (125). An alternative approach has been to attempt to reduce smoking in an entire community, not just among those who come to special programs. One recent effort, using mass media and personal instruction, succeeded in reducing cigarette consumption in the community by 24 percent over a period of two years (126).

Very little information is available about attempts to change the Coronary Prone Behavior Pattern, but preliminary results indicate that a program to train Coronary Prone cardiac patients to recognize and to reduce anxiety states resulted in a significant decrease in their serum lipid levels (127). We believe that efforts to change or to avert the Coronary Prone Behavior Pattern will be more successful and beneficial if directed at teenagers and young adults, rather than at middle-aged cardiac patients whose coronary arteries already have suffered considerable irreversible damage. Many young people appear to adopt the Coronary Prone Behavior Pattern only at times when they are under pressure, especially pressure arising from competition for the limited number of highly rewarding jobs available (Waldron, Butensky, Faralli and Heebner, unpublished data). Thus, a major cause of the development of the Coronary Prone Behavior Pattern appears to be the scarcity of satisfying jobs and the large differentials in pay and intrinsic rewards for the jobs which are available. This suggests that fewer people would develop this behavior pattern if more institutions were restructured along the lines already accomplished by a variety of businesses, with substantial increases in the sharing of responsibility and profits. This type of restructuring leads to increased satisfaction for most employees and a decrease in hierarchical differentials (40). Such changes could reduce the competitive pressures which currently contribute to men's excess mortality; they could also open the way for women to obtain the benefits which more and more of them are seeking in jobs, without the excessive pressures and elevated mortality which men currently suffer.

These are but some examples of the types of social and behavioral changes which are suggested by our analysis. Many of these changes will be difficult to achieve; however the potential benefits include not only decreased mortality but also improvements in the quality of life.

NOTE

This article was written with the assistance of Susan Johnston.

Acknowledgements—We are happy to thank Joseph Eyer, Jean Gerth, Deborah Heebner, and Kimberly Schmidt for their help in finding useful materials. We are grateful to many friends and colleagues, particularly C. D. Jenkins, for their helpful comments on an earlier version of the manuscript.

REFERENCES

For references see Peter Conrad and Rochelle Kern, eds. The Sociology of Health and Illness: Critical Perspectives (New York: St. Martin's Press, 1981).

4

A Tale of Two States

Victor R. Fuchs

In the western United States there are two contiguous states that enjoy about the same levels of income and medical care and are alike in many other respects, but their levels of health differ enormously. The inhabitants of Utah are among the healthiest individuals in the United States, while the residents of Nevada are at opposite end of the spectrum. Comparing death rates of white residents in the two states, for example, we find that infant mortality is about 40 percent higher in Nevada. And lest the reader think that the higher rate in Nevada is attributable to the "sinful" atmosphere of Reno and Las Vegas, we should note that infant mortality in the rest of the state is almost exactly the same as it is in these two cities. Rather, . . . infant death rates depend critically upon the physical and emotional condition of the mother.

The excess mortality in Nevada drops appreciably for children because, as shall be argued below, differences in life-style account for differences in death rates, and these do not fully emerge until the adult years. As the following figures indicate, the differential for adult men and women is in the range of 40 to 50 percent until old age, at which point the differential naturally decreases.

The two states are very much alike with respect to income, schooling, degree of urbanization, climate, and many other variables that are frequently thought to be the cause of variations in mortality. (In fact, average family income is actually higher in Nevada than in Utah.) The numbers of physicians and of hospital beds per capita are also similar in the two states.

What, then, explains these huge differences in death rates? The answer almost surely lies in the different life-styles of the residents of the two states. Utah is inhabited primarily by Mormons, whose influence is strong throughout the state. Devout Mormons do not use tobacco or alcohol and in general lead stable, quiet lives. Nevada, on the other hand, is a state with high rates of cigarette and alcohol consumption and very high indexes of marital and geographical instability. The contrast with Utah in these respects is extraordinary.

In 1970, 63 percent of Utah's residents 20 years of age and over had been born in the state; in Nevada the comparable figure was only 10 percent; for persons 35–64 the figures were 64 percent in Utah and 8 percent in Nevada. Not only were more than nine out of ten Nevadans of middle age born elsewhere, but more than 60 percent were not even born in the West.

The contrast in stability is also evident in the response to the 1970 census question about changes in residence. In Nevada only 36 percent of persons 5 years of age and over were then living in the same residence as they had been in 1965; in Utah the comparable figure was 54 percent.

The differences in marital status between the two states are also significant in view of the association between marital status and mortality discussed in the previous section. More than 20 percent of Nevada's males aged 35–64 are single, widowed, divorced, or not living with their spouses. Of those who are married with spouse present, more than one-third had been previously widowed or divorced. In Utah the comparable figures are only half as large.

Table 1.   **Excess of Death Rates in Nevada Compared with Utah, Average for 1959–61 and 1966–68**

Age group	Males	Females
< 1	42%	35%
1–19	16%	26%
20–29	44%	42%
30–39	37%	42%
40–49	54%	69%
50–59	38%	28%
60–69	26%	17%
70–79	20%	6%

The impact of alcohol and tobacco can be readily seen in the following comparison of death rates from cirrhosis of the liver and malignant neoplasms of the respiratory system. For both sexes the excess of death rates from these causes in Nevada is very large.

The populations of these two states are, to a considerable extent, self-selected extremes from the continuum of life-styles found in the United States. Nevadans, as has been shown, are predominantly recent immigrants from other areas, many of whom were attracted by the state's permissive mores. The inhabitants of Utah, on the other hand, are evidently willing to remain in a more restricted society. Persons born in Utah who do not find these restrictions acceptable tend to move out of the state.

Summary

This dramatic illustration of large health differentials that are unrelated to income or availability of medical care helps to highlight the [following] themes . . .

1. From the middle of the eighteenth century to the middle of the twentieth century rising incomes resulted in unprecedented improvements in health in the United States and other developing countries.
2. During most of this period medical care (as distinct from public health measures) played an insignificant role in health, but, beginning in the mid-1930s, major therapeutic discoveries made significant contributions independently of the rise in real income.

Table 2.   **Excess of Death Rates in Nevada Compared with Utah for Cirrhosis of the Liver and Malignant Neoplasms of the Respiratory System, Average for 1966–68**

Age	Males	Females
30–39	590%	443%
40–49	111%	296%
50–59	206%	205%
60–69	117%	227%

3. As a result of the changing nature of health problems, rising income is no longer significantly associated with better health, except in the case of infant mortality (primarily post-neonatal mortality)—and even here the relationship is weaker than it used to be.
4. As a result of the wide diffusion of effective medical care, its marginal contribution to health is again small (over the observed range of variation). There is no reason to believe that the major health problems of the average American would be significantly alleviated by increases in the number of hospitals or physicians. This conclusion might be altered, however, as the result of new scientific discoveries. Alternatively, the *marginal* contribution of medical care might become even smaller as a result of such advances.
5. The greatest current potential for improving the health of the American people is to be found in what they do and don't do to and for themselves. Individual decisions about diet, exercise, and smoking are of critical importance, and collective decisions affecting pollution and other aspects of the environment are also relevant.

These conclusions notwithstanding, the demand for medical care is very great and growing rapidly. As René Dubos has acutely observed, "To ward off disease or recover health, men as a rule find it easier to depend on the healers than to attempt the more difficult task of living wisely."[1]

NOTE

1. René Dubos, *The Mirage of Health* (New York: Harper, 1959), p. 110.

Our Sickening Social and Physical Environments

The past decade has seen an increasing public awareness and concern about health dangers in the social and physical environments in which we live and work. (See for example, Tesh, 1981; Chavkin, 1984; Health and Medicine Policy Research Group, 1983/84; Coye, 1984.) Workers' struggles for occupational health and safety have resulted in changes not only in the physical and social organization of work, but in popular and scientific ideas about the nature and effect of work on ill health. A growing number of communities, including Love Canal and Three Mile Island, have had to face the physical and psychological consequences—sometimes occurring decades after initial exposure—of toxic and radioactive industrial wastes that have been "dumped" into water, land, and air supplies. Often, victims of such "human-made disasters" have become embroiled in prolonged legal and political conflicts over claims for medical and economic assistance (Kliman, Kern, and Kliman, 1982).

There is also growing evidence that the stresses and demands of our "social environments"—both at work and at home—are also factors in disease production (e.g., situations that make us anxious, angry, or frustrated) (Stellman and Daum, 1973; Page and O'Brien, 1973; Chavkin, 1984). Stress has been found to be a contributing factor in the development of a number of chronic diseases, including coronary heart disease, hypertension and cancer; a number of acute diseases, for example, infections; and a range of psychological disorders, for example, mild and major depression, onset of psychotic episodes (Dohrenwend and Dohrenwend, 1981).

Today's major diseases are often slow-developing, chronic, and incurable disorders. This section explores the relation of chronic diseases to the social and physical environments in which they develop.

In the previous section we began exploring the relationship between society and the distribution of disease and death. We saw that in American society diseases are patterned by socio-cultural factors, including social class, gender, and life style. Here we continue to search for an understanding of the interface between diseases and society by examining the sociological contexts of three serious health disorders in the United States today: coronary heart disease, black lung disease, and hypertension (high blood pressure).

Social scientists have little difficulty analyzing the social nature of such problems as homicide, suicide, and automobile accidents. Only rarely, however, have they applied sociological perspectives to understanding the causes and prevention of diseases such as cancer or hypertension. The articles in this section share the theme that at least some of these chronic diseases have developed as a result of modern industrialization, and so are deeply connected to the organization and characteristics of social life.

According to the U.S. Department of Health and Human Services, approximately 47 percent of all deaths in 1980 were caused by diseases of the heart and circulatory system (coronary heart disease, hypertension, and stroke), and an additional 21 percent of deaths in 1980 were the result of some form of cancer (National Center for Health Statistics, 1983). These data give us a general picture of the significant impact of chronic disease on our population's health. Chronic diseases generally develop and persist over a long period of time. Their signs often go unnoticed or unidentified until serious damage is done to the victim's body, and they usually have complex rather than simple or single causes. Medical treatment generally aims to alleviate symptoms, prevent or slow down further organic damage, or minimize physical discomfort, primarily through treatments with medications or surgery. Treatment rather than prevention is the dominant medical approach to these diseases.

Although *prevention* of chronic diseases would seem to be the most logical, safe, and perhaps the most moral approach, few financial resources have been devoted in the United States to the elimination of the physical and social causes of chronic health disorders. (To the contrary, the federal government continues to subsidize the tobacco industry in the United States despite the Surgeon General's warnings that cigarette smoking is the leading cause of death from lung cancer.) The growing recognition of the environmental component in many chronic diseases has led some critics to question the priorities of our current medical care system, as well as the limits of its approach to the treatment, let alone prevention, of these disorders.

For example, Samuel Epstein has argued that the "epidemic" of cancer in the United States is both a medical and social issue, involving as it does a range of political and economic factors, including the use of chemicals in manufacturing to increase profits, the economic and political pressures on industry scientists, and the relatively low priority given to cancer prevention research (Epstein, 1976 and 1979). If many cancers are environmentally produced—and the federal government has estimated that as many as 90 percent may be so—why has medical research and treatment focused on cure rather than prevention?

In "Black Lung: The Social Production of Disease,"[4] Barbara Ellen Smith describes the controversy that has surrounded the identification of black lung disease as an occupational health hazard among coal miners. Like victims of environmental dumping, workers in sickening occupational environments are frequently faced with political and legal resistance to their claims for medical or economic assistance. The resulting "politicization" of health hazards and illness often has drawn physicians into struggles in which their "expert" testimony has been used by industry and government to deny the legitimacy of victims' claims about unsafe living or working conditions. By examining the emergence of black lung disease historically, Smith argues that "scientific" knowledge about the disease, as well as governmental and industrial policies for protecting and compensating workers are all products of social and economic changes.

The second article in this section is "Occupational Stress and Coronary Heart Disease: A Review and Theoretical Integration," by James S. House. It examines the relationship between occupational stress and coronary heart disease. The development of many chronic disorders, including heart disease, seems to be related to both biophysiological and psycho-social processes. Increasingly there is evidence that the distinction between "physical" and "mental" health may not be helpful because it masks the important social and interactional components of disease by isolating physical health from its social components. However, many people get sick because they are physically *and* emotionally stressed, and House reviews the literature on the impact of stress caused by work. He points out the severe limitations in the research and data available in this area. For example, certain groups of people, particularly women and working class people of both sexes, have been overlooked in the research which has examined the impact of work on health. Some studies make the mistake of examining small populations, such as executive level, white men, and generalizing their findings to all populations. House's article suggests the importance of studying stress directly and in all populations in order to learn more about the relationship among stress, work, and health. What we do know, he argues, is that there is considerable evidence that stress contributes to the cause of coronary heart disease and probably to other chronic diseases as well. It is important, therefore, that we unravel the complexities of physical and social variables in order to understand better the impact of stress on health.

These issues are placed within a broader conceptual framework in the article by Peter L. Schnall and Rochelle Kern entitled "Hypertension in American Society: An Introduction to Historical Materialist Epidemiology." In considering the particular problem of hypertension, the authors present the concept of "historical materialist epidemiology" (HME): HME, as one approach to social epidemiology, is " . . . the study of disease as it spreads and involves large groups of people within the context of the social organization of any particular society" (Gaynor et al., 1976:ME/1). HME differs from standard social epidemiology in that it focuses on the disease producing consequences of the social and economic organization of society—an organization which changes historically and differs from society to society—rather than demographic variables. Schnall and Kern expand on this view and use it to examine the problem of hypertension as well as the way that disease has been conceptualized, studied, and treated by medicine. HME provides one approach to integrating an understanding of society with our knowledge of disease, and in so doing makes an important contribution to the critical perspective encouraged throughout this book.

REFERENCES

Chavkin, Wendy, ed. 1984. Double Exposure, Women's Health Hazards on the Job and at Home. New York: Monthly Review Press.
Coye, Molly Joel, Mark Douglas Smith, and Anthony Mazzochi. 1984. "Occupational health and safety." In Victor W. Sidel and Ruth Sidel, Reforming Medicine, Lessons of the Last Quarter Century. New York: Pantheon.

Dohrenwend, Barbara S., and Bruce P. Dohrenwend, eds. 1981. Stressful Life Events and Their Contexts. New York, Prodist.

Epstein, Samuel. 1976. "The political and economic basis of cancer." Technology Review, July/August. See also, Samuel Epstein. 1979. The Politics of Cancer. New York: Anchor/Doubleday.

Gaynor, David, Joseph Eyer, and Howard Berliner. 1976. "Materialist epidemiology." Health Marxist Organization (HMO) Packet #1. (Unpublished paper available from Health/PAC, 17 Murray St., New York, NY 10007).

Health and Medicine Policy Research Group. 1983/84. Health and Medicine. Vol. 2, No. 2, Winter.

Kliman, Jodie, Rochelle Kern, and Ann Kliman. 1982. "Natural and human-made disasters: Some therapeutic and epidemiological implications for crisis intervention." In Uri Rueveni, Ross V. Speck, and Joan L. Speck (eds.). Therapeutic Intervention, Healing Strategies for Human Systems. New York: Human Sciences Press.

National Center for Health Statistics. 1983. Health, United States, 1983. DHHS Publication No. (PHS) 84-1232. U.S. Government Printing Office (December).

Page, Joseph, and M. O'Brien. 1973. Bitter Wages. New York: Grossman.

Stellman, Jeanne M., and Susan M. Daum. 1973. Work Is Dangerous to Your Health. New York: Random House.

Tesh, Sylvia. 1981. "Disease causality and politics." Journal of Health Politics, Policy and Law. 6:369–389.

5

Black Lung: The Social Production of Disease

Barbara Ellen Smith

The recognition that certain forms of ill health are socially produced and therefore possibly preventable is one of the most important sources of progressive political vitality in the United States today. During the past decade, sporadic protest has erupted over hazardous situations in isolated workplaces and communities, from the controversy over toxic waste disposal in the Love Canal area to the protest against use of dioxin-contaminated herbicides in the Pacific Northwest. In some instances, more prolonged and widespread struggles have developed, such as the movement for black lung compensation and the

current mobilization against nuclear power. These phenomena are admittedly quite diverse in their social bases, ideologies, and political goals. However, to varying degrees, all have involved the politicization of health hazards and illness, and thereby have drawn into the arena of political controversy one of the most elite professional domains in the United States—scientific medicine.

These controversies characteristically have originated in the bitter suspicions of lay people who fear that certain of their health problems are caused by industrial practices and products, but who have no scientifically credible proof to substantiate their concern. In some cases, scientists have scornfully dismissed as "housewife data" lay efforts to document these health problems (1). Indeed, health advocates' demands for compensatory or preventive action have often encountered their most formidable ideological opposition from the ranks of the medical establishment, who come armed with the seemingly unassailable authority of "science" and characteristically argue that no action is justified until further evidence is collected. Especially in contexts like that of the petrochemical industry, where workers and sometimes residential communities are exposed to manifold hazards about which little is known and whose effects may not be manifested for decades, health advocates can be forced into a no-win situation: they must prove their case with data that do not exist, using a model of disease causation that is ill suited to multiple and/or synergistic hazards, and which a growing chorus of critics argue is structurally incapable of explaining the major health problems of our place and time, such as heart disease and stress (2).

This article examines one health struggle, the black lung movement, during which the scientific authority of the medical establishment was itself questioned in the course of an intense political controversy over the definition of disease. The movement arose in southern West Virginia in 1968 and had as its initial goal the extension of workers' compensation coverage to victims of "black lung," a generic term for the ensemble of respiratory diseases that miners contract in the workplace. To elucidate the medical politics of this struggle, this article looks at three aspects of the history of black lung. The first section explores the major changes in medical perceptions of black lung and presents evidence suggesting that these shifting perceptions have been occasioned by social and economic factors ordinarily considered extrinsic to science. This section also points out the ideological and political functions of the medical definitions of this disease. The second part focuses on the history of black lung itself and argues that the respiratory disease burden is intimately related to the political economy of the workplace, the site of disease production. The final section describes the recent

battle over black lung compensation, focusing on the strikingly different definitions of disease that miners and the medical establishment elaborated.

Medical Constructions of Black Lung

The history of science is popularly conceived as a continuum of concepts and paradigms evolving through time toward an ever more comprehensive and accurate understanding of a "given" external reality. However, there is a growing tradition of literature that challenges this positivist approach by classifying the scientific knowledge of any society as part of its historically specific belief systems, and viewing scientific concepts as both a consequence of and an influence upon the overall structure of social relations. Efforts to pursue this approach with regard to medical science have been especially fruitful and abundant. Scholarship has focused primarily on the ways in which medical practice has tended to reflect and uphold socially structured inequality (especially that based on class, sex, and race). Some analysts have also begun to investigate the exceedingly complex correspondence between the structures, forces, and dynamics that medical knowledge invests in the human body and the dynamics of social relations in the "body politic."(3)

The case of black lung provides an exceptionally clear example of the ways in which factors external to science have shaped and changed medical knowledge. In the United States, medical perceptions of black lung fall into three periods, bounded by major shifts in the political economy of the coal industry. Observations of miners' unusual respiratory disease burden and speculation as to its workplace origins characterized the first medical construction of black lung. This viewpoint originated in the anthracite coalfields of Pennsylvania during a period when medical knowledge and practice, health care delivery arrangements, and industrial relations between miners and operators were all in a state of flux. A completely different concept of black lung emerged in a later period from the expanding bituminous coalfields, where tight corporate control over the health care system, a stark class structure, and other factors were relevant to the medical outlook. A third concept of black lung developed gradually after World War II in the context of a highly unionized, increasingly capital-intensive industry with a union-controlled health plan for miners and their families.

The first written documents concerning miners' unusual respiratory trouble originated from the anthracite region of eastern Pennsylvania; here was located the first large-scale coal mining operations in the United States, dominated by the affiliates of nine railroads. During the 1860s and 1870s, a few physicians acquainted with this region began to publish articles remarking on miners' respiratory difficulties and speculating that they were related to the inhalation of dusts and gases in the workplace. These articles are remarkable for their detailed accounts of unhealthy working conditions and their inclusion of statements by miners themselves on their workplace health (4).

This period prior to the hegemony of scientific medicine was characterized by a relative eclecticism and fluidity in medical knowledge, practice, and health care delivery arrangements. Some medical historians argue that the uncertain financial, professional, and social status of physicians lent more equality and negotiability to the doctor-patient relationship than is customary today (5). In the anthracite coalfields, miners were beginning to finance their health and welfare needs through mutual benefit associations that gave financial assistance in cases of sickness, disability and death (6). This brief period of relative fluidity in the health care system was soon eclipsed, however, by the simultaneous eradication of the benefit associations and the growth of the company doctor system. The most significant episode in this process was the strike of 1874–1875, which led to the famous Molly Maguire murder trials and resulted in the disintegration of the major anthracite trade union, the Miners' and Laborers' Benevolent Association. The powerful Philadelphia and Reading Railroad, whose affiliate Coal and Iron Company was the largest anthracite coal producer, subsequently attempted to replace the union's health and welfare functions with a Beneficial Fund financed by miners and controlled by the company. During the last two decades of the nineteenth century, as mining corporations gradually extended their control over health care delivery through the company doctor system, physicians in the anthracite fields grew silent on the subject of miners' occupational lung disease. The anthracite industry subsequently entered a period of decline from which it never recovered; the center of U.S. coal production shifted to the bituminous fields, where physicians elaborated a completely different concept of black lung.

The bituminous industry of southern Appalachia achieved national economic importance around the turn of the century and by the end of World War I was rapidly becoming the heart of U.S. coal production. In the coal camps of this rural and mountainous region, physicians did not simply ignore the existence of black lung, as many have suggested; rather, they viewed miners' diseased state as normal and nondisabling, and therefore unworthy of scientific investigation. The sources of this perception may be found partly in the political economy of the coal industry, which left a peculiarly repressive stamp on the structure of health care delivery in Appalachia (7).

In the southern bituminous industry, coal operators initially assumed a direct role in establishing, maintaining, and controlling many social and political institutions, such as the public schools, churches, and the police. Their activities derived in part from practical necessity: companies often had to import much of their labor force into this sparsely populated area, and in order to keep these workers had to provide housing, food, and a minimum of public services. However, the operators' role was neither benign nor merely practical. The profits to be made from housing, food, and to a lesser extent medical care were often quite significant to companies attempting to survive in the highly competitive, unstable business environment of bituminous coal. Moreover, totalitarian control of coal communities, including issuance of a separate currency (scrip), domination of the police, and even control of the physical access to the towns, enabled these companies to forestall what they perceived as one of the most pernicious threats to their economic status—unionization.

Health care did not escape the logic of this competitive environment and direct domination of the work force. The company doctor was the only source of medical care in almost all rural Appalachian coal camps. Under this system, the coal company controlled the employment of a doctor, but miners were required as a condition of employment to pay for his services. The company doctors' accountability to the coal operators is one of the most obvious and fundamental reasons for the medical concepts of miners' occupational health developed during this period. Work-related accidents and later diseases spelled economic liability for the coal operators under the workers' compensation system. Any agitation for preventive action would have represented an even greater nuisance. There was instead a uniform tendency to ascribe accidents and diseases to the fault of the miner—his carelessness and personal habits, such as alcoholism. Thus, one physician in 1919, after reciting a litany of occupational safety and health hazards, including dust, gob piles, electricity, poisonous gases, and contaminated water supplies, managed to conclude: "Housing conditions, and hurtful forms of recreation, especially alcoholism, undoubtedly cause the major amount of sickness. The mine itself is not an unhealthful place to work." (8)

The medical ideology surrounding black lung was more complex than this outright denial of occupational causation. Physicians dubbed the widespread breathlessness, expectoration of sputum, and prolonged coughing fits "miners' asthma." These symptoms of lung disease were *constituted as a norm;* as such, they were to be expected and by definition were nondisabling. For example, in 1935, one physician in Pennsylvania wrote (9):

> As far as most of the men in this region are concerned, so called "miners' asthma" is considered an *ordinary* condition that needs cause no worry and therefore the profession has not troubled itself about its finer pathological and associated clinical manifestations (emphasis added).

A miner who complained of disability due to respiratory trouble was diagnosed as a case of "malingering," "compensationitis," or "fear of the mines." The social control aspects of this ideology are obvious: if disease was natural, inevitable, and nondisabling, then prevention

was unnecessary. Moreover, exhibiting disability from a respiratory disease was a medically stigmatized sign of psychological weakness or duplicity (10).

Although the company doctor system provides one explanation for this medical concept, it may also be related to class interactions in the coalfields and to some of the basic precepts of scientific medicine. It may be speculated that the company doctor's social as well as medical perspective on the coal miner and his family was influenced by the relative status of each within the coal camp environment (11). The mono-economy of the Appalachian coalfields produced a rather simple and vivid class structure, in which physicians, lawyers, and a few other professionals formed an island in a working-class sea. On the one hand, the superiority of the doctors' status relative to the working class was everywhere apparent in their standard of living, language, etc. On the other hand, these physicians were in a distinctly inferior position by the standards of the medical profession as a whole, and moreover were denied numerous amenities available in more cosmopolitan surroundings. Their degraded social and physical environment was embodied in and no doubt in many cases attributed to coal miners themselves—their ramshackle houses, coarse language, "lack of culture," and so on. What was "normal" for miners, including even a chronic respiratory condition, was by no means normal for the company doctor (12).

The outlook of scientific medicine, which around the turn of the century was gaining hegemony over other forms of medical theory and practice, is also relevant to the company doctors' conceptualization of black lung. With the rise of scientific medicine, production of medical knowledge gradually became the province of research scientists, divorced from the human patient by their location in the laboratory. Building on the precepts of cell theory and the discovery of bacteria, their efforts focused on the isolation of specific aberrations in cell function, and their correlation with discrete disease agents. The "germ theory" of disease causation, which essentially holds that each disease is caused by a specific bacterium or agent, became the basis of scientific medicine. This theory confounded the microscopic *agent* of disease with the *cause* of disease; it thus implicitly denied a role to social and economic factors in disease causation and displaced the social medicine of an earlier period.

At the level of medical practice, diagnosis became a process of identifying separate disease entities, with confirmation of the diagnosis sought in the laboratory; the patient's own testimony as to his/her condition was relegated to a decidedly secondary status. Indeed, scientific medicine involved what Jewson (5) termed the "disappearance of the sick-man" from the medical world view. The patient increasingly appeared almost incidentally as the medium for disease, eclipsed by the focus on identifying discrete pathologies. In the absence of a verifiable clinical entity, the patient was by definition (health is the absence of disease) pronounced healthy. His/her protestations of feeling ill became a matter for the psychiatrist (13).

These features of the scientific medical outlook dovetailed with previously mentioned factors to produce the company doctors' conceptualization of black lung. To the extent that any company doctor seriously attempted to diagnose a miner's respiratory condition, the effort was informed by the search for previously established clinical entities, especially silicosis and tuberculosis. Up until very recently, silica was considered the only dust seriously harmful to the respiratory system. Moreover, silicosis possesses characteristics that scientific medicine is most conducive to recognizing as a legitimate clinical entity: it is associated with one specific agent; it produces gross pathological change in lung tissue, apparent upon autopsy; and it reveals itself relatively clearly in a characteristic pattern on an X-ray. Most coal miners were not exposed to silica in significant quantity, and their X-rays did not exhibit the classic silicotic pattern. To the extent that their X-rays revealed the pathological changes now associated with coal workers' pneumoconiosis, these too were considered normal—for coal miners (14). Moreover, as a group, miners seemed to experience a low mortality rate from tuberculosis, considered the prime public health problem of this period. Hence developed the perversely ironic "coal dust is good for you" theory: "It is in the highest degree possible that

coal-dust possesses the property of hindering the development of tuberculosis, and of arresting its progress." (15)

The company doctor system did not go unchallenged by coalminers; unrest over its compulsory character occasionally led to strikes and generated the demand for a health care plan organized on the opposite basis—union control and industry financing. Following a protracted strike and federalization of the mines in 1946, miners finally won a contract establishing such a system, the Welfare and Retirement Fund. Financed by a royalty assessed on each ton of mined coal, the Fund provided pensions, hospitalization, and medical care for miners and their families. Although officially directed by a tripartite board composed of representatives from industry, the union, and the public, in reality the Fund was controlled by the United Mine Workers. At the time of its creation, progressives in the health care field almost unanimously viewed the Fund as an innovative leap forward in health care delivery. Contradictions embedded in coal's postwar industrial relations subsequently compromised this vision and constricted the Fund's activities. Nevertheless, in its first decade and heyday, the Fund transformed the structure and quality of health care in the Appalachian coalfields (16).

The establishment of the Fund made possible the beginning of a third period in the medical conceptualization of miners' respiratory disease. Progressive physicians, many organized in prepaid group practice financed through the Fund, undertook clinical research on the respiratory problems of their coal miner patients. The Fund also employed in its central office a physician whose primary responsibility was to educate the medical profession about coal miners' dust disease. These physicians were largely responsible for the trickle of literature on coal workers' pneumoconiosis that began to appear in U.S. medical journals during the early 1950s; of the articles they did not write, most depended on data from Fund-affiliated hospitals and clinics. All argued essentially that "authoritative opinion to the contrary notwithstanding," coal miners suffer from a "disabling, progressive, killing disease which is related to exposure to coal dust." (17)

Despite these efforts, medical recognition of

coal workers' pneumoconiosis did not evolve in an orderly, linear fashion, advanced by the inquiring gaze of these scientists. They remained a minority within the medical establishment, and coal miners in most states continued to be denied workers' compensation for occupational lung disease. The recognition that black lung was rampant among U.S. coal miners did not evolve of its own accord within the boundaries of medical science. It was forced on the medical community by the decidedly political intervention of miners themselves.

Black Lung and the Transformation of the Workplace

Since the changing medical concepts of black lung reveal more about the development of the coal industry and health care delivery systems than the nature and extent of respiratory disease among coal miners, observers may well wonder what the history of black lung actually entails. It is extremely difficult to reconstruct satisfactorily. Epidemiological data on miners' lung disease are simply nonexistent, except for the very recent period. The early commentaries cited previously suggest that pervasive respiratory problems accompanied the growth of the anthracite and bituminous coal industries, a conclusion corroborated by nonmedical sources (18); however, acceptance of "miners' asthma" and a dearth of medical literature swiftly followed. Between 1918 and 1940, a few scattered studies, primarily by the U.S. Public Health Service, uncovered "extraordinary" excess mortality from influenza and pneumonia among anthracite and bituminous coal miners; their susceptibility was likely due to the work-related destruction of their respiratory systems. However, all U.S. Public Health Service research on miners' occupational respiratory disease focused on silicosis; the resulting data were mixed, but the invariable conclusion was that bituminous miners were not exposed to silica in significant quantity and were not seriously disabled by work-related lung disease (19).

Although the lack of statistics precludes documentation of the extent of black lung, it is possible to trace the changing causes of disease by analyzing the site of disease production—the workplace. By "workplace" is meant not only the physical characteristics of the site of coal production but also the social relations that shape and are part of the workplace. The interaction between miners and operators under historically given circumstances has shaped the timing and character of technological innovation, the nature of the work process, the pace of work, and other factors relevant to the production of occupational disease. The history of black lung is thus internally related to the history of the workplace, as a physical site and a social relationship.

This history may be divided into two major periods, distinguished by their different technologies, work organizations, industrial relations, and sources of respiratory disease: handloading and mechanized mining. During the initial handloading era, which persisted until the 1930s, of utmost importance to the production of coal and disease was the highly competitive and labor-intensive character of the industry. Fragmented into thousands of competing companies, bituminous coal suffered from chronic bouts of overproduction, excess capacity, low profit margins, and fluctuating prices. Because labor represented approximately 70 percent of the cost of production, a prime tactic in the competitive struggle was to cut the cost of labor, principally by lowering the piece rate. In addition, the craft nature of the labor process rendered companies relatively powerless to control productivity and output, except by manipulating the miners' wages (20).

These economic dynamics had important implications for the workplace as a site of disease production. The instability of the industry frequently resulted in irregular work and a lowering of the piece rate, both of which forced miners to work faster and/or longer hours in an attempt to maintain their standard of living. The impact on health and safety conditions was almost invariably negative, as miners necessarily reduced nonproductive, safety-oriented tasks, such as roof timbering, to a minimum (21). Working longer hours in mines where "towards quitting time [the air] becomes so foul that the miners' lamps will no longer burn" (22) no doubt increased the respiratory disease risk. Moreover, a financially mandated speedup encouraged miners to re-enter their work areas as soon as possible after blasting the coal loose from the face, an operation that generated clouds of dust and powder smoke (23).

Respiratory hazards often were especially grave in non-gassy mines, where ventilation tended to be poorest. The prospect of losing their entire capital investment in one explosion encouraged mine owners to install better ventilation systems in mines where methane gas was liberated; the non-gassy mines, however, tended to "kill the men by inches." (4, p. 244) Writing around the turn of the century, one mine inspector described in detail the ventilation problem and its implications for miners' health (22, pp. 449–450):

> ... adequate ventilation is not applied in such [non-gassy] mines, because they can be wrought without going to the expense of providing costly and elaborate furnaces or fans, air-courses, stoppings, and brattice. From four to six cents a ton are thus saved in mining the coal that should be applied in ventilating, but saved at the expense of the workmen's health. . . . Constant labor in a badly-aired mine breaks down the constitution and clouds the intellect. The lungs become clogged up from inhaling coal dust, and from breathing noxious air; the body and limbs become stiff and sore, the mind loses the power of vigorous thought. After six years' labor in a badly ventilated mine—that is, a mine where a man with a good constitution may from habit be able to work every day for several years—the lungs begin to change to a bluish color. After twelve years they are black, and after twenty years they are densely black, not a vestige of natural color remaining, and are little better than carbon itself. The miner dies at thirty-five of coal-miners' consumption.

During the 1930s, the introduction of mechanical loading equipment dramatically altered the workplace, while the organizing successes of the United Mine Workers transformed relations between miners and operators. Although mechanical cutting devices were introduced into underground coal mines as early as 1876, their adoption was gradual and associated with only a partial reorganization of the craft work process. The classic changes produced by mechanization and Taylorization, such as elevated productivity, loss of job control, de-skilling, and an increased division of labor, appeared slowly in bituminous coal during the first three decades of the twentieth century. However, the widespread introduction of loading machines in the 1930s broke the craft organization of work once and for all. More technological innovation swiftly followed, with the introduction of continuous mining technology after World War II. This technology did not increase the already specialized division of labor as much as it replaced several tasks (and miners) with one central production worker—the continuous miner operator.

Virtually all sources agree that the mechanization of underground mining greatly increased dust levels and magnified the existing problems with respiratory disease (24). Miners were quick to rename the Joy loaders "man killers" and to protest the unemployment, physical hardships placed on older miners, and health and safety problems that attended their introduction. For example, at the 1934 UMWA convention, miners debated at length a resolution demanding the removal of these machines from the mines; the few delegates who spoke against it were nearly shouted down by the tumultuous convention. One miner argued (25, p. 192):

> I heard one of the brothers say that they don't hire miners over forty years of age in their locality. I want to tell you brothers that there is no miner that can work in the mines under those conveyors [loading machines] and reach the age of forty. Those conveyors are man killers and I believe this convention should do its utmost to find some way whereby those conveyors will be abolished. . . . The young men after they work in the mine six or eight hours daily become sick, either getting asthma or some other sickness due to the dust of the conveyors and they can no longer perform their duty.

Another miner, during debate over continuous mining machinery at a UMWA convention 22 years later, echoed those comments (26):

> . . . [T]hey are putting coal moles [continuous miners] in our mines, and I hope they don't put them in anybody else's mines. We had one man die from the effects of that procedure. We had to give them a 15-minute shift. We have had any number who have had to get off because of health. It seems that someone forgot the miners who have [to operate] the moles. . . . He stands up there and inhales the fumes and the oil and the steam that is

created by the heat from the mole. He doesn't get sufficient oxygen. . . .

It would be mistaken to conclude that because mechanization was associated with increased dust levels, machines themselves were the cause of this problem. Here again, the economic and political circumstances of technological innovation were critical in determining its impact on the workplace. The large coal operators introduced continuous mining technology in the midst of a desperate competitive struggle with oil and natural gas, which by the 1950s had usurped coal's traditional markets in home heating and the railroads. By making coal a capital-intensive industry and vastly increasing labor productivity, the large operators hoped to force the small, labor-intensive producers into bankruptcy and win a respectable share of the growing utility market. Of crucial importance to the pace, nature, and success of this mechanization strategy was the role of the union. Headed by the authoritarian but charismatic John L. Lewis, the United Mine Workers not only accepted but aggressively promoted mechanization, believing that it would lead to institutional security, high wages, and economic prosperity (27). Although there was widespread rank-and-file discontent with mechanization, the very process replaced labor with machinery, rendering miners redundant and their protest ineffective. Despite scattered strikes and other expressions of unrest, miners were unable to modify the policy of their union or exert significant control over the impacts of mechanization on their workplace and communities.

The result was not simply increased respirable dust in the workplace, but social and economic disaster in the coalfields. In the space of 20 years, between 1950 and 1969, the work force shrank by 70 percent. For the unemployed, the monoeconomy of the Appalachian coalfields left no alternative but migration. Coal-dependent communities became ghost towns, as some counties lost half their population in the space of 10 years. Those who managed to keep their jobs in large mines confronted increased dust, noise, high-voltage electricity, and other hazards. Supervision intensified, as the operators attempted to recoup their investments in machinery by pushing productivity higher and higher (28).

The black lung controversy that erupted in 1968 was very much a product of and a challenge to this history. The movement represented an effort by miners and their families to reclaim the political and economic potency denied them for almost 20 years. Black lung disease in a sense became a metaphor for the exploitative social relations that had always characterized the coalfields, but worsened during two decades of high unemployment, social dislocation, and rank-and-file weakness vis-à-vis the coal industry. The goal of black lung compensation represented, in part, a demand for retribution from the industry for the devastating human effects of its economic transformation.

The Battle is Joined

By 1968, when the black lung movement arose, the union's overt cooperation with the large operators had outworn its usefulness to the industry and outlived its tolerability for the rank and file. The major producers had thoroughly mechanized their mines, reduced intraindustry competition from small companies, and held their own against external competition from alternative fuels. Capital was flowing into the industry not only through the enormously increased productivity of its workers, which tripled between 1950 and 1969, but also in the form of investment by the oil industry. Electric utilities seemed to offer unlimited market potential. Threatening the rosy forecasts, however, were an increasingly rambunctious work force and a projected manpower shortage. An enormous turnover was beginning in the work force, as the miners who managed to keep their jobs during postwar mechanization were now retiring en masse, replaced by young workers with no necessary allegiance to the UMWA leadership. The economic prosperity rankled workers already beginning to question the sluggish collective bargaining advances of their union leaders and made strikes a more potent weapon (29).

The first unmistakable evidence that rank-and-file rebellion was afoot erupted in the winter of 1968–1969 with the birth of the black lung movement. Originating in southern West Virginia, the movement was based in the older generation of workers who were leaving the mines. They faced retirement with a sparse pension of $100 per month (if they could meet the Fund's increasingly arbitrary and strict eligibility requirements), without the traditional cushion of the extended family and without compensation for the respiratory disease from which so many suffered (30). Discontent focused on the demand that the West Virginia legislature pass a bill recognizing black lung as a compensable disease under the state's workers' compensation statutes. Opposing the movement were the combined forces of the coal industry and the medical establishment. A member of the latter insisted, "There is no epidemic of devastating, killing and disabling man-made plague among coal workers." (31) Another argued, "The control of coal dust is not the answer to the disabling respiratory disease of our coal miners." (32)

Exasperated by strident opposition and legislative inaction, miners began to quit work in February 1969 in a strike that eventually brought out 40,000 workers and shut off coal production throughout the state. Their solidarity and economic muscle forced a black lung compensation bill through the legislature; although less liberal than what miners had hoped for, they declared a victory and returned to work after the governor signed the bill into law.

This was the most dramatic and widely reported phase of the black lung movement, but it marked only the beginning. Coupled with the death of 78 miners in the violent Farmington mine explosion in November 1968, the black lung movement generated a national political debate over health and safety conditions in U.S. coal mines. In December 1969, the Congress passed a Coal Mine Health and Safety Act, which detailed to an unprecedented degree mandatory work practices throughout the industry and offered compensation to miners disabled by black lung and the widows of miners who died from the disease. Large coal companies vigorously opposed certain, but not all, of the act's provisions. Most notably, they fought the extremely strict respirable dust standard of 3.0 mg/m³, scheduled to drop to 2.0 mg/m³ after three years; this was designed to prevent black lung. The compensation program, by contrast, was to their liking: not only did it seem to promise that the turmoil over black

lung would dissolve, the program also relieved them of liability for compensation by financing benefits with general tax revenues from the U.S. Treasury.

Ironically, passage of the act ensured that the issue of black lung compensation would not die but remain the focus of a continuing movement. In 1970, the Social Security Administration began administering the claims process for compensation benefits; within the program's first week of operation, 18,000 claims poured into agency offices (33). By the fall of the same year, letters of denial began to flow back into the coalfields. The bitterness and confusion that ensued derived partly from a pattern that repeated itself throughout thousands of these rural communities: several disabled miners and widows received black lung benefits, but their brothers or uncles or neighbors down the road were denied, even though by all appearances they were equally or even more disabled by lung disease. In other words, the criteria by which the Social Security Administration judged claimants' eligibility appeared completely arbitrary and violated local perceptions of who was disabled by black lung. Thus miners and their families pitted themselves against Social Security and the medical establishment in a bitter struggle over who would control the definition of disease and disability.

The Social Security Administration initially based its eligibility criteria on the orthodox medical conception of black lung, a view that reflects the rigidity and narrowness of the germ theory. According to this perspective, black lung is limited exclusively to one clinical entity—coal workers' pneumoconiosis (CWP); this is the only lung disease considered occupational in origin and therefore compensable. The agent (and cause) of CWP is, by definition (pneumoconiosis means "dust-containing lung"), the inhalation of respirable coal mine dust, which produces certain pathological changes in one organ (the lungs) and which are revealed in a characteristic pattern on an X-ray. The disease process is linear and quantitative; the stage of CWP is determined by the number and size of opacities on the lung field, as revealed through an X-ray. The first stages of disease, categorized as "simple" pneumoconiosis, are considered compatible with health, whereas advanced or "complicated" pneumoconiosis is severely disabling and sometimes fatal (34).

This conception of black lung has highly significant political and ideological functions. Most important, it minimizes and depoliticizes the problem. If the *cause* of CWP is respirable dust, then prevention is a technical matter of controlling this inanimate object, rather than a political question involving the relations of power in the workplace. Moreover, most surveys find a 3 percent prevalence of complicated CWP; if this is the only stage of disease considered disabling, then a relatively small number of coal miners are functionally impaired by occupational lung disease and deserve compensation. Respiratory disability in miners with simple CWP is attributed to nonoccupational factors, above all the victims themselves and their cigarette smoking. Obviously, this entire train of thought functions to shift medical and political emphasis away from the workplace as a source of disease and onto the worker (35).

The entire diagnostic and claims procedure also functioned to individualize what miners and other activists considered a collective problem. On a practical level, the dominant medical concept of black lung meant that claimants with evidence of complicated CWP, even if they experienced little disability, automatically received compensation; some with lesser stages who met a complex combination of other criteria also received benefits. But thousands of miners and the widows of miners, who by all appearances were equally or more disabled by respiratory disease, were denied compensation.

In the course of their movement to achieve more liberal eligibility criteria, miners and other activists implicitly elaborated a completely different understanding of black lung and its causes. Their view was not articulated by a single spokesperson or written down in a single position paper; it was woven into the culture and ideology of the movement, and in almost all respects ran counter to the dominant medical view of black lung. Indeed, the very act of insisting collectively on the reality of their own disease experience was in itself a challenge to scientific medicine, insofar as the latter tends to individualize health problems and denigrate the patients' perceptions of their own condition.

It should be stressed that the movement's ideology did not involve a wholesale rejection of science and was not based on fundamentalist religion or other anti-scientific sensibilities. Indeed, some activists made skillful use of the scientific arguments of a few physicians who, because of their research findings, lent support to the black lung cause (36). Overall, the movement's ideology was based in the collective experience of its participants. Their skepticism toward the medical establishment had historical roots in the company doctor system, which for many activists was a bitter and living memory. Their view of black lung itself was based in their own holistic experience of disease—its physical as well as psychological, social, and economic aspects. And their understanding of the causes of black lung derived from their experiences with the coal industry, as workers, as widows of men killed by the mines, and as residents of coal towns where "there are no neutrals" (37)—even scientists.

For movement participants, the medical definition of black lung as a single clinical entity principally affecting one organ of the body had little meaning, because black lung meant a transformation in their whole way of life. As one 56-year-old miner, disabled by black lung since the age of 48, described (38):

> Black lung is a cruel disease, a humiliating disease. It's when you can't do what you like to do; that's humiliating. I had to lay down my hammer and saw, and those were the things I got the most pleasure out of. The next thing I liked to do was work in my garden; now my garden's the biggest weed patch in Logan County. There were times in 1971 when I was still working that it was difficult for me to get to the bedroom when I was feeling bad. Now, of course, that's humiliating.

Many miners' analysis of the agents and causes of black lung also contrasted with the orthodox medical view. They argued that many features of the workplace had damaged their lungs, such as working in water over their ankles or breathing the fumes from cable fires. Moreover, they asserted that although respirable dust was the agent of CWP, the cause of the whole disease experience ultimately was economic:

Where do we get the black lung from? The coal companies! They've had plenty of time to lessen the dust so nobody would get it. It's not an elaborate thing to keep it down: spray water. They just don't put enough of it on there. They don't want to maintain enough in materials and water to do that. . . . (39)

Should we all die a terrible death to keep those companies going? (40)

Thus, miners developed a belief that they were *collectively entitled* to compensation, not at all because of individualized medical diagnoses of CWP but because of the common health-destroying experience that defined them as a group: work in the mines. Implicit in this view was the idea that black lung is a destructive process that begins when a miner starts work, not something that acquires legitimacy only when a radiologist can find it on an X-ray.

A disabled coal miner reported (41):

I worked in the cleaning plant, an outside job. I had four conveyors to bring to the storage bin. I had, I'd say, 16 holes in this galvanized pipe, two rows, that's 32 holes in all, little tiny holes, to keep down the dust. I stood many a time across from that conveyor and somebody'd be on the other side, and all you could see was their cap lamp. And that's in the cleaning plant; that's outside! That's not even at the face.

In the Black Lung Association, we're asking due compensation for a man who had to work in the environment he worked in. Not that a man can't choose where he works. But he's due more than just a day's wages. He and his family ought to be compensated for the environment he worked in.

These beliefs found expression in a multitude of political demands concerning the black lung compensation program, eventually and most clearly in the demand for automatic compensation after a specified number of years' work in the mines. Federal legislation to effect this change went down to defeat in 1976. However, medical and legal eligibility requirements for compensation were so liberalized by amendments passed in 1972 and 1978 that most miners and the widows of miners who worked a substantial period of time in the mines are now receiving black lung benefits (42).

The black lung movement has been rightly criticized for its lack of a preventive focus. Despite the clear and widely held perception that the coal companies were to blame for black lung, activists never directed their struggle at the heart of the problem, prevention in the workplace. This was partly due to the initial, erroneous view that the cost of state compensation (financed by industry) would force the companies to improve health conditions in the mines. A lasting and effective prevention campaign would have required a tighter alliance between working miners, disabled miners, and widows; a much firmer conviction that black lung is not inevitable; and, at least eventually, a political vision of how miners might improve their occupational health by asserting greater control over the workplace.

However, the black lung movement suggests that even within the confines of an after-the-fact struggle for compensation, important and intensely political issues may be at stake. This article has explored the history of black lung on many levels—as a medical construct, a product of the workplace, a disease experience, and a political battle. The evidence presented suggests that miners' experientially based view of black lung and challenge to the medical establishment have historical justification. Medical science's understanding of black lung has not derived from observation unencumbered by a social and economic context, but has been profoundly shaped by that context; as a result, it has performed crucial political and ideological functions. In one era, it served to "normalize" and thereby mask the existence of disease altogether; in the more recent period, it has tended to minimize and individualize the problem.

By contrast, black lung activists succeeded in challenging the scientific medical establishment by insisting on the validity of their own definition of disease. They viewed black lung as an experience affecting the whole person in all aspects of life. Rather than focusing on a causal relationship between one discrete agent and one disease, they looked at the workplace as a total environment where the miner confronts an array of respiratory hazards. Finally, activists defined black lung as a collective problem whose ultimate cause was economic. In its entirety, the history of black lung suggests that a similar task of redefinition awaits other health advocates if they wish to challenge effectively the social production of disease.

NOTE

Acknowledgements—This article was written under a research fellowship at the International Institute for Comparative Social Research in Berlin, West Germany. I wish to thank the Institute and its staff for their financial support, friendship, and intellectual stimulation. Conversations and correspondence with Norm Diamond, Gerd Göckenjan, and Meredeth Turshen were also an invaluable part of the process that led to this article.

REFERENCES

1. NOVA. A plague on our children. WGBH Educational Foundation, Boston, 1979, film transcript, p. 35.
2. For a clear presentation of the overall argument, see Doyal, L. (with Pennell, I.). *The Political Economy of Health,* Pluto Press, London, 1979. See also Turshen, M. The political ecology of disease. *Review of Radical Political Economics* 9(1): 45–60, 1977. See also Eyer, J. Hypertension as a disease of modern society. *Int J. Health Serv.* 5(4): 539–558, 1975.
3. Many analysts have pointed out this relationship on a theoretical level, but only a few have attempted to apply it in concrete investigation. See the discussion concerning the relationship between capitalist work relations and technology and the scientific model of brain function (as factory manager, telephone exchange, and, today, computer) in Rose, A. *The Conscious Brain.* Alfred A. Knopf, New York, 1974. For a more general discussion, see Figlio, K. The historiography of scientific medicine: An invitation to the human sciences. *Comparative Studies in Society and History* 19: 262–286, 1977. See also Foucault, M. *The Birth of the Clinic.* Vintage Books, New York, 1975.
4. The most comprehensive discussion I found was Sheafer, H. C. Hygiene of coal-mines. In *A Treatise on Hygiene and Public Health,* edited by A. H. Buck, vol. 2, pp. 229–250. William Wood and Company, New York, 1879. Sheafer wrote: "Any one who has seen a load of coal shot from a cart, or has watched the thick clouds of dust which sometimes envelop the huge coal-breakers of the anthracite region so completely as almost to hide them from sight, can form an idea of the injurious effect upon the health of constant working in such an atmosphere. The wonder is not that men die of clogged-up lungs, but that they manage to exist so long in an atmosphere which seems to contain at least fifty per cent of solid matter" (p. 245). See also Carpenter, J. T. Report of the Schuylkill County Medical Society. *Transactions of the Medical Society of Pennsylvania,* fifth series, part 2, pp. 488–491, 1869.
5. Figlio (3). Jewson, N. D. The disappearance of the sick-man from medical cosmology, 1770–1870. *Sociology* 10(2): 225–244, 1976.
6. On early financing of medical care in the coalfields, see Ginger, R. Company-sponsored welfare plans in the anthracite industry before 1900. *Bulletin of the Business Historical Society* 27(2): 112–120, 1953. See also Falk, L. A. Coal miners' prepaid medical care in the United States—and some British relationships, 1792–1964. *Med. Care* 4(1): 37–42, 1966.
7. A comprehensive survey of health care under the company doctor system was extracted from the U.S. government by the United Mine Workers of America during temporary federalization of the mines in 1946. The result was the so-called Boone report. U.S. Department of the Interior, Coal Mines Administration. *A Medical Survey of the Bituminous-Coal Industry.* Government Printing Office, Washington, D.C., 1947.
8. Hayhurst, E. R. The health hazards and mortality statistics of soft coal mining in Illinois and Ohio. *J. Ind. Hygiene* 1(7): 360, 1919.
9. Rebhorn, E. H. Anthraco silicosis. *Med. Soc. Reporter* 29(5): 15, Scranton, Pennsylvania, 1935.
10. Those who persisted in their complaints of breathlessness were eventually referred to psychiatrists, according to the testimony of miners and their families during interviews with the author. The argument that miners' symptoms of lung disease were psychological in origin may be found in Ross, W. D., et al. Emotional aspects of respiratory disorders among coal miners. *J.A.M.A.* 156(5): 484–487, 1954.
11. My thoughts on this relationship were stimulated and clarified by Figlio, K. Chlorosis and chronic disease in 19th century Britain: The social constitution of somatic illness in a capitalist society. *Int. J. Health Serv.* 8(4): 589–617, 1978.
12. This view persists today. Abundant examples may be found, especially in journalistic and sociological literature on Appalachia. Miners are alternatively romanticized and reviled; in either case, they are "a breed apart."

13. See Brown, E. R. *Rockefeller Medicine Men.* University of California Press, Berkeley, 1979. On the germ theory and its implications for the doctor-patient relationship, see Jewson (5), Figlio (3), and Berliner, H. S., and Salmon J. W. The holistic health movement and scientific medicine: The naked and the dead. *Socialist Review* 9(1): 31–52, 1979.

14. "One radiologist in southern West Virginia says until five years ago he regularly encountered chest X-rays from physicians that showed massive lung lesions labeled 'normal miner's chest.' " Aronson, B. Black lung: Tragedy of Appalachia. *New South* 26(4): 54, 1971.

15. Meiklejohn, A. History of lung disease of coal miners in Great Britain: Part II, 1875–1920. *Br. J. Ind. Med.* 9(2): 94, 1952. This view apparently originated in Britain and was picked up by physicians in the United States.

16. See Seltzer, C. Health care by the ton. *Health PAC Bulletin* 79: 1–8, 25–33, 1977.

17. Martin, J. E., Jr. Coal miners' pneumoconiosis. *Am. J. Public Health* 44(5): 581, 1954. See also Hunter, M. B., and Levine, M. D. Clinical study of pneumoconiosis of coal workers in Ohio river valley. *J.A.M.A.* 163(1): 1–4, 1957. See also the numerous articles by Lorin Kerr in this period, especially Coal workers' pneumoconiosis. *Ind. Med. Surg.* 25(8): 355–362, 1956.

18. Nonmedical literature from all over the world suggests that coal miners have long experienced black lung. Friedrich Engels discusses miners' "black spittle" disease in *The Condition of the Working Class in England.* Alden Press, Oxford, 1971. Emile Zola's character Bonnemort in the novel *Germinal* is clearly a victim of black lung. And John Spargo, a progressive era reformer intent on the prohibition of child labor, discusses the respiratory problems of the anthracite breaker boys in *The Bitter Cry of the Children.* Macmillan Company, New York, 1906, p. 164.

19. U.S. Public Health Service. The health of workers in dusty trades, Part III. Public Health Bulletin Number 208, Government Printing Office, Washington, D.C., 1933; U.S. Public Health Service. Anthraco-silicosis among hard coal miners. Public Health Bulletin Number 221, Government Printing Office, Washington, D.C., 1936; U.S. Public Health Service and Utah State Board of Health. The working environment and the health of workers in bituminous coal mines, non-ferrous metal mines, and non-ferrous metal smelters in Utah, 1940.

20. A lucid discussion of the labor process in this period may be found in Dix, K. *Work Relations in the Coal Industry: The Hand-Loading Era, 1880–1930.* Institute for Labor Studies, West Virginia University, Morgantown, West Virginia, 1977. On the economics of the industry, see Suffern, A. E. *The Coal Miners' Struggle for Industrial Status.* Macmillan Company, New York, 1926. See also Hamilton, W. H., and Wright, H. R. *The Case of Bituminous Coal.* Macmillan Company, New York, 1925.

21. One study actually found an inverse statistical relationship between employment levels and the rate of fatal accidents. See the discussion in Dix (20), pp. 101–104.

22. Roy, A. *History of Coal Miners of the U.S.* J. L. Trauger Printing Company, Columbus, Ohio, 1907, p. 119.

23. In some cases, state law or local practice dictated that coal be shot down at the end of the day, allowing the atmosphere to clear overnight. However, this was not uniform practice throughout the industry.

24. Physicians, miners, and government officials seem to agree on this point; representatives from industry in some cases demur. There is also disagreement about the magnitude of any increase in respiratory disease. See *Papers and Proceedings of the National Conference on Medicine and the Federal Coal Mine Health and Safety Act of 1969.* Washington, D.C., 1970. Debate on these questions also runs through the many volumes of testimony on the 1969 act. See U.S. Senate, Committee on Labor and Public Welfare, Subcommittee on Labor, *Coal Mine Health and Safety.* Hearings, 91st Congress, 1st Session, Government Printing Office, Washington, D.C., 1969.

25. United Mine Workers of America. *Proceedings of the 33rd Consecutive Constitutional Convention.* United Mine Workers of America, Indianapolis, Indiana, 1934, vol. 1.

26. United Mine Workers of America. *Proceedings of the 42nd Consecutive Constitutional Convention.* United Mine Workers of America, Washington, D.C., 1956, see pp. 306–331.

27. Lewis clearly articulated this position in his book, *The Miners' Fight for American Standards.* Bell Publishing Company, Indianapolis, Indiana, 1925.

28. This paragraph compresses an enormous social and economic transformation into a few sentences. For a detailed description of the changed industrial relations in this period, see Seltzer, C. The United Mine Workers of America and the coal operators: The political economy of coal in Appalachia, 1950–1973. Ph.D. dissertation, Columbia University, 1977.

29. See David, J. P. Earnings, health, safety, and welfare of bituminous coal miners since the encouragement of mechanization by the United Mine Workers of America. Ph.D. dissertation, West Virginia University, 1972. David demonstrates how miners fell behind workers in certain other unionized industries during this period.

30. In 1969, the U.S. Surgeon General estimated that 100,000 coal miners were afflicted with CWP. A study of 9,076 miners, conducted between 1969 and 1972, found a 31.4 percent prevalence of the disease among bituminous miners; among those who had worked 30 to 39 years in the mines, prevalence rose to over 50 percent. See Morgan, W.K.C., et al. The prevalence of coal workers' pneumoconiosis in U.S. coal miners. *Arch. Environ. Health* 27: 222, 1973. Current prevalence in the work force runs around 15 percent. These data are all on CWP. Black lung, i.e. the whole disease experience that miners consider occupational in origin, is not considered a legitimate concept by scientific medicine, and its prevalence is unknown. In scientific medical terms, black lung includes CWP, bronchitis, emphysema, and possibly other unrecognized disease processes. The prevalence of this ensemble of diseases is of course higher than that of CWP alone.

31. Dr. Rowland Burns, as quoted in the Charleston (West Virginia) *Daily Mail,* January 15, 1969.

32. Dr. William Anderson, as quoted in the Charleston (West Virginia) *Gazette,* April 16, 1969.

33. U.S. House, Committee on Education and Labor. *Black Lung Benefits Program.* First Annual Report. Government Printing Office, Washington, D.C., 1971.

34. The views of W.K.C. Morgan and his associates represent the dominant position of the medical establishment on CWP. See Morgan, W.K.C. Respiratory disease in coal miners. *Am. Rev. Resp. Dis.* 113: 531–559, 1976.

35. For example: "The presence of severe shortness of breath in a coal miner with simple CWP is virtually always related to a nonoccupationally related disease, such as chronic bronchitis or emphysema, rather than to coal mining. . . . Smoking is by far the most important factor in producing respiratory symptoms and a decrease in ventilatory function." Morgan (34), pp. 540–541.

36. Several physicians took the side of miners in the black lung controversy, arguing that the degree of respiratory disability does not correlate with X-ray stages of CWP and that disabilty in miners with simple CWP is often occupationally related. Some explained this phenomenon by hypothesizing that the disease process is pulmonary vascular in nature, i.e. it affects the small vessels of the lungs, impairing their ability to exchange gases with the bloodstream. See Hyatt, R. E., Kistin, A. D., and Mahan, T. K. Respiratory disease in southern West Virginia coal miners. *Am. Rev. Resp. Dis.* 89(3): 387–401, 1964. See also Rasmussen, D. L., et al. Respiratory impairment in southern West Virginia coal miners. *Am. Rev. Resp. Dis.* 98(10): 658–667, 1968.

37. This is a line from a famous song by Florence Reese, "Which Side Are You On?", inspired by the mine wars in Harlan County, Kentucky, during the 1930s.

38. Author's interview with disabled coal miner, Logan County, West Virginia, September 6, 1978.

39. Author's interview with disabled coal miner, Raleigh County, West Virginia, September 19, 1978.

40. Author's interview with working coal miner, Raleigh County, West Virginia, August 24, 1978.

41. Author's interview with disabled coal miner, Raleigh County, West Virginia, September 19, 1978.

42. By 1978, approved claims exceeded 420,000, and amendments enacted in that year are pushing the total even higher. This does not mean, however, that eligibility requirements will not be tightened in the future. Indeed, the current trend is to do so. See General Accounting Office. *Legislation Allows Black Lung Benefits To Be Awarded without Adequate Evidence of Disability.* Report to the Congress. Government Printing Office, Washington, D.C., 1980.

6

Occupational Stress and Coronary Heart Disease: A Review and Theoretical Integration

James S. House

Empirical Evidence

Two kinds of evidence point to an important role for occupational stress in the etiology of heart disease. First, there are standard epidemiological studies comparing morbidity or mortality rates for different demographic categories such as race, sex, age, occupation, education, ethnicity, region, or place of residence. While an observed difference between demographic categories in incidence of disease is ambiguous with respect to the causal mechanisms that produce it, such data are useful in suggesting hypotheses about the impact of occupational stress on heart disease. Stress is only one of the possible causal mechanisms, and well-designed research should assess relevant competing causes, such as diet, exercise, smoking, or family history. But a second type of research is needed to establish adequately a relationship between occupational stress and heart disease: it must relate specific types of stress to heart disease and show that the differential distribution of stress across demographic categories accounts, at least in part, for observed differences in mortality or morbidity between groups.

This literature review considers both broad demographic comparisons and more focused studies of specific types of occupational stress in relation to heart disease. The more focused studies present the major evidence relating specific objective work conditions and/or subjective perceptions of stress to heart disease. The process by which individual and social situational characteristics condition relationships of objective work conditions and/or subjective perceptions thereof to heart disease is also considered briefly. Unfortunately, no good empirical evidence is available on the influence of response modes upon the relationship between occupational stress and heart disease. This is a problem needing future research.

Demographic Comparisons

Aside from its increase with age, perhaps the most striking fact about the distribution of coronary heart disease (CHD) in the American population of working age is the degree to which it afflicts young and middle-aged males and spares young and middle-aged white females. Throughout the period of peak occupational endeavor (ages 25 to 64 years), the mortality rate from CHD among white males is from 2.75 to 6.50 times greater than the white female rate, while non-white males die from CHD at a rate only 1.35 to 1.91 times greater than the non-white female rate. Among females, those who are black or of lower social status run a significantly greater risk of death from CHD, but there are no sizeable or consistent race or status differences among males (see mortality data for 1959–61 in Moriyama et al., 1971:58–64; also see Antonovsky, 1968; Marks, 1967).

Interestingly, few have speculated about the potential role of occupational stress in producing these sex differences. Moriyama et al. (1971) discount the possibility that the unique female hormonal make-up prior to menopause can account for the difference, since no noticeable increase in female death rates follows the age of menopause. But these same authors then suggest only that we look to differences in diet, physical activity, and smoking as explanations; they do not mention occupational or other social stress. If occupational stress contributes to the sex differences in CHD mortality, there should be evidence of a declining sex difference as female employment and equality increase. And, in fact, Moriyama et al. (1971) report that, between 1940 and the late 1950's, male CHD death rates steadily increased, while white female rates steadily declined; but since then the male rate seems to have levelled off, while the female rate (for ages 35 to 54 years) is rising.

The sizeable occupational differences in CHD morbidity and mortality also suggest the potential etiological importance of occupational stress (Guralnick, 1963). In a number of studies cited here, men in occupations involving "greater stress" showed higher susceptibility to heart disease. Yet, such occupational comparisons have generally produced few interpretable results since little effort has been made to specify types of stresses which might explain occupational differences. As Suchman (1967), Jenkins (1971), and others have suggested, identification of specific stresses and their differential distribution across occupations is *sine qua non* for establishing work-related stress as an explanation of occupational differences in heart disease. Demographic comparisons can suggest the potential relevance of occupational stress to CHD, but more focused studies must demonstrate that relevance.

Focused Studies

Studies of social psychological aspects of work in relation to CHD constitute the largest and most productive body of research relating occupational stress to chronic diseases. The studies to be reviewed here use essentially two measures of health: (1) actual disease entities such as heart attacks; and (2) behavioral and physiological factors known to increase the risk of such disease (high levels of cigarette smoking, obesity, blood sugar, blood pressure, cholesterol, etc.). Studies using actual disease as the dependent variable are of two types—retrospective and prospective. In a retrospective study persons with heart disease are compared on measures of occupational stress with a control group of persons without this disease. A major methodological flaw here is that differences between the heart disease and control groups may be a result rather than a cause of heart disease. In a prospective design asymptomatic persons are interviewed about their lives and work and then followed until some develop heart disease. Here the evidence is more convincing that the social psychological characteristics differentiating those who do and do not incur the disease are, in fact, causes of the disease.

Studies utilizing "risk factors" of heart disease as dependent variables are usually cross-sectional, and occasionally prospective. In a cross-sectional study, occupational stress and risk factors are measured at about the same time and their associations determined. Although correlations cannot establish causality, it is usually more plausible to assume, for example, that job satisfaction affected blood pressure rather than *vice versa*. A number of longitudinal and/or experimental studies clearly demonstrate that changes in work-related variables cause changes in risk factors. Despite the flaws in any single study, a rather convincing pattern of results emerges from the studies considered below.

Job Satisfaction and Self-Esteem

A number of retrospective studies in the United States and other countries found that persons with coronary disease were significantly more dissatisfied with their overall jobs or aspects thereof (e.g., tedious details, lack of recognition, poor relations with co-workers, poor working conditions) and/or had more work "problems" and difficulties (Jenkins, 1971). Three different samples of occupations (N's = 16, 12, and 36, respectively) studied by Sales and House (1971) produced consistently negative and generally very significant correlations across occupations between average levels of job satisfaction and heart disease mortality rates. The relationships were strongest for intrinsic job satisfaction measures and in white collar, as opposed to blue collar, occupations. Relationships between average levels of job dissatisfaction and mortality from a variety of other causes (tuberculosis, cancer, diabetes, influenza, pneumonia, and accidents) were nonexistent. Controlling for occupational status via partial correlation did not seriously diminish the relationship between satisfaction and CHD.

House (1972) reported correlations between a three-item index of job satisfaction and a variety of heart disease risk factors (e.g., smoking, obesity, cholesterol, blood pressure, and blood sugar) for a sample of 288 men representing the full range of occupations in a total community (the Tecumseh Community Health Study of the University of Michigan). Correlations across the total sample were near zero. However, further analyses revealed rather different correlations in specific age and occupational subgroups. As in the Sales and House study, correlations were in the expected negative direction more often among white-collar than among blue-collar workers. Interestingly, the expected relationships generally emerged for men 45 or more years of age, but a positive relationship was found for younger men. Among older men (i.e., 45+ years of age), correlations between satisfaction and a CHD risk summary measure were significantly negative for professionals and salaried managers (r=−.31) and for industrial foremen and workers (r=−.25).

These results highlight a persisting problem in the occupational stress and heart disease literature. The subject population for most studies is restricted to white-collar workers and/or specific organizations. Results from such homogeneous samples often do not replicate across the full range of more heterogeneous populations. The dangers in generalizing from quite limited samples to all employed males (much less females) cannot be overemphasized.

Self-esteem in work is closely related to job satisfaction. House (1972) found occupational self-esteem in work to be even more strongly and negatively associated with heart disease risk than was job satisfaction, again especially among middle-aged and older white-collar workers. However Kasl et al. (1968) and Kasl and Cobb (1970) longitudinally compared male blue-collar workers terminated by factory closings with a steadily employed control group. Self-esteem declined with job loss and rose with reemployment. Significant negative correlations between self-esteem and CHD risk factors emerged both at any given point in time and over time.

In an earlier study, Kasl and French (1962) found that men whose occupational self-esteem was low frequented their company dispensaries much more often than those with higher self-esteem. Perhaps low work self-esteem predisposes men to a wider variety of illnesses than just heart disease. Men who felt their jobs were dull and boring also made more dispensary visits. In contrast, Caplan (1971) and French et al. (1965) found no clear relationships between self-esteem and heart disease risk among professional workers. Nevertheless, evidence is mounting to support a contention that low satisfaction and self-esteem in work predispose men to heart disease and perhaps to other diseases as well.

Job Pressures

The layman's conception of occupational "stress" is reflected best in studies about effects of high levels of work load, responsibility, and role conflict or ambiguity—what will here be termed job "pressures." A series of studies by French and his colleagues have found associations between feelings of work overload and elevated heart disease risk in a variety of populations. Work overload refers to feelings that job demands exceed one's capacities, given one's available times, resources, and abilities. Deadlines are a frequent source of overload. Among 104 university professors, men who felt overloaded had significantly higher cholesterol and significantly lower self-esteem (French et al., 1965). An unpublished study of 22 white-collar employees of the National Aeronautics and Space Administration (NASA) related feelings of overload to higher levels of heart rate and cholesterol (Caplan and French, 1968), but a later study of a large NASA sample failed to replicate that finding (Caplan, 1971). These studies also found significant positive correlations between subjective reports of work overload and more objective measures (ranging from wives' reports of the number of hours their husbands worked to direct observational measures of the demands made on men by others in the organization). These objective measures were also associated with elevated heart disease risk, but the results suggest that the effects of objective job conditions are mediated through the person's subjective experience of overload or "stress" (as has been assumed in the framework developed that is above).

These data are in line with earlier studies relating work load and job pressures to changes in heart disease risk factors. A seminal investigation found marked increases in serum cholesterol in tax accountants as the April 15 deadline for filing Federal income tax returns approached (Friedman et al., 1957). A number of studies have found significantly higher levels of cholesterol in medical students on the day before examinations as compared with times when they were not facing tests (see review by Sales, 1969b). It is plausible that these changes are attributable to increased work load under tax deadline or examination pressures. They also highlight what it is about work overload, as opposed to sheer work load, that makes it stressful—the feeling that one does not have enough time or ability and hence may fail (Pepitone, 1967).

Responsibility for the work of others has recently been implicated as a correlate of selected heart disease risk factors and possibly other illnesses. Caplan (1971) found that NASA managers, scientists, and engineers who spent a higher percentage of their time on such responsibilities smoked more cigarettes and had higher diastolic blood pressure. Studies showing high levels of CHD risk factors among executives (e.g., Montoye et al., 1967) might also support this responsibility hypothesis, although consistently positive relationships have not been found between managerial status and actual CHD (Hinkle, et al., 1968).

House's (1972) total community study produced further support for the role of job pressures in heart disease risk. A composite measure of job pressures (including work overload, responsibility, and role conflict) was associated with significantly greater heart disease risk in virtually the whole range of occupations. As with the findings on job satisfaction and self-esteem in this study, occupational stress effects were much more pronounced among men 45 to 65 years of age.

Several studies have also documented a relationship between occupational pressure or stress and actual coronary heart disease. Russek (1962) asked a number of practicing professionals to rank several categories of practice within the fields of medicine, dentistry, and law by the amount of "occupational stress" involved in each specialty. Regardless of the specific profession involved, individuals in the "high stress" categories reported higher incidences of coronary disease. A second Russek (1965) study compared 100 young coronary patients and 100 controls. Here Russek (1965:189) found that "prolonged emotional strain associated with job responsibility" preceded the heart attacks of 91 percent of the patients, while such strain was evident in only 20 percent of the control group. Further, this between-group difference exceeded those for family history of heart disease, diet, obesity, smoking, and physical exercise. In a similar study (Miles et al., 1954), 50 percent of heart disease patients, but only 12 percent of a control group, reported working long hours with few vacations prior to disease onset. Weiss et al. (1957) and Pearson and Joseph (1963) report similar conclusions.

Thus, there is rather consistent evidence that job pressures (measured both objectively and subjectively), such as work overload, responsibility and role conflict, significantly increase heart disease risk and actual coronary heart disease. Of all findings reviewed here, these have been replicated in the largest number of studies and across the widest range of populations. Further corroboration of these results appears in the data on personality and social situational factors influencing these relationships.

Incongruity and Change

A final set of factors seems increasingly important as sources of occupational stress leading to heart disease, though their exact social psychological meaning is unclear. A variety of evidence is accumulating that a life history of occupational mobility or rapid change in occupational environment predisposes men to heart disease. Caplan (1971), following Terreberry (1968), speaks of "complexification" of occupational environments (or rate at which things change or become increasingly complex) as a form of work overload taxing one's ability to adapt to new demands. Both occupationally or geographically mobile persons who expose themselves to change, complexity, and new demands and those whose environment changes rapidly seem to experience greater heart disease (cf. review by Smith, 1967) and perhaps greater illness of all kinds (e.g., Holmes and Rahe, 1967). The accumulating evidence that persons whose status is incongruent on two dimensions (e.g., men with low education in high status jobs) are more prone to heart disease may reflect effects of work overload (the job demands exceed their capacity) or prior occupational mobility rather than "status incongruity" *per se* (cf. reviews by Smith, 1967; Jenkins, 1971; see also Hinkle et al., 1968). The evidence on the relationship of status consistency to heart disease, however, must be subjected to rigorous methodological scrutiny that has recently been applied to this concept in sociology (see Hodge and Siegel, 1970). Attention must also be paid to the specification of intervening or conditioning variables (cf. House and Harkins, 1973).

Conditioning Variables

Conditioning Personal Characteristics

Thus far, direct relationships between objective aspects of work situations or subjective perceptions thereof and heart disease have been considered. Where the evidence is based on subjective reports of dissatisfaction or job pressures, these subjective reports are presumably the outcome of interactions between objective situational characteristics (role demands or expectations, the nature of the job, and its rewards) and individual characteristics (motives, needs, abilities, etc.). However, attempts to document this empirically are just beginning with at least modest success (e.g., Blood and Hulin, 1967; Caplan, 1971; French et al., in press; Turner and Lawrence, 1965).

More importantly, a large and growing body of literature indicates that men with a certain type of "behavior pattern" are more prone to coronary heart disease. This behavior pattern has been most extensively investigated by Friedman, Rosenman, and Jenkins, who labelled it the "Type A behavior-pattern," characterized by:

> ... excessive drive, aggressiveness, ambition, involvement in competitive activities, frequent vocational deadlines, (and) an enhanced sense of time urgency.... The converse ... pattern, called Type B is characterized by the relative absence of this *interplay of psychological traits and situational pressures* (Jenkins et al., 1967:371, emphasis added).

In a long series of studies (including an ongoing prospective study of 3,400 men now followed for over eight years) the Type A (relative to Type B) has been shown to be significantly higher on known heart disease risk factors and significantly more likely (by a factor of 1.4 to 6.5 in different analyses) to have an actual "heart attack" (see Jenkins, 1971; and Sales, 1969a, 1969b, for thorough reviews of these studies). The risk of recurrent and fatal heart attacks has also been shown to be higher for the Type A. Other investigators have found similar results, and in several studies, the Type A variable has been shown to have significant predictive power even when levels of a whole range of standard physiological risk factors are statistically controlled (Jenkins, 1971). The meaning of these results remains unclear however since the Type A pattern reflects "an interplay of psychological traits and situational pressures." To some extent these results may further demonstrate the importance of work overload and other "job pressures" reviewed above.

What role is played by psychological traits? Sales (1969a) suggested that the Type A person possesses personality traits (e.g., impatience, ambition, competitiveness, aggressiveness) causing self-selection into jobs involving greater "stress" (e.g., "time urgency," "frequent vocational deadlines," etc.), but no direct empirical test of this proposition has yet been made. Similarly, House (1972) suggested that a central psychological trait of the Type A is his "desire for social achievement" (reflected in ambition, competitiveness, aggressiveness, etc.), a trait apparently analogous to what others term "status-seeking" or extrinsic motivation for working (i.e., desire for money, status, recognition) as opposed to intrinsic motivation (i.e., desire for interesting, self-satisfying work). House predicted that persons with extrinsic motivations for working were more likely to choose jobs involving greater occupational stress and, hence, to experience heart disease, while intrinsically motivated persons would avoid highly stressful work and, hence, heart disease. Partial support for these hypotheses was found among white-collar workers, but, among lower blue-collar factory workers, intrinsic motivation was positively related to occupational stress and heart disease risk. These and other findings from that study indicate the difficulty of generalizing from the limited samples usually studied in this field (i.e., white collar, and often professional, workers) to all employed men.

Another approach to the meaning of the Type A behavior pattern asserts that under potentially stressful objective conditions Type A persons are more prone to perceive stress and manifest increases in heart disease or its risk factors. Caplan (1971) found support for this contention in research on NASA professionals. He proposes that the dramatic and consistent results derived from the Freidman et al. program of research may be due to the fact that the classification of a man as Type A indicates that he both possesses certain personality traits and experiences greater situational pressures. The role of personality in leading men into situations of stress and/or in accentuating the effects of such situations deserves further research.

Conditioning Social Characteristics

Just as personality factors may determine whether a person experiences stress and how he reacts to it, so may other characteristics of the work situation. As already noted, social and organizational change are likely to increase the stresses felt by individuals. Existing evidence indicates that individuals in positions involving great contact with external environments (and hence more varied and perhaps changing inputs) suffer greater emotional strain (Kahn et al., 1964) and heart disease risk (Caplan, 1971). Alternatively, the surrounding social environment may provide resources mitigating stress effects on individuals. Prescriptive theories of work organizations suggest that social support from peers, superiors, and subordinates improves the ability of men to cope with job stresses and, therefore, should enhance physical and mental health (e.g., Likert, 1967).

. . . .

Occupational Stress and Longevity

Given the accumulating evidence relating occupational stress to coronary heart disease and the significance of heart disease as a cause of death, occupational stress should also be a potent predictor of general mortality and, conversely, longevity. Evidence from demographic comparisons and from at least one focused study suggests that this is so.

Demographic Comparisons

In general, women, whites, and persons of higher educational or social status live longer and have lower age-adjusted mortality rates from many, though not all, diseases (cf. Palmore and Jeffers, 1971; Kitigawa and Hauser, 1968). Social status differentials are greater among women than men, and larger for communicable diseases than for such major chronic diseases as ulcer, stroke, arthritis, cancer, or heart disease (Kitigawa and Hauser, 1968; Lerner, 1969). Thus, social status and color differentials in general mortality probably stem more from poor living conditions and inadequate medical care or from social stress outside of work than from occupational stresses *per se*. There are, of course, occupational differences in most disease incidences, but in many cases the reasons for them remain unclear. However, the sex difference in longevity, just as that in heart disease mortality discussed above, again suggests a central role of work in the genesis of disease (cf. discussion in Palmore and Jeffers, 1971:284 ff).

Focused Studies

The best evidence that "stress" in life and work determines mortality and longevity comes from the Duke Longitudinal Study of Aging (Palmore 1969a, 1969b; Palmore and Jeffers, 1971). This panel study has been carried out on 268 volunteers, ages 60 to 94 years (median age 70), at the time of their initial interview and physical examination. Although not a random sample, the distribution of volunteers by sex, race, and occupation approximated that of the area from which they were drawn. The dependent variable was a Longevity Quotient—the number of years a person actually lived divided by the actuarially expected number of years remaining at the time of the initial examination.

For the total sample, *work satisfaction* was the strongest predictor of the Longevity Quotient ($r = .26$). It remained one of the three strongest predictors for all subgroups of the sample except for blacks, and was strongest ($r = .38$) among those (males, age 60 to 69 years) most likely to be working full-time. The second best longevity predictor ($r = .26$) in the total sample was the interviewing social worker's rating of the respondent's overall "happiness." These two social psychological measures (1) predicted longevity more accurately than either an overall physical functioning rating by the examining physician ($r = .21$) or a measure of the use of tobacco ($r = .21$); and (2) remained a strong predictor even when the aforementioned physical variables were controlled via multiple regression.

Conclusions

Traditional sociological and epidemiological research on social factors in heart disease has most often involved comparing disease rates across categories of standard demographic variables such as occupation, sex, race, or ethnicity. "Stress" is often presumed to be a mediating variable in such research, but the nature of stress seldom is specified carefully and almost never measured independently. As noted above, such research can at best yield suggestive results. Only when all variables that mediate and/or condition the relationship between objective social conditions and health outcomes are explicitly conceptualized and measured can we have an adequate understanding of the effect of social stress on heart disease.

. . . There is considerable evidence that occupational stress plays a significant role in the etiology of coronary heart disease and probably other chronic diseases as well. Particularly noteworthy is the accumulation of studies documenting a relationship between stress and heart disease even when a variety of more medically recognized variables (e.g., heredity, diet, exercise, etc.) are controlled. However, we are just beginning to understand the complexities in the relationship between occupational stress and heart disease. . . .

NOTE

This paper is based in part on a report prepared for the Secretary's Committee on Work in America, Department of Health, Education and Welfare. I am grateful for the helpful comments and suggestions of the following people on earlier drafts of this paper: Sidney Cobb, John R. P. French, Jr., Elizabeth Bates Harkins, Wendy F. House, Berton Kaplan, George Maddox, Erdman Palmore, and Thomas Regan. Work on this paper has also been supported in part by a Biomedical Sciences Support Grant (5S05RR077007) from the National Institutes of Health and by Public Health Service Research Grant (HD0068) from NICHD.

REFERENCES

Antonovsky, A. 1968. "Social class and the major cardiovascular diseases." Journal of Chronic Diseases 21 (May):65–108.

Appley, Mortimer H., and Richard Trumbull (eds.). 1967. Psychological Stress. New York: Appleton-Century-Crofts.

Blood, M. R., and C. L. Hulin. 1967. "Alienation, environmental characteristics and worker responses." Journal of Applied Psychology 51 (June):284–290.

Caplan, Robert. 1971. Organizational Stress and Individual Strain: A Social-Psychological Study of Risk Factors in Coronary Heart Disease among Administrators, Engineers, and Scientists. Unpublished Ph.D. thesis. Ann Arbor: University of Michigan.

Caplan, Robert, and John R. P. French, Jr. 1968. Final Report to NASA. Unpublished manuscript. Ann Arbor: University of Michigan.

Cobb, Sidney. 1972. A Report on the Health of Air Traffic Controllers Based on Aeromedical Examination Data. Unpublished report to the Federal Aviation Agency. Ann Arbor: University of Michigan.

Coelho, G. V., D. A. Hamburg and J. E. Adams (eds.). In press. Coping and Adaptation: Interdisciplinary Perspectives. New York: Basic Books.

Epstein, F. H. 1965. "The epidemiology of coronary heart disease: A review." Journal of Chronic Diseases 18 (August):735–774.

Felton, J. S., and R. Cole. 1963, "The high cost of heart disease." Circulation 27 (May):957–962.

French, John R. P., Jr., C. John Tupper and Ernst Mueller. 1965. Workload of University Professors. Cooperative Research Project No. 2171, U.S. Office of Education. Ann Arbor: University of Michigan.

French, J. R. P., Jr., W. Rodgers and S. Cobb. In press. "Adjustment as person-environment fit." In G. V. Coelho, D. A. Hamburg and J. E. Adams (eds.), Coping and Adaptation: Interdisciplinary Perspectives. New York: Basic Books.

Friedman, M., R. H. Rosenman and V. Carroll. 1957. "Changes in the serum cholesterol and blood clotting time of men subject to cyclic variation of occupational stress." Circulation 17 (May):852–961.

Graham,S., and L. G. Reeder. 1972. "Social factors in the chronic illness." Pp. 63–107 in Howard E. Freeman, Sol Levine and Leo G. Reeder (eds.), Handbook of Medical Sociology. Englewood Cliffs: Prentice-Hall.

Guralnick, Lillian. 1963. "Mortality by occupation and cause of death among men 20 to 64." National Center for Health Statistics. Vital Statistics Special Reports 53 (September):Number 3.

Hinkle, L. E., Jr. 1961. "Ecological observations on the relation of physical illness, mental illness, and the social environment." Psychosomatic Medicine 23 (July–August):289–297.

Hinkle, L. E., Jr., L. H. Whitney, E. W. Lehman, J. Dunn, B. Benjamin, R. King, A. Platum and B. Flehinger. 1968. "Occupation, education, and coronary heart disease." Science 161 (July):238–246.

Hodge, R W., and P. M. Siegel. 1970. "Nonvertical dimensions of social stratification." Pp. 512–520 in Edward O. Laumann, Paul M. Siegel, and Robert W. Hodge (eds.), The Logic of Social Hierarchies. Chicago: Markham.

Holmes, T. H. and R. H. Rahe. 1967. "The social readjustment rating scale." Journal of Pyschosomatic Research 11 (August):213–225.

House, James S. 1972. The Relationship of Intrinsic and Extrinsic Work Motivations to Occupational Stress and Coronary Heart Disease Risk. Unpublished Ph.D. thesis. Ann Arbor: University of Michigan.

House, James. S., and Elizabeth Bates Harkins. 1973. Why and When Is Status Inconsistency Stressful? Unpublished manuscript. Durham: Duke University.

Jenkins, C. D. 1971. "Psychologic and social precursors of coronary disease." New England Journal of Medicine 284 (February 4, February 11):244–255; 307–317.

Jenkins, C. D., R. H. Rosenman and M. Friedman. 1967. "Development of an objective psychological test for the determination of the coronary-prone behavior pattern." Journal of Chronic Diseases 20 (June):371–379.

Kahn, Robert L., Donald M. Wolfe, Robert P. Quinn, J. Dietrich Snoek and Robert A. Rosenthal. 1964. Organizational Stress: Studies in Role Conflict and Ambiguity. New York: John Wiley.

Kasl, S. V., and J. R. P. French, Jr. 1962. "The effects of occupational status on physical and mental health." Journal of Social Issues 18 (July):67–89.

Kasl, S. V., S. Cobb and G. Brooks. 1968. "Changes in serum uric acid and cholesterol levels in men undergoing job loss." Journal of the American Medical Association 206 (November):1500–1507.

Kasl, S. V., and S. Cobb. 1970. "Blood pressure changes in men undergoing job loss: A preliminary report." Psychosomatic Medicine 32 (January-February):19–38.

Kitigawa, Evelyn M., and P. M. Hauser. 1968. "Educational differentials in mortality by cause of death: United States, 1960." Demography 5 (February):318–353.

Lazarus, Richard S. 1966. Psychological Stress and the Coping Process. New York: McGraw-Hill.

Lerner, M. 1969. "Social differences in physical health." Pp. 69–112 in John Kosa, Aaron Antonovsky and Irvin K. Zola (eds.), Poverty and Health: A Sociological Analysis. Cambridge: Harvard University Press.

Levine, Sol, and Norman Scotch. 1970. Social Stress. Chicago: Aldine.

Likert, Rensis. 1967. The Human Organization: Its Management and Value. New York: McGraw-Hill.

Marks, Renee. 1967. "Factors involving social and

demographic characteristics: A review of empirical findings." Pp. 51–108 in S. Leonard Syme and Leo G. Reeder (eds.), Social Stress and Cardiovascular Disease. Milbank Memorial Fund Quarterly 45 (April): Part 2.

Matsumoto, Y. S. 1970. "Social stress and coronary heart disease in Japan: A hypothesis." Milbank Memorial Fund Quarterly 48 (January):9–13.

McGrath, Joseph E. (ed.). 1970. Social and Psychological Factors in Stress. New York: Holt, Rinehart and Winston.

Mechanic, David. 1962. Students Under Stress. New York: Free Press.

————. 1970. "Some problems in developing a social psychology of adaptation to stress." Pp. 104–123 in Joseph McGrath (ed.), Social and Psychological Factors in Stress. New York: Holt, Rinehart, and Winston.

Miles, H. H. W., S. Waldfogel, E. Barrabee and S. Cobb. 1954. "Psychosomatic study of 46 young men with coronary artery disease." Psychosomatic Medicine 16 (November–December):455–477.

Montoye, H. J., J. A. Faulkner, H. J. Dodge, W. M. Mikkelson, R. W. Willis, III and W. D. Block. 1967. "Serum uric acid concentration among business executives and observations on other coronary heart disease risk factors." Annals of Internal Medicine 66 (May): 838–850.

Moriyama, Iwao M., Dean E. Krueger and Jeremiah Stamler. 1971. Cardiovascular Diseases in the United States. Cambridge: Harvard University Press.

Palmore, E. B. 1969a. "Physical, mental, and social factors in predicting longevity." Gerontologist 9 (Summer):103–108.

————. 1969b. "Predicting longevity: A follow-up controlling for age." Gerontologist 9 (Winter): 247–250.

Palmore, Erdman B., and Frances Jeffers (eds.). 1971. Prediction of Life Span. Boston: D. C. Heath-Lexington.

Pearson, H. E. S., and J. Joseph. 1963. "Stress and occlusive coronary-artery disease." The Lancet 1 (February):415–418.

Pepitone, A. 1967. "Self, social environment, and stress." Pp. 182–199 in Mortimer H. Appley and Richard Trumbull (eds.). Psychological Stress. New York: Appleton-Century-Crofts.

Russek, H. I. 1962. "Emotional stress and coronary heart disease in American physicians, dentists, and lawyers." American Journal of Medical Science 243 (June):716–725.

————. 1965. "Stress, tobacco, and coronary heart disease in North American professional groups." Journal of the American Medical Association 192 (April): 189–194.

Sales, S. M. 1969a. Differences Among Individuals in Affective, Behavioral, Biochemical, and Physiological Responses to Variations in Work Load. Unpublished Ph.D. thesis. Ann Arbor: University of Michigan.

————. 1969b. "Organizational roles as a risk factor in coronary heart disease." Administrative Science Quarterly 14 (September):325–336.

Sales, S. M., and J. House. 1971. "Job dissatisfaction as a possible risk factor in coronary heart disease." Journal of Chronic Diseases 23 (May):861–873.

Seashore, Stanley. 1954. Group Cohesiveness in the Industrial Work Group. Institute for Social Research. Ann Arbor: University of Michigan.

Selye, Hans. 1956. The Stress of Life. New York: McGraw-Hill.

Smith, Thomasina. 1967. "Sociocultural incongruity and change: A review of empirical findings." Pp. 17–46 in S. Leonard Syme and Leo G. Reeder (eds.), Social Stress and Cardiovascular Disease, Milbank Memorial Fund Quarterly 45 (April): Part 2.

Suchman, E. A. 1967. "Factors involving social and demographic characteristics: Appraisal and implications for theoretical development." Pp. 109–116 in S. Leonard Syme and Leo G. Reeder (eds.), Social Stress and Cardiovascular Disease. Milbank Memorial Fund Quarterly 45 (April): Part 2.

Syme, S. L. 1967. "Implications and future prospects." Pp. 175–181 in S. Leonard Syme and Leo G. Reeder (eds.), Social Stress and Cardiovascular Disease. Milbank Memorial Fund Quarterly 45 (April): Part 2.

Syme, S. Leonard and Leo G. Reeder (eds.). 1967. Social Stress and Cardiovascular Disease. Milbank Memorial Fund Quarterly 45 (April): Part 2.

Terreberry, S. 1968. The Organization of Environments. Unpublished Ph.D. thesis. Ann Arbor: University of Michigan.

Turner, A. N., and P. R. Lawrence. 1965. Industrial Jobs and the Worker: An Investigation of the Response to Task Attributes. Harvard University Graduate School of Business Administration, Division of Research. Cambridge: Harvard University.

Weiss, E., B. Dlin, H. R. Rollin, H. K. Fischer and C. R. Bepler. 1957. "Emotional factors in coronary occlusion." Archives of Internal Medicine 99 (April):628–641.

7

Hypertension in American Society: An Introduction to Historical Materialist Epidemiology

Peter L. Schnall and Rochelle Kern

Introduction

The causes of essential hypertension—a disease that afflicts an estimated 50 million American adults—remains a medical mystery despite more than a hundred years of research efforts by scientists and physicians (Freis, 1976). Moreover, in the absence of an adequate medical understanding of the cause(s) of hypertension, millions of dollars are currently spent on extensive education and treatment programs (National HBP Education Program, 1978). This paper examines what medicine has learned about essential hypertension, how it has studied and explained the disease, and the limitations of its explanation and approach. We will describe a relatively new perspective on social epidemiology that is being developed and applied by a growing number of scholars and health providers: "historical materialist epidemiology" (HME). We will then use the perspective of HME to examine what is known about essential hypertension and to suggest new directions for research to understand and prevent this major health problem.

This paper is a preliminary analysis, provocative, we hope, in its questioning of the traditional medical perspective and in its use of the developing historical materialist epidemiology to suggest an alternative, more adequate approach to understanding not only essential hypertension but other health problems as well. HME gives us the beginnings of an explanatory perspective to identify and understand the connections among the organization of society, the nature and distribution of disease within society, and the available methods and dominant modes of treating and explaining diseases. While this is an enormous task, HME and the issues it raises provide a promising direction for future understanding of the relationship between disease and society.

The Problem of Hypertension

What is Hypertension and Why Is It a Problem?

Hypertension, or chronic high blood pressure, has been defined by the medical profession as the presence of a sustained elevation of blood pressure in an individual higher than $140/90$ (HDFP, 1979).[1] What this means is that when blood pressure is measured, the pressure of the blood against the walls of the arteries generated by the pumping of the heart in a normal, healthy adult should be no greater than 140 systolic (the highest pressure generated by the heart during the peak of its contraction) over 90 (the lowest pressure generated by the heart during its relaxation phase). Using this measurement of normal blood pressure, more than 50 million American adults have what is called "essential hypertension" and are seen by the medical profession as candidates for treatment (Relman, 1980). Essential hypertension is distinguished from secondary hypertension in that the latter is known to be caused by, or is secondary to, a particular organic problem, such as kidney disease; in the former, what we will refer to only as *hypertension* throughout the rest of this paper, the causes of the elevated pressure are unknown (or, in the medical view, are as yet "undiscovered") (Harrison, 1977:1307).

Hypertension is a known health problem. Chronic elevation of blood pressure causes serious damage to the human body and may lead, if uncontrolled, to stroke, heart disease and heart attack, kidney disease and renal failure, and other organic problems. These serious consequences of untreated hypertension can be prevented or at least postponed if the blood pressure is lowered to normal. Unfortunately, people with hypertension often experience no symptoms of the disease, leading to its characterization in public service messages as "the silent killer." Nearly half of all deaths in this country are from cardiovascular disease, including coronary heart disease, hypertension-induced heart disease, and stroke (DHEW, 1980).

How Has Hypertension Been Studied by Medicine?

There is a great deal known about hypertension and the organic damage it causes. Medical science has utilized the "medical model" paradigm both to search for the causes of hypertension and to explain its consequences. That paradigm sees hypertension as an organic abnormality caused by some disturbances within the body that results in the physiological alteration of the circulatory system. By and large, as with other diseases, the medical model's perspective of hypertension sees it as *a* disease with one or more identifiable *organic* causes. Ironically, the inability of the medical model to explain the presence of hypertension in so much of the American population results in part from the extraordinary success of its doctrine of specific etiology (Dubos, 1959) for providing explanations for a range of diseases which plagued human populations during the nineteenth and early twentieth centuries. We will review briefly some of the landmark

discoveries of medicine about blood pressure and hypertension.

There is a long tradition of laboratory research on the anatomical and physiological functioning of the human body. As early as 1658, John Jacob Reiter was performing autopsies in order to discover the cause of apoplexy (stroke) and learned that cerebral hemorrhages were caused by ruptured arteries. Throughout the nineteenth century, laboratory research into the physiology of blood circulation made remarkable progress with numerous discoveries about the nature of cardiovascular functioning, and the mechanisms by which the heart and nervous system maintain blood pressure in the arteries. By the end of the nineteenth century it was clinically established that a "hard" pulse and increased blood pressure could result in stroke (Ruskin, 1956).

Scientific technological inventions contributed to the growth of knowledge about hypertension. In the early nineteenth century, Jean Leonard Poisseule developed the mercury hemodyamometer which eventually led to the development of the modern blood pressure cuff, generally credited to Scipione Riva-Rocci in 1896 (Castiglione, 1947: 842). With the development of the blood pressure cuff (a mechanical device which allows a numerical measurement of blood pressure), there was a formative discovery about hypertension. It was generally believed that diseases of the kidneys were responsible for both high blood pressure and stroke until Theodore Janeway noted in 1906 that individuals could have increased blood pressure without evidence of kidney disease (Janeway, 1906).

Throughout the twentieth century, using the medical paradigm, physicians pursued the identification of the causes of increased blood pressure with some important successes. These successes included the identification of the causes of what we earlier distinguished as secondary hypertension. However, evidence soon emerged that a great percentage of the population had elevated blood pressure which could not be attributed to one of the identified causes of secondary hypertension. The realization of the prevalence and patterns of essential hypertension began to take form and give the picture of hypertension we have today. While the predominant scientific hypothesis of the medical model was that hypertension is a disease with a *specific etiology* and that, therefore, people with hypertension constitute a distinct and separable population from those without hypertension, medicine has failed to demonstrate the validity of this hypothesis.

As early as 1931 in a review of available studies, Wetherby (1932) found that the bulk of research on American population groups revealed that blood presure tends to rise continuously with age, is higher in men than in women, until about the age of forty when women's blood pressure tends to exceed and then become significantly higher than men's by the age of about fifty. Other population studies have failed to discover a natural dividing line between those with high blood pressure and those without it (Pickering, 1961). Further evidence that those with hypertension don't constitute a population separate from those without hypertension is found in data from the Actuarial Society of America (1941) that shows mortality (death) rates increase with arterial pressure, and that the relationship is curvilinear, with there being *no point* below which blood pressure is unrelated to mortality.

In 1933 the federal government mandated the keeping of vital statistics for all states in the United States. Hypertension and its consequences such as stroke emerged as the third ranked cause of death for all Americans. The important association between hypertension and coronary heart disease (the nation's number one killer) began to attract scientific attention in the 1940s. At the beginning of that decade Davis and Klainer (1940) published an article noting an association for their patients under the age of fifty between the presence of hypertension and an increased incidence of coronary artery disease.

Following World War II medical research focused on trying to understand the cause of coronary heart disease. Prospective community studies, such as the famous Framingham Study, followed large groups of people over time and monitored their health in order to see what organic problems and behaviors (e.g., cigarette smoking) lead to coronary heart disease. These studies primarily focused on white, middle-class people and they conceptualized hypertension as an independent variable and coronary heart disease as a dependent variable (i.e., hyperten-

sion was seen as something that caused coronary heart disease). The results of these prospective community studies was to show that hypertension was a "risk factor" for the development of coronary heart disease (Kannel, 1969). A "risk factor" is one that, when present, increases the prevalence of the dependent variable, coronary heart disease, in a group by at least twofold as compared to its prevalence in a group in which no risk factor is present.

Medical Explanations of Hypertension

Unfortunately, no prospective study of essential hypertension as a dependent variable has been carried out in the United States. Medical explanations of the cause of hypertension have focused on three variables: (1) aging, (2) genetically inherited susceptibility, and (3) increased salt intake. We will briefly review each of these as possible explanations as well as the data which examine the relationship of a fourth variable, stress, to hypertension.

(1) Some medical explanations posit that hypertension is the *natural* consequence of growing old, and that because people live longer, we're just seeing more of it now. There are two serious problems with this explanation. First, not everybody's blood pressure goes up with age, even within American society. Second, cross-cultural data shows that in other societies (e.g., primitive hunting and gathering societies), there is little or no increase in blood pressure with age. This is true even for some groups having racial and genetic inheritances identical with groups in the United States (Page, 1976).

(2) The genetic explanation of hypertension was given impetus by the finding that blacks had prevalence rates of hypertension two to three times higher than whites in the United States (e.g., DHEW, 1964). Genetic theories of increased susceptibility to hypertension were supported by results of twin studies (Thomas, 1973). As with all twin studies in which the twins are raised in the same household, however, these studies cannot control for the relative influence of the sharing of both genes and environment. In fact, some studies have found that familial influence and not genetic susceptibility accounts

for hypertension in some children (Zinner, 1971).

Several other findings limit the power of genetic theories to explain hypertension. First, there is a rapid rise in the prevalence of high blood pressure in black populations when they migrate from their communities of origin to industrialized urban centers (Eyer, 1975; Page, 1976). Likewise, genetic explanations cannot account for why blacks have the same prevalence rate as whites up to about the age of twenty-four and why only then do black males show a rapid increase in their rates of hypertension compared to their white male counterparts (DHEW, 1978: 13). Inheritance perhaps plays a role via increased susceptibility in some people, but genetic explanations alone cannot account for the development and distribution of hypertension in the American population.

(3) Salt intake appears to be a prerequisite variable in the development of hypertension, but, like genetic variables, it alone cannot explain hypertension. There has been a linear increase in salt consumption in Western societies which parallels the increase in blood pressure in the population. On the other hand, there are a number of primitive communities that use salt in their diets but do not show increased blood pressure with age (Thomas, 1959). Further, those individuals in the United States whose blood pressure does not increase with age have the same salt intake as do those who do develop hypertension. Experimental attempts to induce (cause) hypertension in human subjects with normal blood pressure by giving them salt were not "successful" (Dahl, 1960). Salt may play a contributory role in the development of hypertension, but only in combination with other variables.

In addition to looking at age, genetic susceptibility, and salt intake, a great deal of research has been conducted in the past twenty years to find a specific abnormality of a particular body organ to explain the cause of hypertension. No single abnormality of the body, however, has been identified which can account for the findings regarding the prevalence of hypertension in the United States (Freis, 1976). Before turning to a discussion of an alternative epidemiological perspective on high blood pressure and hypertension, we want to examine briefly a fourth variable which has been broadly identified as a correlate of elevated blood pressure: stress.

(4) There is a range of data that indicates that stress causes increases in human blood pressure. However, there is no adequate research on the relationship of sustained stress to the etiology of hypertension. We note as well that there is disagreement as to the exact definition of stress and how best to measure it (See, for example, Brown, 1974; Dohrenwend, 1974; and Waldron, 1977.) Among the available evidence on stress and hypertension are studies which found elevated blood pressure in men who lost their jobs (Kasl and Cobb, 1970), in populations who live in "deprived" neighborhoods (Harburg et al., 1970), in prisoners forced to live in crowded cells as compared to prisoners in private cells (D'Atri and Ostfeld, 1975), and among air traffic controllers compared to lower-ranking and less-stressed airmen (Cobb and Rose, 1973). Recent evidence indicates that people's blood pressure varies regularly—day by day and minute by minute in response to environmental stimuli (Pickering, 1975). Blood pressure increases during arguments, sex, and exercise, and decreases in relaxation and sleep.

We will return to a discussion of the role of stress in hypertension, but we would like here to point out that there is evidence that stress influences blood pressure but the role of stress in hypertension is not one of the major concerns in the medical literature on hypertension. When data on stress and blood pressure have been incorporated into medical conceptualizations, it has been in terms of *individual* characteristics that correlate with elevated blood pressure—for example, personality types and individual susceptibility. (See, e.g., Shapiro, 1979.) In short, stress is treated in the medical model as an individual characteristic similar to the individual organic variables reviewed above.[2] It is this identification of environmental influences as "psychosocial" characteristics that leads to medical recommendations for individual behavioral adjustments to decreased blood pressure through, for example, bio-feedback and relaxation techniques.

To summarize, medicine conceptualizes the disease of hypertension as the consequence of some disturbance within the individual organism. The various explanations offered by medicine, including age, genetic susceptibility, salt intake, and psychosocial susceptibility to stress all locate both the cause and potential cure of hypertension within the individual. While each of these variables has been studied within this model of individual correlates to elevations in blood pressure, none has provided an adequate explanation for either the cause of hypertension or its distribution.

Historical Materialist Epidemiology

The Context of the Emergence of HME

The serious limitations of scientific medicine's ability to explain or treat chronic diseases has contributed to a growing disenchantment with medicine and a reassessment of the medical paradigm which for so long has dominated American medical care. It has become increasingly clear through careful historical analyses of the decline of mortality over the past hundred years that the elimination of infectious diseases as major causes of mortality was tied to a number of social changes, including improvements in sanitation and nutrition, rather than to the specific treatments of medicine (Dubos, 1959; McKeown, 1971; Powles, 1973; Knowles, 1977). Likewise, it is becoming equally clear that chronic diseases also have a relationship to the organization of society, and in particular, to the physical and social environments in which people live and work (Epstein, 1976; House, 1974).

These recognitions of the social components of disease and the limitations of scientific medicine did not develop in a vacuum, but were fueled and made popular in part by a number of social and political struggles that took place over the past twenty-five years. In this context there emerged a strong leftist health movement in the United States, composed of people who were by and large current or future medical care workers. Through organizations such as The Medical Committee for Human Rights, these progressive health workers contributed to an analysis of the way American society creates and sustains ill health in certain segments of the population, and fails to provide equitable, accessible and adequate medical care to all. (See, for example, Bodenheimer et. al., 1972; Ehrenreich and Ehrenreich, 1970; and all of Health/PAC.) As part of the growing understanding of the relationship of health and medical care to the priorities of American society, the reemergence of Marxism within the newly politicized colleges and universities of the 1960s and 1970s provided the intellectual resources for the development of an examination of the basic societal causes of disease and ill health and the relationship of these causes to the political economy of capitalism in particular. These intellectual and social developments provided the historical context in which HME developed and within which it must be examined and appraised.

The Marxist Analysis of Capitalism and the Health of Citizens

There is long tradition of scholarship documenting the consequences of capitalist production on the health of both its paid labor force and the rest of its citizens. The most explicit analysis of this relationship, and a central work for the historical development of historical materialist epidemiology, is Friedrich Engel's (1845) analysis of the conflict of workers and owners in Great Britain in the nineteenth century. In *The Conditions of the Working Class in England,* Engels examined the social conditions produced by early capitalism and their consequences for the health of the working class. Under early (or primitive) capitalism, an industrial working class, a proletariat, was created for the first time in history with no means of subsistence other than the sale of its labor. Early capitalism mechanized the farm and used land for the grazing of animals, giving rise to enclosures, which meant, ultimately, the creation of a surplus of workers forced to migrate from their farms to urban centers to find work (Engels, 1958 [1845]). The need to accumulate capital (property and money) led businesses to minimize the cost of labor power by providing only the cheapest of shelter, food and working conditions (including wages) for its workers. This process resulted in the rise of the great slums of Britain in the nineteenth century and a range of diseases endemic to those particular living conditions—for example, tuberculosis (which still exists in American slums), typhoid, and other infectious epidemics. These diseases, argued Engels, were the social and physical products of early capitalism.

Capitalism has undergone enormous transformation from its early primitive stages to its current stage of what has been termed advanced monopoly capitalism (O'Connor, 1973; Sweezy, 1968). In the process, the nature of work and social life has been altered in the past 150 years, and these changes have been accompanied by a great improvement in the standard of living for the majority of Americans. With this improved standard of living, early deaths from infectious diseases decreased, but the resultant increase in life expectancy has been accompanied by the rise of chronic diseases, including coronary heart disease, cancer, and hypertension and stroke.

By the economic laws of capitalism and capitalist accumulation, it is necessary for businesses to constantly expand their markets, compete with each other, grow ever-larger or, failing that, be swallowed up by even larger businesses. Twentieth-century capitalism is characterized by enormous corporations—firms like General Motors, IBM, AT&T, and Exxon—which dominate the American economy (Baran and Sweezy, 1966). Declining competition created by increasing control by fewer and fewer firms within an economic sector increases the power of corporations and the dependence of workers. So, modern capitalism is characterized by efforts to increase "worker productivity"—that is, the amount of goods or services produced by workers in a given period of time for a given wage. This can be accomplished by introducing technologies to automate portions of the work process and thus eliminate workers and the wages they earn, by getting workers to work harder and thereby produce more in the same time period for the same wage, or by decreasing wages and benefits for workers. As a result, a continuous struggle emerges in the workplace between the owners' need to increase surplus value and the workers' attempts to keep their wages up with the cost of living and to limit the degree of their exploitation in the job market. This struggle between workers and owners—between the working class and the capitalist class—is seen by Marxists as a central

struggle within capitalist society with significant consequences on the health of workers and their families.

During the past six years a number of politically active, progressive health workers and scholars have utilized the philosophy, economic theory, and methodology of Marxism in conjunction with the findings and methods of social epidemiology to study the nature of health and illness in modern society. By conceptualizing historical materialist epidemiology, they have produced a theoretical perspective that differs from that of traditional social epidemiology in its attempts to relate the patterns of disease in society to the economic and social relations which are the historical underpinnings of that society:

> [Historical] Materialist Epidemiology maintains that the history of a particular human disease is a unique nonrepetitive process, which obeys discoverable laws and results from discoverable relationships. These relationships are essentially social in nature. It is the same social environment which forms the context within which we live that also forms the context within which disease arises. The physics and chemistry of diseases may recur again and again. But the causes of these phenomena and the reason for their spread are socially rooted and historical in nature. (Gaynor et al., 1976)[3]

How then does a Marxist perspective inform the study of epidemiology? First, a Marxist perspective alerts us to the important sociological role of economic relations in society. The organization of work and the work process, the distribution of economic wealth and power, and the creation of particular forms of stratification all emerge from a capitalist political economy.[4] Among the particular features of American capitalism are racism, sexism, the chronic unemployment of large segments of the population, significant movement of the population due to the demands for a mobile labor force, crowded and decaying urban centers, and the stratification of society by social class. While not all of these inequalities are unique to American capitalism, they are all *integral* to it and need to be understood as part of the larger social organization of a capitalist economy. Second, a Marxist perspective gives us empirical and theoretical categories by which to locate significant social variations in the health of citizens—categories which emerge from an understanding of the particular inequalities of capitalism as well as the stresses and conflicts produced by a capitalist mode of production. Marxism gives us not only the categories of analysis, but a theory and methodology by which to understand those social, economic, and psychological categories.[5] That scholarship encourages an historical perspective and an understanding of the conflicts and contradictions which characterize the ongoing process of capitalism (Waitzkin, 1978).

In one example of the use of HME to understand disease patterns, Eyer and Sterling (1977) examined the consequences of unavoidable swings in a capitalist economy. They were concerned with the continuous social disruptions engendered by the American economy with its requirements of mobility and a competitive striving for success. They present evidence that disease and death vary among the population according to the predictable patterns of social mobility, urban living, and swings in the economy, including unemployment and periods of industrial expansion. In another article, Eyer (1977b) looked specifically at the effect of the swings in the American economy—the so-called booms and falls—on the mortality rate. He found that booms in the economy, those periods of increased productivity and increased pressures on workers to produce, were characterized by increased death rates:

> The causes of death involved in this variation range from infectious diseases through accidents to heart disease, cancer and cirrhosis of the liver, and include the great majority of all causes of death. Less than 2% of the death rate—that for suicide and homicide—varies directly with unemployment ... the role of social stress is probably predominant. Overwork and the fragmentation of community through migration are two important sources of stress which rise with the boom, and they are demonstrably related to the causes of death which show this variation. (Eyer, 1977b:125.)

While there is continuing debate about whether these economic swings indeed cause the patterns of death that Eyer claims (Brenner, 1977; Eyer, 1977a), there is no doubt that in order to develop a fully articulated analysis of the relationship of society and disease, we need to examine and understand the particular consequences of changes in the economy on people's health. We cannot present here all the work done within the perspective of HME[6] but we can note a range of health issues that have been examined from and informed by this perspective, including suicide (Hopper and Guttmacher, 1979), violence against women (Stark, Flitcraft, and Frazier, 1979), the epidemic (Stark, 1977b), and occupational health (Turshen, 1977; Gaynor, 1977; Stark, 1977a; HMO Packet #5, 1979; Sterling, 1978). In addition, there is a range of works which utilizes a Marxist paradigm to analyze the features of the medical care system as it relates to the political economy. (See, for example, HMO Packet #6, 1979; Salmon, 1977; Navarro, 1977 and 1978; and Rodberg and Stevenson, 1977.)

An important study of the social origins of hypertension—and a work that did much to stimulate the development of HME—was an early work by Joseph Eyer on "Hypertension as a disease of modern society." In that study, Eyer identifies two features of modern society as being critical to the development of hypertension in the population: (1) the disruption of social communities, and (2) the rise of hierarchically controlled, time-pressured work. For Eyer the central feature of modernization is the

> ... wresting of control over social resources ... from the village communities and craft organizations ... and placing this control in the hands of a new ruling class, either private or state capitalists ... [This] transfer of power entails the destruction of the settled rural kin-based extended family and village community ... delegating socialization and work training to an extra communal educational system (Eyer, 1975: 547).

Eyer concludes that people who are uprooted from stable communities, thrust into hostile, competitive urban environments experience great elevations in their blood pressure. Of equal importance is the continual development of new technology and work organization that characterizes modern society.

> Combined with the accompanying specialization and hierarchical division of labor, this development

necessitates multiple work role adjustments during the life-span, and this in turn means that a higher proportion of people experience a lack of fit between their skills and preparation and the work position they find themselves in. (Eyer, 1975: 548)

While Eyer attempts to relate these changes in modern society to the social relations of capitalism, his analysis is limited by his puzzling conclusion that there ". . . is no relation between the economic level of the population and rates of death from hypertension or between family income and blood pressure . . ." (Eyer, 1975: 548–549). For Eyer, all residents of modern society experience elevations in blood pressure. As we will see, however, specific features of capitalist society (e.g., differentials in income) *are* correlated with differences in both prevalence of hypertension and subsequent morbidity from this disease.

Utilizing Historical Materialist Epidemiology to Understand Hypertension

Drawing on the perspective of historical materialist epidemiology, we would hypothesize that there is an identifiable relationship between the patterns of hypertension in American society and the (historically changing) political economic organization of society. We know that capitalism generates particular inequalities, divisions, conflicts, and stresses among its citizens, although understanding the relationship between these particular social forms and disease patterns is an enormous task. Likewise, it is important to remember that not everybody who is oppressed, stressed, or underpaid develops hypertension (or even gets sick). As social scientists, however, we are interested in trends in the population rather than the "exception to the rule," and so we begin by looking at patterned differences. Ultimately we would need to know a lot more about the details of the effects of both physical and social differences (including the role of personality) before we could develop a fully adequate understanding of the causes of hypertension. We suggest that by examining the variations in the distribution of hypertension in American society according to the social and physical categories

suggested by HME, we can begin to develop this understanding.

This is not an easy task, in part because existing data are usually gathered by researchers who utilize the medical model to design their studies, collect their data, and analyze their findings. These limitations affect the types of analyses we can generate from available research. We present the following as a preliminary evaluation of what HME can tell us about hypertension, an evaluation based on available epidemiological data, with all its limitations. With this in mind, then, we turn to five categories suggested by the HME perspective as relevant social categories for the study of disease: (1) social class, (2) occupation, (3) race/ethnicity, (4) gender, and (5) age.

Social Class and Hypertension

The fact that poverty is associated with increased prevalence rates of all diseases has been well documented (Kitagawa and Hauser, 1973). Interestingly, there is limited information on the relationship of income to hypertension. Social class, by which Marxists mean people's relationship to the economy, is often referred to as "socioeconomic status" and is measured only indirectly in many studies by occupation, level of education, or income.[7] HME leads us to hypothesize that those people with the least economic benefit from work, or those unable to support themselves and their families (i.e., the poor and working class) would show more evidence of hypertension than wealthier populations. To test this hypothesis on available data, however, we will have to look at both income and education as indicators of social class.

> Mean systolic blood pressure levels in the U.S. population are found to be inversely related to the size of the family income. As family income increases from less than $3000 to $10,000 or more per year, the mean systolic pressure of the population age 7–74 decreases [as well] . . . (DHEW, 1977: 15–16.)[8]

Utilizing education as an indicator of socioeconomic status (i.e., higher levels of education represent higher social class), a similar relationship to income is found: "blood pressure shows a significant inverse relationship to education level . . ." (DHEW, 1977: 16). This finding is replicated in another study where "prevalence of hypertension was [found to be] inversely related to level of education among both blacks and whites, i.e., the greater the number of school years completed, the lower the prevalence of hypertension . . ." (HDFP, 1977: 354). The differences between the extremes of education are also quite marked:

> Those completing college had approximately 40 percent lower prevalence rates of hypertension than did those completing less than ten years of school (36.9 percent lower in black college graduates and 41.6 percent lower in white college graduates). (HDFP, 1977: 354.)

This relationship between level of education and prevalence of hypertension holds up in all age groups, although it is more marked in the younger populations and is a "considerably more striking" relationship among blacks than whites. So, for example, among the black population between 30–39 years of age, those with a college education were found to have a hypertension prevalence rate almost 50 percent *lower* than those blacks with less than ten years of formal education (HDFP, 1977: 354).

When income has been studied directly, the strongest relationship between income and prevalence of hypertension was found for the age group 35–49, where the prevalence of hypertension is three times higher in the group whose annual income is less than $5,000 than the group with an annual income of $15,000 or more (Harris, 1973). Interestingly, no large-scale studies of the prevalence of hypertension among the upper class have been carried out. In fact, the National Health Survey (a major source of national health information) lumps together all those who earn more than $14,000 into one group. In addition, no research has carefully analyzed available data on income, education, *and* occupation simultaneously in one analysis. So, the exact relationship of social class to hypertension can only be approximated, although it is clear that there is a relationship between income and prevalence of hypertension.

Occupation and Hypertension

An association between certain occupations and an increased prevalence of hypertension has been demonstrated. However, little can be learned about the national distribution of hypertension by occupational category as there are practically no national data available by occupation. The National Health Survey for 1960–1962 gathered data on hypertension and occupation and found that certain occupations had higher prevalence rates than others. However, no follow-up or long-term prospective study was done to identify the characteristics of the occupations correlated with elevations in blood pressure. In fact, the National Health Survey did not collect data on hypertension again until 1970–1972, but at this time did not collect data on occupation.

In a review of several smaller studies on occupation and hypertension, Mustacchi examines the possible physical causes of hypertension within the workplace. Among the physical characteristics of work associated with high blood pressure are continuous exposure to noise, physical vibrations, extremes of heat and cold, and a range of chemicals and toxins (Mustacchi, 1977).

Recently, Karasek and his co-workers have been developing a more adequate understanding of the relationship among work, stress, and hypertension through a detailed examination of particular features of occupations and rates of hypertension (Karasek et al., 1978). Among the variables they found associated with hypertension are time-pressured work, a lack of freedom over work and the conditions of work, and working under close supervision. Assuming the replicability of these findings, questions arise as to the specific features of occupations which are responsible for elevations in blood pressure. We might ask, for example, whether it is the repetitive nature of certain jobs that causes hypertension, or the lack of worker control over the worksite (as when assembly lines are speeded up by management or work breaks limited to increase worker productivity)? Perhaps it is the workers' lack of control over the future of their jobs which contributes to hypertension (plants may close with little or no notice to workers, moving whole companies to areas or other countries where lower wages can be paid to poorer workers). These issues are raised by utilizing the perspective of HME and by some of the initial findings of correlations between occupation and rates of hypertension, although as yet they have not been specifically investigated. This suggests to the sociologist that there are "natural" experiments possible which might permit a better understanding of what it is about work that contributes to hypertension. For example, by comparing factories or plants organized traditionally (in which workers have little or no control over their work or the work process) with more innovative settings (in which workers collectively own and manage whole plants or have more control than under the traditional work organizations), we might be able to identify and document what we can only hypothesize to be differences in stress and consequent rates of hypertension in different occupational situations.

Race/Ethnicity and Hypertension

As was discussed earlier, the discovery of higher rates of hypertension among American blacks was interpreted (and still is by many medical scientists) as evidence of a genetic etiology of hypertension, at least among blacks. This perspective was initially weakened by data collected in cross-cultural anthropological studies which demonstrated that groups of blacks living in Africa in their original tribal conditions, and with genetic inheritance identical with that of American blacks, did not demonstrate progressive increases in blood pressure with age (Page, 1976). Migration studies as well demonstrate that during the process of adjustment to modern, industralized societies, these groups evidence increases in their levels of blood pressure.

Before looking at variations among blacks, let us look at the data on the difference between hypertension in blacks and whites. There is a systematic difference in the patterns and prevalence of hypertension among whites and blacks in the United States. Without controlling for age or social class (or anything else), one study found that among males, the hypertension prevalence ratio of blacks to whites was 1.9 and for females was a higher 2.2. In comparing the patterns of

age and blood pressure elevations for blacks and whites, studies have found that black and white males have similar levels of blood pressure up until about the age of twenty-four, whereupon the population of black men has progressively greater elevations of blood pressure with increasing age than white men. (HDFP, 1977; DHEW, 1977). A similar pattern for females shows an increase in prevalence of hypertension in black women compared to white women after about the age of twenty-five (DHEW, 1977).

During the past fifteen years a number of researchers have studied patterns of hypertension among blacks while controlling for other variables, including age, social class, and community disruption. By comparing poor blacks with poor whites living under similar social circumstances (e.g., in communities with significant amounts of social stress as measured by high crime and juvenile delinquency rates, high rates of other violence, and high rates of divorce), these researchers have sought to identify the specific influence of race versus other social characteristics on patterns of hypertension. In all these studies, when both socioeconomic status and levels of social or community disruption were controlled for, the differences in prevalence rates between blacks and whites dropped significantly (Harburg, 1973; James and Kleinbaum, 1976; Keil et al., 1977).

The fact that a small but significant difference still persists between blacks and whites even when controlling for social class and community disruption points to the possibility that institutionalized racism with its damaging psychological and social consequences may contribute independently to the stress experienced by blacks, and therefore to the etiology of hypertension. (This would parallel the finding that Reed [1981] reports on the consequences of institutionalized racism on infant mortality in the United States.) Alternatively, the data may be interpreted to mean genetic inheritance does play a small role in the etiology of hypertension among blacks.

Given the pattern of increased hypertension among blacks (i.e., that the difference between whites and blacks increases with age), we might hypothesize that somewhere in their mid-twenties, black people are forced to recognize the reality of their social situation—a reality in this country characterized by high unemployment, poor paying jobs with little prospect for advancement, and persistent patterns of social discrimination based on race. In his study of blacks and whites in Detroit, Harburg found a significantly increased amount of repressed anger in those blacks with elevated blood pressure compared to those blacks with normal levels of blood pressure. Perhaps, Harburg theorized, blacks faced with a bleak future internalize their anger because of their socialization and the fear of the consequences of expressing their rage, resulting in the patterns of hypertension he found (Harburg, 1973).

Hypertension and Gender

For both women and men in the United States, average blood pressure increases with age, but from twenty-five years on, the rate is substantially higher in women than in men (DHEW, 1977). Up until about the age of forty-five, men's (as a population) blood pressure is greater than women's. After that, for both blacks and whites, women's blood pressure surpasses and remains higher than men's (HDFP, 1977; DHEW, 1977; Kannel et al., 1969). While this patterned difference between women and men's rates of hypertension has been shown and replicated for years, little is known beyond this about the differences in blood pressure by gender. In fact, little is known about women's health patterns in general (Olesen, 1977). Much more about variations among different groups of women needs to be learned. However, limitations in the epidemiological data collected about women often prevent such intra-gender comparisons.

In one recently published study of coronary heart disease among women, comparisons between women who worked outside the home with housewives revealed important differences among working women, as well as among women with different numbers of children. Although somewhat limited and not directly a study of hypertension, we can see in this study the potential for important differentiations among groups of women suggested by the findings that numbers of children and type of job

correlated more with coronary heart disease than whether or not a woman worked outside the home *per se* (Haynes and Feinleib, 1980). Without an adequate understanding of the details of women's lives, including their domestic and family arrangements, we cannot really illuminate variations in women's health patterns (Kanter, 1977; Verbrugge, 1979).

One explanation for the pattern of female hypertension has to do with acknowledging the decreasing social and cultural value of women in our society as they age (Stannard, 1971). There is evidence, for example, that when women devote their younger years exclusively to unpaid domestic work, including the raising of children, they are more likely to become ill after their children are grown and leave home (Bart, 1970). For many women, aging means the loss of identity along with the loss of a socially valued role. This would possibly explain the pattern of increased hypertension in middle class women, but since many working class women don't really shift their work patterns with age, such an explanation may be inapplicable to them. Without better data on variations in women's domestic lives, differences by social class between women's patterns of work and health, and more information on women's health patterns in general, any possible explanation of women's patterns of hypertension remain speculative (Lipman-Bluman, 1977).

Age and Hypertension

As mentioned earlier, a consistent finding in studies of prevalence patterns of hypertension is that hypertension increases with the age of the population (DHEW, 1977; Kannel et al., 1969; DHEW, 1978). As seen in Table 1, the prevalence of hypertension increases for both blacks and whites with each age increment.

Although we earlier noted that cross-cultural evidence does not support the hypothesis that increased blood pressure is part of the "natural" process of aging, we can hypothesize that the increasing prevalence of hypertension with age in the United States has a social and economic basis. We suggest there are two interrelated processes that account for the findings concerning age and hypertension. First, stress has a cumulative effect

Table 1.   Prevalence per 100 of Hypertension by Race and Age: United States, 1974

Age	All persons 17 years and over	White	Black
All ages over 17 years	16.8	16.0	24.1
17–24 years	4.2	4.1	5.3
25–44 years	9.5	8.6	17.9
45–64 years	24.2	22.7	39.1
65 years and over	36.3	35.3	47.2

SOURCE: DHEW, 1978. "Characteristics of persons with hypertension: United States, 1974." Edited by Abigail J. Moss. Vital and Health Statistics, Data from National Health Survey. DHEW Publication No. (PHS) 79-1549 [series 10, no. 121], p.4.

over the course of any particular person's lifetime, so that we see a gradual but constant increase in blood pressure with increased age among most Americans. Second, being old in our society is itself a negative experience for many, with its own particular sets of stresses and difficulties. Many old people must live on fixed incomes from inadequate Social Security or retirement benefits; many are forced to live in nursing homes for lack of alternatives; and the elderly are enormously overrepresented among the poor in this country. No longer able to be of "economic value" unless they are wealthy, the elderly find themselves without social or cultural value in a society that honors wealth and gives privilege only to those who can afford to buy it. The point for this discussion is that age, like gender and race, is not simply a physical characteristic (although it is often conceptualized so by medical research), but is a social and psychological one as well. It is in understanding the social nature of aging that we can begin to get some insight into the stresses and problems that the elderly have which can lead to sustained elevations in blood pressure and perhaps explain the American patterns of hypertension by age.

Summary and Conclusions

We have seen that certain groups of people in American society are more likely to have hypertension than others. Hypertension varies with social class (being more prevalent among those with less income and less education), race (being more prevalent among blacks than whites), age (it varies directly with age), occupation (certain

occupations, and particular features of work situations are correlated with higher rates of hypertension), and gender (women have lower prevalence rates than men until their mid-forties when they surpass and exceed men's rates, and after the age of twenty-five, women's rates of hypertension increase more rapidly than do men's).

While a great deal of information has been collected relating these various social categories to prevalence rates of hypertension, each of these correlations treats the social variables as if they were independent of one another. The studies reviewed presented these variables as if they were characteristics of individuals rather than reflections of patterns of society. HME would suggest alternatively that we examine these correlations and categories *simultaneously* in order to identify the broad social and physical context in which hypertension occurs. Social class, occupation, race, age, and gender are interrelated in the organization of society. The political economy of capitalism (with its particular social and cultural characteristics) gives rise to both the organization of American society and the distribution and patterns of disease within it.

Historical materialist epidemiology makes those connections through a social analysis informed by a Marxist perspective. That perspective gives priority to the economic relations in society generated by the organization of production (work) and the distribution of material resources.

Before drawing any further conclusions, we want to reiterate the preliminary nature of HME, point out what we regard as some serious limitations in its perspective, and offer some suggestions for its future direction. Among its limitations are: (1) the overemphasis on wage labor, (2) the need for a feminist perspective and an understanding of the domestic sphere, and (3) the need for original, prospective empirical research.

(1) Traditional Marxist approaches, including HME,[9] focus on the importance of paid (wage) labor and the social relations of production as the crucial processes of society. While it is certainly the case that the organization of work under capitalism produces a range of stressful work conditions as well as an unequal distribution of wealth and power in society, we need to go beyond the organization of paid labor in order to understand all of the patterns of hypertension we find. The widespread existence of hypertension among the chronically unemployed as well as those who perform unpaid labor in the home (most women in our society) are two patterns which, while related to the political economy of capitalism, represent different sorts of stresses than those found within the factory. Perhaps the perception that one lacks control over one's life (true for both the employed and unemployed) is a central factor in the development of hypertension. Likewise, the small but significant percentage of hypertension among blacks that is not explained by their economic situation requires a fuller understanding of the social, psychological, and physical consequences of racism. We suggest that an adequate HME perspective will need to expand the range of social situations examined beyond those most directly related to paid labor in order to develop a full understanding of the processes involved in the development of hypertension in our society.

(2) There is a growing feminist literature that points to the limitations of Marxism to account for either the particular experiences of women in society (including their patterns of morbidity and mortality) or the relationships of men and women. (See, for example, Eisenstein, 1979; Kuhn and Wolpe, 1978; Mitchell, 1971; Firestone, 1970.) A major point of this feminist critique is the serious limitations in the Marxist understanding of the family and the domestic sphere. (See, for example, Poster, 1978; Zaretsky, 1976.) In order to account for the particular patterns of hypertension among women, and the variations among groups of women, we need to expand HME to understand the related but separate effects of the "sex/gender system" (institutionalized male dominance) and capitalism on both women and men (Rubin, 1975).

(3) The last problem reflects the available epidemiological research on chronic disease, so much of which utilizes a traditional medical model to gather and analyze its data. We suggest the critical need for original empirical research that is prospective and incorporates the theoretical and empirical categories of HME (as expanded to include unpaid labor, non-work social and psychological variables, and an adequate understanding of the consequences of sexism, the lives of women, and the role of the domestic sphere). Such research would be able to provide the sort of data we currently lack in order to test the hypothesized relationships between the organization of American society and the patterns of disease among its citizens. While HME helps us to identify possible and significant correlations (e.g., between social class and hypertension), without better data we cannot identify the causal processes that are involved in the etiology of hypertension (or any other chronic disease). Although no perspective can provide the total explanation for a chronic disease, research examining HME's hypotheses will enlighten our understanding of the social production of disease in a new way.

While this article cannot begin to address the complex social and political reasons why medicine has failed to explore the social basis of hypertension, it is easily demonstrable by examining the available medical literature that medicine continues to rely on a paradigm that does not (and cannot) incorporate social structural variables into the explanation and prevention of chronic disease. HME has as an explicit part of its theory the corollary possibility of the prevention of disease by changing those social and political conditions that contribute to its development. So, we would conclude from our examination of hypertension that we need to identify and understand better the social bases of stress as well as the relevant physical conditions which contribute to chronic elevations in blood pressure, and work to eliminate them in order to prevent the continued epidemic of hypertension in our society. This stance unfortunately is exactly the opposite of that of the current campaign of organized medicine, the National Heart, Blood and Lung Institute (part of the Department of Health, Education and Welfare), and the American pharmaceutical industry, which have joined forces to attempt to "cure" hypertension by placing 50 million (or more!) American adults on medications for even mild elevations in blood pressure (Relman, 1980). Indeed, this campaign has taken the direction of seeking increasingly sophisticated methods of ensuring patient "compliance" with medication regimens in order to guarantee the "success" of treatment.

We are certainly not opposed to those with severe hypertension being given the option of taking medications to lower their blood pressure: indeed, they should take such medications. However, in the long run, the most logical and safe approach to eliminating hypertension is to prevent it. This means, of course, identifying and eliminating those sources of both physical and social stress that are causing so many people to be plagued by this chronic and serious disease. Only through an analysis such as HME can we develop an integrated understanding of the relationship between society and disease, and thereby begin to develop insights and recommendations to eliminate hypertension through its prevention.

NOTES

We thank Peter Conrad and Kim Hopper for their extensive conceptual and editorial suggestions, and Gail Garbowski for her background research contributions. We take full responsibility for the ideas presented here. (The order of author listing was determined by the flip of a coin.)

1. Until about five years ago, the higher cutoff of 160/95 was used within medicine as the measurement of "normal" blood pressure. (See, for example, Inter-Society Commission for Heart Disease Resources, 1970.)
2. An early effort to develop a socio-medical analysis of hypertension was by Stahl et al. (1975) and suggested a model in which cognition (or perception) mediates between social structure and the development of hypertension (and other diseases). However, the ultimate suggestion that physicians become involved in the "manipulation of percep-

tion" is not only questionable, but relies once again on an individualistic conceptualization of disease and cure.
3. See also Schnall (1977) for an early introduction to the conceptualization of HME.
4. While non-capitalist societies also have chronic disease (including hypertension), the major focus of HME has been on the particular disease patterns prevalent under capitalism. Certainly, comparative and cross-cultural work needs to be done in order to isolate the particular products of American capitalism from those of other forms of political economic organization. One problem is the increasingly international influence of capitalism through multi-national corporations, so that any analysis of "underdeveloped" Third World countries would necessarily have to address their relationship to capitalist economies.
5. At this point we note that there are limitations in the Marxist perspective, and in HME, and these will be discussed in the last section of this paper.
6. Two valuable published resources of work are: *The Review of Radical Political Economics* (Special Issue on "The Political Economy of Health"), Vol. 9, No. 1, Spring, 1977, available through URPE, 41 Union Square West, Room 901, New York, NY 10003, and *The International Journal of Health Services* (published quarterly and to be found in most university libraries).
7. In one major study of hypertension, the researchers actually gathered data on family income as well as the occupation of the "head of the household," but chose to use only education as a measure of socioeconomic status. Their failure to use family income and occupation, as well as their failure to develop more adequate measures of social class, remains a serious limitation in their study (HDFP, 1977).
8. This citation refers to the findings of the United States National Health Survey.
9. There is variation within the writings of those who see their work as contributing to an historical materialist epidemiology. In particular, some have tried to expand the traditional Marxist emphasis on paid labor and the social relations of production, although this emphasis does dominate the bulk of HME writings. One notable exception is Hopper and Guttmacher (1979).

REFERENCES

Actuarial Society of America and The Association of Life Insurance Medical Directors. 1941. "Supplement to 'Blood Pressure Study.' " New York: Actuarial Society of America and The Association of Life Insurance Medical Directors.

Baran, Paul, and Paul Sweezy. 1966. Monopoly Capital. New York: Monthly Review Press.

Bart, Pauline. 1970. "Portnoy's mother's complaint." Trans-action (November–December).

Bodenheimer, Thomas, Steve Cummings and Elizabeth Harding. 1972. Billions for Bandaids. San Francisco: Medical Committee for Human Rights.

Brenner, Harvey. 1977. "Health costs and benefits of economic policy." International Journal of Health Services 7, 4: 581–623.

Brown, George. 1974. "Meaning, measurement, and stress of life events." Pp. 217–244 in Barbara S. Dohrenwend and Bruce P. Dohrenwend (eds.), Stressful Life Events: Their Nature and Effects. New York: John Wiley and Sons.

Castiglione, Arturo. 1947. A History of Medicine. New York: Alfred A. Knopf.

Cobb, S., and R. M. Rose. 1973. "Hypertension, peptic ulcer, and diabetes in air traffic controllers." The Journal of The American Medical Association 224: 489–492.

Dahl, L. 1960. "Possible role of salt intake in the development of essential hypertension." Pp. 53ff in K. Bock and P. Cottier (eds.), Essential Hypertension. Berlin: Springer-Verlag.

D'Atri, D. A., and A. M. Ostfeld. 1975. "Crowding: Its effects on the elevation of blood pressure in a prison setting." Preventive Medicine 4: 550–566.

Davis, David, and Max Klainer. 1940. "Studies in hypertensive heart disease I. The incidence of coronary atherosclerosis in cases of essential hypertension." American Heart Journal 19: 185–192.

DHEW. 1964. "Hypertension and hypertensive heart disease, United States, 1960–1962." Vital and Health Statistics from the National Center for Health Statistics, Data from National Health Survey. DHEW [series 11, no. 13].

DHEW. 1977. "Blood pressure levels of persons 6–74 years, United States, 1971–1974." Edited by Jean Roberts. Department of Health, Education and Welfare. DHEW No. (HRA) 78-1648 [series 11, number 203].

DHEW. 1978. "Characteristics of persons with hypertension: United States, 1974." Edited by Abigail J. Moss. Vital and Health Statistics, Data from National Health Survey. DHEW Publication No. (PHS) 79-1549 [series 10, no. 121].

DHEW. 1980 "Births, marriages, divorces, and deaths for 1979." Monthly Vital Statistics Report, Provisional Statistics from the National Center for Health Statistics. Department of Health, Education and Welfare. DHEW Publication No. (PHS) 80-1120 [vol. 28, no. 12] (March 14).

Dohrenwend, Bruce P. 1974. "Problems in defining and sampling the relevant populations of stressful life events." Pp. 275–312 in Barbara S. Dohrenwend and Bruce P. Dohrenwend (eds.), Stressful Life Events. New York: John Wiley and Sons.

Dubos, René. 1959. Mirage of Health. New York: Harper and Row.

Ehrenreich, Barbara, and John Ehrenreich. 1970. The American Health Empire: Power, Profits and Politics. New York: Random House.

Eisenstein, Zillah R. (ed.). 1979. Capitalist Patriarchy and the Case for Socialist Feminism. New York: Monthly Review Press.

Engels, Friedrich. 1958. [1845] The Condition of the Working Class in England. Stanford, California: Stanford University Press.

Epstein, Samuel. 1976. "The political and economic basis of cancer." Technology Review 78: 1–7.

Eyer, Joseph. 1975. "Hypertension as a disease of modern society." International Journal of Health Services 5, 4: 539–558.

Eyer, Joseph. 1977a. "Does unemployment cause the death rate peak in each business cycle? A multifactor model of death rate change." International Journal of Health Services 7, 4: 625–662.

Eyer, Joseph. 1977b. "Prosperity as a cause of death." International Journal of Health Services 7, 1: 125–150.

Eyer, Joseph, and P. Sterling. 1977. "Stress-related mortality and social organization." The Review of Radical Political Economics 9, 1 (Spring): 1–44.

Firestone, Shulamith. 1970. The Dialectic of Sex. New York: William Morrow and Co., Inc.

Freis, Edward. 1976. "Salt, volume and the prevention of hypertension." Circulation 53, 4: 589–595.

Gaynor, David, et al. 1976. "Materialist epidemiology." HMO Packet #1: ME/1.

Gaynor, David. 1977. "Materialist epidemiology applied to occupational health and safety." HMO Packet #2: The Social Etiology of Disease (Part I): 23–28.

Harburg, E. W., J. Schull, J. C. Erfurt, and M. A. Schork. 1970. "A family-set method for estimating heredity and stress I. A pilot survey of blood pressure among Negroes in high and low stress areas, Detroit, 1966–1967." Journal of Chronic Disease 23: 69–81.

Harburg, E. W. 1973. "Socio-ecological stress, suppressed hostility, skin color, and black-white male blood pressure." Psychosomatic Medicine 35, 4.

Harris, L. 1973. "The public and high blood pressure." A Survey Conducted for the National Heart and Lung Institute. Department of Health, Education and Welfare 74–356.

Harrison, T. R. 1977. Harrison's Principles of Internal Medicine, Eighth Edition. Edited by George W. Thorn, et al. New York: McGraw-Hill Book Company.

Haynes, Suzanne, and Manning Feinleib. 1980. "Women, work and coronary heart disease: Prospective findings from the Framingham heart study." American Journal of Public Health 70, 2 (February): 133–141.

Health/PAC, 17 Murray Street, New York NY 10007.

HMO Packet #5. 1979. "Work and Health." Unpublished collection of papers.

HMO Packet #6. 1979. "Imperialism, Dependency and Health. The Political and Economic Determinants of Health and Nutrition. Case Studies in Latin America." Unpublished collection of papers available from: Sally Guttmacher, Columbia University School of Public Health, Division of Sociomedical Sciences, 600 W. 168th Street, New York, NY 10032.

Hopper, Kim, and Sally Guttmacher. 1979. "Rethinking suicide: Notes toward a critical epidemiology." International Journal of Health Services 9, 3: 417–438.

House, James. 1974. "Occupational stress and coronary heart disease: A review and theoretical integration." Journal of Health and Social Behavior 15 (March): 17–27.

Hypertension Detection and Follow-up Cooperative Group [HDFP]. 1977. "Race, education and prevalence of hypertension: Hypertension Detection and Follow-up Program Cooperative Group." American Journal of Epidemiology 106, 5 (November): 351–361.

Hypertension Detection and Follow-up Cooperative Group [HDFP]. 1979. "Five-year findings of the Hypertension Detection and Follow-up Program I, Reduction in mortality of persons with HBP, including mild hypertension." and "Five-year findings of the Hypertension Detection and Follow-up Program II, Mortality by race-sex to age." Journal of the American Medical Association [JAMA] 242, 23: 2562–2577.

Inter-Society Commission for Health Disease Resources. 1970. "Primary prevention of the atherosclerotic diseases." Circulation 43: A55.

James, Sherman, and David Kleinbaum. 1976. "Socioecologic stress and hypertension related mortality rates in North Carolina." American Journal of Public Health 66, 4 (April).

Janeway, Theodore. 1906. "The diagnostic significance of persistent high arterial pressure." American Journal of Medical Sciences 131: 772–779.

Kannel, William, et al. 1969. "Blood pressure and risk of coronary heart disease: The Framingham study." Diseases of the Chest 56: 43–52.

Kanter, Rosabeth Moss. 1977. Work and Family in the United States: A Critical Review and Agenda for Research and Policy. New York: Russell Sage.

Karasek, Robert, et al. 1978. "Job decision latitude, job demands and coronary heart disease, A cross-sectional and prospective study of Swedish men." Unpublished paper quoted with author's permission (December).

Kasl, S.V., and S. Cobb. 1970. "Blood pressure changes in men undergoing job loss: A preliminary report." Psychosomatic Medicine 2: 19–38.

Keil, Julian, et al. 1977. "Hypertension: Effects of social class and racial admixture." American Journal of Public Health 67, 7 (July): 634–639.

Kitagawa, E. M., and P. Hauser. 1973. Differential Mortality in the United States: A Study in Socioeconomic Epidemiology. Cambridge, Mass: Harvard University Press.

Knowles, John. 1977. "The responsibility of the individual." Daedalus (Winter).

Kuhn, Annette, and Ann Marie Wolpe (eds.). 1978. Feminism and Materialism, Women and Modes of Production. London: Routledge and Kegan Paul.

Lipman-Bluman, Jean. 1977. "Demographic trends and issues in women's health." Pp. 11–22 in V. Olesen (ed.), Women and Their Health: Research Implications for a New Era. Proceedings of a Conference Held at San Francisco, California, August 1–2. 1975. National Center for Health Services Research.

McKeown, Thomas. 1971. "A historical appraisal of the medical task." In G. McLachlan and T. McKeown (eds.), Medical History and Medical Care: A Symposium of Perspectives. New York: Oxford University Press.

Mitchell, Juliet. 1971. Woman's Estate. New York: Random House.

Mustacchi, Piero. 1977. "The interface of the work environment and hypertension." Medical Clinics of North America 61, 3 (May): 531–545.

National High Blood Pressure Education Program. 1978. "Info-memo." National Heart, Lung and Blood Institute 13 (May).

Navarro, Vicente. 1977. "Political power, the state, and their implications in medicine." The Review of Radical Political Economics 9, 1 (Spring): 61–80.

Navarro, Vicente. 1978. "The crisis of the western system of medicine in contemporary capitalism." International Journal of Health Services 8, 2: 179–211.

O'Connor, James. 1973. The Fiscal Crisis of the State. New York: St. Martin's Press.

Olesen, Virginia (ed). 1977. Women and Their Health: Research Implications for a New Era. Proceedings of a Conference Held at San Francisco, California, August 1–2, 1975. National Center for Health Services Research.

Page, Lot. 1976. "Epidemiological evidence on the etiology of human hypertension and its possible prevention." American Heart Journal 91, 4 (April): 527–534.

Pickering, George W. 1961. The Nature of Essential Hypertension. New York: Grune and Stratton, Inc.

Pickering, George. 1975. "Hypertension: Natural histories and consequences." In J. H. Laragh (ed.), Hypertension Manual: Mechanisms, Methods, Management. New York: Dun-Donnelly Publishing Corporation.

Poster, Mark. 1978. Critical Theory of the Family. New York: Seabury Press.

Powles, John. 1973. "On the limitations of modern medicine." Science, Medicine and Man 1: 1–30.

Reed, Wornie. 1981. "Suffer the children: Some effects of racism on the health of black infants." In Part Two of this volume.

Relman, Arnold S. 1980. "Mild hypertension: No more benign neglect." New England Journal of Medicine 302, 5 (January 31): 293–294.

Rodberg, Leonard, and Gelvin Stevenson. 1977. "The health care industry in advanced capitalism." The Review of Radical Political Economics 9, 1 (Spring): 104–115.

Rubin, Gayle. 1975. "The traffic in women: Notes on the 'political economy' of sex." Pp. 157–210 in Rayna Reiter (ed.), Toward an Anthropology of Women. New York: Monthly Review Press.

Ruskin, Arthur. 1956. Classics in Arterial Hypertension. Charles C. Thomas Publishers.

Salmon, J. Warren. 1977. "Monopoly capital and the reorganization of the health sector." The Review of Radical Political Economics 9, 1 (Spring): 125–133.

Schnall, Peter L. 1977. "An introduction to Historical Materialist Epidemiology." HMO Packet #2, The Social Etiology of Disease (Part I): 1–9.

Shapiro, Alvin (ed.). 1979. "The role of stress in hypertension—A symposium." The Journal of Human Stress 4, 2 (June): 7–26.

Stahl, Sidney M., et al. 1975. "A model for the social sciences and medicine: The case for hypertension." Social Science and Medicine 9: 31–38.

Stannard, Una. 1971. "The mask of beauty." Pp. 187–203 in Vivian Gornick and Barbara K. Moran (eds.), Woman in Sexist Society. New York: Basic Books.

Stark, Evan. 1977a. "The cutting edge in occupational health." HMO Packet #3: The Social Etiology of Disease (Part II), Implications and Applications of HME: 52–62.

Stark, Evan. 1977b. "The epidemic as a social event." International Journal of Health Services 7, 4: 681–705.

Stark, Evan, Anne Flitcraft and William Frazier. 1979. "Medicine and patriarchal violence: The social construction of a 'private' event." International Journal of Health Services 9, 3: 461–493.

Sterling, T. D. 1978. "Does smoking kill workers or working kill smokers? Or the mutual relationship between smoking, occupation, and respiratory disease." International Journal of Health Services 8, 3: 437–452.

Sweezy, Paul. 1968. The Theory of Capitalist Development. New York: Monthly Review Press.

Thomas, C. B. 1973. "Genetic patterns of hypertension in man." In G. Onesti, K. E. Kim, and J. H. Moyer (eds.), Hypertension Mechanism and Management. New York: Grune and Stratton, Inc.

Thomas, E. 1959. The Harmless People. New York: Vintage.

Turshen, Meredeth. 1977. "Worker safety and health." HMO Packet #3: The Social Etiology of Disease (Part II), Implications and Applications of HME: 41–51.

Verbrugge, Lois. 1979. "Marital status and health." Journal of Marriage and Family (May): 267–285.

Waitzkin, Howard. 1978. "A Marxist view of medical care." Annals of Internal Medicine 89: 264–278.

Waldron, Ingrid. 1977. "Society, 'stress' and illness." HMO Packet #2: The Social Etiology of Disease (Part I): 105–107.

Wetherby, Macnider. 1932. "A comparison of blood pressure in men and women." Annals of Internal Medicine 6: 754–770.

Zaretsky, Eli. 1976. Capitalism, the Family and Personal Life. New York: Harper Colophon.

Zinner, S. H., P. S. Levy and E. H. Kass. 1971. "Familial aggregation of blood pressure in childhood." New England Journal of Medicine 284: 401–404.

The Experience of Illness

Disease not only involves the body. It also affects people's social relationships, self-image, and behavior. The social psychological aspects of illness are related in part to the biophysiological manifestations of disease, but are also independent of them. The very act of defining something as an illness has consequences that are independent of any effects of biophysiology.

> When a veterinarian diagnoses a cow's condition as an illness, he does not merely by diagnosis change the cow's behavior; to the cow, illness [disease] remains an experienced biophysiological state, no more. But when a physician diagnoses a human's condition as an illness, he changes the man's behavior by diagnosis: a social state is added to a biophysiological state by assigning the meaning of illness to disease. (Friedson, 1970: 223.)

Much of the sociological study of illness has centered on the *sick role* and *illness behavior*. Talcott Parsons (1951) argued that in order to prevent the potentially disruptive consequences of illness on a group or society, there exists a set of shared cultural rules (norms) called the "sick role." The sick role legitimates the deviations caused by illness and channels the sick into the reintegrating physician-patient relationship. According to Parsons the sick role has four components: (1) the sick person is exempted from normal social responsibilities, at least to the extent it is necessary to get well; (2) the individual is not held responsible for his or her condition and cannot be expected to recover by an act of will; (3) the person must recognize that being ill is undesirable and must want to recover; and (4) the sick person is obligated to seek and cooperate with "expert" advice, generally that of a physician. Sick people are not blamed for their illness, but must work toward recovery. There have been numerous critiques and modifications of the concept of the sick role, such as its inapplicability to chronic illness and disability, but it remains a central sociological way of seeing illness experience (Segall, 1976).

Illness behavior is essentially how people act when they develop symptoms of disease. As one sociologist notes, it includes ". . . the ways in which given symptoms may be differentially perceived, evaluated, and acted (or not acted) upon by different kinds of persons . . . whether by reason of early experience with illness, differential training in respect to symptoms, or whatever" (Mechanic, 1962). Reaction to symptoms, use of social networks in locating help, and compliance with medical advice are some of the activities characterized as illness behavior.

Illness behavior and the sick role, as well as the related concept of *illness career* (Suchman, 1965), are all more or less based on a perspective that all (proper) roads lead to medical care. They tend to create a "doctor-centered" picture by making the receipt of medical care the centerpiece of sociological attention. Such concepts are essentially "outsider" perspectives on the experience of illness. While these viewpoints may be useful in their own right, none of them has the actual subjective experience of illness as a central concern. They don't analyze illness from the sufferer's (or patient's) viewpoint. A few sociologists (e.g., Strauss and Glaser, 1975) have attempted to develop more subjective "insider" accounts of what it is like to be sick. These accounts focus more on individuals' perceptions of illness, interactions with others, the effects of illness on identity, and people's strategies for managing illness symptoms than do the abstract notions of illness careers or sick roles. Recent studies of the experience of epilepsy (Schneider and Conrad, 1983) and the family response to a heart attack (Speedling, 1982), among others, demonstrate an increasing interest in examining the experiential perspectives of illness.

The three selections in this section illuminate several faces of the subjective side of illness. In the first and most general article, "Chronic Illness," Anselm Strauss depicts the experience of chronic illness in the social worlds in which people live. Most of the problems encountered by people with chronic illnesses are apart from medical care. Strauss shows, from the patient's viewpoint, how family interaction, handling medical regimens, and finding ways to "get by" are critical to the personal management of illness and the "disease trajectory."

Uncertainty is an inherent feature of many illnesses and treatments and is a problem for sufferers and professionals alike (cf. Fox, 1957; Davis, 1960). In "Ambiguity and the Search for Meaning: Childhood Leukaemia in a Modern Clinical Context," Jean Comaroff and Peter Maguire show how uncertainty and the search for meaning are pivotal aspects of the experience of sufferers and their families. They argue that in the context of medical progress individual prognosis is still unpredictable and thus a further source of uncertainty. These uncertainties affect both social relations and medical care, and managing them is a central feature of illness experience. In the third article, "In the Closet with Illness: Epilepsy, Stigma Potential and the Control of Information," Joseph W. Schneider and Peter Conrad examine how people manage the stigmatizing potential of epilepsy. It is noteworthy that many sufferers perceive the social stigmas a greater problem than the biomedical disorder (Schneider and Conrad, 1983) and yet are left largely to their own devices to deal with it. Schneider and Conrad show how people with epilepsy manage the stigma potential of the illness by information control strategies, including, ironically, both disclosing and concealing information.

It is important that we see that issues such as uncertainty and stigma are crucial aspects of illness experience independent of disease conceptions or the sick role. When we understand and treat illness as a subjective as well as objective experience we no longer treat patients as diseases but as people who are sick. This is an important dimension of human health care.

REFERENCES

Davis, Fred. 1960. "Uncertainty in Medical Prognosis: Clinical and Functional." American Journal of Sociology 66: 41–47.

Fox, Renee. 1957. "Training for Uncertainty." Pp. 207–241 in R.K. Merton, G. Reader and P.L. Kendall (Eds.) The Student Physician. Cambridge, MA: Harvard University Press.

Freidson, Eliot. 1970. Profession of Medicine. New York: Dodd, Mead.

Mechanic, David. 1962. "The concept of illness behavior." Journal of Chronic Diseases. 15: 189–94.

Parsons, Talcott. 1951. The Social System. New York: Free Press.

Segall, Alexander. 1976. "The sick role concept: Understanding illness behavior." Journal of Health and Social Behavior. 17 (June): 163–70.

Schneider, Joseph W., and Peter Conrad. 1983. Having Epilepsy: The Experience and Control of Illness. Philadelphia: Temple University Press.

Speedling, Edward. 1982. Heart Attack. New York: Methuen.

Strauss, Anselm, and Barney Glaser, 1975. Chronic Illness and the Quality of Life. St. Louis: C. V. Mosby.

Suchman, Edward. 1965. "Stages of illness and medical care." Journal of Health and Social Behavior. 6: 114–28.

8

Chronic Illness

Anselm Strauss

Smallpox, diphtheria, polio, measles—conquered through immunization. Tuberculosis, leprosy, plague, yellow fever, malaria—defeated or checked by santiation, improved living conditions and effective treatment.

In the old days, people who died from diseases contracted them quickly, reached crisis shortly thereafter, and either died or pulled through. Modern medical researchers have changed this dramatic pattern by taming many once-devastating ailments. Improved conditions of living, along with effective medical skills and technology, have altered the nature of illness in scientifically advanced societies. While patients suffering from communicable diseases once filled most hospitals, treatment centers now serve mainly those afflicted with chronic ailments.

Many who would have died soon after contracting a disease now live and endure their affliction. Today most illnesses are chronic dis-

eases—slow-acting, long-term killers that can be treated but not cured. A 1964 survey by the Department of Health, Education and Welfare indicates that about 40 percent of all Americans suffer from one or more chronic diseases; one out of every four so afflicted have lost some days at work because of disabling symptoms.

A large and growing body of medical literature presents detailed discussions of etiology, symptomatology, treatments and regimens. This outpouring of information, however, generally ignores a basic aspect of chronic illness—how to deal with such ailments in terms that are *social*—not simply medical. How can patients and professionals cope with health-related problems of family disruption, marital stress, role destruction and adjustment, stigmatization and even loss of body mobility?

Each chronic condition brings with it multiple problems of living. Among the most pressing are preventing and managing medical crises (that go even to death), managing regimens, controlling symptoms, organizing one's time efficiently, preventing or living with social isolation, adjusting to changes in the disease trajectory, and normalizing interaction and life, despite the disease. To handle those problems, people develop basic strategies which call for an organization of effort (including that of kinsmen, neighbors and health professionals). To establish and maintain this organization requires certain resources (financial, medical, familial and so forth), as well as interactional and social skills in order to make the necessary arrangements.

Medicine and the health professionals are very much included in this scheme but are neither at the scheme's focal point nor even constitute its primary elements. What is primary is simply the question of living: the difference between chronic sufferers and "normal people" merely being that the former must live with their diseases, their symptoms and often with their regimens. Medicine may contribute, but it is secondary to "carrying on."

Coping with Crises

Some chronic diseases carry a constant threat of grave medical crises. Diabetics may fall into insulin coma and die; epileptics can go into convulsions (which of themselves are not lethal) and be killed in a fall or a traffic accident. In order to prevent crises, minimize their effects, get the critically ill person into the hands of a physician or a hospital staff—and if need be actually save him—the person himself and possibly his kinsmen must be organized and prepared to handle all contingencies.

Relevant to the question of crises is how far they can go (to, or short of, death), how fast they appear, the clarity of advance warning signals to laymen or even to health professionals, the probability of recurrence, the predictability of their appearance, the complexity of the saving operations, and the speed and completeness of recovery from them.

The ability to read signs that portend a crisis is the first important step in managing chronic illness. Thus, diabetics or the parents of diabetic children learn how to recognize the signs of oncoming sugar shortage or insulin shock and what to do in case of actual crisis. Likewise, epileptics and sickle cell disease sufferers, if they are fortunate enough to have warning signs before their crises, learn to prepare themselves: if they are in public they get themselves to a place of safety and sit or lie down. Diabetics may carry instructions with them and may also carry those materials, like sugar or candy or insulin, which counteract the crisis; and epileptics may stuff handkerchiefs between their teeth just before convulsions.

When signs aren't properly read, are read too slowly or are interpreted as meaning something else, then people die or come close to dying. This may happen the first time a cardiac patient experiences severe chest pains and doesn't yet know their cause or treatment. (After the first sequence the patient may put his doctor's name close to the telephone for emergency use.) Even physicians may misread signs and so precipitate a crisis—even death. If an unconscious sickle cell anemia sufferer is brought bleeding to a hospital he may die if the natural immediate effort is made to stop his bleeding. Patients who carry instructions with them can sometimes avoid difficulties. Whenever an unconscious individual is brought into the emergency room of the nearest hospital, physicians there understandably may treat him for the wrong disease. Inexperienced patients who are on kidney dialysis machinery may not realize that their machinery is working incorrectly and that their bodies are nearing crisis. The complexity of the human body can cause even experienced persons to misread important signs.

Any breakdown or disruption of the crisis-preventing or crisis-coping organization can be disastrous. Family strain can lead to the abandonment of or lessening control over regimens, and temporary absence of "protective agents" or of "control agents" (such as mothers of diabetic children who are prone to eat too much candy) can also be traumatic. A divorce or separation that leaves an assisting agent (a mother helping her cystic-fibrosis child with absolutely necessary exercises) alone, unrelieved with her task, can gradually or quickly lead to a crisis. (One divorced couple arranged matters so that the father relieved the mother on weekends and some evenings.) Even an agent's illness can lead to the relaxation of regimens or the elimination of activities that might otherwise prevent crisis.

There is also a post-crisis period, in relation to the organization of effort. Some failure of organization right in the hospital can be seen when the staff begins to pull away from a cardiac patient, recently saved from a heart attack, but now judged "less critical" than other patients. Back home, of course, such patients require plenty of family organization to prevent additional attacks. What is not so evident is that the patient and his family may read signs of improvement where few exist, or that contingencies may arise which render faulty the organization for crisis prevention and crisis management. Relevant variables here are the length and rapidity of recovery—since both of these may vary for different disease conditions.

During an extended period of crisis the family may need to make special arrangements about their time (for visiting the hospital, for nursing the patient at home) and their living space (having the bed downstairs rather than upstairs, living near the hospital during the peak of the crisis). They may have to juggle the family's finances or spell each other in nursing the patient during his crisis. Even the patient himself—in trying to get better rather than giving up—may have to contribute to the necessary organization of effort to bring the family through the crisis period.

Unless the physician is absolutely helpless in the face of a given chronic disease, he will suggest or command some kind of regimen. Adhering to regimens, though, is a very complex matter, for regimens can sometimes set problems so difficult that they may present more hardships than the symptoms themselves.

Patients do not adhere to regimens automatically. Those who accept and maintain a regimen must have abiding trust in the physician, evidence that the requirements work without producing distressing or frightening side-effects (or that the side-effects are outweighed by symptom relief or fear of the disease itself), and the guarantee that important daily activities, either of the patient or of the people around him, can continue relatively uninterrupted.

In addition to the time it takes and the discomfort it causes, an important property of a given regimen is whether it is visible to other people, and what visibility may mean to the patient. If the regimen means that a stigmatized disease can be suspected or discovered, the person is unlikely to carry it out in public. (Tuberculosis patients sometimes have this problem.) If the visible regimen is no more than slightly embarrassing or is fully explainable, then its visibility is much less likely to prevent its maintenance in public or private.

Another property is also important: if the regimen appears to work for the patient, then that *may* convince him that he should continue with it. But continuance is problematic, not only because the other properties noted above may counteract his best intentions or his good sense, but because once a regimen has brought symptom relief, the patient may forego the routine—no matter what the physician says. This is exactly what happens when tuberculosis patients see their symptoms disappear, and figure that now they can cut out—partially or totally—their uncomfortable regimen.

The very properties of the regimen, then, constitute contributing conditions for adhering, relaxing or even rejecting the prescribed activities. Thus, if the patient simply denies that he has the disease (as with tuberculosis, where many patients experience no symptoms), he may not carry out his regimen. Instructions for a treatment routine may leave him confused or baffled: cardiac patients told to "rest" or "find their own limits" can be frustrated because they don't really know what "sufficient rest" means.

Patients and kinsmen inevitably enter into negotiations with each other, and sometimes with the physician, over relaxing or otherwise changing (substituting one drug for another, one activity for another) the regimen. They are negotiating not only over such matters as the elimination of discomfort and side-effects, but also the possibility of making the management of ordinary life easier or even possible. Physicians, of course, recognize much of this bargaining, but they may not realize just how high the stakes can be for the patient and his family. If a doctor ignores those factors, his patient may go shopping for another physician or, at the least, he may quietly alter his regimen or substitute part of it with something recommended by an amateur—pharmacist, friend or relative.

Symptom Management

The control of symptoms is obviously linked with adherence to effective regimens. Like adherence to regimen, symptom control is not merely a matter of medical management. Most of the time, the patient is far from medical facilities, so he and his family must rely upon their own judgment, wisdom and ingenuity in controlling symptoms—quite aside from faithfully following the prescribed regimens. Some physicians—probably not many—recognize that need for judgment.

Whatever the sophisticated technical references may be, the person who has symptoms will be concerned primarily with whether he hurts, faints, trembles visibly, has had his mobility or his speech impaired, or is evidencing some kind of disfigurement. How much they interfere with his life and social relationships depends on whether they are permanent or temporary, predictable or unpredictable, publicly visible or invisible; also on their degree (as of pain), their meaning to bystanders (as of disfigurement), the nature of the regimen called for to control the symptom, and of course on the kinds of lifestyle and social relations which the sufferer has been accustomed to.

Even minor, occasional symptoms may lead to some changing of habits, and major symptoms may call for the redesigning or reshaping of important aspects of a patient's life-style. Thus, someone who begins to suffer from minor back pains is likely to learn to avoid certain kinds of chairs and even discover to his dismay that a favorite sitting position is precisely the one he must forego. Major adjustments could include moving to a one-story house, buying clothes that cloak disfigurement, getting the boss to assign jobs that require less strength, using crutches or other aides to mobility. In one case a mailman suffering from colitis lived "on a leash" having arranged never to be very far from that necessary toilet. Emphysema patients learn to have "puffing stations" where they can recoup from lack of breath while looking like they have stopped normally.

Ideas for redesigning activiites may come from others, too. A community nurse taught an emphysema patient how to rest while doing household chores; a sister taught a patient afflicted with brittle bones (because of a destructive drug) how to get up from the toilet, minus a back brace, without breaking bones in her back. Another woman figured out how her cardiac-arthritic grandfather could continue his beloved walks on his farm, by placing wooden stumps at short distances so that he could rest as he reached each one. Unfortunately, kinsmen and health professionals can function in just the opposite fashion: for instance, a woman with multiple sclerosis had carefully arranged her one-room apartment so that every object she needed was literally within arm's reach: but the public health nurse who visited her regarded the place as in a terrible shambles and proceeded to tidy things up herself.

Perhaps inventiveness, just as much as finances or material resources, is what makes the difference between reaching and not reaching some relatively satisfying redesign of life. The cancer patient with lessened energy who can ingeniously juggle her friends' visits and telephone calls can maintain a relatively unimpaired social life. Arthritic farm women who can get neighbors to bring in groceries can live on their farms during the summer although they must move to town for the winter months. One multiple sclerosis patient who is a student not only has rearranged her apartment but persuaded various people to help her manage despite her increasingly restricted mobility. A veritable army of people have come to her aid: the university architect redesigned certain of the public toilets for her wheelchair and also put in some ramps; the handy men around the university help her up and down stairs, by appointment; they also have rebuilt her cupboards so that she can reach them from her wheelchair; and so on.

Lack of imagination about useful redesigning makes symptom control harder. This lack of imaginative forethought can be seen in many homes for the elderly where stiff-jointed or low-energy people must struggle to rise from sitting positions on low sofas and chairs, or must painstakingly pick their way along highly polished corridors—minus handrails.

The reshaping of activities pertains also to the crucial issue of "interaction." A variety of judicious or clever maneuvers can keep one's symptoms as inobtrusive as possible. Sometimes the tactics are very simple: a college teacher with bronchitis, whose peak load of coughing up sputum is in the morning, arranges his teaching schedule so that he can stay at home, or at least in his office, until after lunchtime. Another person who tends continually to have a runny allergic nose always carries tissue in her hand when in public. Another with a tendency to cough carries cough drops with him—especially important when he attends concerts. An epileptic may have to persuade acquaintances that his epileptic fits are not communicable! Emphysema sufferers learn to sit down or lean against buildings in such a fashion that they are not mistaken for drunks or loiterers.

Agents of various kinds can also be useful—wives who scout out the terrain at a public meeting to find the least obtrusive spot, and then pass on the information to their husbands in wheelchairs or on crutches. Spouses may have prearranged signals to warn each other when a chronic symptom (for example, runny nose) starts appearing. In a more dramatic instance a couple was attending a party when the husband noticed his wife's temporarily slurred speech—a sign of her tiredness and pain from cancer. Since they did not want to have their friends know of her illness, he acted quickly to divert the others' attention and soon afterward manufactured an excuse so that they could leave the party.

When visible symptoms cannot easily be disguised, misleading explanations may be offered—fainting, for instance, is explained away by someone "in the know" as a temporary weakness due to flu or to some other reasonable cause. When a symptom cannot be minimized, then a wife may attempt to prepare others for the distressing sight or sound of her husband's affliction. The sufferer himself may do this, as when a cancer patient who had lost much weight warned friends, over the phone, that when they visited they would find her not looking like herself at all. Each friend who visits is very likely, in turn, to warn other friends what to expect.

Various chronic diseases lead to such disruption that they call for some temporal re-ordering.

One all-too-familiar problem is too much time. It may only be temporary, as with persons who are waiting out a post-crisis period, but, for the disabled elderly or victims of multiple sclerosis, it may be a permanent condition. Among the consequences are boredom, decreased social skills, family strains, negative impact on identity and even physical deterioration.

Just as common is not enough time. Not only is time sopped up by regimens and by symptom control, but those who assist the patient may expend many hours on their particular tasks. Not to be totally engulfed, they in turn may need to get assistants (babysitters, housecleaners, cooks) or redistribute the family workload. Occasionally the regimens require so much time, or crises come so frequently (some sickle cell anemia sufferers have been hospitalized up to 100 times), that life simply gets organized around those events; there is not enough time for much of anything else. Even just handling one's symptoms or the consequences of having symptoms may require so much time that life is taken up mainly with handling them. Thus, a very serious dermatological condition forced one woman to spend hour after hour salving her skin; otherwise she would have suffered unbearably. Unfortunately, the people who suffer cannot leave their bodies. Kinsmen and other assisting agents, however, may abandon their charges out of desperation for what the temporal engulfment is doing to their own lives. Abandonment, here, may mean shifting the burdens to a nursing home or other custodial institution, such as a state mental institution.

The term "dying trajectory" means the course of dying as defined by various participants in it. Analogously, one can also think of the course of the chronic disease (downward in most instances). Like the dying trajectory, that course can be conceived as having two properties. First, it takes place over time: it has duration. Specific trajectories can vary greatly in duration. Some start earlier, some end later. Second, a trajectory has shape. It may plunge straight down; it may move slowly but steadily downward; it may vacillate slowly, moving slightly up and down before diving downward radically; it may move slowly down at first, then hit a long plateau, then plunge abruptly even to death. Neither the duration nor shape of a dying trajectory is a purely objective physiological property. Both are perceived properties; their dimensions depend on when the perceiver initially defines someone as diseased and on his expectations of how the disease course will proceed. (We can add further that the dying trajectory consists merely of the last phases of some chronic disease trajectories.) Each type of disease (multiple sclerosis, diabetes and so forth) or subtype (different kinds of arthritis) may have a range of variation in trajectory, but they certainly tend to be patterned in accordance with duration and shape.

It would be much too simplistic to assert that specific trajectories determine what happens to a sense of identity; but certainly they do contribute, and quite possibly in *patterned* ways. Identity responses to a severe heart attack may be varied, but awareness that death can be but a moment away—every day—probably cannot but have a different impact on identity than trajectories expected to result in slow death, or in leaving one a "vegetable" or perfectly alive but a hopeless cripple.

We have alluded to the loss of social contact, even extending to great social isolation, that may be a consequence of chronic disease and its management. This loss is understandable given the accompanying symptoms, crises, regimens and often difficult phasing of trajectories.

It is not difficult to trace some of the impact on social contact of varying symptoms, in accordance with their chief properties. The disfigurement associated with leprosy leads many to stay in leper colonies; they prefer the social ease and normal relationships that are possible there. Diseases which are (or which the sufferer thinks are) stigmatizing are kept as secret as possible. But talking about his illness with friends who may understand can be comforting. Some may find new friends (even spouses) among fellow sufferers, especially through clinic visits or special clubs formed around the illness or disability (such as those formed by kidney failure victims and people who have had ileostomies). Some virtually make careers of doing voluntary work for those clubs or associations. People can also leave circles of friends whom they feel might now be unresponsive, frightened or critical and move to more sympathetic social terrain. An epileptic who has used a warning tactic and has moved to a supportive terrain said:

> I'm lucky, I still have friends. Most people who have epilepsy are put to the side. But I'm lucky that way. I tell them that I have epilepsy and that they shouldn't get scared if I fall out. I go to things at the church—it's the church people that are my friends. I just tell them and then it is okay. They just laugh about it and don't get upset.

Some people may choose to allow their diseases to advance rather than put up with their regimens. One cardiac patient, for instance, simply refused to give up his weekly evening playing cards with "the boys"—replete with smoking, beer drinking and late hours—despite his understanding that this could lead to further heart attacks. Another cardiac patient avoided coffee breaks at work because everyone smoked then. He stayed away from many social functions for the same reasons. He felt that people probably thought him "unsociable," but he was not able to think of any other way to stop himself from smoking. Perhaps the extreme escape from—not minimization or prevention of—social isolation was exhibited by one woman with kidney disease who chose to go off dialysis (she had no possibility of getting a transplant), opting for a speedy death because she saw an endless time ahead, dependence on others, inability to hold down a job, increasing social isolation and a purposeless life. Her physicians accepted her right to make this choice.

Those who cannot face physically altered friends may avoid or even abandon them. One individual who was losing weight because of cancer remarked bitterly that a colleague of his had ducked down the street, across campus, to avoid meeting him. Spouses who have known great intimacy together can draw apart because of an illness: a cardiac husband may fear having sex or may be afraid of dying but cannot tell his wife for fear of increasing *her* anxiety. The awkwardness that others feel about discussing death and fear of it isolates many chronically ill people from their friends—even from their spouses. During the last phases of a disease trajectory, an unbridgeable gap may open up between previously intimate spouses.

Even aside from the question of death fears,

friends may draw apart because the patient is physically isolated from the mainstream of life. One stroke patient who temporarily lost the ability to speak described what happened between himself and his friends: "I felt unguarded and my colleagues—who pretty soon found their conversation drying up in the lack of anything from me—felt bored, or at any rate I thought they were. My wife, who was usually present, saved the conversation from dying—she was never at loss for a word." A cardiac patient hospitalized away from his home town at first received numerous cards and telephone calls, but once his friends had reached across the distance they chose to leave him alone, doubtless for a variety of reasons. He and his wife began to feel slightly abandoned. Later, when he had returned to part-time work, he found that his fellow executives left him relatively alone at first, knowing that he was far from recuperated. Despite his conscious knowledge that his colleagues were trying to help, he still felt out of things.

Friends and relatives may withdraw from patients who are making excessive demands or who have undergone personality changes caused by a crisis or the progress of a disease. Abandonment may be the final result. Husbands desert, spouses separate and adult children place their elderly parents in nursing homes. In some kinds of chronic diseases, especially stigmatic (leprosy) or terribly demanding (mental illness), friends and relatives and even physicians advise the spouse or kinsmen quite literally to abandon the sick person: "It's time to put her in the hospital." "Think of the children." "Think of yourself—it makes no sense." "It's better for her, and you are only keeping her at home because of your own guilt." These are just some of the abandonment rationales that are offered, or which the person offers himself. Of course, the sick person, aware of having become virtually an intolerable burden, may offer those rationales also—though not necessarily alleviating his own sense of estrangement.

The chief business of a chronically ill person is not just to stay alive or to keep his symptoms under control, but to live as normally as possible despite his symptoms and his disease. In the case of chronically ill children, parents work very hard at creating some semblance of a normal life for their offspring. "Closed awareness" or secrecy is the ruling principle of family life. No one tells the child he is dying. Parents of children with leukemia, for example, have a very difficult time. For much of the time, the child actually may look quite well and live a normal life—but his parents have to work very hard at *acting* normal unless they can keep the impending death well at the back of their minds. The parents with children with longer life expectancies need not work so hard to maintain a normal atmosphere in their homes, except insofar as the child may rebel against aspects of a restrictive regimen which he feels makes *his* life abnormal. Some of the difficulties which chronic sufferers experience in maintaining normal interaction are reflected in the common complaint that blind and physically handicapped people make—that people assume they cannot walk and work like ordinary mortals, but rush up to help them do what they are quite capable of doing as anyone else. The non-sick, especially strangers, tend to overemphasize the sick person's visible symptoms, so that they come to dominate the interaction. The sick person fights back by using various tactics to disavow his deviant status: he hides the intrusive symptom—covers it with clothes, puts the trembling hand under the table—or if it can't be hidden, then minimizes its impact by taking attention away from it—like a dying woman who has lost a great deal of weight but who forces visitors to ignore her condition by talking cheerfully and normally about their mutual interests.

Artful Striving

In setting guidelines for "acting normal" there is much room for disagreement between the ill person and those near to him about just how ill he is. The sick person may choose more invalidism than his condition really warrants. After a crisis or a peak period of symptoms, the sick person may find himself rushed by others—including his helping agents—who either misjudge his return to better health—or simply forget how sick he might still be since he does not show more obvious signs of his current condition. All patients who have partial-recovery trajectories necessarily run that hazard. ("Act sicker than you look or they will quickly forget you were so ill" was the advice given to one cardiac patient who was about to return to his executive job.)

The more frequent reverse phenomenon is when the sick person believes his condition is more normal than others believe. His friends and relatives tell him, "Take it easy, don't rush things." His physician warns him that he will harm himself, even kill himself, if he doesn't act in accordance with the facts of his case. But it sometimes happens that the person really has a very accurate notion of just how he feels. One man who had had a kidney transplant found himself having to prove to his fellow workers that he was not handicapped—doing extra work to demonstrate his normality. A slightly different case is the ill person who may know just how ill he is but wishes others to regard him as less ill and allow him to act accordingly. One dying man who was trying to live as normally as possible right down through his last days found himself rejecting those friends, however well intentioned, who regarded him as "dying now" rather than as "living fully to the end."

As the trajectory of the ill person's health continues downward, he may have to come to terms with a lessened degree of normality. We can see this very clearly with those who are slowly dying, when both they and their friends or kinsmen are quite willing to settle for "something less" at each phase of the downward trajectory, thankful at least for small things. It is precisely when the chronically ill cannot settle for lower levels of functioning that they opt out of this life. When their friends and relatives cannot settle for less, or have settled for as much as they can

stand, then they too opt out of his life: by separation, divorce or abandonment. Those who are chronically ill from diseases like multiple sclerosis or other severe forms of neurological illness (or mental illness, for that matter) are likely to have to face this kind of abandonment by others. The chronically ill themselves, as well as many of their spouses, kinsmen and friends, are remarkably able to accommodate themselves to increasingly lower levels of normal interaction and style; they can do this either because of immense closeness to each other or because they are grateful even for what little life and relationship remain. They strive manfully—and artfully—to "keep things normal" at whatever level that has come to mean.

We must not forget, either, that symptoms and trajectories may stabilize for long periods of time, or in fact not change for the worst at all: then the persons so afflicted simply come to accept, on a long-term basis, whatever restrictions are placed on their lives. Like Franklin D. Roosevelt, they live perfectly normal (even super-normal!) lives in all respects except for whatever handicaps may derive from their symptoms or their medical regimens. To keep interaction normal, they need only develop the requisite skills to make others ignore or de-emphasize their disabilities.

Helping those afflicted with chronic diseases means far more than simply displaying compassion or having medical competence. Only through knowledge of and sensitivity to the *social* aspects of symptom control, regimen management, crisis prevention, handling dying and death itself, can one develop truly beneficial strategies and tactics for dealing with specific diseases and chronic illness in general.

9

Ambiguity and the Search for Meaning: Childhood Leukaemia in the Modern Clinical Context

Jean Comaroff and Peter Maguire

"The real hell of this illness is that you just don't know!"

Parent of a leukaemic child

Introduction

The immediate concerns of this paper are the changing social and experiential implications of childhood leukaemia under conditions of modern medical management [1]. In the last decade, developments in the clinical context of the disease have significantly altered its course in most sufferers. Remissions of five or more years are now secured for up to 50% of children in many treatment centres, and a small proportion have survived much longer [2]. Inevitably, such changed patterns of intervention have significant psychological and socio-cultural implications: the very meaning of the disease is undergoing revision, both among clinicians and laypeople. Ironically, apparent clinical gains have heightened immediate medical and experiential uncertainties. Insight into etiology and into variation in response to treatment have not kept pace with chemotherapeutic advance, and prognosis in individual cases remains relatively unpredictable. In fact, knowledge has advanced in piece-meal fashion, its gains highlighting the vastness of remaining ignorance.

The condition of childhood leukaemia is a graphic instance of the state of knowledge on the margins of bio-medical science, of the manner in which the known becomes distinguished from the unknown in this domain. Our concern in this paper is the effect of this process upon the experience of those to whom such changing knowledge is applied. The case of childhood leukaemia shows clearly how advances in empirical knowledge may occur in seemingly uneven fashion—as when, for example, modes of intervention precede knowledge of etiology. These developments imply specific reformulation of the contrast between the certain and the uncertain, the predictable and the random, and the relevant and the irrelevant.

. . . .

Our study of the impact of childhood leukaemia revealed this process in clear detail; the experience of uncertainty and the search for meaning were *the* characteristic features of the impact of the disease upon sufferers and their families. While these features are inherent in the experience of threatening illness itself, their striking form in this case was clearly the result of a particular set of developments in treatment. In this paper, we examine this relationship between advancing medical knowledge, its clinical application and its effects upon the sick. We place this process in its total socio-cultural context, and then discuss its implications for the social role of medical knowledge in general.

· ·

The Study

The data drawn upon here were collected as part of a study of the families of 60 children with acute myoloblastic or lymphoblastic leukaemia, admitted to a regional pediatric oncology unit in England between January 1976 and April 1977 [3]. Research focussed on the psychological and social implications of the disease for close kin and significant others associated with the afflicted children. Of particular concern was the relationship between the disease and its socio-cultural context. We wished to examine both how pre-existing socio-economic and cultural factors contributed to its impact and management and how the challenge of the condition itself, the confrontation with suffering, grief and death, articulated collective conceptions and values.

In this paper we discuss the normal, i.e. typical features of the illness process observed, rather than the minority of cases (some 25%) in which reactions were definable in terms of psychiatric morbidity. However, the structure of the situation described here applied to all families in our study, and focusses doubt on the appropriateness of established criteria for assessing its impact criteria of psycho-social 'normality,' 'coping' and 'adjustment'.

Implications of Therapeutic Advance: Crisis and Remission

· ·

Our own observations reinforced [the] view [that there are] social and psychological effects of improved prognosis. For the most striking feature of the condition is now the *unpredictability* of its course and outcome, which turns upon the starkest of alternatives—life or death. In fact, overall improvement in the length of survival of victims dramatically heightens the perceptions of uncontrollable threat in particular cases. Thus the hope of long-term (perhaps complete) remission becomes the preoccupation of all families [4], despite their awareness that the odds are unfavourable; and this hope is poignantly maintained against counter evidence. The course of the disease now becomes extremely difficult to define and classify. The significance of remission is not easily interpretable at any point in a particular survivor's career; comprehending clinical predictions and translating them into conventional cultural terms is problematic. While the longer the child survives, the better his chances, relapse *can* occur at any time; and statistical attempts to factorize the risk of such occurrence are as yet of little help in particular cases. Hence prognosis is difficult to fix, and the illness is neither clearly 'acute' nor 'chronic' for much of its course, a pattern which does not fit established cultural categories. Like other forms of 'acute' illness, this one is threatening on impact; yet no defined phase of resolution follows. For the very meaning of the term 'remission' (i.e. the retreat of symptoms) is profoundly ambiguous, both clinically and experientially. Is it partial or total? When does long-term survival become apparent 'cure'? Periods of remission in leukaemia and related malignant disease combine both the everpresent threat of relapse with the more mundane uncertainties of chronic illness (such as how to manage the sufferer's ambiguous blend of 'illness' and 'normality'). The condition thus raises problems of meaning, management and communication, both in face-to-face and in less bounded social contexts.

Crisis: The Early Phase of Impact

While the 'typical' course of childhood leukaemia today is difficult to define in clinical and cultural terms, as a social phenomenon it displays regularities which serve to organize our present discussion. The first of these deals with the phase of impact [5], during which the disease is clinically diagnosed and the diagnosis is communicated to close adult kin, and sometimes, to the victim himself. Some aspects of this phase are a function of the impact of threatening disease everywhere;

others are more specifically linked to current advances in leukaemia treatment.

The onset of leukaemia is often insidious. The child displays symptoms—e.g. lack of appetite, tiredness and aches and pains—which are easily attributable to trivial illnesses. Only when these persist, or there is a dramatic change in the child's physical and/or psychological disposition, is the possibility of serious disease usually recognized. Other more distinctive clinical features—pallor, bruising and petechiae, or bone pain—may also be misread by parents; and lack of first-hand knowledge of the condition by the primary practitioner may further impede diagnosis.

Such procrastination has distressing consequences once the nature of the disease becomes known. Parents who delay consulting a doctor feel guilt. If the primary practitioner initially misdiagnoses the condition, parents are resentful and may impugn his clinical judgement. The apparent deficiencies in the primary physician's competence are often heightened by the seemingly dramatic and specialist intervention which follows referral to a hospital. Once the child has been discharged, the problem of primary care is often exacerbated by a lack of confidence (both by the parents and the physician himself) in his ability to treat so special a case. Thus, while the hospital specialist becomes the object of optimistic faith, the primary doctor is frequently devalued, or made the target of anger and guilt. Here the effects of the moving margin of specialist knowledge upon perceptions and social relationships is clearly seen.

Interpreting the Diagnosis

We have suggested that in our culture malignant disease in childhood has particularly distressing emotive connotations, due not only to its inherent implications, but also, to its symbolic marking of the critical frontier of medical science. The most cogent initial response to clinical identification of the disease among the families observed was that they had been singled out to suffer the kind of irreversible misfortune that usually seemed "only to happen to others". Davis [6], in his classic account of the 'passage through crisis' of childhood polio victims, makes a similar

observation: such threatening information taxes a family's sense of sharing in a common universe or experience and implies a position of marginality and collective stigma.

Among the families of leukaemic children, the isolating effects of receiving the diagnosis were modified once contact was made with a new group of reference, comprising others similarly afflicted. Here constructions of the event were reappraised in relation to a universe of comparable experience. As one mother put it:

When you first learn that your child has such a disease, your world collapses. You think: 'It can't happen to us? It only happens to other people!'. Then you get to the hospital and learn that there are others like you and that helps. Not that you are pleased by their suffering; it's just that you're not alone in it. They've been through the same, or worse sometimes . . . But when you go home again, it's difficult. You feel different, and people avoid you. I suppose it's because they don't know how to take you. But it's upsetting—like you've all got the plague or something!

Sociological observations show that participants in ordeals of apparently uncertain course and duration (such as periods of imprisonment and hospitalization) seek to systematize information and construct norms against which to gauge their present state and future prospects [7]. The parents of leukaemic children performed similar activities. It was here that the implications of therapeutic advance and changing prognosis were clearly seen, for predicting the course of the disease in particular cases has become increasingly difficult. Families discovered that 'leukaemia' comprised a category of related clinical conditions, with differing individual implications for treatment and outcome. Moreover, within this category knowledge and technical control were unevenly distributed.

. . . .

The case of childhood leukaemia is an instance of Durkheim's classic assertion that science, inherently fragmentary and incomplete, cannot provide an 'impetus' to everyday action. The theories which make it possible for men to 'live and act' are thus 'obliged to pass science and complete it prematurely' [8]. Doctors in our study were seldom able, on the basis of available knowledge, to provide clear bio-medical guidelines for parents facing the uncharted course of the illness. Thus parents (and frequently, sick children) set about collating all available information in the attempt to formulate timetables and statements of probability for themselves. In doing this, they drew heavily upon knowledge of other laymen with more experience of the disease, and from the case-histories of other victims. A subtle process of cross-referencing occurred whereby parents sought to systematize the range of differing types of data at their disposal. In their efforts, however, they tried to maintain an optimistic definition of their case for as long as possible. They would thus stress similiarities between their child and others who appeared to be doing well, and avoid identification with those who appeared to be failing. Significantly, the quest was not only for prognostic certainty, but for an extension of clinical definitions to include psychological, social and moral dimensions. As time passed, progress of the condition itself often narrowed the limits of expectation; a relapse dispelled the hope of further long-term remission. But the process of classification, and the search for meaning in carefully collated bodies of evidence persisted for as long as the illness lasted. And each case of relapse and death occurring within the reference group presented a fresh challenge to survivors and their families.

The process of systematization also varied with the progress of the disease. At points of crisis—initial diagnosis, relapse and death—there was an expressed need to identify with others who had experienced the same affliction, to ease the isolation of being picked out to suffer irreversible tragedy. But when individual and collective definitions had reached relative stability, referencing often declined and other sufferers were avoided as possible sources of disorienting information.

The attempt to manage communication so as to maintain fragile optimism also reflects another feature of the changing relationship between what is formally 'known' and what is 'unknown'—i.e. the discontinuity between widely held lay images of leukaemia and those current in clinical oncology. In this case, rapid therapeutic advance in recent years has resulted in a significant gap. Lay people generally continue to perceive leukaemia as intractable, short-lived and fatal. Clinical diagnosis presents contrary, but bewildering information about variations in types of disease and treatment and about unpredictable possibilities of survival. Those afflicted now attempt to construct and maintain expectations which counter their own previously pessimistic, common-sense views (still shared by many others in the wider community, including some health care professionals outside the field of oncology).

In assessing how those involved seek a stable understanding of the illness and its implications, we are not dealing with unambiguous, uniform states of awareness, definable as 'realistic acceptance' or 'irrational denial'. States of knowledge which follow in the wake of such crises often display contradiction and situational variation, suggesting that the perception of threat to life (whether in the victim or those close to him) is a developing consciousness. Parents showed that this process often involved oscillation between contradictory responses: repugnance, guilt, optimism and despair. It follows that such processes are not easily reducible to stable descriptive models such as 'awareness context' [9], or to finite and unambiguous communications (often implied in the classic cancer literature on 'telling' or 'not telling' fatal prognoses). The referencing activities through which constructions of the illness process are formed by those caught up in it are expressions of the need to 'complete' seemingly inadequate clinical knowledge—to bring its definitions into line with everyday experience, and to transcend the stark and apparently arbitrary boundary between the formally 'known' and the 'unknown'.

The Meaning of Affliction

An interrelated and crucial feature of the early phase of leukaemia (but one which recurred throughout its course) was the attempt to explain *why* it happened. Again, other sociological accounts of the experience of crisis suggest that this 'stock-taking' (what Davis calls the 'inventory stage') generally occurs once the critical peak and initial shock have passed. However, studies of the social role of Western medicine have not been particularly concerned with this quest for meaning, except to note that our medical knowledge addresses a relatively limited range of causal explanations of disease—the 'how' rather than the 'why' of illness; or its proximate 'cause' rather than its 'meaning' [10]. In the literature on childhood leukaemia all that emerges is that in the post-crisis period, self-searching and guilt give way to resigned acceptance if feelings of personal culpability are effectively allayed [11].

Our observations indeed confirmed that perceptions of guilt were significant in parents' attempts to impose meaning on the illness. The identity of children is generally regarded as a function of that of their parents, who feel practical and moral responsibility for their well-being and their suffering. Threatening illness is frequently seen as an assault on childrearing capacities [12]. Hence the quest for cause and meaning in such illness is closely tied to the attempt to allocate responsibility for its occurrence.

But the search for meaning also reflects the widely observed effects of threatening and seemingly random events upon everyday assumptions and modes of knowledge. All cultures provide repertoires of explanation—theories—to account for and manage such events [13]. We, in the Western industrialized societies, have come to think increasingly in the idiom of 'scientific' explanation, in which 'objective' and 'neutral' principles serve to order the elements of a materially constituted world. Such theories are explicitly impersonal and amoral. They do not relate specific physical causes to more embracing social, moral or spiritual orders. Scientific explanation fails to account for the seeming random occurrence of a wide range of 'natural' events (such as the onset of disease). However, where such affliction strikes to the heart of everyday realities and resists control, it calls into question tacit assumptions about reality and the nature of human control. And it is in such cases—of which childhood leukaemia is typical—that the ambiguities of current bio-medical knowlege are most keenly perceived.

Parents in our study typically tried to bring the stunning diagnosis of leukaemia into relation with perceived medical facts, the experience of others and their own biographies and worldview. While the process was most intense during the initial phase of impact, the quest for a satisfactory explanation was, by its nature, inconclusive and continuous, often asserting itself strongly after relapse and bereavement. One mother remarked after the death of her child:

> Well, now it's all over, and I have time to think again. I find myself going over and over the problem in my mind, just like I did at the beginning: 'Why did he get it? How does it start?'. You can drive yourself crazy with those sort of questions! Could it happen to the other children too? I want to ask the hospital to let us know if they find that out—how it starts. Even if it's in 15 years, I'll still want to know.

In their search for an explanation for the onset of the disease, parents generally sought knowledge at two interrelated levels: first, that of proximate biological and medical cause (what has happened in the child's body?) and second, that of more ultimate cause (Why us? Why now?). In our society, bio-medical science and practice may provide satisfactory explanation and resolution for a wide range of afflictions, often (but not always) seeming to render more thoroughgoing metaphysical speculation redundant. But precisely *because* of its apparent wide applicability in everyday life, particularly in the wake of the decline of overarching cosmological systems, we are especially bereft when we have to face events for which no rational explanation or remedy is forthcoming. The search for meaning, in short, becomes a conscious problem under such conditions. Threatening illness strikes at personal identities and challenges everyday realities, calling for an interpretive framework to order fragmented experience; but the process of 'completing' scientific etiologies is not as automatic as Durkheim [8] and others have suggested. It founders on the essential Western cultural opposition between material and moral realities.

Precisely because this is so, both medical and popular speculation about possible psychological and environmental components in malignant disease serve as a bridge for moving from proximate (clinically framed) explanations to encompassing (cosmologically ordered) explanations. Despite the lack of clinical concern with psycho-social factors, the parents we observed reviewed their own biographies, passing from questions like: "Should I have breast-fed?" and "Could one X-ray in pregnancy have done it?", to more diffuse issues: "Could it be that I work with chemicals?" or "Perhaps it's because we live in such a filthy industrial environment?". The incidence of disease at present suggests no regional or socio-economic bias. Social and environmental factors in etiology were a concern of both working-class and middle-class families. About 10% of parents tentatively invoked metaphysical explanations: "It's a punishment for something we've done". Those who held strong beliefs in divine causation were less concerned with other aspects of etiology. But few found such encompassing reassurance, either from the doctrines or the representatives of the church. For most, nagging concerns about 'hidden' carcinogenic features in the everyday environment remained strong. Problems raised by this search for meaning reveal fundamental features of the structure of knowledge in our culture, and derived from the contradictions which characterize its social role. Parents' reactions express the dilemma of relating the complexity of what is known about the disease to what remains stubbornly unknown, of reconciling, for example, how etiology can remain almost a total mystery while progress is made at the level of intervention (many perceived this as an inversion of common-sense assumptions about the logical priority of causal knowledge). Their problems also stress the contradictory detachment of bio-medical knowledge from the multi-faceted contours of illness experience. And, most fundamentally, they express ambiguous perceptions about efficacy and the absence of control in the everyday exercise of knowledge. Not surprisingly, physicians aware of problems in fixing the cause of the illness found it very difficult to confront them within the parameters of established clinical practice.

The Social Implications of Uncertain Prognosis

The uncertain prognosis of leukaemia victims has considerable impact upon the social relationships which surround them. In the first instance, the symbolic associations of the disease have patent effects upon everyday encounters for the families affected. As Strauss has pointed out, knowledge of potential fatality is disrupting of ordinary social encounters [14]. Others often reacted with embarrassment or emotion when confronting the leukaemic child or his family after hearing of the illness. This could be misinterpreted by the family, who resented being treated as 'contagious' or being patronized with sympathy. And these more usual components of threatening illness were complicated by the uncertain definition of the child's condition.

At the heart of the drama was the relationship between the sick child and his parents, often a source of agonizing difficulty. For parents generally felt it important to conduct as 'normal' a mode of domestic existence as possible and were strongly encouraged by the clinicians to do so. Yet such 'normality' was maintained in a domestic context whose meaning for them had been tragically redefined. Hence, apart from having to deal with the child's own perceptions of the illness and treatment [15], they had to face dilemmas in their relationship to him which stemmed from his own uncertain future [16]. How far a child should be made to conform to normal expectations (based on the premise of socialization of adulthood) or how far he (rather than the disease and treatment) was responsible for his behaviour was not easily resolved. As one mother put it:

> They say: "Take him home and treat him as normal". But it's hardly a normal situation, is it? I mean, he's a different child, for a start. He throws tantrums for the least thing. He can't bear to be crossed. What I don't know is how much of this is due to the treatment and the leukaemia. So, do I punish him? It's hard when you think that it might not be his fault, and when you think of what he's got and all. If he's not going to grow up, what does it matter? But if we don't check him and he pulls through this, he'll be a little monster one day!

Indeed, a series of situational and cultural constraints (such as the child's ignorance of the condition, and the diffuse but widespread sanction in our society against dwelling on issues deemed 'morbid') tend to result in families striving to stifle any overt acknowledgement of the illness. Yet most reveal clearly that the illness radically alters the meaning of their lives, their values and their expectations for the future. And, while most faced the ordeal without manifest sign of collapse, the child's suffering, and the disruption of familial relations and quality of life, raised searching questions about the meaning of survival. Moreover, as noted above, at least one longitudinal study of survivors suggests that these disruptions are a continuing source of emotional distress for children and their families [17].

Remission

Unlike the classic model of acute illness, malignancies such as leukaemia do not, under modern clinical conditions, entail an explicit stage of 'recovery' or resolution after initial crisis. Rather, early crisis is usually followed by a remission phase of uncertain length and status, during which major symptoms of the disease are in abeyance, but its clinical definition remains tentative. The family of the sufferer now has to reconcile their knowledge of the possible future implications of the illness with the seeming absence of serious symptoms. Many of the problematic features of this stage are in the uncertain nature of chronic illness itself—i.e. its protracted course, uncertain outcome and oscillation between apparent 'health' and 'illness' [18]. But the more usual stresses are here exacerbated by the ever-present threat of fatal relapse, a threat whose likelihood does not simply diminish with the passage of time. As one father remarked:

> It's on your mind all the time. In fact, it's worse once the first panic is over and everything is more-or-less back to normal. The heat is off, and other people now have their own lives to lead. And you sit here, when you're alone and wonder: "How is it going to turn out? Will she make it?". The real hell of this illness is that you just don't know. They can be fine for two years and then suddenly relapse.

In fact, the notion of 'remission' as the first clinical hurdle which victims must reach has come to symbolise the fragile balance of threat and hope which their survival connotes. The terms itself, widely associated with the clinical battle against disease which remains fundamentally intractable, entails a range of meanings which combine the notion of divine pardon with the retreat of symptoms. It represents in condensed form the entanglement of control and chaos at the frontiers of medical knowledge.

The Threat of Uncertain Outcome

The phase of remission entails the process of learning to live with the uncertain status and outcome of the illness. Here again, the changing prognosis of leukaemia is important. For the dramatic risks that this represents have to be reconciled with the apparent normality of everyday existence while the child remains symptom free. In theory, the longer the child survives, particularly after the suspension of chemotherapy, the better his overall chances. But, in fact, the proportion who remain in remission after three years remains very small [19]. Relapses thus continue within the reference group, some well after the suspension of active treatment. This, plus the fundamental clinical uncertainties as regards etiology and the effects of treatment mean that the therapy itself comes to be viewed by the families as rather unspecific or 'hit and miss'. It is generally understood as not yet capable of striking at the origins of the disease itself. While these ambiguities become more clearly delineated in parents' perceptions, clinicians and other agents of care tend to encourage short-term optimism. Thus the overall contradictions in the predicament of family and victim become more marked over time, typically inducing oscillations in perception and mood from unreflective hope to fear and depression. As a result, at least one set of recent observers of this situation have characterized the experience in terms of the 'double-bind' hypothesis [20].

Both agents of care and most lay confidantes project strongly positive definitions of the illness and discourage speculation about possible loss. Families in our study percieved strong taboos against raising these issues in clinical encounters. Thus, while it was usually not the result of concerted strategy, both clinicians and lay people systematically deflected the expression of basic anxieties. Those seeking to reconcile the profound ambiguities inherent in the remission phase found little opportunity for ventilating these concerns. Even when parents' discussion groups were formally instituted by clinicians after our observations had ceased, initial reactions of those questions suggested that here too they felt constrained not to "upset those who were more hopeful by dwelling on morbid things". Family practitioners were turned to by some, but most responded by prescribing psychotropic drugs, which were regarded by parents as distressingly inappropriate. Here again, an existing cultural bias within our wider society and our medical practice discourages overt acknowledgement of mortality and related fears. The ambiguous definition of modern childhood leukaemia make projection of unquestioned optimism by doctor and lay person the predictable course of action.

The lack of opportunities for addressing these uncertainties in remission is heightened by the absence of markers intrinsic to illness and treatment which might signal longer-term prospects. The only 'bench-marks' which punctuate the protracted period of remission are regular clinical check-ups, which assume symbolic significance as hurdles, or pointers with which to map out the disease's uncharted course. At such points, families look hopefully toward the doctors for an indication of the relationship between the child's present state and longerterm outcomes.

> I don't sleep before bone marrow day [21]. I still can't get used to it, and it's over a year now that he's been in remission. Even when they tell me that it's all O.K., I'm still down, because I keep hoping to hear more about his real progress. They say it like this: "He's fine at the moment!". And I think: "Dear God, but for how long? What does it mean for his chances?"

Families raised the problems of uncertainty and disorientation during the phase of remission with distressing regularity and symptoms of depression (feelings of despair, helplessness and hopelessness), had not abated in the majority of this 'typical' population eighteen months after the onset of the disease. Attempts to deflect doubt about treatment and concern about outcome exacerbate the effects of uncertainty. In our society, explicit avoidance of the practical and conceptual implications of death coexists with a stress on rational life-planning—both arguably

the outcome of our perception of ourselves as self-determining corporeal individuals. But these cultural values appear to be tragically at odds with certain forms of experience, such as imperfectly controlled, life-threatening illness. The ambiguities of protracted remission are thus the outcome of deeper contradictions which shape the overall predicament: the contrast between the perception of illness and clinical definition; between the values of planning and predictability and seemingly random uncertainty; between technical control and chaos and between an ideology or rational meliorism and the 'meaninglessness' of suffering and mortality. While these contradictions are written into the very structure of our socio-cultural system, they are realized particularly acutely in the context of affliction and serious illness. And the increasingly aggressive intervention of modern bio-medicine in the course of malignant disease has served to sharpen these oppositions, rendering more explicitly problematic both the experience and the management of clinical treatment.

Conclusion: Illness, Uncertainty, and the Provision of Care

The situation of clinicians and patients in the treatment of childhood leukaemia is an expression of fundamental features of our society and culture, which themselves shape the direction and implications of technical advance in this domain. Because the form and direction of clinical knowledge is part and parcel of a more encompassing system of thought and action, it cannot be either evaluated or transformed in any simple, decontextualized manner. Thus, while it is now quite widely acknowledged in the social and health sciences that bio-medical criteria fail in themselves to define and manage the experience of illness, the implications of this for medical research and practice are more complex than is often supposed. As is increasingly being realized, the meaning of illness and medicine—if not defined merely as physical disease and neutral technical intervention—becomes profoundly problematic. It is then open to essential dilemmas of human value and meaning, which exist currently both in applied science and in other spheres of our formal and popular knowledge.

In relation to the predicament of childhood leukaemics and their families, simple remedies are likely to be merely palliative; the etiology of the more thoroughgoing malaise it represents lies in the very logic of our social and cultural forms. It is with the form and function of medical knowledge in our wider society that real consideration of the problems expressed in this study must begin. Like a host of previous social science investigations, the study of childhood leukaemia reveals the contrast between the meanings and values attached to illness by the sufferers and by clinical definitions. But this account suggests also that this relationship is not static; it is not dictated by an unavoidable or constant gap between formal and lay knowledge, a gap clearly justified by the efficacy of the former. It suggests, rather, that the moving frontier of bio-medical science rests upon a set of contradictions that increasingly widens the gulf, *opposes* formal and lay knowledge and raises basic questions about the meaning and value of biomedical science itself. Thus for parents in our study, uncertain physical survival (often at the cost of pain, confusion and distress) gave rise to persistent doubt, not only about the nature of clinical intervention, but also about established professional definitions of health and well-being.

The reality of these concerns has to be acknowledged by those working for clinical progress, if the meaning of hard-won advance is not to become dangerously irrelevant to our perceptions of need. The important implications of intervention in malignant disease cannot merely be defined as 'psychological maladjustments' or failure to 'cope' on the part of a few unfortunate victims. Neither can they be delegated to agents of care ancillary to somatic medicine, such as psychiatrists or social workers, who are expected to assist sufferers in adapting to clinically defined realities. For it is precisely these realities which such illness experience calls into doubt. And failure to recognise this merely aggravates the victim's dilemma.

In practical terms, no neat professional solutions are at hand for the problems discussed here—either those of the sick, or those of the specialists who work to extend biomedical knowledge and advance their treatment. Yet, in an important sense, the solutions to both orders of problem are entailed in one another. For evaluations of technical developments should begin by acknowledging the ambiguous experience of the recipients of new modes of intervention. In the process of understanding the shape and origins of their distress, we gain insight into the complex social effects of uneven shifts in medical knowledge. It is only in this manner that we become aware of the multi-faceted implications of particular courses of technical advance, and the contradictions attendant upon all 'discoveries' in applied science. At the very least, this must engage the specialist in a process of self-consciousness—of seriously questioning whether current bio-medical definitions adequately reflect the parameters of human distress and suffering, and whether current clinical knowledge might not in fact exacerbate problems central to the experience of health and illness.

REFERENCES

1. The research upon which this paper is based was made possible by the interest and cooperation of the doctors, children and families associated with the regional oncology centre upon which the project focussed. Research was funded by the Leukaemia Research Fund of Great Britain, and preparation for publication was assisted by Bio-Medical Research Support Grant (PHS 5 SO7 RR-07029-14) from the Division of Social Science of the University of Chicago.

2. Simone J., Rhomes M. A. A., Husto H. O. and Pinkel D. 'Total therapy' studies of acute lymphocytic leukaemia in children. *Cancer* 30, 1488, 1972; Till M. M., Hardisty R. M. and Pike M. C. Long survivals in acute leukaemia. *Lancet* I 534, 1973; Li F. P. and Stone R. Survivors of cancer in childhoood. *Ann. intern. Med.* 84, 551, 1976.

3. A total of 82 children in these categories were admitted during the period, 9 of whose parents refused to participate in the study, 9 who died before we were able to establish contact with their families, and 4 whose families left the region while the research was in progress. Of the 60 children included in the study, 50 were A.L.L. cases and 10 were A.M.L. cases, roughly the ratio of incidence in the general population. The data were collected largely by means of semi-structured interviews

with parents in their homes, first shortly after diagnosis, and then some 18 months later. Initial contact included an interview with both parents, and one with the mother alone. During home visits, it was possible to observe the ambience of family life, the relationship of the family to the immediate neighborhood, and so on. On-going contact was maintained with families in the clinical setting, where interaction between doctors and patients was observed. A series of lengthy, semi-structured interviews were also conducted with different categories of clinical staff during the research period.

4. This is true only for the families of children with Acute Lymphoblastic Leukaemia, the commonest form of the disease in childhood and the form most responsive to current treatment regimes. It is in this category that dramatic increase in length and overall rate of survival has been achieved.

5. We use the notion of 'impact' in a similar sense to Davis in his discussion of polio in childhood as an existential and social process [6]. However, the obvious differences in the course of the two diseases renders his overall classification (of the structure of *acute* illness) inappropriate here. While leukaemia presents a particularly stark instance of the lack of fit between illness form and conventional cultural categories—both in sociology and everyday life—it is obviously not unique to this disease. All inherently uncertain conditions (and hence much so-called 'chronic' illness) pose similar sorts of problems of classification.

6. Davis F. *Passage Through Crisis*. Bobbs Merrill, New York, 1963.

7. See Roth J. A. *Timetables*. Bobbs Merrill, New York, 1963 and Fox R. C. *Experiment Perilous*. The Free Press, New York, 1959. The construction of interpretations of the illness by clinicians and lay people is examined in detail elsewhere. (Comaroff J. The symbolic constitution of Western medical knowledge. Forthcoming in *Cult. Med. Psychiat.*).

8. Durkheim E. *Elementary Forms of the Religious Life,* trans. by Swain J., 4th edn, p. 431. Allen & Unwin, London, 1915. One parent provided a particularly graphic example of the attempt to 'complete' available information: as a life-insurance broker, he attempted to collate relevant data

on the course of the disease from all available sources—doctors, paramedical personnel and other parents. He devised a multifactorial model of risk and survival for the population at hand, against which he plotted his son's prognosis.

9. See Glaser B. and Strauss A. *Awareness of Dying.* Wiedenfeld & Nicholson, London, 1965.

10. See Powles J. On the limitations of modern medicine. *Sci. Med. Man* 1 1, 1973; Horton R. African traditional thought and Western science. *Africa* 31, 50, 155, 1969; Crick N. *Explorations in Language and Meaning: Towards a Semantic Anthropology*. Malaby Press, London, 1976.

11. See Natterson J. M. and Knudson A. G. Observations concerning fear of death in fatally ill children and their mothers. *Psychosom. Med.* **22**, 456, 1960.

12. See *Pediatrics* 515 1967.

13. See Horton *op. cit.* [11].

14. Strauss A. L. (Ed.), *Chronic Illness and the Quality of Life,* p. 59. Mosby, St. Louis, 1975.

15. While our study did not focus directly upon the perceptions of the sick children, all of the victims over the age of 10 presented direct or indirect signs of anxiety about their condition. However, only in eleven cases did one or both parents suggest that the child might be expressing concern about survival, and in only six cases (all involving children over the age of four) had the full known implications of the child's condition been discussed with him/her.

16. C.f. Bluebond-Langner M. *The Private World of Dying Children*. Princeton Univ. Press, Princeton, 1978.

17. O'Malley J. E. Long-term follow-up of survivors of childhood cancer: psychiatric sequalae. Paper presented to the *85th Annual Convention of the American Psychiatric Association,* San Francisco, 1977.

18. Strauss (Ed.) *op. cit.* [15].

19. See Li and Stone, *op. cit.* [2].

20. Longhofer J. with the collaboration of Floersch J. E. Dying and living: the double bind. *Cult. Med. Psychiat.* **4**, 119, 1980.

21. Bone-marrow aspirations are performed at regular intervals to detect whether leukaemic cells are present, or whether the disease remains in remission.

10

In the Closet with Illness: Epilepsy, Stigma Potential and Information Control

Joseph W. Schneider and Peter Conrad

The metaphor of the closet has been used frequently to discuss how people avoid or pursue "deviant" identities. Formulated originally in the homosexual subculture, to be "in the closet" has meant to be a secret or covert homosexual. Sociologists have adopted the notion of "coming out" of the closet to describe the development of a gay identity, focusing on self-definition and "public" disclosure as important elements in identity formation (Dank, 1971; Humphreys, 1972; Warren, 1974; Ponse, 1976). Kitsuse (1980) recently has extended the concept of coming out to refer to the "social affirmation of the self" for a wide variety of disvalued groups, including feminists, elderly people, blacks, prostitutes, marijuana users, American Nazis, and many others. In arguing against an "oversocialized" view of deviants encouraged by some narrow labeling interpretations, Kitsuse suggests that increasing numbers of disvalued people in American society have "come out" to affirm their identities as legitimate grounds for the dignity, worth and pride they believe is rightfully theirs.

This link between the closet metaphor and the development of identity is premised, however, on the assumption that in "coming out" there is indeed something to come out to; that there are some developed or developing social definitions that provide the core of this new, open and proud self. Certainly in the case of homosexuality, abandoning the closet of secrecy and concealment was facilitated greatly by the availability of a public identity as "gay and proud." But what of those disvalued by some attribute, performance, or legacy for whom there is no alternate new and proud identity? And what of those for whom even the existence of some "old" and "spoiled" identity may be questionable? In such cases where there may be no clear identity to move from or to, the closet metaphor may seem to lack insight and hence be of little use. We believe, however, that this metaphor taps a more fundamental sociological problem that may, but need not, be linked to the formation of identity.

In this paper we argue that the metaphor of the closet, entry into and exit from it, may be used to focus on the more general sociological problem of how people attempt to manage what they see as discreditable information about themselves. We draw on depth interview data from a study of people with epilepsy—a stigmatized illness (see also Schneider and Conrad, 1979). We try to see how people attempt to maintain favorable or at least neutral definitions of self, given a condition for which no "new" readily available supportive identity or subculture yet exists, and which most of the time—except for the occurrence of periodic seizures—is invisible. By extending the metaphor of the closet to describe this situation, we hope both to increase its analytic utility and learn more about how people manage nondeviant yet stigmatized conditions.[1]

Our sample of 80 people is divided roughly equally by sex, ranging in age from 14 to 54. Most of the respondents come from a metropolitan area of the midwest and none have a history of long-term institutionalization for epilepsy. Interviews were conducted over a two and a half year period beginning in mid-1976, and respondents were selected on the basis of availability and willingness to participate. We used a snowball sampling technique, relying on advertisements in local newspapers, invitation letters passed anonymously by common acquaintances, and names obtained from local social agencies, self-help groups, and health workers. No pretense of statistical representativeness is intended nor was it sought. Due to official restrictions and perceived stigma associated with epilepsy, a population listing from which to draw such a sample does not exist. Our intention was to develop a sample from which theoretical insights would emerge (see Glaser and Strauss, 1967).

We will try here to provide an "insider's" view[2] of 1) how people with epilepsy themselves define their condition as undesirable and discreditable, and hence, grounds for being "in the closet"; and of 2) how they attempt to manage this discreditable information in such a way as to protect their reputations and rights as normal members of society. We first discuss epilepsy as a potentially stigmatized condition, then move to illustrations of how people perceive the stigma of epilepsy and adopt various strategies of concealment and (paradoxically) selective disclosure, all directed toward protecting what they believe to be a threatened self.

The Stigma Potential of Epilepsy

We suggest the concept "stigma potential" to emphasize the significance of epilepsy as an attribute discreditable to one's personal identity (cf. Goffman, 1963:157). Description of the stigma as "potential" rests on two assumptions: 1) that knowledge of one's epilepsy be limited to relatively few others, and 2) that if it were to become more widely known, significant redefinition of self, accompanied by various restrictions and regulation of conduct, might well follow. Although Goffman suggests that possession of such discreditable attributes weighs heavily and shamefully on one's own definitions of self, whether others have the same knowledge or not,

we prefer to make that an empirical question. Like Goffman's discreditable person, Becker's (1963, 1973) secret or potential deviant recognizes his or her own acts, qualities and characteristics, *and* is aware of certain relevant prohibitions in the larger cultural and social setting. Given this knowledge, the potential deviant is one who concludes that there is at least some probability that disclosure would lead to discrediting and undesirable consequences. Becker is more equivocal on the issue of self-derogation and shame, requiring only that the actor be aware that rules do exist which may be applied and enforced if others become aware of the hidden practice or attribute. Although shame is an important phenomenon, it is not necessary to the rise of information control strategies. It is of both theoretical and practical interest that epilepsy is an attribute that would seem to create precisely this kind of potentially deviant or stigmatized person.

Like leprosy and venereal disease, epilepsy is an illness with an ancient associated stigma. Furthermore, epileptic seizures—which can range from nearly imperceptible "spacing out" to the more common, dramatic and bizarre grand mal convulsions—constitute violations of taken-for-granted expectations about the competence of actors in social settings, and are thus likely candidates for becoming "deviant behaviors." Although physicians have been defining and treating it for centuries (Temkin, 1971), epilepsy has long been associated with disreputability, satanic possession, and evil (Lennox and Lennox, 1960). Nineteenth century medical and psychiatric research, including that of Maudsley and Lombroso, suggested a causal link between epilepsy and violent crime[3] and encouraged myths about the relation of epilepsy, violent behavior and mental illness. This research supported placing epileptics in colonies and later special hospitals, excluding them from jobs, from entering the United States as immigrants, and sometimes even from marrying and having children.

The advent of anticonvulsant medications (e.g., phenobarbital in 1912 and Dilantin in 1938) allowed for greater medical control of seizures, enabling epileptics to live more conventional lives. Modern medical conceptualizations of epilepsy as a seizure disorder produced by "intermittent electrochemical impulses in the brain" (HEW-NIH, 1975) are far removed from the earlier morally-tinged interpretations. But historical residues of the deviant status of epilepsy remain central to the condition's current social reality. The stigma potential of epilepsy is well-documented. In a fairly recent review of the literature, Arangio (1975, 1976) found that stigma was still pervasive. It was manifested in various forms of social discrimination: difficulty in obtaining a driver's licence; until 1965, prohibitions (in some states) against marrying; discrimination in obtaining employment (e.g., until 1959 epileptics were not hired for federal civil service positions); difficulties in obtaining all types of insurance; laws (in nine states) that permit sterilization of epileptics under some conditions; and laws (in 17 states) that allow for institutionalization of epileptics (Arangio, 1975). Researchers using intermittent Gallup poll data over the 25-year period 1949 to 1974 found a decrease in attitudinal prejudice toward epileptics, although 20 percent of the population in 1974 still maintained that epileptics should not be employed (Caveness *et al.,* 1974).

Such attitudes and official regulations are, of course, not lost on people with epilepsy. A recent nationwide survey found that one quarter of all epileptics do not tell their employers about epilepsy, and half indicated that having epilepsy created problems in getting a job (Perlman, 1977). While these and other "objective" aspects of prejudice and discrimination toward people with epilepsy have been documented, the ways in which such features of the larger cultural and social world are given meaning in people's subjective experience is less accessible and relatively unexplored.

The Perception of Stigma

Stigma is by no means an automatic result of possessing some discreditable attribute. The significance of "having" epilepsy is a product of a collective definitional process in which the actor's perspective occupies a central place. As suggested earlier, a discreditable attribute or performance becomes relevant to self only if the individual perceives it as discreditable, whether or not such perceptions are actually applied by others to self or simply considered as a relevant "object" in the environment that must be taken into account. The actor has an important part in the construction of the meaning of epilepsy and of illness generally. It is of course logically possible that people otherwise deemed "ill" are unaware of what their conditions mean to the others with whom they interact: for example, a person is surprised by sympathetic reactions to his or her disclosure of cancer, or a young "tough" who in polite society wears venereal disease as a badge of sexual prowess.

Most sociological work on stigma assumes that the stigmatized learn the meaning of their attribute or performance primarily through direct exposure to rejection and disapproval from others. Less understood is the place of the *perception of stigma*—of what the putatively stigmatized think others think of them and "their kind" and about how these others might react to disclosure. This brings us back to the situation of Goffman's discreditable actor, but makes actors' definitions central and problematic. Such actor definitions of epilepsy provide the foundation on which the stigma of epilepsy is constructed.

Over and over in our interviews, people with epilepsy told us that they "have" something that others "don't understand," and that this lack of understanding and knowledge of "what epilepsy is" is a fundamental source of what they see as an actual or potentially negative reaction. They believe that what little information others have about epilepsy is probably incorrect and stereotypical, sometimes incorporating elements of madness and evil. Adjectives such as "frightened" and "scared" were used to describe others' views of epilepsy. One woman, whose epilepsy had been diagnosed at middle age and who had lost a teaching job because of seizures at work, said:

Well, I understand it now and *I'm* not afraid of it. But most people are unless they've experienced it, and so you just don't talk to other people about it, and if you do, never use the word "epilepsy." The word itself, I mean job-ways, insurance-ways . . . anything, the hang-ups there are on it. There's just too much prejudice so the less said about it the better.

One man compared others' ignorance and fear of epilepsy to similar reactions to leprosy: "The public is so illy educated toward an epileptic. It's like someone with leprosy walking into a room. You see a leper and you run because you're afraid of it." And another woman spoke of epilepsy's "historical implications":

> The fact of having epilepsy. It isn't the seizures. I think they are a very minor part of it. Its implications are so *enormous*. The historical implications of epilepsy are fantastic. I'm lucky to have been born when I was. If I was born at the beginning of this century I would have been discarded . . . probably locked away somewhere.

In these and similar ways, people recognize that ignorance and fear taint public images of epilepsy. They then take such recognitions into account in their own strategies and decisions about how to control such discrediting information.

Seizures in social situations are an important aspect of this discrediting perception of epilepsy. Seizures might be seen as sociologically akin to such involuntary *faux pas* as breaking wind or belching. Farts or belches, however, are reasonably familiar and normalized in middle-class society, but people with epilepsy believe that others ordinarily consider seizures as beyond the boundaries of undesirable but nevertheless "normal" conduct. One woman suggested seizures are "like having your pants fall down" in public. Another described how she believed others see seizures: "I can't use the word 'horrible,' but they think . . . it's *ugly*. It is. It's strange. It's something you're not used to seeing." People with epilepsy believe that others see the actual behaviors associated with seizures—including unconsciousness, violent muscle contractions, falling to the ground, or simply being "absent" from the social scene—as objective grounds for a more fundamental, "essential" disreputability. The stigma was described in this way by another woman:

> It's one of those fear images; it's something that people don't know about and it has strong negative connotations in people's minds. It's a bad image, something scary, sort of like a beggar; it's dirty, the person falling down and frothing at the mouth and

jerking and the bystanders not knowing what to do. It's something that happens in public which isn't "nice."

As these data suggest, aside from the question of shame or self-labeling, people who have epilepsy perceive the social meanings attached to it and to seizures as threats to their status as normal and competent members of society.

Coaches for Concealment: Learning to be Discreditable

How do people construct these views of others' perceptions? As we suggested, conventional sociological wisdom has emphasized direct disvaluing treatment by others. While this interactive experience is undoubtedly important to study, our data strongly suggest that people with epilepsy also learn such views from significant and supportive others, particularly from parents. Parental training in the stigma of epilepsy is most clear for people who were diagnosed when they were children, but stigma coaches were also identified by those who were diagnosed when they were adults.[4]

Our data indicate that the more the parents convey a definition of epilepsy as something "bad," and the less willing they are to talk about it with their children, the more likely the child is to see it as something to be concealed. One thirty-four year old woman had maintained a strategy of tightly controlled secrecy from the time she was diagnosed as having epilepsy at age fourteen. She recalled her parents' reaction:

> Complete disbelief. You know, "We've never had anything like that in our family." I can remember that it was very plainly said, almost like I was something . . . something was wrong. They did not believe it. In fact, we went to another doctor and then it was confirmed.

These parents proceded to manage their daughter's epilepsy by a combination of silence and maternal "coaching" on how to conceal it from others. When asked if she told her husband about her epilepsy before they were married, the same woman said:

I talked to Mom about it. She said, "Don't tell him because some people don't understand. He may not understand. That's not something you talk about." I asked her, "Should I talk to him about passing out?" She said, "Never say 'epilepsy.' It's not something we talk about."

She had learned her "lesson" well, and concealed her illness for almost twenty years.

Family silence about epilepsy can itself be a lesson in stigma. One middle-aged woman who was just beginning to "break through" (cf. Davis, 1961) such silence, said that her parents had never told her that she had epilepsy: "They just told me I suffered from fainting fits." She had filled this vacuum of silence by concluding that she must be "going mad." Throughout her childhood, and even in her present relationship with her parents, epilepsy had been "brushed under the carpet": "It's not nice to talk about those things." Like sexual variety in the late nineteenth century, epilepsy was obviously something "bad" because it was something "people just didn't [i.e., shouldn't] talk about."

Parents are not the only coaches for secrecy. Close associates, friends, and even professionals sometimes suggest concealment as a strategy for dealing with epilepsy, particularly in circumstances where it is believed to be a disqualifying characteristic. One woman described such advice by a physician-medical examiner who said he "had to" fire her from a teaching job because of her seizures: "He advised me to lie about it. He said, 'If you don't miss work from it and it's not visible to anybody, lie about it.' And I've been doing that since and I've been able to work since."

As the literature on subcultures makes clear, stigmatized people can learn practical survival strategies from each others' experience. A supportive subculture surrounding epilepsy is only in its infancy, as is true for most illnesses,[5] but various self-help groups do exist through which people with epilepsy may learn relevant coping skills (see Borman *et al.*, 1980). In the absence of a developed subculture for people like themselves, some people with epilepsy learn the importance of concealment from people with other illnesses. As one woman said of her diabetic husband's experience.

He didn't know. He hadn't gone through this [or] met other diabetics. He didn't know how to carry out a lie. One of the things that we learned, again from the diabetes, was how [to] lie if they asked for a urine sample. We now have met, through the rap sessions, people who said, "You bring somebody else's urine!" Well, that's a pretty shocking thing to have to do. Yeah, there are times when you gotta lie.

The importance of others as coaches for concealment is clear. Through this "diabetes underground" her husband learned how to lie, then taught it to her.

Some significant others, however, including some parents, adopt strategies of openness, honesty and neutralization. Parents who define their child's epilepsy "just like any other medical problem" and "certainly nothing to be ashamed of" apparently encourage their children to have a much more neutral view and a more open informational control strategy. One successful businessman credited his parents with managing epilepsy so as to minimize it and prevent him from using it as a "crutch" or "excuse":

The parents of an epileptic child are the key to the whole ball of wax, in recognizing that you have a problem in the family but not to let that control the total actions and whole livelihood and whole future of the family. Accept it and go about doing what has to be done to maintain an even keel.

The themes of "taking epilepsy in stride," not "using" it as a "cop-out" are reminiscent of the cautions against the temptation to use medical excuses which Parsons (1951) analyzed (cf. Waitzkin and Waterman, 1974). They were common to the accounts given to us by people who seemed to portray their epilepsy as "no big thing," partly from concern that such comments might be interpreted by others as requests for "sympathy" and "special treatment." Parents who cautioned against such "special pleading" uses of epilepsy also typically were recalled as having taught their children the values of self-reliance, independence and achievement—as another way of overcoming an emphasis on epilepsy and its significance. Learning that epilepsy need not be a barrier to personal or social acceptance led individuals to be more "out" of than "in" the closet of epilepsy; learning to believe that epilepsy was a shameful flaw encouraged, understandably, the development of just the opposite strategy.

Strategies of Selective Concealment: The Closet of Epilepsy Has a Revolving Door

Most discussions of the self and the "closet" assume that one can only be in or out, and that being out must follow a period of being in. As we learned more about how people experience epilepsy, we realized that such a view of the closet of epilepsy was much too simple. Sometimes people conceal their epilepsy, sometimes they do not, and the same persons can be both "open" and "closed" during the same period in their lives. In short, both concealment and disclosure proved to be quite complex and selective strategies of information management.

A part of the "wisdom" of the world of epilepsy is that there are some people you can tell about your illness and others you cannot (cf. Goffman, 1963). Even the most secretive (and twelve of our respondents said we were the first people they had told about their epilepsy except for their physicians and immediate family) had told at least several other people about their condition. Close friends and family members are perhaps the most clear instance of "safe others," but "people I feel comfortable with" and those who "won't react negatively to epilepsy" are also sometimes told. Such persons are often used to test reactions: "I think the first couple of times I mentioned it was with my very closest friends to sort of test the water and when it wasn't any problem, then I began to feel freer to mention it."

The development of more diffuse disclosure or "coming out" seemed contingent on how these early disclosures went. Just as perceived "positive" results may encourage people to come out more, perceived "negative" consequences from trial disclosures may encourage a return to concealment as the predominant way to control personal and social impacts. As one woman put it:

> I tried to get a driver's license when I was 18 or 19, after I was married. We were living in Mississippi and I put it on [the form] that I was epileptic, only

because I was afraid if I pass out and I'm drivin' a car, well, that's dangerous. I took the thing up there and they said, "Epileptics can't—you have to have a doctor's thing." We moved about two months later to California. I got my driver's license and didn't put it down.

Later on she made another attempt at disclosure, this time on an application to live in a college dormitory. After being disqualified from living on campus and then declining a scholarship, she decided that secrecy was the only strategy by which she could minimize the risk of rejection and differential treatment. In retrospect, she concluded: "I don't know if maybe I wasn't testing . . . at the time, you know, well, is it okay? If things had been different, maybe I could have talked about it." When asked if she discusses epilepsy with new people she meets, another woman spoke specifically of this "risk":

> It depends. I still find it hard, but I'm trying to. I have to trust somebody a lot before I'll tell them in terms of a friendship basis. All my close friends know, but in terms of my work, forget it. This is a risk I can't take after the previous experience. I still have great built-in fears about losing a job from it. I'm not ready to put myself at that risk.

An upwardly mobile young administrator said he lost his driver's license as a result of disclosing his epilepsy. He recalled that experience and what he "learned" from it: "I started out tryin' to be honest about it and got burned. So I gave up bein' honest about it in that circumstance." Although this man did disclose his epilepsy to a wide variety of others, including his employer, he said he regularly lied about it on driver's license forms.

Such data clearly suggest that people can and do maintain carefully segregated and selective strategies of managing the stigma potential of epilepsy. Some situations were considered considerably more "high risk" than others. In employment, for example, concealment, including lying on initial employment applications, was thought to be the best general strategy. Because they thought there would be reprisals if their employers subsequently learned of their epilepsy, respondents who advocated such concealment typically said they adopted a monitoring or "see how it's going" approach to possible later disclosure. If they saw approval in others' reactions to them during initial contacts, they could attempt disclosure. One young woman who said she had not had a seizure for 19 years and took no medication was still very sensitive about her "past" when applying for a job:

> Well, employers are the only thing I haven't been open with. On an application, I will not write it. If I feel I have a chance for a job and I'm gonna make it, I'll bring it up. But to put it on that application—because employers, they look at it, they see that thing checked; it just gives me a feeling that they don't give you a chance.

Although she said she had never experienced discriminatory treatment in employment, this woman says she usually waits "until I get into that interview and sell myself first. Then I'll come out and say, 'There's one more point'. . . ." Another respondent said he would wait until "I have my foot in the door and they said, 'Hey, he's doing okay' " before disclosing his epilepsy to employers. People who had tried this strategy of gradual disclosure after employer approval of their work were often surprised that others made so little of their condition. As a result of such experiences they proceeded to redefine some aspects of their own "theories" of others' reactions to epilepsy.

Finally, concealing epilepsy—staying in the closet—was believed important in situations where others might be predisposed to criticize. One woman, who said she was open to friends, commented that she wouldn't want others "in the neighborhood" to know. She explained: "At this point I'm not involved in quarrels. I would think that if I got into a quarrel or feuding situation, it [the epilepsy] would be something that would be used against me." The same view of epilepsy as ammunition for critics was expressed by a man who defined his work as "very political." He thought that if others learned of his epilepsy, they would "add that on as an element of [my] character that makes [me] undesirable." Sometimes this "closing ranks" against adversaries can even exclude those who would otherwise be told. One woman said that because her brother married a woman "I don't particularly care for," she had decided simply not

to tell him of her diagnosis. Her sister-in-law was "the type that would say, you know, 'You're crazy because you have it,' or 'There's something wrong with you.' And she would probably laugh." Even a physician may be seen more as a gatekeeper than an advocate and counselor. One man expressed this theme in many of our interviews quite clearly:

> If he is going to go running to the state and tell the state every time I have a seizure, I don't feel I can be honest with that doctor. He is not keeping his part of the bargain. Everything on my medical records is supposed to be sacred.

Taken together, these data suggest that the process of information management used by people with epilepsy is much more complex than the now-familiar metaphor of being either "in or out of the closet" would lead us to believe. They also indicate that, in strategies of disclosure and concealment of potentially stigmatizing attributes, being out of or in the closet of *epilepsy* may often have much less to do with one's "identity" than with the more practical matter of preventing others from applying limiting and restrictive rules that disqualify one from normal social roles. Epilepsy is something to be hidden at some times and in some places and disclosed quite readily at other times and in other places. Such disclosure and concealment appear contingent upon a complex interaction of one's learned perceptions of the stigma of epilepsy, actual "test" experiences with others before and/or after disclosure, and the nature of the particular relationship involved.

Instrumental Telling: Disclosing As a Management Strategy

Information management may include disclosure as well as concealment, even when the information is potentially discreditable. Except for the respondents who adopted rigidly secretive strategies, the people we spoke to said they "usually" or "always" told certain others of their epilepsy under certain circumstances. In this final section we discuss two types of such telling that emerged in our data: telling as "therapy" and "preventive telling." Both involve disclosure but, like concealment, are conscious attempts to mitigate the potentially negative impact of epilepsy on one's self and daily round.

Telling as Therapy

Disclosing feelings of guilt, culpability, and self-derogation can be cathartic, as we know from a variety of social science research. Particularly for those who have concealed what they see as some personal blemish or flaw, such telling can serve a "therapeutic" function for the self by sharing or diffusing the burden of such information. It can free the energy used to control information for other social activities. Such relief, however, requires a properly receptive audience: that is, listeners who are supportive, encouraging, empathetic, and nonjudgmental. Such occasions of telling and hearing can not only be cathartic, they also can encourage people with epilepsy to define their condition as a nonremarkable and neutral facet of self, perhaps even an "interesting" one, as one man told us. This sort of "telling as therapy" is akin to what Davis (1961) described as the relief associated with breaking through the collectively created and negotiated silence surrounding the physical disabilities of polio victims when they interacted with normals.

Such therapeutic telling seems instrumental primarily in its impact on the actor's self-definition: at the minimum, it simply externalizes what is believed to be significant information about self that has been denied one's intimates and associates. Many of the people we interviewed, in recalling such experiences of "coming out" to select and safe audiences, emphasized the importance of talk as therapy. One woman said of such talking: "It's what got me together about it [the epilepsy]." And a man recalled how telling friends about epilepsy allowed him to minimize it in his own mind:

> I think in talking to them [friends] I would try to convince myself that it didn't have to be terribly important. Now that I think more about it, I was probably just defiant about it: "I ain't gonna let this God-damned thing get in my way, period."

For a final example, one of the few respondents, who in keeping with her mother's careful coaching had told virtually no one, insightfully suggested how she might use the interview itself as grounds for redefining her epilepsy and self:

> It just seems so weird now that I've—because I'm talking to you about it, and I've never talked to anybody about it. It's really not so bad. You know it hasn't affected me that much, but no one wants to talk about it. . . . [Talking about epilepsy] makes me feel I'm not really so bad off. Just because I can't find answers to those questions, cuz like I think I feel sorry for myself. I can sit around the house and just dream up all these things, you know, why I'm persecuted and [all].

Such selective disclosure to supportive and nonjudgmental others can thus help "banish the ghosts" that flourish in secrecy and isolation. It allows for feedback and the renegotiation of the perception of stigma. Through externalizing what is believed to be a potentially negative feature of self, people with epilepsy *and* their audiences can redefine this attribute as an "ordinary" or "typical" part of themselves (Dingwall, 1976). As we have already indicated, however, this strategy appears to be effective primarily among one's intimates and close friends. When facing strangers or those whose reactions cannot be assumed supportive, such as prospective employers, the motor vehicle bureau, or virtually any bureacracy's application form, such openness can be set aside quite quickly.

Preventive Telling

Another kind of instrumental telling we discovered in our data could be called "preventive": disclosure to influence others' actions and/or ideas toward self and toward epileptics in general. One variety of such preventive telling occurs when actors think it probable that others, particularly others with whom they share the same routine, will witness their seizures. The grounds cited for such disclosure are that others then "will know what it is" and "won't be scared." By "knowing what it is," respondents mean others define "it"—the epilepsy and seizure—as a *medical* problem, thereby removing blame and responsibility from the actor for the aberrant conduct in question. The actors assume that others should not be "frightened" if they too learn that "it" is a medical problem.

To engage in such anticipatory preventive telling is to offer a kind of "medical disclaimer" (cf. Hewitt and Stokes, 1975) intended to influence others' reactions should a seizure occur. By bringing a blameless, beyond-my-control medical interpretation to such potentially discrediting events, people attempt to reduce the risk that more morally disreputable interpretations might be applied by naive others witnessing one's seizures. One young woman recalled that she felt "great" when her parents told her junior high teachers about epilepsy, because "I'd rather have them know than think I was a dummy or something . . . or think I was having . . . you know, *problems*." Reflecting the power of medical excuses (as well as a relative hierarchy of legitimacy among medical excuses), a middle-aged man who described himself as an "alcoholic" told of how he would disclose his epilepsy to defuse others' complaints about his drinking:

I'd say, "I have to drink. It's the only way I can maintain . . . I have seizures you know" . . . and this kind of thing. People would then feel embarrassed. Or you'd say, "I'm epileptic," then they'd feel embarrassed and say, "Oh, well, gee, we're sorry, that's right. We forgot about that."

Such accounts illustrate the kind of social currency that medical definitions possess in general and in particular with respect to epilepsy. As with all currency, however, its effectiveness as a medium of acceptable exchange rests on its mutual validation by those who give and receive it; what others in fact think of such accounts remains largely unknown.

Beyond providing a medical frame of reference through which others may interpret seizures, such preventive telling may also include specific instructions about what others should do when seizures do occur. Because people with epilepsy believe others are almost totally ignorant of what seizures are, they similarly assume that others have little idea of how to react to seizures. By providing what in effect are directions for others to follow, people who do preventive telling

believe they are protecting not only their body but their self. As the young administrator we quoted earlier put it:

Down the road, I'll usually make a point to tell someone I'm around a lot because I know it's frightening. So I will, partly for my own purposes, tell them I've got it; if I have one [seizure] that it's nothing to worry about. And don't take me to the hospital even if I ask you to. I always tell people that I work with because I presume I'll be with them for some long period of time. And I may have a seizure and I want them to know what *not* to do, in particular.

Through such telling, people solve some of the problems that a seizure represents for naive others. While these others then have the task of carrying out such instructions—which typically are "do nothing," "make me comfortable," "don't call the ambulance," and "keep me from hurting myself"—the authority, and therefore responsibility, for such reaction rests with the individual giving the instructions.

Disclosure of one's epilepsy may depend also on the anticipation of rejection at some subsequent telling or disclosure occasion. "Coming out" to those who appear to be candidates for "close" relationships is a strategy for minimizing the pain of later rejection. As one man said, "If they're going to leave [because of epilepsy], better it be sooner than later." Another spoke of such telling as a "good way of testing" what kind of friend such persons would be: "Why go through all the trauma of falling in love with someone if they are going to hate your guts once they find out you're an epileptic?"

We discovered that people also disclose their epilepsy when they feel it necessary or important to "educate" others. While this strategy is sometimes mediated and supported through participation in various self-help groups, some individuals initiated it themselves. One young man who became active in a local self-help group described his "rap" on epilepsy as follows:

It's a good manner. I use it quite a bit. I'll come through and say epilepsy is a condition, not a disease. I can throw out all the statistics. I usually say most people are not in wheelchairs or in bed because of epilepsy, they're walking the streets just like I am and other people. Anything like that to make comparisons, to get a point across.

Another respondent, who believed she had benefited greatly by an early talk with a veteran epileptic, spoke of the importance of such education: "That's why I think it is important to come out of the closet to some extent. Because once people have met an epileptic and found out that it's a *person* with epilepsy, that helps a lot." Exposure to a person who "has epilepsy" but is conventional in all other ways may stimulate others to redefine their image of "epileptics."

Conclusion

Illness is an individualizing and privatizing experience. As Parsons (1951) argued, occupants of the sick role are not only dissuaded from "enjoying" the exemptions associated with their state but are segregated and separated from other sick people. When individuals desire to be "normal" and lead conventional lives the potential of stigma is isolating; persons fear disclosure of discreditable information and may limit their contacts or connections with others. As Ponse observes, "The veils of anonymity are often as effective with one's own as with those from whom one wishes to hide. Thus, an unintended consequence of secrecy is that it isolates members from one another" (1976:319). Persons with stigmatized illnesses like epilepsy, and perhaps with other illness as well, are doubly insulated from one another, at least in one very important sense. Because there is no illness subculture they are separate, alone and unconnected with others sharing the same problems (for an unusual exception, see Gussow and Tracey, 1968). And this very desire to lead conventional and stigma-free lives further separates and isolates them from each other. It is not surprising that the vast majority of people with epilepsy we interviewed did not know a single other epileptic.

Returning to our metaphor of the closet, we can now see that the potential of stigma certainly leads some people to create the closet as a secret and safe place. And usually, whether with homosexuality or epilepsy, people are in the closet alone. There are important differences, however. Few people in the closet with epilepsy even have any idea where other closets may be. Because there is usually no supportive subculture (a few recent and important self-help groups are notable exceptions) there is no place for a person with epilepsy to get insider information or to test the possible effects of coming out. Since most people with epilepsy want to be considered conventional people with a medical disorder, there is little motivation to come out and develop an epileptic identity. It is little wonder, then, that the closet of epilepsy has a revolving door.

To summarize: for those who possess some discreditable feature of self, some generally hidden "fact" or quality, the disclosure of which they believe will bring undesired consequences, the attempt to control information is a major strategy. We have described several ways people with epilepsy engage in such management work. Our data have suggested that the idea of being "in the closet" and that of being a "secret deviant" need to be extended to incorporate the complex reality of how people very selectively disclose or withhold discreditable information about themselves. Finally, we have shown how disclosing can serve the same ends as concealing. In addition, we suggest that sociological explorations into the experience of illness may well lend new dimensions to old concepts and give us greater understanding of the ways people manage such discomforting and vulnerable parts of their lives.

NOTES

A version of this paper was presented at the 75th annual meetings of the American Sociological Association, New York, August 1980. Thanks to Irving Kenneth Zola and anonymous reviewers for helpful comments on a previous draft. The research was supported by grants from the National Institutes of Mental Health, Small Grants Section (MH 30818-01), the Epilepsy Foundation of America, and the Drake University Research Council.

1. The moral parallel between illness and deviance has been well-recognized in the sociological literature. Parsons (1951) first noted that illness and crime are analytically similar because they both represent threats to effective role performance and are "dysfunctional" for society, calling forth ap-

propriate mechanisms of social control. Freidson (1966, 1970) addressed this moral parallel more directly, by arguing that both illness and deviance are disvalued and disvaluing attributes variously attached to actors and situations believed to challenge preferred and dominant definitions of appropriate conduct and "health." More recently, Dingwall (1976) has advocated a phenomenological, insider's approach to illness as lived experience. He suggests that illness might be considered deviance (1) to the extent that it involves behavior perceived by others as "out of the ordinary" or unusual, and (2) if sufficient intentionality or willfulness can be attributed to the ill/deviant actor for the conduct in question (see also Conrad and Schneider, 1980). While we stop short of concluding that epilepsy is "deviant," it seems clear from our data that it is stigmatized, at least in the eyes of those who have it.

2. While there is a relative imbalance of sociological "insider" accounts of being deviant, such work is even more rare for the experience of illness. We have few sociological studies of what it is like *to be* sick, to *have* cancer, diabetes, schizophrenia, heart disease, and so on (for exceptions see Davis, 1961; Gussow and Tracey, 1968; Strauss and Glaser, 1975). This may be due in part to the historic dominance of professional medical definitions of health and illness. We agree with Dingwall (1976), Fabrega (1972, 1979), and Idler (1979), that more research is needed into how these and other illnesses are experienced as social phenomena.

3. For a more current version of the argument linking the biophysiology of the brain and violence, see Mark and Ervin (1970).

4. See West's (1979a, b) discussion of 24 British families containing a child with epilepsy and how parents managed negative stereotypes of epilepsy in light of their child's diagnosis.

5. For an interesting discussion of some exceptions, see Anspach's (1979) analysis of the "identity politics" of the physically disabled and former mental patients. As we suggest, the availability of a new and positive identity is crucial to the development of the kind of politics Anspach describes.

REFERENCES

Anspach, Renee R.
1979　"From stigma to identity politics: Political activism among the physically disabled and former mental patients." Social Science and Medicine 13A: 766–73.

Arangio, Anthony J.
1975　Behind the Stigma of Epilepsy. Washington, D.C.: Epilepsy Foundation of America.
1976　"The stigma of epilepsy." American Rehabilitation 2 (September/October): 4–6.

Becker, Howard S.
1963　Outsiders. New York: Macmillan.
1973　"Labeling theory reconsidered." Pp. 177–208 in Howard S. Becker, Outsiders. New York: Free Press.

Borman, Leonard D., James Davies and David Droge
1980　"Self-help groups for persons with epilepsy." In B. Hermann [ed.], A Multidisciplinary Handbook of Epilepsy. Springfield, Ill.: Thomas.

Caveness, W. F., H. Houston Merritt and G. H. Gallup, Jr.
1974　"A survey of public attitudes towards epilepsy in 1974 with an indication of trends over the past twenty-five years." Epilepsia 15: 523–36.

Conrad, Peter and Joseph W. Schneider
1980　Deviance and Medicalization: From Badness to Sickness. St. Louis, Missouri: Mosby.

Dank, Barry M.
1971　"Coming out in the gay world." Psychiatry 34 (May): 180–97.

Davis, Fred
1961　"Deviance disavowal: The management of strained interaction by the visibly handicapped." Social Problems 9 (Fall):120–32.

Dingwall, Robert
1976　Aspects of Illness. New York: St. Martin's.

Fabrega, Horacio, Jr.
1972　"The study of disease in relation to culture." Behavioral Science 17:183–200.
1979　"The ethnography of illness." Social Science and Medicine 13A:565–76.

Freidson, Eliot
1966　"Disability as social deviance." Pp. 71–99 in M. Sussman [ed.], Sociology and Rehabilitation. Washington, D.C.: The American Sociological Association.
1970　Profession of Medicine. New York: Dodd, Mead.

Glaser, Barney G. and Anselm L. Strauss
1967　The Discovery of Grounded Theory. Chicago: Aldine.

Goffman, Erving
1963　Stigma. Englewood Cliffs, N.J.: Prentice-Hall.

Gussow, Zachary and George S. Tracey
1968   "Status, ideology and adaptation to stigmatized illness: A study of leprosy." Human Organization 27(4):316–25.
Hewitt, John P. and Randall Stokes
1975   "Disclaimers." American Sociological Review 40:1–11.
Humphreys, Laud
1972   Out of the Closets. Englewood Cliffs, N.J.: Prentice-Hall.
Idler, Ellen L.
1979   "Definitions of health and illness in medical sociology." Social Science and Medicine 13A:723–31.
Kitsuse, John I.
1980   "Coming out all over: Deviants and the politics of social problems." Social Problems 28, 1.
Lennox, Gordon W. and Margaret A. Lennox
1960   Epilepsy and related disorders, Volume 1. Boston: Little, Brown
Mark, Vernon H. and Frank R. Ervin.
1970   Violence and the Brain. New York: Harper and Row.
Parsons, Talcott
1951   The Social System. New York: Free Press.
Perlman, Leonard G.
1977   The Person With Epilepsy. Life Style, Needs, Expectations. Chicago: National Epilepsy League.
Ponse, Barbara
1976   "Secrecy in the lesbian world." Urban Life 5 (October):313–38.

Schneider, Joseph W. and Peter Conrad
1979   "Medical and sociological typologies: The case of epilepsy." Unpublished manuscript, Drake University, Des Moines, Iowa.
Strauss, Anselm L. and Barney G. Glaser
1975   Chronic Illness and the Quality of Life. St. Louis, Missouri: Mosby.
Temkin, Oswei
1971   The Falling Sickness. Second edition. Baltimore, Maryland: Johns Hopkins Press.
U.S. Department of Health Education and Welfare—National Institute of Health
1975   The NINCDS Epilepsy Research Program. Washington, D.C.: U.S. Government Printing Office.
Waitzkin, H. K. and B. Waterman
1974   The Exploitation of Illness in Capitalist Society. Indianapolis: Bobbs-Merrill.
Warren, Carol A. B.
1974   Identity and Community in the Gay World. New York: Wiley.
West, Patrick B.
1979a   "Making sense of epilepsy." Pp. 162–69 in D. J. Osborne, M. M. Gruneberg and J. R. Eiser (eds.), Research in Psychology and Medicine, Volume 2. New York: Academic.
1979b   "An investigation into the social construction and consequences of the label epilepsy." Sociological Review 27: 719–41.

The Social Organization
of Medical Care

In Part Two we turn from the production of disease and illness to the social organizations created to treat it. Here we begin to examine the institutional aspects of health and illness—the medical care system. We look at the social organization of medical care historically, structurally, and, finally, interactionally. We seek to understand how this complex system operates and how its particular characteristics have contributed to the current health care crisis.

Creating and Maintaining the Dominance of Medicine

Physicians have a professional monopoly of medical practice in America. They have an exclusive state-supported right, manifested in the "licensing" of physicians, to medical practice. With their licenses, physicians can legally do what no one else can, including cutting into the human body and prescribing drugs.

Until the latter part of the nineteenth century various groups and individuals (homeopaths, midwives, botanical doctors, etc.) competed for the "medical turf." By the second decade of this century virtually only M.D. physicians had the legal right to practice medicine in this country. One might suggest that physicians achieved their exclusive rights to the nation's medical territory because of their superior scientific and clinical achievements, a line of reasoning which suggests that physicians demonstrated superior healing and curative skills and the government therefore supported their rights against less effective healers and quacks. But this seems not to have been the case. As we noted earlier, most of the improvement in the health status of the population resulted from social changes, including better nutrition, sanitation, and a rising standard of living rather than from the interventions of clinical medicine. Medical techniques were in fact rather limited, often even dangerous, until the early twentieth century. As L. J. Henderson observed, ". . . somewhere between 1910 and 1912 in this country, a random patient, with a random disease, consulting a doctor chosen at random, had, for the first time in the history of mankind, a better than fifty-fifty chance of profiting from the encounter" (quoted in Blumgart, 1964).

The success of the American Medical Association (AMA) in consolidating medical power in its own organizational hands was central to the securing of a monopoly for M.D. physicians. Although the AMA has lost some power recently to the "corporate rationalizers" in medicine (e.g., health insurance industry, hospital organizations [Alford, 1972]), its monopoly over professional practice remains intact. (The creation and maintenance of this medical monopoly has been more of a political than a scientific achievement.) By virtue of their monopoly of medical practice, physicians have been able to gain dominance over the entire field of medicine, including the right to define what constitutes disease and how to treat it. As Freidson (1970a:251) has observed, "The medical profession has first claim to jurisdiction over the label illness and *anything* to which it may be attached, irrespective of its capacity to deal with it effectively."

Physicians also gained "professional dominance" over the organization of medical services in the United States (Freidson: 1970b). This monopoly gave the medical profession functional autonomy and a structural insulation from outside evaluations of medical practice. In addition, professional dominance includes not only the exclusive right to treat disease, but also the right to limit and evaluate the performance of most other medical-care workers. Finally, the particular vision of medicine that became institutionalized included a "clinical mentality" (Freidson, 1970a) which focused on medical responsibility to *individual* patients rather than to the community or public.

In the first essay in this section, "Professionalization, Monopoly, and the Structure of Medical Practice," Peter Conrad and Joseph W. Schneider present a brief review of the historical development of this medical monopoly. They examine the case of abortion in the nineteenth century to highlight how specific medical interests were served by a physician-led crusade against abortion. By successfully outlawing abortion and institutionalizing their own professional ethics, "regular" physicians were able to eliminate effectively some of their competitors and secure greater control of the medical market.

Richard W. Wertz and Dorothy C. Wertz expand on this theme of monopolization and professional dominance in "Notes on the Decline of Midwives and the Rise of Medical Obstetricians." They investigate the medicalization of childbirth historically and the subsequent decline of midwifery in this country. Female midwifery, which continues to be practiced in most industrialized and developing countries, has been virtually eliminated in the United States. Wertz and Wertz show that it was not merely professional imperialism that led to the exclusion of midwives (although this played an important role), but also a subtle and profound sexism within and outside the medical profession. They postulate that the physicians' monopolization of childbirth resulted from a combination of a change in middle-class women's views of birthing, physicians' economic interests, and the development of sexist notions which suggested that women weren't suitable for attending births. Physicians became increasingly interventionist in their childbirth practice partly due to their training (they felt they had to "do" something) and their desire to use instruments "to establish superior status" and treat childbirth as an illness rather than a natural event. In recent years we have seen the reemergence of nurse midwives, but their work is usually limited to hospitals under medical dominance (Rothman, 1982). Also, there are presently a small number of "lay" midwives whose practice is confined to quasi-illegal situations outside of medical control (See Arms, 1975). See Barbara Katz Rothman's article in this volume for a description of how modern midwives' clinical perspectives were transformed through their experiences attending homebirths.

In the third article in this section, "Professional Dominance and the Ordering of Health Services: Some Consequences," Eliot Freidson analyzes some of the effects of professional monopolization. He first describes medicine as having an "organized autonomy" and then shows how it also has a professional dominance over the medical division of labor. He describes how professional practice, rather than bureaucratic organization, contributes to the discomfort and dissatisfaction patients experience in medical encounters. Freidson notes that the jurisdiction of medicine is widening and that the profession exerts an unwarranted influence on the planning and financing of services in the health field.

Professional dominance, while still powerful, is being challenged by the increasing corporatization of medicine (Starr, 1982). This corporatization of medicine—as evidenced by the rise of for-profit hospital chains, emergicenters, and HMOs—is creating a transformation in the organization of medicine (see articles by Relman and Waitzkin in this volume). Professional sovereignty is declining and commercial interest and investment in the health sector is rising. One analyst has suggested this is due in part to the new existence of an actual "surplus" of doctors in this country and the increasing power of "third parties" in financing of medical care (Starr, 1982; see also section on "Financing Medical Care" in this volume).

In the final article, "Transitions in Pediatrics: A Segmental Analysis," Dorothy Pawluch demonstrates how in a changing social environment pediatricians were able to adapt their orientations so as to maintain their practices. With improved standards of living, public health measures, and preventive vaccinations, there were fewer sick children for pediatricians to treat. Pawluch shows how pediatricians weathered this professional crisis by changing the focus of their practice first by becoming "baby feeders" and recently by including children's troublesome behavior in their domain. The new "behavioral pediatrics" enabled pediatricians to maintain and enhance their medical dominance by expanding their professional territory. This consequently led to the medicalization of numerous childhood problems (e.g., Conrad, 1975).

REFERENCES

Alford, Robert. 1972. "The political economy of health care: Dynamics without change." Politics and Society. 2: 127–164.

Arms, Suzanne. 1975. Immaculate Deception. Boston: Houghton Mifflin Company.

Blumgart, H. L. 1964. "Caring for the patient." New England Journal of Medicine. 270:449–56.

Conrad Peter. 1975. "The discovery of hyperkinesis: Notes on the medicalization of deviant behavior." Social Problems 23: 12–21.

Freidson, Eliot. 1970a. Profession of Medicine. New York: Dodd, Mead.

———. 1970b. Professional Dominancc. Chicago: Aldine.

Rothman, Barbara Katz. 1982. In Labor. New York: Norton.

Starr, Paul. 1982. The Social Transformation of American Medicine. New York: Basic Books.

11

Professionalization, Monopoly, and the Structure of Medical Practice

Peter Conrad and Joseph W. Schneider

. . . .

Medicine has not always been the powerful, prestigious, successful, lucrative, and dominant profession we know today. The status of the medical profession is a product of medical politicking as well as therapeutic expertise. This discussion presents a brief overview of the development of the medical profession and its rise to dominance.

Emergence of the Medical Profession: up to 1850

In ancient societies, disease was given supernatural explanations, and "medicine" was the province of priests or shamans. It was in classical Greece that medicine began to emerge as a separate occupation and develop its own theories, distinct from philosophy or theology. Hippocrates, the great Greek physician who refused to accept supernatural explanations or treatments for disease, developed a theory of the "natural" causes of disease and systematized all available medical knowledge. He laid a basis for the development of medicine as a separate body of knowledge. Early Christianity depicted sickness as punishment for sin, engendering new theological explanations and treatments. Christ and his disciples believed in the supernatural causes and cures of disease. This view became institutionalized in the Middle Ages, when the Church dogma dominated theories and practice of medicine and priests were physicians. The Renaissance in Europe brought a renewed inter-

est in ancient Greek medical knowledge. This marked the beginning of a drift toward natural explanations of disease and the emergence of medicine as an occupation separate from the Church (Cartwright, 1977).

But European medicine developed slowly. The "humoral theory" of disease developed by Hippocrates dominated medical theory and practice until well into the 19th century. Medical diagnosis was impressionistic and often inaccurate, depicting conditions in such general terms as "fevers" and "fluxes." In the 17th century, physicians relied mainly on three techniques to determine the nature of illness: what the patient said about symptoms; the physician's own observations of signs of illness and the patient's appearance and behavior; and more rarely, a manual examination of the body (Reiser, 1978, p. 1). Medicine was by no means scientific, and "medical thought involved unverified doctrines and resulting controversies" (Shryock, 1960, p. 52). Medical practice was a "bedside medicine" that was patient oriented and did not distinguish the illness from the "sick man" (Jewson, 1976). It was not until Thomas Sydenham's astute observations in the late 17th century that physicians could begin to distinguish between the patient and the disease. Physicians possessed few treatments that worked regularly, and many of their treatments actually worsened the sufferer's condition. Medicine in colonial America inherited this European stock of medical knowledge.

Colonial American medicine was less developed than its European counterpart. There were no medical schools and few physicians, and because of the vast frontier and sparse population, much medical care was in effect self-help. Most American physicians were educated and trained by apprenticeship; few were university trained. With the exception of surgeons, most were undifferentiated practitioners. Medical practices were limited. Prior to the revolution, physicians did not commonly attend births; midwives, who were not seen as part of the medical establishment, routinely attended birthings (Wertz and Wertz, 1977). William Rothstein (1972) notes that "American colonial medical practice, like European practice of the period, was characterized by the lack of any substantial body of usable scientific knowledge" (p. 27). Physicians, both educated and otherwise, tended to treat their patients pragmatically, for medical theory had little to offer. Most colonial physicians practiced medicine only part-time, earning their livelihoods as clergymen, teachers, farmers, or in other occupations. Only in the early 19th century did medicine become a full-time vocation (Rothstein, 1972).

The first half of the 19th century saw important changes in the organization of the medical profession. About 1800, "regular," or educated, physicians convinced state legislatures to pass laws limiting the practice of medicine to practitioners of a certain training and class (prior to this nearly anyone could claim the title "doctor" and practice medicine). These state licensing laws were not particularly effective, largely because of the colonial tradition of medical self-help. They were repealed in most states during the Jacksonian period (1828–1836) because they were thought to be elitist, and the temper of the times called for a more "democratic" medicine.

The repeal of the licensing laws and the fact that most "regular" (i.e., regularly educated) physicians shared and used "a distinctive set of medically invalid therapies, known as 'heroic' therapy," created fertile conditons for the emergence of *medical sects* in the first half of the 19th century (Rothstein, 1972, p. 21). Physicians of the time practiced a "heroic" and invasive form of medicine consisting primarily of such treatments as bloodletting, vomiting, blistering, and purging. This highly interventionist, and sometimes dangerous, form of medicine engendered considerable public opposition and resistance. In

this context a number of medical sects emerged, the most important of which were the homeopathic and botanical physicians. These "irregular" medical practitioners practiced less invasive, less dangerous forms of medicine. They each developed a considerable following, since their therapies were probably no less effective than those of regulars practicing heroic medicine. The regulars attempted to exclude them from practice; so the various sects set up their own medical schools and professional societies. This sectarian medicine created a highly *competitive* situation for the regulars (Rothstein, 1972). Medical sectarianism, heroic therapies, and ineffective treatment contributed to the low status and lack of prestige of early 19th-century medicine. At this time, medicine was neither a prestigious occupation nor an important economic activity in American society (Starr, 1977).

The regular physicians were concerned about this situation. Large numbers of regularly trained physicians sought to earn a livelihood by practicing medicine (Rothstein, 1972, p. 3). They were troubled by the poor image of medicine and lack of standards in medical training and practice. No doubt they were also concerned about the competition of the irregular sectarian physicians. A group of regular physicians founded the American Medical Association (AMA) in 1847 "to promote the science and art of medicine and the betterment of public health" (quoted in Coe, 1978, p. 204). The AMA also was to set and enforce standards and ethics of "regular" medical practice and strive for exclusive professional and economic rights to the medical turf.

The AMA was the crux of the regulars' attempt to "professionalize" medicine. As Magali Sarfatti Larson (1977) points out, professions organize to create and control *markets*. Organized professions attempt to regulate and limit the competition, usually by controlling professional education and by limiting licensing. Professionalization is, in this view, "the process by which producers of special services sought to constitute *and control* the market for their expertise" (Larson, 1977, p. xvi). The regular physicians and the AMA set out to consolidate and control the market for medical services. As we shall see in the next two sections, the regulars were successful in professionalization, eliminating competition and creating a medical monopoly.

Crusading, Deviance, and Medical Monopoly: The Case of Abortion

The medical profession after the middle of the 19th century was frequently involved in various activities that could be termed social reform. Some of these reforms were directly related to health and illness and medical work; others were peripheral to the manifest medical calling of preventing illness and healing the sick. In these reform movements, physicians became medical crusaders, attempting to influence public morality and behavior. This medical crusading often led physicians squarely into the moral sphere, making them advocates for moral positions that had only peripheral relations to medical practice. Not infrequently these reformers sought to change people's values or to impose a set of particular values on others. . . . We now examine one of the more revealing examples of medical crusading: the criminalization of abortion in American society.[1]

Most people are under the impression that abortion was always defined as deviant and illegal in America prior to the Supreme Court's landmark decision in 1973. This, however, is not the case. American abortion policy, and the attendant defining of abortion as deviant, were specific products of medical crusading. Prior to the Civil War, abortion was a common and largely legal medical procedure performed by various types of physicians and midwives. A pregnancy was not considered confirmed until the occurrence of a phenomenon called "quickening," the first perception of fetal movement. Common law did not recognize the fetus before quickening in criminal cases, and an unquickened fetus was deemed to have no living soul. Thus most people did not consider termination of pregnancy before quickening to be an especially serious matter, much less murder. Abortion before quickening created no moral or medical problems. Public opinion was indifferent, and for the time it was probably a relatively safe medical procedure. Thus, for all intents and purposes, American women were free to terminate their pregnancies before quickening in the early 19th century. Moreover, it was a procedure relatively free of the moral stigma that was attached to abortion in this century.

After 1840 abortion came increasingly into public view. Abortion clinics were vigorously and openly advertised in newspapers and magazines. The advertisements offered euphemistically couched services for "women's complaints," "menstrual blockage," and "obstructed menses." Most contemporary observers suggested that more and more women were using these services. Prior to 1840 most abortions were performed on the unmarried and desperate of the "poor and unfortunate classes." However, beginning about this time, significantly increasing numbers of middle- and upper-class white, Protestant, native-born women began to use these services. It is likely they either wished to delay childbearing or thought they already had all the children they wanted (Mohr, 1978, pp. 46–47). By 1870 approximately one abortion was performed for every five live births (Mohr, 1978, pp. 79–80).

Beginning in the 1850s, a number of physicians, especially moral crusader Dr. Horatio Robinson Storer, began writing in medical and popular journals and lobbying in state legislatures about the danger and immorality of abortion. They opposed abortion before and after quickening and under Dr. Storer's leadership organized an aggressive national campaign. In 1859 these crusaders convinced the AMA to pass a resolution condemning abortion. Some newspapers, particularly *The New York Times,* joined the antiabortion crusade. Feminists supported the crusade, since they saw abortion as a threat to women's health and part of the oppression of women. Religious leaders, however, by and large avoided the issue of abortion; either they didn't consider it in their province or found it too sticky an issue to discuss. It was the physicians who were the guiding force in the antiabortion crusade. They were instrumental in convincing legislatures to pass state laws, especially between 1866 and 1877, that made abortion a criminal offense.

Why did physicians take the lead in the antiabortion crusade and work so directly to have abortion defined as deviant and illegal?

Undoubtedly they believed in the moral "rightness" of their cause. But social historian James Mohr (1978) presents two more subtle and important reasons for the physicians' antiabortion crusading. First, concern was growing among medical people and even among some legislators about the significant drop in birthrates. Many claimed that abortion among married women of the "better classes" was a major contributor to the declining birthrate. These middle- and upper-class men (the physicians and legislators) were aware of the waves of immigrants arriving with large families and were anxious about the decline in production of native American babies. They were deeply afraid they were being betrayed by their own women (Mohr, 1978, p. 169). Implicitly the antiabortion stance was classist and racist; the anxiety was simply that there would not be enough strong, native-born, Protestant stock to save America. This was a persuasive argument in convincing legislators of the need of antiabortion laws.

The second and more direct reason spurring the physicians in the antiabortion crusade was to aid their own nascent professionalization and create a monopoly for regular physicians. . . . The regulars had formed the AMA in 1847 to promote scientific and ethical medicine and combat what they saw as medical quackery. There were, however, no licensing laws to speak of, and many claimed the title "doctor" (e.g., homeopaths, botanical doctors, eclectic physicians). The regular physicians adopted the Hippocratic oath and code of ethics as their standard. Among other things, this oath forbids abortion. Regulars usually did not perform abortions; however, many practitioners of medical sects performed abortions regularly, and some had lucrative practices. Thus for the regular AMA physicians the limitation of abortion became one way of asserting their own professional domination over other medical practitioners. In their crusading these physicians had translated the social goals of cultural and professional dominance into moral and medical language. They lobbied long and hard to convince legislators of the danger and immorality of abortion. By passage of laws making abortion criminal any time during gestation, regular physicians were able to legislate their code of ethics and get the

state to employ sanctions against their competitors. This limited these competitors' markets and was a major step toward the regulars' achieving a monopolization of medical practice.

In a relatively short period the antiabortion crusade succeeded in passing legislation that made abortion criminal in every state. A by-product of this was a shift in American public opinion from an indifference to and tolerance of abortion to a hardening of attitudes against what had until then been a fairly common practice. The irony was that abortion as a medical procedure probably was safer at the turn of the 20th century than a century before, but it was defined and seen as more dangerous. By 1900 abortion was not only illegal but deviant and immoral. The physicians' moral crusade had successfully defined abortion as a deviant activity. This definition remained largely unchanged until the 1973 Surpeme Court decision, which essentially returned the abortion situation to its pre-1850 condition.

. . . .

Growth of Medical Expertise and Professional Dominance

Although the general public's dissatisfaction with heroic medicine remained, the image of medicine and what it could accomplish was improving by the middle of the 19th century. There had been a considerable reduction in the incidence and mortality of certain dread diseases. The plague and leprosy had nearly disappeared. Smallpox, malaria, and cholera were less devastating than ever before. These improvements in health engendered optimism and increased people's faith in medical practice. Yet these dramatic "conquests of disease" were by and large *not* the result of new medical knowledge or improved clinical medical practice. Rather, they resulted from changes in social conditions: a rising standard of living, better nutrition and housing, and public health innovations like sanitation. With the lone exception of vaccination for smallpox, the decline of these diseases had nearly nothing to do with clinical medicine (Dubos, 1959; McKeown, 1971). But despite lack of effective treatments, medicine was the beneficiary of much popular credit for improved health.

The regular physicians' image was improved well before they demonstrated any unique effectiveness of practice. The AMA's attacks on irregular medical practice continued. In the 1870s the regulars convinced legislatures to outlaw abortion and in some states to restore licensing laws to restrict medical practice. The AMA was becoming an increasingly powerful and authoritative voice representing regular medical practice.

But the last three decades of the century saw significant "breakthroughs" in medical knowledge and treatment. The scientific medicine of the regular physicians was making new medical advances. Anesthesia and antisepsis made possible great strides in surgical medicine and improvements in hospital care. The bacteriological research of Koch and Pasteur developed the "germ theory of disease," which had important applications in medical practice. It was the accomplishments of surgery and bacteriology that put medicine on a scientific basis (Freidson, 1970a, p. 16). The rise of scientific medicine marked a death knell for medical sectarianism (e.g., the homeopathic physicians eventually joined the regulars). The new laboratory sciences provided a way of testing the theories and practices of various sects, which ultimately led to a single model of medical practice. The well-organized regulars were able to legitimate their form of medical practice and support it with "scientific" evidence.

With the emergence of scientific medicine, a unified paradigm, or model, of medical practice developed. It was based, most fundamentally, on viewing the body as a machine (e.g., organ malfunctioning) and on the germ theory of disease (Kelman, 1977). The "doctrine of specific etiology" became predominant: each disease was caused by a specific germ or agent. Medicine focused solely on the internal environment (the body), largely ignoring the external environment (society) (Dubos, 1959). This paradigm proved fruitful in ensuing years. It is the essence of the "medical model".…

The development of scientific medicine accorded regular medicine a convincing advantage in medical practice. It set the stage for the achievement of a medical monopoly by the AMA regulars. As Larson (1977) notes, "Once scientific medicine offered sufficient guarantees of its superior effectiveness in dealing with disease, the state willingly contributed to the creation of a monoply by means of registration and licensing" (p. 23). The new licensing laws created regular medicine as a *legally enforced monopoly of practice* (Freidson, 1970b, p. 83). They virtually eliminated medical competition.

The medical monopoly was enhanced further by the Flexner Report on medical education in 1910. Under the auspices of the Carnegie Foundation, medical educator Abraham Flexner visited nearly all 160 existing medical schools in the United States. He found the level of medical education poor and recommended the closing of most schools. Flexner urged stricter state laws, rigid standards for medical education, and more rigorous examinations for certification to practice. The enactment of Flexner's recommendations effectively made all nonscientific types of medicine illegal. It created a near total AMA monopoly of medical education in America.

In securing a monopoly, the AMA regulars achieved a unique professional state. Medicine not only monopolized the market for medical services and the training of physicians, it developed an unparalleled "professional dominance." The medical profession was *functionally autonomous* (Freidson, 1970b). Physicians were insulated from external evaluation and were by and large free to regulate their own performance. Medicine could define its own territory and set its own standards. Thus, Eliot Freidson (1970b) notes, "while the profession may not everywhere be free to control the *terms* of its work, it is free to control the *content* of its work" (p. 84).

The domain of medicine has expanded in the past century. This is due partially to the prestige medicine has accrued and its place as the steward of the "sacred" value of life. Medicine has sometimes been called on to repeat its "miracles" and successful treatments on problems that are not biomedical in nature. Yet in other instances the expansion is due to explicit medical crusading or entrepreneurship. This expansion of medicine, especially into the realm of social problems and human behavior, frequently has taken medicine beyond its proven technical competence (Freidson, 1970b). . . .

The organization of medicine has also expanded and become more complex in this century. In the next section we briefly describe the structure of medical practice in the United States.

Structure of Medical Practice

Before we leave our discussion of the medical profession, it is worthwhile to outline some general features of the structure of medical practice that have contributed to the expansion of medical jurisdiction.

The medical sector of society has grown enormously in the 20th century. It has become the second largest industry in America. There are about 350,000 physicians and over 5 million people employed in the medical field. The "medical industries," including the pharmaceutical, medical technology, and health insurance industries, are among the most profitable in our economy. Yearly drug sales alone are over $4.5 billion. There are more than 7000 hospitals in the United States with 1.5 million beds and 33 million inpatient and 200 million outpatient visits a year (McKinlay, 1976).

The organization of medical practice has changed. Whereas the single physician in "solo practice" was typical in 1900, today physicians are engaged increasingly in large corporate practices or employed by hospitals or other bureaucratic organizations. Medicine in modern society is becoming bureaucratized (Mechanic, 1976). The power in medicine has become diffused, especially since World War II, from the AMA, which represented the individual physician, to include the organizations that represent bureaucratic medicine: the health insurance industry, the medical schools, and the American Hospital Association (Ehrenreich and Ehrenreich, 1970). Using Robert Alford's (1972) conceptualizations, corporate rationalizers have taken much of the power in medicine from the professional monopolists.

Medicine has become both more specialized and more dependent on technology. In 1929 only 25 percent of American physicians were fulltime specialists; by 1969 the proportion had grown to 75 percent (Reiser, 1978). Great advances were made in medicine, and many were directly related to technology: miracle medicines like penicillin, a myriad of psychoactive drugs, heart and brain surgery, the electrocardiograph, CAT scanners, fetal monitors, kidney dialysis machines, artifical organs, and transplant surgery, to name but a few. The hospital has become the primary medical workshop, a center for technological medicine.

Medicine has made a significant economic expansion. In 1940, medicine claimed about 4 percent of the American gross national product (GNP); today it claims about 9 percent, which amounts to more than $150 billion. The causes for this growth are too complex to describe here, but a few factors should be noted. American medicine has always operated on a "fee-for-service" basis, that is, each service rendered is charged and paid for separately. Simply put, in a capitalist medical system, the more services provided, the more fees collected. This not only creates an incentive to provide more services but also to expand these medical services to new markets. The fee-for-service system may encourage unnecessary medical care. There is some evidence, for example, that American medicine performs a considerable amount of "excess" surgery (McCleery and Keelty, 1971); this may also be true for other services. Medicine is one of the few occupations that can create its own demand. Patients may come to physicians, but physicians tell them what procedures they need. The availability of medical technique may also create a demand for itself.

The method by which medical care is paid for has changed greatly in the past half-century. In 1920 nearly all health care was paid for directly by the patient-consumer. Since the 1930s an increasing amount of medical care has been paid for through "third-party" payments, mainly through health insurance and the government. About 75 percent of the American population is covered by some form of medical insurance (often only for hospital care). Since 1966 the government has been involved directly in financing medical care through Medicare and Medicaid. The availability of a large amount of federal money, with nearly no cost controls or regulation of medical practice, has been a major factor fueling our current medical "cost crisis." But the ascendancy of third-party payments has effected the expansion of medicine in another way: more and more human problems become defined as "medical problems" (sickness) because that is the only way insurance programs will "cover" the costs of services. . . .

In sum, the regular physicians developed control of medical practice and a professional dominance with nearly total functional autonomy. Through professionalization and persuasion concerning the superiority of their form of medicine, the medical profession (represented by the AMA) achieved a legally supported monopoly of practice. In short, it cornered the medical market. The medical profession has succeeded in both therapeutic and economic expansion. It has won the almost exclusive right to reign over the kingdom of health and illness, no matter where it may extend.

NOTE

1. We rely on James C. Mohr's (1978) fine historical account of the origins and evolution of American abortion policy for data and much of the interpretation in this section.

REFERENCES

Alford, R. The political economy of health care: dynamics without change. *Politics and Society* 1972 2 (2), 127–64.

Cartwright, F. F. *A Social History of Medicine*. New York: Longman, 1977.

Coe, R. *The Sociology of Medicine*. Second edition. New York: McGraw-Hill, 1978.

Dubos, R. *Mirage of Health*. New York: Harper and Row, 1959.

Ehrenreich, B., and Ehrenreich, J. *The American Health Empire*. New York: Random House, 1970.

Freidson, E. *Profession of Medicine*. New York: Dodd, Mead, 1970a.

Freidson, E. *Professional Dominance*. Chicago: Aldine, 1970b.

Jewson, N.D. The disappearance of the sick-man from medical cosmology, 1770–1870. *Sociology*, 1976, 10, 225–44.

Kelman, S. The social nature of the definition of health. In V. Navarro, *Health and Medical Care in the U.S.* Farmingdale, N.Y.: Baywood 1977.

Larson, M. S. *The Rise of Professionalism*. Berkeley: California, 1977.

McCleery, R. S., and Keelty, L. T. *One Life-One Physician: An Inquiry into the Medical Profession's Performance in Self-regulation*. Washington, D.C.: Public Affairs Press, 1971.

McKeown, T. A historical appraisal of the medical task. In G. McLachlan and T. McKeown (eds.), *Medical History and Medical Care: A Symposium of Perspectives*. New York: Oxford, 1971.

McKinlay, J. B. The changing political and economic context of the physician-patient encounter. In E. B. Gallagher (ed.), *The Doctor-Patient Relationship in the Changing Health Scene*. Washington, D.C.: U.S. Government Printing Office, 1976.

Mechanic, D. *The Growth of Bureaucratic Medicine*. New York: Wiley, 1976.

Mohr, J. C. *Abortion in America*. New York: Oxford, 1978.

Reiser, S. J. *Medicine and the Reign of Technology*. New York: Cambridge, 1978.

Rothstein, W. G. *American Physicians in the Nineteenth Century: From Sects to Science*. Baltimore: Johns Hopkins, 1972.

Shryock, R. H. *Medicine and Society in America: 1660–1860*. Ithaca, N.Y.: Cornell, 1960.

Starr, P. Medicine, economy and society in nineteenth-century America. *Journal of Social History*, 1977, 10, 588–607.

Wertz, R., and Wertz, D. *Lying-In: A History of Childbirth in America*. New York: Free Press, 1977.

12

Notes on the Decline of Midwives and the Rise of Medical Obstetricians

Richard W. Wertz and Dorothy C. Wertz

. . . .

The Americans who were studying medicine in Great Britain [in the late eighteenth century] discovered that men could bring the benefits of the new midwifery to birth and thereby gain income and status. In regard to the unresolved question of what medical arts were appropriate, the Americans took the view of the English physicians, who instructed them that nature was usually adequate and intervention often dangerous. From that perspective they developed a model of the new midwifery suitable for the American situation.

From 1750 to approximately 1810 American doctors conceived of the new midwifery as an enterprise to be shared between themselves and trained midwives. Since doctors during most of that period were few in number, their plan was reasonable and humanitarian and also reflected their belief that, in most cases, natural processes were adequate and the need for skilled intervention limited, though important. Doctors therefore envisaged an arrangement whereby trained midwives would attend normal deliveries and doctors would be called to difficult ones. To implement this plan, Dr. Valentine Seaman established a short course for midwives in the New York (City) Almshouse in 1799, and Dr. William Shippen began a course on anatomy and midwifery, including clinical observation of birth, in Philadelphia. Few women came as students, however, but men did, so the doctors trained the men to be man-midwives, perhaps believing, as Smellie had contended, that the sex of the practitioner was less important than the command of new knowledge and skill.[1]

As late as 1817, Dr. Thomas Ewell of Washington, D.C., a regular physician, proposed to establish a school for midwives, connected with a hospital, similar to the schools that had existed for centuries in the great cities of Europe. Ewell sought federal funding for his enterprise, but it was not forthcoming, and the school was never founded. Herein lay a fundamental difference between European and American development of the midwife. European governments provided financial support for medical education, including the training of midwives. The U.S. government provided no support for medical education in the nineteenth century, and not enough of the women who might have aspired to become midwives could afford the fees to support a school. Those who founded schools turned instead to the potentially lucrative business of training the many men who sought to become doctors.[2]

Doctors also sought to increase the supply of doctors educated in America in the new midwifery and thus saw to it that from the outset of American medical schools midwifery became a specialty field, one all doctors could practice.

The plans of doctors for a shared enterprise with women never developed in America. Doctors were unable to attract women for training, perhaps because women were uninterested in studying what they thought they already knew and, moreover, studying it under the tutelage of men. The restraints of traditional modesty and the tradition of female sufficiency for the management of birth were apparently stronger than the appeal of a rationalized system for a more scientific and, presumably, safer midwifery system.

Not only could doctors not attract women for training in the new science and arts, but they could not even organize midwives already in practice. These women had never been organized among themselves. They thought of themselves as being loyal not primarily to an abstract medical science but to local groups of women and their needs. They reflected the tradition of local self-held empiricism that continued to be very strong in America. Americans had never had a medical profession or medical institutions, so they must have found it hard to understand why the European-trained doctors wished to organize a shared, though hierarchical, midwifery enterprise. How hard it was would be shown later, when doctors sought to organize themselves around the new science of midwifery, in which they had some institutional training. Their practice of midwifery would be governed less by science and professional behavior than by empirical practice and economic opportunity.

In the years after 1810, in fact, the practice of midwifery in American towns took on the same unregulated, open-market character it had in England. Both men and women of various degrees of experience and training competed to attend births. Some trained midwives from England immigrated to America, where they advertised their ability in local newspapers.[3] But these women confronted doctors trained abroad or in the new American medical schools. They also confronted medical empirics who presented themselves as "intrepid" man-midwives after having imbibed the instrumental philosophy from Smellie's books. American women therefore confronted a wide array of talents and skills for aiding their deliveries.

Childbirth in America would not have any neat logic during the nineteenth century, but one feature that distinguished it from childbirth abroad was the gradual disappearance of women from the practice of midwifery. There were many reasons for that unusual development. Most obvious was the severe competition that the new educated doctors and empirics brought to the event of birth, an event that often served as entrance for the medical person to a sustained practice. In addition, doctors lost their allegiance to a conservative view of the science and arts of midwifery under the exigencies of practice; they came to adopt a view endorsing more extensive interventions in birth and less reliance upon the adequacy of nature. This view led to the conviction that a certain mastery was needed, which women were assumed to be unable to achieve.

Women ceased to be midwives also because of a change in the cultural attitudes about the proper place and activity for women in society. It came to be regarded as unthinkable to confront women with the facts of medicine or to mix men and women in training, even for such an event as birth. As a still largely unscientific enterprise, medicine took on the cultural attributes necessary for it to survive, and the Victorian culture found certain roles unsuitable for women. Midwives also disappeared because they had not been organized and had never developed any leadership. Medicine in America may have had minimal scientific authority, but it was beginning to develop social and professional organization and leadership; unorganized midwives were an easy competitive target for medicine. Finally, midwives lost out to doctors and empirics because of the changing tastes among middle- and upper-class women; for these women, the new midwifery came to have the promise of more safety and even more respectability.[4]

Midwives therefore largely ceased to attend the middle classes in America during the nineteenth century. Except among ethnic immigrants, among poor, isolated whites, and among blacks, there is little significant evidence of midwifery. This is not to say that there were no such women or that in instances on the frontier or even in cities when doctors were unavailable women did not undertake to attend other women. But educated doctors and empirics penetrated American settlements quickly and extensively, eager to gain patients and always ready to attend birth. The very dynamics of American mobility contributed to the break-up of those communities that had sustained the midwives' practices.

Because of continued ethnic immigration, however, by 1900 in many urban areas half of the women were still being delivered by immigrant midwives. The fact that ethnic groups existed largely outside the development of American medicine during the nineteenth century would pose a serious problem in the twentieth century.

Native-born educated women sought to become doctors, not midwives, during the nineteenth century. They did not want to play a role in birth that was regarded as inferior and largely nonmedical—the midwife's role—but wished to assume the same medical role allowed to men.

It is important to emphasize, however, that the disappearance of midwives at middle- and upper-class births was not the result of a conspiracy between male doctors and husbands. The choice of medical attendants was the responsibility of women, upon whom devolved the care of their families' health. Women were free to choose whom they wished. A few did seek out unorthodox practitioners, although most did not. But as the number of midwives diminished, women of course found fewer respectable, trained women of their own class whom they might choose to help in their deliveries.

In order to understand the new midwifery [i.e. medical obstetrics], it is necessary to consider who doctors were and how they entered the medical profession. The doctors who assumed control over middle-class births in America were very differently educated and organized from their counterparts in France or England. The fact that their profession remained loosely organized and ill-defined throughout most of the nineteenth century helps to explain their desire to exclude women from midwifery, for often women were the only category of people that they could effectively exclude. Doctors with some formal education had always faced competition from the medical empirics—men, women, and even freed slaves—who declared themselves able to treat all manner of illnesses and often publicly advertised their successes. These empirics, called quacks by the orthodox educated doctors, offered herbal remedies or psychological comfort to patients. Orthodox physicians objected that the empirics prescribed on an individual, trial-and-error basis without reference to any academic theories about the origins and treatment of disease. Usually the educated physician also treated his patients

empirically, for medical theory had little to offer that was practically superior to empiricism until the development of bacteriology in the 1870s. Before then there was no convincing, authoritative, scientific nucleus for medicine, and doctors often had difficulty translating what knowledge they did have into practical treatment. The fundamental objection of regular doctors was to competition from uneducated practitioners. Most regular doctors also practiced largely ineffective therapies, but they were convinced that their therapies were better than those of the empirics because they were educated men. The uneducated empirics enjoyed considerable popular support during the first half of the nineteenth century because their therapies were as often successful as the therapies of the regulars, and sometimes less strenuous. Like the empirics, educated doctors treated patients rather than diseases and looked for different symptoms in different social classes. Because a doctor's reputation stemmed from the social standing of his patients, there was considerable competition for the patronage of the more respectable families.

The educated, or "regular," doctors around 1800 were of the upper and middle classes, as were the state legislators. The doctors convinced the legislators that medicine, like other gentlemen's professions, should be restricted to those who held diplomas or who had apprenticed with practitioners of the appropriate social class and training. State licensure laws were passed, in response to the Federalist belief that social deference was due to professional men. The early laws were ineffectual because they did not take into account the popular tradition of self-help. People continued to patronize empirics. During the Jacksonian Era even the nonenforced licensing laws were repealed by most states as elitist; popular belief held that the practice of medicine should be "democratic" and open to all, or at least to all men.[5]

In the absence of legal control, several varieties of "doctors" practiced in the nineteenth century. In addition to the empirics and the "regular" doctors there were the sectarians, who included the Thomsonian Botanists, the Homeopaths, the Eclectics, and a number of minor sects of which the most important for obstectrics were the Hydrotherapists.

The regular doctors can be roughly divided into two groups: the elite, who had attended the better medical schools and who wrote the textbooks urging "conservative" practice in midwifery; and the great number of poorly educated men who had spent a few months at a proprietary medical school from which they were graduated with no practical or clinical knowledge. (Proprietary medical schools were profit-making schools owned by several local doctors who also taught there. Usually such schools had no equipment or resources for teaching.) In the eighteenth century the elite had had to travel to London, or more often Edinburgh, for training. In 1765, however, the Medical College of Philadelphia was founded, followed by King's College (later Columbia) Medical School in 1767 and Harvard in 1782. Obstetrics, or "midwifery," as it was then called, was the first medical specialty in those schools, preceding even surgery, for it was assumed that midwifery was the keystone to medical practice, something that every student would do after graduation as part of his practice. Every medical school founded thereafter had a special "Professor of Midwifery." Among the first such professors were Drs. William Shippen at Philadelphia, Samuel Bard at King's College, and Walter Channing at Harvard. In the better schools early medical courses lasted two years; in the latter half of the nineteenth century some schools began to increase this to three, but many two-year medical graduates were still practicing in 1900.

A prestigious medical education did not guarantee that a new graduate was prepared to deal with patients. Dr. James Marion Sims, a famous nineteenth-century surgeon, stated that his education at Philadelphia's Jefferson Medical College, considered one of the best in the country in 1835, left him fitted for nothing and without the slightest notion of how to treat his first cases.[6] In 1850 a graduate of the University of Buffalo described his total ignorance on approaching his first obstetrical case:

> I was left alone with a poor Irish woman and one crony, to deliver her child . . . and I thought it necessary to call before me every circumstance I had learned from books—I must examine, and I did— But whether it was head or breech, hand or foot, man or monkey, that was defended from my uninstructed finger by the distended membranes, I was as uncomfortably ignorant, with all my learning, as the foetus itself that was making all this fuss.[7]

Fortunately the baby arrived naturally, the doctor was given great praise for his part in the event, and he wrote that he was glad "to have escaped the commission of murder."

If graduates of the better medical schools made such complaints, those who attended the smaller schools could only have been more ignorant. In 1818 Dr. John Stearns, President of the New York Medical Society, complained, "With a few honorable exceptions in each city, the practitioners are ignorant, degraded, and contemptible."[8] The American Medical Association later estimated that between 1765 and 1905 more than eight hundred medical schools were founded, most of them proprietary, money-making schools, and many were short-lived. In 1905 some 160 were still in operation. Neither the profession nor the states effectively regulated those schools until the appearance of the Flexner Report, a professional self-study published in 1910. The report led to tougher state laws and the setting of standards for medical education. Throughout much of the nineteenth century a doctor could obtain a diploma and begin practice with as little as four months' attendance at a school that might have no laboratories, no dissections, and no clinical training. Not only was it easy to become a doctor, but the profession, with the exception of the elite who attended elite patients, had low standing in the eyes of most people.[9]

. . . .

Nineteenth-century women could choose among a variety of therapies and practitioners. Their choice was usually dictated by social class. An upper-class woman in an Eastern city would see either an elite regular physician or a homeopath; if she were daring, she might visit a hydropathic establishment. A poor woman in the Midwest might turn to an empiric, a poorly-educated regular doctor, or a Thomsonian botanist. This variety of choice distressed regular doctors, who were fighting for professional and economic exclusivity. As long as doctors were organized only on a local basis, it was impossible to exclude irregulars from practice or even to set enforceable standards for regular practice. The American Medical Association was founded in 1848 for those purposes. Not until the end of the century, however, was organized medicine able to re-establish licensing laws. The effort succeeded only because the regulars finally accepted the homeopaths, who were of the same social class, in order to form a sufficient majority to convince state legislators that licensing was desirable.

Having finally won control of the market, doctors were able to turn to self-regulation, an ideal adopted by the American Medical Association in 1860 but not put into effective practice until after 1900. Although there had been progress in medical science and in the education of the elite and the specialists during the nineteenth century, the average doctor was still woefully undereducated. The Flexner Report in 1910 revealed that 90 percent of doctors were then without a college education and that most had attended substandard medical schools.[10] Only after its publication did the profession impose educational requirements on the bulk of medical practitioners and take steps to accredit medical schools and close down diploma mills. Until then the average doctor had little sense of what his limits were or to whom he was responsible, for there was often no defined community of professionals and usually no community of patients.

Because of the ill-defined nature of the medical profession in the nineteenth century and the poor quality of medical education, doctors' insistence on the exclusion of women as economically dangerous competitors is quite understandable. As a group, nineteenth-century doctors were not affluent, and even their staunchest critics admitted that they could have made more money in business. Midwifery itself paid less than other types of practice, for many doctors spent long hours in attending laboring women and later had trouble collecting their fees. Yet midwifery was a guaranteed income, even if small, and it opened the way to family practice and sometimes to consultations involving many doctors and shared fees. The family and female friends who had seen a doctor "perform" successfully were likely to

call him again. Doctors worried that, if midwives were allowed to deliver the upper classes, women would turn to them for treatment of other illnesses and male doctors would lose half their clientele. As a prominent Boston doctor wrote in 1820, "If female midwifery is again introduced among the rich and influential, it will become fashionable and it will be considered indelicate to employ a physician."[11] Doctors had to eliminate midwives in order to protect the gateway to their whole practice.

They had to mount an attack on midwives, because midwives had their defenders, who argued that women were safer and more modest than the new man-midwives. For example, the *Virginia Gazette* in 1772 carried a "LETTER on the present State of MIDWIFERY," emphasizing the old idea that "Labour is Nature's Work" and needs no more art than women's experience teaches, and that it was safer when women alone attended births.

> It is a notorious fact that more Children have been lost since Women were so scandalously indecent as to employ Men than for Ages before that Practice became so general. . . . [Women midwives] never dream of having recourse to Force; the barbarous, bloody Crochet, never stained their Hands with Murder. . . . A long unimpassioned Practice, early commenced, and calmly pursued is absolutely requisite to give Men by Art, what Women attain by Nature.

The writer concluded with the statement that men-midwives also took liberties with pregnant and laboring women that were "sufficient to taint the Purity, and sully the Chastity, of any Woman breathing." The final flourish, "True Modesty is incompatible with the Idea of employing a MAN-MIDWIFE," would echo for decades, causing great distress for female patients with male attendants. Defenders of midwives made similar statements throughout the first half of the nineteenth century, Most were sectarian doctors or laymen with an interest in women's modesty.[12] No midwives came forward to defend themselves in print.

The doctors' answer to midwives' defenders was expressed not in terms of pecuniary motives but in terms of safety and the proper place of women. After 1800 doctors' writings implied that women who presumed to supervise births had overreached their proper position in life. One of the earliest American birth manuals, the *Married Lady's Companion and Poor Man's Friend* (1808), denounced the ignorance of midwives and urged them to "submit to their station."[13]

Two new convictions about women were at the heart of the doctors' opposition to midwives: that women were unsafe to attend deliveries and that no "true" woman would want to gain the knowledge and skills necessary to do so. An anonymous pamphlet, published in 1820 in Boston, set forth these convictions along with other reasons for excluding midwives from practice. The author, thought to have been either Dr. Walter Channing or Dr. Henry Ware, another leading obstetrician, granted that women had more "passive fortitude" than men in enduring and witnessing suffering but asserted that women lacked the power to act that was essential to being a birth attendant:

> They have not that power of action, or that active power of mind, which is essential to the practice of a surgeon. They have less power of restraining and governing the natural tendencies to sympathy and are more disposed to yield to the expressions of acute sensibility . . . where they become the principal agents, the feelings of sympathy are too powerful for the cool exercise of judgment.[14]

The author believed only men capable of the attitude of detached concern needed to concentrate on the techniques required in birth. It is not surprising to find the author stressing the importance of interventions, but his undervaluing of sympathy, which in most normal deliveries was the only symptomatic treatment necessary, is rather startling. Clearly, he hoped to exaggerate the need for coolness in order to discountenance the belief of many women and doctors that midwives could safely attend normal deliveries.

The author possibly had something more delicate in mind that he found hard to express. He perhaps meant to imply that women were unsuited because there were certain times when they were "disposed to yield to the expressions of acute sensibility." Doctors quite commonly believed that during menstruation women's limited bodily energy was diverted from the brain,

rendering them, as doctors phrased it, idiotic. In later years another Boston doctor, Horatio Storer, explained why he thought women unfit to become surgeons. He granted that exceptional women had the necessary courage, tact, ability, money, education, and patience for the career but argued that, because the "periodical infirmity of their sex . . . in every case . . . unfits them for any responsible effort of mind," he had to oppose them. During their "condition," he said, "neither life nor limb submitted to them would be as safe as at other times," for the condition was a "temporary insantiy," a time when women were "more prone than men to commit any unusual or outrageous act."[15]

The author of the anonymous pamphlet declared that a female would find herself at times (i.e., during menstruation) totally unable to manage birth emergencies, such as hemorrhages, convulsions, manual extraction of the placenta, or inversion of the womb, when the newly delivered organ externally turned itself inside out and extruded from the body, sometimes hanging to the knees. In fact, an English midwife, Sarah Stone, had described in 1737 how she personally had handled each of these emergencies successfully. But the author's readers did not know that, and the author himself could have dismissed Stone's skill as fortuituous, exercised in times of mental clarity.[16]

The anonymous author was also convinced that no woman could be trained in the knowledge and skill of midwifery without losing her standing as a lady. In the dissecting room and in the hospital a woman would forfeit her "delicate feelings" and "refined sensibility"; she would see things that would taint her moral character. Such a woman would "unsex" herself, by which the doctors meant not only that she would lose her standing as a "lady" but also, literally, that she would be subject to physical exertions and nervous excitements that would damage her female organs irreparably and prevent her from fulfilling her social role as wife and mother.[17]

· ·

The exclusion of women from obstetrical cooperation with men had important effects upon the "new practice" that was to become the dominant tradition in American medical schools. American obstetric education differed significantly from training given in France, where the principal maternity hospitals trained doctors clincally alongside student midwives. Often the hospital's midwives, who supervised all normal births, trained the doctors in normal deliveries. French doctors never lost touch with the conservative tradition that said "Dame Nature is the best midwife." In America, where midwives were not trained at all and medical education was sexually segregated, medicine turned away from the conservative tradition and became more interventionist.

Around 1810 the new midwifery in America appears to have entered a new phase, one that shaped its character and problems throughout the century. Doctors continued to regard birth as a fundamentally natural process, usually sufficient by itself to effect delivery without artful assistance, and understandable mechanistically. But this view conflicted with the exigencies of their medical practice, which called upon them to demonstrate skills. Gradually, more births seemed to require aid.

Young doctors rarely had any clinical training in what the theory of birth meant in practice. Many arrived at birth with only lectures and book learning to guide them. If they (and the laboring patient) were fortunate, they had an older, experienced doctor or attending woman to explain what was natural and what was not. Many young men were less lucky and were embarrassed, confused, and frightened by the appearances of labor and birth. Lacking clinical training, each had to develop his own sense of what each birth required, if anything, in the way of artful assistance; each had to learn the consequence of misdirected aids.[18]

If the doctor was in a hurry to reach another patient, he might be tempted to hasten the process along by using instruments or other expedients. If the laboring woman or her female attendants urged him to assist labor, he might feel compelled to use his tools and skills even though he knew that nature was adequate but slow. He had to use his arts because he was expected to "perform." Walter Channing, Professor of Midwifery at Harvard Medical School in the early nineteenth century, remarked about the doctor, in the context of discussing a case in which forceps were used unnecessarily, that he "must do something. He cannot remain a spectator merely, where there are too many witnesses and where interest in what is going on is too deep to allow of his inaction." Channing was saying that, even though well-educated physicians recognized that natural processes were sufficient and that instruments could be dangerous, in their practice they also had to appear to *do* something for their patient's symptoms, whether that entailed giving a drug to alleviate pain or shortening labor by using the forceps. The doctor could not appear to be indifferent or inattentive or useless. He had to establish his identity by doing something, preferably something to make the patient feel better. And if witnesses were present there was perhaps even more reason to "perform." Channing concluded: "Let him be collected and calm, and he will probably do little he will afterwards look upon and regret."[19]

If educated physicians found it difficult in practice to appeal before their patients to the reliability of nature and the dangers of instruments, one can imagine what less confident and less competent doctors did with instruments in order to appear useful. A number of horror stories from the early decades of the century have been retailed by men and women who believed that doctors used their instruments unfairly and incompetently to drive midwives from practice.[20] Whatever the truth may be about the harm done, it is easy to believe that instruments were used regularly by doctors to establish their superior status.

If doctors believed that they had to perform in order to appear useful and to win approval, it is very likely that women, on the other hand, began to expect that more might go wrong with birth processes than they had previously believed. In the context of social childbirth, which . . . meant that women friends and kin were present at delivery, the appearance of forceps in one birth established the possibility of their being used in subsequent births. In short, women may have come to anticipate difficult births whether or not doctors urged that possibility as a means of selling themselves. Having seen the "best," perhaps each woman wanted the "best" for her delivery, whether she needed it or not.

Strange as it may sound, women may in fact have been choosing male attendants because they wanted a guaranteed performance, in the sense of both guaranteed safety and guaranteed fashionableness. Choosing the best medical care is itself a kind of fashion. But in addition women may have wanted a guaranteed audience, the male attendant, for quite specific purposes; namely, they may have wanted a representative male to see their pain and suffering in order that their femininity might be established and their pain verified before men. Women, then, could have had a range of important reasons for choosing male doctors to perform: for themselves, safety; for the company of women, fashion; for the world of men, femininity.

So a curious inconsistency arose between the principle of noninterference in nature and the exigencies of professional practice. Teachers of midwifery continued to stress the adequacy of nature and the danger of instruments. Samuel Bard, Dean of King's College Medical School, wrote a text on midwifery in 1807 in which he refused even to discuss forceps because he believed that interventions by unskilled men, usually inspired by Smellie's writings, were more dangerous than the most desperate case left to nature. Bard's successors made the same points in the 1830s and 1840s. Dr. Chandler Gilman, Professor of Obstetrics at the College of Physicians and Surgeons in New York from 1841 to 1865, taught his students that "Dame Nature is the best midwife in the world. . . . Meddlesome midwifery is fraught with evil. . . . The less done generally the better, Non-interference is the cornerstone of midwifery."[21] This instruction often went unheeded, however, because young doctors often resorted to instruments in haste or in confusion, or because they were poorly trained and unsupervised in practice, but also, as we have indicated, because physicians, whatever their state of knowledge, were expected to do something.

What they could do—the number of techniques to aid and control natural processes—gradually increased. In 1808, for example, Dr. John Stearns of upper New York State learned from an immigrant German midwife of a new means to effect the mechanics of birth. This was ergot, a powerful natural drug that stimulates uterine muscles when given orally. Ergot is a fungus that grows on rye and other stored grains. It causes powerful and unremitting contractions. Stearns stressed its value in saving the doctor's time and in relieving the distress and agony of long labor. Ergot also quickens the expulsion of the placenta and stems hemorrhage by compelling the uterus to contract. Stearns claimed that ergot had no ill effects but warned that it should be given only after the fetus was positioned for easy delivery, for it induced an incessant action that left no time to turn a child in the birth canal or uterus.

There was in fact no antidote to ergot's rapid and uncontrollable effects until anesthesia became available in later decades. So if the fetus did not move as expected, the drug could cause the uterus to mold itself around the child, rupturing the uterus and killing the child. Ergot, like most new medical arts for birth, was a mix of danger and benefit. Critics of meddlesome doctors said that they often used it simply to save time. However true that was, ergot certainly fitted the mechanistic view of birth, posed a dilemma to doctors about wise use, and enlarged the doctors' range of arts for controlling birth. Doctors eventually determined that using ergot to induce labor without an antidote was too dangerous and limited its use to expelling the placenta or stopping hemorrhage.[22]

Despite the theory of the naturalness of birth and the danger of intervention, the movement in midwifery was in the opposite direction, to less reliance on nature and more reliance on artful intervention. The shift appeared during the 1820s in discussions as to what doctors should call themselves when they practiced the new midwifery. "Male-midwife," "midman," "man-midwife," "physician man-midwife," and even "androboethogynist" were terms too clumsy, too reminiscent of the female title, or too unreflective of the new science and skill. "Accoucheur" sounded better but was French. The doctors of course ignored Elizabeth Nihell's earlier, acid suggestion that they call themselves "pudendists" after the area of the body that so interested them. Then an English doctor suggested in 1828 that "obstetrician" was as appropriate a term as any. Coming from the Latin meaning "to stand before," it had the advantage of sounding like other honorable professions, such as "electrician" or "geometrician," in which men variously understood and dominated nature.[23]

The renaming of the practice of midwifery symbolized doctors' new sense of themselves as professional actors. In fact, the movement toward greater dominance over birth's natural processes cannot be understood unless midwifery is seen in the context of general medical practice. In that perspective, several relations between midwifery and general practice become clearly important. In the first place, midwifery continued during the first half of the nineteenth century to be one of the few areas of general practice where doctors had a scientific understanding and useful medical arts. That meant that practicing midwifery was central to doctors' attempts to build a practice, earn fees, and achieve some status, for birth was one physical condition they were confident they knew how to treat. And they were successful in the great majority of cases because birth itself was usually successful. Treating birth was without the risk of treating many other conditions, but doctors got the credit nonetheless.

In the second place, however, birth was simply one condition among many that doctors treated, and the therapeutic approach they took to other conditions tended to spill over into their treatment of birth. For most physical conditions of illness doctors did not know what processes of nature were at work. They tended therefore to treat the patient and the patient's symptoms rather than the processes of disease, which they did not see and were usually not looking for. By treating his or her symptoms the doctors did something for the patient and thereby gained approbation. The doctors' status came from pleasing the patients rather than from curing diseases. That was a risky endeavor, for sometimes patients judged the treatment offered to relieve symptoms to be worthless or even more disabling than the symptoms themselves. But patients expected doctors to do something for them, an expectation that carried into birth also. So neither doctors nor patients were inclined to allow the natural processes of birth to suffice.

There is no need to try to explain this contradiction by saying that doctors were ignorant, greedy, clumsy, hasty, or salacious in using medical arts unnecessarily (although some may have been), for the contradiction reflects primarily the kind of therapy that was dominant in prescientific medicine.

The relations between midwifery and general medical practice become clearer if one considers what doctors did when they confronted a birth that did not conform to their understanding of birth's natural processes. Their mechanistic view could not explain such symptoms as convulsions or high fevers, occasionally associated with birth. Yet doctors did not walk away from such conditions as being mysterious or untreatable, for they were committed to the mastery of birth. Rather, they treated the strange symptoms with general therapies just as they might treat regular symptoms of birth with medical arts such as forceps and ergot.

Bloodletting was a popular therapy for many symptoms, and doctors often applied it to births that seemed unusual to them. If a pregnant woman seemed to be florid or perspiring, the doctor might place her in a chair, open a vein in her arm, and allow her to bleed until she fainted. Some doctors bled women to unconsciousness to counter delivery pains. A doctor in 1851 opened the temporal arteries of a woman who was having convulsions during birth, "determined to bleed her until the convulsion ceased or as long as the blood would flow." He found it impossible to catch the blood thrown about during her convulsions, but the woman eventually completed her delivery successfully and survived. Bloodletting was also initiated when a woman developed high fever after delivery. Salmon P. Chase, Lincoln's Secretary of the Treasury and later Chief Justice, told in his diary how a group of doctors took 50 ounces of blood from his wife to relieve her fever. The doctors gave careful attention to the strength and frequency of her pulse, debating and deliberating upon the meaning of the symptom, until finally Mrs. Chase died.[24]

For localized pain, doctors applied leeches to draw out blood from the affected region. A distended abdomen after delivery might merit the application of twelve leeches; a headache, six on the temple; vaginal pain also merited several.[25]

Another popular therapy was calomel, a chloride of mercury that irritated the intestine and purged it. A woman suffering puerperal fever might be given extended doses to reduce swelling by purging her bodily contents. If the calomel acted too violently, the doctors could retard it by administering opium. Doctors often gave emetics to induce vomiting when expectant women had convulsions, for they speculated that emetics might be specifics for hysteria or other nervous diseases causing convulsions.

An expectant or laboring woman showing unusual symptoms might be subjected to a battery of such agents as doctors sought to restore her symptoms to a normal balance. In a famous case in Boston in 1833 a woman had convulsions a month before her expected delivery. The doctors bled her of 8 ounces and gave her a purgative. The next day she again had convulsions, and they took 22 ounces of blood. After 90 minutes she had a headache, and the doctors took 18 more ounces of blood, gave emetics to cause vomiting, and put ice on her head and mustard plasters on her feet. Nearly four hours later she had another convulsion, and they took 12 ounces, and soon after, 6 more. By then she had lapsed into a deep coma, so the doctors doused her with cold water but could not revive her. Soon her cervix began to dilate, so the doctors gave ergot to induce labor. Shortly before delivery she convulsed again, and they applied ice and mustard plasters again and also gave a vomiting agent and calomel to purge her bowels. In six hours she delivered a stillborn child. After two days she regained consciousness and recovered. The doctors considered this a conservative treatment, even though they had removed two-fifths of her blood in a two-day period, for they had not artificially dilated her womb or used instruments to expedite delivery.[26]

Symptomatic treatment was intended not simply to make the patient feel better—often the treatment was quite violent, or "heroic"—but to restore some balance of healthy appearances. Nor were the therapies given to ailing women more intrusive or different from therapies given to suffering men. The therapies were not, in most instances, forced upon the patients without their foreknowledge or consent. People were often eager to be made healthy and willing to endure strenuous therapies to this end. Doctors did believe, however, that some groups of people were more susceptible to illness than others and that different groups also required, or deserved, different treatments.

These views reflected in large part the doctors' awareness of cultural classifications of people; in other words, the culture's position on the relative social worth of different social classes influenced doctors' views about whose health was likely to be endangered, how their endangered health affected the whole society, and what treatments, if any, were suitable. For birth this meant, for example, that doctors believed it more important for them to attend the delivery of children by middle- and upper-class women than the delivery of children by the poor. It meant that doctors expected "fashionable" women to suffer more difficult deliveries because their tight clothing, rich diet and lack of exercise were unhealthy and because they were believed to be more susceptible to nervous strain. It also meant that doctors thought it fitting for unmarried and otherwise disreputable mothers not to receive charitable care along with other poor but respectable women.

There is abundant evidence that doctors came to believe in time that middle- and upper-class women typically had more difficult deliveries than, for example, farm women. One cannot find an objective measure of the accuracy of their perception, nor, unfortunately and more to the point, can one find whether their perception that some women were having more difficult deliveries led doctors consistently to use more intervention in attending them than in attending poorer women with normal deliveries. Doctors' perception of the relative difficulty of deliveries was part of their tendency to associate different kinds of sickness with different social classes. They expected to find the symptoms of certain illnesses in certain groups of people, and therefore looked for those particular symptoms or conditions. In the nineteenth century upper-class urban women were generally expected to be sensitive and delicate, while farm women were expected to be robust. Some doctors even believed that the evolutionary result of education was to produce smaller pelves in women and larger heads in babies, leading to more difficult births among civilized women. There is no evidence that these beliefs were medically accurate. Whether a doctor considered a patient "sick" or "healthy" depended in part upon class-related standards of health and illness rather than on objective scientific standards of sickness.

Treatment probably varied according to the doctor's perception of a woman's class and individual character. At some times and places the treatment given probably reflected the patient's class as much as her symptoms. Thus some doctors may have withheld the use of instruments from their upper-class patients in the belief that they were too fragile to undergo instrumental delivery. The same doctors may have used instruments needlessly on poor patients, who were considered healthy enough to stand anything, in order to save the doctor's time and permit him to rush off to the bedside of a wealthier patient. On the other hand, some doctors may have used instruments on the upper-class women in order to shorten labor, believing that they could not endure prolonged pain or were too weak to bring forth children unassisted, and also in order to justify higher fees. The same doctors may have withheld forceps from poor women whom they considered healthy enough to stand several days of labor. Unfortunately, there is no way of knowing exactly how treatments differed according to class, for very few doctors kept records of their private patients. The records now extant are for the small number of people, perhaps 5 percent of the population, who were treated in hospitals in the nineteenth century. Only poor women, most unmarried, delivered in hospitals, so the records do not cover a cross-section of classes. These hospital records do indicate a large number of instrumental deliveries and sometimes give the reasons as the patient's own "laziness" or "stupidity" in being unable to finish a birth. It is likely that doctors' expectations of lower-class performance are reflected here. Hospital records also reflect the use of poor patients for training or experimentation, another reason for a high incidence of instrumental deliveries.

The fact that doctors' tendency to classify patients according to susceptibility did not lead to consistent differences in treatment is an important indication that they were not merely slavish adherents to a mechanistic view of nature or to cultural and class interests. Doctors were still treating individual women, not machines and not social types. The possibility of stereotypical classification and treatment, however, remained a lively threat to more subtle discernments of individual symptoms and to truly artful applications of treatment in birth.

At the same time, it was possible that patients would find even unbiased treatments offensively painful, ineffective, and expensive, or would doubt that the doctor had a scientific reason for giving them. Such persons could seek other treatments, often administered by laypeople or by themselves. Yet those treatments, including treatments for birth, were also directed toward symptoms. At a time when diseases were unrecognized and their causes unknown, the test of therapy was the patient's whole response, not the curing of disease. So patients who resented treatments as painful, ineffective, or officious rejected the doctor and the treatments. A woman who gave birth in Ohio in 1846 recalled that the doctor bled her and then gave her ergot even though the birth was proceeding, in her view, quite normally. She thought he was simply drunk and in a hurry and angrily judged him a "bad man."[27]

The takeover of birth by male doctors in America was an unusual phenomenon in comparison to France and England, where traditional midwifery continued as a much more significant part of birth. Practice developed differently in America because the society itself expanded more rapidly and the medical profession grew more quickly to doctor in ever new communities. American mobility left fewer stable communities than in France or England, and thus networks of women to support midwives were more often broken. The standards of the American medical profession were not so high or so strictly enforced as standards in other countries, and thus there were both more "educated" doctors and more self-proclaimed doctors in America to compete with midwives. So American midwives disappeared from view because they had less support from the stable communities of women and more competition from male doctors.

The exclusion of women from midwifery and obstetrics had profound effects upon practice. Most obviously, it gave obstetrics a sexist bias; maleness became a necessary attribute of safety, and femaleness became a condition in need of male medical control. Within this skewed view of ability and need, doctors found it nearly impossible to gain an objective view of what nature could do and what art should do, for one was identified with being a woman and the other with being a man.

The bias identified functions, attributes, and prerogatives, which unfortunately could become compulsions, so that doctors as men may have often felt that they had to impose their form upon the processes of nature in birth. Obstetrics acquired a basic distortion in its orientation toward nature, a confusion of the need to be masterful and even male with the need for intervention.

Samuel Bard, one of the few doctors to oppose the trend, remarked that the young doctor, too often lacking the ability to discriminate about natural processes, often became alarmed for his patient's safety and his own reputation, leading him to seek a speedy instrumental delivery for both. A tragedy could follow, compounded because the doctor might not even recognize that he had erred and might not, therefore, learn to correct his practice. But doctors may also have found the "indications" for intervention in their professional work—to hurry, to impress, to win approval, and to show why men rather than women should attend births.

The thrust for male control of birth probably expressed psychosexual needs of men, although there is no basis for discussing this historically. The doctor appears to history more as a ritualistic figure, a representative man, identifying and enforcing sexual roles in critical life experiences. He also provided, as a representative scientist, important rationalizations for these roles, particularly why women should be content to be wives and mothers, and, as a representative of dominant cultural morality, determined the classifications of women who deserved various kinds of treatment. Thus the doctor could bring to the event of birth many prerogatives that had little to do with aiding natural processes, but which he believed were essential to a healthy and safe birth.

Expectant and laboring women lost a great deal from the exclusion of educated female birth attendants, although, of course, they would not have chosen men if they had not believed men had more to offer, at least in the beginning decades of the century. Eventually there were only men to choose. Although no doubt doctors were often sympathetic, they could never have the same point of view as a woman who had herself borne a child and who might be more patient and discerning about birth processes. And female attendants would not, of course, have laid on the male prerogatives of physical and moral control of birth.

. . . .

REFERENCES

1. Valentine Seaman, *The Midwives' Monitor and Mother's Mirror* (New York, 1800); Lewis Scheffey, "The Early History and the Transition Period of Obstetrics and Gynecology in Philadelphia," *Annals of Medical History,* Third Series, 2 (May, 1940), 215–224.
2. John B. Blake, "Women and Medicine in Ante-Bellum America," *Bulletin of the History of Medicine* 34, No. 2 (March-April 1965): 108–109; see also Dr. Thomas Ewell, *Letters to Ladies* (Philadelphia, 1817) pp. 21–31.
3. Julia C. Spruill, *Women's Life and Work in the Southern Colonies* (New York: Norton, 1972), pp. 272–274; Jane Bauer Donegan, "Midwifery in America, 1760–1860: A Study in Medicine and Morality." Unpublished Ph.D. dissertation, Syracuse University, 1972, pp. 50–52.
4. Alice Morse Earle (ed.), *Diary of Anna Green Winslow, a Boston Schoolgirl of 1771* (Detroit: Singing Tree Press, 1970), p. 12 and n. 24.
5. William G. Rothstein, *American Physicians in the Nineteenth Century: From Sects to Science* (Baltimore: Johns Hopkins Press, 1970), pp. 47–49.
6. J. Marion Sims, *The Story of My Life* (New York, 1888), pp. 138–146.
7. *Buffalo Medical Journal* 6 (September, 1850): 250–251.
8. John Stearns, "Presidential Address," *Transactions of the New York State Medical Society* 1:139.
9. Sims, *Story of My Life*, pp. 115–116.
10. Abraham Flexner, *Medical Education in the United States and Canada: A Report to the Carnegie Foundation for the Advancement of Teaching* (New York, 1910).
11. Anonymous, *Remarks on the Employment of*

Females as Practitioners in Midwifery, 1820, pp. 4–6. See also Samuel Gregory, *Man-Midwifery Exposed and Corrected* (Boston, 1848) pp. 13, 49; Donegan, "Midwifery in America," pp. 73–74, 240; Thomas Hersey, *The Midwife's Practical Directory; or, Woman's Confidential Friend* (Baltimore, 1836), p. 221; Charles Rosenberg, "The Practice of Medicine in New York a Century Ago," *Bulletin of the History of Medicine* 41 (1967):223–253.

12. Spruill, *Women's Life and Work,* p. 275; Gregory, *Man-Midwifery Exposed,* pp. 13, 28, 36.

13. Samuel K. Jennings, *The Married Lady's Companion and Poor Man's Friend* (New York, 1808), p. 105.

14. Anonymous, *Remarks,* p.12.

15. Horatio Storer, M.D., *Criminal Abortion* (Boston, 1868), pp. 100–101n.

16. Sarah Stone, *A Complete Practice of Midwifery* (London, 1737).

17. Anonymous, *Remarks,* p. 7.

18. Harold Speert, M.D., *The Sloane Hospital Chronicle* (Philadelphia: Davis, 1963), pp. 17–19; Donegan, "Midwifery in America," p. 218.

19. Walter Channing, M.D., *A Treatise on Etheriza-tion in Childbirth, Illustrated by 581 Cases* (Boston, 1848), p. 229.

20. Gregory, *Man-Midwifery Exposed,* pp. 13, 28, 36; Hersey, *Midwife's Practical Directory,* p. 220; Wooster Beach, *An Improved System of Midwifery Adapted to the Reformed Practice of Medicine . . .* (New York, 1851), p. 115.

21. Speert, *Sloane Hospital Chronicle,* pp. 31–33, 77–78.

22. Palmer Findlay, *Priests of Lucina: The Story of Obstetrics* (Boston, 1939), pp. 220–221.

23. Elizabeth Nihell, *A Treatise on Art of Midwifery: Setting Forth Various Abuses Therein, Especially as to the Practice with Instruments* (London, 1760), p. 325; Nicholson J. Eastmen and Louis M. Hellman, *Williams Obstetrics,* 13th Ed. (New York: Appleton-Century-Crofts, 1966), p. 1.

24. Rothstein, *American Physicians,* pp. 47–49.

25. *Loc. cit.*

26. Frederick C. Irving, *Safe Deliverance* (Boston, 1942), pp. 221–225.

27. Harriet Connor Brown, *Grandmother Brown's Hundred Years, 1827–1927* (Boston, 1929), p. 93.

13

Professional Dominance and the Ordering of Health Services: Some Consequences

Eliot Freidson

A great many words have been spoken in discussions of what a profession is, or rather, what the best definition of "profession" is. Unfortunately, discussion has been so fixed on the question of definition that not much analysis has been made of the significance and conse-quences of some of the elements common to most definitions. The most critical of such underex-amined elements are organizational in character and are related to the organization of practice and the division of labor. Such elements are critical because they deal with facets of professional occupations that are independent of individual motivation or intention, and that may, as Carlin has suggested for law,[1] minimize the importance to behavior of the personal qualities of intelligence, ethicality, and trained skill imputed to professionals by most definitions. The key to such institutional elements of professions, I believe, lies in the commonly invoked word "autonomy." Autonomy means "the quality or state of being independent, free, and self-directing."[2] In the case of professions, autonomy apparently refers most of all to control over the content and the terms of work. That is, the professional is self-directing in his work.

From the single condition of self-direction or autonomy I believe we can deduce or derive virtually all the other institutional elements that are included in most definitions of professions. For example, an occupational group is more likely to be self-directing in its work when it has obtained a legal or political position of privilege that protects it from encroachment by other occupations. This is one of the functions of licensure, which provides an occupation with a legal monopoly over the performance of some strategic aspect of its work and effectively prevents free competition from other occupations. In the United States, for example, the physician is virtually the only one who can legally prescribe drugs and cut into the body. Competitors are left with being able to talk to patients and to lay hands *on* the body, but they may not penetrate the body chemically or physically.

Second, an occupational group is not likely to be able to be self-directing if it cannot control the production and particularly the application of knowledge and skill in the work it performs. This is to say, if the substance of its knowledge and skill is known to and performed by others, the occupation cannot be completely autonomous because those others can legitimately criticize and otherwise evaluate the way it carries out its work. The extended period of education controlled by the profession in an exclusively segregated professional school rather than in a variegated liberal arts school and a curriculum that includes some *special* theoretical content (whether scientifically proven or not) may represent a declaration that there is a body of special knowledge and skill necessary for the occupation

that is not represented in colleges of arts and sciences or their specialized departments. The existence of such self-sufficient schools in itself rules out as *legitimate* arbiters of the occupation's work those with specialized training in the same area who received their training from some other kind of school. The professional school and its curriculum, of course, also constitute convenient institutional criteria for licensure, registration, or other exclusionary legal devices.

Third, a code of ethics or some other publicly waved banner of good intentions may be seen as a formal method of declaring to all that the occupation can be trusted, and so of persuading society to grant the special status of autonomy. The very existence of such a code implies that individual members of the occupation have the personal qualities of professionalism, the imputation of which is also useful for obtaining autonomy. Thus, most of the commonly cited attributes of professions may be seen either as consequences of their autonomy or as conditions useful for persuading the public and the body politic to grant such autonomy.

Autonomy and Dominance in the Division of Labor

Clearly, however, autonomy is not a simple criterion. One can think of many occupations that are autonomous merely by virtue of the esoteric character of their craft or the circumstances in which they work. Nightclub magicians and circus acrobats, for example, form autonomous occupations by virtue of their intensive specialization in an area of work that is itself narrowly specialized without at the same time constituting part of an interdependent division of labor. Other occupations, like cab drivers or lighthouse keepers, are fairly autonomous because their work takes place in a mobile or physically segregated context that prevents others from observing, and therefore evaluating and controlling, performance. In all these cases we have *autonomy by default*. An occupation is left wholly to its own devices because there is no strong public concern with its work, because it works independently of any functional division of labor, and because its work (in complexity, specialization, or observability) precludes easy evaluation and control by others.

Where we find autonomy by default, we find no formal institutions in existence that serve to protect the occupation from competition, intervention, evaluation, and direction by others. Should interest in such an autonomous occupation be aroused among other workers or in society, its autonomy would prove to be fragile indeed without the introduction of such institutions. In short, *organized autonomy* is most stable and relevant to professions.

When we look at occupations engaged in such a complex division of labor as is found in the field of health, however, we find that with the exception of dentistry the only occupation that is truly autonomous is medicine itself.[3] It has the authority to direct and evaluate the work of others without in turn being subject to formal direction and evaluation by them. Paradoxically, its autonomy is sustained by the *dominance* of its expertise in the division of labor. It is true that some of the occupations it dominates—nursing for example—claim to be professions, as do other groups that lack either organized autonomy or dominance, such as schoolteachers and social workers. But surely there is a critically significant difference between dominant professions and those others that claim the name but do not possess the status. While the members of all may be committed to their work, may be dedicated to service, and may be specially educated, the dominant profession stands in an entirely different structural relationship to the division of labor than does the subordinate profession. To ignore that difference is to ignore something major. One might call many occupations "professions" if one so chooses, but there is a difference between the dominant profession and the others. In essence the difference reflects the existence of a *hierarchy of institutionalized expertise*. That hierarchy of expertise, which is almost as definite as the hierarchy of office to be found in rational-legal monocratic bureaucracies,[4] can have the same effect on the experience of the client as bureaucracy is said to have. Let me briefly indicate how.

The Client in the Health Organization

Unlike education, where most services are given within complex organizations, most personal services in the field of health have been given in settings that are, organizationally, analogous to small shops. For a number of reasons, however, the proportion of personal health services given in complex organizations like hospitals seems to be increasing. It is the service in these complex organizations that has been most criticized for dehumanizing care, but is it bureaucratic office or institutionalized expertise that produces the client experience underlying that criticism?

Some complaints, like the cost of hospitalization, reflect the method of financing medical care in the United States rather than organization as such. Other complaints—such as those about poor food, noise, and general amenities—reflect the economic foundation and capital plant of the institution rather than its organization. For our present question, two sets of complaints seem most important—those related to the physical treatment for sickness and those related to the discomforts of being in a patient role in medical organizations.

Clearly, many complaints about the depersonalization of the client in the medical organization concern what some technical, ostensibly therapeutic, procedures do to people.[5] Simply to be strapped on a rolling table and wheeled down corridors, into and out of elevators, and, finally, into an operating room for the scrutiny of all is to be treated like an object, not a person. To be anesthetized is to become literally an object without the consciousness of a person. And to be palpated, poked, dosed, purged, cut into, probed, and sewed is to find oneself an object. In such cases, it is the technical work of the profession, not bureaucracy, that is responsible for some of the unpleasantness the client experiences in health organizations. That unpleasantness is partly analogous to what the industrial worker suffers when the machine he works on requires him to make limited, repetitive motions at some mechanically paced speed. It is directly analogous to what is suffered by the raw materials shaped by worker and machine in industry.

Such discomfort may easily be excused by the outcome—that is, improvement or cure is generally thought to be a product well worth the discomfort of being treated like an object. The problem, though, is to determine exactly how much of that treatment has any necessary bearing at all on the technical outcome. There is no doubt that some of the management of the patient has little or no bearing on the purely technical requirements for treatment.[6] Some practices bear on the bureaucratic problem of administering services to a number of individuals in a manner that is fair, precise, predictable, and economical. Other practices bear on the convenience of the staff, medical or otherwise, and while they may be justified by reference to staff needs as workers, such justification has no bearing on staff expertise as such. Without denying the role of formal bureaucratic organization in creating some of the problem, it is the role of the professional worker himself I wish to examine more closely, if only because, in medical and other organizations, the professional worker is specifically antibureaucratic, insisting on controlling the management of treatment himself. The question is, how do professional practices contribute to the unhappy experience of the patient?

The best way of beginning to answer this question lies in recalling the distinction I made between an object and a person. An object does not possess the capacity for understanding, and its behavior cannot be influenced by its understanding. When a person is treated *as if* he were an object, he will nonetheless behave on the basis of his understanding of that treatment. Naturally, his understanding is formed in part by what he brings with him into the treatment setting. It is also formed by the sense he himself can make of what is happening to him in the treatment setting. Since the treatment setting is presumably dominated by specialized, expert procedures, however, the most critical source of his information and understanding lies in the staff and its ability and inclination to communicate with the patient. If the staff does not communicate to the patient the meaning of and justification for what is done to him, it in essence refuses him the status of a responsible adult or of a person in the full sense of the word.

The extent to which the staff withholds information from the patient and avoids communicative interaction with him has been a common criticism of the operation of such medical organizations as hospitals.[7] The complaint is that no one tells the client what is going to be done to him, why, and when. And after he has been

treated no one tells him why he feels the way he does, what can be expected subsequently, and whether or not he will live or die. The charge is that so little information is provided him that the patient cannot evaluate why he is being treated in a certain manner. Experience is mysteriously meaningless when it includes long waits for something unknown to happen or for something that does not happen, being awakened for an apparently trivial reason, being examined by taciturn strangers who enter the room unintroduced, perceiving lapses in such routines as medication and feeding without knowing whether error or intent is at issue. Surely this experience is little different from that of Kafka's antibureaucratic hero of *The Castle.*

Explanation by the staff constitutes acknowledgment of the client's status as a responsible adult capable of intelligent choice and self-control. In commercial organizations such acknowledgment does occur, however superficially, by "personalized" forms. Why does it not occur in hospitals? Part of the reason may stem from the necessity to treat clients in batches standardized by their technical status and by the services required. Some reason may also be found in understaffing and overwork, which excuses the minimization of interaction with some in order to maximize it with those with more "serious" problems. But these reasons do not explain why *bureaucratic* solutions to the problem of communication are not adopted—for example, distributing brochures explaining and justifying hospital routines, describing the experience of "typical" cholycystectomies, mastectomies, or heart patients from the first day through convalescence, and including answers to "commonly asked questions." The prime reason for the failure to communicate with the patient does not, I believe, lie in underfinancing, understaffing, or bureaucratization. Rather, it lies in the professional organization of the hospital and in the professional's conception of his relation to his clients.

Professional Control of Information

In the medical organization the medical profession is dominant. This means that all the work done by other occupations and related to the service of the patient is subject to the order of the physician.[8] The profession alone is held competent to diagnose illness, treat or direct the treatment of illness, and evaluate the service. Without medical authorization little can be done for the patient by paraprofessional workers. The client's medication, diet, excretion, and recreation are all subject to medical orders. So is the information given to the patient. By and large, without medical authorization paramedical workers are not supposed to communicate anything of significance to the patient about what his illness is, how it will be treated, and what the chances are for improvement. The physician himself is inclined to be rather jealous of the prerogative and is not inclined to authorize other workers to communicate information to the patient. Consequently, the paraprofessional worker who is asked for information by a patient is inclined to pass the buck like any bureaucrat. "You'll have to ask your doctor," the patient is told.

The dominant professional, then, is jealous of his prerogative to diagnose and forecast illness, holding it tightly to himself. But while he does not want anyone else to give information to the patient, neither is he himself inclined to do so. A number of reasons are advanced for this disinclination—the difficulty of being sure about diagnosis and precise about prognosis being perhaps the most neutral and technical of them all. Another reason is the physician's own busy schedule; he does not have the time to talk with the patient, and more serious cases need his attention. But the reasons of uncertainty and time-pressure are rather too superficial to dwell on. In the former case, the fact of uncertainty can constitute communication, though as Davis has shown[9] it can be asserted to avoid communication; in the latter case, surely the task can be delegated if time is lacking the doctor. For our present purposes, the most revealing argument against communication is based on characteristically professional assumptions about the nature of their clients. The argument, which goes back at least as far as Hippias' defensive remarks in the Hippocratic Corpus, asserts that, lacking professional training, the client is too ignorant to be able to comprehend what information he gets and that he is, in any case, too upset at being ill to be able to use the information he does get in a

manner that is rational and responsible.[10] From this it follows that giving information to the patient does not help him, but rather upsets him and creates additional "management problems" for the physician. Thus, the patient should not be treated like an adult, but rather like a child, given reassurance but not information. To do otherwise would only lead to the patient being upset and making unnecessary trouble for the staff. Characteristically, the professional does not view the client as an adult, responsible person.

In addition, it is worth pointing out the implications of the professional insistence on faith or trust rather than persuasion. The client, lacking professional training, is thought to be unequipped for intelligent evaluation or informed cooperation with his consultant. Essentially, he is expected either to have faith in his consultant and do what he is told without searching question or else to choose another consultant in whom he does have faith. To question one's doctor is to show lack of faith and is justifiable grounds for the doctor to threaten to withdraw his services. Such insistence on faith, I believe, rests on more than the purely functional demands of an effective therapeutic or service relationship. It also neutralizes threat to status. The very special social position of institutionalized privilege that is the profession's is threatened as well as demeaned by the demand that advice and action be explained and justified to a layman. If he must justify himself to a layman, the professional must use grounds of evidence and logic common to both professional and layman and cannot use esoteric grounds known and subscribed to by the profession alone. Insistence on faith constitutes insistence that the client give up his role as an independent adult and, by so neutralizing him, protect the esoteric foundation of the profession's institutionalized authority.[11]

Other Workers in the Professional Organization

Thus far I have pointed out that in medical organizations, the source of a client's alienation is professional rather than bureaucratic authority.[12] Some alienating characteristics of professional authority may lead to practices with a curiously bureaucratic look to them, including such notorious practices as passing the buck and such a notorious problem as (in the form of requiring doctors' orders) red tape. In this organization the client's position is similar to his position in civil service bureaucracies—he is handled like an object, given little information or opportunity for choice, and made to feel less than a responsible adult. And what of the subordinate worker in this setting dominated by a profession?

. . . many writers have felt that the worker as well as the client suffers from the bureaucratization of production by a monocratic administration. Lacking identification with the prime goals of the organization, lacking an important voice in setting the formal level and direction of work, and performing work that has been so rationalized as to become mechanical and meaningless, a minute segment of an intricate mosaic of specialized activities that he is in no position to perceive or understand, the worker is alienated. In contrast to the bureaucratized worker, however, the professional is said to be committed to and identified with his work so that it retains meaning for him, becoming in fact a central life interest. This may be true for dominant professions, but what of the other occupations working in the organization that the professional dominates? Are they not prone to alienation?

By and large, this question has not been asked in past studies, for the emphasis has been more on the positive response of "professionalism" than on the negative responses of alienation. What evidence there is, however, indicates that there are serious problems of worker morale in professional settings. Available studies are fairly clear about the existence of hierarchy in the professional health organization and about a decrease of participation in decision making the farther down the hierarchy one goes. Neither the ends nor the means of their work seem to be a matter for legitimate determination by lower-level workers, though, of course, they do sometimes have a very strong informal influence on such determination. Furthermore, even in situations where the stated official expectation is free participation by all workers in conferences about the running of such units as wards, participation has been observed to be quite unequal.[13]

The paraprofessional worker is, then, like the industrial worker, subordinated to the authority of others. He is not, however, subordinated solely to the authority of bureaucratic office, but also to the putatively superior knowledge and judgment of professional experts. In some studies this authority is characterized as a kind of stratification,[14] in others as a function of status.[15] In very few, if any, studies is that status or stratification said to be of administrative or bureaucratic origin. It is instead largely of professional origin. In a few studies the notion of alienation has been specifically cited.[16] Clearly, while there is no comparative evidence to allow us to determine whether more or fewer workers are alienated from professional than from bureaucratic organizations, neither hierarchical nor authoritarian tendencies are missing in the professional organization of the division of labor, nor are alienation, absenteeism, low morale, and high turnover insignificant problems. It is as true for the worker as for the patient that the professionally organized division of labor has pathologies similar to those stemming from bureaucracy.

Substantive Bias in Client Services

Thus far I have compared the influence of professional authority with the influence of bureaucratic authority on the experience of both client and worker in the physically limited corporate body we usually call an organization. However, because interorganizational relations may themselves be seen as organization and since the production of particular goods and services is rarely limited to the confines of a single corporate body requiring a variety of functions from outside "the" organization, it seems useful to continue my comparison in the rather broader context of planning and coordinating service as such. I have already noted that the common assumption is that expert authority has a neutral, functional foundation rather than, like bureaucratic authority, the foundation of arbitrary office. If this is so, we should expect the influence of expert authority on the support and planning of services to be highly functional, lacking arbitrary bias from the special vantage of bureaucratic office. Our expectation is not met in health services. There, the dominant profession exercises great influence on the disposition of resources that makes services available for clients. The character of that influence does stem from professional views of the purely functional considerations of what service is needed to accomplish some desired end, but *those views have been distorted by the lenses of a special occupational perspective.*

To understand how resources get distributed to the varied health services sought or required by the client, we must keep in mind the fact that the *medical* division of labor is not functionally complete. It is composed solely of those occupations and services controlled by the dominant profession. Outside it are some performing work that is functionally and substantively related to the profession but not subject to the profession's authority. In matters of health in the United States, such occupations as dentistry, optometry, chiropracty, and clinical psychology exemplify by their independent existence the functional incompleteness of the medically ordered division of labor. Furthermore, there are occupational groups whose work is often at least partly related to health problems but which are not recognized medical occupations; schoolteachers, specialized training and guidance personnel, social workers, and even ministers may be cited here. These are not part of the medically ordered division of labor either. Thus, while the profession stands as the supreme authority in the medical division of labor, the medical division of labor does not encompass all health-related activities of the larger health-related division of labor. Nonetheless, the distribution of support and resources tends to move disproportionately through the medical division of labor.

I have argued for the distinction of a type of profession that has ultimate authority over its work in such a way that it is self-directing or autonomous and dominant in a division of labor. In the case of medicine, a strategic facet of its authority is its delineation of pathology, the definitions of health and illness that guide the application of knowledge to human ills. The physician is the ultimate expert on what is health and what illness and on how to attain the former and cure the latter. Indeed, his perspective leads him to see the world in terms of health and

illness, and the world is presently inclined to turn to him for advice on all matters related to health and illness regardless of his competence. Given the highly visible miracles medicine has worked over the past century, the public has even been inclined to ask the profession to deal with problems that are not of the biophysical character for which success was gained from past efforts. What were once recognized as economic, religious, and personal problems have been redefined as illness and have therefore become medical problems.[17] This widening of medical jurisdiction has had important consequences for the allocation of resources to client services.

No philanthropies today seem to be able to attract more financial support than those devoting themselves to illness, particularly those of children. If the label of illness can be attached to a problem it receives extensive support and also becomes dominated by medical institutions even when there is no evidence that medical institutions have any especially efficacious way of dealing with the problem. By virtue of controlling the notions of illness and health, medicine has in fact become a giant umbrella under which a disparate variety of workers (including sociologists) can be both financed and protected from overly close outside scrutiny merely through their semantic connection with health. But those who do not or cannot choose to huddle under the umbrella, even though their work is health-related, tend to find it difficult to obtain support.

One rather obvious consequence is the uneven distribution of resources to health-related activities. For example, it was pointed out recently that heavy financing has been given to medical research into mental deficiency, only a small amount of which is biologically or genetically caused, while *educational* facilities for the training and teaching of mental deficients have been sorely underfinanced.[18] Less obvious and more important to public welfare is the extent to which this uneven distribution of resources emphasizes some hypotheses and investigatory and therapeutic models at the expense of others equally plausible. For example, it was recently noted that work in rehabilitation has come under medical supervision, resulting in an inappropriate emphasis on the traditional authoritarian therapeutic relationship of medicine that I have already discussed.[19] It has also been noted that the disease model has dominated the approach to mental illness.[20] By and large, within the well-financed division of labor dominated by the profession and under its protective umbrella, most work is limited to that which conforms to the special perspective and substantive style of the profession—a perspective that emphasizes the individual over the social environment, the treatment of rare and interesting over common and uninteresting disorders, the cure rather than the prevention of illness, and preventive medicine rather than what might be called "preventive welfare"—social services and resources that improve the diet, housing, way of life, and motivation of the people without their having to undertake clinical consultation with a practitioner. In short, I suggest that by virtue of its position in the public esteem and in its own division of labor, the dominant profession of the field of health exerts a special and biased influence on planning and financing services of the general field within which it is located. The prime criterion for determining that emphasis is not necessarily functional in character, but social and structural—whether or not the services can be dominated by or be put under the umbrella of the dominant profession. The consequence for the client is an array of differentially supported services that may not be adequate for his needs and interests.

Finally, I might point out that given this array of health-related services differentially developed and supported by functional and other considerations, still further qualification of the kind of service a client is likely to get is exercised by the dominant profession. In general, I wish to suggest that when some of the relevant services lie outside the medical division of labor and some inside, serious problems of access to care and of the rational coordination of care are created by the barriers that the profession erects between that segment of the division of labor it does dominate and that segment it does not.[21]

Perhaps the simplest way of discussing these barriers is to examine the process by which clients move through the division of labor. They move in part by their own choice and selection of consultants and in part by their consultants' choice of and referral to other consultants or technicians. To the extent that the client moves through the division of labor by his own volition, he is responsible for his own care and his consultants are dependent on him for relevant information about his problem. But to the extent to which the client is being guided by consultants, the character of his experience and care is dependent on the substantive direction of his consultants' referrals and on the exchange of information bearing on treatment among them. Here is where the professionally created barrier is found. Within the general health division of labor, the referral of clients tends to go in only one direction—into the smaller medical division of labor, without also going from the medical into the larger system. This is also generally true of the transmission of information about the client. To put it more bluntly, teachers, social workers, ministers, and others outside the medical division of labor refer to physicians and communicate information about the client to them, but physicians are not likely either to refer clients to them or to provide them with the results of medical investigation.[22]

By the same token, physicians do not routinely refer to clinical psychologists, optometrists, chiropractors, and others outside the medical division of labor but clearly within the health division of labor. They are likely to refer only when they are sure that the limited services they may order—psychological testing rather than psychotherapy, spectacle fitting and sales rather than refractions, and minor manipulations for medically untreatable muscular-skeletal complaints rather than for other complaints—will be performed, and no more. They are also, wittingly or not, likely to discourage such workers' referrals to them by reciprocating neither referrals nor information about their findings. And from at least one study there is evidence that medically oriented workers are prone to reject the patient if he comes to them from the wrong source.[23]

By and large, physicians refer to and communicate extensively with only those who, within the medical division of labor, are subject to their prescription, order, or direction. Indeed, physicians are likely to be very poorly informed about any institutional and occupational resources that lie outside their own jurisdiction. And, as is quite natural for people who have developed commitment to their work, they are likely to be suspicious of the value of all that lies outside their domain, including the competence and ethicality of those working outside. Their commitment leads them to deprecate the importance of extramedical services, and their position as professionals encourages them to restrict their activities to the medical system they control. So long as this is all their clients need or want, no harm is done save for the possibility that the professional's response to outside services may encourage those outside to avoid or delay in referring clients to the physician. Even when outside services are necessary for the client's well-being, referral to them may be delayed or never undertaken and the client's interests left unprotected.

NOTES

1. Jerome Carlin, *Lawyers' Ethics* (New York: Russell Sage Foundation, 1966). It should be noted that Carlin's findings also were that a stable individual attribute of ethicality influenced behavior independently of the setting. A recent study of college students found the same thing. See William J. Bowers, "Normative Constraints on Deviant Behavior in the College Context," *Sociometry, 31* (December, 1968), 370–385.

2. *Webster's Third New International Dictionary* (Springfield, Mass.: C. & C. Merriam Co., 1967), p. 148.

3. See Eliot Freidson, "Paramedical Personnel," in *International Encyclopedia of the Social Sciences* (New York: Macmillan and Free Press, 1968), Vol. 10, pp. 114–120, for more discussion on the medical division of labor.

4. A recent article argues persuasively against the value of using the idea of formal bureaucratic organization to analyze settings in which professionals work, pointing out that even in industrial settings the idea does not faithfully reflect observed behavior. See Rue Bucher and Joan Stelling, "Characteristics of Professional Organization," *Journal of Health and Social Behavior,* 10 (1969), 3–15. The same point may be made for the division of labor I describe. However, formal bureaucratic organization and formal occupational jurisdiction and authority do provide limits of a fairly definite nature; just as a stenographer cannot negotiate with her employer over who will chair a policy making meeting, so a nurse cannot

negotiate with a surgeon over who will perform an operation.

5. Important in this context is Erving Goffman's "The Medical Model and Mental Hospitalization," in Erving Goffman, *Asylums* (Garden City, N.Y.: Doubleday, 1961), pp. 321–386.

6. For an extended analysis of the substance of expertise which tries to indicate what is genuine and what spurious in medical work, see Eliot Freidson, *Profession of Medicine: A Study of the Sociology of Applied Knowledge* (New York: Dodd-Mead, 1970), Chapter 15.

7. For example, see the following: Julius A. Roth, "The Treatment of Tuberculosis as a Bargaining Process," in A. M. Rose, ed., *Human Behavior and Social Processes* (Boston: Houghton Mifflin, 1962), pp. 575–588; Jeanne C. Quint, "Institutionalized Practices of Information Control," *Psychiatry, 28* (1965), 119–132.

8. For example, see Albert F. Wessen, "Hospital Ideology and Communication Between Ward Personnel" in E. G. Jaco, ed., *Patients, Physicians, and Illness* (New York: Free Press, 1958), pp. 448–468.

9. Fred Davis, "Uncertainty in Medical Prognosis, Clinical and Functional," *American Journal of Sociology, 66* (1960), 41–47.

10. See, for example, the material in Barney G. Glaser and Anselm L. Strauss, *Awareness of Dying* (Chicago: Aldine, 1965).

11. For a more extensive discussion of the professional ideology see Freidson, *Profession of Medicine,* Chapter 8.

12. For a rare study of patients using a measure of alienation, see John W. Evans, "Stratification, Alienation, and the Hospital Setting," *Engineering Experiment Station Bulletin* No. 184, Ohio State University, 1960.

13. For example, see the findings in William Caudill, *The Psychiatric Hospital as a Small Society* (Cambridge, Mass.: Harvard University Press, 1958), and William A. Rushing, *The Psychiatric Professions* (Chapel Hill: University of North Carolina Press, 1964), pp. 258–259.

14. See M. Seeman and J. W. Evans, "Stratification and Hospital Care," *American Sociological Review, 26* (1961), 67–80, 193–204, and Ivar Oxaal, "Social Stratification and Personnel Turnover in the Hospital," *Engineering Experiment Station Monograph* No. 3, Ohio State University, 1960.

15. See E. G. Mishler and A. Tropp, "Status and Interaction in a Psychiatric Hospital," *Human Relations, 9* (1956), 187–205, and William R. Rosengren, "Status Stress and Role Contradic-

tions: Emergent Professionalization in Psychiatric Hospitals," *Mental Hygiene, 45* (1961), 28–39.

16. See Rose L. Coser, "Alienation and the Social Structure: Case Study of a Hospital," in E. Freidson, ed., *Hospital in Modern Society* (New York: Free Press, 1963), pp. 231–265, and L. I. Pearlin, "Alienation from Work: A Study of Nursing Personnel," *American Sociological Review, 27* (1962), 314–326.

17. For an extended discussion of the relative place of notions of health and illness in modern society, see Freidson, *Profession of Medicine,* Chapter 12.

18. George W. Albee, "Needed—A Revolution in Caring for the Retarded," *Trans-action, 5* (1968), 37–42.

19. Albert F. Wessen, "The Apparatus of Rehabilitation: An Organizational Analysis," in Marvin B. Sussman, ed., *Sociology and Rehabilitation* (Washington, D. C.: American Sociological Association, 1966), pp. 148–178.

20. See Marline Taber et al., "Disease Ideology and Mental Health Research," *Social Problems, 16* (1969), 349–357, for a recent statement.

21. See the discussion in William L. Kissick, "Health Manpower in Transition," *The Milbank Memorial Fund Quarterly, 46* (January 1968), Part 2, pp. 53–91, for this and many other relevant points.

22. For work bearing on these statements see Elaine Cumming et al., *Systems of Social Regulation* (New York: Atherton, 1968), and Eugene B. Piedmont, "Referrals and Reciprocity: Psychiatrists, General Practitioners, and Clergymen," *Journal of Health and Social Behavior, 9* (1968), 29–41.

23. See David Schroder and Danuta Ehrlich, "Rejection by Mental Health Professionals: A Possible Consequence for Not Seeking Appropriate Help for Emotional Disorders," *Journal of Health and Social Behavior, 9* (1968), 222–232.

14

Transitions in Pediatrics: A Segmental Analysis

Dorothy Pawluch

As part of the medical profession, pediatricians share with other doctors certain goals and interests. But as pediatricians, they have a unique identity and sense of mission that can and often does bring them into conflict with their medical colleagues. Moreover, pediatrics is itself comprised of different groupings or segments: there are pediatricians who teach and do research, pediatricians in clinical practice who offer specialized services on a consulting basis to referring doctors, and, in the United States, pediatricians who deliver general primary care to children. The interests and identities of these segments are not necessarily complementary and do not always converge. Diversity, rather than a common purpose, characterizes pediatrics and, indeed, all professions. Bucher and Strauss (1961:326) made this observation when they defined professions as loose amalgamations of segments "pursuing different objectives in different manners and more or less delicately held together under a common name at a particular period in history."

Bucher and Strauss (1961:332) stressed also that professional segments are not fixed but undergo continual modification in response to changes in the context of their work. The most significant catalyst of ferment and change for pediatrics in the industrialized world through the 20th century has been the dramatic reduction in infant and child mortality[1] and drastic changes in the nature of childhood morbidity. Pediatricians have had to adjust to fewer sick children and to childhood illnesses that are minor and self-correcting.[2] This has been easier for some pediatricians than for others. There is always need for academic pediatricians to teach pediatric principles and methods, and to study those serious illnesses that do threaten the life and health of children. There is also need for the consulting pediatrician and pediatric subspecialist to treat the rare case of serious childhood illness. But by 1950, the need for a large contingent of primary care doctors with expert knowledge of children's diseases had diminished substantially. In European countries and in Australia, where pediatricians functioned primarily as academicians and consulting specialists,[3] pediatrics adapted smoothly to new patterns of practice. But in the United States, where the majority of pediatricians were in general primary care, the declining mortality and morbidity threatened to destroy the largest segment of the specialty.

Primary care pediatricians in the United Staes survived by broadening the scope of pediatric practice to incorporate the management of children's troublesome behavior. Parents had always sought medical counselling on child rearing, and their concern for children's behavioral difficulties may have increased with the decline of serious physical illness. But prior to 1950, troublesome behavior was seen largely in non-medical terms and controlled by parents themselves, school officials, or juvenile authorities. After 1950, parents found the primary care pediatrician increasingly willing to apply a medical model to children's problems which were not necessarily biological in nature. Thus, pediatricians began to appropriate the behaviorial, emotional, and social problems of children. Pediatricians today treat not only physical conditions but poor school performance, hyperactivity, shyness, aggressive and anti-social behavior, temper tantrums, and peer rejection (Gabel, 1981).

In this paper I use documentary, historical material to show how primary care pediatricians in the United States came to espouse and promote the medicalization of children's troublesome behavior. I begin by describing the emergence and development of the specialty in the United States. Then I look at the declining mortality rate and its implications for pediatrics. I describe the crisis experienced by primary care pediatricians and the new directions they forged in response. Finally, I consider the likelihood of continued pediatric involvement in the management of children's troublesome behavior.

The Birth of a Specialty

Pediatrics became an organized branch of medicine in the United States in the late 19th century when the rates of infant and child mortality were exceedingly high. The rapid urbanization that resulted from industrial expansion and mass immigration after 1820 produced living conditions that few children survived. In the last half of the 19th century, more than a quarter of all children in the United States died before the age of five (Cone, 1979:112), most from intestinal infections such as dysentery, cholera, and cholera infantum, and infectious diseases such as diptheria, scarlet fever, pneumonia, and tuberculosis (Faber and McIntosh, 1966:3). Humanitarian, economic, and political interests around the turn of the 19th century heightened public awareness of these problems and led to intense activism on behalf of children. The child-saving movement, as it was known in the United States, produced child labor laws, compulsory education, juvenile courts and reforms in the health and welfare services for children (Zietz, 1969:55). It also produced a new medical specialty: pediatrics.

After the 1850s, a group of fewer than 50 doctors, practicing independently, developed a special interest in the diseases of children and began concentrating their practices heavily, though not exclusively, on the young. Until then, the care of sick children was largely the responsibility of women and marginal practitioners such as homeopaths. Regular doctors had little interest in treating children; when they did they made few distinctions between children and adults. They applied the same drastic therapies including phlebotomy, or bleeding, and the administration of massive doses of mineral medications, often with disastrous consequences for children (Coulter, 1969:113; Gittings, 1928:1; Jacobi, 1911:3).

The doctors who initially called themselves pediatrists or pedologists, and later pediatricians,[4] claimed children should be given unique medical attention and fought for recognition and study of the special health problems of children. They condemned their medical colleagues for treating children as if they were miniature adults, and for approaching childhood illness as if it was the same class of disease in smaller bodies. "There are anomalies and diseases," wrote Abraham Jacobi, the father of U.S. pediatrics, in 1890, "which are met in the infant and child only" (Bremner, 1971:817). Children could not be treated by simply reducing dosages, the pediatricians argued, nor could child anatomy and physiology be deduced backwards from studies of adults. Pediatricians proclaimed a new and independent branch of medicine.

The Organizational Growth of Pediatrics

The first formal recognition of pediatrics in the United States came in 1879, when the American Medical Association (AMA) formed a Section on Diseases of Children, headed by Dr. Abraham Jacobi and Dr. Samuel Busey. But the AMA was oriented toward the generalist in medicine. As the professional identity of pediatricians coalesced, they, like other emerging specialists, felt the AMA did not provide sufficient leadership (Stevens, 1971:52). Schultz (1933:417) claims the section's early years were "marked by a struggle for existence and independent identity." In 1888, 42 physicians formed the American Pediatric Society (APS). The organizers at first considered a loose affiliation with the AMA, but then decided that the new society should "steer clear of medical cliques" and "guard against entangling alliances" (APS, 1938:xi). Membership was restricted to researchers who had made an important contribution to the study of the children, but included just about every clinician and academician in the United States and Canada with a declared interest in pediatrics (Faber and McIntosh, 1966:311; Morse, 1935:305).

Between 1880 and 1935, pediatrics consolidated its position in medicine. After 1900, some doctors began restricting their practices exclusively to children. According to the directories of the AMA, the number of doctors who limited their practices exclusively to pediatrics grew to 138 in 1914, 664 in 1921, and 1,734 in 1934 (Veeder, 1935:6). No other specialty experienced such a rapid increase. A study of doctors who graduated between the years 1915 and 1920 found that while the percentage of graduates limiting themselves to surgery, internal medicine, and diseases of the eye, ear, nose, and throat decreased over the five-year period, the percentage of those specializing in pediatrics increased nearly 100 percent from 5.8 in 1915 to 11.1 in 1920 (Veeder, 1935:7). Several pediatric journals appeared, including the *Archives of Pediatrics* in 1884, published by William Perry Watson, the *Transactions of the American Pediatric Society* in 1889, *Pediatrics* in 1896, published by Dillon Brown, and the *American Journal of Diseases of Children* in 1911, published by the AMA. Local and regional societies of pediatricians were formed. Medical schools included pediatrics in undergraduate curricula and introduced residency programs in pediatrics. Those interested in graduate work in pediatrics were no longer obliged to travel abroad.[5] Gradually, pediatrics and pediatric research achieved respectability. In 1930, Alexander Blackader remarked: "[During the 1880s and 1890s] the care of children was considered hardly worth the attention of an experienced intern, or of a physician of repute. How changed is the position of pediatrics today" (Faber and McIntosh, 1966:161). Two more national pediatric associations were formed: in 1930 clinical pediatricians formed the American Academy of Pediatrics (AAP) and, in 1931, young pediatric researchers who were having difficulty penetrating the new exclusive APS, founded the Society for Pediatric Research (SPR).

By the 1930s, pediatricians were concerned that there were no standards of pediatric training (Pease, 1952:109). Following the example of ophthalmologists in 1917, and otolaryngologists, obstetricians, and gynecologists in the early 1930s, pediatricians formed the American Board of Pediatrics (ABP). The board was composed of representatives from the AAP, the APS, and the

Section of the Diseases of Children in the AMA. It set standards of training and issued certificates to those who successfully completed board examinations, thereby formally entrenching pediatrics as a specialty.

Declining Mortality Rates

The organizational growth of pediatrics was paralleled by plummeting infant and child mortality rates in the United States. The rates for infants dropped from approximately 273 per 1,000 live births in 1885, to 162.4 in 1900, 92.3 in 1920, and 69 in 1930, a drop of 75 percent over 45 years (U.S. Bureau of the Census, 1975:60). Mortality rates for children one to four years old declined from 19.8 in 1900, to 9.9 in 1920, and 5.6 in 1930, a drop of 72 percent over 30 years. For children age five to 14, the rates dropped from 3.9 per 1,000 in 1900, to 2.6 in 1920, and 1.7 in 1930, a drop of 57 percent over 30 years (U.S. Bureau of the Census, 1975:60).

There were at least five factors responsible for the decline in mortality rates:

1. The most significant factor was improved living conditions. The great cholera, smallpox, and yellow fever epidemics in the United States between 1800 and 1870 alerted people to the medical dangers of an unsanitary environment (Smillie, 1952:58). But the real impetus for improved sanitation came with the discovery of bacteria. During the 1860s and 1870s, Louis Pasteur in France and Robert Koch in Germany firmly established that diseases were not spontaneously generated but caused by germs. Their work provided a basis for the further study of bacteria, the diseases they produce, and the mechanisms by which they are transmitted. Through the late 19th and early 20th centuries, research progressed rapidly. The application of the new knowledge through the public health movement resulted in vast improvements in urban living conditions, especially in overcrowding, bad housing, inadequate sewage and sanitation facilities, polluted water supplies, and contaminated food and milk. Mortality rates for all age groups fell sharply after 1900, but the effects were particularly noticeable among infants and children. The improvements were so dramatic that urbanization, the key factor in rising infant mortal-

ity rates at the end of the 19th century, became in the 20th century the most significant factor in their decline (Lawson, 1960:14).

2. Pasteur also established the basis for immunology which led to the development and dissemination of vaccines for many child-killing diseases. Edward Jenner first conceived of the idea of inoculating people against smallpox by injecting the more benign cowpox virus, and introduced the vaccine in England in 1796. But Jenner had no understanding of the principles of immunization. Pasteur established these in 1885, with his discovery of a vaccine for rabies. During the 1890s and early 1900s, scientists extended Pasteur's work to diphtheria, tetanus, typhoid fever, cholera, the plague, and meningitis (Ackerknecht, 1982:175; Parish, 1965; Winslow, 1923:177).

3. Nutrition research around the turn of the century and the identification of vitamins in 1912 led to the control of deficiency diseases such as scurvey, rickets, and pellagra (Jeans, 1950:363).

4. The discovery that many infant deaths were related to poor maternal health led to increased hospital deliveries, development of better programs in obstetrics for both obstetricians and general practitioners, screening programs for pregnant women, and intensive supervision and specialized obstetrical care for women who showed significant abnormalities during pregnancy. Better maternal health was reflected in lower maternal mortality rates and lower infant mortality rates (Shapiro *et al.,* 1968:159).

5. The reformers of the child-saving movement played a key role in reducing mortality rates by initiating specific health reforms based on new knowledge about infectious diseases and nutrition, and by improving the general welfare of mothers and their children. At first privately, and then with public support, the reformers established—between 1890 and 1930—milk depots that dispensed information as well as pure milk, courses for expectant and new mothers on the care and proper feeding of children, visiting public health nurse programs, and health supervision and compulsory immunization in schools (Rosen, 1958:349).

Though pediatricians supported the reformers and participated in the programs they established, they neither figured prominently, nor assumed positions of leadership, in reform activities. Pediatricians defined their role in fighting infant and child mortality in more narrow medical terms. Until 1930, the single most important concern for pediatricians in the United States was the artificial feeding of infants.

The Role of Pediatricians: Baby Feeders

While pediatrics was emerging as a specialty, the leading causes of death among children under five years of age were intestinal infections such as cholera infantum, cholera morbus, diarrhea, dysentery, cholera, and enteritis. Close to 23 percent of all infant deaths in 1850 were due to intestinal infections or their complications (Smillie, 1952:70). In 1880, 75 percent of deaths among children under five years were due to intestinal infections (Faber and McIntosh, 1966:4). Most of these deaths occurred during the summer among children fed with cow's milk. Until the 1920s, 80 to 90 percent of childhood deaths due to intestinal infections occurred among bottle-fed children (Cone, 1979:152). The prime mission of pediatricians between 1870 and 1930 was to overcome the problems of artificial feeding.

Since the precise relationship between milk and disease had not yet been specified, scientists and pediatric researchers in the last half of the 19th century focused on the nutritional deficiencies of cow's milk, rather than its cleanliness. They sought ways of compensating for deficiencies in the composition of cow's milk by varying proportions of fat, sugar, and protein. The simple, fixed formulae developed by pediatricians such as Arthur V. Meigs were replaced during the 1890s with Thomas Rotch's more elaborate percentage-feeding method which modified the cow's milk according to the age, nutritional requirements, and digestive capabilities of individual children. Percentage computations and milk adjustment became the pediatricians "chief stock in trade" (Powers, 1939:4). The formulae for calculating variations in milk were complex and, according to pediatrician Herman F. Meyer, required "almost the equivalent of an advanced degree in higher mathematics" (Cone, 1979:137). The pediatricians' mastery of the formulae and skill in applying them were a source of status and prestige among their medical colleagues who called them "baby feeders" (Lawson, 1960:14). General practitioners referred the most difficult feeding problems to pediatricians. It took "a master's touch to avoid the Scylla of indigestion and the Charybdis of inanition" (L. Emmett Holt, quoted in Evans, 1967:315).

The success of the pediatricians' formulae, however, was due in large part to their use of a cleaner quality of milk than was generally available. Before bacteria were recognized as the cause of disease and raw milk as an ideal culture for the growth of germs, milk was obtained under uncontrolled and unhygienic conditions from cows that were poorly kept and often diseased. Bettman (1974:115) describes cows in New York in 1870, so enfeebled from tuberculosis that "they had to be raised on cranes to remain milkable until they died." Dealers sometimes added water, flour, chalk, or plaster of Paris to increase the quantity or improve the color of the product. The milk was hauled in large tin containers to homes where it was kept without refrigeration or cooling (Wain, 1970:251).

Towards the end of the 19th century scientists identified the harmful properties of contaminated milk and Pasteur developed pasteurization, a process which destroys pathogenic bacteria in liquids. In 1886, Franz von Soxhlet applied the process to milk and, in 1890, Denmark became the first country to pasteurize milk on a commercial basis. In 1889, Abraham Jacobi introduced pasteurization in the United States. But the value of pasteurization was not immediately recognized. For many years experts in the United States debated the relative merits of pasteurization and certification as solutions to the problem of contaminated milk. Pasteurization treats the milk itself. Certification controls the conditions under which the milk is produced. A pediatrician named Henry Leber Coit developed certification in 1889; over the first decade of the 20th century, medical milk commissions certified 63 farms across the United States. The raw, unaltered milk produced on these farms was sold mainly to pediatricians who used it for clinical treatment of children experiencing gastro-intestinal difficulties.

But certification was difficult to apply on a large scale and, by 1910, it became apparent that the cleanliness of a milk source could not be guaranteed because of the ever-present threat of the well-carrier. (A carrier is an individual or animal who harbors a disease organism in its body without manifesting the symptoms of the disease, thereby distributing the infection.) Pasteurization was the only assured method of safe-guarding milk. In 1908, Chicago became the first U.S. city to require pasteurization of its milk supply, followed by New York in 1910. The certification movement waned in popularity; by 1920, it had disappeared and pasteurized milk was readily available across the United States.

Rubber nipples and safe, commercially prepared infant food were also available after the 1870s. As a result of advertisements in newspapers and domestic magazines, these easy-to-use patent food preparations became popular among women and were even recommended by pediatricians, who were growing increasingly frustrated with the complexity of percentage-method feeding. Despite the rising popularity of artificial feeding after 1900, the incidence and severity of gastro-intestinal infections in children dropped markedly. In Connecticut, for example, the percentage of infant deaths due to intestinal infections dropped from 23.1 in 1916 to 5.9 in 1930 (Powers, 1939:8) Pediatricians and other doctors who treated children continued to supervise artificial feeding after the 1920s, but only because their association with the manufacturers of infant food assured them a monopoly over the information needed to use the products (Apple, 1980).

Changing Patterns of Practice

By 1930, infant feeding had become largely routine, and the pediatricians' function as baby-feeders redundant. Those pediatricians not connected with universities and teaching hospitals moved progressively into primary care, where they functioned less as specialists for difficult feeding problems and complex childhood illnesses and more as general practitioners within a limited age range. Pediatricians in private, primary care practices were still available to general practitioners in their communities for consultation, but few general practitioners turned to them for fear of losing the patient to the pediatrician altogether (AAP, 1950:509).

The pediatric research and teaching elite predicted that with improved child health and better pediatric training for general practitioners, pediatrics would disappear as a primary care speci-

alty and become restricted to a small group of researchers, teachers, and consulting specialists (Veeder, 1935:9). In 1936, pediatrician John Morse made this sullen pronouncement to the Philadelphia Pediatric Society:

> Forty years ago pediatrics was a virgin field; now it is overcultivated. The other end of life now offers the greatest field of development. My advice to young pediatricians . . . is to take up geriatrics, not pediatrics (Morse, 1937:532).

The gloomy forecasts were incorrect. The need for primary care pediatricians may have diminished after 1930, but the demand and opportunities did not. Primary care pediatrics continued to grow. In 1930, there were less than 1,000 doctors in the United States who identified themselves as pediatricians. By 1948, there were about 4,000, 3,500 of whom were in private, general pediatric practice (AAP, 1950:514). The number of hospitals approved for residency training by the AMA's Council on Medical Education and Hospitals increased from 105 in 1939 to 211 in 1949, and the number of approved residency positions from 330 in 1939 to 959 in 1949 (*Journal of the AMA*, 1949:157).

The growth of primary care pediatrics was made possible largely by a demand that pediatricians themselves created. Preventive medicine had always been a distinguishable feature of pediatrics. But during the late 1920s and 1930s, pediatricians, with the help of the Children's Bureau and popular literature, convinced mothers that the well-being of their children depended on continuous medical supervision, preferably by a pediatrician (Rothman, 1978:148). It became fashionable, among those mothers who could afford it, to seek the services of a pediatrician not only to treat their children in times of illness but to monitor their normal growth as well. Preventive and routine care constituted as much as 30 to 40 percent of the average pediatric practice during the 1930s (Aldrich, 1934:1062; Boulware, 1958:555; London, 1937:770). But sufficient, serious childhood illnesses remained to stimulate and challenge pediatricians. Infections of all sorts predominated, including tuberculosis, pneumonia, upper respiratory tract infections, meningitis, otitis media, and organ abscesses. Though generally less fatal than they had been earlier in the 20th century, respiratory and intestinal infections continued to be the leading killers of children through the 1940s (Vaughan *et al.*, 1979:4).

In 1928, Alexander Fleming accidentally discovered penicillin, and in 1938 Ernest Chain and Howard Florey developed penicillin for use in the treatment of human bacterial infections. Over the next 15 years several antibiotics and sulfonamides came into general use in the treatment of tuberculosis and other serious infections. So effective were these drugs that doctors would often administer them for several days before examining the patient and diagnose only those patients who showed no sign of improvement (Davison, 1952:537; Washburn, 1951:304). The incidence and severity of measles, mumps, and rubella were also reduced during the 1940s with the development of gamma globulin.

The impact of these developments was staggering. The infant mortality rate dropped from 60.9 deaths per 1,000 live births in 1935 to 33 in 1950. Childhood mortality dropped from 4.4 deaths per 1,000 to 1.4 for children between one and four years and from 1.5 to 0.6 for children between five and 14 years (U.S. Bureau of the Census, 1975:60). After 1950, accidents surpassed infectious diseases as the leading cause of death among children (Vaughan *et al.*, 1979:4). Comparing lists of causes of childhood death in 1850 and 1950, one observer wrote:

> The picture has entirely changed in 100 years. Every single one of the ten important causes of illness and death in infancy and early childhood in 1850 has been wiped out. The slate is clean. Childhood has become a period of abundant health and of preparation for a full and satisfactory adult life, free from invalidism and from the scars of early acute infections (Smillie, 1955:207).

For practicing pediatricians, the trends meant an even greater emphasis on prevention. A national survey conducted by the AAP (1950) showed that, in 1948, 54 percent of all visits to general pediatricians were for health supervision. The remaining 46 percent consisted primarily of self-correcting or easily treated minor infections. Serious medical problems were referred to various pediatric subspecialties such as pediatric cardiology and pediatric neurology that had

emerged between 1920 and 1940 around specific organ systems (Holt, 1961:672). The age of curative pediatrics had indeed ended. One pediatrician suggested that the Department of Pediatrics at his institution change its name to the Department of Child Life, as at the University of Edinburgh (Davison, 1952:538).

Problems for Primary Care Pediatricians

As prevention gradually displaced treatment as the pediatrician's primary task, the heavy emphasis on prevention itself created problems. After 1950, pediatricians began to complain openly to each other, and in letters to leading pediatric journals, about boredom, a lack of prestige, and the unprofitability of a medical practice concentrated on health supervision rather than the treatment of illness. In 1960, the median income for pediatricians in the United States was $20,700, the lowest of nine medical specialties surveyed, including dermatology, internal medicine, and psychiatry, and only $700 more than the net earnings of the average general practitioner (*Medical Economics*, 1961:90).

Letters to the journals suggested that pediatricians were leaving pediatrics either for general practice or for other specialties:

> I seldom saw a really interesting medical problem. Anxious mothers and running noses are not what I was trained for. (Levine, 1960:651).

> It is inconceivable that any physician with intelligence and interest in the unusual can long survive the routine of playing grandmother for years on end in a well-baby practice. My former pediatric practice was monotonous in the extreme. Upper respiratory infections, infant feeding, the endless discussions with endless mothers of problems that are self-righting anyhow, all of it except the occasional emergency situation was not sufficiently stimulating for a steady diet. There are no longer enough surprises in the package. The pediatrician is indeed low man on the totem pole (Tabrah, 1957:745).

> To admit that we are in a field that has less to offer than we have been taught is distressing. To continue to mislead fine young men into a specialty that does not exist is even more unfortunate (Wineberg, 1959: 1008).

Many wanted to relieve the boredom of routine care by encouraging independence among mothers, but recognized that this might be "poor economics." "The pediatrician would do better financially," one pediatrician admitted, "if he permitted the parents to have a little anxiety and encourage them to depend on him through frequent office visits" (Coddington, 1959:1008).

The discontent was not isolated. A survey conducted by *Medical Economics* (1956) showed that pediatrics was medicine's most frustrated specialty and confirmed that pediatricians were switching to other areas of medicine. Ninety-five percent of the pediatricians were glad they chose medicine as a career, but only 63 percent were satisfied with their chosen specialty, the lowest proportion of satisfied practitioners among the specialists surveyed. Holt (1961:675) summarized the pediatricians' dilemma:

> They were intrigued by medicine; they wanted to treat sick children and they were trained to do just that. Now they find that the sick child is the exceptional one they are asked to see.

Pediatrics was also losing its appeal among medical school graduates. By the 1950s, hospitals were having difficulty filling their available pediatric residency positions (Levine, 1960). Through the 1960s, pediatrics—along with other such low-status specialties as general practice, anesthesiology, pathology, internal medicine, and psychiatry—had one of the highest number of vacant residency positions (AMA, 1964–1969).

Another ominous trend was the resurgence of the pediatrician's major competitor in the area of primary child care: the general practitioner. With the rise of specialization, general practitioners had been declining steadily through the 20th century, both in status and numbers. The decline was highlighted during the Second World War when practitioners were at a disadvantage next to doctors certified by specialty boards. Board-certified doctors received higher ranks and all the benefits that accrued from them. General practitioners came out of the war protesting vociferously (APA, 1950:515). In 1947, 150 general practitioners formed the American Academy of General Practitioners. The academy launched a

campaign to reverse the trend towards increasing specialization. The spirit of the new generalist movement was captured in the insignia the American Board of Family Practice eventually adopted: the phoenix, a mythical bird who sets itself ablaze only to rise again from its ashes. Promoting themselves as purveyors of family health, the general practitioners aggressively sought to better equip themselves in pediatric methods and demanded greater emphasis on pediatrics in their training programs (Deisher, 1958:579). Some pediatricians agreed that it made more sense to channel resources toward better training in pediatrics for general practitioners than to produce more pediatricians (Davison, 1952; Veeder, 1950; Wineberg, 1959). In 1948, after all, general practitioners cared for 75 percent of the total child population, in contrast to pediatricians who cared for only 11 percent (AAP, 1950).

The "New Pediatrics"

Anticipating the dilemma future pediatricians faced, Stafford (1936:378) warned that practicing pediatricians would disappear if they did not recognize "the volume of work before [them] that remained untouched." He urged pediatricians to look out for borderline problems: "shades of difference between health and disease, conditions whereby the child is not invalided, but his social and individual efficiency is decreased." Primary care pediatricians followed his advice. After 1950 they increasingly defined their specialty not in traditional terms of childhood illness, its treatment, and prevention, but in broader terms of the active promotion of child health in all its aspects. They stressed in particular the child's mental, emotional, and social development. Nelson (1955:112) claimed the goal of pediatrics was not only to prevent disease, but "to assist the child to become an adult able to compete at a level approaching his optimal capacity and to assume his share of responsibility within the community." Joseph Stokes, in his 1962 presidential address to the APS, argued that pediatrics was "deeply obliged to concern itself with the mental and social as well as the physical well-being of the child in his family setting." Pediatrics' new image must encourage "concern with social science, psychology, and psychiatry. Inescapably, it must include also the development of character" (Faber and McIntosh, 1966:285). Pediatricians were cast as child advocates who had a vital role to play in anything connected with the welfare of their young patients.

Using this broader definition of their mandate, pediatricians began to point to the "unmet needs" of the child as a potential source of satisfaction for practitioners. They referred not only to children with chronic handicaps, but also to those whose optimal functioning was impaired by school problems, juvenile delinquency, adoption, accidents, parental abuse, or neglect, and behavioral problems of all sorts. These problems were not always life-threatening, nor were they as spectacular as the infectious diseases of a previous era. But they did compromise the quality of a child's life. The proponents of this view pointed to disturbing social trends and surveys indicating that 12 out of every 100 individuals examined for the U.S. armed services during the Second World War were rejected because of mental deficiency (Talbot, 1963:910), that the rates of mental and emotional difficulties and juvenile delinquency among the population were high, and that the suicide rate was rising (Richmond, 1967:652). Many of these problems, the pediatricians argued, stemmed from the experiences of childhood; intervention was required during the formative years. Pediatricians were in a strategic position to influence the mental, emotional, and social development of children and had a "moral obligation" to do so (Washburn, 1951:304).

Such was the nature of medicine: the natural progression of a specialty from one set of conquered diseases to another, and a constant refocusing of medical attention (Fischer, 1957:594). Pediatricians waxed eloquent with colorful images of multi-headed hydra (Cole, 1959:642) and referred increasingly to the "new pediatrics," "comprehensive pediatrics," "restorative pediatrics," "social or community pediatrics," and "the new morbidity in pediatrics." They also urged pediatricians to pay more serious attention to the problems of adolescents (Gallagher, 1954; Garell, 1965; Levine, 1960; Smith, 1951; Wheatley, 1961) and to extend the age limit of their practices

beyond 16 and 18 years.[6] If pediatricians were willing to broaden their definition of pediatrics and accept a wider scope of practice, Levine (1960:653) argued, their task could be "far more challenging, exciting, and important than it ever was even in the heyday of curative pediatrics." More importantly, the "new pediatrics" was a way for pediatricians to distinguish themselves from general practitioners. Pediatricians contrasted their new, comprehensive approach with what they called the pill-peddling, mass production, and quick-turnover care delivered by general practitioners, and debated how best to educate the public to this distinction (Ambuel, 1959; Cutler, 1959; May, 1959:254).

Was the "new pediatrics" merely the hopeful rhetoric of a declining professional segment or were general pediatricians in fact widening their therapeutic scope? Practicing pediatricians at a Ross Pediatric Research Conference in 1956 estimated that 50 to 85 percent of their practices concerned preventive psychological or emotional care (Butler, 1956:432). Other studies noted that although psycho-social problems and counselling appeared infrequently as primary diagnoses, the amount of time pediatricians spent providing counselling traditionally given by relatives, friends, and clergy had increased markedly (Aldrich, 1960; Bergman *et al.,* 1966; Deisher *et al.,* 1960). A controlled, time-motion study of four Washington pediatricians corroborated the trends: emotional and behavioral difficulties accounted for an average of 5 percent of their time, but ranked fourth after preventive health supervision, respiratory infections, and accidents (Bergman *et al.,* 1966:257).

Adjusting Educational Programs

Pediatric training programs did not reflect the concerns of the "new pediatrics." Curricula continued to focus on the physical conditions that affected a comparatively small number of children and that were of interest primarily to subspecialists. These conditions included diseases of the newborn, leukemia, congenital heart disease, genetic defects, rheumatic and renal diseases, and metabolic and endocrine disorders. Pediatric academicians felt that the "new pediatrics" involved elements that were not strictly medical and feared that by forging directions away from physical disease, primary care pediatricians were damaging rather than elevating the status of pediatrics as a specialty. "Has the practicing pediatrician completely mined the medical aspects of his practice so that he must now turn to the paramedical?" asked Harned (1959:860). Another academician warned:

> The pediatrician, as a member of the medical profession, must not allow his ambitions to outstrip his abilities. [Pediatricians] must not delude themselves by supposing they can become a priestly class of counsellors on all things. Let those who choose to be primarily counsellors set themselves apart or enter the ranks of professions other than medicine (May, 1960:662).

Academicians were more concerned with maintaining pediatrics' legitimacy and respectability in the eyes of other branches of medicine than they were with deciding which medical group would deliver the bulk of child health services. They resisted pressure to adjust pediatric training programs, recommended that the number of pediatric residencies be severely curtailed, and advised pediatric researchers who were beginning to explore the behavioral and functional disorders of children to set limits on the types of "medical problems" they studied.

Educational programs in pediatrics, therefore, became a major target for those promoting an expanded role for the specialty. Pediatricians accused educators of being "unrealistic about life outside the Ivory Tower" (Senn, 1956:613), and of having too narrow a vision of what pediatrics had become. They scorned the academicians' condescending attitudes toward preventive care and the management of non-organic or psychosomatic problems (Cole, 1959). They criticized the pediatric curricula for being "no more designed to prepare the physician for pediatric practice than a life of ease would prepare a man for duty on the frontline trenches" (Ambuel, 1959:1008). And they called for greater emphasis on an understanding of common pediatric problems (Ambuel, 1959; Deisher, 1953, 1955; Eisenberg, 1967; Haggerty and Janeway, 1960; Hansen, 1954; Levine, 1960; Poncher and Richmond, 1950; Richmond, 1959). Many pediatri-

cians belived that if trainees received adequate preparation in these areas they would have more realistic expectations about practice and experience less frustration and boredom.

Through the late 1950s and 1960s, academicians responded to these criticisms by redesigning pediatric programs to incorporate courses on normal growth and development, and care of the non-hospitalized and healthy child. Many programs included practical experience in preventive care. Preceptorships, a scheme which placed trainees with pediatric practitioners in outpatient and private clinics, became common (Deisher, 1955; Green and Stark, 1957; Rose and Ross, 1960; Senn, 1956). Training programs also began to pay more attention to the psychosocial aspects of child development. During the 1960s, courses on behavior, taught mostly by psychiatrists, were introduced into pediatric curricula. With the introduction of a fellowship program in behavioral pediatrics at the University of Rochester in 1978, pediatrics began to generate its own instructors. The findings of the Task Force on Pediatric Education (1978), a committee of 17 societies responsible for pediatric education, research, and services in the United States, provided additional impetus. A survey conducted for the task force confirmed that bio-social and behavioral problems of children and adolescents constituted a substantial portion of pediatric practice, and found that 54 percent of recent graduates from pediatric residency programs were disatisfied with their training in these areas (Kempe, 1978:1150). The task force strongly recommended that training institutions pay more attention to bio-social and developmental aspects of pediatrics, including the wide range of behavioral disorders. By 1981 there were 20 programs in U.S. medical schools in behavioral pediatrics and several more with plans in the works (Hoekelman, 1981:xiv).

The Future

While the precise extent of pediatric involvement in the behavioral difficulties of children is unclear,[7] it is clear that pediatricians play a considerably larger role than they once did and that their role is increasing. In a survey conducted for the AAP in 1978, 59.6 percent of all pediatricians reported an increase in time spent on school problems and 38.1 percent reported an increase in general counselling (Burnett and Bell, 1978:647).

This increased involvement has been accompanied by much hand-wringing about the appropriate role for pediatricians (Bergman, 1974:533; Budetti, 1981:604; Cantwell, 1979:8; Charney, 1974:3; Haggerty *et al.*, 1975; Olmsted, 1979:11; Pless, 1974). The ambivalence is rooted in the paucity of objectively validated techniques for effective intervention (Rogers *et al.*, 1981). Most behavioral disorders are treated with counselling and behavioral management techniques whose efficacy in restoring optimal functioning cannot be precisely measured. Some experts admit that strategies of intervention have little to offer in the way of effective control, but reject this as a basis for abdication (Eisenberg, 1977:16).

The pressures for pediatricians to continue, indeed to extend, their involvement in the psycho-social problems of children are great. Birth and fertility rates are still comparatively low. The number of pediatricians continues to rise and the majority of these pediatricians are concentrated in general primary care practice (Budetti, 1981:598). The Graduate Medical Education National Advisory Committee predicts an over-supply of 7,500 primary care pediatricians in the United States by 1990 (U.S. Department of Health and Human Services, 1980). Pediatricians are concerned about the rising number, and assertiveness, of pediatric nurse associates, child health associates, pediatric nurse practitioners, and other groups of allied child health workers that emerged during the 1960s to assist in routine and preventive care. But as allied health professionals, these groups are subject to supervision and control by pediatricians.

Developments in family practice pose a more serious threat. Since the establishment of the American Board of Family Practice in 1969, the number of U.S. residency programs in family practice have increased from 15 in 1969 to 358 in 1977, and the number of residents from 0 in 1969, to 290 in 1970, and 6,033 in 1978 (Geyman, 1979:862). In 1976, for the first time since the 1920s, the number of doctors engaged

in general or family practice increased (Willard and Ruhe, 1978). Primary care pediatricians can no longer hope to survive by simply off-setting declining numbers of general practitioners. Despite claims that family practice graduates cannot match the quality of care provided by pediatricians (Olmsted, 1979:11; Van Gelder, 1977:8), family practitioners are perceived as viable contenders for the child health market. The National Commission on the Cost of Medical Care (1979) recommended an acceleration in the proportion of family practitioners as a less expensive way of providing primary medical services for children.

In 1981, the AAP established a Task Force on the Promotion of Pediatrics (AAP, 1981:3) and launched an on-going publicity campaign promoting pediatricians. A strong selling point now, and in the future, will be pediatricians' willingness to deal with a wider spectrum of child health needs. Pediatricians' unique interest in growth and development is their single distinguishing feature, and the most persuasive argument they can make in convincing parents that the health needs of their children are better served by pediatricians.

Discussion

Bucher and Strauss (1961) argued that professional segments have many characteristics of a social movement. Segments form around stated goals or purposes, develop, modify themselves in response to changes in their work situation, and disappear. Bucher's (1962) analysis of pathology demonstrated that threatened segments can survive if they hit upon a "revitalization formula," a means of incorporating new elements into the traditional mission of the segment. The history of pediatrics in the United States offers an example of the changes that professional segments are forced to make and the strategies they adopt to survive. Through the first half of the 20th century, pediatrics witnessed the virtual elimination of the medical problems that first gave rise to the specialty. For some pediatric segments this meant a refocusing of research and clinical interest towards the physical conditions that continued to compromise the life and health of children. These segments faced new medical problems, but their mission, the study and cure of childhood illness, remained the same.

The threat for primary care pediatricians was more serious. The original mission of the segment was exhausted. Children still got sick, of course, but they did so less often and in less life-threatening ways. Primary care pediatricians were over-qualified for preventive and routine child care and not qualified enough to treat the remaining serious illnesses of childhood. Parents might still be persuaded to take their children to pediatricians but primary care pediatricians lost the scientific rationale for their continued existence.

They survived by discovering a new mission or at least by retrospectively redefining the old mission in a way that allowed expansion into new areas of care. The mandate of pediatrics was extended beyond the treatment and prevention of childhood disease to include the positive promotion of child health in all its dimensions. This involved not only the physical well-being of children, but their mental, emotional, and social functioning as well. The rhetoric and manoeuverings of primary care pediatricians after 1950 resembled not the strategies of a threatened or declining segment, but those of an emerging segment or specialty. They proclaimed the mission of the "new pediatrics" and argued that the pediatrician was uniquely suitable to monitor the growth and development of children; they reshaped their institutions and educational programs to reflect the new mission; and they launched public campaigns to promote the new image of the primary care pediatrician as child counsellor and child advocate.

The redefinition of primary care pediatrics has extended pediatrics beyond the traditional limits of medicine. This has created problems for some pediatricians who feel uncomfortable with the new categories of illness, either because they may not conform to models of organic illness or because pediatricians have few effective strategies to control children's behavioral problems. It has also brought primary care pediatricians into conflict with other segments of the specialty. The academic and research segments were sympathetic as long as they were not implicated in the survival strategies of primary care pediatricians.

But they were among the first to predict the demise of the primary care pediatrician, and when primary care pediatricians began demanding that educational and research programs reflect pediatrics' new mission, academicians resisted. They feared that their own status in the scientific community would be compromised if pediatric programs were diluted with "paramedical" material. They have acknowledged begrudgingly the significance of the "new pediatrics" but, thus far, have made little more than token efforts to incorporate behavioral pediatrics into the pediatric curriculum.

The "new pediatrics," then, is still in an emerging state. It will be interesting to see how firm an institutional position it can secure and how much power and prestige it will eventually be able to garner within the specialty. The extent to which it succeeds will determine the fate of primary care pediatricians in the United States.

NOTES

This is a revised version of a paper presented at the 32nd annual meeting of the Society for the Study of Social Problems, in San Francisco, September 1982. The author thanks Malcolm Spector, John Gilmore, Joseph Schneider, Rue Bucher, Joan Stelling, Peter New, Ilze Kalnins, Ian Coulter, and the anonymous *Social Problems* reviewers for their comments.

1. Infant mortality refers to the mortality of liveborn children who have not yet reached their first birthday. Childhood mortality, unless otherwise specified, refers to the mortality of children between one and 14 years of age (Hogarth, 1976:199).
2. The experience of the developing nations of the world is radically different. The health problems of children continue to be striking and mortality rates remain high. An estimated 20 million children under the age of five die annually in developing countries; the corresponding figure for the developed world is half a million. More than 97 percent of all deaths in the world among children under the age of five years occur in the developing nations (Morley 1973:ix). Living conditions are poor and health services inadequate. Pediatricians in these nations generally treat children up to 12 years of age and face challenges very

different from those in the industrialized world (Achar, 1973; Ransome-Kuti, 1981:115).

3. An oversupply of pediatricians in Australia has pushed some pediatricians into the primary care field, where they have come into conflict with general practitioners and community nurses (Butler *et al.*, 1981:453). Canada represents a cross between the English model, where pediatrics is a consulting specialty, and the U.S. model, where it is mainly a primary care specialty. Those Canadian pediatricians who practice as primary care specialists in large, urban areas, where they compete with other primary care specialists and general practitioners, experience problems similar to those of their U.S. counterparts.

4. Around 1875, doctors first began referring to the study and treatment of diseases of children as *pediatry* or *pedology*. These terms were derived from the Greek word *pais, paidos* meaning child. Doctors who treated children were called *pediatrists*. These terms persisted until the early 20th century when they were replaced with *pediatrics* and *pediatrician,* probably to prevent confusion with the terms *podiatry* and *podiatrist* which refer to the study and treatment of diseases of the foot (Cone, 1979:70, 102; Funk and Wagnalls, 1974:624, 929, 974).

5. The French dominated pediatric research for the first half of the 19th century. But after 1850, Germany took the lead in establishing scientific teaching and investigation of the medical problems of children. The Germans were the first to develop a laboratory approach to pediatrics and formulated the first exact classification of children's diseases. The Pediatric Clinic and Polyclinic at the Charité in Berlin under the directorship of Eduard Henoch, between 1872 and 1893, attracted a steady stream of foreign students, many of whom were from the United States. After 1925, the United States assumed the leadership in pediatric research (Cone, 1979:101, 196).

6. Eighteen years was the age limit adopted as official policy by the AAP in 1938 (AAP, 1938a, b). In 1969, the AAP's Council of Pediatric Practice requested that the policy be updated to reflect practice patterns. In 1972, the AAP extended the limit to 21 years of age (AAP, 1972).

7. Estimates of the proportion of pediatric visits for behavioral problems run from five to 40 percent. Starfield *et al.* (1980:16*.*) account for the variability in terms of differences in diagnostic nomenclature, population characteristics, reimbursement schemes for providing such services, and physician propensity to recognize psycho-social problems.

REFERENCES

Achar, S. T.
1973   Pediatrics in Developing Tropical Countries. Bombay: Orient Longman.

Ackerknecht, Erwin H.
1982   A Short History of Medicine. Baltimore: John Hopkins Press.

Aldrich, C. A.
1934   "The composition of private pediatric practice." American Journal of Diseases of Children 47(5): 1051–1064.

Aldrich, R.
1960   "Discussion." Pp. 75–76 in R. H. Spitz (ed.), Careers in Pediatrics. Ross Conference on Pediatric Research. Columbus, Ohio: Ross Laboratories.

Ambuel, J. Philip
1959   "Letter to the editor." Pediatrics 23(5): 1008–1010.

American Academy of Pediatrics
1938a   "Proceedings." Journal of Pediatrics 3(1): 127.
1938b   "Proceedings." Journal of Pediatrics 3(2): 266–267.
1950   "Child health services and pediatric education: Report of the Committee for the Study of Child Health Services." Pediatrics 6(3): 509–556.
1972   "Age limits of pediatrics." Pediatrics 49(3): 463.
1981   News and Comments 32(12):3.

American Medical Association
1964-   Directory of Approved Internships and
1969   Residencies. Chicago: American Medical Association.

American Pediatric Society
1938   Semi-Centennial Volume of the American Pediatric Society, 1888–1938. Menasha, Wisconsin: Privately published.

Apple, Rima D.
1980   "To be used only under the direction of a physician: Commercial infant feeding and medical practice, 1870–1940." Bulletin of the History of Medicine 54(3):402–417.

Bergman, A. B.
1974   "Pediatric turf." Pediatrics 54(5):533–534.

Bergman, A. B., S. W. Dassel, and R. J. Wedgwood
1966   "Time-motion study of practicing pediatricians." Pediatrics 38(2):254–263.

Bettman, O. L.
1974   The Good Old Days: They Were Terrible. New York: Random House.

Boulware, J. R.
1958   "The composition of private pediatric practice in a small community in the south of the United States: A 25-year survey." Pediatrics 22(3):548–558.

Bremner, R. H. (ed.)
1971   Childhood and Youth in America: A Documentary History. Volume 2, 1866–1932. Cambridge, Massachusetts: Harvard University Press.

Bucher, Rue
1962   "Pathology: A study of social movements within a profession." Social Problems 10(Fall):40–51.

Bucher, Rue, and Anselm Strauss
1961   "Professions in process." American Journal of Sociology 66:325–334.

Budetti, Peter P.
1981   "The impending pediatric 'surplus': Causes, implications, and alternatives." Pediatrics 67(5):597–606.

Burnett, R. D., and L. S. Bell
1978   "Projecting pediatric patterns: A survey of the American Academy of Pediatrics, Committee on Manpower." Pediatrics 62(4): 627–680.

Butler, Allan
1956   "Quo vadis pediatrics." A.M.A. Journal of Diseases of Children 92:431–437.

Butler, D. L., N. Buchanan, and S. Clarke
1981   "Whither pediatrics." Medical Journal of Australia 1:452–453.

Cantwell, Ronald J.
1979   "Letters." American Academy of Pediatrics, News and Comments 30(8):8.

Charney, Evan
1974   "Forward." Pediatric Clinics of North America 21(1):3–4.

Coddington, R. Dean
1959   "Letter to the editor." Pediatrics 23(5): 1008–1009.

Cole, W. C. C.
1959   "Pediatrics in the space age." Journal of the American Medical Association 171(6):641–643.

Cone, Thomas E.
1979   History of American Pediatrics. Boston: Little, Brown and Company.

Coulter, H. L.
1969   Political and Social Aspects of 19th Century Medicine in the United States. Unpublished Ph.D. dissertation, Columbia University.

Culter, Charles H.
1959   "Letter to the editor." Pediatrics 23(5): 1005–1007.

Davison, W. C.
1952   "The pediatric shift." Journal of Pediatrics 40(4):536–538.

Deisher, Robert W.
1953   "Use of the child health conference in the training of medical students." Pediatrics 11(5):538–543.
1955   "Pediatric residency program." Pediatrics 16(4):541–543.
1958   "Survey of G.P.'s opinions on pediatric education." Journal of Medical Education 33(8):579–584.

Deisher, Robert W., Alfred J. Derby, and Melvin J. Sturman
1960   "Changing trends in pediatric practice." Pediatrics 25(4):711–716.

Eisenberg. L.
1967   "The relationship between psychiatry and pediatrics: A disputatious view." Pediatrics 39(5):645–647
1977   "Controversial issues in health care for children." Pp. 3–21 in Harvard Child Health Project, Task Force on Children's Medical Care, Needs and Treatment. Volume 2. Cambridge, Massachusetts: Ballinger Publishing Co.

Evans, Philip R.
1967   "Fashions in infant feeding." Pp. 307–317 in J. A. Askin, R. E. Cooke, and J. A. Haller Jr. (eds.), A Symposium on the Child. Baltimore: Johns Hopkins Press.

Faber, H. K., and R. McIntosh
1966   History of the American Pediatric Society. New York: McGraw-Hill.

Fischer, C. C.
1957   "The pediatrician and his changing world." Journal of Pediatrics 51(5):593–605.

Funk and Wagnalls
1974   Standard Dictionary of the English Language, International Edition, Volumes 1 and 2. New York: Funk and Wagnalls.

Gabel, Stewart
1981   Behavioral Problems in Childhood: A Primary Care Approach. New York: Grune and Stratton.

Gallagher, J. R.
1954   "Adolescent Unit of Children's Hospital Medical Center." Children 1:165–170.

Garell, D. G.
1965   "Adolescent medicine." American Journal of Diseases of Children 109:314–317.

Geyman, John P.
1979   "Graduate education in family practice: A ten-year view." Journal of Family Practice 9(5):859–871.

Gittings, John C.
1928 "Pediatrics of one hundred years ago." American Journal of Diseases of Children 36:1–15.
Green, Morris, and Mary Stark
1957 "A post-graduate program for the longitudinal health supervision of infants." Pediatrics 19(2):499–503.
Haggerty, R. J., and C. A. Janeway
1960 "Evaluation of a pediatric house officer program." Pediatrics 26(5):858–861.
Haggerty, R. J., K. J. Roghmann, and I. B. Pless (eds.)
1975 Child Health and the Community. New York: John Wiley and Sons.
Hansen, Arild E.
1954 "Pediatricians' reactions regarding residency training." Pediatrics 14(1):82–84.
Harned, H. S.
1959 "A challenge to practitioners." Pediatrics 24(5):859–862.
Hoekelman, Robert A.
1981 "Forward." Pp. xiii–xv in Stewart Gabel, Behavioral Problems in Childhood. New York: Grune and Stratton.
Hogarth, James
1976 Glossary of Health Care Terminology. Copenhagen: World Health Organization.
Holt, L. Emmett Jr.
1961 "Pediatrics at the delta." American Journal of Diseases of Children 102(5):671–676.
Hudson, P.
1963 "Letter to the editor." Pediatrics 31(1): 161–162.
Jacobi, Abraham
1911 "Introduction." American Journal of Diseases of Children 1(1):1–5.
Jeans, Philip C.
1950 "Application of nutrition research to everyday practice." American Journal of Diseases of Children 80(3):363–369.
Journal of the American Medical Association
1949 "Approved internships and residencies in the United States." 140(2):157–160.
Kempe, C. H.
1978 "The future of pediatric education." Pediatric Research 12:1149–1151.
Lawson, Robert B.
1960 "Historical perspectives of pediatrics in the United States." Pp. 14–16 in R. H. Spitz (ed.), Careers in Pediatrics, Ross Conference on Pediatric Research. Columbus, Ohio: Ross Laboratories.
Levine, S. Z.
1960 "Pediatric education at the crossroads." American Journal of Diseases of Children 100:651–656.

London, Arthur H.
1937 "The composition of an average pediatric practice." Journal of Pediatrics 10(6):762–771.
May, Charles D.
1959 "Can the new pediatrics be practiced?" Pediatrics 23(2):253–254.
1960 "The future of pediatricians as medical specialists." A.M.A. Journal of Diseases of Children 100:661–668.
Medical Economics
1956 "Medicine's most frustrating specialty." 33 (November):68–74.
1961 "How the specialties compare financially." 38 (March):88–93.
Morley, David
1973 Pediatric Priorities in the Developing World. London: Butterworths.
Morse, J. L.
1935 "Recollections and reflections of forty-five years of artificial feeding." Journal of Pediatrics 7(3):303–324.
1937 "The future of pediatrics." Journal of Pediatrics 10(4):529–532.
National Commission on the Cost of Medical Care
1978 Report. Monroe, Wisconsin: American Medical Association.
Nelson, W. E.
1955 "Trends in pediatrics." Journal of Pediatrics 47(1):109–123.
Olmsted, Richard W.
1979 "A perspective: Pediatrics today and tomorrow." American Academy of Pediatrics, News and Comments 30(8):9–11.
Parish, H. J.
1965 A History of Immunization. Edinburgh: E. and S. Livingstone Ltd.
Pease, M. C.
1952 The American Academy of Pediatrics: June 1930 to June 1951. New York: Privately published.
Pless, I. B.
1974 "The changing face of primary pediatrics." Pediatric Clinics of North America 21(1): 223–244.
Poncher, Henry G., and Julius B. Richmond
1950 "Some midcentury reflections on pediatric education." Pediatrics 5(5):893–898.
Powers, Grover F.
1939 "Developments in pediatrics in the past quarter century." Yale Journal of Biology and Medicine 12(1):1–12.
Ransome-Kuti, O.
1981 "Health services research in developing

countries." Pp. 115–123 in Norman Krechmer and Jo Anne Brasel, Biomedical and Social Bases of Pediatrics. New York: Masson Publishing.

Richmond, Julius B.
1959   "Some observations on the sociology of pediatric education and practice." Pediatrics 23(6):1175–1178.
1967   "Child development: A basic science for pediatrics." Pediatrics 39(5):649–658.

Rogers, David E., Robert J. Blendon, and Ruby P. Hearn
1981   "Some observations on pediatrics: Its past, present, and future." Pediatrics 67(5):776–784.

Rose, J. A., and D. C. Ross
1960   "Comprehensive pediatrics: Postgraduate training for practicing physicians." Pediatrics 25(1):135–144.

Rosen, George
1958   A History of Public Health. New York: MD Publications.

Rothman, Sheila M.
1978   Women's Proper Place: A History of Changing Ideals and Practices, 1870 to the Present. New York: Basic Books.

Schultz, F. W.
1933   "First half century of the Section on Pediatrics." Journal of the American Medical Association 101(6):417–420.

Senn, M. J. E.
1956   "An orientation for instruction in pediatrics." Journal of Medical Education 31(9):613–619.

Shapiro, Sam, Edward R. Schlesinger, and R. E. L. Nesbitt Jr.
1968   Infant, Perinatal, Maternal, and Childhood Mortality in the United States. Cambridge, Massachusetts: Harvard University Press.

Smillie, W. G.
1952   "The periods of great epidemics in the United States." Pp. 52–73 in F. H. Top, The History of American Epidemiology. St. Louis: Mosby.
1955   Public Health, Its Promise for the Future. New York: Macmillan.

Smith, Richard M.
1951   "Medicine as a Science: Pediatrics." New England Journal of Medicine 244:176–181.

Stafford, Henry E.
1936   "The changing pediatric practice." Journal of Pediatrics 8(3):375–380.

Starfield, Barbara, Edward Gross, Maurice Wood, Robert Pantell, Constance Allen, I. Bruce Gordon, Patricia Moffat, Robert Drachman, and Harvey Katz
1980   "Psychosocial and psychosomatic diagnoses in primary care of children." Pediatrics 66(2):159–167.

Stevens, Rosemary
1971   American Medicine and the Public Interest. New Haven, Connecticut: Yale University Press.

Tabrah, Frank L.
1957   "Letter to the editor." Journal of Pediatrics 51(6):745–747.

Talbot, N.
1963   "Has psychologic malnutrition taken the place of rickets and scurvey in contemporary pediatric practice?" Pediatrics 31(6):909–918.

Task Force on Pediatric Education
1978   The Future of Pediatric Education. Denver, Colorado: Hirschfeld Press.

U.S. Bureau of the Census
1975   Historical Statistics of the United States: Colonial Times to 1970, Bicentennial Edition, Part 1. Washington, D.C.: U.S. Government Printing Office.

U.S. Department of Health and Human Services
1980   Report of the Graduate Medical Education National Advisory Committee to the Secretary, Volume 1. Washington, D.C.: U.S. Government Printing Office.

Van Gelder, David W.
1977   "Primary care: Pediatrician or family physician." American Academy of Pediatrics, News and Comments 28(5):8.

Vaughn, Victor C., R. James McKay, and Richard E. Behrman (eds.)
1979   Nelson Textbook of Pediatrics. Philadelphia: W. B. Saunders Co.

Veeder, Borden
1935   "Trends of pediatric education and practice." American Journal of Diseases of Children 50(1):1–10.
1950   "Letter to the editor." Pediatrics 5(4):739–741.

Wain, Harry
1970   A History of Preventive Medicine. Springfield, Illinois: Charles C. Thomas.

Washburn, Alfred H.
1951   "Pediatric potpourri." Pediatrics 8(2):299–306.

Wheatley, George M.
1961   "Adolescents." Pediatrics 27(1):159–160.

Wilcox, Herbert B.
1940   "The pediatrician in the councils of the

nation." American Journal of Diseases of Children 60(1):1–10.

Willard, W. A., and C. H. W. Ruhe
1978 "The challenge of family practice reconsidered." Journal of the American Medical Association 240(5):454–458.

Wineberg, Julius J.
1959 "Letter to the editor." Pediatrics 23(5): 1007–1008.

Winslow, C. E. A.
1923 The Evolution and Significance of the Modern Public Health Campaign. New York: Yale University Press.

Zietz, Dorothy
1969 Child Welfare: Service and Perspectives. New York: John Wiley and Sons Inc.

The Social Organization of Medical Care Workers and Services

Medical care in the United States is an enormous and complex industry, involving thousands of organizations, the expenditure of billions of dollars each year, and the employment of millions of workers. There are discernible patterns in the types and distribution of medical services available in any society. These patterns reflect and reinforce the socio-cultural context in which they are found, including the political, economic, and cultural priorities of a society (Waitzkin and Waterman, 1974: 8). The composition of the labor force in most sectors of society reflects that society's distribution of power and privilege. This section examines (1) the organization and distribution of medical care services; and (2) the nature of the medical care labor force in this country.

(1) Our medical care system has been described as ". . . acute, curative, [and] hospital-based . . ." (Knowles, 1977: 2). That is, we have a *medical* care system (as distinguished from a *health* care system)[1] organized around the cure and/or control of serious diseases and the repairing of physical injuries rather than the "caring" for the sick or prevention of disease. The American medical care system is highly technological, specialized and, increasingly, centralized. More and more medical care is delivered in large bureaucratic institutions, many of them hospitals. And these organizations now employ more than 75 percent of all medical care workers (DHHS, 1983: 242). Our medical care system is becoming increasingly hospital-centered.

From 1900 to 1975 there was a gradual increase in the number of hospitals in the United States, reaching a total of over 6300. In the past decade there has been a slight decline in the number of hospitals although the number of hospital beds has increased slightly (DHHS, 1983:248). The trend seems to be toward fewer yet larger hospitals, which threatens the existence of some community hospitals. Approximately 50 percent of all hospitals in 1981 were owned by nonprofit organizations, with another 33 percent owned either by federal, state, or local governments. The remaining 14 percent were owned by profit-making organizations; in addition, 81 percent of all nursing homes at that time were profit-making institutions (National Center for Health Statistics, 1983). The number of for-profit hospitals, especially in the form of hospital chains, has increased dramatically in the past decade (see article by Relman in this volume).

The first article in this section, "Health Care and Medical Care in the United States," by Victor W. Sidel and Ruth Sidel addresses the issue of how and why medical care services are organized and distributed the way they are in the United States. The authors find a serious maldistribution of medical services, coupled with a set of economic and political priorities that has produced a medical care system unresponsive to the health needs of many of its citizens. Why this should be so in a country that invests so much money in medical care—more than any other country in the world—remains a central question in their article and throughout this book.

(2) The growth and expansion of medical care institutions has engendered a rapid expansion of the medical labor force. The number of people employed between 1970 and 1982 in the medical care industry in the United States expanded 86 percent—from 4.2 million to 7.8 million. Medical care workers constitute about 7 percent of the total American labor force. Approximately 55 percent of all medical care workers are employed by hospitals, 15 percent by convalescent institutions (nursing homes), 11 percent in doctors' offices, 5 percent in dentists' offices, and the remainder in offices of other health practitioners and at other medical service sites. Some of these workers are physicians, but the vast majority are not. In fact, physicians make up 6 *percent* of the entire medical labor force (DHHS, 1983:242–243).

Approximately half of the total medical labor force provides nursing-related services. Only about 4 percent of the hospital workforce are physicians. As Caress (1976: 178) notes, "There are about the same number of physicians as there are maintenance men in American hospitals." Among hospital workers there is an enormous range in the level of education and skill required to carry out their jobs.

> Of all hospital employees 43.5 percent are either RN's [registered nurses] (16.2 percent), LPN's [licensed practical nurses] and LVN's [licensed vocational nurses] (7.4 percent) or aides, orderlies and attendants (19.9 percent). The remainder of hospital workers are in clinical technology (3.2 percent), pharmacy (0.8 percent), administration (0.6 percent), dentistry (0.6 percent) and even smaller representations in other categories. (Caress, 1976: 178.)

Medical care workers include some of the highest paid employees in our nation (physicians) and some of the lowest paid (until the early 1970s many hospital workers were not even covered by minimum wage laws). More than 75 percent of all medical workers are women, although more than 85 percent of all physicians are men. Many of these women are members of Third World and minority groups, and most come from working-class and lower-middle class backgrounds. Almost all physicians are white and upper middle class. In short, the structure of the medical workforce reflects the inequalities of American society in general.

This medical care workforce structure can be pictured as a broad-based triangle, with a small number of highly paid physicians and administrators at the very top. These men (and they are mostly men) by and large control the administration of medical care services *within* institutions. As one moves toward the bottom of the triangle, there are increasing numbers of significantly lower-paid female workers with little or no authority in the medical delivery organization. This triangle is layered with a growing number of licensed occupational categories of workers, a number currently close to 300 different medical occupations (Caress, 1976: 168). There is practically no movement of workers from one category to another, since each requires its own specialized training and qualifications, requirements which are largely controlled through licensing procedures authorized by the American Medical Association's Committee on Education. Professional dominance, as discussed in the previous section, is highly evident throughout the division and organization of medical labor.

The development of this rigidly layered or *stratified* medical labor force is the result of a complex historical process, deeply connected to the development of the hospital as a central site of American medical care delivery. Susan Reverby explores this connection in the second article in this section, "Reforming the Hospital Nurse: The Management of American Nursing." She traces the relationship of the development of the division of labor within nursing, the efforts of nursing to gain professional power, and the changing organizational needs of the hospital administrators.

In the final article, "The Health Labor Force: The Effects of Change," Nancy Aries and Louanne Kennedy examine factors shaping the health labor force. The number of workers employed in the health field has increased dramatically in the past three decades, making the medical care industry one of America's largest employers. We can see how the organization of medicine, especially professional dominance, and the growth of technology have affected the growth of "manpower" in the health field. This is especially evident in the proliferation of jobs at lower wage levels (including a wide variety of medically oriented "assistants," "technicians," and "technologists"). The composition of the health labor force reflects the inequities of American society: white males are overwhelmingly in the highest and most powerful positions; women and minorities predominate the lower ones. Aries and Kennedy propose there are two strategies for increasing power and autonomy for health workers: professionalization or unionization. It is not yet clear which route, if any, most workers will choose and which will be most successful in changing the status of workers in the health field.

NOTE

1. The distinction between "medical" and "health" care is one made by Sidel and Sidel in their article in this section.

REFERENCES

Caress, Barbara. 1976. "The health workforce: Bigger pie, smaller pieces." Pp. 163–170 in David Kotelchuck, Prognosis Negative. New York: Vintage Books. [Reprinted from Health/PAC Bulletin, January/February, 1975.]

Department of Health and Human Services. 1983. Health, United States 1983. DHHS Publication No. (PHS) 84-1232. Washington D.C.; U.S. Government Printing Office.

Knowles, John. 1977. "Introduction." John Knowles (ed.), Doing Better and Feeling Worse: Health in the United States. Daedalus. 106, 1: Winter.

National Center for Health Statistics, 1983. Vital and Health Statistics: Nursing and
  Related Care Homes. DHHS Publication No. (PHS) 84-1824. Washington D.C.:
  U.S. Government Printing Office.
Waitzkin, Howard, and Barbara Waterman, 1974. The Exploitation of Illness in
  Capitalist Society. Indianapolis: The Bobbs-Merrill Co., Inc.

15

Health Care and Medical Care in the United States

Victor W. Sidel and Ruth Sidel

. . . .

Although in one sense the U.S. medical care system is highly structured—for the benefit of those who control it and of some of those who work in it—in another sense it is so fragmented, the responsibilities so diffuse, the levels of control so manifold, the communication and coordination between its parts so haphazard, that—except for the euphemisms "pluralistic" and "pragmatic"—the system almost defies brief description.

One type of analysis, analogous in some ways to the classifications of levels of prevention, is the definition of various levels of care as "primary," "secondary" and "tertiary" according to the severity of the illness and the nature of the medical response that is required.

At the first level, the patient with relatively minor symptoms or who is worried about his health may seek reassurance or care in a number of different ways. Self-care, often with medications available without prescription ("over the counter"), is the most frequent response to common symptoms or anxiety which an individual feels on a given day. Such an individual may turn to members of his family for advice and care, or to nonprofessional people within his community. Teachers or fellow workers are often consulted on various types of health problems. In some cultures spiritualists, herbalists or other well-defined individuals within the culture are consulted at times of minor illness, or even illness of greater severity.

The first contact with the professional medical system is often with a professional other than a physician. Pharmacists, for example, play an important role in first-contact professional care. If a physician is to be consulted as the point of first-contact professional care, the choice of the type of physician to be contacted is quite different from country to country. In most countries the physician of first contact will be a "primary-care physician," which, as we define the term, signifies a physician based in the community rather than in a hospital; a physician people first turn to, who does not regularly see referrals from other physicians; who provides continuing care rather than episodic care; and who serves the function of integrating the work of referral specialists and other community resources in relation to the patient's care.

In this sequence, "secondary care" is that which is provided by specialists, either on an ambulatory basis or in the hospital, and "tertiary care" is that which is provided in specialized hospitals by highly specialized or subspecialized personnel. In the United States, however, first-contact primary care is often provided by specialists, by emergency rooms and by hospital outpatient departments—resources which in other societies are largely reserved for secondary or even tertiary care.

Beyond these three levels of medical care is that of long-term care for the chronically ill or disabled. In the United States, long-term care is often provided in chronic hospitals or in nursing homes for those whose illnesses are so severe that function outside of an institution is impossible or, in an increasing number of instances, for those who have no alternative place with either family or friends in which they can be given the care they need while continuing to function within the society.

Another framework for analysis is based on the nature of the controlling institution. These institutions are usually divided into three basic groups, one conventionally defined as "public" (meaning governmental) and two defined as "private," although the distinctions increasingly have less and less meaning.

Let us begin with the elements of the system in the "public" sector. All levels of government play a role in health care and in medical care, with a complex mix of direct operating responsibility for some elements, funding for others, and regulation for yet others. The federal government directly *operates* medical-care delivery programs for military personnel and their families, for veterans and for native Americans on reservations. It *finances* medical care for the aged and for a limited group of other disabled people through Medicare and indirectly pays a major part of the cost of medical care for the poor through Medicaid; it is the major funding agency for the construction of medical facilities and for medical research; and it provides a large part of the funding for medical education directly to medical schools and indirectly through scholarships and loan funds for medical students. Finally, the federal government has important *regulatory* authority over health and medical affairs involving "interstate commerce," such as food and drugs, occupational health and safety,

and environmental pollution. Overall, federal money accounts for nearly 30 percent of all U.S. health expenditures. These include about 25 percent of all funds spent on personal health and medical-care services, 65 percent of the investment in biomedical research and development, and over 45 percent of the revenues of the nation's medical schools.

State governments provide medical care directly for many of the mentally ill and, until recently, those with tuberculosis; they administer and contribute to the financing of health care for the poor through Medicaid; they conduct state-wide public health programs; they operate medical schools, usually through a state university, and contribute to the financing of others; and they license hospitals and a wide range of health workers.

Local governments, at the county and municipal levels, often provide inpatient and ambulatory-care services directly for the poor. They also carry out a wide variety of public health functions, including the collecting of vital statistics and statistics on reportable illnesses; controlling communicable diseases, including tuberculosis and venereal diseases; monitoring environmental sanitation, including water quality and supervision of foods and eating places; providing maternal and child health services, including school health services; and conducting programs of health education.

In short, almost all "public health services" in the United States and many personal medical-care services are directly provided by government agencies, and many other personal medical-care services are financed by government.

The two parts of the "private" sector are defined as "profit-making" (sometimes called, for historical reasons, "proprietary" or, for public-relations reasons, "investor-owned") and "nonprofit-making" (sometimes termed "voluntary" or "eleemosynary").

Examples of parts of the system almost entirely in the profit-making sector are nursing homes; pharmaceutical research, manufacture, distribution and sale; and commercial health-insurance companies. For the United States as a whole, most ambulatory medical and dental care is in the profit-making part of the private sector, although the situation is different in the centers of some of our largest cities where many of these services are provided by government or by voluntary hospitals. Only a small fraction of U.S. hospital beds lie in profit-making hospitals, many of which are owned by groups of physicians.

The "nonprofit" sector includes the voluntary hospitals, which contain over 60 percent of the country's acute-general-care beds; many of the nation's medical schools, including some of its most prestigious ones; and insurance organizations in each state affiliated with each other under the name of Blue Cross and Blue Shield, providing insurance respectively for hospitalization costs and for doctors' fees.

In sum, a large part of the U.S. medical-care system—as contrasted with its health-care system—is controlled by the private sector, even though, as we have seen, large amounts of it are financed publicly. Furthermore, the fact that medical care is largely controlled by the private sector and that health care is largely controlled by the public sector is surely one of the major reasons for the overwhelmingly greater investment in treatment rather than in prevention. This is especially true for ambulatory care. Of the 1.1 billion patient visits made annually in the United States (an average of five visits per person per year), two-thirds are made to private medical practitioners and private group practices, almost all on a fee-for-service basis. Another 18 percent of the visits nationwide—though a far higher percent in the inner cities—are made to hospital outpatient departments and emergency rooms, many of them also in the "private" (albeit "nonprofit") sector.

The situation shifts markedly when one looks at inpatient hospital care. Mainly because of the large number of long-stay beds in mental hospitals owned by state and local governments, and to a lesser extent the number of beds in the federal government's Veterans Administration, Armed Services, and Public Health Service hospitals, approximately half the U.S. hospital beds are in government-owned and -operated hospitals. Only 5 percent of the beds are in proprietary hospitals, owned and operated for profit. The remaining 45 percent are in voluntary hospitals, operated on a nonprofit basis by churches, other organized groups, or by self-elected and self-perpetuated boards of trustees.

It is of interest that since 1946 the ratio of hospital beds of all kinds to population has decreased, from one bed for every 100 people to one for every 130 people. The decrease has occurred largely in federal hospitals and in psychiatric, tuberculosis and other long-term hospitals. At the same time, however, there has been an increase in the bed/population ratio for short-term general hospitals. There are now approximately 4.5 short-term general medical and surgical beds per 1000 population (one for every 225 people); of these, in contrast to the situation for long-stay beds, only about one-third are operated by government. There has also been a trend over this period to larger hospitals, with a reduction in the number of hospitals having less than 100 beds. Despite the fact that hospitals have increased in size in the name of efficiency and despite the net movement of people from rural areas to metropolitan areas where hospitals are larger, the level of bed occupancy has changed almost not at all from 1946 (75 percent) to 1975 (76 percent).

The training and practice of the health workers in the system are also fragmented and there is little accountability to the public. Patterns for education of physicians are largely set by nongovernmental bodies, such as the Association of American Medical Colleges, and by the medical schools themselves. Although there is an increasing attempt at coordination of criteria for licensure and the use of a standardized national examination, licensure standards are set on a state-by-state basis, almost in every case by physician-dominated boards with little public accountability. Except for the internal standards set by hospitals and other medical institutions, which vary widely and are often unenforced, any physician, whatever his or her training, can legally do anything in medical practice: perform neurosurgery, counsel people with marital problems or read X rays. For physicians who practice largely outside institutions, fear of malpractice suits is almost the only deterrent—other than conscience—to undertaking procedures in which they have had only minimal training or experience.

Of the approximately 375,000 active physicians in the United States (one for every 550 people), almost 8 percent are employed by the federal government and approximately 20 per-

Figure 1. *Distribution of Physicians by Specialization Status in the United States, 1949–1972*

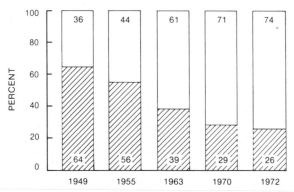

☐ FULL-TIME SPECIALISTS

▨ "GENERAL PRACTITIONERS" AND "PART-TIME SPECIALISTS"

SOURCE: Modified by the authors from a figure prepared by the University of Michigan School of Public Health from data published by the U.S. Public Health Service (before 1970) and the National Center for Health Statistics (1970 and 1972). The data include only M.D.s in private practice.

cent are in salaried hospital practice; some of the former and most of the latter are in training programs, usually as interns and residents. Approximately another 10 percent are employed in teaching, administration, research and other activities not directly related to patient care. The remaining 60 percent of active doctors are employed in "office-based" patient care, most of them practicing on a fee-for-service basis.

Physicians are largely free to choose their own form of postgraduate training and their own form of practice. As a result over the past quarter-century there has been a major shift away from primary care—first-contact, continuing integrated care for the patient—and a major shift toward specialist practice, as shown in Figure 1. Even if one includes doctors who say they "limit their practice" to internal medicine and pediatrics, the supply of primary-care doctors in the United States has fallen sharply from 1930, when there was approximately one for every 1000 people, to 1970, when there was one for every 2000.

There has been somewhat of a reversal in the 1970s, due in part to the efforts of the federal

and state governments, but the number of specialist physicians still far exceeds the number of primary-care physicians. In fact, the United States probably exceeds all other countries in the world in the extent to which medical care is given by physicians who consider themselves specialists rather than generalists or even, as is the increasing trend in the United States, as "specialists" in "family practice."

The result, of course, of this specialization and of the benefit coverage of most health-insurance policies, which cover hospital care but rarely ambulatory care and even more rarely continuing and preventive care, is a medical-care system devoted largely to technological diagnosis and treatment for serious acute illness and relatively little to care for less serious acute illness and to care for chronic illness and disability.

Similar kinds of analyses can be applied to nurses and other health workers. Among the major differences is that most nurses, for example, are salaried rather than fee-for-service entrepreneurs, that a far higher percentage of them are women, and that their incomes are far lower than those of doctors. But there are also vast similarities: a fragmentation of training patterns with little public control, an increasing emphasis in training (the "university-trained" nurse) and in practice (the "nurse-clinician") on technology rather than care, and gross geographic and social maldistribution.

The gross maldistribution of health workers in the United States can be seen by a regional, a state-by-state, or a community-by-community analysis. In 1973 there was, for example, one doctor for every 1343 people in South Dakota, compared to one for every 432 people in New York . . . The differences among states are not simply a result of differences in population density; Vermont and Iowa, for example, have approximately the same population density, but there is one physician for every 565 people in Vermont compared to one for every 999 in Iowa. The wealth of the state, and its desirability to physicians as a place to live and work, appear to be the major attractions.

The same is true for other types of health workers. There is one registered nurse, for example, for every 400 to 500 persons in the South Central states while in the New England states there is one nurse for every 150 to 200 people; an average person in the South, in other words, has available less than half the number of nurses than does his counterpart in the Northeast.

Not only is there gross maldistribution among regions and among states, but there is similar maldistribution within states and within cities. In a study performed in the Appalachian states in 1967, the ratio of physicians to population in counties with a median disposable income of more than $5000 per family was, with the exception of one state, consistently higher than the ratio in counties with an income of $5000 or less per family . . . In Maryland, Tennessee and Alabama, for example, there were almost three times as many doctors per capita in the rich counties as in the poor counties, and in Virginia, West Virginia and North Carolina, there were about twice as many per capita for the wealthy counties as for the poor.

Individual small, relatively isolated communities often have severe difficulty in recruiting or in keeping a physician. The National Health Service Corps estimated in 1976 that there were 748 U.S. communities that lacked a physician. These doctorless communities were located in 46 states; every one of the United States, with the exception of Hawaii, Massachusetts, New Jersey and Rhode Island, had at least one town needing a doctor.

Inside the large cities the maldistribution of physicians is equally severe, but it is harder to demonstrate statistically because many of the teaching hospitals, with their large numbers of doctors, are located in the midst of what have become the poorest urban areas. However, because they limit their practice to specialties or subspecialties or because they are in training for these specialties, most of these hospital-based doctors are unavailable to meet the general medical-care needs of the poor who surround them. A study performed in Boston, for example, showed that the number of general-care physicians per capita was twice as high in affluent areas studied as in poor ones.

Even when general-care doctors are available— often grudgingly—in outpatient departments and in the emergency rooms of the hospitals (and, because of the inaccessibility of general medical care elsewhere, the emergency room is becoming the place in which much primary medical care is currently being given), there are great barriers to access by the poor. Members of the New York City Department of Health in the mid-1960s described some of the remaining barriers, even when those imposed by cost of care are removed, which keep poor people from equitable access to medical care. These include inadequate transportation, complex and imposing institutions, difficulty in taking time off from work or in finding someone to take care of the children, and the fragmentation and repeated visits common in such care.

Medicaid, which was intended to ameliorate some of the inequity of access, has indeed brought physicians into the urban ghetto, but the nature of the financial incentives which brought them in have led to other forms of abuse. One is the promotion of brief and unnecessarily frequent visits, with the "ping-ponging" of patients from one physician to another, often in a shared facility known as a "Medicaid mill." This is done so that each physician may charge a separate fee for the partial service rendered. For the same reason—receipt of extra fees—the number of lab tests and number of prescriptions seem far in excess of the number needed. There are exceptions, of course, both among some principled and therefore in fact self-sacrificing individual doctors operating in fee-for-service practice and in those few instances where Medicaid has been used to support forms of practice different from fee-for-service care.

Paradoxically, programs like Medicaid themselves produce limited access to care, due to their reimbursement levels and their bureaucratic structure. Patients in New York State are required to reregister for Medicaid monthly, no matter how sick or how poor they are. Delays of up to six months or longer in payments to providers of care are common, and limitations on reimbursement often have little or no relationship to actual costs, causing many physicians, pharmacists and other providers to refuse to accept Medicaid patients.

. . . .

Interestingly, the distribution of hospital beds in the United States is much more equitable than that of physicians. In 1948 some states had as few as two general medical and surgical hospital beds per 1000 population. Since that year, however, the Hill-Burton program, a federal hospital-construction program, has spent more than $12 billion, in addition to even greater amounts of local funds, for hospital construction and modernization. As a result of these vast expenditures the distribution of hospital beds throughout the country has become much more balanced. States such as Mississippi, Alabama, Georgia and Tennessee, which had the lowest bed/population ratios in 1948, are now at the national average or above it. Some of the states with particularly high bed/population ratios in 1948 have experienced a decrease, and within states there is also evidence of a more equitable distribution of hospital facilities between rich and poor areas. In some ways hospital-bed distribution is used to "make up for" shortages of physicians; states, like South Dakota, which have low physician-to-population ratios, have relatively high hospital bed/population ratios. While part of the object of the Hill-Burton program was to "lure" physicians into rural areas by building hospitals there, the strategy has largely been a failure.

There is indeed gross maldistribution and social misuse of hospital resources, but it takes a different form than that of physicians and other health workers. The maldistribution and misuse occur in the competition among hospitals, particularly in urban areas, for prestige-enhancing equipment and for patients to keep the beds full.

Examples of needless and dangerous duplication of expensive equipment are ubiquitous. It was estimated in 1971, for example, that the number of teletherapy units (containing X-ray equipment used for treating certain kinds of cancer) concentrated on Chicago's near-South Side could, if properly distributed, take care of the needs of the entire state of Illinois. There were teletherapy units in Chicago that had never even been used since their installation because no one knew how to operate the equipment. Furthermore, the Chicago Regional Hospital Study estimated that a more rational distribution of teletherapy and coronary-care units might cut the operating costs of Chicago hospitals by as much as 10 percent.

The most commonly cited examples of expensive and hazardous duplication of services lie in the field of open-heart surgery, in which complex and costly heart-lung machines are used to maintain the patient's blood flow while surgeons repair or replace valves or other parts of the heart. The duplication of such units is so extensive that, despite intense competition for patients, many hospitals manage to attract only a few candidates for such surgery and thus perform extremely few such operations. The Inter-Society Commission for Heart Disease Resources reported that in 1969, 360 U.S. hospitals were equipped to do open-heart surgery. Of these, 220 average 50 operations or less a year—less than one per week. The commission, composed of experts in heart disease, advises that an open heart surgery unit can maintain its skills and function efficiently only if it does a minimum of 200 operations a year, a minimum of 4 on the average per week. Of the 360 U.S. hospitals with units, only 15 actually performed 200 or more in 1969.

. . . .

The most recent rush to duplicate facilities has been for computed tomographic (CT) scanners which can diagnose conditions that previously could only be found by exploratory surgery or other invasive techniques. The machines cost an average of $500,000 to purchase and install and $100,000 annually to run. In mid-1976 there were over 300 CT scanners in operation in the United States and over 500 more approved for installation. The hospital portion of the private sector is now under some control by federally mandated Health Systems Agencies and other hospital planning bodies, so the hospital competition is somewhat constrained. Private offices and group practices are not so constrained and there is some evidence that an extraordinarily expensive piece of technology will move into areas of use in which there is even less quality and utilization control than in hospitals; almost 20 percent of CT installations are already in private offices.

In short, the fragmentation and the lack of accountability of the U.S. medical-care system have led to severe inequities, inefficiency and

Figure 2. *Number of Health Workers in the United States, 1900–1974*

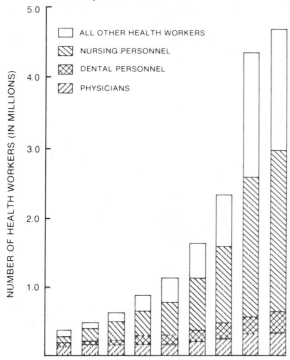

SOURCE: Prepared by the authors from data published by the National Center for Health Statistics.

danger. In all areas of medical care, with the possible exception of hospitalization, the poor and nonwhite, who by almost every measure have far greater needs for care than do the more affluent, have less than equitable access to medical care. And the duplications and overlapping areas of high technology in medicine vastly increase the cost of care and undermine the competence in its use.

. . . .

Health care is not only a huge industry when measured by the amount of money and technology poured into it, it is also huge in terms of the number of people employed in it. As shown in Figure 2, almost five million people work in health care—some 5 percent of the employed population of the United States.

Of these health workers, approximately one-half—some two and a half million—are employed in providing what are called "nursing services," including registered nurses, licensed practical nurses, nurses' aides, orderlies and home health aides. About 375,000 (8 percent) are physicians, most with the M.D. degree, but also including a much smaller number with the degree of doctor of osteopathy, who in all states are licensed to do anything that a physician with an M.D. degree can do. The remainder are employed in approximately 100 other skilled and unskilled occupations, including such varied roles as ambulance attendants, laboratory technicians, pharmacists, receptionists, radiologic technicians, dieticians, secretaries, dental assistants and research scientists.

Over the panoply of facilities and people that is the U.S. medical-care system, the physician has reigned supreme. His or (rarely, but increasingly) her dominance over the U.S. health system has been derived, at least in part, from his authority over and dominance of his patients, a phenomenon which has existed since prehistoric times when the practice of medicine originated in magic and was a priestly art.

There are, of course, still elements of the priesthood in the physician's role, in how he sees himself and how he is viewed by patients and co-workers alike. The authority of the physician today is still based both on the "authority of office" (that is, on the fact that he is a member of the guild), on the "authority of knowledge" (that is, on the assumption that he has special technical competence) and on the "authority of class" (that is, on the often vast social-class difference between him and other health workers or patients). Because the technical competence is more complex and more powerful than ever before, and because the income and prestige differences are huge and increasing, today more than ever his authority takes precedence over all others in the health field.

The physician guards the powers conferred on him, in part by controlling the information made available to patients and to the general public, a control as rigid in its technological form as was the ancient guarding of priestly rituals. A fictionalized account of one physician's internship vividly conveys this withholding of information and its function:

I didn't show her the X-rays; none of us ever showed parents the studies themselves. It was a kind of informal tradition that you were to interpret what the lab results revealed, not show the tests. The idea was not to make the parents nervous with technical details they were not prepared to understand. That it could also be a device to keep control, to keep the mystery—and patient respect—alive and working, had not occurred to me then.

But there are even larger issues at stake than the mystification of the individual patient and family. The physician is now in a position to control vast resources—resources for medical-care services, for medical education and for research. In an age when billions of dollars are spent at the bidding of technologists and technocrats and when the vast majority of the people in every society possesses insufficient knowledge and information (as opposed to intelligence and judgment) on which to base sound decisions, physicians and other technocrats of medicine become extraordinarily powerful in the technological decision-making process.

Furthermore, the process itself becomes self-perpetuating, the technology becomes an end in itself, and the only ones who can discuss the technology with adequate understanding (who have the tools to deal with the issues) are those who control it. What should be a political decision, in its original sense—made with the good of the polity in view—often becomes a narrow technical decision made by those whose judgment must at least in part be colored by their view of what's in it for them.

Between the macrocosm of social policy and the microcosm of the doctor's office, the modern U.S. hospital has come more and more to resemble a modern industrial plant with its elaborate division of labor and the increasing alienation of the hospital worker. Most hospital workers remain at their entry-level jobs unless they acquire more formal training or other credentials even though they often learn skills on the job and perform tasks at a higher level.

The result is a rigid occupational hierarchy with an elaborate system of rank identifications such as uniforms and titles and an equally rigid social-class system. In 1970, 98 percent of U.S. physicians were white, 91 percent were male and predominantly from middle- and upper-middle-

class families; while 92 percent of nurses were white, 98 percent were female and from predominantly middle- and lower-middle-class families. Of the total enrolled in training programs administered by hospitals in 1973–74, 86 percent of practical-nurse trainees were white and 96 percent were female; while 64 percent of nurse's-aide trainees were white and 87 percent were female, and 64 percent of orderly-trainees were white and 14 percent were female.

Thus it is clear that in general as income and power drop, the domination by white males ends and medical professions become overwhelmingly female and increasingly nonwhite. As one practical nurse described the hierarchy in the hospital where she worked, "You have to see this place as a giant bureaucracy. I'm at the bottom of it, or maybe the patients are, and there's not a lot an individual can do."

The physician is of course at the top of the medical-care structure, earns the most money . . . and has the most power. . . . The income differentials between those at the top and those at the bottom have markedly increased over the past two decades.

The nurse is typically subordinate to both the physician and the hospital, and early in her training learns to play what one observer has called the "doctor-nurse game," the object of which is that the nurse "be bold, have initiative and be responsible for making significant recommendations, while at the same time [appearing] passive." She must "make her recommendations appear to be initiated by the physicians," taking care not to disturb the physician's narcissism or feelings of omnipotence.

The doctor's role vis-à-vis other health professionals and paraprofessionals is even more distant and authoritarian. In hospital settings those persons who are in continuous and intimate contact with patients are workers with the lowest status and least power in the institution. Eliot Freidson's description of the alienated industrial worker seems to fit the medical paraprofessional as well:

Lacking identification with the prime goals of the organization, lacking an important voice in setting the formal level and direction of work, and performing work that has been so rationalized as to become mechanical and meaningless, a minute segment of an intricate mosaic of specialized activities that he is in no position to perceive or understand, the worker is alienated.

In spite of this alienation, more and more of the caring functions of medicine are left to the nurse's aides, the LPNs, the orderlies. Furthermore, since workers in the primarily female caring professions of nursing and social work have been awakened to their low staus by the women's movement, members of these professions have in significant numbers attempted to "move up" into traditionally male and therefore higher-status teaching or administrative roles, leaving the caring function increasingly to powerless paraprofessionals with still lower status.

Thus we may view the typical structure of a large medical institution as a pyramid with the usually white, male physician on top, his orders carried out by middle-level professionals who are generally women, and with the patients and the "dirty work" left to low-paid, frequently alienated, largely black female paraprofessionals at the bottom of the pyramid.

Although acceptance into medical school has shifted somewhat in recent years toward the female (24 percent of the entering class in 1975 compared to 6 percent 20 years earlier) and toward "minority" students (8 percent of the entering class in 1975), the more pronounced trend has been toward higher and higher intellectual requirements; the percentage of students with A averages in medical school has increased from 13 percent in 1965 to 44 percent in 1975. This, together with the rapid increase in medical school (and college) tuition—in one medical school now over $10,000 per year for four years—discriminates more and more against the socially and educationally disadvantaged. Yet, there is absolutely no evidence that intellectual attainment beyond a given level is necessary for technical proficiency or that intellectual attainment at any level is correlated with skill in providing humane medical care. Furthermore, the emphasis on grades, particularly in science courses, and the intense competition for the limited number of medical school places, has led to enormous anxieties among premedical stu-

dents and a profound distortion of the undergraduate learning experiences.

Furthermore, once in medical school, the educational pattern is largely irrelevant—and actually seems to be inimical—to the practice of medicine, particularly of primary medical care. Much of the work in the preclinical sciences is based on the needs and desires of a "science" faculty and has little use meeting patients' needs. A very large percentage of the clinical work is done on (the word "on" is usually more appropriate than "with") hospitalized patients in large teaching hospitals. In most medical schools well over 50 percent of the teaching is done on "horizontal" rather than "vertical" patients. As Jack Geiger has commented, "It's like teaching forestry in a lumber yard." Moreover, while studies of how patients actually need and use medical care indicate that patients' needs lie largely outside the hospital, the teaching nevertheless concentrates on the small fraction of care that takes place not only in a hospital, but in the university medical center tertiary-care hospital.

Inappropriate intellectualization and academization of training occurs among other health workers as well. A recent report by the secretary of education of Massachusetts states that he finds absolutely no evidence that registered nurses who hold bachelor's degrees are any more competent in patient care than are those who have graduated from hospital-based schools, yet diploma nurses find it difficult to get jobs at comparable pay to baccalaureate nurses. Registered nurses with diplomas, the report stated, find themselves "squeezed" between the registered nurses with bachelor's degrees, on one hand, and the licensed practical nurses, who have lesser levels of technical skills and thus command far less salary, on the other. At all of these levels, nurses, like other health workers, are judged more by how academic their training was and by their degrees and licenses than by what they can actually do for the patient.

New categories of personnel are constantly being added to the system, both in response to the demands of technology and to the demands of patient care. One response over the past ten years to the shortage and inappropriate use of health personnel has been the development of physician's assistant programs. The effort has been highly publicized, but the number of new workers trained is still quite small.

The term "physician's assistant" includes a range of health workers—variously called physician's associates, MEDEX (for "medical extenders"), clinical associates, child-health associates and others. "Assistant to the primary-care physician," for example, is a generic term used for an assistant who performs certain specified tasks under the direction and supervision of a physician in a number of settings, from a physician's office to a hospital. The assistant has a wide range of duties which include taking patients' case histories, performing physical examinations, drawing blood samples, giving intravenous injections and infusions, providing immunizations, suturing and caring for wounds, and other specific tasks usually performed by doctors.

Programs to train PAs (the abbreviation is in part a way of avoiding the problem of whether they should be called "assistants" or "associates") were begun in the mid-1960s at a time when the Vietnam War was annually producing thousands of military medical corpsmen whose knowledge and experience were being lost to the civilian world after their discharge. Because the PA concept was originally seen as a way to utilize those trained in the military medical corps and at the same time provide needed medical manpower, the new medical professionals were expected to be predominantly male. The nursing profession, not unreasonably, saw the development as yet another device of the medical establishment to undercut the predominantly female nursing profession, and in response the new professional role of "nurse practitioner" has been developed.

Since the first PA program at Duke University in 1965, some 4000 students have graduated from the roughly 60 training programs now accredited by the AMA. The programs, which now graduate about 1300 PAs a year, vary enormously in their requirements and even in the length of the program. Some 40 states have enacted legislation governing the use of PAs.

Severe problems have developed. There are conflicts between PA and nurse-practitioner programs in determining status, hierarchy and which training programs will receive how much money

from the federal government. Although most PAs are trained in primary care, some are already reflecting the specialization of the medical profession; they are being trained in such diverse medical specialties as anesthesiology, pathology, surgery, obstetrics and orthopedics, and in these roles the PAs are adding to the specialization within medicine rather than providing additional primary care.

And, of course, for the PA, as for the nurse practitioner, the nurse, the nurse's aide and other health workers, there is usually almost no chance to become a physician. The only pathway to advancement is through administration, supervision and teaching, with the result that the most skilled health workers either feel trapped and frustrated in their subsidiary roles or are forced to move further and further away from direct patient care.

Another, perhaps even more basic, criticism is that PAs and nurse practitioners may become the physicians for the poor while the rich are able to purchase and demand care by "real" doctors. While this criticism is still for the most part more theoretical than real, the danger in an unregulated, fee-for-service system certainly exists. The issue is how the medical-care system chooses to use these new workers—as part of an effort to bring greater equity to the system, or to further stratify the already highly stratified provision of health care.

Up to this point PAs are not changing the nature of American medicine but rather shoring up its current organization and priorities. Nationally, 77 percent of PA graduates are absorbed into private practices. The physicians who add PAs to their practice often charge their regular fees for a visit conducted entirely or largely by a PA, and pocket the difference between the PA's salary (from $7500 to $22,500 a year, relatively modest compared to a doctor's income) and the fee charged.

In short, these new health roles act to further the physician's control of the health-care system.

There are some areas, however, in which the physician's dominance of the medical-care system is being effectively threatened. The increasing size, complexity and corporate structure of the hospital give its professional managers new power over the workshop in which a large share of the physician's income is generated. The increasing cost of medical care and its major financing through insurance companies and tax levy funds give regulators and claims examiners new power over the physician's income and therefore over his pattern of practice.

The response of many physicians is to join together in what they view as—and sometimes call—"physician's unions." Strikes have been threatened, and over some issues, such as malpractice insurance rates, have even been partially carried out in some areas. While some physicians question the "ethics" of such actions—which, to be effective, will leave patients without a source of continuing or even emergency care—it seems likely that when the provocation is seen as large enough a significant percentage of physicians will be willing to use methods traditionally identified with the working class.

Some critics see unionization of physicians as a step forward, a breaking down of some of the elitist pretensions of the physician, even as a "proletarianization" of physicians. One major difference, of course, is that the threat to withhold services is often the only significant leverage available to workers wishing to improve their wages or working conditions, while most doctors already have other powerful resources and methods for control and change at their disposal. Another is that most workers are economically damaged by even a short strike, while most doctors can afford to strike for a prolonged period either because of their accumulated wealth or their expectation of future large incomes.

Others therefore fear that the elitist attitudes will not change but simply be further expressed through the power of organized deprivation of services, a deprivation which will become the ultimate weapon in the hands of an already powerful group.

Postscript 1983

Specialization and Maldistribution

As the number of physicians in the United States has continued to increase relative to population (see below), there has been an increase in the number of generalists and in the geographic distribution of both generalists and specialists. There are still far fewer of the former than the latter, and there are still many areas of the United States (poor urban as well as poor rural areas) where access to a physician remains difficult. The average number of physician visits annually by poor people remained almost constant from 1974 to 1979 (5.3 visits per person for those with family incomes less than $7000) while visits for the well-off actually decreased (from 5.2 in 1974 to 4.7 in 1979 for those with family incomes over $25,000). But the larger number of visits by the poor still does not match the greater amount of illness and disability among poor people. The average number of physician visits per person fell for both whites and blacks from 1974 to 1979 and blacks, despite their much higher illness and disability rates, continued to have fewer annual visits (4.5) than whites (4.8).[1] Recent studies also continue to show significant differences in specific types of care based on class, race or geography. A study of coronary artery bypass surgery in the Buffalo, New York, area, for example, showed that people living in poor areas had significantly fewer of these operations than did those living in well-off areas.[2]

. . . .

Health Workers

In 1980 there were 7.2 million people employed in health work in the United States compared to 4.2 million in 1970. The number of professionally active physicians (including MDs and DOs) increased from 323,000 in 1970 (one doctor for every 650 people) to 450,000 in 1980 (one for every 500 people). At current rates of medical school graduation, there will be approximately 590,000 doctors in 1990 (one for 410 people) and 705,000 in 2000 (one for 370).[3]

Physicians' assistants and nurse practitioners continue to be trained and widely used. There has been little change in their status, although an apparently greater percentage of physicians, concerned about the "competition" posed by the increasing number of doctors, have called for a limitation on the number and scope of practice of "mid-level" health workers. Nurses, now in short supply in many areas of the U.S., have grown increasingly militant, and there have been a number of strikes by hospital-based nurses for higher wages and better working conditions. Despite these efforts, the incomes of physicians, on the average, are still vastly greater than those of other health workers.

NOTES

A recent detailed and comprehensive description of the United States health-care and medical-care system, with an extensive bibliography, may be found in Steven Jonas and others, *Health Care Delivery in the United States* (New York: Springer Publishing Co., 1977). Detailed data on distribution of hospitals and health workers, on physicians' visits and on health problems may be found in *Health United States 1975,* DHEW Publication no. (HRA) 76-1232. Detailed data on the geographic distribution of doctors, nurses and other health workers are presented in *Health Resources Statistics,* issued annually by the National Center for Health Statistics; the most recent volume, for 1975, in DHEW Publication no. (HRA) 76-1509.

An analysis of barriers to health care for the poor was made by L. Bergner and A. S. Yerby, "Low Income and Barriers to Use of Health Services," *New England Journal of Medicine* 278 (March 7, 1968): 541–6. The study of teletherapy units in the city of Chicago and the report of the Inter-Society Commission were discussed by Spencer Klaw in *The Great American Medicine Show,* (New York: Viking Press, 1975).

Data on the current numbers of health workers in the United States may be found in the annual editions of *Health Resources Statistics,* cited above. Distribution of health workers in 1970 and projections to 1990 were presented in *The Supply of Health Manpower,* DHEW Publication no. (HRA) 75–38. An analysis of the authority of the physician has been presented by Eliot Freidson in *Professional Dominance: The Social Structure of Medical Care* (New York: Atherton Press, 1970), pp. 108–9.

The quotation on the withholding of information is from Ronald J. Glasser, *Ward 402* (New York: Pocket Books, 1974), p. 69.

A discussion of characteristics and roles of health workers can be found in Barbara Ehrenreich and John H. Ehrenreich, "Hospital Workers: Class Conflicts in the Making," and in Carol A. Brown, "Women Workers in the Health Service Industry," published, respectively, in the *International Journal of Health Services* 5, no. 1 (1975): 43–51; no. 2 (1975): 173–84;

and in Vicente Navarro, "Women in Health Care," *New England Journal of Medicine* 292 (February 20, 1975): 398–402. A series of articles describing nurse-doctor relationships is presented in Bonnie Bullough and Vern Bullough, eds., *New Directions for Nurses* (New York: Springer Publishing Co., 1971), particularly Leonard I. Stein, "The Doctor-Nurse Game," pp. 129–37. Further analysis of these relationships can be found in Shirley A. Smoyak, "Problems in Interprofessional Relations," *Bulletin of the New York Academy of Medicine* 53 (January–February 1977): 51–9. The quotation describing the alienated worker is taken from Freidson's *Professional Dominance,* p. 144.

Data on the characteristics of U.S. medical students are published regularly in the *Journal of Medical Education* and annually in the medical-education issue of the *Journal of the American Medical Association;* the December 27, 1976, issue gives data for the classes entering and graduating in 1975.

Further material on the development of the "intermediate" categories of health personnel and the issues surrounding their training can be found in the following sources: Donald M. Pitcairn and Daniel Flahault, eds., *The Medical Assistant: An Intermediate Level of Health Care Personnel,* Public Health Paper no. 60 (Geneva: World Health Organization, 1974); Alfred M. Sadler, Jr., Blair L. Sadler, and Ann A. Bliss, *The Physician's Assistant: Today and Tomorrow* (Cambridge, Mass.: Ballinger Publishing Co., 1975); Susan Reverby, "The Sorcerer's Apprentice," in Kotelchuck, ed., *Prognosis Negative* (New York: Vintage, 1976): 215–229; Margaret E. Mahoney, "The Future Role of Physician's Assistants and Nurse Practitioners," in John Z. Bowers and Elizabeth Purcell, eds., *National Health Services: Their Impact on Medical Education and Their Role in Prevention* (New York: Josiah Macy, Jr., Foundation, 1973), pp. 124–42; and Anthony Robbins, "Allied Health Manpower—Solution or Problem?" *New England Journal of Medicine* 286 (April 27, 1972): 918–23. Examples of studies on their effectiveness and acceptance include Charles E. Lewis and others, "Activities, Events and Outcomes in Ambulatory Patient Care," *New England Journal of Medicine* 280 (March 20, 1969): 645–9; Evan Charney and Harriet Kitzman, "The Child-Health Nurse (Pediatric Nurse Practitioner) in Private Practice: A Controlled Trial," *New England Journal of Medicine* 285 (December 9, 1971): 1353–8. Eugene C. Nelson, Arthur R. Jacobs, and Kenneth G. Johnson, "Patients' Acceptance of Physicians' Assistants," *Journal of the American Medical Association* 228 (April 1, 1974): 63–7; and Lawrence S. Linn, "Patient Acceptance of the Family Nurse Practitioner," *Medical Care* 14 (April 1976): 357–64. Marianne G. Dekker documents "First Doctor Opposition to Physician's Assistants" in *Medi-*

cal Economics, September 6, 1976. Warnings that the use of nonphysician personnel to provide primary care is likely to further the two-class nature of medical care in the United States, with the poor cared for by those with less training, were sounded by Milton Terris, "False Starts and Lesser Alternatives," *Bulletin of the New York Academy of Medicine* 53 (January–February 1977): 129–40, and Milton I. Roemer, "Primary Care and Physician Extenders in Affluent Countries," *International Journal of Health Services* 7 (Fall 1977): 545–55.

The decrease in home visits, demonstrated by the National Health Interview Survey, was summarized in *Forward Plan for Health FY 1978–82.*

NOTES TO POSTSCRIPT

1. *Health, United States, 1981,* DHHS Publication No. (PHS) 82–1232 (Hyattsville, Md.: U.S. Department of Health and Human Services, December 1981), pp. 157.
2. R. L. Dickman and S. Bukowski, "Epidemiology and Ethics of Coronary Artery Bypass Surgery in an Eastern County," *Journal of Family Practice* 14 (1982): 233–39.
3. *Health, United States, 1981,* pp. 176–77.

16

Re-forming the Hospital Nurse: The Management of American Nursing

Susan Reverby

The labyrinthine hospital, filled with multitudes of personnel in a rainbow assortment of uniforms, is the norm for the contemporary medical institution in the United States. But the hospital has not always been a huge specialized acute care institution with a complex staffing pattern. For most of its history, the institution was run by relatively few people and served a generalized social welfare function. As the hospital's purpose and function have changed, so has its division of labor. This article is a brief overview of this transformation as it has affected and was effected by the largest segment of the hospital workforce: the nurses. It explores the impact of the confluence of the professional aspirations of nursing and the managerial thrusts of the hospital administrations.[1]

Until the early twentieth century, most people, even when acutely ill, were cared for not in the hospital, but at home by relatives, friends or a neighborhood nurse. The hospital was more an institution primarily for the very poor or transients in need of food and shelter as much as medical and surgical attention. Conditions in many hospitals, as in the most disreputable nursing homes of today, were often abominable: dirty, unkempt, understaffed, places of little hope and much despair. Alcohol, considered an important medicine, was dispensed as frequently to the staff as to the patients.

Many of the women who provided what nursing care there was were either patients themselves, inmates of an adjacent prison or almshouse, or women hired almost off the streets. Strength, in particular a strong back, and a somewhat pleasing disposition, were the major job requirements. Thus, for example, the matron of a Boston hospital placed this ad in the newspaper in 1874: "Wanted, a nurse for the Boston Lying-In Hospital, Experience not required."[2] When she couldn't find someone to take the job (she reported the applicants weren't prepossessing enough), she had one of the recuperating patients become the hospital laundress, and she moved the laundress up to nurse. Similarly, in 1913, a survey of New York hospitals noted that ". . . in the absence of other institutions where the periodic and semi-respectable drunks can live and work, they can, to the best advantage to themselves and to the City, be supported as workers in the City's hospitals."[3]

But not all the nurses, even in the worst of hospitals, were the immoral and inexperienced semi-alcoholics so bitingly satirized by Dickens in Sairey Gamp and Betsy Prig in his novel *Martin Chuzzlewitt.* Many women (and much of the hospital workforce was women) became permanent employees and stayed at their jobs for many years. They learned and accumulated some skills on the job and gained what one historian has called an "ad hoc" professionalism.[4] These women often did everything in the institution: washing dishes, mending the linen, cleaning hoppers and bedpans, but also careful watching, skilled bandaging, bathing, and assisting in operations and deliveries.

The hospital's major decisions were made primarily by the administrator, called a superintendent, and the board of trustees. As medical care was less important in the hospital, the medical staff's power over decisions was not as large as it is today.[5] But in a hospital world in which stays were measured in weeks and months, not days, many of the patients were more convalescent than acutely ill, and doctor and trustee visits more rituals than daily occurrences. Thus a strong hospital culture developed which linked the patients and workers together in a web of both class and circumstance. Frequent clashes between the rules of the institution and its daily life were common.[6]

Beginning in 1873, as part of general reform effort in social welfare and the necessity for finding more respectable work for the daughters of the lower middle classes, several nurses' training schools, attached to hospitals, were founded in this country. Several of the early schools were independent institutions with their own funds and boards, but by the 1880s, most schools were organized and controlled by the hospitals, which realized the "students" could be used as a source of more docile, "non-wage" labor. The early schools, despite the efforts of nursing reformers, were primarily hiring halls for the hospitals in which student drop-outs were replaced on an individual basis whenever the necessity arose, with no concern for organized classes or a graded curriculum.[7]

Student nurses became the key nursing workers in the hospitals and made possible the rapid expansion in the number of hospitals in the late nineteenth and early twentieth centuries. Graduate nurses were sometimes used in supervisory positions, but it was more common to find such positions filled by a senior nursing student. The hospital administrations were quick to realize that the nursing students were not only cheaper, but as employees were preferable to either untrained attendants or graduate nurses for several reasons.

First, students could be trained into the exact routine of the hospital and would not bring the knowledge of different routines from other hospitals with them. Second, since training lasted for two to three years, the students became a relatively permanent workforce who could be depended upon to stay longer than other employees, if they did not die or break down from the overwork. Any time lost to illness, however, had to be made up before the student received her diploma. Third, management could exert more discipline and control over students than it could over employees who, not seeing the work as something to be endured until graduation, might quit more readily. The nursing leadership, anxious to develop the proper "character" in their charges and to shed the image of the nurse as an intemperate lowlife, saw the necessity for strict disciplining. Their emphasis on the hierarchy and military-like obedience, however, in the face of their lack of control over the schools, left the students easily open ideologically and in practice to exploitation by the hospitals. Lavinia Dock, one of the early leaders of American nursing, stated succinctly: "Discipline and strict subordination of the school makes it possible for the hospital to exact from [the nursing students] an amount of work it would be quite impossible to exact from women over whom it had no special hold. . . ."[8]

Since the nursing students were pushed onto the wards with almost no training and were expected to do everything, strict supervision of these unskilled women was necessary if any degree of quality care was to be obtained. Nursing leaders rightly believed that good supervision would help with the on-the-job training of the nursing students. The system was far from flawless. An Iowa physician lamented: "We are entirely too careless in the operating rooms, and too many pupil nurses are put into operating rooms who are too stupid ever to learn operating technic, too many who are too careless, and who have not been long enough in the school to have acquired the proper mental attitude toward the profession of nursing."[9]

Since the hospital was also a school, control over the nurses was sanctioned by the ideology of *in loco parentis* as well. Adherence to such strict control over work meant that the hospitals could admit virtually any warm body to the nursing school knowing that the supervision and teaching of strict routines would largely make up for the deficit in knowledge and training. Consequently, the public often viewed the hospital nursing school as ". . . a sort of respectable reform school where its mental or disciplinary cases can be sent," as a 1928 nursing reform report noted.[10]

For the graduate nurse conditions of labor were quite different. After graduation, most nurses left the hospital to become private duty nurses. They were hired by patients and worked individually in the home. Hiring took place either by word of mouth or through registries established in the major cities by the nursing alumnae associations, commerical businesses, the hospitals, and medical societies. For a small fee, nurses could register, give their prices and their preferences for work.[11]

In private duty nursing, the only real supervision was that given by doctors, and this was at best haphazard and uneven. Nurses were still expected to kowtow and cover for the physicians and their mistakes. Dr. William L. Richardson, for example, told the graduating class at the Boston Training School for Nurses on June 18, 1886 to "always be loyal to the physician." He warned them not to be "tempted" to impress the doctor with their knowledge because "what error can be more stupid?"[12] Although the private duty nurse was technically working "independently," she was in fact dependent on the physicians for her reputation and often for her actual case loads. The difference in the situation for nurses and physicians was clearly reflected in the language used to describe their respective positions: a doctor out on his own was in private *practice,* the nurse was working on private *duty.*

Graduate nurses increasingly in the 1920s worked in hospitals as private duty or special nurses for the paying patients in their private rooms. Hospitals usually kept registries, mostly of their own graduates, but patients could obtain private duty nurses anywhere they pleased. The presence of the private duty nurse was a constant problem for both the nursing supervisors and the hospital administrators. She was independent of the rules, discipline and supervision of the hospital and its nursing hierarchy. Often her patients were not considered to be "that sick" and the fact that she worked less diligently than the other nurses was deeply resented.[13] Moreover, she was not responsible for anything but the care of her one patient. Because she was usually older than the students and out of school, she often used older or different techniques, a practice which clearly disturbed nursing supervisors bent on teaching the students their own particular or more modern ways of doing things.[14]

Hospital administrators were even more concerned about the behavior of private duty nurses who could tell their patients about failings in the hospitals. Since their patients were usually well-to-do people in the community, the hospitals could ill afford to have their problems or limitations revealed to them.[15] Where they could, hospitals retaliated against these nurses, limiting their registry lists and using these as blacklists to keep out particularly troublesome nurses. Nurses frequently complained about discrimination on the part of the hospitals.[16]

The outbreak of World War I and the flu pandemic of 1918 were critical events which helped shape personnel relations within the hospitals. Both made the hospitals more acutely aware of shortages, the cost of labor turnover, and the need for better trained workers. Problems of quality and the division of labor intensified in the 1920s.

This new concern for quality in the workforce was closely related to the change in the nature of patients using the hospital. As the institutions expanded and the scientific and sanitary basis for care improved, more middle and upper class patients began to use the hospital. By 1931, the income from private, paying patients, rather than public funds or private donations, was the most important source of hospital income.

Because of the difference in the kind of patient hospitals served and their importance to hospital income, administrators began increasingly to worry about the quality of the workforce and the impressions they made on the patients. Thus during the 1920s and 1930s the hospital managers moved both to downgrade the scope of authority of their workers through increasing the division of labor and to upgrade their quality through better selection and standardization of training and through the provision of better ancillary benefits. In direct patient care areas, in particular, nursing, the changes were made in training and the types of workers.

The administrators' first line of attack was upon the stratum in the hospital which would be equivalent to lower middle management or foremen in industry: the head nurses and matrons in charge of the housekeeping departments. As administrators tried to chart lines of authority and make concrete rules about procedures, these "foremen" quickly sensed a threat to their authority. They clearly understood that the development of bureaucratic rules and the clear demarcation of authority would limit their control over their work.

Henry Hurd, one of the editors of *The Modern Hospital,* editorialized that matrons and nurses sometimes had "the impulse" or an "overwhelming desire" to organize or supervise the work in departments that were not their own. He was particularly concerned that these women did not want to give up the power of purchasing to a central authority. "The result of all this," he pointed out, "is a confusion of duty, a mingling of responsibilities, and a loss of efficiency, costly to the institution, all of which are most unwise." Such plans led to increased departmental dependence on centralized planning and control of the administrators.[17]

The nurses and matrons realized this and fought as best they could. Counseling and cajoling on the part of the administrators did not always result in cooperation. When department heads refused to give up their broader decision-making powers, *The Modern Hospital* counseled firings, and letters to the journals make it clear that dismissals were common.[18] At the same time the administrators moved to increase the division of labor. The extent to which this division of labor and increasing substitution of lower-skilled workers occurred varied depending upon both the hospital's size and funding source.[19] Regardless of the speed of substitution, however, increasing division of labor in the direct patient care areas resulted from the convergence and delicate balance of professional pressures and scientific management principles. The establishment of nurse's aides illustrates this tension.

During the shortages of the First World War and the flu pandemic many hospitals briefly introduced nurse's aide programs. Toward the end of the period 1910–1919, the expansion of these programs and other quick nursing courses produced an oversupply rather than a shortage of nurses.[20] With funding from the Rockefeller Foundation, a commission was established in 1918 to study nursing and nursing education.[21] When the report, known as the Goldmark Report after its principle investigator, Josephine Goldmark, was issued in 1922, it established two principles which were to become more generally accepted in subsequent years: (1) subsidiary grades of nurses serving patients with mild cases and serving as nurses' assistants in the hospitals should be licensed, and (2) such workers should be trained in the hospitals, apart from regular nursing students. The report also recommended that nurses increasingly be trained in universities and transformed into hospital foremen.[22]

The Goldmark report was not greeted with hosannas from most physicians and administrators. They were unwilling to give up the cheaper nursing students or to upgrade to any higher professional status the "uppity nurses."[23] Other doctors, notably Charles Mayo of the Mayo Clinic, went as far as to accuse the nursing profession of being the most "autocratic closed shop" in the country and to suggest that professional nurses could be done away with completely and "100,000 country girls could be trained as subnurses."[24] With such powerful opposition, while numerous hospitals began setting up training programs for aides in the 1920s and 1930s, widespread use of aides did not occur until the shortages of World War II.

Most of the hospitals in the 1920s and 1930s were, however, more concerned about the nature of their nursing staff than they were with the question of aides. Long debates ensued during these years over who the nursing worker should be, how she should be trained and who should control her work. Decisions about the kind of nursing worker necessary were based in part upon attempts to determine a nurse's productivity and how many patients she could care for in an hour. How to "scientifically" ascertain this number was and still is a question which is extremely difficult to answer.

A survey of nurses in the New York City hospitals in 1913, concluded: ". . . no recognized standards of the numbers of nurses that should be employed to a given number of beds and admissions existed."[25] The problem was based in part on the fact that, while the hospitals could regularize the number of beds they had, the occupancy rate of those beds always was variable. It was difficult for hospitals to know their staffing needs from day to day.

Among nursing's more educated leadership, there was a real willingness to experiment with different forms of work organization. This leadership also hoped that better training and planning could upgrade the nurse's status and dignity. Many of the early leaders worked with the scientific management movement in an attempt to apply its principles to nursing. Minnie Goodnow, a nursing superintendent and nurse historian, informed the 1914 annual hospital convention that nurses were training students "as Mr. Gilbreth does his bricklayers, and as all the efficiency engineers are doing in factories and business offices."[26] M. Adelaide Nutting, the first full professor of nursing at Columbia University, became interested in scientific management and efficiency schemes through her work in the American Home Economics Association.[27] By the 1920s, the National League for Nursing Educa-

tion introduced some of the first time-and-motion studies of nursing work.[28]

The 1932 report of a study conducted by the League had important implications for the changes in nursing in the 1930s. The study documented the variability in both patient census and nursing load which made it necessary to shift nurses from one service to another. When these nurses were students, however, their education and ultimately the quality of nursing care suffered. The researchers concluded that nursing students could not provide enough quality care and that "a supplementary general duty graduate nursing staff . . . [was] essential."[29] The study also found that one-third of the nurses' time was spent in "extratreatment activities or non-nursing duties." This finding laid the basis for further consideration of the introduction of ward clerks and nurse's aides to take over these functions.

The move toward the employment of graduate nurses was encouraged by the work of yet another major nursing study which issued several reports between 1928 and 1934.[30] The first report urged the closing of some nursing schools and the upgrading of training in those that remained. The national nursing groups began to reconsider their focus on private duty and to look increasingly at the hospital as a place to work.

It was not time and motion studies or the actions of the American Nurses' Association, however, which determined the gradual introduction of the graduate nurse to the hospital.[31] The expansion of nursing in the early 1920s had led to an oversupply; by 1928 the depression had already begun in nursing.[32] The plight of private duty nurses became even more acute as the Depression wore on and patients began to cut back on use of their services. The American Nurses' Association moved exceedingly slowly in assisting their members through pressure for shorter hours or relief.[33] By 1932, the national nursing groups reluctantly drafted an appeal letter to the trustees of American hospitals asking them to remember nurses in their hour of need and to begin to employ graduate nurses. The letter also noted that the dilemma for nursing was not just the result of the Depression but was due ". . . to a weakness of a system of accepting students primarily as workers in the hospital. . . ."[34]

Hospitals were at first reluctant to employ more graduate nurses. A 1927 questionnaire sent to five hundred supervisors questioning them on which type of worker they preferred showed that 76 percent wanted students; only 24 percent wanted graduate nurses.[35] The nursing supervisors were fearful of employing women used to working independently because ". . . they find even kindly direction irksome," as one nursing supervisor explained.[36]

Hospitals had been convinced by economics and by earlier demands of the nursing profession to use trained nursing students. They now seemed reluctant to give up their free labor in exchange for the graduate nurse, even if the Depression made her cheaper and more available. The 1928 nursing report remarked: "It is an extraordinary thing, but it seems to be a fact that hospitals regard the suggestion that they pay for their own nursing service as unreasonable . . . the student nurse is seen as an inalienable right. . . ."[37]

As the Depression wore on, however, more and more small hospitals were forced to close their nursing schools. The number of schools dropped from 1,885 in 1929 to 1,311 in 1940. Studies began to appear in the journals to show that nursing students were not cheaper, because of their high maintenance and supervision costs.[38] By 1934 a new study of nursing superintendents concluded that their position on the use of graduate nurses had shifted positively.[39]

Some hospitals at first experimented with a form of private group nursing, which allowed a group of private duty nurses to care for several private patients at once. The nursing associations, finally coming to understand that this meant allowing the graduate nurse to become the general floor duty nurse, attacked the group nursing plans as ". . . merely another attempt on the part of the hospital to saddle the patient with nursing costs the hospital itself should meet, if this is not merely one more attempt to bolster up an inadequate nursing service."[40]

By the end of the 1930s it became clear that graduate nurses could provide better quality nursing service, could function as supervisors for auxiliary personnel, and, if they were not cheaper than students, neither were they that much more expensive. The hospital nurse became more common than private duty or public health nurse by 1937 and the number of graduate nurses within hospitals climbed from 4,000 in 1929 to 28,000 in 1937.[41]

The nurses also slowly began to accept the idea of nurses' aides in the hospital, as long as the training programs followed the dictates of the Goldmark Report, limiting the training of aides and constantly reminding them ". . . that they are not and will not be nurses."[42] The attempt to develop a subsidiary nursing worker who was cheaper but could provide quality care caught the hospitals in a contradiction which they have yet to resolve. If aides were to be given less responsibility and pay than the nurses, then their duties had to be different and more narrowly circumscribed. Yet because they were going to be handling sick patients, not machine parts, they had to be taught to understand basic procedures and to cope with many different kinds of emergencies. It is therefore understandable that they would want to improve their skills and to grow into more responsible positions. Yet the credentialing barrier established by the nursing profession in its quest for status and control prevented this happening through a job ladder in the hospital.[43]

A report on a nurse's aide program from Cleveland City Hospital makes this point candidly from the perspective of the administration: ". . . There is keen resentment on the part of several students because they feel that there is too much class distinction in the hospital. Probably it is inevitable that in so large a group a few would lose perspective regarding their place. On the other hand, perhaps, we, in our enthusiasm for the experiment, painted too glowing a picture of the joys of domestic work on our wards. After all, there is not much glamour to cleaning and bed making, even if they are an expression of devotion. Undoubtedly the continuance of their interest will be one of our perplexing situations. . . ."[44]

Hospitals met this dilemma in several ways. First, the training programs emphasized again and again the limited role of the aide. She had to be socialized " . . . to continue to try and perfect herself in the skills that her assignments permit rather than to forge ahead to new accomplishment."[45] Second, nurses were shifted to paperwork and supervisory tasks and nurse's aides and practical or vocational nurses were left to do much of the direct patient care.[46] Since neither of these solutions really solved the "perplexing situation" for the hospitals, the aides responded in classic ways—shirking greater responsibilities, fighting with other workers, or quitting.[47]

Thus by the 1920s, turnover in hospitals relying heavily on aides first surfaced as a major issue. This dilemma was and continues to be unsolved by the hospital management. On the one hand, high turnover controlled the resentment of the workers, allowed the hospitals to continue to pay low wages and yet keep an unskilled workforce. On the other hand, such high turnover meant that new workers had to be constantly taught the routines and integrated into the hospitals, making the workforce less efficient—the goal the administrators were trying so hard to achieve.

As the hospital became the center of the health system, scientific medicine necessitated a skilled as well as a controlled labor force; more than this, hospitals needed employees who were socially acceptable to paying patients upon whom they were becoming increasingly dependent. Poor men and women from almshouses were neither skilled nor acceptable. Students, although at first socially compatible, were expensive to maintain and inadequate to the tasks. While graduate nurses meet the two former objections, they presented a threat to the institutional integrity of the hospital.

The graduate nurses, therefore, had to be incorporated into the hospital hierarchy. First, they were separated from their potential source of power—the paying patient. A new level of workers, aides, was introduced to take over many of the traditional nursing chores. Aides could be employed in nursing without risk to the administration. They had no collective memory of control over patient care, and were more easily contained because of differences in training, class and race from graduate nurses. Additionally, they were cheaper to employ.

Second, nurses were further removed from the bedside by being made supervisors. This served two purposes: it made clear to the aides that there was more to nursing than bedside care, and it seemingly elevated the RN by making her someone else's boss. Once incorporated into the administration of the hospital, nurses quickly gained a stake in its smooth functioning. Advancement in nursing consisted of climbing up the hospital hierarchy and meant implicit acceptance of the institution's terms.

In the face of institutionalization, however, nurses were not merely passive recipients of bureaucratic whims. Often they saw the dangers inherent in their situation. Unfortunately, many of their responses were inadequate to meet the challenge and ironically played into the hands of the very forces they needed to combat. Imitating the earlier, successful thrust of doctors for professional status, nurses called upon their own unique abilities to cope with the nursing demands of scientific medicine, inadvertently conferring their stamp of approval on the ideology of high technology medicine. Thus, the more professional the nurse, the further removed she became from the patients and the more vulnerable she became to administrator's control. Like the insect in the spider's web, the more the nurses fought, the more entwined they became.

Prior to World War II, the transformation of nursing from direct patient care to a variety of specialized roles, including administration, was accomplished with few changes in technology. Rather, it was effected by the division of nursing into subsections with the imposition of a multi-leveled hierarchy. For graduate nurses, it meant an end to the possibility of being autonomous practitioners who set their own work rules and controlled their own time. Unlike doctors, nurses became employees of institutions and were dependent upon and subject to those institutions' needs.

Thus, RN journals today are filled with articles about the threat to the existence of nursing coming from technicians below and doctors' assistants above. This pincer-like grip on the nursing profession is most frequently attributed to the technological proliferation within some aspects of nursing care and the complexity of hospital administration. Thus on the one hand, nurses are being replaced by lesser paid, lesser skilled people operating machines, and on the other, by clerical workers and computers. It is also becoming clearer that nurses cannot succeed in making demands on the institutions if they do it alone. In 1976 the nurses went on strike in Seattle, Washington. During the strike, the hospitals were able to replace them: aides, lpn's, pharmacy mates, supervisors took over their jobs. At the end of the strike, the hospitals were able to replace them with more lower level workers; nurses were clearly not indispensable.[48]

The nurses' responses are often to either recite the catalog of nurses' skills or to insist upon some mystical healing quality inherent in the nurse's touch. But, as the history of nursing demonstrates, the extinction of the profession, if it happens, will result from the increasing division of labor mystified and speeded up by high technology medicine. It can only be resisted and reversed through a critique of the "science" of medicine and nursing and the "science" of management. They go hand in hand.

REFERENCES

For a more detailed and analytic study of the historical development of nursing, see my dissertation, "Apprenticeship to Duty: Nursing and Hospital Reform in the United States, 1860–1940" (Boston University, 1981). The research for this article was originally done under a grant from the Milbank Memorial Fund.

1. The history of the American hospital is just beginning to be written. See, for recent examples, Morris J. Vogel, *The Invention of the Modern Hospital, Boston 1870–1930* (Chicago: University of Chicago Press, 1980); David Karl Rosner, "A Once Charitable Enterprise: Health Care in Brooklyn, 1890–1914" (Unpublished dissertation, Harvard University, 1978); Charles E. Rosenberg, "And Heal the Sick: The Hospital and the Patient in 19th Century America," *Journal of Social History,* 1977, 10: 428–448, and "Inward Vision & Outward Glance: The Shaping of the American Hospital, 1880–1914," *Bulletin of the History of Medicine,* 1979, 53: 346–391.
2. "Diary of Eliza Higgins," Matron of Boston Lying-In Hospital, Volume I, June 1, 1874, Boston Hospital for Women, Public Relations Office.
3. Henry C. Wright, *Report of the Committee on Inquiry into the Departments of Health, Charities, and Bellevue and Allied Hospitals in the City of New York* (New York: Board of Estimate and Apportionment, 1913), p. 78.
4. Rosenberg, "And Heal the Sick . . . ," p. 434; and

G. L. Sturtevant, "Personal Recollections of Hospital Life," *The Trained Nurse and Hospital Review,* 1917, 58: 129–131.
5. See Rosenberg, "Inward Vision & Outward Glance . . . ," passim.
6. See Rosenberg, "And Heal the Sick . . . ," *op. cit.* passim; and chapter two of my dissertation.
7. JoAnn Ashley, *Hospitals, Paternalism and the Role of the Nurse* (New York: Teachers' College Press, 1976).
8. Lavinia Dock, "The Relation of Training Schools to Hospitals," *Nursing of the Sick, 1893,* ed. Isabel Hampton (New York: McGraw-Hill, 1949), p. 20; and Bonnie and Vern Bullough, *The Emergence of Modern Nursing* (New York: Macmillan, 1964), p. 144.
9. Iowa physician, "Pupil Nurses a Hazard to Patients," Letter in *Modern Hospital,* Vol. 3, No. 5, November, 1914, p. 314.
10. May Ayres Burgess, *Nurses, Patients and Pocketbooks* (New York: Committee on Grading of Nursing Schools, 1928), p. 347.
11. See Susan Reverby, " 'Neither for the Drawing Room Nor for the Kitchen,' Private Duty Nursing 1880–1914." Paper presented at the Organization of American Historians Meetings, April 15, 1978.
12. "Address on the Duties and Conduct of Nurses in Private Nursing" (Boston: Press of George H. Ellis, 1886), p. 22 (Box 8, Folder 3, Boston University Nursing Archives).
13. H. B. J., "The Special Nurse," Letter in *The Trained Nurse and Hospital Review,* Vol. 54, No. 2, February, 1915, p. 107.
14. *Ibid.*
15. John A. Hornsby and Richard E. Schmidt, *The Modern Hospital: Its Inspiration; Its Architecture; Its Equipment; Its Operation* (Philadelphia and London: W. B. Saunders and Company, 1913), passim.
16. Janet Geister, "Hearsay and Facts in Private Duty," *American Journal of Nursing,* Vol. 26, No. 7, July, 1926, pp. 515–528; Burgess, *op. cit.* pp. 80–93.
17. "Another Source of Friction in Hospital Administration," *Modern Hospital,* Vol. 6, No. 2, February, 1916, p. 112.
18. "Team Work in the Hospital," *Modern Hospital,* Vol. 4, No. 3, March, 1915, p. 220; "The Usual Duties of a Matron," *Modern Hospital,* Vol. 6, No. 6, June 1916, pp. 460–61.
19. Norman Metzger and Dennis Pointer, *Labor-Management Relations in the Health Services Industry: Theory and Practice* (Washington, D.C.:

Science and Health Publications, Inc., 1972),
p. 13.

20. Kathleen Canning and William Lazonick, "The Development of the Nursing Workforce in the United States: A Basic Analysis," *International Journal of Health Services,* November, 1975, p. 21.

21. Committee for the Study of Nursing Education, *Nursing and Nursing Education in the United States* (New York: Macmillan, 1923).

22. *Ibid.,* pp. 16, 26, 28.

23. Richard O. Beard, "The Report of the Rockefeller Foundation on Nursing Education, A Review and Critique," *American Journal of Nursing,* Vol. 23, No. 5, February, 1923, pp. 358–365; No. 6, March, 1923, pp. 460–466; No. 7, April, 1923, pp. 550–554; Canning and Lazonick, *op. cit.,* p. 23.

24. "Are Nurses Self-Seeking?" *American Journal of Nursing,* Vol. 21, No. 2, November, 1921, pp. 73–74.

25. Wright, "Report . . . ," *op. cit.,* p. 407.

26. "Efficiency in the Care of the Patient," *Transactions of the American Hospital Association,* 16th Annual Conference, 1914, p. 210.

27. Helen E. Marshall, *Mary Adelaide Nutting, Pioneer of Modern Nursing* (Baltimore: Johns Hopkins University Press, 1972), p. 158.

28. Elizabeth Greener, "A Study of Hospital Nursing Service," *Modern Hospital* 16 (January 1921): 99–102; A. Owens et al., "Some Times Studies," *American Journal of Nursing* 27 (February 1927): 99–101; Blanche Pfefferkorn and Marion Rottman, *Clinical Education in Nursing* (New York: Macmillan, 1932); for a review of the more contemporary literature on this, see Myrtle Aydelotte, *Nurse Staffing Methodology, A Review and Critique of Selected Literature* (Washington, D.C.: Government Printing Office, 1970).

29. Pfefferkorn and Rottman, *op. cit.,* p. 59.

30. May Ayres Burgess' *Nurses, Patients and Pocketbooks,* published in 1928, was the first report in this research study. The final report was published as *Nursing Schools: Today and Tomorrow, The Final Report of the Committee on the Grading of Nursing Schools* (New York: Committee on the Grading of Nursing Schools, 1934).

31. *Ibid.,* p. 24.

32. Burgess, *op. cit.,* p. 83.

33. Canning and Lazonick, *op. cit.,* pp. 24–25; Bullough and Bullough, *op. cit.,* Chap. 5.

34. "National Nursing Groups Appeal to Hospital Trustees," *Modern Hospital,* Vol. 34, No. 1, July, 1932, p. 108.

35. Burgess, *op. cit.,* p. 290.

36. *Ibid.,* p. 531.

37. *Ibid.,* p. 434.

38. Malcolm MacEachern, "Which Shall We Choose—Graduate or Student Service?" *Modern Hospital,* Vol. 38, No. 6, June, 1932, pp. 94–104; Anna Wolf, "Is the Use of Graduate Nurses for Floor Duty Justified?" *Modern Hospital,* Vol. 33, No. 5, November, 1929, pp. 140–142; "How Many Students Can a Graduate Nurse Replace?" *Modern Hospital,* Vol. 41, No. 2, August, 1933, p. 86; J. C. Geiger, "An Important Change in Policy," *American Journal of Nursing,* Vol. 32, No. 2, February, 1932, p. 180; R. B. Brisbane, "Should the Small Hospital Employ Graduate or Student Nurses?," *Modern Hospital,* Vol. 28, No. 6, June, 1927, pp. 142–144.

39. *Nursing Schools: Today and Tomorrow, op. cit.,* p. 117.

40. Shirley Titus, "The Significance of General Duty Nursing to Our Profession," *American Journal of Nursing,* Vol. 31, No. 2, February, 1931, pp. 197–207, and "Group Nursing and How It Affects the Welfare of Patients," *Modern Hospital,* Vol. 35, No. 6, December, 1930, pp. 120–128.

41. Canning and Lazonick, *op. cit.,* p. 26.

42. A. C. Jensen, "Training Nursing Attendants," *Modern Hospital,* Vol. 51, No. 5, November, 1938, p. 68.

43. Emily Spieler, "Division of Laborers," *Health/ PAC BULLETIN,* No. 45, November, 1972, pp. 3–17; and Susan Reverby, "From Aide to Organizer, the Oral History of Lillian Roberts," in Carol Berkin and Mary Beth Norton, eds., *Women of America, A History* (Boston: Houghton-Mifflin, 1979) pp. 289–317.

44. Winifred Shepler et al., "Standardized Training Course for Ward Aids," *Modern Hospital,* Vol. 51, No. 6, December, 1938, pp. 68–69.

45. *Ibid.,* p. 70; A. K. Haywood, "The Status of the Nursing Attendant," *Modern Hospital,* Vol. 19, No. 3, September, 1922, pp. 226–227.

46. Everett Hughes et al., *20,000 Nurses Tell Their Story* (Philadelphia: J. B. Lippincott, 1948), pp. 131–146.

47. M., "The Attendant, Her Place and Work," Letter in *American Journal of Nursing,* Vol. 20, No. 2, November, 1919, pp. 154–155.

48. Margaret Levi, "Functional Redundancy and the Process of Professionalization: The Case of Registered Nurses in the United States," paper presented to the 1978 International Sociological Association Meetings in Uppsala, Sweden, July 1978.

17

The Health Labor Force: The Effects of Change

Nancy Aries and Louanne Kennedy

Introduction: Physicians, Technology, and Finance

This article examines the ways in which the organization of the health labor force is shaped by three factors: the dominant role of physicians in medical care; medical technology; and health care financing. Most analyses of the health labor force explain its organization in terms of the first two of these variables. The result is that the existing structure of the health care system appears to be the "natural" result of scientific progress (Banta, 1981).

Physician role and technology are important but they are only a part of the explanation. The organization of work in a market economy is also related to the method by which it is financed. Therefore an analysis of the organization of health employment must also include an examination of the role of health care financing.

Physicians, for better or worse, are the central figures in defining the limits of health and disease and the scope of medical practice. (For a more complete discussion of these issues see Starr, 1982.) Following the Second World War, an apparent "explosion" of medical science and technology made available new tools, techniques, and facilities. As new equipment for diagnosis and treatment developed, physicians readily incorporated them into standard practice. The new technology, in turn, transformed medical care from an individual, office based occupation to an increasingly centralized, hospi-

tal based, high-technology industry. Hospitals became the locus of medical services in part because they were capable of marshalling the necessary resources to transform the health services industry from one which relied on labor to one which currently also depends on complex medical equipment.

Medical technology not only affected the method and location of physician practice, it also influenced the shape of the health labor force. Unlike most industries where capital investment decreases labor intensity (and therefore labor costs), in the health industry, the greater the reliance on new equipment, the greater the need for additional support staff. The development of hospital intensive care units is a case in point. These units use highly sophisticated and expensive equipment which require higher nursing to patient ratios than a medical or surgical floor. Thus, the last thirty years has seen an explosion in nursing and technologic support occupations with the percentage increase in personnel reaching as high as 1000 percent.

The impact of technology and physician practice on the health labor force can only be understood in the context of the larger economics of health care production. The central economic feature of American health care has been the fee-for-service payment system which dominates most of medical practice. Under this arrangement doctors and hospitals generate income by providing services. Thus, there is an implicit economic incentive to maximize the volume of services in order to maximize revenue. Third-party payers (i.e., private insurors and the government) reinforce this incentive because they reimburse at the higher rate for services performed in hospitals than those done in offices and clinics. Until recently, third-party reimbursement to hospitals has been based on their costs. Under this system, an institution that reduces its costs reduces its income, since the record of past costs affects future reimbursement levels. Institutions with higher costs received greater reimbursements. Hospitals were encouraged to solve financial problems by maximizing reimbursement rather than minimizing costs. Thus, under fee-for-service, cost-based reimbursement, hospitals increased their services and the personnel necessary to provide them.

Beginning in the late 1970s, cost containment became the dominant theme in policy making concerning the health care system. A variety of restrictions on reimbursement were introduced, all with the purpose of removing incentives for hospitals to provide a greater volume of services. The most dramatic change occurred in 1983 when Medicare introduced a new system of reimbursement based on Diagnostically Related Groups (DRG) under which a hospital is paid a flat fee per patient based on diagnosis. The DRG system reverses the incentive of the fee-for-service system; under DRGs the fewer services provided a patient, the greater the profit to the hospital.

One response of hospital managers to cost containment has been the developemnt of strategies to cut costs. Because 60 percent of the hospital costs are attributed to labor inputs, labor costs are the most likely source of savings. Unlike most industries, the nature of health care services has not permitted the substitution of capital for labor. Accordingly, hospital management is attempting to cut labor costs by breaking down work tasks into ever simpler components that can be done by lower paid individuals; and to increase productivity, for example, by increasing the number of procedures performed by a worker in a given period of time. The result of this strategy has been the proliferation of jobs at the lower wage levels, reduction of opportunity for advancement, and increased management-labor tensions.

The Size and Organization of the Health Labor Force

Estimates of the size of the health labor force range from 5 to 8 million workers, depending on whether or not workers with or without health related training are included. The Bureau of the Census uses an inclusive definition of the health labor force as all people who work within the health care industry. The critical factor here is the location of work. Thus physicians, nurses, laboratory technologists, orderlies, and receptionists are all defined as health workers although the receptionist may have no skills relevant to the industry. The National Center for Health Statistics is only concerned with those personnel who have explicit training for health related jobs. While the Center's definition includes all health personnel regardless of the industry in which they are employed, its definition tends to be the more exclusive since a large proportion of the health labor force does not consist of workers trained in health care.

For the purposes of this article we will use the more limited definition of health personnel to examine the effects of changing technology and medical organization on those workers who have knowledge and skills which are unique to the health industry. It is those workers who are specifically trained for the health field that determine the shape of the industry.

The structure of the health labor force resembles a layered pyramid-like structure (McTernan and Leiken, 1982). Physicians are at the apex followed by other independent practitioners such as dentists and podiatrists. Together, these two groups are responsible for directing the work of support personnel such as nurses, technologists, and aides who comprise the majority of the labor force. The importance of the pyramid is that it is indicative of the labor intensive nature of the industry. Monetarily, almost two-thirds of the value of health services is accounted for by the labor of medical workers (Sorkin, 1977, p. 1).

While the pyramid generally describes who controls the organization of the medical care system, it fails to recognize the lack of unity within occupational groups. One of the consequences of a hospital based medical care system which relies on advanced technology has been a split in the nature of physician practice. There are the technically trained specialists who can perform complex medical procedures using state of the art technology such as computerized laser and x-ray technology; for example, pathologists, radiologists, and anesthesiologists. These physicians are hospital based and have a limited and circumscribed relationship with the patient. They tend to lead teams of highly trained technologists and technicians who work under close physician supervision.

Other physicians generally practice in primary care and are literate about the new diagnostic tools and techniques. They perform routine examinations of patients as in the past. Their new role requires them to order the proper diagnostic tools and to consult with the technically trained physicians about the appropriate use of surgical and medical interventions. These physicians with less technical skills are case managers who have an ongoing relationship with their patients as did the idealized general practitioners of a bygone era. But these case managers are not general practitioners in the old sense of the term. They are usually specialists in fields such as internal medicine, obstetrics, gynecology, and pediatrics.

Of course not all physicians fall neatly into these two categories, but an increasing division in the profession appears to be underway. As a result of the increased reliance by physicians on the diagnostic and therapeutic techniques delivered by new "high tech" oriented nurses and technologists, employment in these fields has grown more rapidly than employment in the health field in general. As with the diversity among physicians, the diverse roles and pressures within nursing and technologists are masked by the broader level.

Physicians

Physicians include doctors of medicine (MD) and doctors of osteopathy (DO). In the period between 1950 and 1970 the number of physicians remained relatively constant. In 1950 there were 232,000 and in 1970, 280,000 physicians, but between 1970 and 1980, there was a 54 percent increase in the overall number of physi-

cians, to 433,000 (see Tables 1 and 2). Despite the increase in the numbers of physicians, their ratio to other health workers has declined markedly. In 1900, 1 out of 3 health workers was a physician. Now only 1 out of 16 health workers is a physician (Ginsberg, 1983, 483).

This sharp increase in physicians in the 1970s was due to a number of factors. In the late sixties, there were projections of a physician shortage. The labor force projections indicated that the shortage would be concentrated by specialty and geographic location. There was a two-part strategy to address the shortage and concentration of physicians. The first sought to increase supply and allow the market to resolve problems of distribution. Large sums of federal monies went to educating physicians. A number of new medical schools were formed and established schools were expanded. The second strategy was based on incentives. Funds were made available in programs such as the National Health Service Corps to encourage the training of primary care physicians and to encourage their practice in medically underserved areas. Although the number of physicians increased, geographic and specialty maldistribution has persisted. The increased supply of physicians has intensified competition in some large urban areas and in some specialties such as surgery (44 percent of all practicing physicians in 1977 were surgeons). Rural areas and low-income communities continue to suffer shortages. Primary care physicians (obstetrics-gynecology, pediatrics, and family practice) are also in short supply (Huet-Cox, 1984).

Non-Physician Practitioners

Non-physician practitioners consist of three groups: (1) those who have been empowered to maintain independent practices, (2) those who have not, and (3) those where the lines are not so clearly drawn. The first includes dentists, podiatrists, psychologists, chiropractors, and optometrists. The second group is referred to as dependent allied health professionals because their practice is circumscribed by physicians. These are the nurse practitioners (NP) and physician assistants (PA). Other categories such as physical

Table 1.   Number of Persons Employed in Selected Health Occupations: 1950–1980

Occupation	1950	1960	1970	1980
Physicians (1)	232,700	274,800	280,929	433,255
Dentists	87,200	101,900	90,801	125,291
Podiatrists, Chiropractors, Optometrists, Veterinarians	60,700	70,000	56,409	66,741
Pharmacists	101,100	117,000	109,642	145,637
Therapists (2)	11,100	22,400	75,161	150,865
Nurse Practitioners, Physician Assistants	—	—	—	26,000
Registered Nurses	375,000	504,000	829,691	1,285,299
Laboratory Technologists and Technicians	30,000	68,000	117,606	243,982
Radiologic Technologists and Technicians	30,800	70,000	52,230	96,311
Dental Auxiliaries (3)	62,200	96,196	103,980	204,309
Medical Records	12,000	28,000	11,164	15,147
Dieticians	22,000	26,000	40,131	67,270
Practical Nurses	137,000	206,000	237,133	435,176
Nursing Aides and Orderlies	225,000	482,074	717,968	1,378,118
Administrators	8,600	12,000	84,139	110,881

(1) Doctors of Medicine, Doctors of Osteopathy
(2) Physical Therapists, Occupational Therapists, Respiratory Therapists, Speech Therapists
(3) Dental Hygienists, Dental Assistants
Sources: US Census Bureau, *Reports for 1980*
        US Census Bureau, *Decennial Census Data—1970*
        US Census Bureau, *1960 Special Census Report*

therapists, nurse-midwives, and social workers may be independent or dependent practitioners. They have attempted to establish independent practices but are increasingly coming under the control of the medical profession.

With the exception of dentists, the number of independent non-physician practitioners has remained fairly constant. Between 1950 and 1980, dentists experienced a 44 percent increase in their overall numbers while podiatrists, chiropractors, optometrists and veterinarians experienced only a 10 percent increase (see Table 2). The increase among dentists, as opposed to the other independent practitioners, was a by-product of the general investment in physicians training in the 1970s. At that time, money was also made available for dental schools and dental traineeships.

The group of non-physician practitioners with less certain boundaries in terms of independence of practice have increased dramatically over the last thirty years. Therapists including respiratory,

occupational, physical, and speech have increased by more than 1000 percent (see Table 2). The explanation for the growth of this group is related to the changing basis of medical practice and financing. Therapists, for example, offer services that are beyond the scope of physician practice but fall within the domain of medicine. They hold out the promise of rehabilitation in much the same way that a technical procedure holds out the promise of cure. Given the increased pressure for rehabilitation in a system which will reimburse services prescribed by a physician, it is logical for a physician to order therapy if there is the slightest evidence that it will be efficacious. Thus, the demand for services has generated the growth of occupations where there are limited barriers to access, such as the cost of training.

The development of new types of practitioners (NPs and PAs) emerged in the 1960s as a response to possible physician shortages, particularly in low-income areas. The new practitioners

Table 2.   Percentage Change in Selected Health Occupations: 1950–1980

Occupation	1950–60	1960–70	1970–80	1950–80
Physicians (1)	18%	2%	54%	86%
Dentists	17	−12	38	44
Podiatrists, Chiropractors, Optometrists, Veterinarians	15	−24	18	10
Pharmacists	16	−7	33	44
Therapists (2)	102	236	101	1,259
Nurse Practitioners, Physician Assistants	n.a.	n.a.	n.a.	n.a.
Registered Nurses	34	65	55	243
Laboratory Technologists and Technicians	127	73	108	714
Radiologic Technologists and Technicians	127	−34	84	213
Dental Auxiliaries (3)	55	8	96	228
Medical Records	133	−151	36	26
Dieticians	18	54	68	206
Practical Nurses	50	15	84	218
Nursing Aides and Orderlies	114	49	92	512
Administrators	40	601	32	1,189

(1) Doctors of Medicine, Doctors of Osteopathy
(2) Physical Therapists, Occupational Therapists, Respiratory Therapists, Speech Therapists
(3) Dental Hygienists, Dental Assistants
Source: Table 1

provided care under limited physician supervision. In addition, the utilization of NPs and PAs by health care providers held out the promise of improved productivity and decreased costs. Finally, these new practitioner occupations emerged in part as a response to other pressures in the labor market. For example, physician assistants were seen as an appropriate position for trained Vietnam medics returning to the United States. Nurse practitioners provided an occupational opportunity by which nurses could achieve greater autonomy (Backup and Molinaro, 1984).

Despite the attention given to NPs and PAs their numbers are relatively small in relation to the health labor force. In 1970 there were no nurse practitioners or physician assistants listed in the census. As of 1980 there were 25,000 NPs and PAs combined (see Table 1). This is less than one percent of all workers in the health labor force. Furthermore, this group of workers is unevenly distributed throughout the system.

Given the rapidly expanding physician supply, organized medicine has begun resisting the independent practitioners who are perceived to threaten physical autonomy and economic power. This objection is expressed in terms of quality of care. When physicians are able to maintain control or their economic interests are not threatened, they are less likely to object to PAs and NPs and find the quality of care delivered by the latter to be excellent. For example, in rural areas, PAs and NPs work miles from the nearest physicians and may call on them as little as once a month to have them sign prescriptions and review records (Backup and Molinaro, 1984). Thus, the power and autonomy of NPs and PAs in the medical care system emerges only in those geographic locations characterized by low-income or medically underserved communities (Ostow, 1981).

Medical Technologists and Technicians

The groups of workers made up of technologists and technicians has seen the most dramatic growth in the last thirty years. Not only have their numbers increased, but there has also been a proliferation of new job categories related to the development of new technologies. The major classifications of health technologists and technicians include clinical, laboratory, radiologic, dental, and medical record workers.[1] In addition, the classification includes those men and women who run specialized equipment such as EKG machinery.

The emergence and rapid growth of this segment of the health labor force is a function of the changing nature of medical care. At the turn of the century, physician diagnosis was limited to history taking and physical examination. Similarly, medical intervention was of a limited nature. Now innumerable laboratory and diagnostic procedures are part of the diagnostic process. As diagnosis and treatment have both become based on active intervention, there has been a rise in the number of support personnel to operate the machinery and staff the laboratories.

The delegation of tasks to the new occupations serves multiple purposes. Besides assigning the least interesting aspects of care, it allows physicians to increase patient load and therefore income (Starr, 1982). At one time it was possible for physicians to provide the full range of ancillary services themselves without affecting the size of their patient load; this becomes more difficult as the number of services increases. Delegation, therefore, enables physicians to increase patient loads by having a technologist assume responsibility for the most routinized aspects of care.

The numbers bear out the postulation that tasks are being delegated by independent professionals in order to increase patient load or the quantity of services provided to each patient. As previously stated, between 1950 and 1980 there was only a 44 percent increase in the number of dentists. The number of dental assistants and hygienists, however, increased by 228 percent (see table 2). This is a clear case where delegation can be documented in terms of changing office practice. A similar increase is also apparent in the practice of radiology. Formerly carried out by physicians, now a great number of the tasks have been delegated to technologists and technicians. The number of radiologic technologists and technicians increased by 85 percent between 1970 and 1980. While there has been an increase

in support personnel who provide services most directly linked to medical practice, the most dramatic increase has been the area of laboratory sciences. Laboratory technicians and technologists increased by 714 percent between 1950 and 1980. Their increase points to the changing basis of medical practice.

Nurses

Registered nurses (RNs) are the largest occupational group in the health labor force. In 1980, there were 1,285,299 RNs, about one-fifth of all health workers. Registered nurses are the original "physician assistants." Nursing was a career path fashioned to permit women to work in the health field along side the "men of medicine" without challenging physicians' occupational dominance (Melosh, 1982).

For years nursing leadership has struggled to find an occupational niche within the "science" of medical care and traditional medical practice. To that end, nursing education has been moving away from hospital based diploma programs towards university based baccalaureate and graduate training programs. The advanced training of nurses can be seen in the development of a wider range of nursing positions. At the upper end of the nursing hierarchy are the specialists: intensive care unit, cardiac unit, and operating room nurses. At the lower end of the nursing hierarchy are those nurses whose jobs involve more routine bedside activities. The dilemma which faces the profession as a result of this shift is that as the training becomes more technically and biologically grounded within scientific medicine, the limits imposed by physicians on nursing practice produce conflicts and contradictions for those newly educated nurses. They must confront occupational expectations that devalue, ignore, and even contradict what is now nursing's own expertise.

As one consequence of these pressures, nursing leadership has been willing to pass on the more routine bedside tasks to licensed practical nurses (LPNs), aides, orderlies, and ward clerks. Delegation is part of the nursing profession's strategy to enhance occupational power within the medical care labor force. This causes a dilemma because hospital administrators also share the goal of task delegation as a means to expand managerial control over the work in hospitals by replacing more skilled with less skilled workers. While both administrators and nursing leadership agree on this outcome they have very different reasons for pursuing these ends. For managers it is to limit the occupational control by higher paid nurses; for nurses it is seen as enhancing their professional status.

Replacing professional nurses with less skilled workers may result in adverse effects on quality. RNs, trained in medical and biological science, understand the symptoms and interventions that patients require in the absence of a physician. When bedside care is partially removed from the direct responsibility of RNs, the RN becomes more of a manager supervising lesser trained personnel who actually provide the direct patient care.

Health Care Managers

Before 1960, hospital administrators were typically physicians. As medical care became increasingly technological and hospital based, and with the advent of complex reimbursement systems that followed the introduction of Medicare and Medicaid, health care management became redefined as a distinct occupation. Administrators needed training in management and financing in order to manage the increasingly complex hospitals and health care organizations. Health care management has become identified as the occupation which is responsible for controlling the rising costs of medical care. Within the last twenty years there has been a growth of graduate programs that train health care managers in the areas of financial control and productivity. Health administration has grown from 8,600 personnel in 1950 to 110,881 in 1980, a change of 1,189 percent (see Tables 1 and 2).

An additional pressure on health care managers has come as a result of the growth of for-profit hospitals and hospital chains. Proprietary organizations reflect a conscious orientation to "business" practices and view hospital and health care organizations like any other industry. Corporate chains, both profit and nonprofit, stress marketing of health care services, productivity management, and maximization of profits. This orientation has affected management of all hospitals including proprietary, voluntary, and public facilities. Health care marketing stresses attracting well-insured patients as a primary goal, and productivity management stresses reducing labor costs by hiring less expensive and less skilled technologists. When combined with controls on reimbursement and a lessening of entitlement for poor people, the continuation of this trend may limit access and increase pressure on physicians and other workers to practice medicine with a sharper focus on profits (Kennedy, 1981).

Race, Gender, and Class

Employment in the health industry reflects inequalities within American society; occupational power and wealth are predominantly concentrated among white men. In contrast, the lowest level jobs are often filled by black women. A society with unequal wealth and power generates jobs by race, sex, and social class. Thus, even within the category of white men, those from upper social and economic strata will have easier access to the jobs which command the most wealth and status. In this context, class can be thought of as the relative ability to control one's own life. The higher an individual's social class the more resources are at that person's command. Upper-class people will have easy access to the elite colleges and medical schools. This gives them entrance into the most desired specialty residencies, which in turn leads to dominant positions within the health care hierarchy. This is not to say that a poor child might not become a prominent heart surgeon through a rare combination of talent, ambition, and luck. But the number of these exceptional success stories is irrelevant to the normal operation of social and professional power. As a result of racism, sexism, and social class distinctions, the distribution of workers in the hierarchy of jobs in the health care industry reflects the discriminations of the larger society (Navarro, 1976).

Women make up the majority of workers in the health services industry. Although women

Table 3.   Selected Health Occupations by Total Employment, Percent Black, Percent Female: 1980

	Total Employed	Percent Black	Percent Female
Physicians (1)	433,255	3.1%	13.4%
Dentists	125,291	2.5	6.7
Podiatrists, Chiropractors, Optometrists, Veterinarians	66,741	1.2	10.9
Pharmacists	145,637	3.2	24.0
Therapists (2)	150,865	7.2	74.5
Nurse Practitioners, Physician Assistants	n.a.	—	—
Registered Nurses	1,285,299	7.4	95.9
Laboratory Technologists and Technicians	243,982	11.5	97.0
Radiologic Technologists and Technicians	96,311	8.2	71.6
Dental Auxiliaries (3)	204,309	3.6	98.0
Medical Records	15,147	9.7	91.3
Dieticians	67,270	21.4	89.9
Practical Nurses	435,176	18.0	96.6
Nursing Aides and Orderlies	1,378,118	27.0	87.8
Administrators	110,881	8.5	50.8

(1) Doctors of Medicine, Doctors of Osteopathy
(2) Physical Therapists, Occupational Therapists, Respiratory Therapists, Speech Therapists
(3) Dental Hygienists, Dental Assistants
Sources: US Census Bureau, *Reports for 1980*

constitute 42 percent of the national work force, they are 75 percent of all health industry workers (Sekscenski, 1981). There are still marked differences between job categories occupied by men and women. Medicine, dentistry, and optometry are still predominantly male occupations. Only 13 percent of physicians are women whereas 96 percent of nurses are women. The other occupations where women are underrepresented are pharmacology and administration. In both cases these have been traditional male jobs because they were equated with independent practice or a strong controlling presence (see Table 3).

The predominance of women in the industry is considered to be one of the reasons for the lower average earnings of health service workers (Ginsberg, 1983). Women employed as health therapists and registered nurses earn about 85 percent of the average weekly earnings of men in the same occupational categories. The same earnings ratio by sex applies to LPN's, nurses aides, and nonprofessional health service workers (Sekscenski, 1981).

Black workers also constitute a large percentage of health service employees. Blacks make up 10 percent of the national work force but 13 percent of the health labor force. If jobs within the medical care system were ranked by status, an inverse relation would exist between the job and the percentage of blacks who hold that position. Even after enormous media attention and institutional efforts to meet affirmative action obligations in the 1970s, only 3.1 percent of all physicians were black. This can be contrasted to lower status job categories such as practical nursing, nursing aides, and orderlies. Black workers are overrepresented in these positions: 18 percent of practical nurses and 27 percent of nursing aides and orderlies are black (see Table 3).

Black women are primarily workers in the nonprofessional health occupations. Even registered nursing, while a women's profession, has a smaller percentage of black workers than does the industry as a whole. Black men are also primarily workers in the nonprofessional positions but they have slightly increased their participation in the technical health occupations (Sekscenski, 1981). This overrepresentation in the lowest status job categories is an indication of the degree of discrimination and reduced opportunity in the industry.

Strategies for Occupational Power

Health workers have two options before them to increase their power and autonomy within the medical care system. One choice is to seek professional status similar to that held by physicians. This has typically been the choice of higher status health workers such as nurses. The second choice is to unionize. In this case workers seek power through their unity with other workers regardless of position within the medical care hierarchy. Both options, however, must be seen as routes to the same goal.

The pressure to seek professional recognition is in response to a number of factors, most important of which is the workers' struggle to be recognized as competent practitioners exercising independent judgment. Professional status is believed to be derived from the possession of specialized knowledge which qualifies and entitles workers to control the content and organization of their work. This knowledge serves to define workers' power in decision making about patient care (Freidson, 1970). Professionalization, then, is an ideology and set of activities intended to upgrade the status of health workers; thereby serving as a mechanism for protecting the workers' "turf" despite continuing specialization and rationalization of work. Professionalization has been a strategy of nurses and newly trained technicians. These workers organized professional associations and published professional journals in order to establish a mechanism for internal control. Such organizational forms facilitated communication between workers who otherwise had no access to one another. The primary topics under consideration are the standardization of tasks and the definition of the boundaries of practice (McCready, 1982). Once in place, the associations moved to establish firmly their professional identity through licensure. For any occupation, licensure provides a

means to control the supply of practitioners and the scope of their practice. For individuals, licensure provides legal protection and in some cases, access to third-party reimbursement. Where licensure has not been possible, the associations have striven for certification as a means of protecting their professional status.

The strategy of professionalization, however, has largely failed to accomplish the goal which the allied health workers had set for themselves. It has not given them the control over their work or the recognition and status in the health care hierarchy they sought. With the exception of nursing, the professional associations of allied health workers are controlled by the AMA's Committee on Education. In addition, these workers do not control the technology with which they work. Some labor analysts project that allied health workers will be further de-skilled as the operation of technological equipment continues to be broken down into simplified tasks (Falk, 1983; Friedman, 1983). Finally, the use of medical technology is determined by physician practice. Again, allied health workers do not control any aspect of medical practice or their own roles in the process. The physician remains firmly in control, the "Captain of the Team" (Fuchs, 1974). Thus, allied health professionals cannot approach professional recognition on a level with physicians.

Unionization of medical workers raises sharply differing questions for unskilled and semiskilled workers and for other employees who self-identify as professionals. For many unskilled and semiskilled hospital workers, the organization of trade unions has been a logical response to the increasing industrialization of the health care system. Since the early 1960s, 25 percent of health workers have joined unions. The growth of unions was triggered by a series of major strike actions and, in 1974, by first-time coverage under federal collective bargaining laws for hospital workers. For unskilled and semiskilled hospital workers with no claim to professionalism, unionization has brought dramatic change, greatly improving pay and job security.

Unionization of occupations with professional identities has proceeded more slowly. These occupations are already organized in their own associations (i.e., the American Nursing Association, the National Association of Social Workers). These workers are often fearful that unionization will result in loss of prestige and decline of professional status. Traditionally, union membership has been associated with the low paid, semiskilled or unskilled worker. Trade unionists are seen as staunch group members, whereas the epitome of the professional is the autonomous individual practitioner (Transue, 1980).

The tension between professionalism and unionism is reflected in three different patterns of worker participation. Some workers have declined participation in unions and depend solely on their associations despite the associations' inability to intervene in workplace issues. A relatively small number of higher status workers have joined traditional unions. Nurses, for example, have joined District 1199, National Hospital Workers Union, AFL-CIO; and social workers have joined AFSCME (American Federation of State, County and Municipal Employees). Both nurses and social workers are also part of SWIU (Service Workers International Union). Finally, some membership associations have begun to act as collective bargaining agents. Challenged by traditional unions, organizations like the American Nursing Association have become bargaining units that argue nurses should be represented by a separate association because these workers have special interests such as standards of practice, licensure, and peer review that cannot be adequately addressed by trade unions.

The union strategy has met increased resistance from hospital managers. Management consulting firms with anti-union skills are often hired by hospitals at the first suggestion of a union drive. They have pioneered in the use of agency nurses hired on a per diem basis including a new "flying nurse" category. ("Flying nurses" are hired on a contractual basis with no fringe benefits to fly literally into an area and staff a hospital for a short period of time.) Such management strategies limit the possibility of workers' collective action since high turnover is built into the system. Proprietary (i.e., for-profit) hospitals have been the most successful in keeping unions out of their organizations. They have accomplished this in part because of their concentration in the south and southwest, areas with a strong anti-union bias.

The effectiveness of the two strategies for organizational power will depend upon the ways in which the organizational structure of health care evolves in the future. The fact that neither provides a perfect solution is demonstrated by the case of physicians. As an increasing number of physicians receive larger portions of their incomes as employees of institutions, rather than from independent practice, the same tension between professionalization and unionization is emerging (Sclar, 1984). About 2.5 percent of physicians are now members of unions. These physicians have determined that their prospects are brighter if they behave more like trade unionists and less like independent professionals (Braverman, 1974; Sarfatti-Larsen, 1977). Whether or not increased numbers of professionals will move toward unionization is unclear. The trends which we must follow are the growing number of physician/employees, especially within the burgeoning field of for-profit health care and the ways in which the new DRG system of third-party reimbursement effects the organization of work in the health care industry.

Conclusions

The division of work in the field of health is shaped by three forces: the nature and organization of physician practice, the value attributed to technology, and the modes of financing. Physicians' occupational dominance includes the power to define what medical services will be legitimated as necessary. This power in turn justifies changes in the number, types, and work tasks of the health labor force. Although physician practice has changed over time, the medical model of physician control remains dominant. Physicians control the labor process by defining the boundaries of medical "need" and doing so within existing organizational and technical resources. This thereby limits possibilities for change, in particular a challenge to the fundamental power distribution.

Physician practice is increasingly dependent on technology for both diagnosis and treatment. The increased reliance on technology has led to escalating costs and the proliferation of new occupations to employ the technology. The availability of funding to pay for the new technologies influences the quantity and quality of the services provided through the physician dominated health system. This system creates pressure upon health workers to define as concretely as possible the particular work they do and then to defend the boundaries of that work against encroachments by other health specialists. The result is the proliferation of health occupational specialties, and tensions between and within the different occupational groups.

There is an absence of career ladders bridging the various health occupations. As a result of licensing laws or established patterns of division of labor, a practical nurse cannot be promoted to the position of registered nurse by virtue of work experience.

Similarly, a registered nurse cannot become a physician without eight additional years of training, many of which may be redundant. This results in a system in which average salaries for experienced health workers do not differ by more than about 25 percent from average starting salaries (Nassif, 1980). There is little incentive to stay in fields which do not pay well, causing high turnover and adding high costs for continually training new personnel. A health care system in which rational career ladders existed would tend to be more efficient, more professional, and more accountable than the present one. As matters presently stand, however, such a system is a distant hope. Instead, we are likely to see a continuous proliferation of jobs and professions as health technology continues to change. Workers will be pressured to strive either for enhancement of professional status or the formation of unions in order to protect their positions within the health field.

The absence of career ladders in most of the health occupations has its most severe impact on women and minorities. These groups are disproportionately at the lowest ends of the occupational strata and are least likely to have the resources to retrain in the more autonomous, well-paying professions. The stratification in health occupations reflects the stratification in American society with women and minorities at the lower ends of the occupational scale.

Are there any forces at work to counter physician dominance and the technological imperative that drives the system? Controls on technology and reimbursement have existed since the 1970s but have gained strength in the 1980s as both the government and the private sector have sought to limit health care expenditures. The introduction of Diagnostically Related Groups, the growth of the proprietary sector, and emphasis on managerial decision making are examples of regulatory and market attempts at controlling costs. As a result of these changes the position of health care manager, now charged with the task of controlling costs, has become more powerful. Each of these movements poses a possible threat to the continued hegemony of physician control. The growing strength of managerial decisions, however, does not necessarily auger well for the health occupations. Management emphasis on productivity levels is likely to further the pressures toward the deskilling of labor and continuation of the breakdown in tasks to be done by lower paid and more vulnerable employees. Management control is reflected in pressures to prohibit unions in the name of lowering cost through lowered wages. Management also seeks to limit length of stay and ancillary services in hospitals thereby permitting reductions in force.

These changes in the organization and economics of health care are unlikely to result in a more equitable distribution of occupational groups or their tasks and salaries. Nor are they likely to result in a more equitable arrangement for patients. Current controls on health care spending have a negative effect on the most vulnerable groups of workers and patients: the elderly, the poor, women, and minorities.

NOTES

We want to thank Elliott Sclar and Herbert Semmel for their helpful comments on earlier drafts of the paper. Pamela Wiesen assisted with the data collection.

1. Technologists and technicians are usually grouped together although they differ in terms of status and tasks. In general, technologists are licensed through voluntary associations, e.g., medical technologists are licensed through the American Society of Clinical Pathologists, and bear the title M.T. after their name. Technicians may carry out the same tasks but lack the status and often the salaries of technologists.

REFERENCES

Backup, Molly, and John Molinaro. "New Health Professionals: Changing the Hierarchy." in V. Sidel and R. Sidel, (eds.), *Reforming Medicine*. New York: Pantheon, 1984, pp. 201-219.

Banta, David, and Clyde Behney, and Jane Willems. *Toward Rational Technology in Medicine*. New York: Singer, 1981.

Braverman, Harry. *Labor and Monopoly Capital: The Degradation of Work in the Twentieth Century*. New York: Monthly Review Press, 1974.

Falk, Dennis S. "The Challenge of Change: Specialized Professions Share the Need to Adapt to Constant Change." *Hospitals* (April 1, 1983) pp. 92–98.

Freidson, Eliot. *Profession of Medicine: A Study of the Sociology of Applied Knowledge*. New York: Dodd, Mead and Co., 1970.

Friedman, Emily. "Ebb Tide for Allied Health." *Hospitals* (February 1, 1983) pp.66–71.

Fuchs, Victor, R. *Who Shall Live? Health, Economics and Social Change*. New York: Basic Books, 1974.

Ginsberg, Eli. "Allied Health Resources." in David Mechanic (ed.), *The Handbook of Health, Health Care, and the Health Professions*. New York: Basic Books, 1983, pp. 479–494.

Goldstein, Harold M., and Morris A. Horowitz. *Entry-Level Health Occupations: Development and Future*. Baltimore: Johns Hopkins University Press, 1977.

Goldstein, Harold M., and Morris A. Horowitz. *Health Personnel Meeting the Explosive Demand for Medical Care*. Germantown, MD: Aspens Systems Corp., 1977.

Huet-Cox, Rocio. "Medical Education: New Wine in Old Wine Skins." in V. Sidel and R. Sidel, (eds.), *Reforming Medicine*. New York: Pantheon, 1984, pp. 129–149.

Kennedy, Louanne. "Hospitals in Chains: The Transformation of American Health Institutions", *Health/PAC Bulletin*. 12:8, (Fall 1981) pp. 9–36.

McCready, Linda A. "Emerging Health Care Occupations: The System under Siege." *Health Care Management Review*. (Fall 1982) pp. 71–76.

McTernan, Edmund J., and Alan M. Leiken. "A Pyramid Model of Health Manpower in the 1980's." *Journal of Health Politics, Policy and Law*. 6:4 (Winter, 1982) pp. 739–751.

Melosh, Barbara. *The Physicians Hand: Nurses and Nursing in the Twentieth Century*. Philadelphia: Temple University Press, 1982.

Nassif, Janet Z. *Handbook of Health Careers: A Guide to Employment Opportunities*. New York: Human Sciences Press, 1980.

Navarro, Vincente. *Medicine Under Capitalism*. New York: Prodist, 1976.

Ostow, Miriam, and Michael L. Millman. "The Demographic Dimensions of Health Manpower Policy." *Public Health Reports*. 96:4 (July/August 1981) pp. 304–309.

Sarfatti-Larsen, Magali. *The Rise of Professionalism*. Berkeley: University of California Press, 1977.

Sclar, Elliott. "For-Profit Health Care: The Planners' Dilemma." Paper presented at the Annual Meeting of the New York Academy of Medicine, May 1984.

Sekscenski, Edward S. "The Health Services Industry: A Decade of Expansion." *Monthly Labor Review*. 104:5 (May 1981) pp. 9–16.

Sorkin, Alan L. *Health Manpower: An Economic Perspective*. Lexington: Lexington Books, 1977.

Starr, Paul. *The Social Transformation of American Medicine*. New York: Basic Books, 1982.

Strelnick, Hal, and Richard Younge. "Affirmative Action in Medicine." in V. Sidel and R. Sidel, (eds.), *Reforming Medicine*. New York: Pantheon, 1984, pp. 150–175.

Transue, Judith. "Collective Bargaining on Whose Terms." *Catalyst*. 5 (1980) pp. 25–37.

Medical Industries

The medical industries have "commodified" health in a number of ways. They have turned certain goods and services into products or commodities that can be marketed to meet "health needs" created by the industry itself. A recent and commonplace example of "commodification" was the promotion of Listerine as a cure for the "disease" of "halitosis" (bad breath). A wide range of products have been marketed to meet commodified health needs such as products designed to alleviate feminine hygiene "problems" and instant milk formulas to meet the "problem" of feeding infants.

In the late twentieth century medical care is a profitable investment, at least for stockholders and corporations. With the increase in medical technology and the growth of for-profit hospitals, medicine itself is becoming increasingly a corporate industry. The 1960s saw the rise of a large nursing home industry (Vladeck, 1980), in the 1970s there were huge increases in investment in for-profit hospital chains, and in the 1980s new free-standing emergency rooms are dotting the suburban landscape. The nonprofit, and especially the public, sector of medicine has decreased while the for-profit sector continues to increase. The closing of many urban, public hospitals is a piece of this change (Sager, 1983). As Starr (1982) notes, this corporatization of medicine presents a threat to the long-standing physician sovereignty. This is part of a shift of power in medicine from the "professional monopolists" (AMA physicians) to the "corporate rationalizers" (Alford, 1972).

Technology has long been central to medicine. In recent years medical technology has become a major industry. Innovations such as CT scanners, hemodialysis machines, electronic fetal monitors, neonatal infant care units, among many others, have transformed medical care. These medical technologies contribute significantly to the increasing costs of medical care, although this is usually justified by claims of saving lives or reducing maladies. But medical technologies usually are adopted before they are adequately tested, and become "standard procedures" without sufficient evidence of their efficacy (McKinlay, 1981). This proliferation of medical technology is very expensive and often unnecessary. It is doubtful that every hospital needs a CT scanner, a cardiac care unit, or open heart surgery suite, but most states have exerted little control over the spread of such technology. Further, the medical technological imperative of "can do, should do" has frequently bypassed issues of cost-effectiveness or efficacy.

The articles in this section examine two predominant examples of change in the medical industries, increasing corporate control of medical care and expanding medical technology. The articles show the importance of the profit motive in the growth of medical industry; the authors see real problems with the increases in profit-making medical care. In a sense, medical care itself is becoming more overtly commodified.

In the first article, Arnold S. Relman, a physician and editor of the prestigious *New England Journal of Medicine,* describes the emergence of "The New Medical-Industrial Complex." Relman portrays the development of the enormous new industry, with a gross income of $40 billion, that supplies medical services for a profit. He points out that medical care cannot be treated just like any other commodity in a free enterprise system. He sees the roots of the growth of the medical-industrial complex in the uncontrolled third-party reimbursement system and contends that physicians should not derive financial benefits except through professional services. Relman argues that the medical profession and an informed public can control "profiteering" in medicine, although there is as yet no evidence to suggest that this is true.

Howard Waitzkin, a physician as well as a sociologist, presents in the second article "A Marxian Interpretation of the Growth and Development of Coronary Care Technology." He examines how coronary care units (CCUs) gained acceptance despite high costs and contradictory evidence of effectiveness. Waitzkin argues that this apparently "irrational" health policy becomes understandable when viewed in the context of a capitalist society. He shows the complex interactions among medicine, industry, and philanthropy in the development and desemination of the technology (cf. Bell, 1985), and raises the issue of corporate profit verses the cost-effectiveness of technology.

REFERENCES

Alford, Robert L. 1972. "The political economy of health care: Dynamics without changes." Politics and Society (Winter): 127–164.

Bell, Susan. 1985. "A new model of medical technology development: A case study of DES." In Julius Roth and Sheryl Ruzek (eds.), Research in the Sociology of Health Care, Vol. 4. Greenwich, Ct.: JAI Press.

McKinlay, John B. 1981. "From 'promising report' to 'standard procedure': Seven stages in the career of a medical innovation." Milbank Memorial Fund Quarterly/Health and Society 59: 374–411.

Sager, Alan. 1983. "The reconfiguration of urban hospital care: 1937–1980." In Ann Lennarson Greer and Scott Greer (eds.), Cities and Sickness: Health Care in Urban America, Urban Affairs Annual Review, Vol. 26, Chapter 3. Beverly Hills, Ca.: Sage.

Starr, Paul. 1982. The Social Transformation of American Medicine. New York: Basic Books.

Vladeck, Bruce. 1980. Unloving Care: The Nursing Home Tragedy. New York: Basic Books.

18

The New Medical-Industrial Complex

Arnold S. Relman

In his farewell address as President on January 17, 1961, Eisenhower warned his countrymen of what he called "the military-industrial complex," a huge and permanent armaments industry that, together with an immense military establishment, had acquired great political and economic power. He was concerned about the possible conflict between public and private interests in the crucial area of national defense.

The past decade has seen the rise of another kind of private "industrial complex" with an equally great potential for influence on public policy—this time in health care. What I will call the "new medical-industrial complex" is a large and growing network of private corporations engaged in the business of supplying health-care services to patients for a profit—services heretofore provided by nonprofit institutions or individual practitioners.

I am not referring to the companies that manufacture phramaceuticals or medical equipment and supplies. Such businesses have sometimes been described as part of a "medical-industrial complex," but I see nothing particularly worrisome about them. They have been around for a long time, and no one has seriously challenged their social usefulness. Furthermore, in a capitalistic society there are no practical alternatives to the private manufacture of drugs and medical equipment.

The new medical-industrial complex, on the other hand, is an unprecedented phenomenon with broad and potentially troubling implications for the future of our medical-care system. It has attracted remarkably little attention so far (except on Wall Street), but in my opinion it is the most important recent development in American health care and it is in urgent need of study.

In the discussion that follows I intend to describe this phenomenon briefly and give an idea of its size, scope, and growth. I will then examine some of the problems that it raises and attempt to show how the new medical-industrial complex may be affecting our health-care system. A final section will suggest some policies for dealing with this situation.

In searching for information on this subject, I have found no standard literature and have had to draw on a variety of unconventional sources: corporation reports; bulletins and newsletters; advertisements and newspaper articles; and conversations with government officials, corporation executives, trade-association officers, investment counselors, and physicians knowledgeable in this area. I take full responsibility for any errors in this description and would be grateful for whatever corrections readers might supply.

The New Medical Industrial Complex

Proprietary Hospitals

Of course proprietary hospitals are not new in this country. Since the past century, many small hospitals and clinics have been owned by physicians, primarily for the purpose of providing a workshop for their practices. In fact, the majority of hospitals in the United States were proprietary until shortly after the turn of the century, when the small doctor-owned hospitals began to be replaced by larger and more sophisticated community or church-owned nonprofit institutions. The total number of proprietary hospitals in the country decreased steadily during the first half of this century. In 1928 there were 2435 proprietary hospitals, constituting about 36 per cent of hospitals of all types; by 1968 there were only 769 proprietary hospitals, 11 per cent of the total.[1] However, there has been a steady trend away from individual ownership and toward corporate control. During the past decade the total number of proprietary hospitals has been increasing again, mainly because of the rapid growth of the corporate-owned multi-institutional hospital chains.

There are now about 1000 proprietary hospitals in this country; most of them provide short-term general care, but some are psychiatric institutions. These hospitals constitute more than 15 percent of nongovernmental acute general-care hospitals in the country and more than half the nongovernmental psychiatric hospitals. About half the proprietary hospitals are owned by large corporations that specialize in hospital ownership or management; the others are owned by groups of private investors or small companies. In addition to the 1000 proprietary hospitals, about 300 voluntary nonprofit hospitals are managed on a contractual basis by one or another of these profit-making hospital corporations.

The proprietary hospitals are mostly medium-sized (100 to 250 beds) institutions offering a broad range of general inpatient services but few outpatient facilities other than an emergency room. Some are smaller than 100 beds and a few are larger than 250 beds, but none would qualify as major medical centers, none have residency programs, and few do any postgraduate teaching. Most are located in the Sunbelt states in the South, in the Southwest, and along the Pacific Coast, in relatively prosperous and growing small and medium-sized cities and in the suburbs of the booming big cities of those areas. Virtually none are to be found in the big old cities of the North or in the states with strong rate-setting commissions or effective certificate-of-need policies.

Although there are no good, detailed studies comparing the characteristics and performance of proprietary and voluntary hospitals, there is a generally held view that proprietary hospitals have more efficient management and use fewer employees per bed. It is also said that fewer of the patients in proprietary hospitals are in the lower income brackets and that fewer are funded through Medicaid. One prominent hospital official told me that proprietary hospitals generally have per diem rates that are comparable to those in the voluntary hospitals, but that their ancillary charges are usually higher. However, this official stressed the lack of good data on these questions.

Last year the proprietary-hospital business generated between $12 billion and $13 billion of gross income—an amount that is estimated to be growing about 15 to 20 per cent per year (corrected for inflation). A major area of growth is overseas—in industrialized Western countries as well as underdeveloped countries—where much of the new proprietary-hospital development is now taking place. Of the two or three dozen sizable United States corporations now in the hospital business the largest are Humana and Hospital Corporation of America, each of which had a gross revenue of over $1 billion last year. Others are American Medical International (AMI) and Hospital Affiliates International (a unit of the huge INA Corporation), with gross revenues last year of approximately $0.5 billion each.

Proprietary Nursing Homes

Proprietary nursing homes are even bigger business. In 1977 there were nearly 19,000 nursing-home facilities of all types, and about 77 per cent were proprietary. Some, like the proprietary hospitals, are owned by big corporations, but most (I could not find out exactly how many) are owned by small investors, many of them physicians. The Health Care Financing Administration estimates that about $19 billion was expended last year for nursing home care in the United States. Assuming that average revenues of proprietary and nonprofit facilities are about equal, this means that about $15 billion was paid to proprietary institutions. This huge sum is growing rapidly, as private and public third-party coverage is progressively extended to pay for this kind of care.

Home Care

Another large and rapidly expanding sector of the health-care industry, but one that is even less well defined than the nursing-home business, is home care. A wide variety of home services are now being provided by profit-making health-care businesses. These services include care by trained nurses and nurses' aides, homemaking assistance, occupational and physiotherapy, respiratory therapy, pacemaker monitoring, and other types of care required by chronically ill house-bound patients. The total expenditures for these services are unknown, but I have been told that the market last year was at least $3 billion. Most of these services are provided by a large array of small private businesses, but there are about 10 fairly large companies in this field at present, and their combined sales are probably in excess of $0.5 billion. The largest corporate provider of home care is said to be the Upjohn Company. About half the total cost of home health care in this country is currently paid by Medicare. As Medicare and private third-party coverage broadens, this health-care business can be expected to grow apace.

Laboratory and Other Services

Last year, about $15 billion was spent on diagnostic laboratory services of all kinds. The number of laboratory tests performed each year in this country is huge and growing at a compound rate of about 15 per cent each year.[2] About a third of the diagnostic laboratories are owned by profit-making companies. Most of these are relatively small local firms, but there are a dozen or more large corporations currently in the laboratory business, some with over $100 million in sales per year. Some of these corporations operate laboratories in the voluntary non-profit hospitals, but most of the proprietary laboratories are outside hospitals and use an efficient mail or messenger service. Including all proprietary laboratories, large and small, in and out of hospitals, probably some $5 billion or $6 billion worth of services were sold last year.

A large variety of services are being sold by newly established companies in the medical-industrial complex. Included are mobile CAT scanning, cardiopulmonary testing, industrial health screening, rehabilitation counseling, dental care, weight-control clinics, alcohol and drug-abuse programs, comprehensive prepaid HMO programs, and physicians' house calls. Two markets that deserve special mention are hospital emergency-room services and long-term hemodialysis programs for end-stage renal disease.

With the decline in general practice and the virtual disappearance of physicians able and willing to make house calls, the local hospital emergency room has become an increasingly important source of walk-in medical and psychiatric services in urban and suburban areas. The use of emergency rooms has increased rapidly in the past two decades and has stimulated the development of emergency medicine as a specialty. Most third-party payers reimburse for services rendered in hospital emergency rooms at a higher rate than for the same services provided by physicians in their private offices. The result has been a vigorous new industry specializing in emergency services. Many large businesses have been established by entrepreneurial physicians to supply the necessary professional staffing for emergency rooms all over the country, and this has proved to be a highly profitable venture. In some cases, large corporations have taken over this function and now provide hospitals with a total emergency-care package. Once an appropriate financial arrangement is made, they will organize and administer the emergency room, see to its accreditation, recruit and remunerate the necessary medical and paramedical personnel, and even arrange for their continuing education. At least one large corporation that I learned about has such arrangements with scores of hospitals all over the country and employs hundreds of emergency physicians. I do not know exactly how much money is involved or how many physicians and hospitals participate in such schemes around the country, but I am under the impression that this is a very large business.

Hemodialysis

Long-term hemodialysis is a particularly interesting example of stimulation of private enterprise by public financing of health care. In 1972 the Social Security Act was amended to bring the treatment of end-stage renal disease under Medicare funding. When the new law was enacted, only about 40 patients per million population were receiving long-term hemodialysis treatment in this country, almost entirely under the auspices of nonprofit organizations. Forty per cent of these dialyses were home based, and renal transplantation was rapidly becoming an alternative form of treatment. The legislation provided for reimbursement for center-based or hospital-based dialysis without limit in numbers. The result was an immediate, rapid increase in the total number of patients on long-term dialysis treatment and a relative decline in home dialysis and transplantations. The number of patients on dialysis treatment in the United States is now over 200 per million population (the highest in the world), and only about 13 per cent are being dialyzed at home.

Proprietary dialysis facilities began to appear even before public funding of end-stage renal disease but the number increased rapidly thereafter. These facilities were usually located outside hospitals and had lower expenses than the hospital units. Many were purely local units, owned by nephrologists practicing in the area, but one corporation, National Medical Care, soon became preeminent in the field.[3] This company was founded by nephrologists and employs many local nephrologists as physicians and medical directors in its numerous centers around the country. It currently has sales of over $200 million annually and performs about 17 per cent of the long-term dialysis treatments in the country. It has recently expanded into the sale of dialysis equipment and supplies and the provision of psychiatric hospital care, respiratory care, and centers for obesity treatment, but its main business is still to provide dialysis for patients with end-stage renal disease in out-of-hospital facilities that it builds and operates. According to data obtained from the Health Care Financing Administration, nearly 40 per cent of the hemodialysis in this country is now provided by profit-making units. This figure suggests that total sales are nearly $0.5 billion a year for this sector of the health-care industry.

Income and Profitability

This, in barest outline, is the present shape and scope of the "new medical-industrial com-

plex," a vast array of investor-owned businesses supplying health services for profit. No one knows precisely the full extent of its operations or its gross income, but I estimate that the latter was approximately $35 billion to $40 billion last year—about a quarter of the total amount expended on personal health care in 1979. Remember that this estimate does not include the "old" medical-industrial complex, i.e., the businesses concerned with the manufacture and sale of drugs, medical supplies, and equipment.

The new health-care industry is not only very large, but it is also expanding rapidly and is highly profitable. New businesses seem to be springing up all the time, and those already in the field are diversifying as quickly as new opportunities for profit can be identified. Given the expansive nature of the health-care market and the increasing role of new technology, such opportunities are not hard to find.

The shares of corporations in the health-care business have done exceedingly well in the stock market, and many Wall Street analysts and brokers now enthusiastically recommend such investments to their clients. According to an article in the *Wall Street Journal,* of December 27, 1979, the net earnings of health-care corporations with public stock shares rose by 30 to 35 per cent in 1979 and are expected to increase another 20 to 25 per cent in 1980. A vice-president of Merrill Lynch appeared a few months ago on "Wall Street Week," the public television program, to describe the attractions of health-care stocks. According to this authority, health care is now the basis of a huge private industry, which is growing rapidly, has a bright future, and is relatively invulnerable to recession. He predicted that the health business would soon capture a large share of the health-care market and said that the only major risk to investors was the threat of greater government control through the enactment of comprehensive national health insurance or through other forms of federal regulation.

Why Have Private Businesses in Health Care?

Let us grant that we have a vast, new, rapidly growing and profitable industry engaged in the direct provision of health care. What's wrong with that? In our country we are used to the notion that private enterprise should supply most of the goods and services that our society requires. With the growing demand for all kinds of health care over the past two decades and the increasing complexity and cost of the services and facilities required, wasn't it inevitable that businesses were attracted to the new market? Modern health-care technology needs massive investment of capital—a problem that has become more and more difficult for the voluntary nonprofit institutions. How appropriate, then, for private entrepreneurs to come forward with the capital needed to build and equip new hospitals, nursing homes, and laboratories, and to start new health-care businesses. The market was there and a good profit ensured; the challenge was simply to provide the necessary services efficiently and at an acceptable level of quality.

In theory, the free market should operate to improve the efficiency and quality of health care. Given the spur of competition and the discipline exerted by consumer choice, private enterprise should be expected to respond to demand by offering better and more varied services and products, at lower unit costs, than could be provided by nonprofit voluntary or governmental institutions. Large corporations ought to be better managed than public or voluntary institutions; they have a greater incentive to control costs, and they are in a better position to benefit from economies of scale. We Americans believe in private enterprise and the profit motive. How logical, then, to extend these concepts to the health-care sector at a time when costs seem to be getting out of control, voluntary institutions are faltering, and the only other alternative appears to be more government regulation.

That, at least, is the theory. Whether the new medical-industrial complex is in fact improving quality and lowering unit cost in comparison with the public or private voluntary sectors remains to be determined. There are no adequate studies of this important question, and we will have to suspend judgment until there are some good data. But even without such information, I think that there are reasons to be concerned about this new direction in health care.

Some Issues

Can we really leave health care to the marketplace? Even if we believe in the free market as an efficient and equitable mechanism for the distribution of most goods and services, there are many reasons to be worried about the industrialization of health care. In the first place, health care is different from most of the commodities bought and sold in the marketplace. Most people consider it, to some degree at least, a basic right of all citizens. It is a public rather than a private good, and in recognition of this fact, a large fraction of the cost of medical research and medical care in this country is being subsidized by public funds. Public funds pay for most of the research needed to develop new treatments and new medical-care technology. They also reimburse the charges for health-care services. Through Medicare and Medicaid and other types of public programs, more and more of our citizens are receiving tax-supported medical care.

The great majority of people not covered by medical-care programs have third-party coverage through private insurance plans, most of which is provided as a fringe benefit by their employers. At present almost 90 per cent of Americans have some kind of health insurance, which ensures that a third party will pay at least part of their medical expenses. Federal programs now fund about 40 per cent of the direct costs of personal health care, and a large additional government subsidy is provided in the form of tax exemptions for employee health benefits. Thus, a second unique feature of the medical-care market is that most consumers (i.e., patients) are not "consumers" in the Adam Smith sense at all. As Kingman Brewster recently observed,[4] health insurance converts patients from consumers to claimants, who want medical care virtually without concern for price. Even when they have to pay out of their own pockets, patients who are sick or worried that they may be sick are not inclined to shop around for bargains. They want the best care they can get, and price is secondary. Hence, the classic laws of supply and demand do not operate because health-care consumers do not have the usual incentives to be prudent, discriminating purchasers.

There are other unique features of the medical

marketplace, not the least of which is the heavy, often total, dependence of the consumer (patient) on the advice and judgment of the physician. Kenneth Arrow, in explaining why some of the economist's usual assumptions about the competitive free market do not apply to medical care, referred to this phenomenon as the "informational inequality" between patient and physician.[5] Unlike consumers shopping for most ordinary commodities, patients do not often decide what medical services they need—doctors usually do that for them. Probably more than 70 per cent of all expenditures for personal health care are the result of decisions of doctors.[6]

All these special characteristics of the medical market conspire to produce an anomalous situation when private business enters the scene. A private corporation in the health-care business uses technology often developed at public expense, and it sells services that most Americans regard as their basic right—services that are heavily subsidized by public funds, largely allocated through the decisions of physicians rather than consumers, and almost entirely paid for through third-party insurance. The possibilities for abuse and for distortion of social purposes in such a market are obvious.

Health care has experienced an extraordinary inflation during the past few decades, not just in prices but in the use of services. A major challenge—in fact, *the* major challenge—facing the health-care establishment today is to moderate use of our medical resources and yet protect equity, access, and quality. The resources that can be allocated to medical care are limited. With health-care expenditures now approaching 10 per cent of the gross national product, it is clear that costs cannot continue to rise at anything near their present rate unless other important social goals are sacrificed. We need to use our health-care dollars more effectively, by curbing procedures that are unnecessary or inefficient and developing and identifying those that are the best. Overuse, where it exists, can be eliminated only by taking a more critical view of what we do and of how we use our health-care resources.

How will the private health-care industry affect our ability to achieve these objectives? In an ideal free competitive market, private enterprise may be good at controlling unit costs, and even at improving the quality of its products, but private businesses certainly do not allocate their own services or restrict the use of them. On the contrary, they "market" their services; they sell as many units as the market will bear. They may have to trim their prices to sell more, but the fact remains that they are in business to increase their total sales.

If private enterprise is going to take an increasing share of the health-care market, it will therefore have to be appropriately regulated. We will have to find some way of preserving the advantages of a private health-care industry without giving it free rein and inviting gross commercial exploitation. Otherwise, we can expect the use of health services to continue to increase until government is forced to intervene.

The Role of the Medical Profession

It seems to me that the key to the problem of overuse is in the hands of the medical profession. With the consent of their patients, physicians act in their behalf, deciding which services are needed and which are not, in effect serving as trustees. The best kind of regulation of the health-care marketplace should therefore come from the informed judgments of physicians working in the interests of their patients. In other words, physicians should supply the discipline that is provided in commercial markets by the informed choices of prudent consumers, who shop for the goods and services that they want, at the prices that they are willing to pay.

But if physicians are to represent their patients' interests in the new medical marketplace, they should have no economic conflict of interest and therefore no pecuniary association with the medical-industrial complex. I do not know the extent to which practicing physicians have invested in health-care businesses, but I suspect that it is substantial. Physicians have direct financial interests in proprietary hospitals and nursing homes, diagnostic laboratories, dialysis units, and many small companies that provide health-care services of various kinds. Physicians are on the boards of many major health-care corporations, and I think it is safe to assume that they are also well represented among the stockholders of these corporations. However, the actual degree of physician involvement is less important than the fact that it exists at all. As the visibility and importance of the private health-care industry grow, public confidence in the medical profession will depend on the public's perception of the doctor as an honest, disinterested trustee. That confidence is bound to be shaken by any financial association between practicing physicians and the new medical-industrial complex. Pecuniary associations with pharmaceutical and medical supply and equipment firms will also be suspect and should therefore be curtailed.

What I am suggesting is that the medical profession would be in a stronger position, and its voice would carry more moral authority with the public and the government, if it adopted the principle that practicing physicians should derive no financial benefit from the health-care market except from their own professional services. I believe that some statement to this effect should become part of the ethical code of the AMA. As such, it would have no legal force but would be accepted as a standard for the behavior of practicing physicians all over the country.

. . . .

If the AMA took a strong stand against any financial interest of physicians in health-care businesses, it might risk an antitrust suit. Its action might also be misconstrued as hostile to free enterprise. Yet, I believe that the risk to the reputation and self-esteem of the profession will be much greater if organized medicine fails to act decisively in separating physicians from the commercial exploitation of health care. The professional standing of the physician rests no less on ethical commitment than on technical competence. A refusal to confront this issue undermines the moral position of the profession and weakens the authority with which it can claim to speak for the public interest.

A brochure published by Brookwood Health Services, Inc., one of the many new corporations that owns and operates a chain of proprietary hospitals, says that it "views each physician as a business partner." (In evidence of this commercial partnership, the company recruits young physicians and subsidizes their start in private

practice.) That sentiment may make for good working relations between hospital administration and medical staff, but it sounds precisely the wrong note for a private market in which the hospital is the seller, the physician is the purchasing agent for the patient, and the public pays the major share of the bill.

Critics of the position argued here will probably point out that even without any investment in health-care businesses, physicians in private fee-for-service practice already have a conflict of interest in the sense that they benefit from providing services that they themselves prescribe. That may be true, but the conflict is visible to all and therefore open to control. Patients understand fee-for-service and most are willing to assume that their doctor's professional training protects them from exploitation. Furthermore, those who distrust their physicians or dislike the fee-for-service system have other alternatives: another physician, a prepayment plan, or a salaried group. What distinguishes the conflict of interest that I have been discussing are its invisibility and a far greater potential for mischief.

Other Problems

The increasing commercialization of health care generates still other serious problems that need to be mentioned. One is the so-called "cream-skimming" phenomenon. Steinwald and Neuhauser discussed this problem with reference to proprietary hospitals 10 years ago, when the new health-care industry was just appearing on the scene. "The essence of the cream-skinning argument," they said, "is that proprietary hospitals can and do profit by concentrating on providing the most profitable services to the best-paying patients, thereby skimming the cream off the market for acute hospital care and leaving the remainder to nonprofit hospitals."[1] According to these authors, there are two types of "cream-skimming": elimination of low-frequency and unprofitable (though necessary) services, and exclusion of unprofitable patients (e.g., uninsured patients, welfare patients, and those with complex and chronic illnesses). The nonprofit hospitals could not employ such practices, even if they wished to do so, because they have community obligations and are often located in areas where there are many welfare patients. Another form of "skimming" by proprietary hospitals, whether intentional or not, is their virtual lack of residency and other educational programs. Teaching programs are expensive and often oblige hospitals to maintain services that are not economically viable, simply to provide an adequate range of training experience.

Although these arguments seem reasonable, there are no critical studies on which to base firm conclusions about the extent and implications of the skimming phenomenon in the proprietary sector. One has the sense that the larger teaching institutions, particularly those that serve the urban poor, will be feeling increasing competitive economic pressure not only from the proprietary hospitals but also from the medium-sized community hospitals in relatively well-to-do demographic areas. Their charges are generally lower than those of the teaching centers, they take patients away from the centers, and they put the centers in a difficult position in negotiating with rate-setting agencies.

Another danger arises from the tendency of the profit-making sector to emphasize procedures and technology to the exclusion of personal care. Personal care, whether provided by physicians, nurses, or other health-care practitioners, is expensive and less likely to produce large profits than the item-by-item application of technology. Reimbursement schedules are, of course, a prime consideration in determining what services will be emphasized by the health-care industry, but in general the heavily automated, highly technical procedures will be favored, particularly when they can be applied on a mass scale. Just as pharmaceutical firms have tended to ignore "orphan" drugs, i.e., drugs that are difficult or expensive to produce and have no prospect of a mass market,[7] the private health-care industry can be expected to ignore relatively inefficient and unprofitable services, regardless of medical or social need. The result is likely to exacerbate present problems with excessive fragmentation of care, overspecialism, and overemphasis on expensive technology.

A final concern is the one first emphasized by President Eisenhower in his warning about the "military-industrial complex": "We must guard against the acquisition of unwarranted influence." A private health-care industry of huge proportions could be a powerful political force in the country and could exert considerable influence on national health policy. A broad national health-insurance program, with the inevitable federal regulation of costs, would be anathema to the medical-industrial complex, just as a national disarmament policy is to the military-industrial complex. I do not wish to imply that only vested interests oppose the expansion of federal health-insurance programs (or treaties to limit armaments), but I do suggest that the political involvement of the medical-industrial complex will probably hinder rather than facilitate rational debate on national health-care policy. Special-interest lobbies of all kinds are of course a familiar part of the American health-care scene. The appearance of still one more vested interest would not be a cause for concern if the newcomer were not potentially the largest, richest, and most influential of them all. One health-care company, National Medical Care, has already made its political influence felt, when Congress was considering a revision of the legislation supporting the end-stage renal disease program in 1978.[3,8]

Some Proposals

The new medical-industrial complex is now a fact of American life. It is still growing and is likely to be with us for a long time. Any conclusions about its ultimate impact on our health-care system would be premature, but it is safe to say that the effect will be profound. Clearly, we need more information.

. . . .

The private health-care industry is primarily interested in selling services that are profitable, but patients are interested only in services that they need, i.e., services that are likely to be helpful and are relatively safe. Furthermore, everything else being equal, society is interested in controlling total expenditures for health care, whereas the private health-care industry is interested in increasing its total sales. In the health-care marketplace the interests of patients and of society must be represented by the physician, who alone has the expertise and the authority to decide which services and procedures should be used in any given circumstance. That is why I have urged that physicians should totally separate themselves from any financial involvement in the medical-industrial complex. Beyond that, however, physicians must take a more active interest in assessing medical procedures. Elsewhere I have argued for a greatly expanded national program of evaluation of clinical tests and procedures.[9] Such a program would provide an excellent means by which to judge the social usefulness of the private health-care industry, which depends heavily on new technology and special tests and procedures.

If we are to live comfortably with the new medical-industrial complex we must put our priorities in order: the needs of patients and of society come first. If necessary services of acceptable quality can be provided at lower cost through the profit-making sector, then there may be reason to encourage that sector. But we should not allow the medical-industrial complex to distort our health-care system to its own entrepreneurial ends. It should not market useless, marginal, or unduly expensive services, nor should it encourage unnecessary use of services. How best to ensure that the medical-industrial complex serves the interests of patients first and of its stockholders second will have to be the responsibility of the medical profession and an informed public.

NOTE

Based on the 171st Annual Discourse, delivered before the Massachusetts Medical Society on May 21, 1980.

REFERENCES

1. Steinwald B, Neuhauser, D. The role of the proprietary hospital. Law Contemp Prob. (1970); 35:817–38.
2. Bailey RM. Clinical laboratories and the practice of medicine: an economic perspective. Berkeley, Calif.: McCutchan, 1979.
3. Kolata GB. NMC thrives selling dialysis. Science, 1980; 208:379–82.
4. Brewster K. Health at any price? Proc R Soc Med. 1979; 72:719–23.
5. Arrow KJ. Uncertainty and the welfare economics of medical care. Am Econ Rev. 1963; 53:941–73.
6. Relman AS. The allocation of medical resources by physicians. J Med Educ. 1980; 55:99–104.
7. Finkel MJ. Drugs of limited commercial value. N Engl J Med. 1980; 302:643–4.
8. Greenberg, DS. Renal politics. N Engl J Med. 1978; 298:1427–8.
9. Relman AS. Assessment of medical practices: a simple proposal. N Engl J Med. 1980; 303:153–4.

19

A Marxian Interpretation of the Growth And Development of Coronary Care Technology

Howard Waitzkin

The financial burden of health care has emerged as an issue of national policy. Legislative and administrative maneuvers purportedly aim toward the goal of cost containment. New investigative techniques in health services research, based largely on the cost-effectiveness model, are entering into the evaluation of technology and clinical practices. My purposes in this paper are to document the analytic poverty of these approaches to health policy and to offer an alternative interpretation that derives from Marxian analysis.

In the Marxian framework, the problem of costs never can be divorced from the structure of private profit in capitalist society. Most non-Marxian analyses of costs either ignore the profit structure of capitalism or accept it as given. But the crisis of health costs intimately reflects the more general fiscal crisis, including such incessant problems as inflation and stagnation, that advanced capitalism is facing worldwide. Wearing blinders that limit the level of analysis to a specific innovation or practice, while not perceiving the broader political-economic context in which costly and ineffective procedures are introduced and promulgated, will only obscure potential solutions to the enormous difficulties that confront us.

In this paper I focus on coronary care, having selected this topic merely as one example of apparent irrationalities of health policy that make sense when seen from the standpoint of the capitalist profit structure. The overselling of many other technologic advances such as computerized axial tomography and fetal monitoring (which have undeniable usefulness for a limited number of patients) reflects very similar structural problems.

One cautionary remark is worthwhile. The Marxian framework is not a conspiratorial model. The very nature of capitalist production necessitates the continuing development of new products and sales in new markets. From the standpoint of potential profit, there is no reason that corporations should view medical products differently from other products. The commodification of health care and its associated technology is a necessary feature of the capitalist political-economic system.[1-3] Without fundamental changes in the organization of private capital, costly innovations of dubious effectiveness will continue to plague the health sector. It is the structure of the system, rather than decision-making by individual entrepreneurs and clinicians, that is the appropriate level of analysis.

Historical Development of Intensive Coronary Care

Early Claims

Intensive care emerged rapidly during the 1960s. The first major reports of coronary care units

(CCUs) were written by Day, who developed a so-called "coronary care area" at the Bethany Hospital in Kansas City, with financial help from the John A. Hartford Foundation.[4] From these early articles until the mid-1970s, claims like Day's were very common in the literature. Descriptions of improved mortality and morbidity appeared, based totally on uncontrolled data from patients with myocardial infarction (MI) admitted before and after the introduction of a CCU. Until the 1970s, no major study of CCUs included a randomized control group.

However, Day's enthusiasm spread. In 1967, the classic descriptive study by Lown's group at the Peter Bent Brigham Hospital in Boston appeared.[5] This study was supported by the U.S. Public Health Service, the Hartford Foundation, and the American Optical Company, which manufactured the tape-loop recall memory system that was used in the CCU. The CCU's major objective, as the article pointed out, was to anticipate and to reduce early heart rhythm disturbances, thereby avoiding the need for resuscitation. The paper cited several other articles showing before-after decreases in mortality with a CCU, but never with randomization or other forms of statistical control introduced, and certainly never with a random controlled trial.

This publication led to a conference in 1968, sponsored by the Department of Health, Education, and Welfare (HEW), in which greater development and support of CCUs were advocated, despite clear-cut statements within the conference that the effectiveness of CCUs had not been demonstrated. For example, at the conference the Chief of the Heart Disease Control Program of the Public Health Service claimed: "An attempt was made a few years ago to make some controlled studies of the benefits of CCU efforts, but it was not possible to carry out those investigations for many reasons, some of them fiscal. Therefore, we do not have proper studies for demonstrating the advantages of CCUs. But now that these opportunities and occasions to prevent heart rhythm disturbances have become a great deal more common, we can be assured that our efforts are worthwhile. . . . Upon advice of our colleagues in the profession, we have not considered it ethically acceptable, at this time, to make a controlled study which

Table 1. Growth of Coronary Care Units in the United States, by Region, 1967-1974

Regions	Coronary Care Units (% of hospitals)	
	1967	1974
United States	24.3	33.8
New England	29.0	36.8
Mid-Atlantic	33.8	44.2
East North Central	31.0	38.2
West North Central	17.0	25.3
South Atlantic	23.3	38.2
East South Central	13.4	30.1
West South Central	15.3	24.3
Mountain	21.4	29.3
Pacific	32.7	37.8

SOURCE: Reference 8

would necessitate shunting of patients from a facility without a CCU (but with the support that CCUs provide) to one with a CCU."[6]

So, despite the lack of controlled studies showing effectiveness, there were many calls for the expansion of CCUs to other hospitals and increased support from the federal government and private foundations. In 1968 HEW also issued a set of Guidelines for CCUs.[7] Largely because of these recommendations, CCUs grew rapidly in the following years. Table 1 shows the expansion of CCUs in the United States between 1967 and 1974.[8]

Later Studies of Effectiveness*

Serious research on the effectiveness of CCUs did not begin until the 1970s. As several critics have pointed out, the "before-after" studies during the 1960s could not lead to valid conclusions about effectiveness, since none of these studies had adequate control groups or randomization.[9-13]

Several later studies compared treatment of MI patients in hospital wards vs. CCU settings.[14-17] Patients were "randomly" admitted to the CCU or the regular ward, simply based on the availability of CCU beds. Ward patients were the

*A more detailed review of research summarized in this section is available from the author.

Table 2. Recent Studies Comparing Coronary Care Unit and Ward Treatment for Myocardial Infarction

Studies	No CCU		CCU	
	N	% Mortality	N	% Mortality
Prospective				
Hofvendahl[14]	139	35	132	17
Christiansen[15]	244	41	171	18
Hill[16]				
<65 yrs	186	18	797	15
≥65 yrs	297	32	200	31
Retrospective				
Astvad[17]	603	39	1108	41

"control" group; CCU patients were the "experimental" group. Table 2 reviews the findings of these studies, which are very contradictory. From this research it is unclear, at this late date, that CCUs improve in-hospital mortality.

More recent research contrasted home vs. hospital care (Table 3). One major study was the prospective, random controlled trial by Mather and his colleagues in Great Britain.[18,19] This was an ambitious and couragcous study, of the type that was not considered possible by HEW in the 1960s.[6] Although some methodologic problems arose concerning the randomization of patients to home vs. hospital care, the cumulative 1-year mortality was not different in the home and hospital groups, and there was no evidence that MI patients did better in the hospital. A second random controlled trial of home vs. hospital treatment tried to correct the methodologic difficulties of the Mather study by achieving a higher rate of randomization and strict criteria for the entry and exclusion of patients from the trial. The preliminary findings of this later study, conducted by Hill's group in Great Britain, confirmed the earlier results: the researchers concluded that for the majority of patients with suspected MI, admission to a hospital "confers no clear advantage."[20] A third study of the same problem used an epidemiologic approach in the Teesside area of Great Britain. This investigation was not a random controlled trial but simply a 12-month descriptive epidemiologic study of the incidence of MIs, how they were treated in practice, and the outcomes in terms of mortality.

Both the crude and age-standard rates were better for patients treated

In summary, these issues are far even now. The thrust of recent research that home care is a viable treatment altern hospital or CCU care for many patients w. Early CCU promotion used unsound cl al research. More adequate research has not confirmed CCU effectiveness. One other question is clear—if intensive care is not demonstrably more effective than simple rest at home, how can we explain the tremendous proliferation during the past two decades of this very expensive form of treatment?

From a Marxian perspective, these events cannot be chance phenomena. Nor are they simply another expression of the Pollyanna-like acceptance of high technology in industrial society. People are not stupid, even though the enormously costly development of CCUs occurred without any proof of their effectiveness. Therefore, we must search for the social, economic, and political structures that fostered their growth.

The Political Economy of Coronary Care

The Corporate Connection

To survive, capitalist industries must produce and sell new products. Expansion is an absolute necessity for capitalist enterprises. The economic surplus (defined as the excess of total production over "socially essential production") must grow continually larger. Medical production also falls in this category, although it is seldom viewed in this way. The economist Mandel emphasizes the contradictions of the economic surplus: "For capitalist crises are incredible phenomena like nothing ever seen before. They are not crises of scarcity, like all pre-capitalist crises; they are crises of over-production."[23] This scenario also includes the health-care system, where an over-production of intensive care technology contrasts with the fact that many people have little access to the most simple and rudimentary medical services.

Large profit-making corporations in the United States participated in essentially every

Table 3. Recent Studies Comparing Hospital and Home Care for Myocardial Infarction

Studies	Hospital		Home	
	N	% Mortality	N	% Mortality
Prospective Randomized				
Mather[18,19]				
<60 yrs	106	18	117	17
≥60 yrs	112	35	103	23
TOTAL	218	27	220	20
Hill[20]	132	11	132	13

	Hospital CCU		Hospital Ward		Home	
	N	%Mortality	N	%Mortality	N	%Mortality
Epidemiologic						
Dellipiani[22]	248	13	296	21	193	9

phase of CCU research, development, promotion, and proliferation. Many companies involved themselves in the intensive care market. Here I consider the activities of two such firms: Warner-Lambert Pharmaceutical Company and the Hewlett-Packard Company. I selected these corporations because information about their participation in coronary care was relatively accessible and because they have occupied prominent market positions in this clinical area. However, I should emphasize that many other firms, including at least 85 major companies, also have been involved in coronary care.[24]

Warner-Lambert Pharmaceutical Company (W-L) is a large multinational corporation, with $2.1 billion in assets and over $2.5 billion in annual sales during recent years.[25] The corporation comprises a number of interrelated subsidiary companies: Warner-Chilcott Laboratories, the Parke-Davis Company, and Warner-Lambert Consumer Products (Listerine, Smith Brothers [cough drops], Bromo-Seltzer, Chiclets, DuBarry, Richard Hudnut, Rolaids, Dentyne, Certs, Coolray Polaroid [sunglasses], and Oh Henry! [candy]).[26] Warner-Lambert International operates in more than 40 countries. Although several divisions of the W-L conglomerate participated actively in the development and promotion of coronary care, the most prominent division has been the American Optical Company (AO), which W-L acquired during 1967.

By the early 1960s, AO already had a long history of successful sales in such fields as optometry, ophthalmology, and microscopes. The instrumentation required for intensive coronary care led to AO's diversification into this new and growing area. The profitable outcomes of AO's research, development and promotion of coronary care technology are clear from AO's 1966 annual report: "In 1966, the number of American Optical Coronary Care Systems installed in hospitals throughout the United States more than tripled. Competition for this market also continued to increase as new companies, both large and small, entered the field. However, we believe that American Optical Company . . . will continue a leader in this evolving field."[27]

After purchasing AO in 1967, W-L maintained AO's emphasis on CCU technology and sought wider acceptance by health professionals and medical centers. Promotional materials contained the assumption, never proven, that the new technology was effective in reducing morbidity and mortality from heart disease. Early products and systems included the AO Cardiometer, a heart monitoring and resuscitation device; the first direct current defibrillator; the Lown Cardioverter; and an Intensive Cardiac Care System that permitted the simultaneous monitoring of 16 patients by oscilloscopes, recording instruments, heart rate meters, and alarm systems.[28] In 1968, after introducing a new line of monitoring instrumentation and implantable demand pacemakers, the company reported that "acceptance has far exceeded initial estimates" and that the Medical Division was doubling the size of its plant in Bedford, Massachusetts.[29] By 1969, the company introduced another completely new line of Lown Cardioverters and Defibrillators.[30] The company continued to register expanding sales throughout the early 1970s.

Despite this growth, W-L began to face a typical corporate problem: the potential saturation of markets in the United States. Coronary care technology was capital-intensive. The number of hospitals in the United States that could buy coronary care systems, although large, was finite. For this reason, W-L began to make new and predictable initiatives to assure future growth. First, the company expanded coronary care sales into foreign markets, especially the Third World. Subsequently, W-L reported notable gains in sales in such countries as Argentina, Canada, Colombia, France, Germany, Japan, and Mexico, despite the fact that during the 1970s "political difficulties in southern Latin America slowed progress somewhat, particularly in Chile and Peru."[31]

A second method to deal with market saturation was further diversification within the coronary care field with products whose intent was to open new markets or to create obsolescence in existing systems. For example, in 1975 the AO subsidiary introduced two new instruments. The "Pulsar 4," a light-weight portable defibrillator designed for local paramedic and emergency squads, created "an exceptionally strong sales demand." The Computer Assisted Monitoring System used a computer to anticipate and control changes in cardiac patients' conditions and replaced many hospitals' CCU systems that AO had installed but that lacked computer capabilities. According to the company's 1975 annual report, these two instruments "helped contribute to record sales growth in 1975, following an equally successful performance in the previous year."[32]

A third technique to assure growth involved the modification of coronary care technology for new areas gaining public and professional attention. With an emphasis on preventive medicine, AO introduced a new line of electrocardiogram telemetry instruments, designed to provide early warning of MI or rhythm disturbance in ambulatory patients. In addition, AO began to apply similar monitoring technology to the field of occupational health and safety, after the passage of federal OSHA legislation in 1970.[33]

W-L is only one of many companies cultivating the coronary care market. Another giant is the Hewlett-Packard Company (H-P), a firm that in 1977 held more than $1.1 billion in assets and reported over $1.3 billion in sales. Since its founding in 1939 H-P has grown from a small firm, manufacturing analytical and measuring instruments mainly for industry, to a leader in electronics. Until the early 1960s, H-P's only major product designated for medical markets was a simple electrocardiogram machine. Along with pocket computers, medical electronic equipment has since become the most successful of H-P's product groups. During the 1960s, H-P introduced a series of innovations in coronary care (as well as perinatal monitoring and instrumentation for respiratory disease) that soon reached markets throughout the world.

Initially the company focused on the development of CCU technology. H-P aggressively promoted CCU equipment to hospitals, with the consistent claim that cardiac monitors and related products were definitely effective in reducing mortality from MI and rhythm disturbances. Such claims as the following were unambiguous: "In the cardiac care unit pictured here at a Nevada hospital, for example, the system has alerted the staff to several emergencies that might otherwise have proved fatal, and the cardiac mortality rate has been cut in half."[34] Alternatively, "hundreds of lives are saved each year with the help of Hewlett-Packard patient monitoring systems installed in more than 1,000 hospitals throughout the world. . . . Pictured here is an HP system in the intensive care ward of a hospital in Montevideo, Uruguay."[35]

Very early, H-P emphasized the export of CCU technology to hospitals and practitioners abroad, anticipating the foreign sales that other companies like W-L also later enjoyed. In 1966, the H-P annual report predicted that the effects of a slumping economy would be offset by "the great sales potential for our products, particularly medical instruments, in South American, Canadian and Asian markets. These areas should support substantial gains in sales for a number of years."[36] In materials prepared for potential investors, H-P made explicit statements about the advantages of foreign operations. For example, because H-P subsidiaries received "pioneer status" in Malaysia and Singapore, income generated in these countries remained essentially tax-free during the early 1970s: "Had their income been taxed at the U.S. statutory rate of 48 per cent in 1974, our net earnings would have been reduced by 37 cents a share."[37] By the mid-1970s, H-P's international medical equipment business, as measured by total orders, surpassed its domestic business. More than 100 sales and service offices were operating in 64 countries.

Like W-L, H-P also diversified its products to deal with the potential saturation of the coronary care market. During the late 1960s, the company introduced a series of complex computerized systems that were designed as an interface with electrocardiogram machines, monitoring devices, and other CCU products. For example, a computerized system to analyze and interpret electrocardiograms led to the capability of processing up to 500 electrocardiograms per 8-hour day: "This and other innovative systems recently introduced to the medical profession contributed to the substantial growth of our medical electronics business during the past year. With this growth has come increasing profitability as well."[38] Similar considerations of profitability motivated the development of telemetry systems for ambulatory patients with heart disease and battery-powered electrocardiogram machines designated for regions of foreign countries where electricity was not yet available for traditional machines. In 1973, H-P provided a forthright statement of its philosophy: "Health care expenditures, worldwide, will continue to increase significantly in the years ahead, and a growing portion of these funds will be allocated for medical electronic equipment. Interestingly, this growth trend offers the company . . . the unique opportunity to help shape the future of health care delivery."[39] From the corporate perspective, spiraling health-care expenditures, far from a problem to be solved, are the necessary fuel for desired profit.

The Academic Medical Center Connection

Academic medical centers have played a key role in the development and promotion of costly innovations like those in coronary care. This role has seldom attracted attention in critiques of technology, yet both corporations considered here obtained important bases at medical centers located in geographic proximity to corporate headquarters.

Before its purchase by W-L, American Optical—with headquarters in Southbridge, Massachusetts—had established ties with the Peter Bent Brigham Hospital in Boston. Specifically, the company worked with Bernard Lown, an eminent cardiologist who served as an AO consultant, on the development of defibrillators and cardioverters. Lown pioneered the theoretical basis and clinical application of these techniques; AO engineers collaborated with Lown in the construction of working models. As previously discussed, AO marketed and promoted several lines of defibrillators and cardioverters that bore Lown's name.

AO's support of technologic innovation at the Peter Bent Brigham Hospital is clear. The CCU developed in the mid-1960s received major grants from AO that Lown and his group acknowledged.[5] AO also used data and pictures from the Brigham CCU in promotional literature distributed to the medical profession and potential investors.[40] Lown and his group continued to influence the medical profession through a large number of publications, appearing in both the general and cardiologic literature, that discussed CCU-linked diagnostic and therapeutic techniques (Table 4). In these papers, Lown emphasized the importance of automatic monitoring. He also advocated the widespread use of telemetry for ambulatory patients and computerized data-analysis systems, both areas into which AO diversified during the late 1960s and early 1970s. AO's relationship with Lown and his colleagues apparently proved beneficial for everybody concerned. The dynamics of heightened profits for AO and prestige for Lown were not optimal conditions for a detached, systematic appraisal of CCU effectiveness.

H-P's academic base has been the Stanford University Medical Center, located about one-

Table 4.   Publications Concerning Coronary Care from Peter Bent Brigham Hospital and Stanford University Medical Center Groups, 1965-1975

Year	Peter Bent Brigham Hospital	Stanford University Medical Center
1965	1	1
1966	3	1
1967	3	4
1968	7	4
1969	11	3
1970	6	1
1971	7	2
1972	3	4
1973	4	5
1974	3	5
1975	2	4

SOURCE: *Index Medicus*, citations listing B Lown or DC Harrison as author or co-author and dealing specifically with diagnostic or therapeutic techniques in coronary care units.

half mile from corporate headquarters in Palo Alto, California. For many years William Hewlett, H-P's chief executive officer, served as a trustee of Stanford University. In addition, as I will discuss later, a private philanthropy established by Hewlett was prominent among the University's financial benefactors.

Since the late 1960s, Donald Harrison, professor of medicine and chief of the Division of Cardiology, has acted as H-P's primary consultant in the development of coronary care technology. Harrison and his colleagues at Stanford collaborated with H-P engineers in the design of CCU systems intended for marketing to both academic medical centers and community hospitals. H-P helped construct working models of CCU components at Stanford University Hospital, under the direction of Harrison and other faculty members. Stanford physicians introduced these H-P systems into clinical use.

Innovations in the treatment of patients with heart disease had a profound impact on the costs of care at Stanford. As documented in a general study of the costs of treatment for several illnesses at Stanford, Scitovsky and McCall stated: "Of the conditions covered by the 1964–1971 study, the changes in treatment in myocardial infarction had their most dramatic effect on costs. This was due principally to the increased costs of intensive care

units. In 1964, the Stanford Hospital had a relatively small Intensive Care Unit (ICU). It was used by only three of the 1964 coronary cases. . . . By 1971, the hospital had not only an ICU but also a Coronary Care Unit (CCU) and an intermediate CCU. Of the 1971 cases, only one did not receive at least some care in either the CCU or the intermediate CCU."[41]

During the late 1960s and early 1970s, many articles from the Harrison group described new technical developments or discussed clinical issues tied to intensive care techniques (Table 4). Several articles directly acknowledged the use of H-P equipment and assistance. These academic clinicians also participated in continuing medical education programs on coronary care, both in the United States and abroad. The Stanford specialists thus played an important role in promoting technology in general and H-P products in particular.

Private Philanthropies

Philanthropic support figured prominently in the growth of CCUs. Humanitarian goals were doubtless present, but profit considerations were not lacking, since philanthropic initiatives often emerged from the actions of corporate executives whose companies produced medical equipment or pharmaceuticals.

Primary among the philanthropic proponents of CCUs was the American Heart Association (AHA). The AHA sponsored research that led to the development of CCU products, especially monitoring systems. In addition, the AHA gave financial support directly to local hospitals establishing CCUs. "The underlying purpose" of these activities, according to the AHA's 1967 annual report, was "to encourage and guide the formation of new [CCU] units in both large and small hospitals."[42] Justifying these expenditures, the AHA cited some familiar "data": "Experience with the approximately 300 such specialized units already established, mostly in large hospitals, indicated that a national network of CCUs might save the lives of more than 45,000 individuals each year."[42] The source for this projected number of rescued people, though uncited, presumably was a "personal communication" from an HEW official to which Day referred in his 1963 article.[4] Later in the 1960s, the AHA's annual number of estimated beneficiaries rose still higher, again with undocumented claims of effectiveness. According to the 1968 annual report, "only about one-third of hospitalized heart attack patients are fortunate enough to be placed in coronary care units. If all of them had the benefits of these monitoring and emergency service facilities, it is estimated that 50,000 more heart patients could be saved yearly."[43] This unsubstantiated estimate, raised from the earlier unsubstantiated figure of 45,000, persisted in AHA literature into the early 1970s. During this same period the AHA cosponsored, with the U.S. Public Health Service and the American College of Cardiology, a series of national conferences on coronary care whose purpose was "the successful development of the CCU program" in all regions of the United States.[42]

Other smaller foundations also supported CCU proliferation. For example, the John A. Hartford Foundation gave generous support to several hospitals and medical centers during the early 1960s to develop monitoring capabilities. The Hartford Foundation's public view of CCU effectiveness was unequivocal: the Kansas City coronary care program "has demonstrated that a properly equipped and designed physical setting staffed with personnel trained to meet cardiac emergencies will provide prophylactic therapy which will materially enhance the survival of these patients and substantially reduce the mortality rates."[44] Another foundation that supported CCU growth, although somewhat less directly, was the W. R. Hewlett Foundation, founded by H-P's chief executive officer. The Hewlett Foundation earmarked large annual grants to Stanford University which chose H-P equipment for its CCU and other intensive-care facilities.[45]

The commitment of private philanthropy to technologic innovations is a structural problem that transcends the personalities that control philanthropy at any specific time. The bequests that create philanthropies historically come largely from funds generated by North American industrial corporations, that are highly oriented to technologic advances. Moreover, the invest-

ment portfolios of philanthropic organizations usually include stocks in a sizable number of industrial companies. These structural conditions encourage financial support for technological advances, like those in coronary care.

In addition, it is useful to ask which people made philanthropic decisions to fund CCU development. During the mid-1960s, the AHA's officers included eight physicians who had primary commitments in cardiology, executives of two pharmaceutical companies (L. F. Johnson of American Home Products Corporation's drug subsidiaries and Ross Reid of Squibb Corporation), a metals company executive (A. M. Baer of Imperial Knife Associated Companies), a prominent banker (W. C. Butcher, president of Chase Manhattan Bank), and several public officials (including Dwight Eisenhower). At the height of CCU promotion in 1968, the chairman of the AHA's annual Heart Fund was a drug company executive (W. F. Laporte, president of American Home Products Corporation, former chief of its phramaceutical subsidiaries, and director of several banks).[43] During the 1960s and early 1970s, bankers and corporate executives also dominated the board at the Hartford Foundation. The Hewlett Foundation remained a family affair until the early 1970s, when R. W. Heyns—former chancellor of the University of California, Berkeley, and also a director of Norton Simon, Inc., Kaiser Industries, and Levi-Strauss—assumed the Foundation's presidency. It is not surprising that philanthropic policies supporting CCU proliferation showed a strong orientation toward corporate industrialism.

The Role of the State

Agencies of government played a key role in CCU growth. Earlier I discussed the financial support that the U.S. Public Health service provided to clinicians in the early 1960s for CCU development. An official of HEW provided an "estimate" of potential lives saved by future CCUs[4]; without apparent basis in data, this figure became a slogan for CCU promotion. Conferences and publications by HEW during the late 1960s specified guidelines for adequate CCU equipment, even though the effectiveness of this approach admittedly remained unproven by random controlled trial.

In these activities, three common functions of the state in capitalist societies were evident.[2] First, in health policy the state generally supports private enterprise by encouraging innovations that enhance profits to major industrial corporations. The state does not enact policies that limit private profit in any serious way. Recognizing the high costs of CCU implementation, state agencies could have placed strict limitations on their number and distribution. For example, HEW could have called for the regionalization of CCU facilities and restrictions on their wider proliferation. Subsequently, studies of CCU mortality rates generally have shown better outcomes in larger, busier centers and have suggested the rationality of regionalized policies.[46] HEW's policies supported just the opposite development. By publishing guidelines that called for advanced CCU technology and by encouraging CCU proliferation to most community hospitals, HEW assured the profitability of corporate ventures in the coronary-care field.

A second major function of the state is its legitimation of the capitalist political-economic system.[2,3] The history of public health and welfare programs shows that state expenditures usually increase during periods of social unrest and decrease as unrest becomes less widespread. The decade of the 1960s was a time of upheaval in the United States. The civil rights movement called into question basic patterns of injustice. Opposition to the war in Indochina mobilized a large part of the population against government and corporate policies. Labor disputes arose frequently. Under such circumstances, when government and corporations face large-scale crises of legitimacy, the state tends to intervene with health and welfare projects. Medical technology is a "social capital expenditure" by which the state tries to counteract the recurrent legitimacy crises of advanced capitalism.[47] Technologic innovations like CCUs are convenient legitimating expenditures, since they convey a message of deep concern for the public health, while they also support new sources of profit for large industrial firms.

Thirdly, government agencies provide market research that guides domestic and foreign sales efforts. The Global Market Survey, published by the U.S. Department of Commerce, gives a detailed analysis of changes in medical facilities, hospital beds, and physicians throughout the world. The Survey specifies those countries that are prime targets for sales of biomedical equipment. For example, the 1973 Survey pointed out that "major foreign markets for biomedical equipment are expected to grow at an average annual rate of 15 per cent in the 1970s, nearly double the growth rate predicted for the U.S. domestic market."[48] The same report predicted that West Germany (which would emphasize CCU construction), Japan, Brazil, Italy, and Israel would be the largest short-term markets for products manufactured in the United States. According to the report "market research studies identified specific equipment that present [sic] good to excellent U.S. sale opportunities in the 20 [foreign] markets"; "cardiological-thoracic equipment" headed the list of products with high sales potential.[48] Market research performed by state agencies has encouraged the proliferation of CCUs and related innovations, whose capacity to generate profits has overshadowed the issue of effectiveness in government planning.

Changes in the Health Care Labor Force

Intensive care involves workers as well as equipment. Throughout the twentieth century, a process of "deskilling" has occurred, by which the skilled trades and professions have become rationalized into simpler tasks that can be handled by less skilled and lower paid workers.[49] In medicine, paraprofessionals take on rationalized tasks that can be specified by algorithms covering nearly all contingencies. This deskilling process applies equally to CCUs and other intensive care facilities, where standard orders—often printed in advance—can deal with almost all situations that might arise.

The deskilling of the intensive care labor force has received support from professional, governmental, and corporate planners. During the late 1960s and early 1970s, the training of allied health personnel to deal with intensive care technology became a priority of educators and administrators. According to this view, it was

Figure 1. *Overview of the Development, Promotion, and Proliferation of CCUs and Similar Medical Advances.*

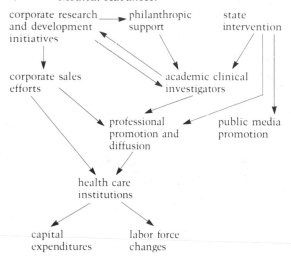

important to train a "cadre of health workers capable of handling routine and purely functional duties."[50] The linkage between allied health workers and new technology was a clear assumption in this approach. There were limits on "the extent to which a markedly greater delegation of tasks can be achieved without the introduction of new technology" that compensates for aides' lack of "decisional training."[51] The availability of monitoring equipment in CCUs made this setting adaptable to staffing partly by technicians who could receive lower wages than doctors or nurses.[52] Paramedical training programs, focusing on intensive care, became a goal of national policy makers, even though they recognized the "built in obsolescence of monitoring equipment" and the tendency of industrial corporations to "capitalize" in this field.[53, 54]

Conclusions

Although not exhaustive, an overview helps clarify the history of CCUs and other technologic "advances" (Figure 1). Corporate research and development leads to the production of new technology, pharmaceuticals, and related innovations. The guiding motivation for corporations is

profit; in this sense the commodification of health care resembles non-medical goods and services. Closely linked to corporations, philanthropies support research and clinical practices that enhance profits. Agencies of the state encourage innovation by grants for investigation, financial assistance to medical centers adopting new technology, and advocacy of new practices. While state intervention benefits private enterprise, it also enhances the faltering legitimacy of the capitalist political-economic system. Academic clinicians and investigators, based in teaching hospitals, help develop technology and foster its diffusion through professional publications and pronouncements in the public media. Corporate sales efforts cultivate markets in health institutions, both domestic and foreign. Technologic change generates the need for allied health workers who are less skilled than professionals. The cyclical acceptance of technologic innovations by medical institutions involves capital expenditures that drive up the overall costs of health care.

Cost containment activities that do not recognize these dynamics of the capitalist system will remain a farce. During the last decade, sophisticated methodologies to analyze costs and effectiveness have emerged in medical care research. These techniques include clinical decision analysis and a variety of related methods.[55-58] Ironically, economists first developed this type of analysis at the Pentagon, to evaluate technologic innovations like new missiles.[59] This methodology led to disastrous policy decisions in Indochina, largely because the cost-effectiveness approach did not take into account the broader, so-called "imponderable" context. This analysis did not predict accurately the political response of the Indochinese people to such technologies as napalm and mechanized warfare. Ironically, many of the same people who developed cost-effectiveness research at the Department of Defense now are moving into the health field, where this approach has become quite fashionable.[60]

In health care as in other areas, cost-effectiveness methodology restricts the level of analysis to the evaluation of specific innovations.[61-65] Studies using this framework generally ignore, or make only passing reference to, the broader structures of capitalism.[66] As a result, this approach obscures one fundamental source of high costs and ineffective practices: the profit motive. Because of this deficiency, cost-effectiveness analysis mystifies the roots of costly, ineffective practices in the very nature of our political-economic system.

Defects of research, however, are less dangerous than defects of policy. Cost containment has become a highly touted national priority. In a climate of fiscal crisis, an ideology of austerity is justifying cutbacks in health and welfare programs. Services whose effectiveness is difficult to demonstrate by the new methodologies are prime candidates for cutbacks and therefore face a bleak future. Poor people and minority groups, historically victimized by the free enterprise system, will be the first to suffer from this purported rationalization of policy. Meanwhile, private profit in health care, a major fuel for high costs, continues unabated. Just as it eludes serious attention in research, the structure of profit evades new initiatives in health policy.

Cost containment will remain little more than rhetoric in the United States unless we begin to address the linkages between cost and profit. It is foolish to presume that major restrictions on profit in the health system can succeed without other basic changes in the political-economic system. On the other hand, working toward progressive alternatives in health care is part of longer-term efforts aimed at social reconstruction.

An initial step involves support for policies that curtail private profit. Unlimited corporate involvement in medicine must end. The corporations that develop and successfully promote ineffective innovations like those in coronary care must cease these activities. Because this will not happen voluntarily, we need compulsory restriction of profit in health care and eventual public ownership of medical industries, especially pharmaceutical and medical equipment manufacturing.[67] A national formulary of permitted drugs and equipment, like that established in several socialist countries, would reduce costs by eliminating the proliferation of unneeded products. Socialization of medical production is no more fanciful than public ownership of utilities, transportation facilities, or schools.

In summary, CCU development and promotion may seem irrational when analyzed in terms of proven medical effectiveness. These trends appear considerably more rational when viewed from the needs of a capitalist system in crisis. By questioning what capitalism does with our hearts, we get closer to the heart of many of our other problems.

REFERENCES

1. Waitzkin H, Waterman B: The Exploitation of Illness in Capitalist Society. Indianapolis, Bobbs-Merrill, 1974.
2. Waitzkin H: A Marxist view of medical care. Ann Intern Med 89:264–278, 1978.
3. Navarro V: Medicine Under Capitalism. New York, Prodist, 1976.
4. Day HW: An intensive coronary care area. Dis Chest 44:423–427, 1963.
5. Lown B, Fakhro AM, Hood WB, et al: The coronary care unit: new perspectives and directions. JAMA 199:188–198, 1967.
6. United States Department of Health, Education, and Welfare: Heart Disease Control Program: Proceedings of the National Conference on Coronary Care Units. DHEW Pub. No. 1764. Washington, DC, Govt Printing Office, 1968.
7. United States Department of Health, Education and Welfare: Heart Disease and Stroke Control Program: Guidelines for Coronary Care Units. DHEW Pub. No. 1824. Washington, DC, Govt Printing Office, 1968.
8. Geographical distribution of coronary care units in the United States. Metropolitan Life Insurance Company Statistical Bulletin 58:7–9, July–August 1977.
9. Peterson OL: Myocardial infarction: unit care or home care? Ann Intern Med 88:259–261, 1978.
10. Martin SP, Donaldson MC, London CD, et al: Inputs into coronary care during 30 years: a cost effectiveness study. Ann Intern Med 81:289–293, 1974.
11. Anti-dysrhythmic treatment in acute myocardial infarction (editorial). Lancet 1:193–194, 1979.
12. Coronary-care units—where now? (editorial). Lancet 1:649–650, 1979.
13. Waitzkin H: How capitalism cares for our coronaries: a preliminary exercise in political economy. In The Doctor-Patient Relationship in the Changing Health Scene, Gallagher EB (ed.) DHEW Pub. No. (NIH) 78-183. Washington, DC, Govt Printing Office, 1978.
14. Hofvendahl S: Influence of treatment in a CCU on prognosis in acute myocardial infarction. Acta Med Scand (Suppl) 519:1–78, 1971.

15. Christiansen I, Iversen K, Skouby AP: Benefits obtained by the introduction of a coronary care unit: a comparative study. Acta Med Scand 189:285–291, 1971.

16. Hill JC, Holdstock G, Hampton JR: Comparison of mortality of patients with heart attacks admitted to a coronary care unit and an ordinary medical ward. Br Med J 2:81–83, 1977.

17. Astvad K, Fabricius-Bjerre N, Kjaerulff J, et al: Mortality from acute myocardial infarction before and after establishment of a coronary care unit. Br Med J 1:567–569, 1974.

18. Mather HG, Morgan DC, Pearson NG, et al: Myocardial infarction: a comparison between home and hospital care for patients. Br Med J 1:925–929, 1976.

19. Mather HG, Pearson NG, Read KLQ, et al: Acute myocardial infarction: home and hospital treatment. Br Med J 3:334–338, 1971.

20. Hill JC, Hampton JR, Mitchell JRA: A randomized trial of home-versus-hospital management for patients with suspected myocardial infarction. Lancet 1:837–841, 1978.

21. Colling A, Dellipiani AW, Donaldson RJ: Teesside coronary survey: an epidemiological study of acute attacks of myocardial infarction. Br Med J 2:1169–1172, 1976.

22. Dellipiani AW, Colling WA, Donaldson RJ, et al: Teesside coronary survey—fatality and comparative severity of patients treated at home, in the hospital ward, and in the coronary care unit after myocardial infarction. Br Heart J 39:1172–1178, 1977.

23. Mandel E: An Introduction to Marxist Economic Thought. New York, Pathfinder, 1970.

24. DeSalvo RJ: Medical marketing mixture—update. Med Marketing & Media 13:21–35, September, 1978.

25. Warner-Lambert Pharmaceutical Company: Annual Report. Morris Plains, NJ, 1977.

26. Idem: Annual Report. Morris Plains, NJ, 1969, p 8.

27. American Optical Company: Annual Report. Southbridge, MA, 1966, p 9.

28. Warner-Lambert Pharmaceutical Company: Annual Report. Morris Plains, NJ, 1967, p 7.

29. Idem: Annual Report. Morris Plains, NJ, 1968, p 25.

30. Idem: Annual Report. Morris Plains, NJ, 1969, pp 18-19.

31. Idem: Annual Report. Morris Plains, NJ, 1970, p 19.

32. Idem: Annual Report. Morris Plains, NJ, 1975, p 5.

33. Idem: Annual Report. Morris Plains, NJ, 1970, p 16.

34. Hewlett-Packard Company: Annual Report. Palo Alto, CA, 1966, p 11.

35. Idem: Annual Report. Palo Alto, CA, 1969, p 11.

36. Idem: Annual Report. Palo Alto, CA, 1966, p 4.

37. Idem: Annual Report. Palo Alto, CA, 1974, p 2.

38. Idem: Annual Report. Palo Alto, CA, 1971, p 5.

39. Idem: Annual Report. Palo Alto, CA, 1973, pp 18–19.

40. Warner-Lambert Pharmaceutical Company: Annual Report. Morris Plains, NJ, 1967, p 7.

41. Scitovsky AA, McCall N: Changes in the Costs of Treatment of Selected Illnesses, 1951–1964–1971. DHEW Pub. No. (HRA) 77-3161. Washington, DC, Govt Printing Office, 1977.

42. American Heart Association: Annual Report. New York, 1967, p 11.

43. Idem: Annual Report. New York, 1968, pp 2, 13-14.

44. John A. Hartford Foundation: Annual Report. New York, 1963, p 58.

45. W.R. Hewlett Foundation: Annual Report to the Internal Revenue Service. Palo Alto, CA, 1967, 1971.

46. Bloom BS, Peterson OL: End results, cost and productivity of coronary-care units. N Engl J Med 288:72–78, 1974.

47. O'Connor J: The Fiscal Crisis of the State. New York, St. Martin's Press, 1973.

48. United States Department of Commerce, Domestic and Internal Business Administration: Global Market Survey: Biomedical Equipment. USDC Pub., unnumbered. Washington, DC, Govt Printing Office, 1973.

49. Braverman H: Labor and Monopoly Capital. New York, Monthly Review Press, 1974.

50. Rosinski EF: Impact of technology and evolving health care systems on the training of allied health personnel. Milit Med 134:390–393, 1969.

51. Moore FJ: Information technologies and health care: the need for new technologies to offset the shortages of physicians. Arch Intern Med 125:351–355, 1970.

52. Foster FL, Casten GG, Reeves TJ: Nonmedical personnel and continuous ECG monitoring. Arch Intern Med 124:110–112, 1969.

53. Sanazaro PJ: Physician support personnel in the 1970s. JAMA 214:98–100, 1970.

54. Barnett GO, Robbins A: Information technology and manpower productivity. JAMA 209:546–548, 1969.

55. McNeil BJ, Keeler E., Adelstein SJ: Primer on certain elements of medical decision making. N Engl J Med 293:211–215, 1975.

56. Schoenbaum SC, McNeil BJ, Kavet J: The swine-

influenza decision. N Engl J Med 295:759–765, 1976.

57. Costs, Risks, and Benefits of Surgery. JP Bunker, BA Barnes, F Mosteller (eds.) New York, Oxford University Press, 1977.

58. Abrahms HL, McNeil BJ: Medical implications of computed tomography ("CAT scanning"). N Engl J Med 289:255–261, 310–318, 1978.

59. Hitch CJ, McKean RN: The Economics of Defense in the Nuclear Age. New York, Atheneum, 1967.

60. Enthoven AC: Consumer-choice health plan. N Engl J Med 298:650–658, 709–720, 1978.

61. Cochrane AL: Efficiency and Effectiveness: Random Reflections on Health Services. London, Nuffield Hospitals Trust, 1972.

62. Illich I: Medical Nemesis. New York, Pantheon, 1976.

63. Rose G: The contribution of intensive coronary care. Br J Prev Soc Med 29:147–150, 1975.

64. Mechanic D: Approaches to controlling the costs of medical care: short-range and long-range alternatives. N Engl J Med 298:249–254, 1978.

65. United States Congress, Office of Technology Assessment: Development of Medical Technology: Opportunities for Assessment (OTA Pub. unnumbered). Washington, DC, Govt Printing Office, 1976.

66. Stevenson G: Laws of motion in the for-profit health industry: a theory and three examples. Internat J Health Serv 8:235–256, 1978.

67. Dellums RV, et al: Health Service Act (H.R. 11879). Washington, DC, Govt Printing Office, 1978.

Financing Medical Care

Medical care is big business in the United States. Billions of dollars are spent each year on medical services, with nearly half of each dollar coming from public funds. Medical costs are a significant factor in the economy's inflationary spiral and, until quite recently, were practically unregulated. Most of the money spent on medical care in the United States is spent via *third-party payments* on a fee-for-service basis.[1] As differentiated from *direct* (or *out-of-pocket*) payments, third-party payments are those made through some form of insurance or charitable organization for someone's medical care. Third-party payments have increased steadily over the past thirty years; in 1950, 32 percent of personal health care expenditures were made via third-party payments; in 1965 that figure was up to 48 percent; and by 1974 the ratio of third-party payments had increased to 65 percent (*Medical Care Chart Book*, 1976: 117). The 1985 estimate was that third-party payments would be nearly 75 percent. Almost all third-party payments are made by public or private insurance. The insurance industry, thus, is central to the financing of medical care services in this country. This section examines the role of insurance in financing medical care and the influence of the insurance industry on the present-day organization of medical services.

The original method of paying for medical services directly or individually, in money or in kind, has today been replaced by payment via insurance. Essentially, insurance is a form of "mass financing" that ensures that medical care providers will be paid and people will be able to obtain or pay for the medical care they need. Insurance involves the regular collection of small amounts of money (premiums) from a large number of people. That money is put into a pool, and when any of the insured people get sick, that pool (the insurance company) pays for their medical services either directly or indirectly by sending the money to provider or patient.

Although most people in the United States are covered by some form of third-party insurance, many millions of Americans are not. In addition, even having an insurance plan does not mean that all of one's medical costs are paid for by that plan.

The United States has both private and public insurance programs. Public insurance programs, including Medicare and Medicaid, are funded primarily by monies collected by federal, state, or local governments in the form of taxes. The nation has two types of private insurance organizations: *nonprofit* tax-exempt Blue Cross and Blue Shield plans and for-profit *commercial* insurance companies.

Blue Cross and Blue Shield emerged out of the Great Depression of the 1930s as mechanisms to assure the payment of medical bills to hospitals (Blue Cross) and physicians(Blue Shield). The Blues (Blue Cross and Blue Shield) were developed as community plans through which people made small "pre-payments" on a regular (generally monthly) basis. If they became sick their hospital bills were paid directly by the insurance plan.

Although there were commercial insurance companies as early as the nineteenth century, it wasn't until after World War II that the commercials really expanded in this country. Blue Cross and Blue Shield originally set the price of insurance premiums by what was called "community rating," giving everybody within a community the chance to purchase insurance at the same price. Commercials, on the other hand, based their price on "experience rating." Experience rating bases the price of insurance premiums on the statistical likelihood of the insured needing medical care. People less likely to need medical care are charged less for premiums than people more likely to need it. Experience rating allowed the commercials to undercut the Blues and capture a large segment of the labor union insurance market in the 1950s and 1960s by offering younger, healthier workers lower rates than could the Blues. In order to compete with the commercials, Blue Cross and Blue Shield eventually abandoned community rating and began using experience rating as well. One unfortunate result of the spread of experience rating has been that those who most need insurance coverage—the old, the sick—are least able to afford or obtain it (Bodenheimer et al., 1974: 583–584).

Medicare and Medicaid were passed by Congress in 1965 as amendments to the Social Security Act. Medicare pays for the medical care of people over sixty-five years of age (and of other qualified recipients of Social Security) and Medicaid pays for the care of those who qualify as too poor to pay their own medical costs. However, commercial and nonprofit insurance companies act as intermediaries in these government programs. Instead of the providers of medical care being paid directly by public funds, these funds are channeled through the (private) insurance industry. For example, 93 percent of Medicare payments to hospitals and 53 percent of Medicare payments to nursing homes are administered by Blue Cross. The Blues also act as intermediaries in most Medicaid programs (which are state controlled). Public funding via private insurance companies has resulted in enormous increases in the costs of both of these public insurance programs, high profits for the insurance intermediaries and their beneficiaries (e.g., physicians, hospitals), and near exhaustion of available public funds for the continuation of Medicare and Medicaid. Before 1965 the federal government paid about 10 percent of all medical expenditures. By 1982 it paid for nearly 30 percent of health care costs or $87 billion. The federal contribution to Medicare alone had risen from a couple of billion dollars in 1965 to 52 billion in 1982 and is still rising.

The Medicare-Medicaid response had a number of consequences. Medicare has provided basic medical insurance coverage for 99 percent of Americans over sixty-five. While there are still significant out-of-the-pocket expenses, this widespread coverage is a stark contrast when compared with the elderly's lack of coverage before 1965 (Davis, 1975). Medicaid has been much less comprehensive. Because it is a federal-state matching program, coverage varies from state to state. While the poor may receive more coverage than before Medicaid, because of severe restrictions in eligibility many poor people are not covered by Medicaid. Utilization of services has increased under

Medicaid so that the poor, who are generally sicker than the nonpoor, visit medical services more frequently. The major impact of Medicaid has been on maternal and child health.

Although federal programs have surely helped some sick people and reduced inequality and inaccessability of medical services, their effect is limited. Under the Reagan administration there were a number of cutbacks in these programs. But even before these cutbacks Medicare covered less than half the elderly's health expenses, and Medicaid covered only a third of that of the poor (Starr, 1982: 374).

The intent of Medicare and Medicaid is certainly worthy, even if the results are limited. But these programs also created new problems. They put billions of new dollars into the health system with no cost controls, so it was clear by the 1970s that Medicare and Medicaid were fueling escalating health costs, which now comprise more than 10 percent of the GNP. Some people were reaping enormous profits from the system, especially owners of shoddy nursing homes and so-called "medicaid mills." Tightening restrictions eliminated the worst offenders, but medical costs continued to soar.

In the early 1970s the federal government began to mandate a series of programs aimed at reducing spiraling costs, especially with Medicare. In 1972 utilization review boards—hospital-based committees—were instituted to review the appropriateness of medical utilization. These were followed by Professional Standard Review Organizations (PSRO) which were meant to monitor both quality and cost of care. In the middle 1970s the nation was divided up into dozens of Health System Agencies (HSAs), which were to be regionalized health planning agencies. HSAs attempted to regulate uncontrolled hospital and technological growth by requiring a "certificate of need" approval before there could be any new investment over $100,000. There were even attempts to put a "cap" (ceiling) on the total amount that could be allocated to a program. While a few cost control programs had limited effects in specific situations, the federal attempt to control costs so far has been generally a failure.

The newest federal attempt to control costs is a complex reimbursement system called "Diagnostically Related Groups" (DRGs). Mandated in 1984 for Medicare, this program replaces the fee-for-service system with a form of "prospective reimbursement" whereby the government will pay only a specific amount for a specified medical problem. The prices of 467 specific diagnoses are established in advance. Medicare will pay no more, no less. If a hospital spends less than the set amount, it gets to pocket the difference. The hope is that hospitals will have the incentive to be efficient and save money. The concern is that patients will get poorer treatment.

The articles in this section examine the origins and consequences of financing medical care in the particular way the American medical system has evolved. In the first selection, "Blue Cross—What Went Wrong?," Sylvia A. Law traces the historical development of Blue Cross and its close connection with the hospital industry. That history, she concludes, is one of unchecked growth and unnecessary expenditures in which, despite its public status as a tax-exempt corporation, Blue Cross has been able to make millions of dollars without public accountability or control. In large measure this has resulted from the administrative domination of Blue Cross by representatives of the American Hospital Association and other medical care providers. She outlines suggestions for reform within the current Blue Cross structure and raises as well the more fundamental question of to whom Blue Cross should be accountable.

Paul Starr examines the expansion of the private, for-profit insurance industry in "The Commercial Edge and the Accommodation of Insurance." Competition from the commercial insurance industry eroded Blue Cross's community orientation and made the distinction between for-profit and non-profit insurance companies almost meaningless. Starr shows how physicians were able to maintain their professional dominance by turning the increase in third-party payments from a threat to an economic benefit.

Starr notes how private insurance worsened the situation of those who were left out. Even with the emergence of Medicare and Medicaid a substantial portion of the population is without any health insurance. Karen Davis and Diane Rowland describe the fate of this uninsured population, estimated as over 25 million people, in "Uninsured and Underserved: Inequities in Health Care in the United States." Davis and Rowland review the successes and limitations of Medicaid and their conclusions are disturbing. We often assume that Medicaid covers at least the basic health needs of the poor, but the largest group of uninsured are the approximately 60 per cent of the poor who are ineligible for Medicaid benefits. Most typically the uninsured are black and live in the South, although they are found among all races and in all regions. The tragic irony is there is evidence that the uninsured are sicker than the insured and thus more in need of services. But as this article shows, one of the consequences of the financing structure of our medical care system is to leave the poor and unemployed without insurance coverage or protection against sickness. And with cutbacks in recent years the situation is getting worse.

NOTES

1. Fee-for-service is a central feature of the economic organization of medicine in our society. Since medical providers are paid a fee for every service they provide, many critics argue that a fee-for-service system creates a financial incentive to deliver unnecessary services, making medical care more profitable and costly.

REFERENCES

Bodenheimer, Thomas, Steven Cummings, and Elizabeth Harding. 1974. "Capitalizing on illness: The health insurance industry." International Journal of Health Services 4, 4: 583–598.

Davis, Karen. 1975. "Equal treatment and unequal benefits: The Medicare program." Milbank Memorial Fund Quarterly 53, 4: 449–88.

Medical Care Chart Book. Sixth Edition. 1976. School of Public Health, Department of Medical Care Organization, University of Michigan. Data on third-party payments computed from Chart D-15: 117.

Starr, Paul. 1982. The Social Transformation of American Medicine. New York: Basic Books.

20

Blue Cross—What Went Wrong?

Sylvia A. Law

....

It is widely acknowledged that the American health care crisis is primarily one of organization, administration, and accountability. Blue Cross is at the heart of the administration of the present medical care delivery system.[1] Over $22 billion a year, about one-third of the national health care dollar, are spent in hospitals.[2] Blue Cross provides about half of hospital revenues, administering over $11 billion in 1970. Public funds comprised over half of Blue Cross payments to hospitals—$4.9 billion under Medicare, $1.2 billion under Medicaid, and $545 million under other federally financed programs.[3]

Blue Cross is a complex animal, impossible to characterize in a few words. For example, it may be seen as the financing arm of American hospitals, with a primary obligation to provide them, on an equitable basis, with a stable source of income to be utilized as they judge necessary. If this is regarded as its primary role, then Blue Cross's responsibilities to subscribers and to the public are to offer hospital insurance benefits at competitive rates, to maintain a financially sound rate structure, and to pay hospitals promptly for services provided to subscribers. Alternatively, Blue Cross may be seen as a quasi-public agency with primary responsibility to the public and to its subscribers. If this is its primary role, then its

obligations are to offer benefits that will enable subscribers to obtain quality health care services economically, to monitor the quality of care provided subscribers in participating hospitals, to utilize the collective power of its payments to encourage hospitals to establish programs that will best meet subscribers' health needs, and to refuse to reimburse hospitals for charges that are excessive or do not meet subscribers' needs. Finally, with respect to the public funds it administers, Blue Cross may legitimately be viewed as an agent of the government, with an obligation to carry out the policies of Congress and of the administrative agencies responsible for publicly financed medical programs. Confusion as to the proper role of Blue Cross is common and pervades the organization itself, the state regulatory agencies, Congress, and the Department of Health, Education and Welfare.

In a nutshell . . . Blue Cross is most accurately characterized today as the financing arm of American hospitals. . . .

A Unique American Institution

Blue Cross is the child of the Depression and the American Hospital Association. The period from 1875 to 1915 was one of major development of medical institutions in this country, and by 1920 the now familiar pattern of community voluntary hospitals and local autonomy in health matters was established.[4] During the 1920s there was growing recognition of the need for some mechanism by which middle income people could finance the extraordinary costs of hospitalization. Hospital insurance was virtually nonexistent.[5] In October 1927, the president of the American Hospital Association described the organization's "ultimate objective" as

> providing hospitalization for the great bulk of people of moderate means . . . [who are] confronted with the necessity of amassing a debt or the alternative of casting aside all pride and accepting the provisions that are intended for the poor . . . Let us keep in mind the *raison d'être* of our existence, vis.: the provision of hospitalization for the patient of moderate means, consisting of 80 percent of the entire population. The wise solution of this great problem will inscribe the name of the American Hospital Association in the hearts of the people for all time.[6]

The solution most often proposed then was public education; people should be taught to save for large medical expenses.[7] The Depression, however, provided the impetus for a movement away from public education toward the development of the comprehensive Blue Cross network. Hospitals were hard hit by the Depression. In one year, from 1929 to 1930, the average hospital receipts per patient fell from $236.12 to $59.26. Average percent of occupancy fell from 71.28 percent to 64.12 percent. Average deficits as a percentage of disbursements rose from 15.2 percent to 20.6 percent.[8] The hospitals had an immediate interest in developing a stable source of payment for services and also had the technical and financial resources to create such a program. Of 39 Blue Cross plans established in the early 1930s, 22 obtained all of their initial funds from hospitals, and five were partially financed by hospitals.[9]

There was by that time a variety of small, voluntary plans for the prepayment of medical expenses, including the predictable expenses incident to childbirth.[10] The largest of these plans, and the one generally credited as the progenitor of Blue Cross, was initiated in 1929 by Dr. Justin Ford Kimball in Dallas, Texas. An executive vice president of Baylor University, Dr. Kimball found the unpaid bills of many local schoolteachers among the accounts receivable of the university's medical facilities. In order to assure payment to the university, he enrolled 1,250 teachers in a program to prepay fifty cents a month for 21 days of semi-private hospitalization at the Baylor University Hospital.[11]

Under the Baylor plan and other early programs, subscribers could receive services only at the hospital that had organized the prepayment program. Most state insurance commissioners regarded these single hospital programs as group contracts for the sale of services by the hospitals to subscribing members and hence not subject to legal requirements applicable to insurance companies.[12] However, in some states insurance officials ruled that single hospital prepayment plans presented serious limitations to individuals and physicians by forcing them to select a hospital at the time of enrollment rather than at the time of illness. Consequently, during 1932 and 1933 "free choice" plans that covered care at a number of hospitals were organized in several cities. While the applicability of insurance laws to single hospital prepayment plans was an open question, the free choice plans were more clearly a form of insurance. The legal issue came sharply into focus when the United Hospital Fund of New York and the Cleveland Hospital Council were told that they would have to establish either a mutual or stock insurance company before making prepaid care available to the public.[13]

In response to this problem, the American Hospital Association and local hospital organizations sought state legislation to create a special class of nonprofit corporation and of hospital insurance. In 1932, Dr. C. Rufus Rorem, associate director of the Julius Rosenwald Fund, studied the existing group hospital prepayment programs. He was also retained by the AHA to promote hospital prepayment and to seek the necessary enabling legislation. The following year the AHA promulgated seven "standards which should characterize group hospitalization plans." The standards were: (1) emphasis on public welfare, (2) limitation to hospital services, (3) freedom of choice of hospital and physician by subscriber, (4) nonprofit sponsorship, (5) compliance with legal requirements, (6) economic soundness, and (7) dignified and ethical administration.[14] In 1936, the AHA obtained a grant from the Rosenwald Fund to finance a special Committee on Hospital Service, and Dr. Rorem became its first executive director. In 1938 the committee established fourteen standards for nonprofit hospital care plans, including, for the first time, the requirement that the plan be approved by the AHA.[15]

The special enabling legislation sought by the AHA conferred the following advantages and privileges on the proposed hospital service corporations: exemption from the general insurance laws of the state; status as a charitable and benevolent organization; exemption from the obligation of maintaining the reserves required of commercial insurers; and tax exemption. The major justification offered in support of the special enabling legislation was the promise of service to the community, and particularly to low income families.[16] The AHA House of Delegates, in a 1939 resolution supporting the development of hospital service plans, cited the need for a program that would provide hospitalization "among the low income groups" and noted that such plans "would reduce the need for taxation and philanthropy."[17] Dr. Rorem explained:

Hospital service plans are unique, historically and geographically.... They deal with a service which has long been recognized as a community responsibility. *Hospital care must be provided for all persons regardless of their ability to pay.* Such a responsibility cannot and should not be assumed by a private insurance company, the first concern of which should be the financial interests of the policyholders and stockholders ... Government controlled hospitalization or health insurance is a second alternative to the nonprofit hospital service plan.... *But low-cost hospital service plans may reach many persons employed at low incomes who would otherwise require the aid of philanthropy or taxation.*[18] (Emphasis added.)

In 1934 the first hospital service plan enabling act was adopted by the New York state legislature.[19] With the support of the AHA, the bill had been promoted by the New York United Hospital Fund—a coalition of civic leaders, hospital administrators, hospital trustees, and physicians.[20] The New York act served as a model for other states, and by 1945 similar laws had been adopted in 35 states.[21] Currently 48 states have special enabling legislation for hospital service organization,[22] and in 20 states such corporations are exempt from taxation.[23] Individual Blue Cross plans and the Blue Cross Association (BCA), the national trade association, are also exempt from the payment of federal taxes.[24]

. . . .

From the 1930s on, the American Hospital Association sought to promote and control the development of monopolistic Blue Cross organizations. Preferred corporate status and tax treatment were important in the growth of Blue Cross and these publicly conferred advantages were intensified by the private policy and control of the AHA. The enabling acts do not refer to Blue Cross by name but rather allow the establishment of "hospital service corporations." Although theoretically there could be several competing hospital service corporations in any one area, the enabling acts typically require that the corporation establish cooperative agreements with the majority of hospitals in the area served. Furthermore, AHA policy has required that, in order to use the Blue Cross emblem, a hospital service corporation must establish agreements with 75 percent of the area hospital,[25] and the AHA generally authorized use of the emblem by only one hospital service corporation in any given area.[26] Thus, historically, the combination of public enabling legislation and the private power of the AHA has assured that there is only one Blue Cross organization in any given area and that it is, to some degree, controlled by the hospitals.

By 1938, 1.4 million people in the United States had enrolled in 38 Blue Cross plans. Private insurance companies provided hospital insurance to only 1 million people. During the forties Blue Cross expanded at a rapid pace; the private health insurance industry also grew, but more slowly. Several factors contributed to the rapid growth of Blue Cross: it began writing contracts with employers and contracts having nationwide coverage; health insurance increasingly became a matter for collective bargaining, with labor supporting Blue Cross; and employment and wages mushroomed during World War II.[27] In 1945 Blue Cross claimed 61 percent of the hospital insurance market, compared with the insurance companies' 33 percent. But in 1951, for the first time, the number of people with private commercial hospital insurance (40.0 million) surpassed the number enrolled in Blue Cross plans (37.4 million),[28] and throughout the fifties and sixties Blue Cross was unsuccessful in competing with the commercial companies. At the end of 1969 Blue Cross had an enrollment of 67.2 million, or 37 percent of the civilian population under 65, while the commercial insurance companies provided hospital coverage to 100 million people, or 57 percent of the civilian population under 65.[29] The passage of Medicare and Medicaid legislation in 1965, however, gave Blue Cross a boost that reestablished its dominance in terms of hospital payments as a whole.

Two major characteristics have distinguished Blue Cross from most commercial insurance companies: payment of service benefits to hospitals rather than cash benefits to the individual insured; and community rating, that is, the provision of benefits to all members of the community at the same rate, rather than higher rates to high risk groups.

The Blue Cross commitment to the payment of service benefits to hospitals means, simply, that while commercial insurers generally pay the individual a fixed dollar amount per day or period of hospitalization, and the individual bears primary responsibility for the payment of the hospital bill, Blue Cross gives the subscriber the assurance it will settle his bill with the hospital, with the subscriber bearing responsibility only for the coinsurance, or deductible, specified in the policy. The original American Hospital Association standards for the approval of hospital service plans required that, "Benefits in member hospitals should be expressed in 'service contracts,' which describe specifically the types and amounts of hospital services to which the subscribers are entitled."[30] Over the years, however, as a result of competitive pressures, an increasing number of Blue Cross plans have offered subscribers indemnity rather than service contracts.[31]

The second major distinction between Blue Cross and commercial insurers was the Blue Cross promise of service to the community. Initially all Blue Cross plans offered hospital insurance to all members of the community at uniform rates,[32] one rate for individuals and one rate for families, while commercial companies offered more favorable rates to those groups and individuals who were actuarially less likely to make claims.[33] Since low income families and the aged tend to utilize hospital services more than the general population, these groups are helped by community rating.[34] During World War II, as organized labor began to press for more adequate health benefits and other insurance companies began to compete for this growing business, Blue Cross, after a decade of internal struggle, abandoned its commitment to community rating.[35] Today most Blue Cross plans offer group experience-rated contracts, particularly for larger group policies, as well as community-rated policies for those individuals who are not able to obtain a group policy through their work or otherwise.[36]

The adoption of experience rating was probably inevitable if Blue Cross was to compete successfully with the commercial insurers for the business of the low risk customer.[37] The alternatives were to persuade low risk groups that Blue Cross was so useful as an organization serving the entire community that low risk customers should subsidize the costs of the higher risk groups or to offer a service so excellent that high risk groups could be subsidized without fatal competitive disadvantage.[38] Either of these alternatives would have been very difficult. Since a return to strict community rating is unlikely, the current major issue is whether Blue Cross deserves its favored status under state and federal law.

. . . .

Local Plans, the Blue Cross Association and the American Hospital Association

Membership in the national Blue Cross organization is critical to a local Blue Cross plan. The advantages of membership include: use of the official Blue Cross emblem and seal; the right to exclusive provision of Blue Cross benefits within a territorial area; the national advertising, public relations, and lobbying; the use of information gathering, processing, and dissemination apparatus; and mechanisms for coordination of national accounts and for the transfer and acceptance of subscribers who move from one plan's territory to another's. With the advent of Medicare, membership in the national organization became even more valuable. The national Blue Cross Association (BCA) contracted with the Social Security Administration for the administration of the Medicare program, and the BCA now serves as protector and interpreter for local plans vis-à-vis the federal government.

The name "Blue Cross" and the Blue Cross insignia were owned by the American Hospital Association until 1972.[39] The relationship between the AHA and Blue Cross plans has been close throughout Blue Cross history, as we have seen. In 1936, as part of its effort to promote the establishment of prepaid hospitalization plans, the AHA created a Committee on Hospital Services, which in 1946 became the Blue Cross Commission of the AHA.[40] Until 1957, the commission performed the national coordinating function among Blue Cross plans. In 1960, most of the commission's functions were transferred to the Blue Cross Association, a nonprofit Illinois corporation. The BCA and AHA maintained close coordination through interlocking directorates, with the AHA designating three members on the BCA board and BCA designating two members on the AHA board. Other functions, including the administration of the approval program for use of the Blue Cross insignia, were retained by the AHA. In 1971, the AHA and Blue Cross agreed in principle that the ownership of the Blue Cross name and insignia should be transferred to the BCA, and this transfer became effective on June 30, 1972.[41] The two groups also agreed to eliminate their interlocking directorates and substitute a joint committee to facilitate communication between them.[42] AHA officials stated that the change was made as a "response to changing public attitudes" and emphasized that it did not represent a "cooling off" in the close relationships between Blue Cross and the AHA.[43]

In 1971, the Subcommittee on Antitrust and Monopoly of the Senate Committee on the Judiciary heard extensive testimony on the operation of BCA review of local plan performance, with particular reference to the Richmond, Virginia, plan. The hearings revealed that BCA's claim of national review of local plans is predominantly public relations puffing. Testimony showed that throughout the late sixties the administrative costs of the Virginia plan were among the highest of any Blue Cross plan in the nation.[44] Subsequent investigations prompted by public and congressional concern revealed gross mismanagement. For example, the plan had 119 rented automobiles and could not account for their use.[45] It paid for staff memberships in various country clubs and owned stock in a country club.[46] Two years after Medicare began, the plan moved into an $8 million office building. One million dollars was spent to decorate and furnish the building, and most of the purchases were made, without competitive bidding, from a firm whose sales manager was chairman of the Building Committee of the Blue Cross board.[47] The plan paid $198,000 to a profit-making data processing organization but received no identifiable service. The assistant general manager of the plan was also a member of the board of the data processing organization, but he never revealed this relationship, because he believed that there was no conflict of interest.[48]

In October 1968, while these policies were in effect, the Richmond plan was given a "Total Plan Review" by the BCA. This review was described as

a review and analysis of the overall corporate structure of the plan, its organization, objectives, future plans and management controls, especially as they related to the effectiveness of the administrative system. Particular emphasis was given to the support function of data processing and financial activities.[49]

The final report, while noting low productivity and high cost per claim, was laudatory.

The team was particularly impressed with the overall corporate structure and organization of the plan ... The executive management group of the Richmond plan displays a progressive and confident attitude. ....There is an atmosphere which is conducive to innovation and change aimed at improvement. ...

It was favorably noted that a good start has been made toward greater refinement of the budget, cost accounting, etc. in the financial area. The Richmond plan has made great strides toward attracting and retaining qualified personnel. This is true with respect to physical surroundings, progressive atmosphere, etc.[50]

Despite this clean bill of health, by early 1970 public attention prompted the BCA to reexamine the plan. Internal BCA memos subpoenaed by the Senate committee revealed that the 1970 investigation was primarily concerned with public appearances. One national official recommended that a BCA team be sent "in the interest of preserving the National reputation as opposed to assisting the Plan." Another BCA official visiting Richmond concluded that BCA should

refrain from moving in since we know the bad news that might erupt. ... Richmond could blow up. It is a real "can of worms." But we know enough bad things without necessarily sending in a team to get more information. However, I also recognize that the National Associations must preserve their dignity and be prepared to answer questions. ... Nevertheless, this is another case of "locking the barn door after the horse has departed."[51]

It seems that local malfeasance is a subject for national concern only when it approaches the level of scandal or illegality. Even then BCA efforts are directed first toward preventing adverse publicity, then toward correcting the problems.

. . . .

While corporate waste through high administrative costs is significant, it is not the central issue in evaluating Blue Cross performance. In Richmond, administrative costs represented only 5.4 percent of the earned subscriber income, the balance being payments to hospitals.[52] The key

issue of public concern should be what Blue Cross does to ensure that hospital costs are reasonable. Not surprisingly, the evidence was that the Richmond plan did not pursue any form of hospital cost control. The executive director of the plan was asked, "What if your audit [of hospital books] indicated clearly wasteful practices? What do you do?" He responded, "Well, Mr. Chairman, I am not aware of our audits ever uncovering wasteful charges, and I really wouldn't know what we would do if we ran into them."[53]

Because of the difficulty in obtaining information about the internal operations of Blue Cross, it is not possible to know whether the Richmond operation is typical. Probably it is not.[54] However, such mismanagement is not unique. For example, the General Accounting Office and a subcommittee of the House Committee on Government Operations found that during 1966–67, Washington, D.C., Blue Cross kept an average of more than $10 million in federal funds in noninterest-bearing accounts in Washington banks. Larger amounts, estimated in excess of $15 million, were kept in noninterest-bearing accounts from 1961–1965.[55] Several members of the Blue Cross board, including the treasurer, were officers and board members of the banks in which the monies were deposited.[56] From 1963 until 1971 Illinois Blue Cross had between $7 and $15 million deposited in noninterest-bearing accounts in a bank at which the chairman of the board served as senior vice president and an additional $2 million in noninterest-bearing accounts in a second bank, one of the officers of which was also on the Blue Cross board.[57]

Periodic investigations by congressional committees are obviously an ineffective means to discover whether plans operate efficiently or to encourage such operation. As the facts concerning the mismanagement of the Richmond plan unfolded, the Subcommittee on Antitrust and Monopoly grappled to find some mechanism of public accountability—some means by which the interests of the public and of subscribers could be protected. Senator Hart asked, "There isn't any outside discipline, either the Virginia Corporation Commission or legislative body or the National Blue Cross, that could do other than sort of wonder. Nobody could correct, is that right, the absent internal discipline?" The chief executive officer responded, "Mr. Chairman, I would say you are absolutely right, but that responsibility rests purely on the shoulders of the boards of directors. . . . The moment they found the level of spending which they couldn't quite stand, they acted immediately."[58]

It is extraordinarily difficult to obtain concrete information about Blue Cross operations. The BCA and published materials do not provide even basic information on the practices of various plans with respect to reimbursement of hospitals, claims review, determination of subscriber rates, governance, or state and federal regulation. Because of the lack of public information and the importance of concrete data on which to base an analysis and evaluation of Blue Cross, the author, on January 20, 1972, distributed a twelve-page questionnaire, covering the subjects listed above, to each Blue Cross plan. On February 1, 1972, D. Eugene Sibery, executive vice president of the BCA, wrote that the national association would be responding to the questionnaire on behalf of the local plans. Its response to most questions was that information was unavailable.[59] The questionnaire had originally been directed to the local plans precisely because the author was unable to obtain the information sought from the BCA and understood that the BCA did not have the data. Local plans may have been reluctant to provide information even if the BCA had not intervened.[60] BCA intervention assured the unavailability of the information.

Blue Cross Boards of Directors

The local Blue Cross board has the primary—and often the sole—responsibility for determining policy and assuring accountability within the plan. For example, the local board determines whether the plan shall offer community rates to all subscribers or experience rates based on the particular utilization patterns of groups of subscribers. It decides whether the plan shall offer benefits only for inpatient hospital services or provide more comprehensive benefits, including coverage for less expensive forms of care. It determines whether the plan shall pay hospitals whatever they ask or use the economic power of payments to force cost control and otherwise shape local hospital planning. It is responsible for establishing procedures for subscriber complaints and for determining the governing structure of the organization.

In the 1960s, the assertion that Blue Cross boards were publicly responsive was a major selling point in persuading Congress to give Blue Cross a key role in the Medicare program.[61] Although citizen control of local Blue Cross policy has always been emphasized in Blue Cross rhetoric, it is only within the past few years that there has been serious scrutiny of the actual composition of Blue Cross boards. Two major issues have been raised. First, what role, if any, should providers of service have on the board? Second, do the standards and procedures for the selection of public members of the board adequately ensure that they will represent public and subscriber interests.

Hospital representatives currently dominate Blue Cross boards. The AHA Standards for Approval, now taken over by the BCA, require that at least one-third of the board members represent the contracting hospitals, and some enabling acts require hospital representatives on the board.[62] In 1970, according to BCA figures, 56 percent of the members of local boards were health care providers, 42 percent representing hospitals and 14 percent representing the medical profession.[63]

A case can be made that hospital representatives have no proper role on Blue Cross boards. Because the federal and state governments have delegated to Blue Cross the public functions of: (1) paying for publicly financed hospital care; (2) determining the reasonableness of hospital costs; and (3) using payment processes to encourage rational planning and utilization patterns, the place of provider representatives on Blue Cross boards can certainly be questioned. For example, the chairman of the Massachusetts Rate Setting Commission and special counsel for health affairs commented:

> If we regard Blue Cross as having a responsibility to "regulate" hospital costs—and I most certainly do—then we can look upon this arrangement as

those who are regulated actually being the regulators of themselves. The counterbalancing and resolution of discrete interests which should be the heart of any regulatory process is lacking.[64]

. . . .

The criticism of provider members on Blue Cross boards is not primarily that they are self-dealing or necessarily incapable of avoiding conflicts of interest.[65] Rather, the problem is that provider representatives are primarily responsible to hospitals rather than to subscribers or the public. It is unrealistic to expect that, as Blue Cross board members, hospital representatives will challenge hospital policies on cost control, area planning, or reorientation of services, when these are policies they have developed. Hospital representatives will seek to maintain the autonomy of the hospital.[66]

. . . .

As presently constituted, even the public board members often do not protect or reflect subscriber interests. Although in 1970, 44 percent of the members of local plan boards were "public" representatives, examination reveals that under present structures public representatives are an elite group with little resemblance to subscribers. In most Blue Cross plans public representatives are selected by the incumbent board.[67] In twenty-one plans they are selected by the hospital representatives.[68] In Washington, D.C., the public representatives are appointed by the commissioner of the district. Subscribers elect public representatives in only eight plans, including the Philadelphia plan.[69]

Compared to other plans the Philadelphia board has democratic selection procedures. Subscribers have always been able to vote for a small minority of board members. However, in 1970 and 1971 the plan bylaws were amended to allow subscribers to vote for all but four of the 34 board members, with nominations being made by the incumbent board or by petition with 300 subscriber signatures. In 1971 and 1972 subscribers nominated candidates to run against nominees of the board. Through advertisements in local newspapers and through contacts with large organizations holding group contracts, the plan management solicited proxy votes for the board's candidates. In both years the plan refused subscriber requests to publish a ballot that would allow subscribers to cast votes for the insurgent candidates and to publish information about the position of various candidates on questions of plan policy. In 1971, the subscriber candidates received over 1,000 votes, but the management slate won with about 3,000 votes. In 1972, the subscriber candidates received over 4,000 votes, but management had increased its effort and obtained 16,000 proxy votes.[70] During the intervening year there had been substantial adverse publicity about Blue Cross, as Insurance Commissioner Herbert Denenberg criticized the plan for failure to hold down hospital costs. It is difficult to believe that the fivefold jump in votes for the incumbent board reflected a vote of confidence or popularity. The number of votes obtained by the management appears to reflect the amount of management resources devoted to the collection of proxies rather than subscriber endorsement of management policy and competence. The subscriber candidates had no financial support but depended on volunteer efforts of those concerned about Blue Cross policy. There are no limitations on the resources which the plan can devote to insuring the election of a board that will support current policies and management.[71]

The Philadelphia plan directors are not representative of the plan's subscribers. Twelve of the 34 directors are directors of banking and financial institutions. Two sit on the boards of major real estate companies, one is the president of a company with major interests in hospital supply, and others are business executives.[72] Two directors represent organized labor. The typical board member is white, male, over 40, and wealthy; departures from this norm are few. The Philadelphia board does not even reflect the broad range of the city's hospitals; in 1970 five of the city's most influential hospitals had more than one representative on the board.[73]

The pattern in Philadelphia is typical of the rest of the country. Blue Cross Association data show that the 824 members of local plan boards designated as public and consumer representatives include: 311 business executives, 116 physicians and surgeons, 90 retired people, 73 bankers, 54 lawyers, 39 labor leaders, 34 university and school officials, 23 investment advisers, 17 religious leaders, 8 real estate men, and 59 people in a variety of other positions.[74] Of these public representatives, only 18 are women.

Labor representatives on Blue Cross boards are often cited as the representatives of ordinary subscribers. There is no evidence that they have played such a role.[75] Further examination of labor members of Blue Cross boards is needed. One hypothesis is that labor representatives have been content to obtain relatively favorable rate treatment for their own members.[76] Blue Cross critics charge that community-rated subscribers, who pay substantially higher rates, subsidize the organized experience-rated subscribers.[77] No one would be the wiser if a plan were to offer favorable group rates based not on experience but on political influence, representation on the plan board, or other extraneous factors. Only Blue Cross has the information needed to determine whether such discriminatory rate setting exists. Insurance commissioners do not obtain sufficient information to know whether experience rates are justified on the basis of actual experience and administrative savings resulting from the group contract; certainly community-rated subscribers do not have access to such information.[78] Aggressive scrutiny of Blue Cross policies and pursuit of institutional reform would require enormous effort and tenacity and could quickly put labor representatives into direct conflict with plan administration and board members from the hospitals. Given that labor representatives constitute such a small minority on a Blue Cross board and given that they are accountable to a constituency that is probably not demanding reforms in the Blue Cross structure, it would not be surprising to find labor members playing a quiet role in Blue Cross governance.[79]

Within the present Blue Cross board structures, there are some reforms that can and should be instituted. It would be a fairly simple matter for the BCA, state insurance departments, or the federal government as administrator of Medicare to gather and publicize information on the affiliations of Blue Cross directors and on the major organizations with which the plan contracts and banks. Simply gathering such information and making it public would do much to curb the more flagrant abuses of Blue Cross power.

The more fundamental question of who governs Blue Cross, and to whom it should be accountable, requires a more comprehensive solution. It is an illusion to believe that effective public control of an institution as complex and influential as Blue Cross could be achieved easily or with minor reforms. . . .

REFERENCES

For references see Peter Conrad and Rochelle Kern, eds. The Sociology of Health and Illness: Critical Perspectives (New York: St. Martin's Press, 1981).

21

The Commercial Edge and the Accommodation of Insurance

Paul Starr

After World War II, commercial indemnity insurance enjoyed the most rapid expansion of any form of health coverage. By the early 1950s, not only did commercial insurers have more subscribers than Blue Cross and Blue Shield, but they were also forcing the Blues to do business on their terms. And, paradoxically, by that very process, they were pushing the system ultimately toward some form of government intervention, as voluntary health insurance became increasingly incapable of providing protection to high-risk groups like the aged.

But this contradiction was barely evident during the period of rapid growth after the war. Between 1945 and 1949 commercial group hospital insurance policies jumped from 7.8 to 17.7 million; individual coverage climbed to 14.7 million. Minus duplication, the total number of people covered solely by commercial insurers in 1949 was estimated at 28 million, compared to over 31 million enrolled in Blue Cross. (Independent plans covered about 4 million people for hospital care.) Commercial insurers were then far ahead of Blue Shield in coverage of surgical bills (22.7 versus 12 million people), and two years later, they pulled ahead of Blue Cross in hospital coverage as well. As of 1953 commercial carriers provided hospital insurance to 29 percent of Americans, Blue Cross to 27 percent, and independent plans to 7 percent.[1]

As commercial health insurance expanded, the character of the industry changed. Before the 1940s there had been a relatively small number of firms, mainly casualty insurers and specialized health and accident companies, which sold policies primarily to individuals. Between 1942 and 1949 the number of firms offering insurance against hospital expenses increased from 28 to 101. Commercial insurers continued to sell more individual policies than the Blues, but as employee benefit plans expanded, their business tilted toward group insurance. That meant a shift in industry leadership from the casualty to the life insurance companies, such as Metropolitan and Prudential, which dominated the group market.[2] The campaign that they had waged thirty years earlier against a government program was finally paying off.

The difference between the insurance companies and the Blues involved more than a contrast between for-profit and nonprofit enterprise. Indeed, whether any clear distinction can be drawn on that basis is doubtful. On the one hand, some of the leading insurance firms, such as Metropolitan, were mutual insurance companies nominally owned by their policy-holders; all "surpluses" were supposedly returned to them. (In fact, the mutual form guaranteed that a self-perpetuating board of directors would have control of the companies' huge financial assets.) On the other hand, the allegedly nonprofit medical society plans were clearly aimed at increasing the income of the physicians who controlled them. Only the law said they were not for profit. As in the case of hospitals, providers preferred the nonprofit form of organization because of the advantages of tax exemption and the desire to avoid any alienation of control or the extraction of any profit from their services. Probably for the same reason, the provider-controlled Blue plans were more successful in holding down the proportion of income retained for administration, commissions, and "surplus." Of every dollar of premium income on health insurance, Blue Cross retained about 6 cents, Blue Shield about 10 cents, and commercial insurers 21 cents.[3] (However, the higher retention rate for the latter was due partly to a greater proportion of individual policies.) The Blues cited the fact that they distributed more of their income in benefits as evidence of their community orientation. But since they mainly provided service benefits (payments to providers), the pattern is sufficiently explained by the interests of their principals.

Despite their lower overhead, the Blue plans had several decided disadvantages in competing with commercial insurers. While the commercial carriers could provide employers one-stop service for a variety of types of insurance, the Blues were restricted by their enabling laws to provision of health insurance only. The Blue plans were also locally controlled and loosely coordinated, which impeded their ability to offer national coverage. And many employers preferred indemnity plans because they were more flexible in the range of benefits and costs; also, indemnity plans could be organized to give the employer a direct administrative role and hence the opportunity to enjoy the gains in good will from making payments to workers at times of adversity. But probably the most important attraction to employers was that the insurance companies were willing to give them a lower price on healthy, low-risk workers.

This was called "experience rating," and it stood in sharp contrast to the way in which social insurance systems and even Blue Cross distributed the costs of health care. Under government programs of health insurance, premiums may be progressively scaled by income. Under Blue Cross, subscribers generally paid the same "community" rate, at least for group policies. (Individual policies cost more.) But under commercial insurance, every employee group was charged according to its "experience." A young, relatively healthy group received a reduced rate because the

costs it experienced were low. By the same token, an older, relatively unhealthy group had to pay more because its costs were likely to be high.

Each of these practices was justified by a different theory of equity, and each was linked to specific social conditions. Social insurance redistributes costs from high- to low-risk groups, but such redistribution is possible only when the state legally requires contributions. Otherwise, the low-risk groups will not participate. Any voluntary health plan has a limited capacity to redistribute costs because it cannot compel low-risk groups to accept higher rates than their level of risk demands. If it "overcharges" them, they may be offered a cheaper rate by a competitor or simply decide to self-insure (that is, to set aside money in their own insurance fund). When the Blue plans began, they were relatively free from competition and were able to adopt uniform rates as part of their effort to make voluntary insurance available to the whole population and to forestall a compulsory program. Though hardly progressive, community rates keep down costs for high-risk groups. But in the prevailing norms of commercial insurance, equity consists in charging every group according to its risk. In this view, a community rate that charges everyone the same is inequitable because it costs healthy people too much—that is, more than they would have to pay for insurance in a competitive market.[4] Equity here is indistinguishable from the logic of competition.

Experience rating allowed the commercial insurers to undersell the Blues in competing for low-risk employee groups. Although many unions as well as employers heeded the commercial carriers' appeal to get the most out of their "welfare dollar," other unions, like the auto and steel workers, were faithful to Blue Cross because of their commitment to service benefits. Many Blue Cross leaders were reluctant to accept experience rating because it seemed to contradict their ideals and undermine their claim on subscriber loyalty. Though some plans had experience rated a few large employee groups as early as 1940, the practice became a subject of controversy when many more adopted it in the fifties. In 1952, when only 4 percent of the Blue Cross enrollment was experience rated, the directors of plans in four Midwestern industrial states introduced a resolution at an annual Blue Cross conference condemning the practice as "contrary to the community service ideal" and likely to "destroy the voluntary, non-profit prepayment plans throughout the United States." A study conducted in response to the resolution urged Blue Cross plans "to make an honest effort to withstand the pressures" for experience rating.[5]

But the logic of competition played itself out almost inexorably. As the commercial insurers began to pick off the low-risk employee groups, they threatened to leave the high-cost population to the Blues. Had this process continued indefinitely, Blue Cross and Blue Shield would have been forced to raise their rates so high that even average-risk groups would have found it cheaper to buy commercial insurance. Eventually, the Blue plans would have become "dumping grounds" for the aged and the poor. This, however, was a function they preferred to leave to the government, and so, despite their reluctance, they, too, moved toward experience rating. By the end of the fifties, a majority of the plans were experience rating at least some employee groups—and as a spokesman for California Physicians Service pointed out, "Once you experience rate the good groups, you have to experience rate the bad groups too."[6]

The commitment of Blue Cross to service benefits also began to erode. As the costs of medical care and health insurance increased, the plans sought ways to keep down their premiums. One way was to raise the share of the costs borne directly by the consumer. Between 1945 and 1953, the proportion of Blue Cross enrollees with service benefits fell from 96 to 76 percent.[7]

So the competition between commercial insurers and the Blues produced a tendency toward convergence. Ironically, though Blue Cross had developed a form of insurance that insurance companies themselves were not originally willing to offer, its success invited imitators and unleashed forces that undermined the principles on which it began. But this, in a sense, was true of the entire health insurance system: While growing rapidly, it was unleashing forces that would eventually help bring about the government intervention its leadership hoped to avoid.

The Accommodation of Insurance

America had taken a different road to health insurance from the one taken by European societies, and it arrived at a different destination. The original European model began with the industrial working class and emphasized income maintenance; from that base, it expanded in both its coverage of the population and its range of benefits. The original Progressive proposals for compulsory health insurance had shared much of this orientation, except that the American Progressives had a distinctive interest in reorganizing medical care on more efficient and rational lines. The defeat of that early conception meant there was no prior institutional structure for health insurance when the middle class encountered its problems of paying for hospital costs during the 1920s and when the hospitals encountered problems meeting their expenses during the Depression. So instead of an insurance system founded originally to relieve the economic problems of workers, America developed an insurance system originally concerned with improving the access of middle-class patients to hospitals and of hospitals to middle-class patients. The Progressive interest in group practice, capitation payment, and incentives for prevention was rejected, and an insurance system developed under the control of the hospitals and doctors that sought to buttress the existing forms of organization. This was the basis for the accommodation of private insurance.

Commercial insurance companies entered the field almost by the back door. Their initial business in the field involved disability insurance for the middle class. Indemnity coverage for hospital expenses, as one insurance expert puts it, "began as a frill on the accident form."[8] Only after Blue Cross had demonstrated its feasibility did the commercial carriers become significantly involved. Indemnity plans, like the provider-controlled service-benefit plans, offered no threat of control to private practitioners. Indeed, the AMA actually preferred commercial indemnity plans to Blue Shield because cash benefits meant no interference in the individual doctor's right to set his own fees.

The system then evolved through a process of

restricted competition. The competition between the Blues and the commercial plans resulted in a broader range of benefits, but it also forced the Blues to adopt experience rating. The competition that might have come from direct-service plans was a factor only in a few areas of the country, such as California. Through boycotts and other techniques, the medical profession inhibited the industry from developing in the direction of comprehensive, direct-service plans, or consumer-controlled service-benefit plans. The only way a lay-controlled program could protect itself from provider boycotts was to insulate itself through the self-contained structure of prepaid group practice, but because of the start-up costs this entailed, the lack of any government assistance, and the legal barriers in more than half the states (in contrast to the favorable enabling laws given to Blue Cross and Blue Shield), the plans could not escape from a marginal position.

Just as European health insurance reflected the earlier sickness funds and friendly societies, so American private insurance was "piggy-backed" on preexisting organizations. In the United States these were the voluntary hospitals, the medical profession, and the life insurance industry. Some of the regional differences in development show this piggy-back pattern. Blue Cross plans held an edge in the older sections of the country, the Northeast and North Central States, where voluntary hospitals were strongest. On the other hand, where hospitals were primarily proprietary and governmental, commercial insurance did better.[9] Independent plans, such as Kaiser, made the most progress in the West, benefiting from an earlier tradition of comprehensive industrial medical care in isolated communities.

Although physicians were not solely responsible for this system of health insurance, they greatly benefited from it. By deflecting insurance first into the private sector and then away from direct services and lay control, the profession was able to turn the third-party insurer from a potential threat into a source of greatly increased income. The evolution of hospitals had followed the same pattern. Initially, the rise of hospitals threatened to take income away from the general practitioners who were cut off from hospital privileges. But because of the hospitals' financial

need to keep their beds filled, they opened up access to physicians on generous terms and became dependent on the physicians' good will. Similarly, government health insurance and lay-controlled prepayment threatened to limit physicians' incomes by restricting fees or the number of patients a doctor could serve. But through the use of political influence and economic power, in conjunction with insurance companies and other powerful interests, doctors were able to avoid the dangers of hierarchical control and competition. The insurance system accommodated their interests, and on those terms they accommodated health insurance.

The rise of private insurance added to the market power of the profession. Although licensing laws were the original means of restricting entry into medical practice, eligibility for reimbursement now became the chief obstacle for any competing group of practitioners. Even if midwives or chiropractors could circumvent licensing laws, they usually could not get reimbursement from Blue Shield, nor could their patients get reimbursed under indemnity plans. The insurance companies used the doctors as gatekeepers to benefits. In this respect, the insurance companies' interest in controlling costs strengthened the profession's authority.

Channeling health insurance through employment helped satisfy many interests simultaneously. As a fringe benefit, health insurance benefited the employer as well as the worker, solved problems in the marketing of private insurance, gave the providers protection against a government program, and offered the unions an alternative to national health insurance and a means of demonstrating concern for their members. Yet while serving these powerful interests, the fringe-benefit system clearly did not serve the interests of those who were retired, out of work, self-employed, or obliged to take a low-paying job without fringes. Those who had to buy insurance individually had to pay more for the same coverage than those who received it as a fringe benefit. While Blue Cross retained about 7 percent of income for administrative expenses in group insurance during the 1950s, it retained 22 percent on individual policies. And this was much better than the commercial insurers, which retained 50 percent on individual policies[10]—

about as much as they had for industrial life insurance. And, of course, because the companies competed partly by seeking the best risks, they avoided many of the chronically ill and the poor altogether. The health insurance system was set up in a highly regressive fashion: first, because it was based on employment; second, because of the practices of community and experience rating; and third, because of the favorable tax treatment of private insurance. (The Internal Revenue Code of 1954 confirmed that employers' contributions to health benefit plans were tax exempt; indirectly, this exemption constituted a massive subsidy to people who had private insurance policies.) In leaving out millions of Americans, the insurance system actually worsened their position because of the inflationary effect that insurance had on the cost of medical care. Private social security was not a neutral force on those left out; it hurt them, and much government intervention was required just to redress the inequities it created.

The distribution of health insurance was a direct outcome of the sort of private system that developed in America. By mid-1958 nearly two thirds of the population had some coverage for hospital costs, the most common type of insurance. A family's chances for insurance depended on its income and the employment situation of its main earner. If a family's income were among the highest rather than the lowest third of the population, it was twice as likely to have some insurance (about 80 versus 40 percent). When the main earner was fully employed, the probability of having some insurance was 78 percent. When the main earner had only a temporary job, the probability was only 36 percent; if retired, 43 percent; if a housewife, just 32 percent; if disabled, only 29 percent. Where the main earner was employed in manufacturing, the chance of having insurance was 91 percent; where employed in construction, 65 percent; and where in agriculture, forestry, or fishing, only 41 percent. If the family lived in a metropolitan area, its chances of having insurance were 75 percent; if they lived in a farm area, 44 percent. Two thirds of those who lived in the Northeast, the Midwest, or the West had some insurance, but only about half of those who lived in the South.[11]

Yet whatever its distributive inequities, the private insurance system provided enough protection for the groups that held influence in America to prevent any great agitation for national health insurance in the 1950s. Oddly enough, although labor favored a compulsory system, its success in pursuing health benefits through collective bargaining had undermined the movement for a government program. The use of collective bargaining had created, in Garbarino's phrase, "a semicompulsory substitute for compulsory health insurance." The union shop, which in the early fifties made union membership mandatory for over two thirds of the production work force, enabled the unions to establish a "private fiscal system" able to levy a "tax" for health insurance.[12] The government supported this private tax system by making employers' contributions into it exempt from the government's own taxes. Private, voluntary insurance was neither strictly voluntary, nor strictly private, but its compulsory and public features were hardly noticed.

This new system of financing increased the share of national income going to health care and stabilized the financing of the whole industry. Prior to insurance, doctors and hospitals had to wait for months or years to be paid for their services. Money for health care came last in a family's budget, after food, rent, and other necessities had been covered. Now, most of the money for medical care was taken out of employees' paychecks before they received them. The result was that Americans did not much reduce spending for medical care during recessions. So even though government insurance was defeated, health care succeeded, as an industry, in winning a guaranteed income. In the prosperity of the postwar years, this income grew very large indeed.

NOTES

1. U.S. Senate, Committee on Labor and Public Welfare, *Health Insurance Plans in the United States,* Report No. 359, pt. 2, 82nd Cong., 1st sess., 1951 (henceforth cited as 1951 Senate Report), 80–81; Odin W. Anderson, Patricia Collette, and Jacob J. Feldman, *Changes in Family Medical Expenditures and Voluntary Health Insurance: A Five-Year Resurvey,* (Cambridge: Harvard University Press, 1963), 8–9. The relative

standing of the commercial insurers, Blue Cross, and the independent plans stayed about the same between 1953 and 1958. However, Blue Shield increased its share of the market significantly.

2. 1951 Senate Report, 74–79, 99–106.

3. Duncon M. MacIntyre, *Voluntary Health Insurance and Rate Making,* (Ithaca, N.Y.: Cornell University Press, 1962), 58. The data refer to 1959, but the pattern was the same earlier. See 1951 Senate Report, 110–11, and Hermon N. Somers and Ann R. Somers, *Doctors, Patients and Health Insurance,* (Washington, D.C.: The Brookings Institution, 1961), 300, 326–27.

4. MacIntyre, *Voluntary Health Insurance and Rate Making,* 26–49, and Somers and Somers, *Doctors, Patients and Health Insurance,* 309–11.

5. Ibid., 155–61.

6. Joseph W. Garbarino, *Health Plans and Collective Bargaining,* (Berkeley: University of California Press, 1960), 228.

7. Somers and Somers, *Doctors, Patients and Health Insurance,* 304.

8. Ibid., 261–62, citing C.A. Culp.

9. Other factors, such as per capita income, were positively related to Blue Cross development. But in the Pacific states, as Reed pointed out, per capita income was high, but the hospitals were not "strongly voluntary," many having recently converted from proprietary status. Blue Cross had made relatively slow progress there. See Louis S. Reed, *Blue Cross and Medical Service Plans* (Washington, D.C.: Federal Security Agency, 1949), 28–30.

10. Somers and Somers, *Doctors, Patients and Health Insurance,* 300.

11. Anderson, Collette and Feldman, *Changes in Family Medical Expenditures,* 4–6, 171.

12. Garbarino, *Health Plans and Collective Bargaining,* 22.

22

Uninsured and Underserved: Inequities in Health Care in the United States

Karen Davis and Diane Rowland

The United States has one of the highest quality and most sophisticated systems of medical care in the world. Most Americans take for granted their access to this system of care. In times of emergency or illness, they can call upon a vast array of health resources—from a family physician to a complex teaching hospital—assured that they will receive needed care and that their health insurance coverage will pick up the tab for the majority of bills incurred.

For a surprisingly large segment of the United States population, however, this ease of access to care does not exist. At any point in time, over 25 million Americans have no health insurance coverage from private health insurance plans or public programs (Kasper et al. 1978). Without health insurance coverage or ready cash, such individuals can be and are turned away from hospitals even in emergency situations (U.S. Congress. House. Committee on Energy and Commerce 1981). Some neglect obtaining preventive or early care, often postponing care until conditions have become life-threatening. Other struggle with burdensome medical bills. Many come to rely upon crowded, understaffed public hospitals as the only source of reliable, available care.

The absence of universal health insurance coverage creates serious strains in our society. Those strains are felt most acutely by the uninsured poor, who must worry about family members—a sick child, an adult afflicted with a deteriorating chronic health condition, a pregnant mother—going without needed medical assistance. It strains our image as a just and humane society when significant portions of the population endure avoidable pain, suffering, and even death because of an inability to pay for health care. Those physicians, other health professionals, and institutions that try to assist this uninsured group also incur serious strain. Demands typically far outstrip available time and resources. Strain is also felt by local governments whose communities include many uninsured persons, because locally funded public hospitals and health centers inevitably incur major financial deficits. In recent years, many of the public facilities that have traditionally been the source of last-resort care have closed, thereby intensifying the stresses on other providers and the uninsured poor.

As serious as these strains have been in the last five years, the years ahead promise to strain the fabric of our social life even more seriously. Unemployment levels today are the highest since the Great Depression. With unemployment, the American worker loses not only a job but also health insurance protection. As unemployment rises and the numbers of the uninsured grow, fewer and fewer resources are available to fill the gaps in health care coverage. Major reductions in funding for health services for the poor and uninsured have been made in the last year; further reductions are likely. Deepening economic recession, high unemployment, and declining sales revenues are strapping the fiscal resources of state and local governments. Their ability to offset federal cutbacks seems limited. Nor can the private sector be expected to bridge this gap. The health industry is increasingly becoming an entrepreneurial business endeavor—with little room for charitable actions.

It is especially timely, therefore, to review what we know about the consequences of inadequate health insurance coverage for certain segments of our population. The first section of this paper presents information on the number and charac-teristics of the uninsured, while the second section describes patterns of health care utilization by the uninsured. The third section assesses the policy implications of these facts and offers recommendations for future public policy to ensure access to health care for all.

Who are the Uninsured?

The 1977 National Medical Care Expenditure Survey (NMCES) provides extensive information on the health insurance coverage of the U.S. population. Six household interviews of a nationwide sample of over 40,000 individuals were conducted over an 18-month period during 1977 and 1978. By following the interviewed population for an entire year, NMCES provided a comprehensive portrait of health insurance coverage, including changes in health insurance status during the course of that year.

Although the scope of the NMCES survey provides extensive information on the characteristics and utilization patterns of the uninsured, it should be noted that the profile of the uninsured presented here describes the portion of the population without insurance in 1977. Recent changes in health insurance coverage due to unemployment and cutbacks in eligibility for Medicaid have increased the size of the nation's uninsured population, but are not reflected in the statistics in this paper.

In the NMCES results, individuals classified as insured are those who were covered throughout the year by Medicaid, Medicare, the Civilian Health and Medical Program of the Uniformed Services (Champus), Blue Cross/Blue Shield or commercial health insurance, or who were enrolled in a health maintenance organization. Differences in scope of coverage among the insured were not available, although further analysis of the NMCES data will address this issue. Therefore, many individuals in the insured category may have actually had very limited health insurance coverage, leaving them basically uninsured for most services. For example, many individuals classified as insured have coverage for inpatient hospital care, but are not covered and are, therefore, essentially uninsured for primary care in a physician's office. In contrast, insured individuals also include those enrolled in a health maintenance organization offering comprehensive coverage for both inpatient and ambulatory care.

The uninsured fall into two groups: the always uninsured and the sometimes uninsured. The always uninsured are individuals without Medicare, Medicaid, or private insurance coverage for the entire year. Individuals using Veterans Administration hospitals and clinics or community health centers are classified as uninsured unless they have third-party coverage. The sometimes uninsured are those who were covered by public or private insurance part of the year but were uninsured the remainder of the year. The sometimes uninsured include the medically needy individuals who qualify for Medicaid coverage during periods of large medical expenses, but are otherwise uninsured. Changes in insurance status during the year are generally the result of loss of employment, change in employment, change in income or family situation that alters eligibility for Medicaid, or loss of private insurance when an older spouse retires and becomes eligible for Medicare.

A snapshot view of the uninsured at a given point in time understates the number of people who spend some portion of the year uninsured. At any one time, there are over 25 million uninsured Americans, but as many as 34 million may be uninsured for some period of time during the year. Approximately 18 million are without insurance for the entire year, and 16 million are uninsured for some portion of the year (Wilensky and Walden 1981; Wilensky and Berk 1982).

The 34 million uninsured are persons of all incomes, racial and ethnic backgrounds, occupations, and geographic locations. In some cases whole families are uninsured, while in others coverage is mixed depending on employment status and eligibility for public programs (Kasper et al. 1978). However, the poor, minorities, young adults, and rural residents are more likely than others to be uninsured. As noted in table 1, over one-quarter of all blacks and minorities are uninsured during the year—a rate 1½ times that of whites. This disparity holds across the demographic and social characteristics of the uninsured (Wilensky and Walden 1981; Institute of Medicine 1981).

Age

The uninsured population, whether covered for all or part of a year, is almost entirely under age 65. Nearly one-fifth of the non-aged population is uninsured for some or all of the year. Less than 1 percent of the aged, barely 200,000 persons, are uninsured during the year (table 1). This is attributable primarily to Medicare which provides basic coverage for hospital and physician services to most older Americans. The success of Medicare in providing financial access to health care for the elderly is demonstrated by the extensive coverage of the elderly today in contrast to the dramatic lack of insurance prior to implementation of Medicare in 1966 (Davis, 1982). Medicaid and private insurance help to fill the gap for those elderly persons ineligible for Medicare because they lack sufficient Social Security earnings contributions. The uninsured elderly are primarily individuals with incomes above the eligibility levels for welfare assistance and Medicaid.

Examination of the uninsured by age group reveals that young adults are the group most likely to be uninsured. As highlighted in table 2, almost one-third of all persons aged 19 to 24 are uninsured during the course of a year. Roughly 16 percent of this age group are without coverage all year, and an additional 14 percent lack coverage at least part of the year. This rate is nearly double that of other age groups. A variety of factors undoubtedly contribute to this situation. Young adults frequently lose coverage under their parents' policies at age 18. Many young adults may elect to forego coverage when it is available, since coverage is costly and they assume themselves to be relatively healthy. High youth unemployment, as well as employment in marginal jobs without health benefits, make insurance difficult to obtain or afford for this group.

Employment

Employment status and occupations are important factors in assessing the likelihood of being uninsured for all or part of a year. Most

Table 1.   Insurance Status during Year by Age and Race, 1977

Age and Race	Total	Always Uninsured	Uninsured Part of Year	Always Insured
		Numbers in millions		
Total, all persons	212.1	18.1	15.9	178.1
Persons under age 65	189.8	18.0	15.8	156.0
White	163.7	14.5	12.5	136.7
Black and Other	26.1	3.5	3.3	19.3
Persons age 65 and over	22.3	0.1	0.1	22.1
White	20.2	0.07	0.09	20.0
Black and Other	2.1	0.03	0.01	2.1
		Percentage		
All persons	100%	8.6%	7.5%	83.9%
Persons under age 65	100	9.5	8.3	82.2
White	100	8.9	7.6	83.5
Black and Other	100	13.3	12.7	74.0
Persons age 65 and over	100	0.4	0.5	99.1
White	100	0.3	0.5	99.2
Black and Other	100	1.0	0.8	98.2

Source: Data from the U.S. Department of Health and Human Services, National Center for Health Services Research, National Medical Care Expenditure Survey.

American workers receive their health care coverage throughout the workplace, but insurance coverage varies widely depending on the type of employer (Taylor and Lawson 1981). Employees of small firms are less likely to be insured than employees of large firms. For example, 45 percent of employees of firms of 25 or fewer employees do not have employer-provided health insurance compared with only 1 percent in firms with more than 1,000 employees. Yet, small firms employ over 20 percent of all workers. Unionized firms are six times more likely to have employee health insurance than are nonunionized firms.

Insurance status varies by type of employment (table 2). Nearly one-quarter of all agricultural workers are uninsured during the year, with 16 percent uninsured for the entire year. As expected, white collar workers are the most likely to be insured, while blue collar and service workers fare only somewhat better than agricultural workers (Wilensky and Walden 1981). Among blue collar and service workers, insurance coverage is low in the construction industry,

wholesale and retail trades, and service industries, and high in manufacturing. Of manufacturing employees, 96 percent have health insurance through their place of employment (Davis 1975).

Residence

These trends in coverage by employment are reflected in the regional picture of insurance status. In the heavily industrial and unionized Northeast and north central regions of the country, the percentage of uninsured during the year is half that of the South and the West. In these areas where agricultural interests are strong and unionization less extensive, over 20 percent of the population is uninsured during the course of a year. Of those living in the South and West, 11 percent are uninsured throughout the year compared with 5 percent in the Northeast and north central regions. Similarly, people in metropolitan areas are more likely to be insured than people living outside metropolitan areas (Wilensky and Walden 1981).

Table 2.   Percent Uninsured during Year by Selected Population Characteristics, 1977

Population Characteristic	Percent Uninsured during Year	Percent Always Uninsured	Percent Uninsured Part of Year
All persons	16.1%	8.6%	7.5%
Age			
Under age 65	17.8	9.5	8.3
less than 6 years	19.6	8.3	11.3
6 to 18 years	16.1	8.6	7.5
19 to 24 years	30.3	16.0	14.3
25 to 54 years	16.1	8.7	7.4
55 to 64 years	12.6	8.2	4.4
Age 65 and over	0.9	0.4	0.5
Occupation			
Farm	22.3	15.9	6.4
Blue collar	19.8	11.3	8.5
Services	20.8	11.9	8.9
White collar	12.6	5.6	7.0
Region			
Northeast	10.7	5.4	5.3
North Central	12.5	5.7	6.8
South	20.5	11.6	8.9
West	20.8	11.7	9.1

Source: Wilensky and Walden (1981), and data from the U.S. Department of Health and Human Services, National Center for Health Services Research, National Medical Care Expenditure Survey.

Income and Race

However, while nature of employment and unionization may explain some of the regional variations, a critical underlying factor in the analysis is the distribution in the population of poverty and minorities. Residents of the South comprise 32 percent of the total population under age 65. Yet 48 percent of the nation's minorities live in the South (Department of Health and Human Services 1982a). The higher concentration of poor and minority persons in the South in comparison with other parts of the country helps explain the high level of uninsured individuals.

Poverty and lack of insurance are strongly correlated. Of poor families with incomes below 125 percent of the poverty line, 27 percent are uninsured. The near-poor, with incomes between 125 and 200 percent of poverty, fare only slightly better, with 21 percent uninsured during the year. The poor are always more likely to be uninsured than the middle and upper income groups (table 3) (Wilensky and Walden 1981).

The limited health insurance coverage for the poor and near-poor demonstrates the limits of coverage of the poor under Medicaid (Wilensky and Berk 1982). Many assume that Medicaid finances health care services for all of the poor. However, many poor persons are ineligible for Medicaid due to categorical requirements for program eligibility and variations in state eligibility policies. Two-parent families are generally ineligibile for Medicaid and single adults are covered only if they are aged or disabled (Davis and Schoen 1978). Moreover, many states have established income eligibility cutoffs well below the poverty level. Many states have not adjusted income levels to account for inflation, resulting in a reduction in the number of individuals covered over the last few years (Rowland and Gaus 1983). As a result of the restrictions on Medicaid coverage, about 60 percent of the poor are not covered by Medicaid. Of the 35 million

Table 3. Percent Uninsured during Year by Ethnic/Racial Background and Income, 1977*

Ethnic/Racial Background	Percent Uninsured during Year	Percent Always Uninsured	Percent Uninsured Part of Year
White, all incomes	14.0	7.0	7.0
Poor	27.1	13.5	13.6
Other low income	21.0	10.9	10.1
Middle income	12.6	6.3	6.3
High income	8.8	4.2	4.6
Black, all incomes	23.2	9.7	13.5
Poor	32.2	10.6	21.6
Other low income	26.6	11.9	14.7
Middle income	17.4	8.6	8.8
High income	12.4	7.1	5.3
Hispanic, all incomes	24.3	12.8	11.5
Poor	29.6	9.5	20.1
Other low income	32.0	18.2	13.8
Middle income	17.7	12.4	5.3
High income	20.0	12.3	8.0

Source: Wilensky and Walden (1981).

*In 1977, the poverty level for a family of 4 was $8,000. Poor are defined as those whose family income was less than or equal to 125 percent of the 1977 poverty level. Other low income includes those whose income is 1.26 to 2 times the poverty level; middle income is 2.01 to 4 times the poverty level; and high income is 4.01 times the poverty level or more.

poor and near-poor in 1977, almost 5 million or about 15 percent had no insurance throughout 1977. Approximately 35 percent were on Medicaid for at least part of the year (Wilensky and Berk 1982). This situation can only be expected to worsen as the recession swells the numbers of poor and near-poor while cutbacks in social programs and Medicaid further erode the health coverage available to some of the poor.

Thus, while the poor are obviously the least able to pay for care directly, they are the most likely to be without either Medicaid or private insurance. The poor are twice as likely to be uninsured as the middle class and three times as likely as those in upper income groups. Lack of insurance is inversely related to ability to bear the economic consequences of ill health.

Blacks, Hispanics, and other minorities are also more likely to be uninsured than whites regardless of their income; poor blacks are the most likely to be uninsured. As noted in table 3, nearly one-third of poor blacks are uninsured during a year. If you are poor and a member of a minority group, your chances of being uninsured are four times as great as for a high income white.

Yet this relationship between race and income (table 3) actually understates this situation because the aged are included in the population analyzed. The aged are overrepresented in the lower income groups, but, as noted in table 1, almost all of the aged are insured. Thus, inclusion of the aged in table 3 tends to overstate the insured status of the nonelderly poor.

Regional and racial differences in insurance coverage for the population under age 65 are enumerated in table 4. When the aged are excluded from the analysis, the differentials become even more striking. Southerners are nearly 1½ times as likely to be uninsured as those from other parts of the country. But blacks in the South are 1½ times more likely to be uninsured as are whites from the South or nonsouthern blacks. Southern blacks are twice as likely to be uninsured as nonsouthern whites.

Similarly, when differences in insurance status are assessed from the perspective of metropolitan versus nonmetropolitan areas, blacks fare much

Table 4.   Percent of Persons under Age 65 Uninsured during Year by Race and Residence, 1977

Race and Residence	Population (in millions)	Percent Uninsured during Year	Percent Always Uninsured	Percent Uninsured Part of Year
Total, all persons				
Under 65	189.8	17.8%	9.5%	8.3%
South	60.5	22.4	12.7	9.7
White	47.9	20.4	11.8	8.6
Black and Other	12.6	30.0	16.2	13.8
Non-South	129.3	15.7	8.0	7.7
White	115.8	14.9	7.7	7.2
Black and Other	13.5	22.2	10.7	11.5
SMSA	132.6	16.3	8.2	8.1
White	111.3	14.9	7.6	7.3
Black and Other	21.3	23.2	11.1	12.1
Non-SMSA	57.2	21.4	12.5	8.9
White	52.5	19.9	11.6	8.3
Black and Other	4.7	38.2	23.3	14.9

Source: Data from the U.S. Department of Health and Human Services, National Center for Health Services Research, National Medical Care Expenditure Survey.

worse than whites. Over 16 percent of nonelderly residents of Standard Metropolitan Statistical Areas (SMSAs) are uninsured compared with over 21 percent of those residing in non-SMSA areas. But, for minorities living outside SMSAs, almost 40 percent are uninsured—a rate twice that of whites residing in non-SMSA areas and 2½ times that of whites in SMSAs.

Thus, health insurance coverage in the U.S. is to some extent a matter of luck. Those fortunate enough to be employed by large, unionized, manufacturing firms are also likely to be fortunate enough to have good health insurance coverage. Those who are poor, those who live in the South or in rural areas, and those who are black or minority group members are more likely to bear the personal and economic effects of lack of insurance and the consequent financial barriers to health care.

Utilization of Health Services by the Uninsured

With the investment in primary care made by federal programs in the late 1960s and 1970s, significant progress in improving access to primary care for the poor and other disadvantaged

groups was achieved. Virtually all of the numerous studies examining trends in access to health care conclude that differentials in utilization of physician services and preventive service by income have narrowed (Davis et al. 1981).

In the early 1960s the nonpoor visited physicians 23 percent more frequently than the poor even though the poor, then as now, were considerably sicker than the nonpoor. By the 1970s the poor visited physicians more frequently than the nonpoor, and more in accordance with their greater need for health care services. Blacks and other minorities also made substantial gains over this period. Utilization of services by rural residents also increased relative to urban residents (Davis and Schoen 1978).

However, use of preventive services by the poor, minorities, and rural residents continues to lag well behind use by those not facing similar barriers to health care. Some studies have also found that these differentials continue to exist for all disadvantaged groups even when adjusted for the greater health needs of the disadvantaged (Davis et al. 1981).

The major difficulty with past studies, however, is that they have not examined insurance coverage of subgroups of the poor to detect the cumulative impact of lack of financial and physical access to care. How do uninsured blacks in rural areas fare in obtaining ambulatory care services? Can nearly all disadvantaged persons get care from public hospitals or clinics, or do those facing multiple barriers to care simply do without?

Data and Methodology

New data from the 1977 National Medical Care Expenditure Survey (NMCES) shed some light on the cumulative effect of multiple barriers to care. Insured persons are those covered during the entire year; the uninsured are those uninsured for the entire year. Those insured for part of the year are excluded; presumably their utilization resembles that of the insured for the portion of the year in which they are insured and that of the uninsured for the portion of the year in which they are uninsured.

The NMCES sample was designed to produce statistically unbiased national estimates that are representative of the civilian noninstitutionalized population of the United States. Since the statistics presented here are based on a sample, they may differ somewhat from the figures that would have been obtained if a complete census had been taken. Tests of statistical significance are indicated in the tables included below (see Department of Health and Human Services 1982d, Technical Notes, for further detail on methodology). Particular caution should be taken in interpreting those data items for which the noted relative standard error is equal to or greater than 30 percent.

The statistics presented here show utilization differentials between insured and uninsured individuals under age 65. Analysis of age-specific differentials between the insured and uninsured showed patterns similar to the general pattern of the nonelderly population. The elderly were excluded from the analysis since the majority of the elderly population is insured.

Ambulatory Care

Most striking is the extent to which insurance coverage affects use of ambulatory care. Table 5 presents data on use of physicians' services from NMCES for the population under age 65; the insured average 3.7 visits to physicians during the year compared with 2.4 visits for the uninsured. That is, the insured receive 54 percent more ambulatory care from physicians than do the uninsured. However, the differential between the insured and uninsured for physician visits may understate the actual differential because variations in scope of coverage among the insured population are not accounted for. Some of the insured may only have insurance coverage for inpatient hospital care, not ambulatory care. Thus, although their utilization pattern is considered in the insured category, such individuals are actually uninsured for physician visits. Better data on ambulatory-care insurance coverage of the insured population therefore might indicate even greater differentials in use of ambulatory care.

Residence and race also affect utilization of ambulatory services. The lowest utilization of ambulatory care occurs for uninsured blacks and other minorities, including Hispanics. These persons use far less than more advantaged groups. For example, uninsured blacks and other minorities in the South make 1.5 physician visits per person annually, compared with 3.7 physician visits for insured whites in the South. That is, to be advantaged multiply leads to a utilization rate almost 2.5 times that of individuals who are disadvantaged multiply.

These data point to the importance of financial and physical barriers to access. It is not the case that the uninsured manage to obtain ambulatory care comparable in amount to that obtained by the insured by relying on public clinics, teaching hospital outpatient clinics, nonprofit health centers, or the charity of private physicians. Without insurance, many simply do without care.

The patterns of utilization for different groups provide some insight into the relative importance of financial, physical, and racial barriers to care. Financial access to care is clearly the most important factor affecting use. Insurance coverage reduces much but not all of the differential in use of ambulatory services. Insured blacks in the South, for example, average 2.8 physician visits annually, compared with 3.7 for insured whites

Table 5. Physician Visits per Person under Age 65 per Year, by Insurance Status, Residence, and Race, 1977

Insurance Status, Residence, and Race	Uninsured	Insured	Ratio
Total	2.4	3.7	1.54*
South	2.1	3.5	1.67*
White	2.3	3.7	1.61*
Black and Other	1.5	2.8	1.87*
Non-South	2.6	3.8	1.46*
White	2.7	3.8	1.41*
Black and Other	1.9	3.5	1.84*
SMSA	2.4	3.8	1.58*
White	2.6	3.9	1.50*
Black and Other	1.7	3.2	1.88*
Non-SMSA	2.3	3.3	1.43*
White	2.4	3.4	1.42*
Black and Other	1.6	2.9	1.81

*indicates values for insured and uninsured are significantly different at the .05 level.
Source: Data from the U.S. Department of Health and Human Services, National Center for Health Services Research, National Medical Care Expenditure Survey.

in the South. That is, whites average about 30 percent more ambulatory care than blacks and other minorities even if both are insured. But this differential is substantially smaller than the 2½ times greater use of physicians between insured southern whites and uninsured southern blacks.

Location remains an important determinant of use of physician services. Lack of insurance coverage is more predominant in rural areas; however, even among the insured, urban residents are more likely to receive ambulatory care than are rural residents, whether white or black (see table 5). Among insured groups, rural whites receive 3.4 physician visits annually compared with 3.9 visits for urban whites. Rural blacks and other minorities with insurance make 2.9 physician visits compared with 3.2 visits for their insured counterparts in urban areas. That is, a 10 to 15 percent differential in use between urban and rural areas occurs even when financial access to care is not a problem. It should be noted, however, that the quality of insurance for ambulatory care may not be as good in rural areas as in urban areas.

Racial differentials in utilization of ambulatory care are also ameliorated with insurance coverage. Insurance is particularly helpful in improving access to care for minorities. Insured minori-

ties receive 80 to 90 percent more ambulatory care than do uninsured minorities, in both rural and urban areas. But even with insurance, strong racial differences persist.

Hospital Care

Despite the common perception that all disadvantaged persons can obtain hospital care from some charity facility, tremendous differentials in use of hospital care also exist by insurance status, residence, and race. The insured receive 90 percent more hospital care than do the uninsured (see table 6). Differentials by insurance status are particularly marked in the South and in rural areas. In the South, insured persons receive three times as many days of hospital care annually as uninsured persons, régardless of race or ethnic background.

These hospital utilization differentials clearly demonstrate that the insured fare much better than the uninsured in obtaining health care services. Since those with insurance are likely to have basic coverage for hospitalization, the hospital utilization data provide a more accurate assessment of the role of insurance coverage in the use of health care services than do the

Table 6. Hospital Patient Days per 100 Persons under Age 65, by Insurance Status, Residence, and Race, 1977

Insurance Status, Residence, and Race	Uninsured	Insured	Ratio
Total	47	90	1.91*
South	35	104	2.97*
White	33	100	3.03*
Black and Other	40†	119	2.98*
Non-South	56	84	1.50
White	51	81	1.59*
Black and Other	89†	114	1.28
SMSA	50	86	1.72*
White	44	83	1.89*
Black and Other	70†	106	1.51
Non-SMSA	42	99	2.36*
White	43	94	2.19*
Black and Other	39†	175	4.49*

*indicates values for insured and uninsured are significantly different at the .05 level.
†indicates relative standard error is equal to or greater than 30 percent.
Source: Data from the U.S. Department of Health and Human Services, National Center for Health Services Research, National Medical Care Expenditure Survey.

ambulatory care differentials in the previous section.

These differentials remove any complacency about the accessibility of inpatient care. They reinforce similar findings by Wilensky and Berk (1982) who find that the insured poor use more hospital care than the uninsured poor. They find the biggest differences between those always uninsured and those on Medicaid all year. Those on Medicaid part of the year used fewer hospital services than those on Medicaid all year. The uninsured also used less hospital care than those privately insured. The analysis here extends these results to examine racial and regional differentials.

More disaggregated information is essential on the types of conditions for which the insured receive inpatient care and the uninsured do not. Standards for appropriate utilization of hospital services are still the subject of wide debate. Some of the differential between the insured and uninsured seen here may be the result of overutilization of hospital services by the insured. However, this is unlikely to explain the entire differential.

Some of the greater utilization of hospital care by the insured may represent self-selection. Those who expect to be hospitalized may obtain such coverage. Hospitalization may itself result in Medicaid coverage of some of the poor and near-poor. However, this should affect primarily those who are insured part of the year and uninsured for the remainder of the year. Such partially insured persons are excluded from this analysis. These explanations are unlikely to account for a three-fold differential in use.

Some of the results by region and race are surprising. It is interesting to note that outside the South uninsured blacks receive more hospital days per 100 persons than insured whites. Insured blacks have the highest use. This may reflect greater health problems among blacks, or the tendency of blacks to receive care in public hospitals which have longer stays. Another unexpected result is high hospitalization among insured blacks in nonmetropolitan areas. This is one of the smallest population groups in the study and results, in this case, may simply be statistically unreliable.

Barriers to access to hospital services for the uninsured need to be explored. To what extent do hospitals require preadmission deposits for the uninsured? What are the consequences of such policies on access to care? Which hospitals serve the uninsured and the insured? Do the differences between metropolitan and nonmetropolitan areas reflect the role of teaching hospitals and public hospitals in caring for the uninsured in the inner city? Do the uninsured have to travel sizeable distances to obtain services? What are the health problems of the insured and uninsured, for what conditions are the insured hospitalized but not the uninsured, and what are the health consequences of lack of hospital care for the uninsured? To what extent do any or all of these factors influence the use of hospital care by the uninsured? Further exploration is certainly warranted.

Health Status and Use of Services

Lower utilization of ambulatory and inpatient care by the uninsured is not a reflection of lower need for health care services. Instead, as measured by self-assessment of health status, the uninsured tend to be somewhat sicker than the insured. Fifteen percent of the uninsured under age 65 rate their health as fair or poor, compared with 11 percent of the insured. Blacks and other minorities in the South systematically rate their health the worst. Of insured blacks and other minorities in the South, 19 percent assess their health as fair or poor, compared with 9 percent of insured whites outside the South.

One possible explanation of the higher rate of poor or fair health among the uninsured is that the lack of insurance is itself related to health status. Those who rate their health as poor or fair are more likely to be unable to work because of illness than those who rate their health good or excellent. Since insurance coverage in the United States is related to employment, those who are unemployed due to poor health are also likely to be without insurance. Under an employment-based insurance system, the working population enjoys both good health and insurance coverage, while those too ill to work suffer both lack of employment and lack of insurance.

The sick who are uninsured use medical care services less than their insured counterparts. Utilization of ambulatory services, adjusted for health status, shows that the insured in poor health see a physician 70 percent more often than the uninsured in poor health. Physician visits per person under age 65 in fair or poor health average

6.9 among the insured, compared with 4.1 visits for the uninsured with similar health problems (table 7). Blacks and other minorities with fair or poor health who are insured receive twice as much care as their uninsured counterparts.

Among the uninsured in poor or fair health, the differentials in physician visits by race and residence are especially noteworthy. Uninsured whites have greater access to physician services than do uninsured minorities. A southern white in fair or poor health sees a physician twice as often as a southern minority person in fair or poor health. The same relationship exists for utilization of physician services in metropolitan areas. However, the utilization differential between whites and minorities narrows in areas outside the South and in nonmetropolitan areas.

The number of physician visits by the uninsured versus the insured in fair or poor health warrants further examination. It is expected that the individual in fair or poor health would require frequent physician visits for diagnosis and treatment of the condition. The average of five to seven visits annually by the insured would appear to provide a reasonable level of physician contact. But for uninsured minorities in the South in fair or poor health, the average number of visits is two per year. This rate would provide no more than an initial visit and one follow-up visit, which might be insufficient to treat serious or complex illnesses. Thus, lower rates of physician visits could impair adequate treatment and follow-up to promote a rapid recovery.

Dental Care

Dental care, unlike hospital care and most physician services, is not covered under most insurance plans. Therefore, differentials in dental visits between the insured and uninsured are not meaningful. However, the NMCES data do show a striking contrast between dental visits by whites and minorities.

Whites obtain dental care twice as often as minorities, averaging 1.5 visits per year compared to 0.7 visits for minorities. Nonsouthern whites had two times the number of visits as nonsouthern minorities and over three times the number of visits as southern minorities. Rural

Table 7. Physician Visits per Person under Age 65 in Fair or Poor Health per Year, by Insurance Status, Residence, and Race, 1977

Insurance Status, Residence, and Race	Uninsured	Insured	Ratio
Total	4.1	6.9	1.68*
South	3.8	6.1	1.61*
White	4.4	6.4	1.45*
Black and Other	2.2†	5.0	2.27
Non-South	4.5	7.4	1.64*
White	4.6	7.6	1.65*
Black and Other	3.5†	6.5	1.86
SMSA	4.1	7.2	1.76*
White	4.7	7.6	1.62*
Black and Other	2.3†	5.9	2.57
Non-SMSA	4.2	6.3	1.50
White	4.3	6.4	1.49
Black and Other	3.2†	5.4	1.69

*indicates values for insured and uninsured are significantly different at the .05 level.
†indicates relative standard error is equal to or greater than 30 percent.
Source: Data from the U.S. Department of Health and Human Services, National Center for Health Services Research, National Medical Care Expenditure Survey.

minorities appear to have the least access to dental services.

The significant differential between access to dental services for minorities and whites warrants further examination. The extent to which this differential reflects differences in health practices and attitudes toward dental care or differences in availability and accessibility to dental care should be explored. The NMCES data confirm other studies that have found that disadvantaged groups are less likely to have a usual source of ambulatory care and more likely to receive their care from a hospital outpatient department or a clinic than from a physician's office. Table 8, for example, enumerates that 84 percent of the insured have a physician's office as their usual source of care compared with 67 percent of the uninsured. About 50 percent of uninsured blacks and other minorities have a physician's office as their usual source of care. While this percentage is quite low in comparison with other groups, it does not fit the stereotype that all minorities in urban areas receive the bulk of their care from public facilities or hospital outpatient departments.

Uninsured residents of nonmetropolitan areas are more likely to have a physician as a usual source of care than are residents of a metropolitan area. In nonmetropolitan areas, 73 percent of the uninsured have a physician as a usual source of care in contrast to only 63 percent of the uninsured in metropolitan areas. However, nonmetropolitan residents are still likely to have fewer physician visits than their metropolitan counterparts (see table 5). The nonmetropolitan uninsured get more of their care from physicians but receive less total care. These differences in utilization among the uninsured undoubtedly reflect differences between metropolitan and nonmetropolitan areas in the availability of alternatives to physician care. Residents of metropolitan areas are more likely to have access to clinic and outpatient hospital services that can substitute for care in physicians' offices.

The metropolitan and nonmetropolitan differential for physicians as a usual source of care is markedly reduced among the insured. As seen in table 8, 86 percent of insured nonmetropolitan residents and 82 percent of insured metropolitan residents have a physician as a usual source of care. Insurance coverage significantly increases the proportion of minorities who have a physician's office as their usual source of care. Among the minority uninsured 49 percent of those living in metropolitan areas and 52 percent of those in nonmetropolitan areas have a physician as a

Table 8.   Percent of Persons under Age 65 Whose Usual Source of Care Is a Physician's Office, by Insurance Status, Residence, and Race, 1977

Insurance Status, Residence, and Race	Uninsured	Insured	Ratio
Total	67	84	1.25*
South	66	81	1.22*
White	70	82	1.16*
Black and Other	53	76	1.41*
Non-South	68	85	1.25*
White	70	86	1.22*
Black and Other	45	69	1.53*
SMSA	63	82	1.31*
White	66	84	1.27*
Black and Other	49	71	1.43*
Non-SMSA	73	86	1.19*
White	76	87	1.15*
Black and Other	52	79	1.53*

*indicates values for insured and uninsured are significantly different at the .05 level.
Source: Data from the U.S. Department of Health and Human Services, National Center for Health Services Research, National Medical Care Expenditure Survey.

usual source of care. In contrast, for insured minorities, 71 percent in metropolitan areas and 79 percent outside of metropolitan areas have physicians as a usual source of care. This would suggest that Medicaid and private health insurance coverage enable a substantial number of minorities to obtain care in a physician's office.

Convenience of Care

When they are able to obtain care, the uninsured must travel longer distances than the insured to obtain it. As enumerated in table 9, 25 percent of the uninsured travel 30 minutes or more to obtain care compared with 18 percent of the insured. Differentials in travel time between the insured and uninsured are somewhat more marked in rural areas than in urban areas, but travel time is a problem for uninsured persons everywhere. These data suggest not only that the uninsured receive less care, but also that when they do obtain care they do so by searching over a longer distance for providers willing to see them. The effort involved in such a search for care may discourage the use of preventive services, resulting in the uninsured only seeking care for serious illnesses or in crises. This would help explain the lower utilization levels of the uninsured.

When the uninsured arrive at a care provider, they generally have to wait longer for care to be delivered. Regardless of residence, the waiting time for insured blacks and other minorities is longer than the waiting time experienced by uninsured whites. Waiting times are longer in the South. Uninsured southern minority persons experience the longest waiting times. The NMCES data show that they wait one-third longer than do insured southern whites (Department of Health and Human Services 1982a).

Policy Implications

The utilization differentials between the insured and uninsured underscore the importance of financial barriers to health care. Lack of insurance coverage is the major barrier. It markedly affects the amount of both ambulatory and inpatient care received. Without insurance coverage, many individuals obviously do without care. Those able to obtain care incur substantial travel and waiting times.

Lack of insurance coverage has three major consequences: it contributes to unnecessary pain, suffering, disability, and even death among the uninsured; it places a financial burden on those uninsured who struggle to pay burdensome

Table 9. Percent of Persons under Age 65 Traveling More Than 29 Minutes to Receive Medical Care, by Insurance Status, Residence, and Race, 1977

Insurance Status, Residence, and Race	Uninsured	Insured	Ratio
Total	25	18	1.39*
South	29	21	1.39*
White	30	20	1.48*
Black and Other	28	26	1.09
Non-South	21	16	1.29*
White	22	16	1.35*
Black and Other	17	21	.81
SMSA	22	17	1.27*
White	21	16	1.32*
Black and Other	24	24	1.00
Non-SMSA	29	20	1.46*
White	30	20	1.50*
Black and Other	23	19	1.24

*indicates values for insured and uninsured are significantly different at the .05 level.
Source: Data from the U.S. Department of Health and Human Services, National Center for Health Services Research, National Medical Care Expenditure Survey.

medical bills; and it places a financial strain on hospitals, physicians, and other health care providers who attempt to provide care to the uninsured.

Research is limited on both the health of the uninsured and the health consequences of having no insurance. Extensive data on utilization patterns by the uninsured disaggregated by residence and race are presented for virtually the first time in this report. But a number of recent studies have shown that medical care utilization has a dramatic impact on health. A recent Urban Institute report by Hadley (1982) explores the relation between medical care utilization and mortality rates. It contains persuasive evidence that utilization of medical care services leads to a marked reduction in mortality rates. A recent study by Grossman and Goldman (1981) at the National Bureau of Economic Research has found that infant mortality rates have dropped significantly in communities served by federally funded community health centers. This growing body of evidence does provide considerable support to the importance of medical care utilization in assuring a healthy population—and at least indirectly provides a basis for concern that the lower medical care utilization of the uninsured contributes to unnecessary deaths and lowered health status.

Lack of insurance coverage also imposes serious financial burdens on those who try to make regular payments to retire enormous debts incurred in obtaining medical care. With the average cost of a hospital stay in the United States now in excess of $2,000, few individuals can afford to build payments for hospital care into their monthly living allowance (Department of Health and Human Services 1982b). Yet, since the uninsured are more likely to be poor, the economic consequences of lack of insurance fall heaviest on those least able to bear the burden.

In addition to its consequences for the uninsured, lack of insurance also takes its toll on the health care system. One result is that the financial stability of hospitals and ambulatory care providers willing to provide charity care for those unable to pay is jeopardized. Health care providers serving the uninsured—particularly inner city community and teaching hospitals, county and municipal clinics, and community health centers—absorb much of the cost of this as charity care or a bad debt. Yet this burden is not evenly distributed among hospitals and other providers. A recent study by the Urban Institute found that one-seventh of a national sample of hospitals studied provided over 40 percent of the free care (Brazda 1982).

Recent policy measures are likely to exacerbate

this situation. The Omnibus Budget Reconciliation Act of 1981 reduced federal financial participation in Medicaid and curtailed eligibility under the Aid to Families with Dependent Children (AFDC) program. Actions by state governments in response to this legislation could swell the ranks of the uninsured poor by over 1 million people. Coupled with the highest rate of unemployment since the Great Depression and the loss of health insurance coverage frequently occurring with unemployment, the number of uninsured continues to rise. Undoubtedly the situation has worsened rather than improved since the NMCES study in 1977. Today, the access problems of the uninsured should be a pressing concern on the nation's health agenda.

For many of the uninsured, community health centers and migrant health centers have helped to fill the gap in access created by the lack of insurance. This was especially important for those ineligible for Medicaid. However, simultaneously with the cutbacks in Medicaid, major reductions were made in these service delivery programs. Overall funding was reduced by 25 percent in absolute dollars, which may lead to 1.1 million fewer people being served than the 6 million served in 1980. The National Health Service Corps, while not as seriously affected now, will be substantially reduced in future years since no new scholarships are being awarded with commitments for service in underserved areas (Davis 1981).

Financial strains on public hospitals and clinics supported by state and local governments are leading to further curtailment of services. Preadmission deposits, often sizeable in amount, impose serious barriers for many of the uninsured seeking hospital care. Teaching hospitals that have for years maintained an open-door policy are reevaluating the fiscal viability of continuing such a policy. In many areas, hospitals are beginning to transfer nonpaying patients to public facilities, further expanding the charity load of those facilities and reducing their ability to remain solvent (Brazda 1982).

Public hospitals, traditionally the care provider of last resort, are under new pressures to close or reduce services as local governments respond to shrinking revenues. Yet, shifting the responsibility of public hospitals to community hospitals will not solve the problem of caring for the uninsured. Recent hearings have documented the refusal of community hospitals to take uninsured patients, even in emergency situations. This has led to documented cases of deaths that could have been avoided with prompt medical attention (U.S. Congress. House. Committee on Energy and Commerce 1981).

Such disparities in access to care are unacceptable in a decent and humane society. Several actions are required to assure progress toward adequate access for all. Medicaid coverage should be expanded to provide basic insurance coverage for all low-income individuals. The Medicaid programs in southern states have tended to have very restrictive eligibility policies leaving many of the poor uncovered (Department of Health and Human Services 1982c). Expanded coverage of the poor through Medicaid would improve the scope of coverage in the South and could help to alleviate some of the extreme utilization differentials between the South and non-South. A minimum income standard set at some percentage of the poverty level would be an important first step. In 1979, 23 states, including most of the southern states, had income eligibility levels for Medicaid below 55 percent of the poverty level. Texas, Alabama, and Tennessee had the lowest standards in the nation—less than $2,000 for a family of four. Coupled with implementation of a minimum income standard, Medicaid coverage should be broadened to include children and ultimately adults in two-parent families. Such steps would help assure access to care for the nation's poorest families.

Yet, the near-poor and working poor without insurance cannot be forgotten. Today, under Medicaid, only 29 states cover the medically needy to provide health coverage for those with large medical expenses. In effect, this catastrophy coverage provides some measure of protection to working families and is undoubtedly the source of care for many of the "sometimes insured." Coverage for the medically needy is currently very limited in the South; implementation of coverage for the medically needy would be another step toward reducing the disparities between the South and the rest of the country. Expansion of this coverage option is an important component of a positive health care agenda.

Finally, the extensiveness of unemployment in today's economy underscores the need to refine the link between employment and health insurance coverage. "Out of work" ought not to translate to "without health care services." Often, health needs are greatest during periods of stress related to unemployment (Brenner 1973; Lee 1979). Health insurance coverage should be extended through employer plans for a period following unemployment, and guaranteed through public coverage until reemployment. Employers should also be encouraged to provide comprehensive coverage, including prevention and primary care services, to all workers and their families.

These measures would help to provide protection and improved access to care for the 34 million or more Americans now without health care insurance. However, as the metropolitan and nonmetropolitan differentials among the insured demonstrate, financing alone is not enough to correct access differentials. Resources development must be coupled with improved financing in underserved areas to assure that needed providers are available. Continued funding and expansion of the community and migrant health center programs to assure physical access to services for residents of high poverty, medically underserved communities is an essential adjunct to broadened financing for low-income populations. Other important ways to provide expanded insurance coverage without perpetuating the cost inefficiencies of the existing system include: reform of Medicaid, Medicare, and private health insurance plans to encourage ambulatory care in cost-effective primary care programs; and experimentation with capitation payments to individual primary care centers, network of centers, hospitals, or other major primary care providers for providing ambulatory and inpatient services to Medicaid beneficiaries.

This agenda of improved financing and resource development represents a positive strategy that can be employed to reduce major inequities in American health care. Today, some will argue that this agenda is too ambitious and costly and would instead opt for a more targeted and incremental approach. For example, instead of expanding Medicaid coverage, advocates of the incremental approach would favor renewed support to public hospitals and financial aid to hospitals serving large numbers of uninsured to mitigate the worst problems. These approaches are piecemeal, however, and do not address the fundamental problems identified in this paper. Such targeted approaches focus on protecting institutions serving the uninsured rather than protecting the uninsured themselves. Thus, they provide for the continued existence of a source of care for the uninsured seeking care, but do not provide comprehensive coverage to the uninsured to encourage early and preventive services. The poor and uninsured who do without care either because they do not live near an "aided facility" or do not know they could obtain free care from a hospital with a financial distress loan would still suffer inequitable health care differentials.

This paper demonstrates that lack of insurance makes a difference in health care utilization. Studies such as the recent work by Hadley (1982) point out the positive impact of medical care on mortality. Society ultimately bears the burden for care of the uninsured. The choice is between paying up front and directly covering the uninsured or indirectly paying for their care through subsidies to fiscally troubled health facilities, higher insurance premiums, and increased hospital costs to cover the cost of charity care and pay for the ill health caused by neglect and inadequate preventive and primary care. Thus, the best and most pragmatic approach is to provide health insurance coverage to the uninsured and to use targeted approaches to improve resource distribution and to remove remaining differentials. The inequities in health care in the United States described here will deepen unless a positive agenda is pursued.

NOTE

Acknowledgments: This paper was prepared for the President's Commission for the Study of Ethical Problems in Medicine and Biomedical and Behavioral Research. We gratefully acknowledge the assistance of Susan Morgan and Kathryn Kelly of the commission staff, and reviewers for helpful comments. We also thank Gail Wilensky and Daniel C. Walden of the National Center for Health Services Research for supplying requested data and assisting in its interpretation, and Karen Pinkston and Mary Frances leMat of Social and Scientific Systems, Inc. for programming support.

REFERENCES

Brazda, J., ed. 1982. Perspectives: Who Will Care for the Uninsured? (September 27) *Washington Report on Medicine and Health* 36 (38, Sept. 27): unpaged insert.

Brenner, H. 1973. *Mental Illness and the Economy.* Cambridge: Harvard University Press.

Davis, K. 1975. *National Health Insurance: Benefits, Costs, and Consequences.* Washington: Brookings Institution.

———. 1981. Reagan Administration Health Policy. (December). *Journal of Public Health Policy* 2(4):312–32.

———. 1982. Medicare Reconsidered. Paper presented at Duke University Medical Center Private Sector Conference on the Financial Support of Health Care of the Elderly and the Indigent, March 14–16.

Davis, K., and C. Schoen. 1978. *Health and the War on Poverty: A Ten Year Appraisal.* Washington: Brookings Institution.

Davis, K., M. Gold, and D. Makuc. 1981. Access to Health Care for the Poor: Does the Gap Remain? *Annual Review of Public Health* 2:159–82.

Department of Health and Human Services. 1982a. National Medical Care Expenditure Survey, 1977. Unpublished Statistics. Hyattsville, Md.: National Center for Health Services Research.

———. 1982b. *Health Care Financing Trends,* June. Baltimore: Health Care Financing Administration.

———. 1982c. *Medicare and Medicaid Data Book 1981.* Baltimore: Health Care Financing Administration.

———. 1982d. Usual Sources of Medical Care and Their Characteristics, Data Preview 12. Hyattsville, Md.: National Center for Health Services Research.

Grossman, M., and F. Goldman. 1981. The Responsiveness and Impacts of Public Health Policy: The Case of Community Health Centers. Paper presented at the 109th Annual Meeting of the American Public Health Association, Los Angeles, November.

Health Centers. Paper presented at the 109th Annual Meeting of the American Public Health Association, Los Angeles, November.

Hadley, J. 1982. *More Medical Care, Better Health?* Washington: Urban Institute.

Institute of Medicine. 1981. *Health Care in a Context of Civil Rights.* Washington: National Academy Press.

Kasper, J.A., D.C. Walden, and G.R. Wilensky. 1978. *Who Are the Uninsured?* National Medical Care Expenditures Survey Data Preview no. 1. Hyattsville, Md.: National Center for Health Services Research.

Lee, A.J. 1979. *Employment, Unemployment, and Health Insurance.* Cambridge, Mass.: Abt Books.

Rowland, D., and C. Gaus. 1983. Medicaid Eligibility and Benefits: Current Policies and Alternatives. In *New Approaches to the Medicaid Crisis,* ed. R. Blendon and T.W. Moloney. New York: Frost and Sullivan.

Taylor, A.K., and W.R. Lawson. 1981. Employer and Employee Expenditures for Private Health Insurance. National Medical Care Expenditures Survey Data Preview 7. Hyattsville, Md.: National Center for Health Services Research, June.

U.S. Congress. House. Committee on Energy and Commerce, U.S. House of Representatives. 1981. *Hearings on Medicaid Cutbacks on Infant Care.* Washington, 27 July.

Wilensky, G.R., and M.L. Berk. 1982. The Health Care of the Poor and the Role of Medicaid. *Health Affairs* 1(4):93–100.

Wilensky, G.R., and D.C. Walden. 1981. Minorities, Poverty, and the Uninsured. Paper presented at the 109th Meeting of the American Public Health Association, Los Angeles, November. Hyattsville Md.: National Center for Health Services Research.

Racism and Sexism in Medical Care

The suppression of the social, economic, and political desires of American women and racial minorities and the exploitation of their labor are two primary characteristics of American society; despite legislation and judicial decisions, women and minorities continue to be discriminated against. Nowhere is discrimination more prevalent than in the treatment which women and minorities receive at the hands of the health industry. Whether as providers or consumers, they are exploited, abused, and discriminated against. (Weaver and Garett, 1978: 677)

American society is stratified, layered with groups who have differing amounts of power, privilege, access to job and educational opportunities, different incomes, and different conditions of living. This stratification is not a "natural" product of society, nor is it a result of mere chance. Indeed, certain forms of institutionalized inequality are both cause and effect of unequal health care among the populations of American society. This section examines the consequences of racism and sexism on the American medical system and on the health of women and nonwhites.

The medical labor force is a microcosm of social stratification in America, with women and nonwhites kept to the "lower rungs" of the medical hierarchy. Almost all physicians are white (approximately 90 percent). Almost all nurses are women, and most of the higher ranking nurses (RN's) are white. But the lower status and lower paying jobs of nursing aides and orderlies are increasingly being filled by minority women. Almost all men who work in these lower status jobs are nonwhite as well. In 1980 only 3.1 percent of all physicians were black, 4.4 percent were of Spanish heritage (Hispanic) and 13.4 percent were female (Department of Commerce, 1983).[1] On the other hand, 88.8 percent of nursing aides, orderlies, and attendants that same year were female, 26.8 percent of those workers were black, and 5.2 percent were of Spanish heritage (Chicanos or Puerto Ricans) (Department of Commerce, 1983).

While the past decade has seen a great deal of publicity about the impact of "affirmative action" on opening up educational opportunities, the absolute and proportionate numbers of women and nonwhites in the medical profession remain low compared to their numbers in the population as a whole (Weaver and Garrett, 1978: 678). In fact, the percentage of black applicants accepted into medical school actually decreased since the early 1970s, although the potential pool of qualified nonwhite applicants entering colleges and universities increased and the total number of applicants has stabilized (Strelnick and Younge, 1984). Despite evidence to the contrary, medical school personnel continue to promote myths about why medicine has failed to improve the representation of nonwhites and, by and large, blame this state of affairs on those discriminated against. And, according to a report by the United States General Accounting Office, the Department of Health, Education and Welfare has failed to enforce affirmative action and nondiscrimination rules (Strelnick, 1980, citing General Accounting Office, 1975).

One indicator of a medical school's willingness to accept nonwhites and women as students is the composition of its faculty and, in turn, the representation of nonwhites and women on faculty admissions committees. The percentage of black, Hispanic and Native-American medical school faculty has remained the same 2.6 percent since 1971–1972. Women currently constitute about the same 15.2 percent of medical school faculties as they did in 1965–1966 (although the percentage dropped and rose during this period). However, since 70 percent of medical school librarians are women, their representation throughout medical school faculties, and in particular as administrators of medical schools, is quite low. In addition, when women are on medical school faculties, they are disproportionately represented in the lower faculty ranks (Strelnick, 1980).

While women have made greater relative improvements in their representation in medical school classes than nonwhites (they currently constitute about 25 percent of students entering medical school classes), they continue to be underrepresented in proportion to their numbers in the population. Women who manage to complete medical school are concentrated in certain, generally stereotypically "female" specialties, including pediatrics and psychiatry, and are underrepresented in the more prestigious and powerful surgical specialties. Indeed, it has been found that gender stereotypes among young male physicians has been increasing rather than decreasing (Quadagno, 1976). Sadly, while there is good evidence that women and nonwhites are more likely to serve those patient populations who most need medical care, their underrepresentation in certain medical areas and specialties undercuts their potential for mitigating the unequal distribution of medical care.

In addition to racism and sexism, there is a continued underrepresentation of people (of all races, both women and men) from working-class and low economic backgrounds in medical schools. In fact, several studies have found that lower class students have had to have higher grades than upper class students to gain entrance to medical schools, and that children of families who earn more than $50,000 per year are admitted to medical schools at higher rates than any other group (Strelnick, 1980 citing Gee, 1959, and Dagenais and Rosinski, 1977). Class background is also a strong predictor of a medical student's choice of specialization, with children of wealthier families more likely to opt to become specialists and children of poorer backgrounds more likely to become primary care physicians (Strelnick, 1980: 10).

Racism and sexism (and class oppression) combine to deliver a "double whammy" to minority women who work in medical care services. Comparing the salaries of males and females who are relatively low-paid health technicians, for example, we find that nonwhite men have the economic advantage over their nonwhite female counterparts. Such a pay differential between men and women holds for all occupational levels within the medical care labor force. It also holds for all occupations throughout the country as a whole. A Department of Labor study indicated that women earn about 57¢ for every $1.00 earned by men, whether they are professors, janitors, or physicians, a differential that has been growing in recent years (Sexton, 1977).

Until recently there has been little information about the nature and consequences of racism and sexism in the medical care industry. We do know that discrimination works in a number of ways, some more obvious than others. For example, for many years medical schools set "quotas" on the numbers of women and blacks they would accept (if any) each year. Further, informal mechanisms of prejudice and discrimination operate within medical schools. We know, for example, that women are often ignored, harassed and otherwise mistreated and informally denied needed faculty support (Campbell, 1973; Quadagno, 1976). In addition, early patterns of discrimination are evident in the "tracking" of nonwhites and females out of preparatory science sequences as early as junior high school, making it impossible for them to have obtained the academic backgrounds to qualify for admission to medical school should they later decide they want to become physicians. In addition, lack of available scholarships makes it impossible for many people from working class and low economic backgrounds to attend medical schools even if they do have the necessary intellectual capacities and academic qualifications.[2]

Both racism and sexism directly affect the health of women and nonwhites. The most obvious effects of racism can be seen in mortality statistics. In his article, "Suffer the Children: Some Effects of Racism on the Health of Black Infants," Wornie L. Reed points out that there is a relationship between institutionalized racism and the inordinately high death rates for black infants in the United States. Such high death rates serve as a gross but reliable indicator of the generally poor health suffered by many if not most blacks in this country. As Reed notes, even when controlling for the effects of social class, black people are less healthy than whites as a population. One conclusion we might draw from this is that the effects of racism compound the known pathological consequences of poverty.

In addition to the direct effects of racism on health, there are added burdens for nonwhite persons who go into a medical care system in which the primary care-givers are white. The problems stemming from ethnic and racial differences may be compounded by prejudice, as when, for example, large numbers of poor black and Hispanic women are sterilized without their knowledge or permission by white, male physicians (Dreifus, 1977).

Sexism, like racism, has had direct consequences on the health and medical experiences of women. Sexist practices eliminated the early dominance of American women in providing health care for one another and thus contributed to the ignorance of many women (even today) about their own bodies and health needs (Ehrenreich and English, 1973). During the nineteenth century, organized medicine gained a strong dominance over the treatment of women, and proceeded to promulgate erroneous and damaging conceptualizations of women as sickly, irrational creatures who are always at the mercy of their reproductive organs (Barker-Benfield, 1976; Wertz and Wertz, 1977). In the selection in this section, "The Sexual Politics of Sickness," Barbara Ehrenreich and Deirdre English explore the history of the rise of these "scientific" explanations of women's health and illness experiences and of the creation of elitist assumptions about the "fragile" nature of upper class women, a nature first believed to be dominated by reproductive organs and, later, by psychological processes innate to women. The creation of the "cult of invalidism" among upper class women in the nineteenth century—at the same time working class women were considered capable of working long, hard hours in sweatshops and factories—can be seen as an example of physicians' functioning as agents of social control: in this case, by keeping women (of both classes) "in their place," both overtly and subtly, through a socialization process in which many women came to accept being sickly as their proper role and in which many more unquestioningly accepted the physician's claim to "expertise" in treating women's health and sexual problems.

By the late twentieth century the grossest biases about women and their bodies have diminished; the examples of sexism we find now are subtler and more complex. Since the 1930s a significant number of "women's problems" have become "medicalized" including childbirth, birth control, abortion, menopause, and, recently, premenstrual syndrome (see also critical debate on The Medicalization of American Society in Part Three). While the consequences of medicalization for women are probably mixed (Reissman, 1983), various feminist analysts see it as an extension of medicine's social control over women (see, for example, Boston Women's Health Book Collective, 1985). To take one example, premenstrual syndrome or PMS, we see that medicalization can legitimate the real discomforts of many women who had long been told their premenstrual stress or pain was "all in their head." On the other hand, one consequence of the adoption of PMS as a medical syndrome is the legitimation of the view that all women are potentially physically and emotionally handicapped each month by menstruation and thus deemed not fully capable of responsibility. Wide adoption of PMS could undercut some important gains of the contemporary women's movement.

In the final article in this section, Frances B. McCrea examines a specific case of such medicalization in "The Politics of Menopause: The 'Discovery' of a Deficiency Disease." The article highlights the social construction of illness and the potential of medical social control. McCrea shows how a natural life event for women, menopause, became defined as a disease in the 1960s when a medical therapy became readily available to treat it (see also Kaufert, 1982). The treatment, estrogen replacement therapy, promised women they could stay "feminine forever." Feminists challenged this medicalization by arguing that menopause is a part of the normal aging process (thus not a disease) and that the treatment is usually unnecessary and always dangerous.

NOTES

1. We might note that there has been some increase in the proportion of minority physicians from 1970 to 1980. The percentage of blacks increased from 2.2 to 3.1 and of Hispanics from 3.7 to 4.4. Yet the representation of minority student

enrollments in the late 1970s and the 1980s suggest that this upward trend is unlikely to continue and the proportion of minority physicians may actually decrease. The proportion of women increased from 9.4 to 13.4 percent and with women making up more than 25 percent of medical school classes we can expect this trend to continue.

2. For years the American Medical Association fought efforts to establish scholarships for poorer medical students, notwithstanding the fact that most medical schools require their students not hold an outside job while attending school. While some scholarship monies have become available in recent years, scholarships are still extremely limited.

REFERENCES

Barker-Benfield, G. J. 1976. The Horrors of the Half-Known Life. New York: Harper and Row.

Boston Women's Health Book Collective. 1985. The New Our Bodies, Ourselves. New York: Simon and Schuster.

Campbell, Margaret. 1973. "Why Would a Girl Go Into Medicine?" Old Westbury, New York: The Feminist Press.

Dagenais, Fred, and Edwin F. Rosinski. 1977. "Social class level, performance, and values in medical school." Proceedings of the 16th Annual Conference on Research in Medical Education. Washington, D.C. (November).

Dreifus, Claudia. 1977. "Sterilizing the poor." Reprinted from The Progressive, 1975 in Claudia Dreifus (Ed.), Seizing Our Bodies. New York: Random House.

Ehrenreich, Barbara, and Deirdre English. 1973. Witches, Midwives and Nurses. Old Westbury, New York: The Feminist Press.

Gee, Helen H. 1959. "Differential characteristics of student bodies: Implications for the study of medical education." Berkeley, Calif., Field Service Center and Center for the Study of Higher Education.

General Accounting Office. 1975. Comptroller General's Report to the Honorable Ronald V. Dellums, "More assurances needed that colleges and universities with government contracts provide equal employment opportunity." Washington, D.C.: Government Printing Office (August 25).

Kaufert, Patricia A. 1982. "Myth and the Menopause." Sociology of Health and Illness 4: 141–66.

Quadagno, Jill. 1976. "Occupational sex-typing and internal labor market distributions: An assessment of medical specialties." Social Problems 23 (April): 442–445.

Riessman, Catherine K. 1983. "Women and medicalization." Social Policy 14: 3–18.

Sexton, Patricia Cayo. 1977. Women and Work. U.S. Department of Labor, R&D Monograph 46, Employment and Training Administration.

Strelnick, Hal. 1980. "Bakke-ing up the wrong tree." Health/PAC Bulletin 11, 3 (January–February).

Strelnick, Hal, and Richard Younge. 1984. "Affirmative action in medicine: Money becomes the admission criterion of the 1980s." In Victor Sidel and Ruth Sidel, Reforming Medicine. New York: Pantheon.

U.S. Department of Commerce (Bureau of Census). 1983. 1980 Census of Population. Supplementary Report (PC80-S1-8). Washington, D.C.: U.S. Government Printing Office.

Weaver, Jerry, and Sharon Garret. 1978. "Sexism and racism in the American health care industry: A comparative analysis." International Journal of Health Services 8, 4: 677–703.

Wertz, Richard, and Dorothy Wertz. 1977. Lying-In, A History of Childbirth in America. New York: Schocken Books.

23

Suffer the Children: Some Effects of Racism on the Health of Black Infants

Wornie L. Reed

The life expectancy of Americans is greater now than ever before, mostly as a result of the increasing survival rate of infants. From this we may conclude that the overall health status of the population has improved, most probably as the result of improvements in the social environment (e.g., sanitation and nutrition) and developments in medical technology and the delivery of medical services. We may also assume that these improvements in general health and in medical services have occurred similarly for all Americans. However, we cannot assume that these improvements have occurred evenly across all population subgroups. In truth, these improvements in health have not been consistent across the board, especially in regards to black Americans. Although black Americans have benefited from these developments through improved health status, as would be expected, the true test of how these developments have affected this subgroup is to examine how blacks have fared relative to other subgroups, especially white Americans. This kind of examination reveals differential effects, with blacks consistently receiving the short end. The causes of this differentiation can be traced to institutional racism.

Institutional racism is to be distinguished from race prejudice and individual racism which, respectively, refer to individual attitudes and individual behaviors (Jones 1972). Institutional racism is racism inherent in and manifested in the outcomes of institutional operations.

Institutional racism can be defined as those established laws, customs, and practices which systematically reflect and produce racial inequities in American society. If racist consequences accrue to institutional laws, customs, or practices, the institution is racist *whether or not the individuals maintaining those practices have racist intentions*. Institutional racism can be either overt or covert (corresponding to *de jure* and *de facto*, respectively) and either intentional or unintentional. (Jones 1972: 131; emphasis in original.)

Detailed treatments of institutional racism can be found in Carmichael and Hamilton (1967), Knowles and Prewitt (1969), and United States Commission on Civil Disorders (1968).

Several health problems can be used to illustrate the disadvantaged position of blacks, including hypertension, which is 235 percent higher in blacks than in whites, and sickle-cell anemia, a genetic disease found mostly in blacks. The debilitating effects of hypertension in the black community—including major incapacity through increased incidence of strokes—suggest a need for more research and more community screening programs than currently exist. Although the belated attention to sickle-cell anemia over the past decade has resulted in the creation of more basic research programs in this disease, it has also resulted in the creation of a potential mechanism for further racism. Many blacks have expressed considerable concern about the programs' thrust toward mandatory genetic screening programs (Wilkinson 1974).

The health problems of black Americans may best be illustrated, however, by examining infant mortality (i.e., children dying before one year of age).

One of the most critical indices used nationally and internationally to interpret the status of a population group is the infant mortality rate. The infant mortality rate is the number of children dying before one year of age per 1,000 live births. The sensitivity of this index is that it provides clues to the nutritional status of the mother and the family, the housing condition, the health care situation, the income level and the overall socio-economic condition. In other words, a high infant mortality rate is indicative of an overall deprivation which impinges on the health of a population group. (Darity and Pitt, 1979: 128.)

In fact, the largest factor in increasing life expectancy has been the reduction in infant mortality in the general population. Thus, the high black infant mortality rate is to some degree reflected in the differential between life expectancies of blacks and whites.

Infant Mortality

As we look at infant mortality, it may be helpful to remember that it is but the tip of the iceberg and indicative of a more general problem of unhealthy infants. The two primary causes of infant mortality are low birth weight and congenital disorders, with low birth weight leading to other problems, including mental retardation, birth defects, growth and developmental problems, blindness, autism, cerebral palsy, and epilepsy (U.S. Department of Health, Education and Welfare, 1979).

Among selected industrialized countries, the United States ranked 10th in infant mortality in 1971, and 10th in 1976 (see Table 1), even though the rate of infant mortality was declining in all these countries. Why does the United States lag behind nine other industrialized countries in infant mortality rates? Clearly, one major reason is the high death rate among nonwhite infants (Metropolitan Life, 1970).

Table 2 shows that although both white and black infant mortality rates have decreased sub-

Table 1. Infant Mortality Rates: Selected Countries, 1976 (Rates per 1,000 live births)

Country	Infant Mortality Rate
Sweden	8.7
Japan	9.3
Switzerland	10.5
Netherlands	10.5
France	12.5
England and Wales	14.0
German Democratic Republic	14.1
Australia	14.3
Canada	14.3
United States	15.2
German Federal Republic	17.4
Italy	19.1
Israel	22.9

SOURCE: U. S. DHEW. Health-United States 1978. Washington, D.C.: Department of Health, Education and Welfare (DHEW Publication No. 78-1232).

stantially over the period between 1950 and 1976, the gap between black and white rates has increased. In 1950, the black infant mortality rate exceeded the white rate by less than two-thirds; yet, in 1976, the black rate exceeded the white rate by almost one hundred percent. Further, the black rate has not decreased as rapidly as that of other nonwhites. In 1950, the black rate was some 20 percent less than the rate for other nonwhites, yet it was nearly twice as high twenty years later in 1970. The decrease among other nonwhites has been mostly the result of a crash health program among Native Americans, which program's success demonstrates the capability of the Federal Government to further equity when it wishes to do so (Darity and Pitt, 1979).

Race and Infant Mortality

To understand the relationship between racism and infant mortality it is necessary to examine some of the factors related to poor infant health. One factor long associated with poor infant health and infant mortality is social class. Consequently, a common explanation for high black infant mortality is the greater proportion of blacks who are poor. In point of fact, infant mortality rates are known to be sensitive to economic instability (Brenner, 1973). However,

Table 2. Infant Mortality Rates by Race: United States 1950–1974 (Rates per 1,000 live births)

Year	All Races	White	Black	All Races Excluding Black and White	Ratio Black/White
1950	29.2	26.8	43.9	55.2	1.64
1955	26.4	23.6	43.1	38.4	1.83
1960	26.0	22.9	44.3	31.2	1.93
1965	24.7	21.5	41.7	26.0	1.94
1970	20.0	17.8	32.6	16.3	1.83
1975	16.1	14.2	26.8	NA[*]	1.89
1976	15.2	13.3	26.2	NA[*]	1.97

[*]Not Ascertained.
SOURCE: *Health of the Disadvantaged—Chart Book*, DHEW Pub. No. (HRA) 77-628, 1977.

there is an excess of black infant mortality *beyond* that explained by socioeconomic status.

Data in Table 3, which show the inverse relationships between infant mortality and socioeconomic status (SES), also show a race effect over and above the class effect. First, the black infant mortality rate greatly exceeds the white rate in each category of the socioeconomic indices. Further examination of the table shows that the highest SES blacks have higher rates of infant mortality than the lowest SES whites. In fact, blacks with some college education have more infant mortality than whites with no more than an eighth grade education. In addition, the rate for blacks earning greater than $7,000, in 1964–1966, was greater than that of whites earning under $3,000.

To understand the many tentacles of racism and how they affect infant mortality, it is helpful to look at: (1) processes that develop conditions conducive to poor infant health, (2) processes that affect acquisition of requisite health care services, and (3) processes constituting the response of the medical care system to the problem of poor infant health. As we shall see, institutional racism places black infants in "triple jeopardy."

Class Inequity

One of the factors contributing to the high black infant mortality rate is economic discrimination.

One result of economic discrimination/racism is the "placement" of a disproportionately high number of blacks and other nonwhites into the lower socioeconomic status groups. For example, 40 percent of blacks are below the poverty level compared to only 10 percent of whites. As shown above, infant mortality is directly connected with socioeconomic status; and more blacks are poor because of institutional racism, which limits opportunity structures (United States Commission on Civil Disorders, 1968).

Residential Segregation

The development of the so-called black ghettoes is another of the racist processes that contributes to the black population being so greatly "at risk" to infant mortality.

> What white Americans have never fully understood—but what the Negro can never forget—is that white society is deeply implicated in the ghetto. White institutions created it, white institutions maintain it, and white society condones it. (U.S. Commission on Civil Disorders, 1968: 2.)

In 1910, some 73 percent of the black population in the United States were living in rural areas. Fifty years later the proportions reversed; some 73 percent of the black population lived in urban areas (Taeuber and Taeuber 1965). Like the European immigrants of earlier decades, blacks took the lowest status positions in the

Table 3. Infant Mortality Rates by Race and Socioeconomic Status: United States 1964–1966 (Rates per 1,000 Live Births)

Socioeconomic Index	All Races	White	Black
Father's Education			
Grade 8 or Less	33.0	30.3	42.4
Grades 9–11	27.4	23.9	44.8
Grade 12	19.0	17.6	32.2
1–3 Years of College	20.6	19.0	37.6
4 Years College or More	17.4	17.0	*
Mother's Education			
Grade 8 or Less	35.2	32.0	45.9
Grades 9–11	27.7	24.6	41.7
Grade 12	19.5	18.0	34.5
1–3 Years of College	15.9	15.0	32.1
4 Years College or More	20.0	19.6	*
Family Income			
Under $3,000	32.1	27.3	42.5
$3,000–4,999	25.1	22.1	46.8
5,000–6,999	18.1	17.8	22.0
7,000–9,999	19.9	19.2	37.6
10,000 or More	19.9	19.4	*

*Numbers too small for estimation.
SOURCE: National Center for Health Statistics, Series 22, No. 14.

urban social structure. And, also like the European immigrants, blacks were restricted in their opportunities for housing. This residential segregation ("ghettoization") created a new urban underclass, in this case an underclass defined by race.

However, in sharp contrast to the immigrants, blacks remained at the bottom of the social structure. Black ghettoes expanded instead of disappearing. As black populations grew, residential boundaries were redrawn in ever widening circles, consistently circumscribing the area.

The restriction of blacks to circumscribed areas is more than a matter of economics. Regardless of income, blacks have been limited to well-defined housing areas. Taeuber and Taeuber (1965:2–3) studied the patterns of racial residential segregation and reached this conclusion:

The poverty of urban Negroes is often regarded as contributory to their residential segregation. Because low-cost housing tends to be segregated from high-cost housing, any low-income group within the city will be residentially segregated to some extent from those with higher incomes. Economic factors, however, cannot account for more than a small portion of observed levels of racial residential segregation. Regardless of their economic status, Negroes rarely live in "white" residential areas, while whites, no matter how poor, rarely live in "Negro" residential areas. In recent decades Negroes have been much more successful in securing improvements in economic status than in obtaining housing on a less segregated basis. Continued economic gains by Negroes are not likely to alter substantially the prevalent patterns of racial residential segregation.

Taeuber (1968) found that whites and blacks were very highly segregated from each other regardless of social class. Updating these findings and using data from the 1970 United States Census as well as the 1950 and 1960 censuses, Shimkus (1978) found that racial residential segregation was still high regardless of occupation. In fact, racial residential segregation is much higher than gross occupational segregation.

This ghettoization is the result of social processes that clearly represent institutional racism. Blackwell (1975) discusses several techniques that worked to bring about the ghettoization of blacks in the United States. Among these are government policy, the operation of the real estate system, zoning laws, restrictive covenants, and violence against blacks.

The federal government itself has greatly contributed to housing discrimination. The Federal Housing Administration, created during the new deal in the 1930s, had an official policy of redlining and segregating residential areas. Its handbook explicitly discouraged the granting of mortgages for houses located in racially mixed residential areas. Further, although the Housing Act of 1937 brought the beginning of public housing for the poor, few blacks were permitted to occupy this housing. Ironically, a current method of racial exclusion is the establishment of zoning ordinances to keep public housing out of predominately "white" areas, since many blacks now occupy public housing.

Another problem area has been the real estate system. White agents generally refused to sell blacks housing that was located in racially mixed areas. Indeed, for a considerable period of time there were no black real estate agents, and when an association of black real estate agents was eventually formed, they were forbidden to label themselves as "realtors," thus limiting their credibility and acceptability. (They became "realtists"!)

State and local zoning laws were—and are—used as instruments of ghettoization. In the early part of this century, zoning laws dealt explicitly with race, specifically excluding blacks from occupying housing in certain areas. Nowadays, racist zoning ordinances are much more subtle, using such stand-in devices as lot size, unit size, land use, and family size to block entry of blacks into residential areas.

Restrictive covenants, agreements in housing purchase contracts that the property will not be sold to persons in specified racial, religious and ethnic groups, were permitted by the courts until the 1950s, thus giving legal sanction to a very powerful mechanism for racial exclusion.

When all else failed, physical violence was often used to restrict the residential movement of blacks. Although this method of restriction is somewhat less common today, it is by no means a thing of the past, a fact amply testified to by current newspaper reports.

All of these actions have combined to create and to maintain black ghettoized areas and to affect the lives of the residents through socio-environmental and other factors associated with ghettoes. The high mortality rate of black infants is but one consequence, albeit a particularly severe one, of institutional racism.

Ghettoization may indirectly affect infant mortality in several ways. One way is through environmental factors such as overcrowding, poor housing, and lack of sanitary environment. These conditions, typical of black ghettoes, are associated with high rates of infant mortality. Yankauer (1950) found that both white and nonwhite infant mortality rates within ghettoized areas rise as levels of segregation increase. While early infant deaths (neonatal mortality) and fetal deaths are related to the health of pregnant women, infant deaths between the end of the first month of life and the first year (post-neonatal mortality) are related to the environmental health as well as the medical care of infants (Stockwell, 1962; Chabot et al., 1975). Another way that ghettoization affects infant mortality is through subordinating, segregating, and precluding blacks from health facilities. Few medical facilities exist in these areas, and many existing ones are characterized by well-known barriers to access, such as travel time to the facility, waiting time to make appointments, and waiting time in the facility, before seeing a health care provider. These barriers contribute to a tendency to underutilize medical facilities.

The Medical Care System

Since high infant mortality implies inadequate medical care and since some studies find barriers to utilization within the health care delivery system itself (Reissman 1974; Dutton 1978; Bullough 1972), it is instructive to examine the health care delivery system vis-à-vis its response to the high black infant mortality rate.

First, we will look at relative access to prenatal care, and then discuss two developments that illustrate inappropriateness of response by the medical system to black infant mortality: (1) the rapid growth of federally supported family planning clinics, and (2) the suggested cutback in training of new physicians.

Prenatal Care

The infant mortality rate of a community has long been regarded as one of the most sensitive indicators of the general health of the population and of the effectiveness of prevailing medical care. It can also be viewed as an indirect measure of the adequacy of prenatal care programs. (National Center for Health Statistics, 1970: 14.)

Prenatal care is a significant factor in infant birth weight: most evidence shows birth weight and prematurity to be highly associated with high infant morbidity and mortality (National Center for Health Statistics, 1972; Kessner et al., 1973). A national study by the National Center for Health Statistics (1972) showed that infants weighing 2,500 grams or less at birth had an infant mortality rate 17 times higher than that of infants weighing over 2,500 grams. A much smaller percentage of white infants than nonwhite infants are born weighing less than 2,500 grams. For example, in 1970, 13.3 percent of all nonwhite babies had low birth weight compared to only 6.8 percent of white babies. Table 4 provides an estimate of what the infant mortality rate would have been for a given poverty-race group if the proportion of low birth weight babies was the same as in a standard population. The observed low birth weight rate for the total United States in 1960 was 7.8 percent. If the percent of low birth weight babies for nonwhites in poverty areas had been 7.8 instead of the observed 15.1, then the infant mortality rate would have been 22.0 instead of the actual 33.5 per 1,000 live births. Thus, the infant mortality rate of nonwhites in poverty areas would be over 50 percent less (National Center for Health Statistics, 1976).

Birth weight, well established as a factor in infant mortality, is affected by both the timing and the amount of prenatal medical visits. As shown in Table 5, over 22 percent of infants of all races for which no prenatal care is obtained will have low birth weight as against less than 3.3 percent if the pregnant woman has between thirteen and sixteen medical visits. Also, if prenatal care is obtained during the first three months, the percentage of low birth weight babies will be smaller than if prenatal care begins later than the third month.

Table 4. Observed and Birth-Weight-Adjusted Infant Mortality Rates, by Poverty Status of Area of Residence and Race: United States, 1969–1971 Average (Rates per 1,000 live births)

Area and Race	Infant Mortality Rates	
	Observed	*Adjusted*
Poverty Areas		
White	24.2	21.8
Nonwhite	33.5	22.0
Nonpoverty		
White	17.4	18.4
Nonwhite	27.0	20.3

Source: National Center for Health Statistics, 1970:15.

According to standards offered by the American College of Obstetricians and Gynecologists (cited in National Center for Health Statistics, 1978), pregnant women should ideally have approximately thirteen prenatal visits for a full-term pregnancy, with more visits if health problems occur. A minimum standard is nine visits. Yet, on the average, only slightly more than half of black mothers meet this standard compared to three-fourths of white mothers (National Center for Health Statistics, 1978a). Approximately twice the proportion of black mothers in comparison to white mothers received late care (in the third trimester) or no care at all. Obviously, lack of prenatal care among pregnant black women must be viewed as a serious problem.

Family Planning Clinics

From 1970 through 1975 the number of federally supported family planning clinics increased from 890 to 4,940, with an eightfold increase in patients (National Center for Health Statistics, 1978b), a growth rate that has caused some concern. This concern is not an argument against the use of, or the need for, family planning, family planning clinics, or abortion. However, one might question the growth and location of these family planning clinics compared to the growth and location of programs for prenatal care. The question is whether family planning clinics were a greater need than prenatal programs.

Table 5. Percent of Infants of Low Birth Weight, by Number of Prenatal Visits and Race: 37 States and the District of Columbia, 1975

Number of Prenatal Visits	All Races[*]	White	Black
Total	7.4	6.2	13.2
No Visits	22.2	18.9	27.9
1 to 4 Visits	19.6	18.5	22.4
5 to 8 Visits	11.5	10.8	14.0
9 to 12 Visits	4.9	4.3	9.0
13 to 16 Visits	3.3	2.9	7.1

[*]Includes races other than white and black.
SOURCE: National Center for Health Statistics, 1978a, p. 23.

The intended user group for these clinics is suggested by the following data from the National Center for Health Statistics (1979a). Of black women 15–55 years of age in the population, approximately 144 per 1,000 had enrolled by 1976 in family planning clinics compared to only 44 per 1,000 white women in this group. Fewer black women than whites used any kind of family planning services (46.2 percent compared to 59.2 percent), yet proportionately more black women enrolled in these public clinics. The racial breakdown between the users of private physicians and family planning clinics illustrates this further. Seventeen percent of the currently married fecund (physiologically able to reproduce) black women, 15 to 44 years of age, used these clinics compared to only 8.3 percent of white women in the same age group. On the other hand, only 29.1 percent of married fecund black women in the 15–44 age group used private physicians against 50.8 percent of white women in this category (National Center for Health Statistics, 1979b). So, during the period of time in which the gap between black and white infant mortality rates was increasing, and while more prenatal services and a better allocation of resources were being requested, there was a rapid increase in public family planning clinics accessible to black women.

Of course, family planning programs and legalized abortion did result in a reduction in black as well as white infant mortality (Roghmann, 1975; Pakter and Nelson, 1974; Lee et al., 1980). They did so by decreasing the incidence of low birth weight babies, the high risk group. On the other hand, there was no improvement in the weight distribution of live births in the United States between 1950 and 1975. Although proportionately as many low birth weight babies were born in 1975 as in 1950, birth weight specific neonatal mortality declined during this period, and it did so at an accelerated pace after the launching of maternal and infant care projects in 1964. The bulk of the evidence suggests that credit for much of the improvement in birth weight specific mortality should be given to maternal and infant care projects and not to abortion or family planning (Lee et al., 1980). The conclusion one must draw is that more, and better, perinatal care might produce more reductions in infant mortality. This would, of course, be beneficial to the black community, which has twice the rate of low birth weight babies as whites.

Limitations on Training Physicians

In the face of the growing concern for the relative lack of medical services in the ghettoized areas, two recent health-policy pronouncements by federal officials forecast the intention to reverse the policy of encouraging medical schools to increase their enrollments. Secretary of Health, Education and Welfare Califano (cited in Darity and Pitt, 1979), referring to a "glut of doctors," proposed that medical schools reduce the size of their classes. In addition, an official from the Office of Management and Budget discussed proposed drastic cuts in health program financing, including those programs that helped black and other minority students to attend medical schools. Yet, data suggest that the black community is underserved rather than "glutted." To the black community, these proposed cutbacks and the current maldistribution of physicians are unfavorable systematic responses to black infant mortality—and further indications of institutional racism.

Discussion

The approximately 15 percent infant mortality rate of the early 1900s was reduced to about 3 percent in the 1950s (through measures such as improved sanitation, personal hygiene, and nutrition) and to approximately 1½ percent in the mid-1970s. Some health policy investigators (McNamara et al., 1978) suggest that a national goal of 1 percent or less (as in Sweden, Japan, Switzerland and the Netherlands) through intensive public intervention will be difficult and quite costly to achieve. This may very well be true. However, it would surely seem that enlightened public policy should attempt to alleviate the great racial inequities in infant mortality, where the current rate in the black community is approximately equivalent to the white rate in the 1950s. Some 6,000 black infants die each year who would be living if the infant mortality rate observed for black infants in a geographic region was as low as that for white infants in the same area (Kovar, 1979).

Generally, reformers suggest attacks on poverty-related factors. These include nutritional programs for poor pregnant mothers and infants, programs to train paramedical personnel to educate expectant mothers on the benefits of prenatal and preventive care, and, most importantly, the provision of free medical care for all poor expectant mothers and for children up to one year of age (Seham 1970).

Maternity and Infant Care (MIC) projects have been quite successful at reaching vulnerable populations and in bringing about subsequent declines in low birth weight incidence and infant mortality (DHEW, 1979). Some urban MIC programs are attacking the problem by better coordination of programs and by outreach programs, including casefinding and surveillance (Gentry, 1979). One study showed that a community health center with an outreach program in prenatal care was used nearly twice as readily as a hospital-based health center program (Birch and Wolfe, 1976).

While some MIC clinics, properly located and staffed, are having success in reducing local infant mortality, many local prenatal programs are understaffed, fragmented, and unsuccessful at reaching pregnant women early enough. Although maternal and infant care providers tend to be confident that good prenatal care helps, some are pessimistic about major progress without direct efforts to eliminate economic and social problems. For example, one local program director feels that "the most effective thing we could do is raise the employment level among young adults. That might do more than all the new hospitals and prenatal units and doctors combined" (Freivogel, 1979).

This assessment returns to center stage the background issue—racial discrimination in economic and social institutions, or institutional racism. With teenage unemployment reaching epidemic proportions in the black community—currently greater than among any other population group in recent American history—and with no program or social policy to reverse this trend, the prognosis for improvement in the black infant mortality rate looks bleak, even if some of the other problems raised above are solved.

REFERENCES

Birch, J. S., and S. Wolfe, 1976, "New and Traditional Sources of Care Evaluated by Recently Pregnant Women." Public Health Reports 91: 413.

Blackwell, J. 1975. The Black Community. New York: Harper and Row Publishers.

Brenner, M. H. 1973. "Fetal, Infant and Maternal Mortality During Periods of Economic Instability." International Journal of Health Services 3: 145–159.

Bullough, B. 1972. "Poverty, Ethnic Identity and Preventive Health Care." Journal of Health and Social Behavior 13: 347–59.

Carmichael, S., and C. Hamilton. 1967. Black Power: The Politics of Liberation in America. New York: Random House.

Chabot, M., J. Garfinkel, and M. W. Pratt. 1975. "Urbanization and Differentials in White and Nonwhite Infant Mortality." Pediatrics 56: 777–81.

Darity, W. A., and E. W. Pitt. 1979. "Health Status of Black Americans." In National Urban League, The State of Black America–1979. Washington, D.C.: National Urban League.

Dutton, D. B. 1978. "Explaining the Low Use of Health Services by the Poor: Costs, Attitudes, or Delivery Systems?" American Sociological Review 43 (June): 348–68.

Freivogel, M. W. 1979. "Infant Death Rate Stays Grim Statistic Here." St. Louis Post-Dispatch, November 18, Section A, 1R.

Gentry, J. T. 1979. "Approaches to Reducing Infant Mortality." Urban Health 8: 27–30.

Jones, J. M. 1972. Prejudice and Racism. Reading, Mass.: Addison-Wesley Publishing Company.

Kessner, D. M., J. Singer, C. E. Kalk, and E. R. Schlesinger. 1973. Contrasts in Health Status. Vol. I. Infant Death: An Analysis by Maternal Risk and Health Care. Washington: Institute of Medicine, National Academy of Sciences.

Knowles, L. and K. Prewitt. 1969. Institutional Racism in America. Englewood Cliffs, N.J.: Prentice Hall.

Kovar, M. G. 1979. "Mortality of Black Infants in the United States." Phylon XXXVIII: 370–97.

Lee, K., N. Paneth, L. M. Gartner, M. A. Pearlman, and L. Gruss. 1980. "Neonatal Mortality: An Analysis of the Recent Improvement in the United States." American Journal of Public Health 70 (1): 15–21.

McNamara, J. J., S. Blumenthal, and C. Landers. 1978. "Trends in Infant Mortality in New York City Health Areas Served by Children and Youth Projects." Bulletin of the New York Academy of Medicine 54: 484–98.

Metropolitan Life. 1970. Statistical Bulletin. 51: 2.

National Center for Health Statistics. 1970. Selected Vital and Health Statistics in Proverty and Nonpoverty Areas of 19 Large Cities, United States 1969–71. Vital and Health Statistics. Series 21, Number 26. Washington, D.C.: U..S. Department of Health, Education and Welfare.

——— 1972. A Study of Infant Mortality from Linked Records by Birth Weight. Series 20, No. 12 (May).

——— 1976. Selected Vital and Health Statistics in Poverty and Nonpoverty Areas of 19 Large Cities, United States, 1969–71.

——— 1978a. Prenatal Care. United States, 1969–75. Vital and Health Statistics. Series 21, Number 33. Washington, D.C.: U.S. Department of Health, Education and Welfare.

——— 1978b. Background and Development of the National Reporting System for Family Planning Services. Vital and Health Statistics. Series 1, Number 13. Washington, D.C.: U.S. Department of Health, Education and Welfare.

——— 1979a. Office Visits for Family Planning, National Ambulatory Medical Care Survey: United States, 1977. Advance Data from Vital and Health Statistics of the National Center for Health Statistics. Number 49. Washington, D.C.: U.S. Department of Health, Education and Welfare.

——— 1979b. Use of Family Planning Services by Currently Married Women 15–44 Years of Age: United States, 1973 and 1976. Advance Data from Vital and Health Statistics of the National Center for Health Statistics. Number 45. Washington, D.C.: U.S. Department of Health, Education and Welfare.

Pakter, J. and F. Nelson, 1974, "Factors in the Unpredicted Decline in Infant Mortality in New York City." Bulletin of the New York Academy of Medicine 50: 839–68.

Riessman, C. K. 1974. "The Use of Health Services by the Poor." Social Policy 5: 41–9.

Roghmann, K. 1975. "Impact of New York State Abortion Law." Chapter 8 in Child Health and the Community. New York: Wiley.

Seham, M. 1973. Blacks and American Medical Care. Minneapolis: University of Minnesota Press.

Shimkus, A. A. 1978. "Residential Segregation by Occupation and Race in Ten Urbanized Areas, 1950–1970." American Sociological Review 43 (1): 81–93.

Stockwell, E. G. 1962. "Infant Mortality and Socioeconomic Status: A Changing Relation." Milbank Memorial Fund Quarterly 40: 101–11.

Taeuber, K. E., and A. F. Taeuber. 1965. Negroes in Cities. Chicago: Aldine.

Taeuber, K. E. 1968. "The Effect of Income Redistribution on Racial Residential Segregation." Urban Affairs Quarterly 4: 5–14.

U.S. Commission on Civil Disorders. 1968. Report of the National Advisory Commission on Civil Disorders. New York: Bantam Books.

U.S. Department of Health, Education and Welfare. 1979. Healthy People: The Surgeon General's Report on Health Promotion and Disease Prevention. Washington, D.C.: U.S. Government Printing Office (DHEW Publication No. 79–55071).

Wilkinson, D. Y. 1974. "For Whose Benefit? Politics and Sickle Cell." The Black Scholar 8 (5): 26–31.

Yankauer, A. 1950. "The Relationship of Fetal and Infant Mortality to Residential Segregation." American Sociological Review 15: 644–48.

24

The Sexual Politics of Sickness

Barbara Ehrenreich and Deirdre English

When Charlotte Perkins Gilman collapsed with a "nervous disorder," the physician she sought out for help was Dr. S. Weir Mitchell, "the greatest nerve specialist in the country." It was Dr. Mitchell—female specialist, part-time novelist, and member of Philadelphia's high society—who had once screened Osler for a faculty position, and, finding him appropriately discreet in the disposal of cherry-pie pits, admitted the young doctor to medicine's inner circles. When Gilman met him, in the eighteen eighties, he was at the height of his career, earning over $60,000 per year (the equivalent of over $300,000 in today's dollars). His renown for the treatment of female nervous disorders had by this time led to a marked alteration of character. According to an otherwise fond biographer, his vanity "had become colossal. It was fed by torrents of adulation, incessant and exaggerated, every day, almost every hour. . . ."[1]

Gilman approached the great man with "utmost confidence." A friend of her mother's lent her one hundred dollars for the trip to Philadelphia and Mitchell's treatment. In preparation, Gilman methodically wrote out a complete history of her case. She had observed, for example, that her sickness vanished when she was away from her home, her husband, and her child, and returned as soon as she came back to them. But Dr. Mitchell dismissed her prepared history as evidence of "self-conceit." He did not want information from his patients; he wanted "complete obedience." Gilman quotes his prescription for her:

"Live as domestic a life as possible. Have your child with you all the time." (Be it remarked that if I did but dress the baby it left me shaking and crying—certainly far from a healthy companionship for her, to say nothing of the effect on me.) "Lie down an hour after each meal. Have but two hours intellectual life a day. And never touch pen, brush or pencil as long as you live."[2]

Gilman dutifully returned home and for some months attempted to follow Dr. Mitchell's orders to the letter. The result, in her words was—

. . . [I] came perilously close to losing my mind. The mental agony grew so unbearable that I would sit blankly moving my head from side to side. . . I would crawl into remote closets and under beds—to hide from the grinding pressure of that distress. . . .[3]

Finally, in a "moment of clear vision" Gilman understood the source of her illness: she did not want to be a *wife;* she wanted to be a writer and an activist. So, discarding S. Weir Mitchell's prescription and divorcing her husband, she took off for California with her baby, her pen, her brush and pencil. But she never forgot Mitchell and his near-lethal "cure." Three years after her recovery she wrote *The Yellow Wallpaper*[4] a fictionalized account of her own illness and descent into madness. If that story had any influence on S. Weir Mitchell's method of treatment, she wrote after a long life of accomplishments, "I have not lived in vain."[5]

Charlotte Perkins Gilman was fortunate enough to have had a "moment of clear vision" in which she understood what was happening to her. Thousands of other women, like Gilman, were finding themselves in a new position of dependency on the male medical profession—and with no alternative sources of information or counsel. The medical profession was consolidating its monopoly over healing, and now the woman who felt sick, or tired or simply depressed would no longer seek help from a friend or female healer, but from a male physician. The general theory which guided the doctors' practice as well as their public pronouncements was that women were, by nature, weak, dependent, and diseased. Thus would the doctors attempt to secure their victory over the female healer: with the "scientific" evidence that woman's essential nature was not to be a strong, competent help-giver, but to be a *patient*.

A Mysterious Epidemic

In fact at the time there were reasons to think that the doctors' theory was not so farfetched. Women were decidedly sickly, though not for the reasons the doctors advanced. In the mid- and late nineteenth century a curious epidemic seemed to be sweeping through the middle- and upper-class female population both in the United States and England. Diaries and journals from the time give us hundreds of examples of women slipping into hopeless invalidism. For example, when Catherine Beecher, the educator, finished a tour in 1871 which included visits to dozens of relatives, friends and former students, she reported "a terrible decay of female health all over the land," which was "increasing in a most alarming ratio." The notes from her travels go like this:

> Milwaukee, Wis. Mrs. A. frequent sick headaches. Mrs. B. very feeble. Mrs. S. well, except chills. Mrs. L. poor health constantly. Mrs. D. subject to frequent headaches. Mrs. B. very poor health . . .
> Mrs. H. pelvic disorders and a cough. Mrs. B. always sick. Do not know one perfectly healthy woman in the place. . . .[6]

Doctors found a variety of diagnostic labels for the wave of invalidism gripping the female population: "Neurasthenia," "nervous prostra-

tion," "hyperesthesia," "cardiac inadequacy," "dyspepsia," "rheumatism," and "hysteria." The symptoms included headache, muscular aches, weakness, depression, menstrual difficulties, indigestion, etc., and usually a general debility requiring constant rest. S. Weir Mitchell described it as follows:

> The woman grows pale and thin, eats little, or if she eats does not profit by it. Everything wearies her,—to sew, to write, to read, to walk,—and by and by the sofa or the bed is her only comfort. Every effort is paid for dearly, and she describes herself as aching and sore, as sleeping ill, and as needing constant stimulus and endless tonics. . . . If such a person is emotional she does not fail to become more so, and even the firmest women lose self-control at last under incessant feebleness.[7]

The syndrome was never fatal, but neither was it curable in most cases, the victims sometimes patiently outliving both husbands and physicians.

Women who recovered to lead full and active lives—like Charlotte Perkins Gilman and Jane Addams—were the exceptions. Ann Greene Phillips—a feminist and abolitionist in the eighteen thirties—first took ill during her courtship. Five years after her marriage, she retired to bed, more or less permanently. S. Weir Mitchell's unmarried sister fell prey to an unspecified "great pain" shortly after taking over housekeeping for her brother (whose first wife had just died), and embarked on a life of invalidism. Alice James began her career of invalidism at the age of nineteen, always amazing her older brothers, Henry (the novelist) and William (the psychologist), with the stubborn intractability of her condition: "Oh, woe, woe is me!" she wrote in her diary:

> . . . all hopes of peace and rest are vanishing—nothing but the dreary snail-like climb up a little way, so as to be able to run down again! And then these doctors tell you that you will die or *recover!* But you *don't* recover. I have been at these alterations since I was nineteen and I am neither dead nor recovered. As I am now forty-two, there has surely been time for either process.[8]

The sufferings of these women were real enough. Ann Phillips wrote, ". . . life is a burden to me, I do not know what to do. I am tired of suffering. I have no faith in anything."[9] Some thought that if the illness wouldn't kill them, they would do the job themselves. Alice James discussed suicide with her father, and rejoiced, at the age of forty-three, when informed she had developed breast cancer and would die within months: "I count it the greatest good fortune to have these few months so full of interest and instruction in the knowledge of my approaching death."[10] Mary Galloway shot herself in the head while being attended in her apartment by a physician and a nurse. She was thirty-one years old, the daughter of a bank and utility company president. According to the New York *Times* account (April 10, 1905), "She had been a chronic dyspeptic since 1895, and that is the only reason known for her suicide."[11]

Marriage: The Sexual Economic Relation

In the second half of the nineteenth century the vague syndrome gripping middle- and upper-class women had become so widespread as to represent not so much a disease in the medical sense as a way of life. More precisely, the way this type of woman was expected to live predisposed her to sickness, and sickness in turn predisposed her to continue to live as she was expected to. The delicate, affluent lady, who was completely dependent on her husband, set the sexual romanticist ideal of femininity for women of all classes.

Clear-headed feminists like Charlotte Perkins Gilman and Olive Schreiner saw a link between female invalidism and the economic situation of women in the upper classes. As they observed, poor women did not suffer from the syndrome. The problem in the middle to upper classes was that marriage had become a "sexuo-economic relation" in which women performed sexual and reproductive duties for financial support. It was a relationship which Olive Schreiner bluntly called "female parasitism."

To Gilman's pragmatic mind, the affluent wife appeared to be a sort of tragic evolutionary anomaly, something like the dodo. She did not work: that is, there was no serious, productive work to do in the home, and the tasks which were left—keeping house, cooking and minding the children—she left as much as possible to the domestic help. She was, biologically speaking, specialized for one function and one alone—sex. Hence the elaborate costume—bustles, false fronts, wasp waists—which caricatured the natural female form. Her job was to bear the heirs of the businessman, lawyer, or professor she had married, which is what gave her a claim to any share of his income. When Gilman, in her depression, turned away from her own baby, it was because she already understood, in a half-conscious way, that the baby was living proof of her economic dependence—and as it seemed to her, sexual degradation.

A "lady" had one other important function, as Veblen pointed out with acerbity in the *Theory of the Leisure Class*. And that was to do precisely nothing, that is nothing of any economic or social consequence.[12] A successful man could have no better social ornament than an idle wife. Her delicacy, her culture, her childlike ignorance of the male world gave a man the "class" which money alone could not buy. A virtuous wife spent a hushed and peaceful life indoors, sewing, sketching, planning menus, and supervising the servants and children. The more adventurous might fill their leisure with shopping excursions, luncheons, balls, and novels. A "lady" could be charming, but never brilliant; interested, but not intense. Dr. Mitchell's second wife, Mary Cadwalader, was perhaps a model of her type: she "made no pretense at brilliancy; her first thought was to be a foil to her husband. . . ."[13] By no means was such a lady to concern herself with politics, business, international affairs, or the aching injustices of the industrial work world.

But not even the most sheltered woman lived on an island detached from the "real" world of men. Schreiner described the larger context:

Behind the phenomenon of female parasitism has always lain another and yet larger social phenomenon . . . the subjugation of large bodies of other human creatures, either as slaves, subject races, or classes; and as a result of the excessive labors of those classes there has always been an accumulation of unearned wealth in the hands of the dominant class or race. *It has invariably been by feeding on this wealth, the result of forced or ill-paid labor,* that the female of the dominant race or class has in the past lost her activity and has come to exist purely through the passive performance of her sexual functions.[14] (Emphasis in original)

The leisured lady, whether she knew it or not and whether she cared or not, inhabited the same social universe as dirt-poor black sharecroppers, six-year-old children working fourteen-hour days for subsubsistence wages, young men mutilated by unsafe machinery or mine explosions, girls forced into prostitution by the threat of starvation. At no time in American history was the contradiction between ostentatious wealth and unrelenting poverty, between idleness and exhaustion, starker than it was then in the second half of the nineteenth century. There were riots in the cities, insurrections in the mines, rumors of subversion and assassination. Even the secure business or professional man could not be sure that he too would not be struck down by an economic downturn, a wily competitor, or (as seemed likely at times) a social revolution.

The genteel lady of leisure was as much a part of the industrial social order as her husband or his employees. As Schreiner pointed out, it was ultimately the wealth extracted in the world of work that enabled a man to afford a more or less ornamental wife. And it was the very harshness of that outside world that led men to see the home as a refuge—"a sacred place, a vestal temple," a "tent pitch'd in a world not right," presided over by a gentle, ethereal wife. A popular home health guide advised that

> . . . [man's] feelings are frequently lacerated to the utmost point of endurance, by collisions, irritations, and dissappointments. To recover his equanimity and composure, home must be a place of repose, of peace, of cheerfulness, of comfort; then his soul renews its strength, and will go forth, with fresh vigor, to encounter the labor and troubles of the world.[15]

No doubt the suffocating atmosphere of sexual romanticism bred a kind of nervous hypochondria. We will never know, for example, if Alice James's lifelong illness had a "real" organic basis. But we know that, unlike her brothers, she was never encouraged to go to college or to develop her gift for writing. She was high-strung and imaginative, but *she* could not be brilliant or

productive. Illness was perhaps the only honorable retreat from a world of achievement which (it seemed at the time) nature had not equipped her to enter.

For many other women, to various degrees, sickness became a part of life, even a way of filling time. The sexuo-economic relation confined women to the life of the body, so it was to the body that they directed their energies and intellect. Rich women frequented resortlike health spas and the offices of elegant specialists like S. Weir Mitchell. A magazine cartoon from the eighteen seventies shows two "ladies of fashion" meeting in an ornately appointed waiting room. "What, *you* here, Lizzie? Why, ain't you well?" asks the first patient. "Perfectly thanks!" answers the second. "But what's the matter with *you*, dear?" "Oh, nothing whatever! I'm as right as possible dear."[16] For less well-off women there were patent medicines, family doctors, and, starting in the eighteen fifties, a steady stream of popular advice books, written by doctors, on the subject of female health. It was acceptable, even stylish, to retire to bed with "sick headaches," "nerves" and various unmentionable "female troubles," and that indefinable nervous disorder "neurasthenia" was considered, in some circles, to be a mark of intellect and sensitivity. Dr. Mary Putnam Jacobi, a female regular physician, observed impatiently in 1895:

> . . . it is considered natural and almost laudable to break down under all conceivable varieties of strain—a winter dissipation, a houseful of servants, a quarrel with a female friend, not to speak of more legitimate reasons. . . . Women who expect to go to bed every menstrual period expect to collapse if by chance they find themselves on their feet for a few hours during such a crisis. Constantly considering their nerves, urged to consider them by well-intentioned but short-sighted advisors, they pretty soon become nothing but a bundle of nerves.[17]

But if sickness was a reaction, on women's part, to a difficult situation, it was not a way out. If you have to be idle, you might as well be sick, and sickness, in turn, legitimates idleness. From the romantic perspective, the sick woman was not that far off from the ideal woman anyway. A morbid aesthetic developed, in which sickness was seen as a source of female beauty, and beauty—in the high-fashion sense—was in fact a source of sickness. Over and over, nineteenth-century romantic paintings feature the beautiful invalid, sensuously drooping on her cushions, eyes fixed tremulously at her husband or physician, or already gazing into the Beyond. Literature aimed at female readers lingered on the romantic pathos of illness and death; popular women's magazines featured such stories as "The Grave of My Friend" and "Song of Dying." Society ladies cultivated a sickly countenance by drinking vinegar in quantity or, more effectively, arsenic.[18] The loveliest heroines were those who died young, like Beth in *Little Women,* too good and too pure for life in this world.

Meanwhile, the requirements of fashion insured that the well-dressed woman would actually be as frail and ornamental as she looked. The style of wearing tight-laced corsets, which was *de rigeur* throughout the last half of the century, has to be ranked somewhere close to the old Chinese practice of foot-binding for its crippling effects on the female body. A fashionable woman's corsets exerted, on the average, twenty-one pounds of pressure on her internal organs, and extremes of up to eighty-eight pounds had been measured.[19] (Add to this the fact that a well-dressed woman wore an average of thirty-seven pounds of street clothing in the winter months, of which nineteen pounds were suspended from her tortured waist.[20] Some of the short-term results of tight-lacing were shortness of breath, constipation, weakness, and a tendency to violent indigestion. Among the long-term effects were bent or fractured ribs, displacement of the liver, and uterine prolapse (in some cases, the uterus would be gradually forced, by the pressure of the corset, out through the vagina).

The morbidity of nineteenth-century tastes in female beauty reveals the hostility which never lies too far below the surface of sexual romanticism. To be sure, the romantic spirit puts woman on a pedestal and ascribes to her every tender viture absent from the Market. But carried to an extreme the demand that woman be a *negation* of man's world left almost nothing for women to actually *be:* if men are busy, she is idle; if men are rough, she is gentle; if men are strong, she is frail; if men are rational, she is irrational; and so on. The logic which insists that femininity is negative

masculinity necessarily romanticizes the moribund woman and encourages a kind of paternalistic necrophilia. In the nineteenth century this tendency becomes overt, and the romantic spirit holds up as its ideal—the *sick* woman, the invalid who lives at the edge of death.

Femininity as a Disease

The medical profession threw itself with gusto on the languid figure of the female invalid. In the home of an invalid lady, "the house physician like a house fly is in chronic attention"[21] and the doctors fairly swarmed after wealthy patients. Few were so successful as S. Weir Mitchell in establishing himself as *the* doctor for hundreds of loyal clients. Yet the doctors' constant ministrations and interventions—surgical, electrical, hydropathic, mesmeric, chemical—seemed to be of little use. In fact, it would have been difficult, in many cases, to distinguish the *cure* from the *disease.* Charlotte Perkins Gilman of course saw the connection. The ailing heroine of *The Yellow Wallpaper,* who is being treated by her physician-husband, hints at the fearful truth:

> John is a physician, and *perhaps*—(I would not say it to a living soul, of course, but this is dead paper and a great relief to my mind)—*perhaps* that is one reason I do not get well faster.[22]

In fact, the theories which guided the doctor's practice from the late nineteenth century to the early twentieth century held that woman's *normal* state was to be sick. This was not advanced as an empirical observation, but as physiological fact. Medicine had "discovered" that female functions were inherently pathological. Menstruation, that perennial source of alarm to the male imagination, provided both the evidence and the explanation. Menstruation was a serious threat throughout life—so was the lack of it. According to Dr. Engelmann, president of the American Gynecology Society in 1900:

> Many a young life is battered and forever crippled on the breakers of puberty; if it crosses these unharmed and is not dashed to pieces on the rock of childbirth, it may still ground on the ever-recurring

shallows of menstruation, and lastly upon the final bar of the menopause ere protection is found in the unruffled waters of the harbor beyond reach of sexual storms.[23]

Popular advice books written by physicians took on a somber tone as they entered into "the female functions" or "the diseases of women."

It is impossible to form a correct opinion of the mental and physical suffering frequently endured from her sexual condition, caused by her monthly periods, which it has pleased her Heavenly Father to attach to woman. . . .[24]

Ignoring the existence of thousands of working women, the doctors assumed that every woman was prepared to set aside a week or five days every month as a period of invalidism. Dr. W. C. Taylor, in his book *A Physician's Counsels to Woman in Health and Disease,* gave a warning typical of those found in popular health books of the time:

We cannot too emphatically urge the importance of regarding these monthly returns as periods of ill health, as days when the ordinary occupations are to be suspended or modified. . . . Long walks, dancing, shopping, riding and parties should be avoided at this time of month invariably and under all circumstances. . . .[25]

As late as 1916, Dr. Winfield Scott Hall was advising:

All heavy exercise should be omitted during the menstrual week . . . a girl should not only retire earlier at this time, but ought to stay out of school from one to three days as the case may be, resting the mind and taking extra hours of rest and sleep.[26]

Similarly, a pregnant woman was "indisposed," throughout the full nine months. The medical theory of "prenatal impressions" required her to avoid all "shocking, painful or unbeautiful sights," intellectual stimulation, angry or lustful thoughts, and even her husband's alcohol and tobacco-laden breath—lest the baby be deformed or stunted in the womb. Doctors stressed the pathological nature of childbirth itself—an argument which also was essential to

their campaign against midwives. After delivery, they insisted on a protracted period of convalescence mirroring the "confinement" which preceded birth. (Childbirth, in the hands of the medical men, no doubt was "pathological," and doctors had far less concern about prenatal nutrition than they did about prenatal "impressions.") Finally after all this, a woman could only look forward to menopause, portrayed in the medical literature as a terminal illness—the "death of the woman in the woman."

Now it must be said in the doctor's defense that women of a hundred years ago *were,* in some ways, sicker than the women of today. Quite apart from tight-lacing, arsenic-nipping, and fashionable cases of neurasthenia, women faced certain bodily risks which men did not share. In 1915 (the first year for which national figures are available) 61 women died for every 10,000 live babies born, compared to 2 per 10,000 today, and the maternal mortality rates were doubtless higher in the nineteenth century.[27] Without adequate, and usually without any, means of contraception, a married woman could expect to face the risk of childbirth repeatedly through her fertile years. After each childbirth a woman might suffer any number of gynecological complications, such as prolapsed (slipped) uterus or irreparable pelvic tear, which would be with her for the rest of her life.

Another special risk to women came from tuberculosis, the "white plague." In the mid-nineteenth century, TB raged at epidemic proportions, and it continued to be a major threat until well into the twentieth century. Everyone was affected, but women, especially young women, were particularly vulnerable, often dying at rates twice as high as those of men of their age group. For every hundred women aged twenty in 1865, more than five would be dead from TB by the age of thirty, and more than eight would be dead by the age of fifty.[28]

So, from a statistical point of view, there was some justification for the doctors' theory of innate female frailty. But there was also, from the doctors' point of view, a strong commercial justification for regarding women as sick. This was the period of the profession's most severe "population crisis." The theory of female frailty obviously disqualified women as healers. "One shudders to think of the conclusions arrived at by female bacteriologists or histologists," wrote one doctor, "at the period when their entire system, both physical and mental, is, so to speak, 'unstrung,' to say nothing of the terrible mistakes which a lady surgeon might make under similar conditions."[29] At the same time the theory made women highly qualified as patients. The sickly, nervous women of the upper or middle class with their unending, but fortunately non-fatal, ills, became a natural "client caste" to the developing medical profession.

Meanwhile, the health of women who were *not* potential patients—poor women—received next to no attention from the medical profession. Poor women must have been at least as susceptible as wealthy women to the "sexual storms" doctors saw in menstruation, pregnancy, etc.; and they were definitely much more susceptible to the hazards of childbearing, tuberculosis, and, of course, industrial diseases. From all that we know, sickness, exhaustion, and injury were routine in the life of the working-class woman. Contagious diseases always hit the homes of the poor first and hardest. Pregnancy, in the fifth- or sixth-floor walk-up flat, really was debilitating, and childbirth, in a crowded tenement room, was often a frantic ordeal. Emma Goldman, who was a trained midwife as well as an anarchist leader, described "the fierce, blind struggle of the women of the poor against frequent pregnancies" and told of the agony of seeing children grow up "sickly and undernourished"—if they survived infancy at all.[30] For the woman who labored outside her home, working conditions took an enormous toll. An 1884 report of an investigation of "The Working Girls of Boston," by the Massachusetts Bureau of Statistics of Labor, stated:

> ...the health of many girls is so poor as to necessitate long rests, one girl being out a year on this account. Another girl in poor health was obliged to leave her work, while one reports that it is not possible for her to work the year round, as she could not stand the strain, not being at all strong.[31]

Still, however sick or tired working-class women might have been, they certainly did not have the time or money to support a cult of

invalidism. Employers gave no time off for pregnancy or recovery from childbirth, much less for menstrual periods, though the wives of these same employers often retired to bed on all these occasions. A day's absence from work could cost a woman her job, and at home there was no comfortable chaise lounge to collapse on while servants managed the household and doctors managed the illness. An 1889 study from Massachusetts described one working woman's life:

> Constant application to work, often until 12 at night and sometimes on Sundays (equivalent to nine ordinary working days a week), affected her health and injured her eyesight. She ... was ordered by the doctor to suspend work ... but she must earn money, and so she has kept on working. Her eyes weep constantly, she cannot see across the room and "the air seems always in a whirl" before her ... [she] owed when seen three months' board for self and children ... She hopes something may be done for working girls and women, for, however strong they may be in the beginning, "they cannot stand white slavery for ever."[32]

But the medical profession as a whole—and no doubt there were many honorable exceptions—sturdily maintained that it was affluent women who were most delicate and most in need of medical attention. "Civilization" had made the middle-class woman sickly; her physical frailty went hand-in-white-gloved-hand with her superior modesty, refinement, and sensitivity. Working-class women were robust, just as they were supposedly "coarse" and immodest. Dr. Lucien Warner, a popular medical authority, wrote in 1874, "It is not then hard work and privation which make the women of our country invalids, but circumstances and habits intimately connected with the so-called blessings of wealth and refinement."

Someone had to be well enough to do the work, though, and working-class women, Dr. Warner noted with relief, were *not* invalids: "The African negress, who toils beside her husband in the fields of the south, and Bridget, who washes, and scrubs and toils in our homes at the north, enjoy for the most part good health, with comparative immunity from uterine disease."[33] And a Dr. Sylvanus Stall observed:

At war, at work, or at play, the white man is superior to the savage, and his culture has continually improved his condition. But with woman the rule is reversed. Her squaw sister will endure effort, exposure and hardship which would kill the white woman. Education which has resulted in developing and strengthening the physical nature of man has been perverted through folly and fashion to render woman weaker and weaker.[34]

In practice, the same doctors who zealously indulged the ills of wealthy patients had no time to spare for the poor. When Emma Goldman asked the doctors she knew whether they had any contraceptive information she could offer the poor, their answers included, "The poor have only themselves to blame; they indulge their appetites too much," and "When she [the poor woman] uses her brains more, her procreative organs will function less."[35] A Dr. Palmer Dudley ruled out poor women as subjects for gynecological surgery on the simple ground that they lacked the leisure required for successful treatment:

... the hardworking, daily-toiling woman is not as fit a subject for [gynecological surgery] as the woman so situated in life as to be able to conserve her strength and if necessary, to take a long rest, in order to secure the best results.[36]

So the logic was complete: better-off women were sickly because of their refined and civilized lifestyle. Fortunately, however, this same lifestyle made them amenable to lengthy medical treatment. Poor and working-class women were inherently stronger, and this was also fortunate, since their lifestyle disqualified them from lengthy medical treatment anyway. The theory of innate female sickness, skewed so as to account for class differences in ability to pay for medical care, meshed conveniently with the doctors' commercial self-interest.

The feminists of the late nineteenth century, themselves deeply concerned about female invalidism, were quick to place at least part of the blame on the doctors' interests. Elizabeth Garrett Anderson, an American woman doctor, argued that the extent of female invalidism was much exaggerated by male doctors and that women's natural functions were not really all that debilitating. In the working classes, she observed,

work went on during menstruation "without intermission, and, as a rule, without ill effects."[37] Mary Livermore, a women's suffrage worker, spoke against "the monstrous assumption that woman is a natural invalid," and denounced "the unclean army of 'gynecologists' who seem desirous to convince women that they possess but one set of organs—and that these are always diseased."[38] And Dr. Mary Putnam Jacobi put the matter most forcefully when she wrote in 1895, "I think, finally, it is in the increased attention paid to women, and especially in their new function as lucrative patients, scarcely imagined a hundred years ago, that we find explanation for much of the ill-health among women, freshly discovered today...."[39]

The Dictatorship of the Ovaries

It was medicine's task to translate the [nineteenth-century] evolutionary theory of women into the language of flesh and blood, tissues and organs. The result was a theory which put woman's mind, body and soul in the thrall of her all-powerful reproductive organs. "The Uterus, it must be remembered," Dr. F. Hollick wrote, "is the *controlling* organ in the female body, being the most excitable of all, and so intimately connected, by the ramifications of its numerous nerves, with every other part."[40] Professor M. L. Holbrook, addressing a medical society in 1870, observed that it seemed "as if the Almighty, in creating the female sex, *had taken the uterus and built up a woman around it*."[41] (Emphasis in original.)

To other medical theorists, it was the ovaries which occupied center stage. Dr. G. L. Austin's 1883 book of advice for "maiden, wife and mother" asserts that the ovaries "give woman all her characteristics of body and mind."[42] This passage written in 1870 by Dr. W. W. Bliss is, if somewhat overwrought, nonetheless typical:

Accepting, then, these views of the gigantic power and influence of the ovaries over the whole animal economy of woman,—that they are the most powerful agents in all the commotions of her system; that on them rest her intellectual standing in society, her physical perfection, and all that lends beauty to those fine and delicate contours which are constant objects of admiration, all that is great, noble and beautiful, all that is voluptuous, tender, and endearing; that her fidelity, her devotedness, her perpetual vigilance, forecast, and all those qualities of mind and disposition which inspire respect and love and fit her as the safest counsellor and friend of man, spring from the ovaries,—*what must be their influence and power over the great vocation of woman and the august purposes of her existence when these organs have become compromised through disease!*[43] (Emphasis in original.)

According to this "psychology of the ovary" woman's entire personality was directed by the ovaries, and any abnormalities, from irritability to insanity, could be traced to some ovarian disease. Dr. Bliss added, with unbecoming spitefulness, that "the influence of the ovaries over the mind is displayed in woman's artfulness and dissimulation."

It should be emphasized, before we follow the workings of the uterus and ovaries any further, that woman's total submission to the "sex function" did not make her a *sexual* being. The medical model of female nature, embodied in the "psychology of the ovary," drew a rigid distinction between reproductivity and sexuality. Women were urged by the health books and the doctors to indulge in deep preoccupation with themselves as "The Sex"; they were to devote themselves to developing their reproductive powers and their maternal instincts. Yet doctors said they had no predilection for the sex act itself. Even a woman physician, Dr. Mary Wood-Allen wrote (perhaps from experience), that women embrace their husbands "without a particle of sex desire."[44] Hygiene manuals stated that the more cultured the woman, "the more is the sensual refined away from her nature," and warned against "any spasmodic convulsion" on a woman's part during intercourse lest it interfere with conception. Female sexuality was seen as unwomanly and possibly even detrimental to the supreme function of reproduction.

The doctors themselves never seemed entirely convinced, though, that the uterus and ovaries had successfully stamped out female sexuality. Underneath the complacent denials of female sexual feelings, there lurked the age-old male fascination with woman's "insatiable lust," which, once awakened, might turn out to be uncontrollable. Doctors dwelt on cases in which women were destroyed by their cravings; one doctor claimed to have discovered a case of "virgin nymphomania." The twenty-five-year-old British physician Robert Brudenell Carter leaves us with this tantalizing observation on his female patients:

> . . . no one who has realized the amount of moral evil wrought in girls . . . whose prurient desires have been increased by Indian hemp and partially gratified by medical manipulations, can deny that remedy is worse than disease. I have . . . seen young unmarried women, of the middle class of society, reduced by the constant use of the speculum to the mental and moral condition of prostitutes; seeking to give themselves the same indulgence by the practice of solitary vice; and asking every medical practitioner . . . to institute an examination of the sexual organs.[45]

But if the uterus and ovaries could not be counted on to suppress all sexual strivings, they were still sufficiently in control to be blamed for all possible female disorders, from headaches to sore throats and indigestion. Dr. M. E. Dirix wrote in 1869:

> Thus, women are treated for diseases of the stomach, liver, kidneys, heart, lungs, etc.; yet, in most instances, these diseases will be found on due investigation, to be, in reality, no diseases at all, but merely the sympathetic reactions or the symptoms of one disease, namely, a disease of the womb.[46]

Even tuberculosis could be traced to the capricious ovaries. When men were consumptive, doctors sought some environmental factor, such as overexposure, to explain the disease. But for women it was a result of reproductive malfunction. Dr. Azell Ames wrote in 1875:

> It being beyond doubt that consumption . . . is itself produced by the failure of the [menstrual] function in the forming girls . . . one has been the parent of the other with interchangeable priority. [Actually, as we know today, it is true that consumption may *result* in suspension of the menses.][47]

Since the reproductive organs were the source of disease, they were the obvious target in the treatment of disease. Any symptom—backaches, irritability, indigestion, etc.—could provoke a medical assault on the sexual organs. Historian Ann Douglas Wood describes the "local treatments" used in the mid-nineteenth century for almost any female complaint:

This [local] treatment had four stages, although not every case went through all four: a manual investigation, "leeching," "injections," and "cauterization." Dewees [an American medical professor] and Bennet, a famous English gynecologist widely read in America, both advocated placing the leeches right on the vulva or the neck of the uterus, although Bennet cautioned the doctor to count them as they dropped off when satiated, lest he "lose" some. Bennet had known adventurous leeches to advance into the cervical cavity of the uterus itself, and he noted, "I think I have scarcely ever seen more acute pain than that experienced by several of my patients under these circumstances." Less distressing to a 20th century mind, but perhaps even more senseless, were the "injections" into the uterus advocated by these doctors. The uterus became a kind of catch-all, or what one exasperated doctor referred to as a "Chinese toy shop": Water, milk and water, linseed tea, and "decoction of marshmellow . . . tepid or cold" found their way inside nervous women patients. The final step, performed at this time, one must remember, with no anesthetic but a little opium or alcohol, was cauterization, either through the application of nitrate of silver, or, in cases of more severe infection, through the use of much stronger hydrate of potassa, or even the "actual cautery," a "white-hot iron" instrument.[48]

In the second half of the century, these fumbling experiments with the female interior gave way to the more decisive technique of surgery—aimed increasingly at the control of female personality disorders. There had been a brief fad of clitoridectomy (removal of the clitoris) in the sixties, following the introduction of the operation by the English physician Isaac Baker Brown. Although most doctors frowned on the practice of removing the clitoris, they tended to agree that it might be necessary in cases of nymphomania, intractable masturbation, or "unnatural growth" of that organ. (The last clitoridectomy we know of in the United States

was performed in 1948 on a child of five, as a cure for masturbation.)

The most common form of surgical intervention in the female personality was ovariotomy, removal of the ovaries—or "female castration." In 1906 a leading gynecological surgeon estimated that there were 150,000 women in the United States who had lost their ovaries under the knife. Some doctors boasted that they had removed from fifteen hundred to two thousand ovaries apiece.[49] According to historian G. J. Barker-Benfield:

Among the indications were troublesomeness, eating like a ploughman, masturbation, attempted suicide, erotic tendencies, persecution mania, simple "cussedness," and dysmenorrhea [painful menstruation]. Most apparent in the enormous variety of symptoms doctors took to indicate castration was a strong current of sexual appetitiveness on the part of women.[50]

The rationale for the operation flowed directly from the theory of the "psychology of the ovary": since the ovaries controlled the personality, they must be responsible for any psychological disorders; conversely, psychological disorders were a sure sign of ovarian disease. Ergo, the organs must be removed.

One might think, given the all-powerful role of the ovaries, that an ovaryless women would be like a rudderless ship—desexed and directionless. But on the contrary, the proponents of ovariotomy argued, a woman who was relieved of a diseased ovary would be a *better* woman. One 1893 advocate of the operation claimed that "patients are improved, some of them cured; . . . the moral sense of the patient is elevated . . . she becomes tractable, orderly, industrious, and cleanly."[51] Patients were often brought in by their husbands, who complained of their unruly behavior. Doctors also claimed that women—troublesome but still sane enough to recognize their problem—often "came to us pleading to have their ovaries removed."[52] The operation was judged successful if the woman was restored to a placid contentment with her domestic functions.

The overwhelming majority of women who had leeches or hot steel applied to their cervices, or who had their clitorises or ovaries removed, were women of the middle to upper classes, for after all, these procedures cost money. But it should not be imagined that poor women were spared the gynecologist's exotic catalog of tortures simply because they couldn't pay. The pioneering work in gynecological surgery had been performed by Marion Sims on black female slaves he kept for the sole purpose of surgical experimentation. He operated on one of them thirty times in four years, being foiled over and over by postoperative infections.[53] After moving to New York, Sims continued his experimentation on indigent Irish women in the wards of New York Women's Hospital. So, though middle-class women suffered most from the doctors' actual practice, it was poor and black women who had suffered through the brutal period of experimentation.

. . . .

Subverting the Sick Role: Hysteria

The romance of the doctor and the female invalid comes to full bloom (and almost to consummation) in the practice of S. Weir Mitchell. But . . . there is a nastier side to this affair. An angry, punitive tone has come into his voice; the possibility of physical force has been raised. As time goes on and the invalids pile up in the boudoirs of American cities and recirculate through the health spas and consulting rooms, the punitive tone grows louder. Medicine is caught in a contradiction of its own making, and begins to turn against the patient.

Doctors had established that women are sick, that this sickness is innate, and stems from the very possession of a uterus and ovaries. They had thus eliminated the duality of "sickness" and "health" for the female sex; there was only a drawn-out half-life, tossed steadily by the "storms" of reproductivity toward a more total kind of rest. But at the same time, doctors *were* expected to cure. The development of commercial medicine, with its aggressive, instrumental approach to healing, required some public faith that doctors could *do something,* that they could fix things. Certainly Charlotte Perkins Gilman had expected to be cured. The husbands, fathers,

sisters, etc. of thousands of female invalids expected doctors to provide cures. A medical strategy of disease by decree, followed by "cures" which either mimicked the symptoms or caused new ones, might be successful for a few decades. But it had no long-term commercial viability.

The problem went deeper, though, than the issue of the doctors' commercial credibility. There was a contradiction in the romantic ideal of femininity which medicine had worked so hard to construct. Medicine had insisted that woman was sick *and* that her life centered on the reproductive function. But these are contradictory propositions. If you are sick enough, you cannot reproduce. The female role in reproduction requires stamina, and if you count in all the activities of child raising and running a house, it requires full-blown, energetic *health.* Sickness and reproductivity, the twin pillars of nineteenth-century femininity, could not stand together.

In fact, toward the end of the century, it seemed that sickness had been winning out over reproductivity. The birth rate for whites shrank by a half between 1800 and 1900, and the drop was most precipitous among white Anglo-Saxon Protestants—the "better" class of people. Meanwhile blacks and European immigrants appeared to be breeding prolifically, and despite their much higher death rates, the fear arose that they might actually replace the "native stock." Professor Edwin Conklin of Princeton wrote:

> The cause for alarm is the declining birth rate among the best elements of a population, while it continues to increase among the poorer elements. The descendants of the Puritans and the Cavaliers . . . are already disappearing, and in a few centuries at most, will have given place to more fertile races. . . .[54]

And in 1903 President Theodore Roosevelt thundered to the nation the danger of "race suicide":

> Among human beings, as among all other living creatures, if the best specimens do not, and the poorer specimens do, propagate, the type [race] will go down. If Americans of the old stock lead lives of celibate selfishness . . . or if the married are afflicted by that base fear of living which, whether for the

sake of themselves or of their children, forbids them to have more than one or two children, disaster awaits the nation.[55]

G. Stanley Hall and other expert observers easily connected the falling WASP birth rate to the epidemic of female invalidism:

> In the United States as a whole from 1860–'90 the birth-rate declined from 25.61 to 19.22. Many women are so exhausted before marriage that after bearing one or two children they become wrecks, and while there is perhaps a growing dread of parturition or of the bother of children, many of the best women feel they have not stamina enough. . . .[56]

He went on to suggest that "if women do not improve," men would have to "have recourse to emigrant wives" or perhaps there would have to be a "new rape of the Sabines."

The genetic challenge posed by the "poorer elements" cast an unflattering light on the female invalid. No matter whether she was "really" suffering, she was clearly not doing her duty. Sympathy begins to give way to the suspicion that she might be deliberately *malingering*. S. Weir Mitchell revealed his private judgment of his patients in his novels, which dwelt on the grasping, selfish invalid, who uses her illness to gain power over others. In *Roland Blake* (1886) the evil invalid "Octapia" tries to squeeze the life out of her gentle cousin Olivia. In *Constance Trescot* (1905) the heroine is a domineering, driven woman, who ruins her husband's life and then relapses into invalidism in an attempt to hold on to her patient sister Susan:

> By degrees Susan also learned that Constance relied on her misfortune and her long illness to insure to her an excess of sympathetic affection and unremitting service. The discoveries thus made troubled the less selfish sister. . . .[57]

The story ends in a stinging rejection for Constance, as Susan leaves her to get married and assume the more womanly role of serving a man. Little did Dr. Mitchell's patients suspect that his ideal woman was not the delicate lady on the bed, but the motherly figure of the nurse in the background! (In fact, Mitchell's rest cure was implicitly based on the idea that his patients were malingerers.) As he explained it, the idea was to provide the patient with a drawn-out experience of invalidism, but without any of the pleasures and perquisites which usually went with that condition.

> To lie abed half the day, and sew a little and read a little, and be interesting and excite sympathy, is all very well, but when they are bidden to stay in bed a month and neither to read, write, nor sew, and to have one nurse,—who is not a relative,— then rest becomes for some women a rather bitter medicine, and they are glad enough to accept the order to rise and go about when the doctor issues a mandate . . .[58]

Many women probably *were* using the sick role as a way to escape their reproductive and domestic duties. For the woman to whom sex really was repugnant, and yet a "duty," or for any woman who wanted to avoid pregnancy, sickness was a way out—and there were few others. The available methods of contraception were unreliable, and not always that available either.[59] Abortion was illegal and risky. So female invalidism may be a direct ancestor of the nocturnal "headache" which so plagued husbands in the mid-twentieth century.

The suspicion of malingering—whether to avoid pregnancy or gain attention—cast a pall over the doctor-patient relationship. If a woman was really sick (as the doctors said she ought to be), then the doctor's efforts, however ineffective, must be construed as appropriate, justifiable, and of course reimbursable. But if she was *not* sick, then the doctor was being made a fool of. His manly, professional attempts at treatment were simply part of a charade directed by and starring the female patient. But how could you tell the real invalids from the frauds? And what did you do when no amount of drugging, cutting, resting, or sheer bullying seemed to make the woman well?

Doctors had wanted women to be sick, but now they found themselves locked in a power struggle with the not-so-feeble patient: Was the illness a construction of the medical imagination, a figment of the patient's imagination, or something "real" which nevertheless eluded the mightiest efforts of medical science? What, after all, was behind "neurasthenia," "hyperesthesia," or the dozens of other labels attached to female invalidism?

But it took a specific syndrome to make the ambiguities in the doctor-patient relationship unbearable, and to finally break the gynecologists' monopoly of the female psyche. This syndrome was hysteria. In many ways, hysteria epitomized the cult of female invalidism. It affected middle- and upper-class women almost exclusively; it had no discernible organic basis; and it was totally resistant to medical treatment. But unlike the more common pattern of invalidism, hysteria was episodic. It came and went in unpredictable, and frequently violent, fits.

According to contemporary descriptions, the victim of hysteria might either faint or throw her limbs about uncontrollably. Her back might arch, with her entire body becoming rigid, or she might beat her chest, tear her hair or attempt to bite herself and others. Aside from fits and fainting, the disease took a variety of forms: hysterical loss of voice, loss of appetite, hysterical coughing or sneezing, and, of course, hysterical screaming, laughing, and crying. The disease spread wildly, not only in the United States, but in England and throughout Europe.

Doctors became obsessed with this "most confusing, mysterious and rebellious of diseases." In some ways, it was the ideal disease for the doctors: it was never fatal, and it required an almost endless amount of medical attention. But it was not an ideal disease from the point of view of the husband and family of the afflicted woman. Gentle invalidism had been one thing; violent fits were quite another. So hysteria put the doctors on the spot. It was essential to their professional self-esteem either to find an organic basis for the disease, and cure it, or to expose it as a clever charade.

There was plenty of evidence for the latter point of view. With mounting suspicion, the medical literature began to observe that hysterics never had fits when alone, and only when there was something soft to fall on. One doctor accused them of pinning their hair in such a way that it would fall luxuriantly when they fainted. The hysterical "type" began to be characterized as a "petty tyrant" with a "taste for power" over her husband, servants, and children, and, if possible, her doctor.

In historian Carroll Smith-Rosenberg's interpretation, the doctor's accusations had some truth to them: the hysterical fit, for many women, must have been the only acceptable outburst—of rage, of despair, or simply of *energy*—possible.[60] Alice James, whose lifelong illness began with a bout of hysteria in adolescence, described her condition as a struggle against uncontrollable physical energy:

> Conceive of never being without the sense that if you let yourself go for a moment . . . you must abandon it all, let the dykes break and the flood sweep in, acknowledging yourself abjectly impotent before the immutable laws. When all one's moral and natural stock-in-trade is a temperament forbidding the abandonment of an inch or the relaxation of a muscle, 'tis a never-ending fight. When the fancy took me of a morning at school to *study* my lessons by way of variety instead of shrieking or wiggling through the most impossible sensations of upheaval, violent revolt in my head overtook me, so that I had to "abandon" my brain as it were.[61]

On the whole, however, doctors did continue to insist that hysteria was a real disease—a disease of the uterus, in fact. (Hysteria comes from the Greek word for uterus.) They remained unshaken in their conviction that their own house calls and high physician's fees were absolutely necessary; yet at the same time, in their treatment and in their writing, doctors assumed an increasingly angry and threatening attitude. One doctor wrote, "It will sometimes be advisable to speak in a decided tone, in the presence of the patient, of the necessity of shaving the head, or of giving her a cold shower bath, should she not be soon relieved." He then gave a "scientific" rationalization for this treatment by saying, "The sedative influence of fear may allay, as I have known it to do, the excitement of the nervous centers. . . ."[62]

Carroll Smith-Rosenberg writes that doctors recommended suffocating hysterical women until their fits stopped, beating them across the face and body with wet towels, and embarrassing them in front of family and friends. She quotes Dr. F. C. Skey: "Ridicule to a woman of sensitive mind, is a powerful weapon . . . but there is not an emotion equal to fear and the threat of personal chastisement. . . . They will listen to the voice of authority." The more women became hysterical, the more doctors became punitive toward the disease; and at the same time, they began to see the disease everywhere themselves until they were diagnosing every independent act by a woman, especially a women's rights action, as "hysterical."

With hysteria, the cult of female invalidism was carried to its logical conclusion. Society had assigned affluent women to a life of confinement and inactivity, and medicine had justified this assignment by describing women as innately sick. In the epidemic of hysteria, women were both accepting their inherent "sickness" *and* finding a way to rebel against an intolerable social role. Sickness, having become a way of life, became a way of rebellion, and medical treatment, which had always had strong overtones of coercion, revealed itself as frankly and brutally repressive.

But the deadlock over hysteria was to usher in a new era in the experts' relationship to women. While the conflict between hysterical women and their doctors was escalating in America, Sigmund Freud, in Vienna, was beginning to work on a treatment that would remove the disease altogether from the arena of gynecology.

Freud's cure eliminated the confounding question of whether or not the woman was faking: in either case it was a mental disorder. Psychoanalysis, as Thomas Szasz has pointed out, insists that "malingering *is* an illness—in fact, an illness 'more serious' than hysteria."[63] Freud banished the traumatic "cures" and legitimized a doctor-patient relationship based solely on talking. His therapy urged the patient to confess her resentments and rebelliousness, and then at last to accept her role as a woman. Freud's insight into hysteria at once marked off a new medical speciality: "Psychoanalysis," in the words of feminist historian Carroll Smith-Rosenberg, "is the child of the hysterical woman." In the course of the twentieth century psychologists and psychiatrists would replace doctors as the dominant experts in the lives of women.

For decades into the twentieth century doctors would continue to view menstruation, pregnancy, and menopause as physical diseases and intellectual liabilities. Adolescent girls would still

be advised to study less, and mature women would be treated indiscriminately to hysterectomies, the modern substitute for ovariotomies. The female reproductive organs would continue to be viewed as a kind of frontier for chemical and surgical expansionism, untested drugs, and reckless experimentation. But the debate over the Woman Question would never again be phrased in such crudely materialistic terms as those set forth by nineteenth-century medical theory—with brains "battling" uteruses for control of woman's nature. The psychological interpretation of hysteria, and eventually of "neurasthenia" and the other vague syndromes of female invalidism, established once and for all that the brain was in command. The experts of the twentieth century would accept woman's intelligence and energy: the question would no longer be what a woman *could* do, but, rather, what a woman *ought* to do.

REFERENCES

1. Anna Robeson Burr, *Weir Mitchell: His Life and Letters* (New York: Duffield and Co., 1929), p. 289.
2. Charlotte Perkins Gilman, *The Living of Charlotte Perkins Gilman: An Autobiography* (New York: Harper Colophon Books, 1975), p. 96.
3. Gilman, loc. cit.
4. Charlotte Perkins Gilman, *The Yellow Wallpaper* (Old Westbury, New York: The Feminist Press, 1973).
5. Gilman, *Autobiography,* p. 121.
6. Catherine Beecher, "Statistics of Female Health," in Gail Parker (ed.), *The Oven Birds: American Women on Womanhood 1820–1920* (Garden City, New York: Doubleday/Anchor, 1972), p. 165.
7. Ilza Veith, *Hysteria: The History of a Disease* (Chicago and London: The University of Chicago Press, 1965), p. 216.
8. Quoted in F. O. Matthiessen, *The James Family* (New York: Alfred A. Knopf, 1961), p. 272.
9. Quoted in Irving H. Bartlett, *Wendell Phillips: Brahmin Radical* (Boston: Beacon Press, 1961), p. 78.
10. Quoted in Leon Edel (Ed.), *The Diary of Alice James* (New York: Dodd, Mead, 1964), p. 14.
11. We thank medical historian Rick Brown for sharing this story with us.

12. Thorstein Veblen, *Theory of the Leisure Class* (New York: Modern Library, 1934).
13. Burr, op. cit., p. 176.
14. Olive Schreiner, *Woman and Labor* (New York: Frederick A. Stokes, 1911), p. 98.
15. John C. Gunn, M.D., *Gunn's New Family Physician* (New York: Saalfield Publishing, 1924), p. 120.
16. New York Public Library Picture Collection, no source given.
17. Dr. Mary Putnam Jacobi, "On Female Invalidism," in Nancy F. Cott (ed.), *Root of Bitterness: Documents of the Social History of American Women* (New York: E. P. Dutton, 1972), p. 307.
18. John S. Haller, Jr., and Robin M. Haller, *The Physician and Sexuality in Victorian America* (Urbana, Illinois: University of Illinois Press, 1974), pp. 143–44.
19. Ibid., p. 168.
20. Ibid., p. 31.
21. Ibid., p. 28.
22. Gilman, *The Yellow Wallpaper*, pp. 9–10.
23. Quoted in G. Stanley Hall, *Adolescence, Vol. II* (New York: D. Appleton, 1905), p. 588.
24. Gunn, op. cit., p. 421.
25. W. C. Taylor, M.D., *A Physician's Counsels to Woman in Health and Disease* (Springfield: W. J. Holland and Co., 1871), pp. 284–85.
26. Winfield Scott Hall, Ph.D., M.D., *Sexual Knowledge* (Philadelphia: John C. Winston, 1916), pp. 202–3.
27. U.S. Bureau of the Census, *Historical Statistics of the United States, Colonial Times to 1957*, Washington, D.C., 1960, p. 25.
28. Rachel Gillett Fruchter, "Women's Weakness: Consumption and Women in the 19th Century," Columbia University of Public Health, unpublished paper, 1973.
29. Haller and Haller, op. cit., p. 59.
30. Emma Goldman, *Living My Life*, Vol. I (New York: Dover Publications, Inc., 1970, first published 1931), pp. 185–86.
31. Carroll D. Wright, *The Working Girls of Boston* (Boston: Wright and Potter Printing, State Printers, 1889), p. 71.
32. Ibid., pp. 117–18.
33. Lucien C. Warner, M.D., *A Popular Treatise on the Functions of Diseases of Woman* (New York: Manhattan Publishing, 1874), p. 109.
34. Quoted in Dr. Alice Moqué, "The Mistakes of Mothers," *Proceedings of the National Congress of Mothers Second Annual Convention*, Washington, D.C., May 1898, p. 43.
35. Goldman, op. cit., p. 187.
36. Quoted in G. J. Barker-Benfield, *The Horrors of the Half-Known Life: Male Attitudes Toward Women and Sexuality in Nineteenth-Century America* (New York: Harper & Row, 1976), p. 128.
37. Quoted in Elaine and English Showalter, "Victorian Women and Menstruation," in Martha Vicinus (ed.), *Suffer and Be Still: Women in the Victorian Age* (Bloomington: Indiana University Press, 1972), p. 43.
38. "Mary Livermore's Recommendatory Letter," in Cott, op. cit., p. 292.
39. Mary Putnam Jacobi, M.D., in Cott, op. cit., p. 307.
40. Frederick Hollick, M.D., *The Diseases of Women, Their Cause and Cure Familiarly Explained* (New York: T. W. Strong, 1849).
41. Quoted in Ann Douglas Wood, "The 'Fashionable Diseases': Women's Complaints and their Treatment in Nineteenth-Century America," *Journal of Interdisciplinary History* 4, Summer 1973, p. 29.
42. Quoted in Rita Arditti, "Women as Objects: Science and Sexual Politics," *Science for the People*, September 1974, p. 8.
43. W. W. Bliss, *Woman and Her Thirty-Years' Pilgrimage* (Boston: B. B. Russell, 1870), p. 96.
44. Quoted in Haller and Haller, op. cit., p. 101.
45. Quoted in Veith, op. cit., p. 205.
46. M. E. Dirix, M.D., *Woman's Complete Guide to Health* (New York: W. A. Townsend and Adams, 1869), pp. 23–24.
47. Quoted in Fruchter, op. cit.
48. Wood, op. cit., p. 30.
49. Barker-Benfield, op. cit., pp. 121–24.
50. Ben Barker-Benfield, "The Spermatic Economy: A Nineteenth Century View of Sexuality," *Feminist Studies* 1, Summer 1972, pp. 45–74.
51. It is unlikely that the operation had this effect on a woman's personality. It would have produced the symptoms of menopause, which do not include any established personality changes. Barker-Benfield, *Horrors of the Half-Known Life*, p. 122.
52. Ibid., p. 30.
53. Ibid., pp. 96–102.
54. Quoted in Theodore Roosevelt, "Birth Reform, From the Positive, Not the Negative Side," in *Complete Works of Theodore Roosevelt*, Vol. XIX (New York: Scribner, 1926), p. 163.
55. Roosevelt, op. cit., p. 161.
56. Hall, op. cit., p. 579.
57. S. Weir Mitchell, *Constance Trescot* (New York: The Century Co., 1905), p. 382.
58. Quoted in Veith, op. cit., p. 217.
59. See Linda Gordon, *Woman's Body, Woman's Right: A Social History of Birth Control in America* (New York: Grossman, 1977).

60. Carroll Smith-Rosenberg, "The Hysterical Woman: Sex Roles in Nineteenth Century America," *Social Research,* 39, Winter 1972, pp. 652–78.

61. Quoted in Matthiessen, op. cit., p. 276.
62. Dirix, op. cit., p. 60.
63. Thomas S. Szasz, *The Myth of Mental Illness* (New York: Dell, 1961), p. 48.

25

The Politics of Menopause: The "Discovery" of a Deficiency Disease

Frances B. McCrea

In the 1960s the medical profession in the United States hailed the contraceptive pill as the "great liberator" of women, and estrogens in general as the fountain of youth and beauty. Prominent gynecologists "discovered" that menopause was a "deficiency disease," but promised women that estrogen replacement therapy would let them avoid menopause completely and keep them "feminine forever." Yet within a few years, U.S. feminists in the vanguard of an organized women's health movement defined the health care system, including estrogen treatment, as a serious social problem. The male-dominated medical profession was accused of reflecting and perpetuating the social ideology of women as sex objects and reproductive organs. Treating women with dangerous drugs was defined as exploitation and an insidious form of social control.

These issues raised several questions: How did such diametrically opposed definitions evolve? How, under what conditions, and by whom does a certain behavior become defined as deviant or sick? In what context does a putative condition become defined as a social problem?

I believe that definitions of health and illness are socially constructed and that these definitions are inherently political. "Deviant behaviors that were once defined as immoral, sinful or criminal," according to Conrad and Schneider (1980:1), "have now been given new medical meanings" which are "profoundly political in nature" and have "real political consequences." Indeed "in many cases these medical treatments have become a new form of social control."

I interpret the definition of menopause from this framework. During the 19th century, Victorian physicians viewed menopause as a sign of sin and decay; with the advent of Freudian psychology in the early 20th century, it was viewed as a neurosis; and as synthetic estrogens became readily available in the 1960s, physicians treated menopause as a deficiency disease (McCrea, 1981). Perhaps more important than these differences, however, are four themes which pervade the medical definitions of menopause. These are: (1) women's potential and function are biologically destined; (2) women's worth is determined by fecundity and attractiveness; (3) rejection of the feminine role will bring physical and emotional havoc; (4) aging women are useless and repulsive.

In this paper I first analyze the rise of the disease definition of menopause and show that this definition reflects and helps create the prevailing ageism and sexism of our times. Then I show how the disease definition has been challenged from inside the medical community. Finally I examine how feminists outside the medical community have also challenged the disease model, claiming that menopause is normal and relatively unproblematic.

Menopause as Disease

The roots of the disease definition of menopause can be traced back to the synthesis of estrogens. The earliest interest in these hormones grew out of efforts to find a cure for male impotence (Buxton, 1944; Page, 1977). In 1889, Charles Édouard Brown-Sequard, a French physiologist, reported to the Société de Biologie in Paris that he experienced renewed vigor and rejuvenation after injecting himself with extracts from animal testicles. Four years later another French scientist, Regis de Bordeaux, used an ovarian extract injection to treat a female patient for menopausal "insanity." And in 1896 a German physician, Theodore Landau, used dessicated ovaries to treat menopausal symptoms at the Landau Clinic in Berlin. In the late 1920s, Edgar Allen and Edward Doisey isolated and crystallized theelin (later known as estrone) from the urine of pregnant women. In 1932 Samuel Geist and Frank Spielman described in the *American Journal of Obstetrics and Gynecology* their efforts to treat menopausal women with theelin. Such treatments, however, were expensive and supplies of the drug limited, since it was derived from human sources. These problems were solved in 1936 when Russell Marker and Thomas Oakwood developed a synthetic form of estrogen known as diethystilbesteral (DES). This cheap and potent hormone substance could be made readily available to a large number of women and paved the way for the development of the contraceptive pill. The last step in the development of hormone therapy occurred in 1943 when James Goodall developed an estrogen extract from the urine of pregnant mares. Termed conjugated equine estrogen and manufactured by Ayerst under the brand name Premarin, it was only about half as potent as synthetic estrogen, but it created fewer unpleasant side effects.

By the early 1960s, exogenous estrogen (that is, estrogen originating outside the human body) was widely available in the United States, and was inexpensive and easy to administer. It was used to treat various conditions of aging. But if estrogens were to become the cure, what was to be the disease?

> [Medicine] is active in seeking out illness. . . . One of the greatest ambitions of the physician is to discover and describe a "new" disease or syndrome and to be immortalized by having his name used to identify the disease. Medicine, then, is oriented to seeking out and finding illness, which is to say that it seeks to create social meanings of illness where that meaning or interpretation was lacking before. And insofar as illness is defined as something bad—to be eradicated or contained—medicine plays the role of what Becker called the "moral entrepreneur" (Friedson, 1970:252).

The moral entrepreneur who, during the 1960s, led the crusade to redefine menopause as a disease was the prominent Brooklyn gynecologist Robert A. Wilson. As founder and head of the Wilson Foundation, established in New York in 1963 to promote estrogens and supported by $1.3 million in grants from the pharmaceutical industry (Mintz and Cohn, 1977), Wilson's writings were crucial to the acceptance of menopause as a "deficiency disease" and the large-scale routine administration of Estrogen Replacement Therapy (ERT). He claimed that menopause was a hormone deficiency similar to diabetes and thyroid dysfunction. In an article published in the *Journal of the American Medical Association,* Wilson (1962) claimed that estrogen prevented breast and genital cancer and other problems of aging. Even though his methodology was weak,[1] this article launched a campaign to promote estrogens for the prevention of menopause and age-related diseases.

A year later, writing with his wife Thelma in the *Journal of the American Geriatrics Society,* Wilson and Wilson (1963) advocated that women be given estrogens from "puberty to grave." Crucial to the popular acceptance of the disease model of menopause was Robert Wilson's widely read book *Feminine Forever* (1966a), which claimed that menopause is a malfunction threatening the "feminine essence." In an article summarizing his book, Wilson described menopausal women as "living decay" (1966b:70) but said ERT could save them from being "condemned to witness the death of their womanhood" (1966b:66). He further proclaimed that menopause and aging could be allayed with ERT and listed 26 physiological and psychological symptoms that the "youth pill" could avert—including hot flashes, osteoporosis (thinning of bone mass), vaginal atrophy (thinning of vaginal walls), sagging and shrinking breasts, wrinkles, absent-mindedness, irritability, frigidity, depression, alcoholism, and even suicide.

Wilson also was aware of the physician's potential and even mandate for social control. The first paragraph of a chapter titled "Menopause—The Loss of Womanhood and Good Health" states:

> I would like to launch into the subject of menopause by discussing its *effect on men.* Menopause covers such a wide range of physical and emotional symptoms that the implications are by no means confined to the woman. *Her husband, her family, and her entire relationship to the outside world* are affected almost as strongly as her own body. Only in this broader context can the problem of menopause—as well as the benefits of hormonal cure—be properly appreciated (emphasis added, 1966a:92).

Wilson gives an example of how he helped a distressed husband who came to him for help with the following complaint:

> She is driving me nuts. She won't fix meals. She lets me get no sleep. She picks on me all the time. She makes up lies about me. She hits the bottle all day. And we used to be happily married (1966a:93).

This man's wife, Wilson says, responded well to "intensive" estrogen treatment and in no time resumed her wifely duties (1966a:94). In another chapter Wilson conjures up visions of Ira Levin's (1972) novel *The Stepford Wives:*

> In a family situation, estrogen makes women adaptable, even-tempered, and generally easy to live with. Consequently, a woman's estrogen carries significancy beyond her own well-being. It also contributes toward the happiness of her family and all those with whom she is in daily contact. Even frigidity in women has been shown to be related to estrogen deficiency. The estrogen-rich woman, as a

rule, is capable of far more generous and satisfying sexual response than women whose femininity suffers from inadequate chemical support (Wilson, 1966:64).

From Wilson's own words it is obvious that the disease label is not neutral. This label, like any disease label, decreases the status and the autonomy of the patient while increasing the status and power of the physician. When seen as part of a political process,

> knowledge and skill are claimed by a group to advance its interests. True or false the knowledge, disinterested or interested the motive, claims of knowledge function as ideologies. . . . insofar as claims to knowledge and skill are essential elements in a political process . . . it is highly unlikely that they can remain neutrally descriptive (Freidson, 1971:30).

By individualizing the problems of menopause, the physician turns attention away from any social structural interpretation of women's conditions. The locus of the solution then becomes the doctor-patient interaction in which the physician is active, instrumental, and authoritative while the patient is passive and dependent. The inherent authority of physicians is institutionalized in ways that minimize reliance on explanation and persuasion. This clinical mentality is "intrinsically imperialistic, claiming more for the profession's knowledge and skill, and a broader jurisdiction than in fact can be justified by demonstrable effectiveness" (Freidson, 1971:31). Such imperialism is independent of the particular motivation of the physician. Not only could it function as "crude self-interest," but also as "a natural outcome of the deep commitment to the value of his work developed by the thoroughly socialized professional" (1971:31).

A number of prominent U.S. physicians supported Wilson's claims. Robert Greenblatt (1974), former president of the American Geriatrics Society, claimed that about 75 percent of menopausal women are acutely estrogen-deficient and advocated ERT for them, even if they were without symptoms. Another crusader for ERT, Helen Jern, a gynecologist at the New York Infirmary, wrote a book of case studies proclaiming the miraculous recoveries made by elderly women placed on ERT:

> I know the remarkably beneficial effect of estrogen as energizer, tranquilizer and anti-depressant. I know that it stimulates and maintains mental capacity, memory, and concentration, restores zest for living, and gives a youthful appearance.... Hormone therapy, once begun, should be continued throughout a woman's lifetime. It is my firm belief that many female inmates of nursing homes and mental institutions could be restored to full physical and mental health through adequate hormone therapy (Jern, 1973:156).

David Reuben proclaimed in his best-selling book *Everything You Wanted To Know About Sex:*

> As estrogen is shut off, a woman comes as close as she can to being a man. Increased facial hair, deepened voice, obesity, and decline of breasts and female genitalia all contribute to a masculine appearance. Not really a man but no longer a functional woman, these individuals live in a world of intersex. Having outlived their ovaries, they have outlived their usefulness as human beings (Reuben, 1969:287).

But women need not despair. Reuben (1969:290) proclaimed that with estrogen replacements women can "turn back the clock," and adequate amounts of estrogen throughout their lives will protect them against breast and uterine cancer.

Throughout the late 1960s and early 1970s, Wilson's book was excerpted widely in traditional women's journals, and over 300 articles promoting estrogens appeared in popular magazines (Johnson, 1977). During the same period an aggressive advertising campaign, capitalizing on the disease label, was launched by the U.S. pharmaceutical industry. ERT products were widely advertised in medical literature and promotional material as amelioratives for a variety of psychological, as well as somatic, problems. One advertisement depicted a seated woman clutching an airline ticket, with her impatient husband standing behind her glancing at his watch. The copy read:

> Bon Voyage? Suddenly she'd rather not go. She's waited thirty years for this trip. Now she doesn't

have the "bounce." She has headaches, hot flashes, and she feels tired and nervous all the time. And for no reason she cries (Seaman and Seaman, 1977:281).

Another advertisement promoted ERT "for the menopausal problems that bother him the most" (Seaman and Seaman, 1977:281). Yet another advertisement stated; "Any tranquilizer might calm her down . . . but at her age estrogen may be what she really needs" (Seaman and Seaman, 1977:281). Such advertisements paid off: between 1963 and 1973 dollar sales in the United States for estrogen replacements quadrupled (U.S. Bureau of the Census, 1975). As one Harvard researcher stated, "few medical interventions have had as widespread application as exogenous estrogen treatment in post-menopausal women" (Weinstein, 1980). By 1975, with prescriptions at an all-time high of 26.7 million (Wolfe, 1979), estrogens had become the fifth most frequently prescribed drug in the United States (Hoover *et al.*, 1976). A 1975 survey in the Seattle-Tacoma area of Washington State revealed that 51 percent of all post-menopausal women had used estrogens for at least three months, with a median duration of over 10 years (Weiss *et al.*, 1976).

Indeed, 1975 was a watershed year for estrogen therapy; sales were at an all-time high and physicians routinely used estrogens to treat a wide variety of purported menopausal symptoms. Yet within a few years this trend changed as estrogen therapy came under attack from inside and outside the medical community.

Medical Controversy

Researchers had suspected an association between estrogens and cancer since the 1890s (Johnson, 1977). Experimental animal studies, conducted in the 1930s and 1940s, claimed that estrogenic and progestinic substances were carcinogenic (Cook and Dodds, 1933; Gardner, 1944; Perry and Gintzon, 1937). Novak and Yui (1936) warned that estrogen therapy might cause a pathological buildup of endometrial tissue.

Most investigators trace the roots of the ERT controversy back to 1947. In that year Dr. Saul Gusberg, then a young cancer researcher at the

Memorial Sloane-Kettering Hospital and Columbia University in New York City, made a histological link between hyperplasia (proliferation of the cells) and adenocarcinoma in the female endometrium (lining of the uterus). After finding a significant increase in endometrial cancer among estrogen users, Gusberg (1947: 910) wrote:

> Another human experiment has been set up in recent years by the widespread administration of estrogens to post-menopausal women. The relatively low cost of stilbestrol [synthetic estrogen] and the ease of administration have made its general use promiscuous.

Why was more attention not paid to these early warnings? In addition to the low cost and ease of administering estrogens mentioned by Gusberg, most scientists judged these early cancer studies to be scientifically unsound: those based on animal studies were dismissed as not applicable to humans. Perhaps most importantly, physicians found estrogens to be remarkably effective in alleviating vasomotor disturbances (hot flashes) and vaginal atrophy (Page, 1977:54). In his book *The Ageless Woman*, Sherwin Kaufman (1967:61) described menopausal symptoms as the result of hormone deficiency, and lamented:

> Many women are obviously in need of estrogen replacements but are so afraid of "hormones" that it requires a good deal of explanation to persuade them that estrogen does not cause cancer and may, on the contrary, make them feel much better.

Kaufman regretted that some of his colleagues also share this unwarranted fear of cancer:

> Some doctors prescribe estrogens reluctantly. . . . Historically, and too often hysterically, estrogens have been endowed with malignant potentialities. Paradoxically, it has been pointed out that even conservative physicians may not hesitate to give sedatives or tranquilizers, yet they stop at the suggestion of estrogen replacement therapy. This is baffling to a good many doctors (1967:67).

Kaufman confessed that "Years ago, I used to discontinue such treatment [ERT] after a few months," but "today I am in no rush to stop" (1967:64).

The ERT controversy erupted in 1975 when two epidemiological studies, by research teams from Washington University (Smith *et al.*, 1975) and The Kaiser-Permanente Medical Center in Los Angeles (Ziel and Finkle, 1975), found a link between post-menopausal estrogen therapy and endometrial cancer. The two studies, according to Ziel,[2] were written independently of each other and published side by side in the prestigious *New England Journal of Medicine*. By 1980, nine more studies, all done in the United States, concluded that women on ERT were four to 20 times more likely to develop endometrial cancer than non-users (Ziel, 1980). Moreover, the risk of cancer purportedly increased with the duration and dose of estrogens. Indeed, according to Gusberg (1980:729), endometrial cancer has "superseded cervical cancer as the most common malignant tumor of the female reproductive tract."

At a 1979 Consensus Development Conference on Estrogen Use and Post-Menopausal Women, sponsored by the National Institute on Aging, researchers unanimously concluded that ERT substantially increases the risk of endometrial cancer.[3] The final report of the conference concluded that ERT is only effective in the treatment of hot flashes and vaginal atrophy, and, if used at all, should be administered on a cyclical basis (three weeks of estrogen, one week off), at the lowest dose for the shortest possible time.[4] Any candidate for post-menopausal estrogen, the report recommended, "should be given as much information as possible about both the benefits and risks and then, with her physician, reach an individualized decision regarding whether to receive estrogens" (Gastel *et al.*, 1979:2).

Not only has the treatment of menopause come under criticism, the disease label has also been challenged by medical researchers. Saul Gusberg, who first warned of the ERT-cancer link, called the deficiency disease label for menopause "nonsense," adding "People are beginning to be more sensible about this, and realize that not a great trauma has happened to the average woman going through menopause" (quoted in Reitz, 1977:198). Research presented at the Consensus Development Conference in 1979 claimed that although ovarian production of estrogen declines after the menopause, older women need less estrogen. Moreover, production of the hormone by the adrenal glands partially compensates diminished ovarian production for most women (Ziel and Finkle, 1976). Furthermore, only 10 to 20 percent of women experience severe or incapacitating symptoms, and even those are generally temporary and decline over time (Gastel *et al.*, 1979; McKinley and Jeffreys, 1974).

Researchers have also criticized the disease model on ideological grounds. Ziel and Finkle (1976:737), two well-known cancer researchers, argued that the disease model was based on a traditional view of women's role:

Because they desire the preservation of cosmetic youth and the unflagging libido of the patients, physicians have championed estrogen replacement therapy in the hope of attaining a maximal quality of life for their patients.

The female patient, in turn, "is readily deluded by her wish to preserve her figure and her physician's implication that estrogen promises eternal youth" (1976:739).

Despite a strong consensus in the research community that ERT increases the risk of endometrial cancer, practicing physicians continued to prescribe the drug. As one San Francisco gynecologist stated after the 1975 cancer studies were published:

I think of the menopause as a deficiency disease like diabetes. Most women develop some symptoms whether they are aware of them or not, so I prescribe estrogens for virtually all menopausal women for an indefinite period (quoted in Brody, 1975:55).

Even though U.S. prescriptions for ERT have steadily declined since the 1975 cancer studies, some 16 million were written in 1978 (Wolfe, 1979). Indeed, a 1978 Detroit-area survey showed that two-thirds of all women who saw their physicians about menopausal complaints received estrogens and 50 percent received tranquilizers (Dosey and Dosey, 1980). In fact, a 1978 drug analysis by the U.S. Food and Drug Administration (FDA) concluded that menopausal estrogens, even after a major decline, were

still "grossly overused" (Burke *et al.*, 1978). My analysis[5] of 1979 estrogen replacement prescriptions revealed that 31 percent were still written for such vague diagnostic categories as "symptoms of senility," "special conditions without sickness," and "mental problems"—in violation of FDA specifications.[6]

Other measures of physicians' endorsement of ERT are authoritative references which describe menopause as a morbid condition for which estrogen therapy is indicated. For example, *The Merck Manual* (Berkow, 1980), a book of diagnosis and therapy widely used by physicians, lists menopause under "Ovarian Dysfunction." Modell's (1980) *Drugs of Choice* lists it under "Diseases of the Endocrine system." Both sources advocate estrogens for treatment. *Drugs of Choice* states that "objective studies" evaluating the risks and benefits are "not currently available" (1980:540). Likewise, *Current Medical Diagnosis and Treatment* (Krupp and Chatton, 1980:731) lists menopause under "Endocrine Disorders" and notes that "estrogen therapy has been recommended for life" but "the advisability of this practice remains unsettled." *Current Therapy* (Kantor, 1980:839) lists as benefits of ERT "improvement of disposition and unreasonable outburst of temper" and "avoidance of the shrinking and sagging of breasts." Attention is called to recent cancer claims, but "when doses are small and administration is in interrupted courses, "any potential risk is indeed small and perhaps theoretic." But a patient who has been frightened by "magazine articles" or "Food and Drug Administration bulletins" may "psychologically block the benefits" of ERT (Kantor, 1980:839).

U.S. physicians have viewed the use of ERT as a political issue, and their endorsement of the therapy as an exercise of professional control. Editorials in the *Journal of the American Medical Association* have been critical of outside interference in the doctor-patient relationship. A 1979 editorial criticized the FDA Commissioner for mandating a "biased" warning: "In doing so he has officially expressed his distrust of the medical profession" (Landau, 1979:47). A 1980 editorial castigated the FDA for creating unnecessary "public anxiety." Contradicting almost all the then-current U.S. research, the editorial concluded that "Estrogens already rank among the safest of all pharmaceuticals" (Meier and Landau, 1980:1658).

Menopause as Normal

In the late 1960s and early 1970s, U.S. feminists began to challenge medical authority by questioning the legitimacy of the disease model of menopause. They argued that menopause is not a disease or sickness but a natural process of aging, through which most women pass with minimum difficulty.[7] The medical problems that do arise can be effectively treated or even prevented by adequate nutrition and exercise combined with vitamin supplements. According to feminists, the menstrual and menopausal myths are a form of social control. If women are perceived as physically and emotionally handicapped by menstruation and menopause, they cannot and may not compete with men. The health care system legitimates sexism, under the guise of science, by depicting women's physical and mental capabilities as dependent on their reproductive organs.

Schur (1980:6) calls these struggles over collective definitions "stigma" contests, wherein subordinate groups reject their deviant label. Although economic, legal, and political power are often involved in stigma contests, "what is essentially at stake in such situations is the power of moral standing or acceptability." Thus, stigma contests are always partially symbolic, since prestige and status are important issues (Gusfield, 1966; 1967). Stigmatized individuals must rectify a "spoiled identity" (Goffman, 1963) through collective efforts. In the United States, feminists have tried to neutralize stigma by claiming that menopause is a normal experience of normal women.

On these ideological grounds, feminists have opposed the routine use of ERT. For example, an article, published in *Ms.* in 1972, before strong medical evidence against ERT was uncovered, maintained that menopause was not a traumatic experience for most women. Because menopause freed women from the risk of pregnancy, it was viewed as a sexually liberating event. ERT, seen as an attempt to keep women "feminine forever," was thus viewed as a male exploitation,

relegating women to the status of sex objects (Solomon, 1972). Four years later, offering a feminist interpretation of the menstrual and menopausal taboo, Delaney *et al.* (1976:184) stated that "the main fault of *Feminine Forever* lies not in the medicine but in the moralizing."

After medical evidence became available to strengthen the ideological arguments, feminist criticism became widespread. In *Women and the Crisis in Sex Hormones* (Seaman and Seaman, 1977), the ERT controversy received a 70-page analysis titled "Promise Her Anything But Give Her . . . Cancer." These authors warned against the increasing medicalization of normal female functions:

> Pregnancy or non-pregnancy are hardly diseases; and neither is menopause. The latter is a normal developmental state wherein reproductive capacity is winding down; the temporary hot flashes some women experience may be compared to the high-to-low voice register changes adolescent boys evidence when their reproductive capacity is gearing up. We no longer castrate young boys to preserve their male sopranos, nor should we treat hot flashes with a cancer-and-cholesterol pill (1977:xi).

In a collection of feminist critiques, Grossman and Bart (1979:167), two social scientists, make a similar claim in a chapter entitled "Taking Men Out of Menopause":

> . . . [the] actions of the medical and pharmaceutical groups dramatize the sexism and general inhumanity of the male-dominated, profit-oriented U.S. medical system. A "deficiency disease" was invented to serve a drug that could "cure" it, despite the suspicion that the drug caused cancer in women. That the suspicion has been voiced for so many years before anyone would investigate it is yet another example of how unimportant the well-being of women is to men who control research and drug companies who fund much of it.

The 1981 edition of *The Ms. Guide to a Woman's Health* warns women that "Estrogen replacement therapy (ERT) is a dangerously overused treatment. Avoid it if at all possible" (Cooke and Dworkin, 1981:310). The chapter on menopause repeatedly states that the change of life is not a disease but a normal process. Similarly, *The New Woman's Guide to Health and Medicine* states "The truth is that menopause is a positive or at least neutral experience for many women" (Derbyshire, 1980:269). Several other U.S. feminist publications, such as *Majority Report* (Lieberman, 1977) and *Off Our Backs* (Moira, 1977), have taken strong stances against ERT. *Mother Jones* condemned ERT in an article entitled "Feminine Straight to the Grave" (Wolf, 1978).

Though most of the criticism has been voiced by younger feminists, some older women have also opposed ERT. Reitz (1977:181) referred to ERT as "The No. 1 Middle-Age Con" and proclaimed:

I accept that I'm a healthy woman whose body is changing. No matter how many articles and books I read that tell me I'm suffering from a deficiency disease, I say I don't believe it. I have never felt more in control of my life than I do now and I feel neither deficient nor diseased. I think that people who are promoting this idea—that something is wrong with me because I am 50—have something to gain or are irresponsible or stupid.

Collins (1973:3), in an article in *Prime Time*, a publication devoted to ageist issues, stated:

Even today the literature . . . defines menopause as a deficiency disease. Of course that may sell estrogen, and we'll stay out of the controversy over whether that's a good thing or not. But it certainly echoes once more the male prejudice against menopausal and post-menopausal women.

Health-related associations and consumer groups have also joined feminists in their opposition to ERT. *Consumer Reports* (1976), the official publication of Consumers Union, published a lengthy article warning women of the risks; Citizens Health, Ralph Nader's organization, opposes (and regularly testifies against) ERT (Wolfe, 1979). Smaller groups such as Coalition For the Medical Rights of Women (Brown, 1978), and National Action Forum for Older Women (1979), have all warned women of the risks of ERT and advocated alternate treatment (diet, exercise, and vitamin supplements) for menopause. Menopause workshops and self-help groups have sprung up across the United States (Page, 1977).

After the 1975 cancer studies several feminist and consumer groups, including the National Women's Health Network and Consumers Union, began to pressure the FDA to warn consumers of the dangers of ERT. On July 22, 1977, after two years of public hearings, the FDA issued a ruling that a "patient package insert" (PPI), warning of the risk of cancer and other dangers, be included with every estrogen and progesterine prescription. On October 5, 1977, in an effort to block this regulation, the Pharmaceutical Manufacturing Association—together with the American College of Obstetricians and Gynecologists, the National Association of Chain Drug Stores, the American Society of Internal Medicine, and various state and county medical societies—responded by filing a civil suit in the Wilmington, Delaware, Federal District Court against the FDA. The plaintiffs charged that the FDA lacked statutory authority to require the patient package insert warning, and that such a requirement was an unconstitutional interference with the practice of medicine. They also asserted that such a regulation is "arbitrary, capricious [and] an abuse of discretion" (*Pharmaceutical Manufacturers Association v. Food and Drug Administration*, 1980).

To represent the interests of women patients, the National Women's Health Network, Consumers Union, Consumers Federation of America, and Women's Equity Action League filed as interveners in the lawsuit in support of the FDA. Three years later, in 1980, Federal District Judge Walter K. Stapleton upheld the FDA decision, giving estrogen replacements the distinction of being one of only four classes[8] of drugs which require such patient package inserts in the United States (*Pharmaceutical Manufacturers Association v. Food and Drug Administration*, 1980). Regulation, however, does not mean compliance, and the feminist victory appears more symbolic than instrumental. A 1979 FDA survey of 271 drug stores in 20 U.S. cities revealed that only 39 percent of all ERT prescriptions were accompanied by the required insert (Morris *et al.*, 1980). Moreover, under the administration of President Ronald Reagan, the FDA has suspended all proposed PPI regulations and is reconsidering existing ones (National Women's Health Network, 1981).[9]

Conclusion

In this article I have characterized the medical-feminist struggle over the collective definition of menopause as a stigma contest. Feminists have attempted to show that menopause is not an event that limits women's psychological or physical capacities, but a natural part of aging. Physicians have tried to explain the problems of middle-aged women through a medical model. In so viewing the life course, including menopause, physicians have tended to see problems experienced during menopause as either "all in the head" or the result of a deficiency disease, to be treated with tranquilizers or hormones.

The aging woman has a particularly vulnerable status in our society. She is no longer the object of adoration and romanticism that youthful women frequently are. Menopause usually comes at a time when children leave home, and husbands frequently seek younger sexual partners. Physical changes taking place in her body might be compounded, and negatively interpreted, by the loss of status and primary social role. Clearly, such women are vulnerable to the promise of a "youth" pill which purports to allay the aging process. Yet to blame all the problems that aging women experience on menopause is a classic case of blaming the victim. The medical model individualizes the problem, and deflects responsibility from the social structure which assigns aging women to a maligned and precarious status.

The vulnerable status of women makes fertile ground for medical imperialism. A health care system, based on fee-for-service, is conducive to defining more and more life events as illnesses. A disease definition of menopause has served the interests of both the medical profession and the pharmaceutical industry. Until these structural arrangements change, the hormone deficiency definition of menopause, or some equivalent to it, is likely to prevail.

Feminists, particularly those in the women's health movement (Ruzek, 1979) have exposed the sexism in women's health care. Publications such as *Our Bodies, Ourselves* (Boston Women's Health Collective, 1976) offered a new definition of women's role in health care. No longer passive consumers of male-dominated medicine, women asserted the right to control their own bodies.

Feminists in the health movement have begun to demystify menopause and have made it a topic for discussion. By making their stigma contest part of a broader-based social movement, feminists have been able to define women's health care as a social problem (Mauss, 1975).

....

NOTES

The author thanks Gerald Markle for his collaboration in the research; John Gilmore, Daryl Kelley, Ronald Kramer, Ellen Page-Robin, Ronald Troyer, and the anonymous *Social Problems* reviewers for their criticism of earlier drafts; and Agnes McColley for typing the manuscript.

1. For example, Wilson (1962) stated that 86 of the 304 women had undergone a total hysterectomy either before or during treatment without giving a reason for the hysterectomy (Johnson, 1977).
2. Harry Ziel, February 1, 1983: personal communication.
3. Other U.S. studies claimed that ERT increased the risk of breast cancer, atherosclerosis, myocardial infarction, pulmonary emboli, thrombophlebitis, gall bladder disease, and diabetes (Gastel *et al.*, 1979).
4. In Great Britain researchers are skeptical of the cancer link. They claim that sequential therapy (the addition of progestin for the last five to 13 days of a 20-to-30 day course of estrogen) would eliminate the potential risk of cancer. U.S. researchers claim that sequential treatment may not prevent endometrial cancer (Ziel, 1980:451) and the dangers associated with progestins have not been fully evaluated (Gastel *et al.*, 1979). British researchers also promote ERT for the prevention of osteoporosis (loss of bone mass), but U.S. researchers contend more research is needed on osteoporosis and, at this time, the established cancer risk outweighs the potential benefit of the treatment. For a discussion of the cancer and osteoporosis debates, see McCrea and Markle (In press).
5. The data for this analysis are proprietary, and were obtained from the IMS National Disease and Therapeutics Index, IMS America, Ltd., Ambler, Pennsylvania. IMS collects these data from a representative panel of 1,500 physicians who, four times a year, report case history information on private patients seen over a 48-hour period. For each prescription written, physicians report their diagnosis.

6. The FDA has found menopausal estrogens "effective" only for the treatment of vasomotor symptoms and atrophic vaginitis, and "probably" effective for "estrogen deficiency-induced osteoporosis, and only when used in conjunction with other important therapeutic measures such as diet, calcium, physiotherapy, and good general health-promoting measures." Furthermore, the FDA states that estrogens are not effective for nervous symptoms or depression "and should not be used to treat such conditions" (*Physicians Desk Reference,* 1982:641).

7. Although the majority of U.S. feminists, particularly those in the women's health movement, have defined menopause as unproblematic, there are notable exceptions. For example, Posner (1979:189) charges that feminists " . . . have been led into the ideological trap of denying their own hormones." Lock (1982) argues that physicians ought to pay more attention to physiology, and not dismiss women's medical complaints as psychological. British feminists also want more medical services made available in the treatment of menstruation and menopause (McCrea and Markle, In press; Sayers, 1982).

8. The other three are oral contraceptives, progestational drug products, and isoproterenol inhalation preparations used by asthmatics.

9. This was confirmed by the FDA official in charge of the PPI program, Louis Morris, May 11, 1983: personal communication.

REFERENCES

Berkow, Robert
  1980 The Merck Manual of Diagnosis and Therapy, 13th edition. Rahway, N.J.: Merck and Company.
Boston Women's Health Book Collective
  1976 Our Bodies, Ourselves. New York: Simon and Schuster.
Brody, Jane
  1975 "Physicians' views unchanged on use of estrogen therapy." New York Times, December 5:55.
Brown, Sheryl
  1978 "The second forty years." Second Opinion 1:1–10.
Burke, Laurie, Dianne Crosby, and Chang Lao
  1978 "Estrogen prescribing in menopause." Paper presented at the annual meeting of the American Public Health Association, Washington, D.C., November 2, 1977. Updated June 23, 1978.

Buxton, C.L.
  1944 "Medical therapy during the menopause." The Journal of Endocrinology 12:591–596.
Collins, Marjorie
  1977 "We are witness to ageism in the medical profession." Prime Time 5:3–5.
Conrad, Peter, and Joseph W. Schneider
  1980 Deviance and Medicalization: From Badness to Sickness. St. Louis: Mosby.
Consumer Reports
  1976 "Estrogen therapy: The dangerous road to Shangri La." Consumer Reports 5:642–645.
Cook, J. W., and E. C. Dodds
  1933 "Sex hormones on cancer-producing compounds." Nature 131:205.
Cooke, Cynthia, and Susan Dworkin
  1981 The Ms. Guide to a Woman's Health. New York: Berkeley Publishing.
Delaney, Janice, Mary Lupton, and Emilly Toth
  1976 The Curse. New York: E. P. Dutton and Co.
Derbyshire, Caroline
  1980 The New Woman's Guide to Health and Medicine. New York: Appleton Century Croft.
Dosey, Mary, and Michael Dosey
  1980 "The climacteric women." Patient Counseling and Health Education 2 (First Quarter): 14–21.
Freidson, Eliot
  1970 Profession of Medicine. New York: Harper and Row.
  1971 The Professions and Their Prospects. Beverly Hills: Sage.
Gardner, W.U.
  1944 "Tumors in experimental animals receiving steroid hormones." Surgery 16:8.
Gastel, Barbara, Joan Coroni-Huntley, and Jacob Brody
  1979 "Estrogen use and post-menopausal women: A basis for informed decisions." Summary Conclusion, National Institute on Aging Consensus Development Conference. Bethesda, Maryland, September 13–14.
Geist, Samuel H., and Frank Spielman
  1932 "Therapeutic value of theelin in menopause." American Journal of Obstetrics and Gynecology 23:701.
Goffman, Erving
  1963 Stigma. Englewood Cliffs, N.J.: Prentice Hall.
Greenblatt, Robert
  1974 The Menopausal Syndrome. New York: Medcom Press.

Grossman, Marilyn, and Pauline Bart
    1979   "Taking men out of menopause." Pp. 163–184 in Ruth Hubbard, Mary Sue Henifin, and Barbara Fried (eds.), Women Looking at Biology Looking at Women. Boston: G. K. Hall and Co.

Gusberg, Saul
    1947   "Precursors of corpus carcinoma estrogens and adenomatous hyperplasia." American Journal of Obstetrics and Gynecology 54:905–926.
    1980   "Current concepts in cancer." New England Journal of Medicine 302:729–731.

Gusfield, Joseph
    1966   Symbolic Crusade. Urbana: University of Illinois Press.
    1967   "Moral passage: The symbolic process in public designations of deviance." Social Problems 15:175–188.

Hoover, Robert, Laman Gray, Philip Cole, and Brian MacMahon
    1976   "Menopausal estrogens and breast cancer." New England Journal of Medicine 295:401–405.

Jern, Helen
    1973   Hormone Therapy of the Menopause and Aging. Springfield, Ill.: Charles C. Thomas Publishers.

Johnson, Anita
    1977   "The risks of sex hormones as drugs." Women and Health 1:8–11.

Kantor, Herman
    1980   "Menopause." Pp. 838–840 in Howard F. Conn (ed.), Current Therapy. Philadelphia: W.B. Saunders and Co.

Kaufman, Shirwin
    1967   The Ageless Woman. Englewood Cliffs, N.J.: Prentice Hall.

Krupp, Marcus, and Milton Chatton
    1980   Current Medical Diagnosis and Treatment. Los Altos, Cal.: Lange Medical Publications.

Landau, Richard
    1979   "What you should know about estrogens." Journal of the American Medical Association 241:47–51.

Levin, Ira
    1972   The Stepford Wives. New York: Random House.

Lieberman, Sharon
    1977   "But you will make such a feminine corpse . . ." Majority Report 6 (February 19–March 4):3.

Lock, Margaret
    1982   "Models and practice in medicine: Menopause as syndrome or life transition?" Culture, Medicine and Psychiatry 6:261–280.

McCrea, Frances
    1981   "The medicalization of normalcy? Changing definitions of menopause." Paper presented at the International Interdisciplinary Congress on Women, Haifa, Israel, December 28–January 1, 1982.

McCrea, Frances, and Gerald Markle
    In   "Estrogen replacement therapy in the United States and Great Britain: Different answers to the same questions?" Social Studies of Science.

McKinley, Sonja M., and Margot Jeffreys
    1974   "The menopausal syndrome." British Journal of Preventive and Social Medicine 28:108–115.

Mauss, Armand
    1975   Social Problems as Social Movements. Philadelphia: J.B. Lippincott.

Meier, Paul, and Richard Landau
    1980   "Estrogen replacement therapy." Journal of the American Medical Association 243:1658.

Mintz, Morton, and Victor Cohn
    1977   "Hawking the estrogen fix." The Progressive 41:24–25.

Modell, Walter
    1980   Drugs of Choice, 1980–1981. St. Louis: Mosby.

Moira, Fran
    1977   "Estrogens forever: Marketing youth and death." Off Our Backs (March):12.

Morris, Louis, Ann Meyers, Paul Gibbs, and Chang Lao.
    1981   "Estrogen PPIs: A survey." American Pharmacy 20 (June):318–322.

National Action Forum for Older Women
    1979   "Forum." Newsletter of the National Action Forum for Older Women 2(2):8.

National Women's Health Network
    1981   "Network fights to save PPI program." National Women's Health Network Newsletter 6(6):1–2.

Novak, Emil, and Enmei Yui
    1936   "Relation of endometrial hyperplasia to adenocarcinoma of the uterus." American Journal of Obstetrics and Gynecology 321:596–674.

Page, Jane
    1977   The Other Awkward Age: Menopause. Berkeley, Cal.: Ten Speed Press.

Perry, I.H., and L. L. Ginzton
    1937   "The development of tumors in female mice

treated with 1:2:5:6 dibenzanthracone and theelin." American Journal of Cancer 29:680.

Physicians' Desk Reference
1982   Physicians' Desk Reference. 36th Edition. Oradell, N.J.: Medical Economics Company, Inc.

Posner, Judith
1979   "It's all in your head: Feminist and medical models of menopause (strange bedfellows)." Sex Roles 5:179–190.

Reitz, Rosetta
1977   Menopause: A Positive Approach. Radnor, Penn.: Chilton Book Co.

Reuben, David
1969   Everything You Always Wanted to Know About Sex But Were Afraid To Ask. New York: David McKay Co.

Ruzek, Sheryl Burt
1979   The Women's Health Movement. New York: Praeger.

Sayers, Janet
1982   Biological Politics. London: Tavistock Publications, Ltd.

Schur, Edwin
1980   The Politics of Deviance. Englewood Cliffs, N.J.: Prentice Hall.

Seaman, Barbara, and Gideon Seaman
1977   Women and the Crisis in Sex Hormones. New York: Rawson Association Publishers, Inc.

Smith, Donald D., Prentice Ross, J. Thompson Donovan, and Walter L. Herrmann
1975   "Association of exogenous estrogen and endometrial carcinoma." New England Journal of Medicine 293:1164–1167.

Solomon, Jean
1972   "Menopause: A rite of passage." Ms. (December) 1:16–18.

U.S. Bureau of the Census
1975   Pharmaceutical Preparations, Except Biologicals. Current Industrial Reports, Series Ma28G(73)–1. Washington, D.C.: U.S. Government Printing Office.

Weinstein, Milton
1980   "Estrogen use in post-menopausal women—costs, risks and benefits." New England Journal of Medicine 303:308–316.

Weiss, Noel S., Daniel Szekely, and Donald F. Austin
1976   Increasing incidence of endometrial cancer in the United States. New England Journal of Medicine 294:1259–1262.

Wilson, Robert
1962   "Roles of estrogen and progesterine in breast and genital cancer." Journal of the American Medical Association 182:327–331.
1966a   Feminine Forever. New York: M. Evans
1966b   "A key to staying young." Look (January):68–73.

Wilson, Robert, and Thelma Wilson
1963   "The fate of nontreated post-menopausal woman: A plea for the maintenance of adequate estrogen from puberty to the grave." Journal of the American Geriatrics Society 11:347–361.

Wolfe, Sidney
1978   "Feminine straight to the grave." Mother Jones (May):18–20.
1979   Women in Science and Technology Equal Opportunity Act, 1979. Testimony before the Committee on Labor and Human Resources, Subcommittee on Health and Scientific Research. 96th Congress, 1st session. Washington, D.C.: U.S. Government Printing Office.

Ziel, Harry K.
1980   "The negative side of long-term postmenopausal estrogen therapy." Pp. 450–452 in Louis Lasagna (ed.), Controversies in Therapeutics. Philadelphia: W.B. Saunders.

Ziel, Harry K., and William D. Finkle
1975   "Increased risks of endometrial carcinoma among users of conjugated estrogens." New England Journal of Medicine 293:1167–1170.
1976   "Association of estrone with the development of endometrial carcinoma." American Journal of Obstetrics and Gynecology 134:735–740.

Case cited
Pharmaceutical Manufacturers Association v. Food and Drug Administration, 484 F. Supp. 1179, 1980.

Medicine in Practice

The social organization of medicine is manifested on the interactional as well as the structural levels of society. There is an established and rich tradition of studying medical work "first hand" in medical settings, through participant-observation, interviewing, or both. Researchers go "where the action is"—in this case amongst doctors and patients to see just how social life (i.e., medical care) happens. Such studies are time-consuming and difficult (see Danziger, 1979) but are the only way to penetrate the structure of medical care and reveal the sociological texture of medical practice. For it is here that the structure of medicine shapes the type of care that is delivered.

There are at least three general foci for these qualitative studies. Some studies focus on the organization of the institution itself, such as a mental hospital (Goffman, 1961) or a nursing home (Gubrium, 1975). Others examine the delivery of services or practitioner-patient interaction ranging from childbirth (Shaw, 1974) to dying (Sudnow, 1967). A third general focus is on collegial relations among professionals (e.g., Freidson, 1975; Bosk, 1979). All of these studies give us a window on the backstage world of medical organization. No matter what the focus, they bring to life the processes through which organizations operate and how participants manage in their situations. It is worth noting also that most of these close-up studies end up with the researchers taking a critical stance toward the organization and practice of medicine.

The four articles in this section reveal different aspects of medicine in practice. The papers represent a range of medical settings and situations: outpatient encounters, an emergency room, a physician review committee, and nurse-midwives' experience of home births. As well as illuminating the texture of medical practice, they individually and together raise a number of significant sociological issues.

In her study of the prenatal care of women, "The Uses of Expertise in Doctor-Patient Encounters During Pregnancy," Sandra Klein Danziger shows how the doctor's monopoly of medical knowledge, which manifests itself in an asymmetrical relationship between doctor and patient, is used by the physician to control the medical encounter. The women's health movement, among other health reform movements, has recognized the implications of the use of medical expertise as an instrument of power and has begun to challenge it.

In the second article, "Some Contingencies of the Moral Evaluation and Control of Clientele: The Case of the Hospital Emergency Service," Julius A. Roth demonstrates how everyday "prejudices" and evaluations by the staff of a patient's social worth affect the type of treatment people receive. (For another example of this process, see Sudnow, 1967.) Emergency room staff make moral judgments of patients' worthiness based on their evaluations of the patients' social attributes and the "appropriateness" of their demands on the staff. This not only reinforces and amplifies existing inequalities in medical care and services, but creates new ones.

Marcia Millman's article, "Medical Mortality Review: A Cordial Affair," takes us into the "backrooms" of medicine and describes how physicians deal with medical mistakes among their colleagues. It appears that the mortality review is essentially designed to neutralize physicians' mistakes (although, of course, not their effect on the patient) and to maintain the medical social structure.[1] It is the "professional dominance" of physicians that insulates them from outside review of their mistakes and confines medical errors to the purview of the physician's peers. It is not surprising, especially given the potential for malpractice suits, that physicians try to neutralize the meaning of their mistakes and downplay their importance, but the problem of accountability for medical error remains a central issue in the reform of medical care.

The final article in this section, "Midwives in Transition: The Structure of a Clinical Revolution" by Barbara Katz Rothman, gives us a look at an alternative conception to the dominant model of childbirth. Nurse-midwives attending home births are presented with anomalies to what they expected given the medical conceptions of birth. They found the "timetables" for normal labor and birth to be different in the home birth situation than in the hospital. Rothman argues that the hospital context shaped medical understandings of timetables for birthing. She shows how practice in a nonmedical setting can influence the construction and reconstruction of medical knowledge—in this case, timetables for birth—and create an alternative knowledge for health care.

All four articles highlight the structure of medical practice. Each illustrates how the social organization of medicine constrains and shapes the physician's work. Aside from delivering services, it appears that a very important element of the physician's task is sustaining the medical order in which services are delivered, although there can be meaningful challenges.

NOTE

1. In a recent study, Bosk (1979) conceptualizes different types of medical errors and implies that neutralization of mistakes may be less widespread than indicated by Millman's findings.

REFERENCES

Bosk, Charles L. 1979. Forgive and Remember: Managing Medical Failure. Chicago: University of Chicago Press.

Danziger, Sandra Klein. 1979. "On doctor watching: Fieldwork in medical settings." Urban Life 7 (January): 513–31.

Freidson, Eliot. 1975. Doctoring Together: A Study of Professional Social Control. New York: Elsevier.

Goffman, Erving. 1961. Asylums. New York: Doubleday.
Gubrium, Jabar. 1975. Living and Dying at Murray Manor. New York: St. Martin's Press.
Shaw, Nancy Stoller. 1974. Forced Labor: Maternity Care in the United States. New York: Pergamon.
Sudnow, David. 1967. Passing On: The Social Organization of Dying. Englewood Cliffs, N.J.: Prentice-Hall.

26

The Uses of Expertise in Doctor-Patient Encounters During Pregnancy

Sandra Klein Danziger

Doctor-patient relationships typically bring together two people with very different interests. One is preoccupied with his/her work concerns, while the other is absorbed in his/her own personal well-being. In our society the state of the individual's well-being is largely in the hands of experts, who assess its status and designate ways to improve it. That people turn to others as experts implies that these others are in some sense "special". They have privileged access to knowledge, resources and skills that presumably can benefit the lay person. How such expertise is employed conversationally in the course of delivering medical care to pregnant women is the focus of this paper.

In theory, every interactional encounter between a physician and patient, whether surgery or a blood test is administered, whether contraception or chemotherapy is prescribed, is a situation in which medical information may be exchanged. How much information is given and how closely it approximates the physician's "real" assessment of the situation may depend in part upon two interactional factors: (a) the doctor's expressed interest in imparting expertise to the patient; and (b) the compatibility between this interest of the doctor and that of the patient in receiving the medical information or expertise.

An asymmetry between lay person and expert arises, then, from the former having to satisfy two conditions of the interaction. The lay person wants both to appear compatible with the expert and meet the need for which the expert's help is sought. In other words, suppose person A wants advice from expert B. In order for A to get B to give the desired quality and quantity of advice, A must fit into B's notions of the type of patient with the type of problem that warrants this particular type of advice giving. In contrast to the Parsonian notion of the medical professional's affective/value neutrality, I am suggesting that people in our society may expect doctors to hold rather typified views of their patients. Because of this, they assume a particular patient role when interacting with medical experts. They attempt to defer in a passive or submissive manner. One implication of their taking this role position is that the doctors are permitted a more active role in controlling or structuring the course of an interaction sequence with a patient.

Two major variables, setting of the interaction and behavioral role repertoire of the individuals, obviously contribute to this asymmetry. First, the import of the factor of locale (and social organization thereof) cannot be underestimated. Compare the situation in which all medical encounters take place on the physician's turf, i.e. where the one person practices on a daily, routine basis and the other "visits" only infrequently and/or irregularly, with what may be the case when the doctor makes house calls, visits to settings where patients live and/or work. See Mehl (1) for a discussion of these differences with regard to home vs hospital childbirth. The other important point to be made here is that the amount of deference vs control exhibited during the encounter may or may not be related to what either party does in other situations. The most persistently aggressive patient may turn out to be most compliant in terms of carrying out a prescribed treatment regimen. Likewise, the most submissive patient in an encounter may be the most noncompliant when out of the doctor's office. See Lorber (2) for an analysis of behavioral compliance to the patient role and medical outcomes.

Many other factors influence the degree of asymmetry between the status positions of doctor and patient. Some of these have been addressed elsewhere, such as socioeconomic background in Duff and Hollingshead (3), ethnicity in Shuval (4) and Zola (5), age, marital status and family size in Shaw (6) and gender in Nathanson (7). My interest here is to elucidate some patterns of *effects* of this status discrepancy in terms of one particular product of medical interactions, the information transmitted. In examining what occurs within this frame of interaction, I am characterizing the doctor and patient as engaged in a parry and thrust situation, giving each other cues about the amount of information sharing that is appropriate. The result is based on what the doctor indicates is appropriate and how this coincides with the patient's expressed interest in obtaining the expertise. The model rests on a theoretical assertion of structural asymmetry, the assumption that the doctor wields more power in controlling the course of conversation, that the patient is for two reasons the more deferential interaction partner.

Within this framework, then, we may conceptualize a continuum of interactional postures doctors can assume with respect to providing information and those that patients can assume with reference to seeking or receiving information. First of all, the doctor is in the autonomous position of having a monopoly on the applied uses of medical scientific knowledge, as argued in Freidson (8). In the encounter with the patient, a physician has the prerogative to define what is therapeutic and what is outside the bounds of consideration, what aspects of the case shall be deemed relevant and irrelevant, and what topics are open and what topics are not open for discussion between doctor and patient. Topical autonomy is also demonstrated in Roth (9), Davis (10) and Daniels (11). In this scheme, there are three styles in which doctors can express their orientation toward the imparting of knowledge. They can perform their services as medical experts, as medical counselors, or as medical coparticipants. Ort (12) and Sorenson (13) posit similar continuums. The expert acts as a technician and exhibits little willingness to discuss his/her plan of action and to impart knowledge to the client. The counselor displays more general, rather than merely technical wisdom. He/she is more informative in the doctor-patient encounter, authoritatively guiding the client through the therapeutic process. The coparticipant acts with recognition of the clients' need for valid information about his/her condition and encourages patient involvement in medical decision making.

The client or patient, on the other hand, is in an inferior position *vis-á-vis* the doctor with respect to information. Lacking the professional's knowledge, skills and resources is what presumably brings him/her to professional services in the first place. For other plausible reasons see Zola (14). Patients can interpret their role as recipient of services (see also Haug [15]) in one of three ways: as mere passive recipients; as active-dependent recipients; or as potentially knowledgeable participants. For a variety of reasons, the passive recipient does not seek information from the physician and is unresponsive to any attempt by the physician to impart knowledge. The active-dependent recipient seeks

Table 1. Positions on Information Sharing

	Doctor	Patient
Not interested	Expert	Passive recipient
In limited favor	Counselor	Active-dependent recipient
Strongly in favor	Teaching coparticipant	Potentially knowledgeable participant

assurance that the doctor is reliable and competent. A minimum amount of information is sought, enough to convince the patient satisfactorily of the physician's ability to handle the therapeutic process. This patient is unlike the third type, the potentially knowledgeable participant, whose interest in the doctor's expertise exceeds this minimum, and who exhibits a willingness to share in the responsibility of decision making, provides information and asks for feedback from the doctor. Physicians and patients thus act out the encounter in ways which convey their respective notions of how expert knowledge is to be shared. See Table 1.

Field Data on Pregnancy

To illustrate the various uses of expertise that occur when each party adopts one of these positions, field data on prenatal medical care in a U.S. midwestern city will be presented. Ethnographic observation was conducted over an eight-month period in 1975–1976 in two clinic and three hospital settings where specialist obstetrician-gynecologists and family medical practitioners work. One clinic was a medical-school-based teaching institution, while the other was organized as a private group practice. In studying the activities and interactions of doctors and nurses with "low-risk"[1] patients and spouses of patients, I utilized two observation strategies. First, I followed staff members through the course of a workday or clinic session in which they would see up to 15–20 patients who were at all stages of the childbearing process. Then, I followed longitudinally a subsample of a dozen women, attending all of their medical encounters from mid-pregnancy through their labor and delivery. The data include descriptions and conversations from 100 to 150 episodes of early and

initial-to-late prenatal care provided by a total of seven physicians to more than 30 patients.

Behavior toward expertise may have some special characteristics in the case of medical care during pregnancy. First of all, in obstetrics the doctor-patient relationship is frequently a male-female one. Knowledge is less likely to flow freely between the two participants when the physician's authority is reinforced by his maleness and the woman is in the role of recipient. The feminist literature abounds with descriptions of the way sex role typifications are exacerbated in health care services to women (16–19). Secondly, as McKinlay (20) and others have described it, pregnancy is a unique and ambiguous state for women. Being pregnant is not a usual condition; nor is it a medically pathological state. In pregnancy, compared to other situations in which people utilize doctors' services, relatively little medical intervention takes place. In its place, it is likely that a great deal of emphasis is placed on preventive health education during doctor-patient interactions. Thirdly, child-bearing women seem to feel an increased sense of vulnerability and need for supportive relationships from their families and their physicians (21, 22). Among the sample of women observed as patients in this study, I noticed a consistent avoidance of potential conflict with obstetrical care providers, physicians and nurses. Such avoidance may diminish the patient's efforts to obtain knowledge during encounters.[2]

Finally, certain dramaturgical aspects of prenatal care may further heighten the status asymmetry between doctor and patient. See Emerson (23) for an analysis of these contingencies in gynecological care. In all of these visits, the doctor has some routine technical tasks of monitoring the woman's and baby's vital signs and progressing development. For the most part, the woman was perched on an exam table while the doctor was standing over her performing these physical manipulations. S/he may have examined further for medical risks, such as to check for edema, and/or inquired about symptoms indicative of risk factors or onset of labor. The woman was usually dressed but with her abdomen exposed for physical access. The physician was almost always in medical garb. Toward the end of pregnancy, s/he may perform from one to several internal pelvic examinations, for which the woman is half-naked and draped, braced on stirrups. In these, the doctor assessed a woman's "progress" in terms of whether or not labor was imminent.

The pronouncement on these occasions was invariably ambiguous in this data set, e.g. "well you're probably not going into labor soon", or "you still might go any day now". More precise information about factors that facilitate ease or promote difficulty during labor was obtained and sometimes conveyed to patients, but doctors were generally quite guarded in their predictions. Symbolic aspects of doctor-patient interaction such as clothing and the manner in which tasks are performed are likely to affect the frequency with which participants adopt the various positions on information sharing, as are other background factors of personality and situation.

In examining what actually transpires during a patient's visit to the doctor, it is useful to note first how little time is spent on information transmittal. For example, Waitzkin (24) found in a pretest study that less than a minute of a 20-minute session was devoted on the average to communicating information about illness. Within this portion of each visit, the variability in information outcomes may fall into one of nine categories, given the position of each participant.

Depending on which participant takes the initiative, the informing occasion takes two forms. One instance is that of the patient asking a question or bringing up a topic for discussion. The physician, on the other hand, is likely to initiate information sharing at a juncture in the session between completing one set of tasks and starting another, such as between the routine physical check and the charting of notes on the patient's medical record. S/he may typically comment upon the patient's progress or situation, describe a procedure or physiological development, or ask the patient if s/he has any questions or troubles to present to the doctor.

Each example from the data is thus characterized by either a patient's inquiry for medical information or a doctor's offering of information. Each participant's contribution to the exchange is classified as exemplifying one of the three relative positions of interest in sharing expertise. This is derived from what is said between the participants directly in the encounters and from descriptive accounts of the observer's interactions with either patient or doctor. The range of possible outcomes is presented in Table 2.

Each of the nine cells represents a different conversational use of expertise, five of which will be illustrated with pregnancy data. These five have been chosen because they represent the three cases of compatible expressions and the two cases of incompatibility in the extreme.

Table 2. Conversational Uses of Expertise

| Type of patient behavior | Type of physician behavior | | |
	Expert	*Counselor*	*Coparticipant*
Passive recipient	Perfunctory 1,1	1,2	Hostile: antagonistic 1,3
Active-dependent recipient	2,1	Protective 2,2	2,3
Potentially knowledgeable participant	Hostile: arrogant 3,1	3,2	Educative 3,3

Perfunctory Use

When the doctor[3] acts as a technical expert and the patient as passive recipient (cell 1,1), the doctor's preexisting monopoly of knowledge does not change, and little information is transmitted during the encounter. This situation is characteristic of the perfunctory relationship, in which services are provided in a way similar to the way plumbers fix plumbing and mechanics repair cars. To such experts providing information to the owner of the car is extraneous to the job of getting the engine running. The perfunctory interchange between doctor and patient emphasizes that the service is a technical matter; communication never advances beyond the expert obtaining medical history and physical information and the patient describing symptoms or asking how to take prescribed medication. The person in the recipient status is treated as a work object, that which is to be operated on; the model of the surgical relationship (see Szasz and Hollander's models in Wilson and Bloom [25]) fits most closely into this category of exchange. The following example from the data on prenatal care illustrates perfunctory information sharing. Relatively little knowledge is imparted in this situation, a routine late pregnancy visit by a woman who suspected she was in labor. The doctor determined that it was "just" a case of stomach flu.

> Well, other than that [the flu and the fact that she isn't in labor], everything looks good. Your blood pressure's good, you're growing, the baby's fine. You've lost a pound; that's probably from the flu.... Well, I think you'll probably go in a day or so, but you ought to go ahead and make another appointment for next week. Dr. ——— will want to do a pelvic exam if you don't, so just in case...

No interpretation of the situation was sought or volunteered. He read off the checklist of things he was recording on the chart without responding to the fact that she had been up all night with cramps, nausea and diarrhea. When she came in, the patient told the nurse that she was uncertain whether she was both sick and in labor; she left with the knowledge that she was only sick and still waiting for labor. The doctor pronounced her condition without elaborating and without expressing any personal sympathy. This perfunctory provision of service thus resulted in no transmission of expertise and no patient involvement in the decision or assessment process.

Protective Use

When the doctor acts as a counselor and the patient as an active-dependent recipient (cell 2,2), the result is the sharing of some knowledge in conjunction with a reaffirmation of the doctor's controlling authority. This provision of information-with-reassurance falls in the category of protective outcomes. Services are rendered in a style characteristic of the benefactor-beneficiary relationship. The source of the benefactor's knowledge remains inaccessible to the patient. Many variations in counseling styles from the manner of a high priest or generalized wise man to that of a more mundane problem solver like a tax accountant, are characterized by this information sharing with assurance. The expertise is applied in a way that emphasizes the special importance of the professional and the deficiencies of the lay person. In medicine, reassuring patients is considered to have great therapeutic value; the profession's ethics give higher priority to courtesy and kindliness than to the patient's right to know. The result is that the information given sometimes does not match the doctor's actual perception of the situation. This is especially common during labor and delivery, when patients are often told only how "well" they are doing, despite the fact that the doctor may be worried and may even be planning contingency strategies for intervening in the birth process.

For example, doctors often assume that the question "How am I doing?" carries an implicit answer, i.e. that patients *want* to be told, "You're doing fine". Doctors presume that patients who ask this do not necessarily want to know what the doctor *really* thinks. One physician commented to me about a patient's question, "some people just beg you to lie to them". Such a patient differs from a passive and non-questioning patient in seeking some kind of information from the doctor. Whichever party initiates the imparting of information and/or the provision of reassurance, they both respond compatibly in the protective use of expertise. This may be contrasted with the situations represented by any of the other four cells in the table: 1,2; 2,1; 3,2; and 2,3. In each of these, only one party initiates assurance-provision, and the other acts with more or less interest in sharing information. The result that is negotiated is marred by less acceptance of the doctor's authority to define the situation than in the more compatible protective case. The following exchange between a doctor and a patient's husband during the woman's regular prenatal visit illustrates protective information sharing. At this point in the session, the doctor has just explained her situation by telling them that with suspected preeclampsia,[4] he advises women to get a lot of rest.

> HUSBAND: Why wouldn't they just go ahead and induce her then?
> DOCTOR: Okay . . . her symptoms aren't really clear enough to suggest something like that is warranted . . . (talk of symptoms) . . . You know, if it were really something we were concerned about, we would start to think of her pregnancy as causing excess strain. But my thinking at this point is that everything is really coming along well but that we just want to make sure it stays that way.
> HUSBAND: Well, you know more about this than I do, but I just couldn't understand why wait when this thing seemed, you know, like it was pretty serious.
> DOCTOR: Oh, gee, I hope I didn't alarm you. Were you worried, ———?
> PATIENT: Well, uh . . .
> HUSBAND: She sure was . . .
> DOCTOR: Well we can't have you worried; that defeats the whole purpose. . . . I hope it's clear now that we aren't terribly concerned and there's nothing to be afraid of, but we just want you to stay well. . . .

The doctor expends most of his verbal energy on assuring them that they need not worry. Deferring to the doctor's superior knowledge, the husband is readily convinced not to press for more information. This doctor told me that he purposely did not go into much detail about induction, that he did not want to be too specific in the event that he changed his mind about its necessity. He was protecting his own autonomy to act without having to justify his decision to the patient. Likewise, the patient displays satisfaction in hearing that the doctor has his reasons, but does not persist in being told what they are.

Educative Use

Another category of compatible behaviors occurs when both parties participate in the sharing of expertise: the doctor acts as coparticipant and the patient as potentially knowledgeable participant (cell 3,3). The product of educative relationships is cooperative decision making and a relatively open feedback situation. Like teachers with students, doctors in this type of interaction spend time explaining procedures to patients, emphasizing the importance of the patient's understanding and involvement in the therapeutic process. The patient expresses interest in acquiring his/her own perspective on the problem at hand, rather than merely deferring to the opinion of the professional. Both parties treat the learning process as intrinsic to the provision of service. The following excerpt from the data—a discussion of breastfeeding during a regular prenatal visit—illustrates the mutual sharing of both information and decision making.

> PATIENT: Oh, I have something else. I'm planning to try to breastfeed the thing and . . . when do they have you start, right away or after a day or so?
> DOCTOR: Whenever you want to.
> PATIENT: Well, which is best?
> DOCTOR: Oh, it depends. It's better for the milk coming in to start as soon as possible. But if you're not up to it, you don't have to. . . .
> PATIENT: But then do they give it formula?
> DOCTOR: No, not necessarily. Listen, the whole thing about breastfeeding is *not* to worry about it and to really want to do it. If you have *any* doubts about it, chances are you'll have trouble.
> PATIENT: Well, I'm not hung up over it or anything. I've got a friend who is really uptight and I can't understand that at all. No, that's not for me. But how do the gals over there in the nursery react to it?
> DOCTOR: Well, we have really come full swing. You know, way back when, it used to be that if you didn't breastfeed, it was somehow not right.

Then, it got to if you did breastfeed, it just wasn't nice or something. Now, we're back to if you don't, you're almost bad. It doesn't matter really one way or the other. I've seen healthy babies on both. I've seen psychologically sound, good relationships both ways. So it's really up to you to do what suits you best. Soooo. . . .

PATIENT: So! Okay, that's all my questions, then. . . .

In this instance, the patient is left to decide what to consider therapeutic. The doctor merely presents the choice and suggests that she follow her own emotional feelings about it. She is clearly free to question him further on the issue. The woman's expressed interest in knowing is compatible with the doctor's view of her as the able and competent decision maker with whom the ultimate responsibility for this matter should rest.

Hostile Uses

The previous three categories represent the results of the most compatible behaviors of doctor and patient. The next two types of uses of expertise occur when the doctor and patient act most dissimilarly with respect to information sharing. The situation of the antagonistic type of hostility occurs when the doctor acts as a coparticipant and the patient as the passive recipient (cell 1,3). This occurs, for example, when the patient is unwilling to comply with medical orders and the physician tries to convince the patient of the seriousness of the situation. The information as to severity of condition is perceived by the doctor as intrinsic to the provision of service while it is irrelevant for the patient.

The arrogant type of hostility occurs when the doctor acts as mere technical expert and the patient acts as potentially knowledgeable participant (cell 3,1). Conflict can result from a patient's wanting to know more than the doctor wants to discuss with her/him. Both types of exchanges can result in the doctor's attempting to resolve the conflict and achieve control of the situation by distorting the information given. In both cases, the patient's expressed attitude to-

ward information is defined by the doctor as inappropriate: in the case of antagonism, the doctor may try to convince the patient of the dangers of not following the prescribed medical regimen, perhaps by exaggerating these dangers beyond what the doctor "really" thinks they are; in the case of arrogance, the doctor may put down the patient's expressed wish for medical information by invoking his or her own superior authoritative wisdom, implying that the patient has overstepped his/her limits. Examples of both types are provided from the data. The following exchange illustrates hostile: antagonistic (cell 1,3).

DOCTOR: You obviously didn't do any of the things I told you. Your pressure's up.
PATIENT: (*Sheepish*) I guess I didn't.
DOCTOR: I'll tell you, you keep this up and I'll put you in the hospital. And if you think that's a threat, it's because it is. I'm threatening you to make you realize you just cannot continue like this. Now what kinds of excuses are you going to give me for not doing what you're supposed to? (*Pause*) No excuses?
PATIENT: I've been busy? (*Sheepish giggle again*).
DOCTOR: Busy? You should be busy *resting* and that's all you should be doing! Did you have high blood pressure with your last pregnancy?
PATIENT: No, I don't think so. They didn't make a big deal out of it, so I would think not.
DOCTOR: Well, it is a big deal. It's the way mothers and babies die. Does your husband know you're supposed to be taking it easy?
PATIENT: Well, yes, but . . .
DOCTOR: This has got to stop. You are to do absolutely nothing except rest two hours in the morning, two hours in the afternoon, and be in bed every night by 9 o'clock.
PATIENT: My little girl isn't even in bed by then.
DOCTOR: Well, her father will have to stay up with her but not you. And if you can't do this, I'll put you in the hospital and put nurses on you who won't let you out of bed . . .

The harangue continued at length, with the doctor giving reasons for reacting so strongly, emphasizing that there is little he can do, that only she can do something about it. His reactions were exaggerated from the beginning, when he accused her of not heeding his advice; in fact, he had not previously warned her of her pressure elevation. In this exchange, the patient acted dumbfounded, and the doctor showered her with information on the severity of her situation and on what needed to be done, resulting in hostility and overly negative information. The last example of a situation in prenatal care illustrates the hostile: arrogant exchange (cell 3,1).

PATIENT: The nurse was saying they're doing the Leboyer method at the hospital?

DOCTOR: Leboyer, huh?

PATIENT: Yes. I was wondering what your opinion of it was.

DOCTOR: My opinion? Of Leboyer? It's unscientific. I'm tired of being told I'm cruel to babies! We don't do that bath business; nor would I do deliveries in the dark without gloves. So, I'm not the least bit interested in it.

PATIENT: Well, what about the things like nursing on the table right away? I thought we had talked about that earlier and you seemed to say that it might be okay.

DOCTOR: You can breastfeed whenever you want and as much as you want. I don't care, that's fine with me.

PATIENT: Hmm, okay.

First, the doctor puts the idea completely out of the question by invoking the canons of science. He simply cannot go along with such "nonsense" so she must not press the issue. The patient then tries another angle, which he permits as a reasonable request. The doctor leaves no room for discussion, but rather insists that his authority is unbendable. He later commented to me that "people who want it (Leboyer) are neurotic, and they want me to do some sort of magic that will change things." The patient's question was indicative of the fact that her attitude about participation was incongruous with her doctor's. The result was hostility and truncated communication with him biasing his comments with ridicule of the patient's ideas, thereby refusing to consider her input in the therapeutic process.

Other Uses

The four other outcomes represented in Table 2 occur when only one of the two participants takes a middle-range position on the continuum.

When the patient acts as active-dependent recipient with either an expert-acting doctor (cell 2,1) or a coparticipating doctor (cell 2,3), or when the doctor acts as counselor with either a passive (cell 1,2) or a potentially knowledgeable patient (cell 3,2), the resulting conversational use of expertise is more variable than in the cases of clearly compatible or incompatible expressions. In these situations, more subtle nuances of interaction are likely to determine the outcomes. The positions taken by each member are only slightly different from each other, which makes it probable that a host of other factors influence the results. The cases illustrating these categories might thus be quite dissimilar from one another depending upon who initiates what type of information sharing.

For example, in cell 2,1, the patient could ask for reassurance and receive a negative response from the technician type doctor such as, "Don't be silly, there is nothing to worry about". On the other hand, a doctor could be acting perfunctorily, to which the patient responds by requesting assurance. The result of this could be a polite, efficient "everything's going to be just fine". The products of such interactions are thus more subject to negotiation and less stable than the patterns described in the preceding five cells.

Summary

In summary, I have typologized doctor-patient encounters in terms of the participants' behavior with respect to expertise and the resulting quality and quantity of information exchanged. Of the nine possible classes of outcomes, five were illustrated with data on care during pregnancy. For any single doctor-patient relationship, the type of exchanges that are engaged in can vary over the course of the pregnancy, birth and postpartum period, and can even be mixed within a single encounter. The primary focus here has been to distinguish analytically the ranges of possible uses of expertise that result from the expressions of different interests in sharing knowledge.

In the first category, expertise is used perfunctorily. In the illustration, the doctor seems obliged to conduct some minimal amount of conversation, so he whips out an assessment of the patient's status. The discussion is apparently intrinsic to the rendering of his services. He merely verbalizes some pieces of his assessment while jotting down his notes on the medical record. The patient expresses no further interest in the information.

In the second category, expertise is used protectively. The doctor restricts his answer to a limited patient inquiry to a variation on the theme of "just leave these things to me and everything will be fine". This allows the doctor greater autonomy by asking the patient to entrust her/himself to the physician. The lack of further questioning from the patient, or in the example given the patient's spouse, appears to confirm the fact that this is all the information s/he is interested in obtaining.

In the third category, the transmittal of information is an intrinsic part of the delivery of the expert's services. The expertise is used to enhance the patient's decision-making responsibility for a therapeutic matter. The patient initiates the discussion of medical policy on breastfeeding, and the physician, despite his message about potential problems, conveys that it is primarily a matter of personal choice.

In the fourth and fifth categories of informing interactions, expertise is used to maximize the physician's power over the patient or, put differently, the lay person's dependency on the expert's control. Information is conveyed from the doctor with hostility of two types. In antagonistic situations, s/he provides an assessment of the patient's health status which exaggerates her problems by accusing her of noncompliance and threatening her with a description of the risks she runs by not abiding by doctor's orders. A more balanced assessment would describe the outcome potential both for doing what the doctor suggests and for not complying, thereby leaving the choice and risk taking up to the patient herself. In the illustration, however, the doctor told her only that if she did not heed his advice, she could die. In all likelihood, he was interpreting her passivity in the encounter as a confirmation of her negligence. He framed his expertise in an argument that suggested that she had no choice but to submit to his authority.

Finally, in the arrogant type of hostile ex-change, the physician reacts negatively to a patient's request for information. She asks what he thinks of a procedure; he interprets her interest as troublesome, as a misguided or inappropriate interest in medical expertise. He responds by distorting the weight of scientific evidence and refusing to entertain her request. Actually, the absurdity or merit of the Leboyer procedure has not been conclusively demonstrated. The doctor masks his intolerance of the patient's input by claiming his privileged access to superior knowledge. He uses his expertise to deny the patient the prerogative to question him on his own territory as he defines it.

Implications

The work settings through which the delivery of health care is "produced" have been extensively examined in the literature. Despite this fact, McKinlay (26) notes the lack of "empirical attempts to explore the various ways in which aspects of professional behavior may influence client-professional encounters". One way in which medical work has been illuminated is in terms of the social relations of one of its special resources, knowledge. Throughout the work of Freidson runs this theme of medicine's privileged monopoly on an ever-encroaching arena of expertise.

His analysis of the profession (8) raises the issue of the fine line between technical expertise and privileged social power. Medicine is viewed as a particular case of an occupational group with autonomy over itself as well as control over an enormous range of occupations in the hierarchy of the health industry. This autonomy, granted to the profession by society, is exercised in the practical routines of medical work in a way that violates the very conditions upon which it is guaranteed—that members will be self-regulating. Not only do clinicians practice avoidance of control over each other, but they are also segregated from each other in a way that reinforces this nonregulation and legitimizes it. The consequences are especially dangerous in the case of this type of consulting profession, since the expanding sphere of medical authority is growing at an unprecedented rate with very little pressure for physicians to become accountable to each other, much less to other groups in society.

Some of his suggestions of the dangers of medical control are based upon the work done by Scheff and others on illness as social deviance, particularly those illnesses classified as mental disorders. In *Being Mentally Ill*, Scheff (27) claims that "the medical metaphor of 'mental illness' suggests a determinate process which occurs within the individual: the unfolding and development of disease". This is sometimes a prejudgment of the issue that socially problematic behavior is symptomatic of existing underlying disorder.

The role of physicians in the process of deviance amplification or secondary career is developed as a uniquely biased type of official authority. The prevailing norm for medical decision rules in cases of diagnostic uncertainty is that it is better to judge a well person sick than a sick person well. To the extent that the public and physicians are biased toward diagnosis and treatment, the creation of illness or secondary deviation will occur.

A most recent extension of this argument has been conceptualized by Conrad as the process of "medicalization of deviance" (28). When an issue is discovered to fall within the rubric of the medical model of intervention, it is desocialized and consequently depoliticized. The crux of the issue of the "coming of the therapeutic state" thesis is for me the question of the peculiarity of this form of social control. How the medical model succeeds in controlling behavior is not so much an issue of use of pharmacological agents or surgical implementation. It is a matter of their occasioned legitimation in terms of the definition of the situation.

An understanding of this legitimation process requires an interactional perspective on what transpires in medical settings. Most of the studies of doctor-patient relationships, however, are not characterized by this dynamic orientation. Instead, they seek largely to explain the finding that communication between doctors and patients is problematic and filled with gaps (see for example Duff and Hollingshead [3]). Such "failures" in communication appear to produce patient dissatisfaction and varying degrees of lack of concern among physicians. In general, doctors are said to minimize the importance of the problem or to make excuses for it by referring to the harried nature of their daily clinical work.

Researchers have replied by suggesting the profound potential detriments to patient welfare that can stem from cognitive difficulties with health problems (see Skipper and Leonard [29] and Leventhal [30]). Others have framed the issue in terms of compliance (2) perhaps on the grounds that if doctors are not aroused by the specter of psychosomatic effects, they may "buy" the issue as significant for patients' motivation to carry out courses of therapy. Of most interest are the studies that have located the source of the problem in the attitudes and orientations of physicians toward their work (see for example Shuval [4], Waitzkin and Stoeckle [31], Waitzkin [24] and Comaroff [32]). However, what doctors and patients may want or expect of their interactions with one another is a different issue than: (1) what occurs during ongoing, situated transactions; and (2) how expected-actual discrepancies are resolved. Whether and, more importantly, how patients struggle to obtain more information and doctors actively engage in withholding information are unsubstantiated by a lack of empirical data.

Many theoretical models have been developed that depict this interaction process (Parsons [33], Freidson [34], Wilson and Bloom [25], Waitzkin and Stoeckle [31] and Leventhal [30]). The contributions of Glaser and Strauss (35), Davis (10) and Roth (9, 36, 37) all provide documentation of one processual aspect of these encounters. Each substantiates that information about prognosis is selectively conveyed to patients, resulting in a variety of consequences for the patient's perception and management of his/her illness. None of these, however, provides a framework to examine the way selective conveyances are produced in the course of the interactional encounter. While some even go so far as to categorize the content of what is conveyed, they do not analyze how it is that these information transmissions "work".

The question addressed with this model is thus not why communication "fails", but precisely how it is done and with what contextual implications. I have described both structural and negotiated interactional features that contribute to the power of medical expertise. Several dimensions of this typology lend themselves to further analysis.

Further Applications of the Model

First of all, the model suggests several hypotheses about relative frequencies of various uses of expertise. One could compare interactions in different settings or with patients at different stages of illness or with different types of problems. One could vary the doctor or professional expert variables as well as the patient or context characteristics in order to test for differences in information transmission. Were this particular data set large enough, I could compare the frequency of informing positions taken by the specialists and the family doctors and hold constant the stage of pregnancy, or the social status of the patient, or the number of patient-initiated requests for information. Another application of the model has to do with the way historical and societal pressures affect the quality of these interactions. Changing frequencies of types of exchanges occurring between one type of experts and their clientele might reflect changes in society or in technology.

In terms of longitudinal changes, one might expect that if the feminist movement is having an impact on medicine, it should become evident in a changing frequency of the different types of doctor-patient exchanges in obstetrics and gynecology (see also Kaiser and Kaiser [38]). While the *protective* patterns are currently the most common ones, we would expect feminist women to intensify their assertions of participatory rights in encounters with doctors. This would increase the number of *hostile: arrogant* and/or *educative* relationships, depending on doctors' reactions to the heightened interest of patients in medical knowledge and decision making.

Among other potentially influential factors are the changing technology of obstetrical medical care and the growing advocacy of patient's rights, particularly in the "natural childbirth" movement. These two factors are probably creating opposing pressures on physicians. While the scientific and technological advances encourage them to be more like experts, more medically specialized and problem oriented, the consumer rights groups demand that they be more like counselors or perhaps coparticipants, more family oriented and attuned to social-psychological and emotional considerations. The changing cultural contexts of medicine and of pregnancy and birth provide different notions of the way expertise should be used and thus have implications for the types of doctor-patient relationships that will proliferate and decline.

NOTES

The research for this paper was supported by a predoctoral Health Services Research Traineeship, National Institutes of Health, directed by George Psathas, Boston University, and by a postdoctoral traineeship from N.I.M.H., directed by David Mechanic. The author wishes to acknowledge the excellent comments of Diane Brown, Sol Levine, Camille Smith, Howard Waitzkin and two anonymous journal referees.

1. The term "low risk" designates the absence of well-known risk factors and forecasts these pregnancies as uneventful or uncomplicated.
2. A psychiatrist I spoke with supported this notion, which is also a popular belief: women hold their obstetricians in extraordinary regard and place them on a pedestal. Many reasons could be offered for this perception which are beyond the scope of this paper.
3. In quoted excerpts from the data, all doctors are referred to by the pronoun "he." While a few of the physicians in the study were women, revealing them as such would risk violating their anonymity.
4. Preeclampsia is a pathological condition of late pregnancy, characterized by hypertension, swelling and protein in the urine.

REFERENCES

1. Mehl, L. E. Options in maternity care. *Women and Health* **2**. 29, 1977.
2. Lorber J. Good patients and problem patients: conformity and deviance in a general hospital. *J. Hlth soc. Behav.* **16**, 213, 1975.
3. Duff R. S. and Hollingshead, A. B. *Sickness and Society*. Harper & Row, New York, 1968.
4. Shuval J. T. *Social Functions of Medical Practice*. Jossey-Bass, San Francisco, 1970.
5. Zola I. K. Problems of communication, diagnosis and patient care. *J. med. Educ.* **38**, 829, 1963.

6. Shaw N. S. *Forced Labor: Maternity Care in the United States*. Pergamon Press, New York, 1974.
7. Nathanson C. A. Illness and the feminine role: a theoretical review. *Soc. Sci. Med.* **9**, 57, 1975.
8. Freidson E. *Profession of Medicine*, Dodd-Mead, New York, 1972.
9. Roth J. A. Staff and client control strategies in urban hospital emergency services. *Urban Life Cult.* **1**, 39, 1972.
10. Davis F. Uncertainty in medical prognosis, clinical and functional. *Am. J. Sociol.* **66**, 41, 1960.
11. Daniels A. K. Advisory and coercive functions in psychiatry. *Sociol. Work Occupn* **2**, 55, 1975.
12. Ort R. S. *et al.* The doctor-patient relationship as described by physicians and medical students. *J. Hlth hum. Behav.* **5**, 25, 1964.
13. Sorensen J. R. Biomedical innovation, uncertainty, and doctor-patient interaction. *J. Hlth soc. Behav.* **15**, 366, 1974.
14. Zola I. K. Pathways to the doctor—from person to patient. *Soc. Sci. Med* **7**, 677, 1973.
15. Haug M. R. The deprofessionalization of everyone? *Sociol. Focus* **8**, 201, 1975.
16. Ehrenreich B. and English D. *Complaints and Disorders: The Sexual Politics of Sickness*. The Feminist Press, New York, 1973.
17. Frankfort E. *Vaginal Politics*, Quadrangle, New York, 1972.
18. Chesler P. *Women and Madness*, Doubleday, New York, 1972.
19. Boston Women's Health Collective. *Our Bodies, Ourselves*. Simon & Schuster, New York, 1971.
20. McKinlay J. B. The sick role—illness and pregnancy. *Soc. Sci. Med* **6**, 561, 1972.
21. Benedek T. The psychobiology of pregnancy. In *Parenthood—Its Psychology and Psychobiology* (Edited by Anthony E. J. and Benedek T.) Little-Brown, Boston, 1970.
22. Newton N. Emotions of pregnancy. *Clin. Obstet. Gynec.* **6**, 639, 1963.
23. Emerson J. Behavior in private places: sustaining definitions of reality in gynecological examinations. In *Recent Sociology* No. 2 (Edited by Dreitzel H. P.) p. 74. Macmillan, London, 1970.
24. Waitzkin H. Information control and the micropolitics of health care: summary of an ongoing research project. *Soc. Sci. Med.* **10**, 263, 1976.
25. Wilson R. and Bloom S. Patient practitioner relationships. In *Handbook of Medical Sociology* 2nd edn. (Edited by Freeman H. E. *et al.*) p. 315. Prentice-Hall, Englewood Cliffs, 1972.
26. McKinlay J. B. Some approaches and problems in the study of the uses of services—an overview. *J. Hlth soc. Behav.* **13**, 137, 1972.
27. Scheff T. J. *Being Mentally Ill*, p. 31. Aldine, Chicago, 1966.
28. Conrad P. The discovery of hyperkinesis: notes on the medicalization of deviant behavior. *Social Probl.* **23**, 19, 1975.
29. Skipper J. K. and Leonard R. C. Children, stress, and hospitalization: a field experiment. *J. Hlth soc. Behav.* **9**, 275, 1968.
30. Leventhal H. The consequences of depersonalization during illness and treatment: an information-processing model. In *Humanizing Health Care* (Edited by Howard J. and Strauss A.) p. 119. Wiley-Interscience, New York, 1975.
31. Waitzkin H. and Stoeckle J. D. The communication of information about illness: clinical, sociological, and methodological considerations. *Adv. psychosom. Med.* **8**, 180, 1972.
32. Comaroff J. Communicating information about nonfatal illness: the strategies of a group of general practitioners. *Sociol. Rev.* **24**, 269, 1976.
33. Parsons, T. *The Social System*. Free Press, New York, 1951.
34. Freidson E. *Professional Dominance: The Social Structure of Medical Care*. Atherton, New York, 1970.
35. Glaser B. and Strauss A. Awareness contexts and social interaction. In *Social Psychology Through Symbolic Interaction* (Edited by Stone G. and Farberman H.) p. 336. Blaisdell, New York, 1970.
36. Roth J. A. *Timetables Structuring the Passage of Time in Hospital Treatment and Other Careers*. Bobbs-Merrill, Indianapolis, 1963.
37. Roth J. A. Some contingencies of the moral evaluation and control of clientele: the case of the emergency hospital service. *Am. J. Sociol.* **77**, 839, 1972.
38. Kaiser B. L. and Kaiser I. H. The challenges of the women's movement to American gynecology. *Am. J. Obstet. Gynec.* **120**, 652, 1974.

27

Some Contingencies of the Moral Evaluation and Control of Clientele: The Case of the Hospital Emergency Service

Julius A. Roth

The moral evaluation of patients by staff members has been explored in detail in the case of "mental illness" (Scheff 1966, chap. 5; Strauss et al. 1964, chaps. 8 and 12; Belknap 1956; Scheff 1964; Goffman 1961, pp. 125–70, 321–86; Hollingshead and Redlich 1958; Szasz 1960). The assumption is made by some (especially Thomas Szasz) that mental illness is a special case which readily allows moral judgments to be made because there are no technical criteria to be applied and because psychiatric concepts in their historical development have been a pseudoscientific replacement of moral judgments. Charles Perrow (1965) stresses lack of technology as a factor which forces psychiatric practitioners to fall back on commonsense concepts of humanitarianism which open the way to moral evaluations of the clientele.

I contend that the diagnosis and treatment of mental illness and the "care" of mental patients are not unique in incorporating moral judgments of the clientele, but are only obvious examples of a more general phenomenon which exists no matter what the historical development or the present state of the technology. Glaser and Strauss (1964) put forward such a notion when they demonstrated how the "social worth" of a dying patient affects the nursing care he will receive. I would add that moral evaluation also has a direct effect on a physician's diagnosis and

treatment recommendations. This is obvious in extreme cases, such as when a monarch or the president of the United States is attended by teams of highly qualified diagnosticians to insure a detailed and accurate diagnosis and has outstanding specialists flown to his bedside to carry out the treatment. I will discuss some aspects of this same process as it applies on a day-to-day basis in a routine hospital operation involving more "ordinary" patients.

The data are taken from observations of six hospital emergency services in two parts of the country—one northeastern location and one West Coast location. My co-workers and I spent several periods of time (spread over two or three months in each case) in the emergency department of each of the hospitals. In one hospital we worked as intake clerks over a period of three months. At other times we observed areas in the emergency unit without initiating any interaction with patients, visitors, or personnel. At other points we followed patients through the emergency service from their first appearance to discharge or inpatient admission, interviewing patient and staff during the process. During these periods of observation, notes were also kept on relevant conversations with staff members.

The hospital emergency service is a setting where a minimum of information is available about the character of each patient and a long-term relationship with the patient is usually not contemplated. Even under these conditions, judgments about a patient's moral fitness and the appropriateness of his visit to an emergency service are constantly made, and staff action concerning the patient—including diagnosis, treatment, and disposition of the case—are, in part, affected by these judgments.

The Deserving and the Undeserving

The evaluation of patients and visitors by emergency-ward staff may be conveniently thought of in two categories: (1) The application by the staff of concepts of social worth common in the larger society. (2) Staff members' concepts of their appropriate work role. In this section I will take up the first of these.

There is a popular myth (generated in part by some sociological writing) that persons engaged in providing professional services, especially medical care, do not permit the commonly accepted concepts of social worth in our culture to affect their relationship to the clientele. An on-the-spot description of *any* service profession—medicine, education, law, social welfare, etc.—should disabuse us of this notion. There is no evidence that professional training succeeds in creating a universalistic moral neutrality (Becker et al. 1961, pp. 323–27). On the contrary, we are on much safer ground to assume that those engaged in dispensing professional services (or any other services) will apply the evaluations of social worth common to their culture and will modify their services with respect to those evaluations *unless discouraged from doing so by the organizational arrangements under which they work.* Some such organizational arrangements do exist on emergency wards. The rapid turnover and impersonality of the operation is in itself a protection for many patients who might be devalued if more were known about them. In public hospitals, at least, there is a rule that *all* patients presenting themselves at the registration desk must be seen by a doctor, and clerks and nurses know that violation of this rule, if discovered, can get them into serious trouble. (Despite this, patients are occasionally refused registration, usually because they are morally repugnant to the clerk.) Such arrangements restrict the behavior of the staff only to a limited extent, however. There remains a great deal of room for expressing one's valuation of the patient in the details of processing and treatment.

One common concept of social worth held by emergency-ward personnel is that the young are more valuable than the old. This is exemplified most dramatically in the marked differences in efforts to resuscitate young and old patients (Glaser and Strauss 1964; Sudnow 1967, pp. 100–109). "Welfare cases" who are sponging off the taxpayer—especially if they represent the product of an immoral life (such as a woman with illegitimate children to support)—do not deserve the best care. Persons of higher status in the larger society are likely to be accorded more respectful treatment in the emergency ward just as they often are in other service or customer relationships, and conversely those of lower status are treated with less consideration. (The fact that higher-status persons are more likely to make an effective complaint or even file lawsuits may be an additional reason for such differential treatment.)

Of course, staff members vary in the manner and degree to which they apply these cultural concepts of social worth in determining the quality of their service to the clientele. The point is that they are in a position to alter the nature of their service in terms of such differentiation, and all of them—porters, clerks, nursing personnel, physicians—do so to some extent. Despite some variations, we did in fact find widespread agreement on the negative evaluation of some categories of patients—evaluations which directly affected the treatment provided. Those who are the first to process a patient play a crucial role in moral categorization because staff members at later stages of the processing are inclined to accept earlier categories without question unless they detect clear-cut evidence to the contrary. Thus, registration clerks can often determine how long a person will have to wait and what kind of treatment area he is sent to, and, occasionally, can even prevent a person from seeing a doctor at all. Some patients have been morally categorized by policemen or ambulance crewmen before they even arrive at the hospital—categorization which affects the priority and kind of service given.

In the public urban hospital emergency service, the clientele is heavily skewed toward the lower end of the socioeconomic scale, and nonwhite and non-Anglo ethnic groups are greatly overrepresented. Also, many patients are in the position of supplicating the staff for help, sometimes for a condition for which the patient can be held responsible. With such a population, the staff can readily maintain a stance of moral superiority. They see the bulk of the patients as people undeserving of the services available to them. Staff members maintain that they need not tolerate any abuse or disobedience from patients or visitors. Patients and visitors may be issued orders which they are expected to obey. The staff can, and sometimes does, shout down patients and visitors and threaten them with ejection from the premises. The staff demands protection against possible attack and also against the possibility of lawsuits, which are invariably classified as unjustified. There is no need to be polite to the clientele and, in fact, some clerks frequently engage patients and visitors in arguments. The staff also feels justified in refusing service to those who complain or resist treatment or refuse to follow procedures or make trouble in any other way. From time to time the clients are referred to as "garbage," "scum," "liars," "deadbeats," people who "come out from under the rocks," by doctors, nurses, aides, clerks, and even housekeepers who sweep the floor. When we spent the first several days of a new medical year with a new group of interns on one emergency service, we found that an important part of the orientation was directed toward telling the interns that the patients were not to be trusted and did not have to be treated politely. At another public hospital, new registration clerks were told during their first few days of work that they would have to learn not to accept the word of patients but to treat everything they say with suspicion.

Despite the general negative conception of the clientele, differentiations are made between patients on the basis of clues which they present. Since this is typically a fleeting relationship where the staff member has little or no background information about the patient, evaluations must usually be made quickly on the basis of readily perceivable clues. Race, age, mode of dress, language and accents and word usage, and the manner in which the client addresses and responds to staff members are all immediate clues on which staff base their initial evaluations. A little questioning brings out other information which may be used for or against a patient: financial status, type of employment, insurance protection, use of private-practice doctors, nature of medical complaint, legitimacy of children, marital status, previous use of hospital services. In the case of unconscious or seriously ill or injured patients, a search of the wallet or handbag often provides informative clues about social worth.

Some characteristics consistently turn staff against patients and affect the quality of care given. Dirty, smelly patients cause considerable comment among the staff, and efforts are made to isolate them or get rid of them. Those dresssed as hippies or women with scanty clothing (unless there is a "good excuse," e.g., a woman drowned while swimming) are frowned upon and are more likely to be kept waiting and to be rushed through when they *are* attended to. We observed hints that certain ethnic groups are discriminated against, but this is difficult to detect nowadays because everyone is extremely sensitive to the possibility of accusations of racial discrimination. If a woman with a child is tabbed a "welfare case" (from her dress, speech, and manner, or in the explicit form of a welfare card which she presents), the clerk is likely to ask, "Is there a father in the house?" while better-dressed, better-spoken women with children are questioned more discreetly.

Attributes and Categories: A Reciprocal Relationship

On one level, it is true to say that the staff's moral evaluation of a patient influences the kind of treatment he gets in the emergency room. But this kind of causal explanation obscures important aspects of the network of interrelationships involved. On another, the definition of devalued or favored categories and the attributes of the patient reinforce each other in a reciprocal manner.

Take, for example, patients who are labeled as

drunks. They are more consistently treated as undeserving than any other category of patient. They are frequently handled as if they were baggage when they are brought in by police; those with lacerations are often roughly treated by physicians; they are usually treated only for drunkenness and obvious surgical repair without being examined for other pathology; no one believes their stories; their statements are ridiculed; they are treated in an abusive or jocular manner; they are ignored for long periods of time; in one hospital they are placed in a room separate from most other patients. Emergency-ward personnel frequently comment on how they hate to take care of drunks.

Thus, it might seem that the staff is applying a simple moral syllogism: drunks do not deserve to be cared for, this patient is drunk, therefore, he does not deserve good treatment. *But* how do we know that he is a drunk? By the way he is treated. Police take him directly to the drunk room. If we ask why the police define him as drunk, they may answer that they smell alcohol on his breath. But not all people with alcohol on their breath are picked up by the police and taken to a hospital emergency room. The explanation must come in terms of some part of the patient's background— he was in a lower-class neighborhood, his style of dress was dirty and sloppy, he was unattended by any friend or family member, and so on. When he comes to the emergency room *he has already been defined as a drunk*. There is no reason for the emergency-room personnel to challenge this definition—it is routine procedure and it usually proves correct insofar as they know. There is nothing to do for drunks except to give them routine medications and let them sleep it off. To avoid upsetting the rest of the emergency room, there is a room set aside for them. The police have a standard procedure of taking drunks to that room, and the clerks place them there if they come in on their own and are defined as drunk on the basis, not only of their breath odor (and occasionally there is no breath odor in someone defined as drunk), but in terms of their dress, manner, and absence of protectors. The physicians, having more pressing matters, tend to leave the drunks until last. Of course, they may miss some pathology which could cause unconsciousness or confusion because they believe the

standard proves correct in the great majority of cases. They really do not know *how* often it does not prove correct since they do not check up closely enough to uncover other forms of pathology in most cases, and the low social status of the patients and the fact that they are seldom accompanied by anyone who will protect them means that complaints about inadequate examination will be rare. There *are* occasional challenges by doctors—"How do you know he's drunk?"—but in most cases the busy schedule of the house officer leaves little time for such luxuries as a careful examination of patients who have already been defined as drunks by others. Once the drunk label has been accepted by the emergency-room staff, a more careful examination is not likely to be made unless some particularly arresting new information appears (for example, the patient has convulsions, a relative appears to tell them that he has diabetes, an examination of his wallet shows him to be a solid citizen), and the more subtle pathologies are not likely to be discovered.

Thus, it is just as true to say that the *label* of "drunk" is accepted by hospital personnel because of the way the patient is treated as it is to say that he is treated in a certain way because he is drunk. Occasional cases show how persons with alcohol on their breath will not be treated as drunks. When an obviously middle-class man (obvious in terms of his dress, speech, and demands for service) was brought in after an automobile accident, he was not put in the drunk room, although he had a definite alcohol odor, but was given relatively quick treatment in one of the other examining rooms and addressed throughout in a polite manner.

Most drunks are men. A common negative evaluation for women is PID (pelvic inflammatory disease). This is not just a medical diagnostic category, but, by implication, a moral judgment. There are many women with difficult-to-diagnose abdominal pains and fever. If they are Negro, young, unmarried, lower class in appearance and speech, and have no one along to champion their cause, doctors frequently make the assumption that they have before them the end results of a dissolute sex life, unwanted pregnancy and perhaps venereal disease, illegal abortion, and consequent infection of the reproductive organs. The label PID is then attached and the patient relegated to a group less deserving of prompt and considerate treatment. This is *not* the same thing as saying a diagnosis of PID leads to rejection by medical personnel.

We observed one patient who had been defined as a troublemaker because of his abusive language and his insistence that he be released immediately. When he began to behave in a strange manner (random thrashing about), the police were promptly called to control him and they threatened him with arrest. A patient who was not defined as a troublemaker and exhibited like behavior prompted an effort on the part of the staff to provide a medical explanation for his actions. Here again, we see that the category into which the patient has been placed may have more effect on determining the decisions of medical personnel than does his immediate behavior.

Thus, it is not simply a matter of finding which "objective" pathological states medical personnel like or dislike dealing with. The very definition of these pathological states depends in part on how the patient is categorized in moral terms by the screening and treatment personnel.

The Legitimate and the Illegitimate

The second type of evaluation is that related to the staff members' concept of their appropriate work roles (Strauss et al. 1964, chap. 13). Every worker has a notion of what demands are appropriate to his position. When demands fall outside that boundary, he feels that the claim is illegitimate. What he does about it depends on a number of factors, including his alternatives, his power to control the behavior of others, and his power to select his clientele (more on this later).

Interns and residents who usually man the larger urban emergency services like to think of this assignment as a part of their training which will give them a kind of experience different from the outpatient department or inpatient wards. Here they hope to get some practice in resuscitation, in treating traumatic injuries, in diagnosing and treating medical emergencies. When patients who are no different from those they have seen *ad nauseam* in the outpatient department present themselves at the emergency ward, the doctors in

training believe that their services are being misused. Also, once on the emergency ward, the patient is expected to be "cooperative" so that the doctor is not blocked in his effort to carry out his tasks. Nurses, clerks, and others play "little doctor" and to this extent share the concepts of the boundaries of legitimacy of the doctors. But, in addition to the broadly shared perspective, each work specialty has its own notions of appropriate patient attributes and behavior based on their own work demands. Thus, clerks expect patients to cooperate in getting forms filled out. Patients with a "good reason," unconsciousness, for example, are excused from cooperating with clerical procedures, but other patients who are unable to give requested information or who protest against certain questions bring upon themselves condemnation by the clerks who believe that a person who subverts their efforts to complete their tasks has no business on the emergency ward.

A universal complaint among those who operate emergency services is that hospital emergency rooms are "abused" by the public—or rather by a portion of the public. This is particularly the case in the city and county hospitals and voluntary hospitals with training programs subsidized by public funds which handle the bulk of emergency cases in urban areas. The great majority of cases are thought of as too minor or lacking in urgency to warrant a visit to the emergency room. They are "outpatient cases" (OPD cases), that is, patients who could wait until the outpatient department is open, or if they can afford private care, they could wait until a physician is holding his regular office hours. Patients should not use the emergency room just because it gives quicker service than the outpatient department or because the hours are more convenient (since it is open all the time). Pediatricians complain about their day filled with "sore throats and snotty noses." Medical interns and residents complain about all the people presenting longstanding or chronic diseases which, though sometimes serious, do not belong in the emergency room. In every hospital—both public and private—where we made observations or conducted interviews, we repeatedly heard the same kinds of "atrocity stories": a patient with a sore throat of two-weeks' duration comes in at

3:00 A.M. on Sunday and expects immediate treatment from an intern whom he has got out of bed (or such variations as an itch of 75-days' duration, a congenital defect in a one-year-old child—always coming in at an extremely inconvenient hour).

Directors of emergency services recognize that some of their preoccupation with cases which are not "true emergencies" is not simply a matter of "abuse" by patients, but the result of tasks imposed upon them by other agencies—for example, giving routine antibiotic injections on weekends, caring for abandoned children, giving routine blood transfusions, receiving inpatient admissions, giving gamma globulin, providing venereal disease follow-up, examining jail prisoners, arranging nursing-home dispositions for the aged. But the blame for most of their difficulty is placed upon the self-referred patient who, according to the emergency-room staff, does not make appropriate use of their service.

The OPD case typically gets hurried, routine processing with little effort at a careful diagnostic work-up or sophisticated treatment unless he happens to strike the doctor as an interesting case (in which case he is no longer classified as an OPD case). Thus, pediatric residents move rapidly through their mass of sore throats and snotty noses with a quick look in ears and throat with the otolaryngoscope, a swab wiped in the throat to be sent to the laboratory, and if the child does not have a high fever (the nurse has already taken his temperature), the parent is told to check on the laboratory results the next day, the emergency-ward form is marked "URI" (upper respiratory infection), and the next child moves up on the treadmill. If a patient or a visitor had given anyone trouble, his care is likely to deteriorate below the routine level. Often, doctors define their task in OPD cases as simply a stopgap until the patient gets to OPD on a subsequent day, and therefore a careful work-up is not considered necessary.

Medical cases are more often considered illegitimate than surgical cases. In our public hospital tabulations, the diagnostic categories highest in the illegitimate category were gynecology, genito-urinary, dental, and "other medical." The lowest in proportion of illegitimate cases were pediatrics (another bit of evidence that children

are more acceptable patients than adults), beatings and stabbings, industrial injuries, auto accidents, other accidents, and "other surgical." Much of the surgical work is suturing lacerations and making other repairs. Although these are not necessarily serious in terms of danger to life (very few were), such injuries were seen by the staff as needing prompt attention (certainly within 24 hours) to reduce the risk of infection and to avoid scarring or other deformity.

It is not surprising that in surgical cases the attributes and behavior of the patients are of lesser consequence than in medical cases. The ease with which the condition can be defined and the routine nature of the treatment (treating minor lacerations becomes so routine that anyone thinks he can do it—medical students, aides, volunteers) means that the characteristics and behavior of the patient can be largely ignored unless he becomes extremely disruptive. (Even violence can be restrained and the treatment continued without much trouble.) Certain other things are handled with routine efficiency—high fevers in children, asthma, overdose, maternity cases. It is significant that standard rules can be and have been laid down in such cases so that everyone—clerks, nurses, doctors (and patients once they have gone through the experience)—knows just how to proceed. In such cases, the issue of legitimacy seldom arises.

We find no similar routines with set rules in the case of complaints of abdominal pains, delusions, muscle spasms, depression, or digestive upset. Here the process of diagnosis is much more subtle and complex, the question of urgency much more debatable and uncertain. The way is left open for all emergency-ward staff members involved to make a judgment about whether the case is appropriate to and deserving of their service. Unless the patient is a "regular," no one on the emergency service is likely to have background information on the patient, and the staff will have to rely entirely on clues garnered from his mode of arrival, his appearance, his behavior, the kind of people who accompany him, and so on. The interpretation of these clues then becomes crucial to further treatment and, to the casual observer, may appear to be the *cause* of such treatment.

It is also not surprising that "psychiatric cases"

are usually considered illegitimate. Interns and residents do not (unless they are planning to go into psychiatry) find such cases useful for practicing their diagnostic and treatment skills,[1] and therefore regard such patients as an unwelcome intrusion. But what constitutes a psychiatric case is not based on unvarying criteria. An effort is usually made to place a patient in a more explicit medical category. For example, a wrist slashing is a surgical case requiring suturing. An adult who takes an overdose of sleeping pills is a medical case requiring lavage and perhaps antidotes. Only when a patient is troublesome—violent, threatening suicide, disturbing other patients—is the doctor forced to define him as a psychiatric case about whom a further decision must be made. (In some clinics, psychiatrists are attempting to broaden the definition by making interns and residents aware of more subtle cues for justifying a psychiatric referral and providing them with a consulting service to deal with such cases. However, they must provide a prompt response when called upon, or their service will soon go unused.)

It is no accident either that in the private hospitals (especially those without medical school or public clinic affiliation) the legitimacy of a patient depends largely on his relationship to the private medical system. A standard opening question to the incoming patient in such hospitals is, "Who is your doctor?" A patient is automatically legitimate if referred by a physician on the hospital staff (or the physician's nurse, receptionist, or answering service). If he has not been referred, but gives the name of a staff doctor whom the nurse can reach and who agrees to handle the case, the patient is also legitimate. Howeover, if he does not give a staff doctor's name, he falls under suspicion. The hospital services, including the emergency room, are designed primarily to serve the private physicians on the staff. A patient who does not fit into this scheme threatens to upset the works. It is the receptionist's or receiving nurse's job to try to establish the proper relationship by determining whether the case warrants the service of the contract physician or the doctor on emergency call, and if so, to see to it that the patient gets into the hands of an attending staff doctor for follow-up treatment if necessary. Any patient

whose circumstances make this process difficult or impossible becomes illegitimate. This accounts for the bitter denunciation of the "welfare cases"[2] and the effort to deny admission to people without medical insurance or other readily tappable funds. (Most physicians on the hospital staff do not want such people as patients, and feel they have been tricked if a colleague talks them into accepting them as patients; neither does the hospital administration want them as inpatients.) Also, such hospitals have no routine mechanism for dealing with welfare cases, as have the public hospitals which can either give free treatment or refer the patient to a social worker on the premises. Such patients are commonly dealt with by transferring them to a public clinic or hospital if their condition permits.

The negative evaluation of patients is strongest when they combine an undeserving character with illegitimate demands. Thus, a patient presenting a minor medical complaint at an inconvenient hour is more vigorouslyy condemned if he is a welfare case than if he is a "respectable citizen." On the other hand, a "real emergency" can overcome moral repugnance. Thus, when a presumed criminal suffering a severe abdominal bullet wound inflicted by police was brought into one emergency ward, the staff quickly mobilized in a vigorous effort to prevent death because this is the kind of case the staff sees as justifying the existence of their unit. The same patient brought in with a minor injury would almost certainly have been treated as a moral outcast. Even in the case of "real emergencies," however, moral evaluation is not absent. Although the police prisoner with the bullet wound received prompt, expert attention, the effort was treated simply as a technical matter—an opportunity to display one's skill in keeping a severely traumatized person alive. When the same emergency ward received a prominent local citizen who had been stabbed by thugs while he was trying to protect his wife, the staff again provided a crash effort to save his life, but in this case they were obviously greatly upset by their failure, not simply a failure of technical skills but the loss of a worthy person who was the victim of a vicious act. One may speculate whether this difference in staff evaluations of the two victims may have resulted in an extra effort in the case of the respected citizen despite the appearance of a similar effort in the two cases.

Staff Estimates of "Legitimate" Demands

As is common in relationships between a work group and its clientele, the members of the work group tend to exaggerate their difficulties with the clients when they generalize about them. In conversations, we would typically hear estimates of 70 percent–90 percent as the proportion of patients who were using the emergency service inappropriately. Yet, when we actually followed cases through the clinic, we found the majority were being treated as if they were legitimate. In one voluntary hospital with an intern and residency training program, we classified all cases we followed during our time on the emergency room as legitimate or illegitimate whenever we had any evidence of subjective definition by staff members, either by what they said about the patient or the manner in which they treated the patient. Among those cases suitable for classification, 42 were treated as legitimate, 15 as illegitimate, and in 24 cases there was insufficient evidence to make a classification. Thus, the illegitimate proportion was about 20 percent–25 percent depending on whether one used as a base the total definite legitimate and illegitimate cases or also included the unknowns. In a very active public hospital emergency room we did not use direct observation of each case, but rather developed a conception of what kind of diagnostic categories were usually considered legitimate or illegitimate by the clinic staff and then classified the total consensus for two days according to diagnostic categories. By this method, 23 percent of 938 patients were classified as illegitimate. This constitutes a minimum figure because diagnostic category was not the only basis for an evaluation, and some other patients were almost certainly regarded as illegitimate by the staff. But it *does* suggest that only a minority were regarded as illegitimate.

The number of specific undesirable or inappropriate categories of patients were also consistently exaggerated. Thus, while in the public hospital the interns complained about all the drunks among the men and all the reproductive organ infections among the women ("The choice between the male and the female service is really a choice between alcoholics and PIDs," according to one intern), drunks made up only 6 percent of the total emergency-room population and the gynecology patients 2 percent. Venereal disease was also considered a common type of case by clerks, nurses, and doctors, but in fact made up only about 1 percent of the total E.R. census. Psychiatric cases were referred to as a constant trouble, but, in fact, made up only a little over 2 percent of the total. Some doctors believed infections and long-standing illnesses were common among the E.R. population and used this as evidence of neglect of health by the lower classes. Here again, however, the actual numbers were low—these two categories made up a little more than 3 percent of the total census. In two small private hospitals, the staffs were particularly bitter toward "welfare cases" whom they regarded as a constant nuisance. However, we often spent an entire shift (eight hours) in the emergency rooms of these hospitals without seeing a single patient so classified.

Workers justify the rewards received for their labors in part by the burdens which they must endure on the job. One of the burdens of service occupations is a clientele which makes life hard for the workers. Thus, the workers tend to select for public presentation those aspects of the clientele which cause them difficulty. Teachers' talk deals disproportionately with disruptive and incompetent students, policemen's talk with dangerous criminals and difficult civilians, janitors' talk with inconsiderate tenants. A case-by-case analysis of contacts is likely to demonstrate in each instance that the examples discussed by the staff are not representative of their total clientele.

Control of Inappropriate Demands for Service

When members of a service occupation or service organization are faced with undesirable or illegitimate clients, what can they do? One possible procedure is to select clients they like and avoid those they do not like. The selecting may be done in categorical terms, as when universities admit undergraduate students who meet given grade and test standards. Or it may be done on the basis of detailed information about specific individuals, as when a graduate department selects particular students on the basis of academic record, recommendations from colleagues, and personal information about the student. Of course, such selection is not made on a unidimensional basis and the selecting agent must often decide what weight to give conflicting factors. (Thus, a medical specialist may be willing to take on a patient who is morally repugnant because the patient has a medical condition the specialist is anxious to observe, study, or experiment with.) But there is an assumption that the more highly individualized the selection and the more detailed the information on which it is based, the more likely one is to obtain a desirable clientele. Along with this process goes the notion of "selection errors." Thus, when a patient is classed as a good risk for a physical rehabilitation program, he may later be classed as a selection error if doctors uncover some pathology which contraindicates exercise, or if the patient proves so uncooperative that physical therapists are unable to conduct any training, or if he requires so much nursing care that ward personnel claim that he "doesn't belong" on a rehabilitation unit (Roth and Eddy 1967, pp. 57–61).

Selectivity is a relative matter. A well-known law firm specializing in a given field can accept only those clients whose demands fit readily into the firm's desired scheme of work organization and who are able to pay well for the service given. The solo criminal lawyer in a marginal practice may, for financial reasons, take on almost every case he can get, even though he may despise the majority of his clients and wish he did not have to deal with them (Smigel 1964; Wood 1967). A common occupational or organizational aspiration is to reach a position where one can be highly selective of one's clientele. In fact, such power of selection is a common basis for rating schools, law firms, hospitals, and practitioners of all sorts.[3]

If one cannot be selective in a positive sense, one may still be selective in a negative sense by avoiding some potentially undesirable clients. Hotels, restaurants, and places of entertainment may specifically exclude certain categories of persons as guests, or more generally reserve the right to refuse service to anyone they choose. Cab drivers will sometimes avoid a presumed "bad fare" by pretending another engagement or just not seeing him. Cab driving, incidentally, is a good example of a line of work where judgments about clients must often be made in a split second on the basis of immediate superficial clues—clues based not only on the behavior and appearance of the client himself, but also on such surrounding factors as the area, destination, and time of day (Davis 1959: Henslin 1968, pp. 138–58). Ambulance crewmen sometimes manage to avoid a "bad load," perhaps making a decision before going to the scene on the basis of the call source or neighborhood, or perhaps refusing to carry an undesirable patient if they can find a "good excuse" (Douglas 1969, pp. 234–78).

Medical personnel and organizations vary greatly in their capacity to select clients. Special units in teaching hospitals and specialized outpatient clinics often are able to restrict their patients to those they have individually screened and selected. The more run-of-the-mill hospital ward or clinic is less selective, but still has a screening process to keep out certain categories of patients. Of all medical care units, public hospital emergency wards probably exercise the least selectivity of all. Not only are they open to the public at all times with signs pointing the way, but the rule that everyone demanding care must be seen provides no legal "out" for the staff when faced with inappropriate or repugnant patients (although persons accompanying patients can be, and often are, prevented from entering the treatment areas and are isolated or ejected if troublesome). In addition, the emergency ward serves a residual function for the rest of the hospital and often for other parts of the medical-care system. Any case which does not fit into some other program is sent to the emergency ward. When other clinics and offices close for the day or the weekend, their patients who cannot wait for the next open hours are directed to the emergency service. It is precisely this unselective influx of anyone and everyone bringing a wide spectrum of medical and social defects that elicits the bitter complaints of emergency-service personnel. Of course, they are not completely without selective power. They occasionally violate the rules and refuse to accept a patient. And even after registration, some patients can be so discouraged in the early stages of processing that they leave. Proprietary hospitals transfer some patients to public hospitals. But compared with other parts of the medical-care system, the emergency-service personnel, especially in public hospitals, have very limited power of selection and must resign themselves to dealings with many people that they believe should not be there and that in many cases they have a strong aversion to.

What recourse does a service occupation or organization have when its members have little or no control over the selection of its clients? If you cannot pick the clients you like, perhaps you can transform those you *do* get somewhere closer to the image of desirable client. This is particularly likely to occur if it is a long-term or repeated relationship so that the worker can reap the benefit of the "training" he gives the client. We tentatively put forth this proposition: *The amount of trouble one is willing to go to to train his clientele depends on how much power of selection he has. The easier it is for one to avoid or get rid of poor clients (that is, those clients whose behavior or attributes conflict with one's conception of his proper work role), the less interested one is in putting time and energy into training clients to conform more closely to one's ideal. And, of course, the converse.*

Janitors have to endure a clientele (that is, tenants) they have no hand in selecting. Nor can a janitor get rid of bad tenants (unless he buys the building and evicts them, as happens on rare occasions). Ray Gold (1964, pp. 1–50) describes how janitors try to turn "bad tenants" into more tolerable ones by teaching them not to make inappropriate demands. Tenants must be taught not to call at certain hours, not to expect the janitor to make certain repairs, not to expect him to remove certain kinds of garbage, to expect cleaning services only on given days and in given areas, to expect heat only at certain times, and so on. Each occasion on which the janitor is able to make his point that a given demand is inappropriate contributes to making those demands from the same tenant less likely in the future and increases the janitor's control over his work load and work pacing. One finds much the same long-term effort on the part of mental hospital staffs who indoctrinate inmates on the behavior and demands associated with "good patients"—who will be rewarded with privileges and discharge—and behavior associated with "bad patients"—who will be denied these rewards (Stanton and Schwartz 1954, pp. 280–89; Belknap 1956, chaps. 9 and 10). Prisons and schools are other examples of such long-term teaching of clients.[4]

The form that "client-training" takes depends in part on the time perspective of the trainers. Emergency-ward personnel do not have the longtime perspective of the mental hospital staff, teachers, or janitors. Despite the fact that the majority of patients have been to the same emergency ward previously and will probably be back again at some future time, the staff, with rare exceptions, treats each case as an episode which will be completed when the patient is discharged. Therefore, they seldom make a direct effort to affect the patient's future use of their services. They are, however, interested in directing the immediate behavior of clients so that it will fit into their concept of proper priorities (in terms of their evaluation of the clients) and the proper conduct of an emergency service, including the work demands made upon them. Since they do not conceive of having time for gradual socialization of the clients, they rely heavily on demands for immediate compliance. Thus, patients demanding attention, if not deemed by staff to be urgent cases or particularly deserving, will be told to wait their turn and may even be threatened with refusal of treatment if they are persistent. Visitors are promptly ordered to a waiting room and are reminded of where they belong if they wander into a restricted area. Patients are expected to respond promptly when called, answer questions put to them by the staff, prepare for examination when asked, and cooperate with the examination as directed without wasting the staff's time. Failure to comply promptly may bring a warning that they will be left waiting or even refused further care if they do not cooperate, and the more negative the staff evaluation of the patient, the more likely he is to be threatened.[5]

Nursing staff in proprietary hospitals dealing with the private patients of attending physicians do not have as authoritative a position vis-à-vis their clients as public hospital staff have: therefore, the demands for prompt compliance with staff directions must be used sparingly. In such a case more surreptitious forms of control are used. The most common device is keeping the patient waiting at some step or steps in his processing or treatment. Since the patient usually has no way of checking the validity of the reason given for the wait, this is a relatively safe way that a nurse can control the demands made on her and also serves as a way of "getting even" with those who make inappropriate demands or whom she regards as undeserving for some other reason.

In general, we might expect that: *The longer the time perspective of the trainers, the more the training will take the form of efforts toward progressive socialization in the desired direction; the shorter the time perspective of the trainers, the more the training wil take the form of overt coercion ("giving orders") if the trainers have sufficient power over the clients, and efforts at surreptitious but immediate control if they lack such power.*

Conclusion

When a person presents himself at an emergency department (or is brought there by others), he inevitably sets off a process by which his worthiness and legitimacy are weighed and become a factor in his treatment. It is doubtful that one can obtain any service of consequence anywhere without going through this process. The evidence from widely varying services indicates that the servers do not dispense their service in a uniform manner to everyone who presents himself, but make judgments about the worthiness of the person and the appropriateness of his demands and take these judgments into account when performing the service. In large and complex service organizations, the judgments made at one point in the system often shape the judgments at another.

The structure of a service organization will affect the manner and degree to which the servers can vary their service in terms of their moral evaluation of the client. This study has not explored this issue in detail. A useful future research direction would be the investigation of how a system of service may be structured to control the discretion of the servers as to whom they must serve and how they must serve them. This paper offered some suggestions concerning the means of controlling the inappropriate demands of a clientele. The examples I used to illustrate the relationships of power of selection and the nature of training of clients are few and limited in scope. An effort should be made to determine whether these formulations (or modifications thereof) apply in a wider variety of occupational settings.

NOTES

The study on which this paper is based was supported by National Institutes of Health grants HM 00437 and HM 00517, Division of Hospital and Medical Facilities. Dorothy J. Douglas, currently at the University of Connecticut Health Center, worked with me and made major contributions to this study.

1. The authors of *Boys in White* (Becker et al. 1961, pp. 327–38) make the same point. A "crock" is a patient from whom the students cannot learn anything because there is no definable physical pathology which can be tracked down and treated.
2. "Welfare cases" include not only those who present welfare cards, but all who are suspected of trying to work the system to get free or low-priced care.
3. I am glossing over some of the intraorganizational complexities of the process. Often different categories of organizational personnel vary greatly in their participation in the selection of the clientele. Thus, on a hospital rehabilitation unit, the doctors may select the patients, but the nurses must take care of patients they have no direct part in selecting. Nurses can influence future selection only by complaining to the doctors that they have "too many" of certain kinds of difficult patients or by trying to convince doctors to transfer inappropriate patients. These attempts at influencing choice often fail because doctors and nurses have somewhat different criteria about what an appropriate patient is (Roth and Eddy 1967, pp. 57–61).
4. Of course, my brief presentation greatly oversimplifies the process. For example, much of the teaching is done by the clients rather than directly by the staff. But, ultimately, the sanctions are

derived from staff efforts to control work demands and to express their moral evaluation of the clients.

5. Readers who are mainly interested in what happens on an emergency ward should not be misled into thinking that it is a scene of continuous orders and threats being shouted at patients and visitors. Most directives are matter-of-fact, and most clients comply promptly with directions most of the time. But when the staff's directive power is challenged, even inadvertently, the common response is a demand for immediate compliance. This situation arises frequently enough so that on a busy unit an observer can see instances almost every hour.

REFERENCES

Becker, Howard S., Blanche Geer, Everett C. Hughes, and Anselm Strauss. 1961. *Boys in White.* Chicago: University of Chicago Press.

Belknap, Ivan. 1956. *Human Problems of a State Mental Hospital.* New York: McGraw-Hill.

Davis, Fred. 1959. "The Cab Driver and His Fare." *American Journal of Sociology* 65 (September): 158–65.

Douglas, Dorothy J. 1969. "Occupational and Therapeutic Contingencies of Ambulance Services in Metropolitan Areas." Ph.D. dissertation, University of California.

Glaser, Barney, and Anselm Strauss. 1964. "The Social Loss of Dying Patients." *American Journal of Nursing* 64 (June): 119–21.

Goffman, Erving. 1961. *Asylums.* New York: Doubleday.

Gold, Raymond L. 1964. "In the Basement—the Apartment-Building Janitor." In *The Human Shape of Work,* edited by Peter L. Berger. New York: Macmillan.

Henslin, James. 1968. "Trust and the Cab Driver." In *Sociology and Everyday Life,* edited by Marcello Truzzi. Englewood Cliffs, N.J.: Prentice-Hall.

Hollingshead, August B., and Frederick C. Redlich. 1958. *Social Class and Mental Illness.* New York: Wiley.

Perrow, Charles. 1965. "Hospitals, Technology, Structure, and Goals." In *Handbook of Organizations,* edited by James G. March. Chicago: Rand McNally.

Roth, Julius A., and Elizabeth M. Eddy. 1967. *Rehabilitation for the Unwanted.* New York: Atherton.

Scheff, Thomas J. 1964. "The Societal Reaction to Deviance: Ascriptive Elements in the Psychiatric Screening of Mental Patients in a Midwestern State." *Social Problems* 11 (Spring): 401–13.

——.1966. *Being Mentally Ill.* Chicago: Aldine.

Smigel, Erwin. 1964. *Wall Street Lawyer.* New York: Free Press.

Stanton, Alfred, and Morris Schwartz. 1954. *The Mental Hospital.* New York: Basic.

Strauss, Anselm, Leonard Schatzman, Rue Bucher, Danuta Ehrlich, and Melvin Sabshin. 1964. *Psychiatric Ideologies and Institutions.* New York: Free Press.

Sudnow, David. 1967. *Passing On.* Englewood Cliffs, N.J.: Prentice-Hall.

Szasz, Thomas. 1960. "The Myth of Mental Illness." *American Psychologist* 15 (February): 113–18.

Wood, Arthur Lewis. 1967. *Criminal Lawyer.* New Haven, Conn.: College and Universities Press.

28

Medical Mortality Review: A Cordial Affair

Marcia Millman

A mortality and morbidity conference for doctors bears some resemblance to a wedding or a funeral for members of a family. In all these ceremonies there is some feeling among those who attend that tact and restraint must be exercised if everyone is to leave on friendly terms. But steering a mortality meeting along on a pleasant and even course is occasionally difficult, for as in weddings and funerals, the very nature of the event often prompts participants to come dangerously close to saying to one another those upsetting things that are usually left unsaid.

Mortality meetings are regularly scheduled conferences at Lakeside Hospital[1]; they are held in a large auditorium to accommodate the entire medical staff (private attending physicians, house officers, and teaching staff). Their avowed purpose is to review, in fine detail, those medical cases that ended in an in-hospital patient death, and in which there is some question of error, failure, or general mismanagement on the part of the physicians involved. One of the implicit if unspoken concerns that always underlies the review is the question of whether the patient's death might have been avoided had the medical judgment been more sound, for what is usually involved in these cases is a question of misdiagnosis or of appropriate medical action taken too late.

In consideration of the delicacy of the occasion, the meetings are restricted to the medical staff of the hospital. Even the surgical staff is generally not invited. The surgical service has its own mortality meetings, and a surgeon would be considered meddlesome for attending a medical mortality conference simply out of curiosity. Only those surgeons who were directly involved in a particular case under consideration will be asked to attend a medical mortality meeting. Families are *not* informed that their deceased relative's case has been chosen for review. Although the meetings may be considerably embarrassing for the doctors involved, the Medical Mortality Conference is, at least on the surface, treated as an *educational* rather than a punitive affair. At Lakeside, the conferences are not investigations or formal hearings held to consider the competence of particular doctors, although they are often presented this way on television medical dramas. There are no formal sanctions applied to doctors at the end of these conferences. Rather, Mortality Review Conferences are "educational" sessions organized around reviewing particular cases rather than individual doctors, even though the cases are selected because there is disagreement over the appropriate treatment and often a question of physician error involved.

The Mortality Review Conference has a special quality of high tension, and the meetings are better attended than are those of the other regular teaching conferences. At Lakeside Hospital, the Chief of Medicine stands on the stage and presides over the Mortality Review Conference as a master of ceremonies. As the case is reviewed in chronological order, starting with the time of the patient admission to the hospital, and proceeding to the autopsy report, the chief calls on the various doctors who were involved in the case, asks them to step to the front of the auditorium, and instructs them to recall and explain what they did and what they thought at each moment in time. He counsels them not to jump ahead of the chronological order, nor to divulge information gained at a later time, in order not to spoil the final diagnosis for the members of the audience. As one after another of the staff testifies about how they were led to the same mistaken diagnosis, a convincing case for the justifiability of the error is implicitly presented and the responsibility for the mistake is spread so that no one doctor is made to look guilty of a mistake that anyone else wouldn't have made, and in fact, didn't make. As in a good detective story, the case is reconstructed to show that there was evidence for suspecting an outcome different from the one that turns out to be the true circumstance. Responsibility for the error is also neutralized by making much of unusual or misleading features of the case, or showing how the patient was himself to blame, because of uncooperative or neurotic behavior. Furthermore, by reviewing the case in fine detail the doctors restore their images as careful, methodical practitioners and thereby neutralize the actual sloppiness and carelessness made obvious by the mistake. The doctors' discomfort is further minimized by treating the review as an educational occasion rather than an investigatory event.

In order to appreciate the special atmosphere and significance of the Mortality Review, it is important to understand that doctors who work together ordinarily live by a gentlemen's agreement to overlook each other's mistakes. The aim is not merely to hide errors and incompetence from the patients and the public, but also to avoid interfering in one another's work and to avoid acknowledgment of the injury that has been done to patients. Such a conspiracy to look the other way regarding the failures of one's colleagues is not always recognized by the doctors for what it is, for a blindness to injury done to patients and a convincing set of justifications and excuses for

medical mistakes are carefully built into their training and professional etiquette. Most doctors are therefore capable of comfortably viewing themselves as altruistic and highly responsible practitioners all the while they engage in collective rationalizations for ignoring and condoning each other's errors and incompetence.

Still, there are special occasions in the hospital routine, such as the Mortality Meeting, when doctors are gathered together to examine the sorts of unpleasant facts they would otherwise ignore. At these times a great deal of effort is expended to make the embarrassing facts seem less damaging. For if such medical incompetence or error were fully and publicly (among themselves) acknowledged, physician-colleagues might feel forced to take measures against one another, and this is one of the things they least like to do.

As the Chief of Medicine at Lakeside explained, "Eighty percent of the mistakes made around here are ignored or swept under the rug. I can only pick *certain* cases for mortality review—it's got to be a cordial affair."

Perhaps that description of the selection procedures for mortality review accounts for the curious fact that at Lakeside, most of the medical situations presented at these conferences conveniently seem to involve an illness that would have ended in the patient's death in any case, even if the correct diagnosis had been made immediately. There is a strange absence of cases reviewed in these meetings in which the patient would clearly have lived had it not been for the medical mismanagement. By selecting only those cases in which the physician's error was not fateful in an ultimate sense the discussion of mistakes largely becomes an academic affair.

Practicality rather than sentiment is the key to the tact and reserve with which doctors respond to each other's errors. A doctor's reluctance to criticize a colleague's mistakes to his face at a large meeting is not motivated out of respect or affection. Indeed, many doctors are willing, in small groups, to say that another physician (not present) is a menace or a terrible doctor. And even at the mortality review conferences, those doctors who are not involved in a case may occasionally sit back and enjoy the gentle roasting of a disliked work associate. The reluctance to point out and criticize another doctor's mistakes at an official meeting comes rather out of a fear of reprisal and a recognition of common interests. For each doctor knows that he has made some more or less terrible mistake in his career, and that he is likely to make others—mistakes, moreover, which will be obvious to his colleagues. That is why, in matters of peer regulation, doctors observe the Golden Rule.

So it is that mortality meetings are built upon a simultaneous admission and cover-up of mistakes. For although the avowed purpose of these meetings is to review mistakes and prevent their recurrence, in actuality the meetings are organized and conducted in ways that absolve the doctors from responsibility and guilt and provide the self-assuring but somewhat false appearance that physicians are monitoring each other and their standards of work. In case after case physician errors are systematically excused and justified, and their consequences made to look unimportant.

Before turning to some actual cases, it should be noted that despite the tact and sensitivity with which doctors treat each other's errors, a mortality meeting is not an entirely comfortable situation. Like a family trying collectively to ignore that the father is having an affair, or that the daughter is a drug addict, the doctors at a mortality meeting are often pushed to extreme displays of courtesy to overlook the worst and find good excuses for regrettable behavior.

Case No. 1: Jonathan Thomas

Jonathan Thomas was a thirty-four-year-old insurance salesman who had complained of abdominal pain and black stool (indicating gastrointestinal bleeding). His problem was diagnosed as a gastric ulcer and he was placed on a regimen of tranquilizers and an ulcer diet. His subsequent complaints were explained as being consistent with an ulcer and a neurotic personality. Ten months later Jonathan Thomas died of cancer spread throughout his abdominal cavity.

This was to be a particularly uncomfortable case for the staff to consider in Mortality Review because of a number of factors. First of all, the patient was a young man with a large family, and this made his life more valuable in the eyes of the doctors. Second, mistakes in diagnosis had been made repeatedly, and important information overlooked more than once. Third, a large number of people had been involved in this case, and while this offered the consolation of spreading out the responsibility, it also pointed out the weaknesses of the hospital consulting system. For if not one of a dozen physicians had caught the obvious errors, it was probably because each of the consultants involved in the case had been too accepting of each other's erroneous assumptions instead of carefully doing the diagnostic jobs they were supposed to be doing.

Notices about the mortality meeting had been distributed days beforehand and signs posted around the hospital. The chief's secretary had made sure that all the doctors involved in the case would be there for the review. As always, the meeting was held in the large theaterlike auditorium and members of the staff seated themselves in the rows of seats facing the stage in a steep incline.

The meeting was called to order by the Chief of Medicine, who welcomed everyone and made brief announcements of unrelated matters. Next, an intern described the hospital's mortality profile for the preceding month: he described how many patients had died in the hospital in each major disease category. Finally, the Chief of Medicine, Dr. Tanner, returned to the stage and introduced the Thomas case. As usual, the patient's history was reviewed in chronological order, each doctor being called to the front of the room to recall his thoughts and describe his participation at that moment in time in the case.

The early history was reviewed by Dr. Backman, the specialist in gastrointestinal disorders who had managed the case. Backman was highly respected and well-liked by most of the staff, and so there were no undertones of questioning his competence but rather friendly empathy for the usually careful physician who had made an uncharacteristic mistake. From the beginning, Backman explained, he had assumed that the gastrointestinal bleeding indicated by the black stool was caused by a stress-induced gastric ulcer: "What led us down the garden path last October was the fact that he was taking on added responsibility for his family's business. The sudden pain seemed to coincide with that, so we put him on an ulcer regimen and gave him tranquilizers and released him in satisfactory condition. After discharge, a GI series was negative, but epigastric pain reappeared and in April he reported severe upper left quadrant pains which became persistent."

Dr. Jenkins, one of the supervisors of the teaching program, interrupted: "Was this severe upper left quadrant pain different from the epigastric pain? Was it something new?"

Dr. Backman: "He described it as different. He had it at night, and it wasn't relieved with antacids."

Dr. Jenkins: "Well, didn't that make you uncomfortable with the diagnosis of gastric ulcer?"

Dr. Backman: "No, because he had resumed smoking and drinking now, and we suspected alcoholic hepatitis, because of his abnormal liver function test. He reported clay-colored stools and we readmitted him to the hospital. From the start of his admission he was quite agitated and needed more sedation, so we called in Dr. Sheingold (the Chief of Psychiatry)."

Dr. Sheingold had considered saying something about Dr. Backman's description of the patient as "drinking again." In fact, he knew the patient drank very little, only a few beers when he went bowling once a week, and it seemed unfair to imply that the man was drinking enough to justify a diagnosis of alcoholic hepatitis. The trouble, Sheingold felt, was that once the doctors decided to bring a psychiatrist into the case most of them no longer believed anything the patient said. And so it had been easy for the doctors to regard this patient as an alcoholic. Still, Dr. Sheingold had observed that Backman was one of the few doctors in the hospital who thought that psychiatry had anything to offer them in their treatment of medical patients, so he had refrained from objecting to the imputation of alcoholism.

Sheingold was motioned to the stage to report on his participation in the case. He began: "Yes, I was invited to walk down the garden path with the others. I talked with the patient on his fourth day of admission. His father-in-law had just retired and appointed the patient as director of the family insurance business. Mr. Thomas had never liked the business and found it morbid.

Indeed, he had complicated feelings about his business exacerbated by a long history of depression. Ten years ago he had been responsible for an automobile accident in which his oldest daughter, then three years old, had died. So I was quite sure along with Dr. Backman that this was gastric ulcer disease, and I wrote that in my notes. I also noted that there was an unlikely chance of pancreatic carcinoma (cancer) because I knew that would be considered at some time, but I was quite sure that it was an ulcer."

Dr. Stevens, one of the department chiefs in medicine, had been upset with the reasoning in this case. As he explained, one of his pet peeves was the stupid use of psychiatry, especially by the GI doctors, and he had noticed that Backman was one of the frequent offenders in this regard because as a GI specialist Backman also considered himself something of an expert in the field of psychiatry. As Stevens described the situation, every time one of the GI doctors heard a patient complaint that couldn't be explained he called in a psychiatrist. Stevens wished they would instead just admit to the patient that they didn't know what was wrong, and explain that they would have to wait or do more tests. Instead, complained Stevens, a psychiatrist came in and spoke to the patient and *always* found a psychiatric complication. "And," concluded Stevens, "what did that tell you? That everyone has problems?"

Dr. Rosen, another internist on the hospital staff, was questioning Backman. "Why weren't the clay-colored stools considered? Didn't you believe him?"

Backman replied: "Well, the clay-colored stools could have been caused by the antacids he was taking but to be perfectly frank, I didn't know how much credence I could give to his reports. He was quite upset and had gone into a rage about having to pay for the use of the television in his room. I should also add that he was now complaining about leg pain as well. He was re-endoscoped and a liver scan was taken. It showed an enlarged liver without focal abnormalities and the liver function was not impaired. A liver biopsy was normal, which surprised us. We expected to find alcoholic hepatitis. After the biopsy there was hemoptysis [coughing up blood]. We were concerned because that had never happened and we thought that bleeding from the liver biopsy might have gone into the lung area. We did a cholangiogram and it was normal, but we noted that he had an elevated alkaphosphotase level. We released him from the hospital once again on a bland diet with tranquilizers, and his discharge diagnosis was peptic ulcer."

Dr. Davis, one of the younger internists, directed more questions to Backman: "Why wasn't a surgical exploration done at this time?"

Backman smiled, shaking his head. "I'm not sure. I guess we weren't smart enough." Davis continued: "Why was no attention paid to the calf pain?" Backman answered: "The reason we ignored his complaints of leg pain was that his roommate in the hospital had thrombophlebitis in the leg. So when Thomas complained of it, it just seemed too coincidental and we figured it was just a hysterical reaction."

Dr. Sheingold was afraid that this case was certainly not going to encourage the doctors in the hospital to turn to the psychiatry department for help. It made him angry that the only situation in which most of the doctors considered psychiatry to be useful was for the management of what they considered a "crazy" patient, and once a patient in the hospital was seen by a psychiatrist the doctors would attribute to the patient all sorts of psychological mechanisms that had nothing to do with the patient's personality (in this case they were imputing "hysterical" behavior to a non-hysterical patient) and they wouldn't even read the notes that Sheingold wrote in the patient's chart about which psychological mechanisms were relevant. Also, since they didn't regard psychiatric illness as real, they always disliked patients with psychiatric symptoms. As Sheingold later explained, all the doctors had disliked this patient when they thought that he suffered only from an ulcer, and they had only decided that he was likeable after they realized that he was "really" sick with cancer.

Backman was still explaining why he had released the patient despite abnormal laboratory findings. "Oh, and to finish your question about surgery—his abdominal pains went away after three days, so we didn't consider it any more." He leafed through the pages of the chart and

continued. "He was readmitted the following week with a swollen foot, an enlarged liver, extensive thrombophlebitis." Backman nodded to Cohen, the cardiologist who had been consulted at his point. Cohen stood up and briefly spoke from his place in the audience. "I was asked to say whether the problem was due to pulmonary emboli or from hemoptysis to the lung from the liver biopsy. I thought he had pulmonary emboli."

Attention was now directed to the Chief of Surgery, who described his part in the case: "I saw him at this point and I knew something terrible was going on. He was going downhill rapidly. It looked like an abdominal mass. The plan was now to deal with his phlebitis—so here we were in a bind. We had a GI bleeder who had to be anticoagulated for his emboli [a treatment that would increase bleeding], and now he had shortness of breath. The problem in dealing with this patient was that he was dead opposed to surgery. He had been in the life insurance business all his life, and every time we talked about surgery he would say, 'Now my family's gonna be collecting on my policy.'" The surgeon turned to Davis, who had earlier criticized Backman for not calling a surgeon sooner. "I'll tell you why we didn't do an exploratory laparotomy [surgical investigation] earlier. He was so frantic and had been sick so long. He had abdominal pain, and calf pain and GI bleeding. He dreaded surgery, and frankly I dreaded going in there. His wife kept yelling at me, asking what was wrong, and when I said I didn't know she called me stupid. I guess maybe we *were* stupid. Anyway that's why we didn't do an exploratory earlier." In the back of the auditorium, some of the medical residents were smiling and mumbling that the reason the Chief had delayed surgery was that he hated to operate. Douglas had a reputation among the younger aggressive doctors in the hospital of being too cautious and slow to act. It was not clear whether Douglas noticed their remarks, and he continued. "So we did a venous clip and when we later did an exploratory we saw that there was cancer all over. The patient died three days later, and I just want to add here that according to the chart he was in severe anguish on the last day of his life, and was not given the painkillers we had prescribed, so we can thank our nurses for making the last day of his life as miserable as possible." The surgeon nodded to the pathologist and the lights were switched off. Color slides of the patient's affected organs were flashed on the screen. Each one showed gross abnormalities from the spread of the cancer. Throughout the auditorium murmurs could be heard at the extensiveness of the cancer, as if to emphasize that with so dramatic and pervasive a disease they as doctors could hardly have been expected to stop such an invasion.

When the lights were turned on the surgeon drew the meeting to a close, explaining how at that very moment the patient's brother was waiting in his office; the brother had come to show him an article about a so-called wonder drug, which was illegal, for curing cancer. Douglas added that he had given the brother an appointment so that the man could yell at him for having refused to try this illegal drug. Several doctors in the audience laughed and shook their heads sympathetically, breaking into small groups as they moved into the adjoining room for coffee and doughnuts.

The Thomas case, described above, illustrates how doctors often justify their errors by pointing to misleading or unusual features of the case. By demonstrating that they had good reason (though later shown to be mistaken) for doing what they did, they may avoid censure and discomfort, and save face before their colleagues. Physical symptoms inconsistent with the final diagnosis are the misleading cues which provide the most comforting and persuasive type of excuse for making the wrong diagnosis. However, when physical justifications are unavailable, doctors often resort to psychological and social evidence as the factors which misguided them and justified their behavior. In these cases, the nonphysical evidence is represented as being so convincing as to justify overlooking even physical evidence which should have alerted doctors to the correct diagnosis. In the Thomas case, for example, the doctors overlooked clear symptoms of organic disorder (such as the elevated alkaphosphotase level) because they were so convinced that the patient was neurotic and that his complaints and symptoms could be explained psychologically.

In other cases where physical findings are

overlooked, or erroneously discounted, the physician will often excuse his embarrassing error by blaming the patient. If the patient can be "discredited" as crazy, alcoholic, obnoxious, uncooperative, or otherwise difficult or undeserving, then the responsibility for the medical error can be shifted away from the doctor to the patient. The physician's errors are made to seem understandable and inconsequential in a life fated for disaster by the patient's own doing. The following case illustrates this process.

Case No. 2: Alice McDonald

Mrs. McDonald was a fifty-year-old woman who died in the Emergency Room of a perforated duodenal ulcer which the staff failed to diagnose, despite her complaints of severe abdominal pain.

The case was introduced in the meeting by the intern who had seen her in the Emergency Room. He opened the discussion by describing her as "An obese, alcoholic woman of Irish extraction who was very uncooperative and used very abusive language," thereby fixing her in the minds of the physicians in the audience as the type of patient who is difficult to treat.

In explaining why they had not paid much attention to her complaints of abdominal pain, the doctors involved in the case made much of her appearance of being "mentally disconnected." Asked to be more specific about her mental state, both the intern and the medical doctor covering the Emergency Room that night stated that they remembered noting the smell of alcohol on her breath, and therefore felt they could dismiss her complaints as the ravings of a drunken woman.

Toward the end of the meeting someone in the audience offhandedly asked what the alcohol level in the blood had been at the time of the incident. Now the Chief of Medicine sheepishly admitted a fact that had been previously left unmentioned: although much had been made of this woman's drunkenness, the fact was that the alcohol level in the blood had been zero at the time of her examination.

This embarrassing fact was passed over quickly. No longer able to use her drunkenness as an excuse for their failure to take her complaints seriously, the doctors now turned more exclusively to emphasizing her angry, "disconnected" and uncooperative behavior toward them as the factor responsible for the poor treatment she received.

The power of the doctor's self-justification is highlighted in this case. For even after implicitly acknowledging that drunkenness was falsely attributed to the patient, the doctors continued to blame this woman's death on her own anger and abusive language, and ignored the possibility that such behavior was appropriate for a woman dying in great pain while the doctors around her treated her complaints as the fabrications of a hysterical alcoholic.

The case also illustrates how doctors may overlook important physical findings (which should indicate a serious illness) if they have already discounted the complaints by viewing the patient as a certain kind of neurotic individual. For a "neurotic" individual is viewed by doctors as an unreliable reporter, and once characterized this way, a patient's remarks are likely to be ignored. Indeed, these patients are commonly known among many doctors as "crocks" or "turkeys" and are considered undeserving of serious attention.

It is a complicated problem, for certainly doctors will occasionally meet with an anxious patient who will refuse to believe that he is in good health. But serious errors are often made as a result of characterizing patients as "crocks," for doctors are usually not in a position to correctly guess who is really sick and who isn't, from behavior alone. Furthermore, doctors appear to assign the label "crock" quite often on grounds of personal or prejudiced responses. They are more likely, for example, to dismiss a patient as neurotic and not really sick if the patient seems angry, mistrustful, or disrespectful to the doctor. The label "crock" also seems to be applied erroneously more often to women.

A third case reviewed in the Medical Mortality Conference illustrates another common pattern in neutralizing mistakes. Sometimes the patient may be viewed as so lacking in social value or otherwise so physically deteriorated that the question of a consequential medical mistake hardly occurs to anyone involved in the case. That is, the recognition of, and attention to,

medical mistake depends upon the doctor's seeing the patient as an individual having some value. The very definition of a mistake, by doctors, therefore, rests not on some universal and fixed standard of good or poor practice applied to every case, but the definition of a mistake rather shifts and slides according to the value of the patient as assessed by the doctors.

As this final Mortality Review case illustrates, the patient was viewed as so physically and socially worthless that the audience paid little attention to the one doctor among them who expressed distress at how the case had been handled.

Case No. 3: Freddy Grazzo

Freddy Grazzo had become a well-known patient in Lakeside Hospital, and his case the source of many jokes among the staff. He was a clear example of what many physicians think of as the "garbage" or deadwood of their work and clientele. Elderly, unmarried and unemployed, Freddy Grazzo lived in a rooming house and spent his days drinking beer with his friends. He had an undiagnosed illness that repeatedly brought him to the Emergency Room, close to death and in pulmonary edema (his lungs filled with fluid, and breathing with great difficulty). Each time, the resident or intern on duty would resuscitate him and have to do a "work-up" examination as part of the hospital admission. Within a day or two, "Freddy" (as he was called by doctors thirty years his junior) would be doing well enough to leave the hospital, but his furlough was always short: within a few days he would be back in the Emergency Room in the same condition.

Because of his surprising ability to survive one after another of these emergencies Freddy had acquired a wide reputation in the hospital. Any one of these attacks might have ended his life, so it had become something of a standing hospital joke when his emergency admissions began to number in the twenties. Word would spread in the hospital that Freddy was back, and the interns and residents would laugh bitterly about how they had to waste their fine talents on old broken men who would never get better.

Still, over the course of twenty-five admissions a bit of abstract affection for Freddy Grazzo had developed among the staff. As he would be rushed into the Emergency Room, gasping for air, the nurses would tease him that he should be fixed up with Mary O'Leary, who was the female record-breaking survivor of Emergency Room resuscitations. At daily reports to the Chief of Medicine the residents would describe his condition as the "paddle syndrome": like a ball attached to a paddle, he was released from the hospital, went down the street to the nearest bar and soon bounced back into the hospital again.

If the annoyance that the staff felt for this patient were weighed against the amusement, it would have to be said that annoyance prevailed. When Freddy Grazzo arrived in the Emergency Room for the twenty-third time, the charge nurse openly complained that "they shouldn't have even coded him the last time he came in." When patients have an illness that will never improve and when their continued existence seems unwarranted in the doctors' eyes, either the doctor will note in the chart that the patient should not be resuscitated, or word will get passed informally around the staff that the patient should not again be coded the next time he gets into a life-threatening situation.

There was some feeling in the hospital that Freddy Grazzo had already been granted or burdened with too many codes, but he was still to survive this twenty-third admission. As the interns leisurely carried out the resuscitation like a familiar routine and inserted intravenous lines for his drugs, they argued about which floor of the hospital Freddy should be admitted to because no one wanted to do the work-up examination. It was late at night, and when Dr. Jenkins (a physician covering for Dr. Rosen, who was the regular doctor on the case) arrived in the Emergency Room, the charge nurse asked why he had bothered to come in. Jenkins replied that a decision might have to be made that night about keeping the patient alive. (As he put it: "In case something brews tonight a decision should be made.") Although Freddy Grazzo survived this admission, it was not long after that he was one day declared dead on arrival in the Emergency Room.

But even after his death Freddy Grazzo's name was still often heard, because toward the end of his life his physician became convinced that this was no ordinary case of geriatric decline, no mere piece of "medical garbage" after all. Dr. Rosen felt that he might just have stumbled across an exciting rare disease in Freddy Grazzo.

When the mortality meeting was held a few weeks later, Rosen seemed pleased that the case would be reviewed. He had indicated that he was convinced that Freddy had been an unsalvageable patient and he was happy to have a chance to show off his unusual diagnosis.

Rosen had first come to the hospital as a specialist in internal medicine twenty years before. In the old days he had been considered one of the more highly trained physicians in the hospital, and he had been given a free hand in treating the whole range of medical cases, including the most esoteric ones. But in the last few years the power in the hospital had progressively shifted to the newer "subspecialists" on the staff. Now the most challenging heart cases were referred to the cardiologists, and not to doctors like Rosen.

Furthermore, all the internists (an internist is a specialist in internal medicine, not to be confused with an intern, who is an untrained doctor fresh out of medical school) like himself were now expected to call in the specialists for consultations and special diagnostic tests whenever they had anything but the most routine cases. This meant that the specialists wound up managing all the interesting cases while Rosen was supposed to be satisfied with what he called the "lumps and bumps."

His reluctance to bow to pressure and invite consultation from the experts was not a matter of resentment, Rosen had argued to the house officers. For he believed that most consultation from these subspecialists was pointless because their recommendations were completely predictable. For example, during the previous week one of his patients had been admitted after being found unconscious with symptoms possibly suggesting a subarachnoid (brain) hemorrhage. This diagnosis could only have been positively confirmed by doing a somewhat risky and uncomfortable procedure, a cerebral arteriogram. The resident assigned to the case had been in favor of having the diagnostic procedure done, and knowing that Rosen was opposed to it, he had tactfully asked Rosen if they could get a specialist's opinion before ruling it out. Rosen had refused and explained why it was pointless: he could tell the resident exactly what the consultants would say without bothering to have them look at the patient. If the hospital neurologist (who was known to be conservative) was consulted, he would say, "Don't do anything." And if instead, they invited the opinion of the neurosurgeon, he would be sure to say, "Let's operate." So, as Rosen had argued to the resident, since it was all an arbitrary choice, it was better made by the doctor who knew something about the patient (and Rosen felt she was a nervous woman who would be upset by the diagnostic procedure) than on the basis of the prejudice of either subspecialist.

But to return to the Grazzo case, Rosen had indicated his confidence in the care the patient had received, and he was looking forward to the Mortality Review. In fact, he had asked the Chief of Medicine to let him use the entire meeting for this case, although it was customary to go through two cases in each meeting. The chief had refused but compromised by curtailing the discussion on the first case, explaining to the group that he wanted to leave more time for "Hal Rosen's masterpiece."

As Rosen came cheerfully tripping down the stairs to the front of the auditorium he conceded that the case was perhaps a "masterpiece with flaws." Proudly pointing to the twelve volumes of the patient's chart, he apologized that because of time constraints they would have to begin their review with the patient's eighteenth hospital admission. The facts were as follows: the patient had suffered recurrent dyspnea (breathlessness) and pulmonary edema, would often faint after eating, and they had long suspected that the cause of the symptoms were pulmonary emboli which were causing the edema. To illustrate the symptoms, Rosen entertained the audience with stories of how Freddy Grazzo would collapse on the street but somehow always get to the hospital in time to be resuscitated. On one occasion, Rosen smiled, Grazzo had suffered a coronary arrest (they believed an embolus had triggered a cardiac arrhythmia) on a street corner in the next town, and he would never have made it to the

hospital in time had he not unknowingly reached out and grabbed on to what turned out to be a fire alarm box to steady himself before he collapsed to the ground. A fire truck had arrived within two minutes, and seeing the man collapsed to the ground, the firemen had thrown him on the back of the truck and hauled him into the hospital.

After the laughter subsided Rosen described how they had made their discovery of the suspected rare disease. One day, upon being released from the hospital, Freddy had been waiting in front of the hospital for a taxi to take him home only to collapse, once more, into the arms of Rosen's colleague, Dr. Paul Jenkins, who had been walking by. Grabbing him in his arms, Jenkins had suddenly had the inspiration that the patient might be suffering not from pulmonary emboli but rather from the interesting and unusual central nervous hyperventilation syndrome. And, Rosen concluded with a smile, he concurred.

What followed next was some friendly joking about whether Rosen was only daydreaming to come up with such a diagnosis. Gordon Frank, the Chief of Cardiology, looked annoyed and finally openly expressed his disapproval. Standing up, he interrupted the friendly teasing: "I am deeply disturbed by the levity of this meeting, and I must say it matches the levity with which this patient was admitted every time to the Coronary Care Unit. Each time he came in everyone would giggle 'Guess who's back, ha-ha.' And I think that instead of sending him into our unit each time without knowing what was wrong with him, the patient should have had tests to ascertain what was wrong. The tests might have shown that he had a treatable illness."

As Frank explained, by saying "I don't like the levity with which this case was handled" he was actually saying that he didn't like the way that Rosen had managed the case medically. There had long been tension and disagreement between Rosen and himself. As he described it, Rosen would never come to him for help when he was out of his depth, and so Frank considered Rosen to be a potentially dangerous doctor. But, he admitted, a doctor couldn't come right out at a Mortality Meeting and say that he didn't like the way someone managed a case, so he had criticized the joking. Those who knew how he felt about Rosen would understand the deeper meaning of his remarks, and those who didn't, or who refused to acknowledge the issue, would be spared an unpleasant scene.

At the Mortality Meeting, Rosen met Frank's challenge and defended his refusal to do the diagnostic tests. There would have been no point, he argued, in performing angiography on this patient because even if the test had shown emboli as the cause of edema, the patient would never have consented to corrective surgery anyway. Frank replied, with obvious irritation, that if Rosen had allowed him to perform a diagnostic angiogram, it might have confirmed one of two possible diseases which were treatable even without surgery. He then described some new procedures, unknown to Rosen, which might have allowed them to treat Grazzo's problem without surgery.

The meeting time was coming to an end and so the doctors in the audience called out their final guesses about the true cause of Freddy Grazzo's illness. The intern who had pronounced the patient dead in the Emergency Room placed his bet on aspiration as the cause of death. An older physician in the audience hazarded the guess of atrial myxoma (a tumor in the heart).

The positions having been staked, it was now time for the final verdict. Solemnly, the pathologist stepped to the front of the room to announce what he had found in his autopsy.

To fully appreciate this moment it must be understood that the part of their work that medical doctors enjoy most is the challenging diagnosis. For most surgeons, the excitement and pleasure in the work is in doing a good job in the operating room: it is in the operating room that surgeons get to use their most highly specialized skills. But for medical doctors, the most exciting opportunity in the work is to make a brilliant diagnosis. Surgeons may also enjoy witnessing a dramatic cure as a result of an operation, but a medical doctor is often denied the satisfaction of bringing about a dramatic cure, especially in the treatment of elderly or chronically ill patients. In such cases, the work of internists can only prolong a painful and limited life. Under these circumstances, pleasure and excitement in the work are found, not in what can be done for patients, but rather in being the first one to come up with a brilliant diagnosis. That is why there would be special satisfaction in turning a routine and boring medical case into a good detective story with a surprising turn of events.

The pathologist, who paused before giving the final verdict on the Grazzo case, did not give away the ending all at once. Instead, he eliminated the losing guesses first. Like runners-up at a beauty contest, those who had guessed incorrectly bowed out good-naturedly. No, the death had not been caused by aspiration; the intern who guessed this possibility received the thumbs-down sign from the doctors sitting around him. And no, there had been no myxoma; the older physician who had made that guess shrugged his shoulders in concession. The pathologist turned to Rosen, sympathetically. While there *had* been some reason to suspect central nervous hyperventilation syndrome, not all of the criteria necessary to make that diagnosis were met in this case, and so that rare disorder could not be claimed. Freddy Grazzo had died the most ordinary death after all: his cardiac arrhythmias (irregularities of the heart beat) had been brought on by atherosclerosis (thickening and occlusion of the walls of the coronary arteries), and it was this common condition of the elderly which had triggered the emboli and his pulmonary edema.

As the meeting broke up, several of Rosen's friends patted him on the back for making a valiant effort at finding an exciting disease.

It is difficult to talk about mistakes without thinking about the feelings which mistakes arouse, both in the individual who has made the error and in the others around him. Acknowledging a consequential mistake is a profoundly upsetting experience for many reasons. First, there is the pain of fully knowing that things might have turned out better had one acted the way one should have. Then there is the unbearable self-doubt that follows from admitting to a mistake. The person who has recognized that he is capable of grave errors is suddenly unable to trust his own judgment. Every future act is cast in doubt and every decision agonized over lest it lead to further disaster. Finally, there is the fact, fair or not, that the individual who has made a mistake is somewhat tarnished in the eyes of his associates, and may even be formally punished or sanctioned. There is sad irony here, for the designation "mistake" is meant, at least on the surface, to excuse or pardon the actor. To say "it was just a mistake" signifies that such a wrong act was out of keeping for such an ordinarily trustworthy individual, just a fluke of nature unlikely to happen again. Nevertheless, most people are naturally suspicious of "mistakes," and the reputation of the person who makes them is often permanently stained.

No wonder, then, that most people try to avoid admitting to mistakes and prefer to live with the continued bad consequences of errors than with the distress of admitting to the mistake. But even if an individual is personally prepared to admit to a mistake, those whose lives and fates are tied up with his own are very likely to talk him out of such an admission, for the acknowledgment of a mistake is upsetting for groups as well as for individuals. When one member of a group starts calling attention to mistakes, not only does everyone else become vulnerable to the same exposure, but the entire collective enterprise they have committed themselves to begins to look more and more shabby.

Groups of doctors are not exempt from the upsetting possibility of having mistakes exposed. The works of just one outspoken member are enough to make everyone uncomfortable. The admission of mistakes is especially upsetting in the world of medicine because it is a world that rests and depends upon a faith in science, objectivity and rationality. A mistake in such a world is as disruptive as the commission of a sin in a religious society. It challenges the most cherished beliefs and identities of its members. Furthermore, since self-sufficiency and self-confidence are so highly valued in the medical profession, an admission of uncertainty or error exposes the physician to the kind of self-doubt that is unacceptable among his colleagues. The admission of a mistake is also very difficult in medicine because the stakes are so high. Many doctors, for example, retain disturbing memories for the rest of their lives of how they were responsible for a patient's death when they were residents because they had been too inexperienced to handle a situation properly.

For all of these reasons, it is not surprising that individual doctors are strictly discouraged by their group and their profession from being too willing to point out a mistake, or to openly admit to a feeling of guilt. The likelihood of making a bad mistake is too high and the price of admitting to it too costly to the group to leave the matter open to the discretion and dispositions of individual members. That is why a doctor is carefully taught in training and afterward not to regard as a mistake what most lay people would consider a mistake, and not to make too much of these unfortunate episodes.

A similar point can be made about feelings of guilt in medicine. Given the probability of making a bad mistake sometime in one's career, and given the probability of recognizing that the cynical reality of medical work is dramatically different from the idealistic expectations and self-images that one began with as a young student, the potential for feeling guilty is very high for physicians. That is why there are strong professional and institutional supports for avoiding feelings of guilt. Indeed, if a doctor is still prone to feeling guilty despite all of the supports to the contrary, he will quickly learn to keep his feelings to himself. Nobody wants to hear about a colleague's feelings of guilt, and talking too freely about such feelings with other doctors is considered a very embarrassing faux pas.

So it is that doctors are not likely to dig too deeply into one another's errors nor even to recognize fully the extent to which they collude in covering up each other's mistakes and incompetence. It is easier for them to shift the blame and responsibility for mistakes away from themselves, either to the patient, who becomes discredited in the process, or to surrounding impersonal circumstances such as misleading or unusual evidence in a particular case. Under these circumstances, mistakes are allowed to flourish and be repeated, and incompetence goes unchecked. Clearly it is the patient who pays the highest price in this arrangment for insuring the comfort of physician-colleagues, but some unusually conscientious doctors also pay the smaller price of being left alone with the residual feelings that manage to survive the professional neutralization and justifications.

NOTE

1. All names in this article are pseudonyms—Eds.

29

Midwives in Transition: The Structure of a Clinical Revolution

Barbara Katz Rothman

There has been considerable interest in the United States in recent years in the medical management of the reproductive processes in healthy women. Much of this interest represents a growing recognition by many mothers that hospital births impose structures upon the birth process unrelated to and in many cases disruptive of the process itself.

This paper contends that changing the setting of birth from hospital to home alters the timing of the birth process, a result of the social redefinition of birth. Through an analysis of the medical literature on birth, I compare the social construction of timetables for childbirth—how long normal labor and birth takes—by hospital and home-birth practitioners. I argue that, like all knowledge, this knowledge is socially determined and socially constructed, influenced both by ideology and social setting.

This paper is based on interviews I conducted in 1978 with one subgroup of the home-birth movement: nurse-midwives certified by the State of New York to attend births. I located 12 nurse-midwives in the New York metropolitan area who were attending births in homes and at an out-of-hospital birth center. Nurse-midwives in the United States are trained in medical institutions one to two years beyond nursing training and obtain their formative experience in hospitals. They differ from lay midwives, who receive their training outside of medical institutions and hospitals. Once nurse-midwives are qualified, most of them continue to practice in

hospitals. I use the term *nurse-midwives* throughout this paper to distinguish them from lay midwives. I discuss those parts of the interviews with these nurse-midwives which focus on their reconceptualization of birth timetables as they moved from hospital to home settings.

This sample was selected for two reasons: first, because of the position that nurse-midwives hold in relation to mothers compared with that held by physicians; while physicians in hospital settings control the birth process, nurse-midwives in home settings permit the birth process to transpire under the mother's control. Second, because nurse-midwives have been both formally trained within the medical model and extensively exposed to the home-birth model, data gathered in monitoring their adjustment to and reaction to the home-birth model provide a cross-contextual source for comparing the two birth settings.

Observation of the reactions of nurse-midwives to the home-birth setting demonstrates the degree to which their medical training was based on social convention rather than biological constants. The nurse-midwives did not embrace their non-medical childbirth work as ideological enthusiasts; rather, they were drawn into it, often against what they perceived as their better medical judgment. The nurse-midwives were firmly grounded in the medical model. Their ideas of what a home birth should and would be like, when they first began doing them, were based on their extensive experience with hospital births. While they believed that home birth would provide a more pleasant, caring, and warm environment than that ordinarily found in hospital birth, they did not expect it to challenge medical knowledge. And at first, home births did not. What the nurse-midwives saw in the home setting was screened through their expectations based on the hospital setting. The medical model was only challenged with repeated exposures to the anomalies of the home-birth experience.

The nurse-midwives' transition from one model to another is comparable to scientists' switch from one paradigm to another—a "scientific revolution," in Kuhn's (1970) words. Clinical models, like paradigms, are not discarded lightly by those who have invested time in learning and following them. The nurse-midwives were frequently not prepared for the anomalies in the timetable that they encountered at home. These involved unexpected divergences from times for birthing stages as "scheduled" by hospitals. Breaking these timetable norms without the expected ensuing "complications" provided the nurse-midwives attending home births with anomalies in the medical model. With repeated exposure to such anomalies, the nurse-midwives began to challenge the basis of medical knowledge regarding childbirth.

The medical approach divides the birth process into socially structured stages. Each of these stages is supposed to last a specific period of time. Roth (1963) notes that medical timetables structure physical processes and events, creating sanctioned definitions and medical controls. Miller (1977) has shown how medicine uses timetables to construct its own version of pregnancy. Similarly, medical timetables construct medical births: challenging those timetables challenges the medical model itself.

There are four parts of the birth process subject to medical timetables: (1) term (the end of pregnancy); (2) the first stage of labor; (3) delivery; and (4) expulsion of the placenta. I describe the hospital and home-birth approaches to these four parts and how each part's timetable issues arise. Then I consider the function of these timetables for doctors, hospitals, and the medical model.

1. Term: The End of Pregnancy

The Hospital Approach

In the medical model, a full-term pregnancy is 40 weeks long, though there is a two-week allowance made on either side for "normal" births. Any baby born earlier than 38 weeks is "premature;" after 42 weeks, "postmature." Prematurity does not produce any major conceptual anomalies between the two models. If a woman attempting home birth goes into labor much before the beginning of the 38th week, the nurse-midwives send her to a hospital because they, like physicians, perceive prematurity as abnormal, although they may not agree with the subsequent medical management of prematurity. In fact, few of the nurse-midwives' clients enter labor prematurely.

Post-maturity however, has become an issue for the nurse-midwives. The medical treatment for postmaturity is to induce labor, either by rupturing the membranes which contain the fetus, or by administering hormones to start labor contraction, or both. Rindfuss (1977) has shown that physicians often induce labor without any "medical" justification for mothers' and doctors' convenience.

Induced labor is more difficult for the mother and the baby. Contractions are longer, more frequent, and more intense. The more intense contractions reduce the baby's oxygen supply. The mother may require medication to cope with the more difficult labor, thus further increasing the risk of injury to the baby. In addition, once the induced labor (induction) is attempted, doctors will go on to delivery shortly thereafter, by Cesarian section if necessary.

The Home-Birth Approach

These techniques for inducing labor are conceptualized as "interventionist" and "risky" within the home-birth movement. The home-birth clients of the nurse-midwives do not want to face hospitalization and inductions, and are therefore motivated to ask for more time and, if that is not an option, to seek "safe" and "natural" techniques for starting labor. Some nurse-midwives suggest nipple stimulation, sexual relations, or even castor oil and enemas as means of stimulating uterine contractions. As I interviewed the 12 nurse-midwives about their techniques it was unclear whether their concern was avoiding postmaturity *per se* or avoiding medical treatment for postmaturity.

The nurse-midwives said that the recurring problem of postmaturity has led some home-birth practitioners to re-evaluate the length of pregnancy. Home-birth advocates point out that the medical determination of the length of pregnancy is based on observations of women in medical care. These home-birth advocates argue that women have been systematically malnourished by medically ordered weight-gain limitations. They attribute the high level of premature births experienced by teenage women to malnourishment resulting from overtaxing of their energy reserves by growth, as well as fetal, needs. The advocates believe that very well nourished women are capable of maintaining a pregnancy longer than are poorly nourished or borderline women. Thus, the phenomenon of so many healthy women going past term is reconceptualized in this developing model as an indication of even greater health, rather than a pathological condition of "postmaturity."

The first few times a nurse-midwife sees a woman going past term she accepts the medical definition of the situation as pathological. As the problem is seen repeatedly in women who manifest no signs of pathology, and who go on to have babies, the conceptualization of the situation as pathological is shaken. Nurse-midwives who have completed the transition from the medical to home-birth model, reject the medical definition and reconceptualize what they see from "postmature" to "fully mature."

2. The First Stage of Labor

The Hospital Approach

Childbirth, in the medical model, consists of three "stages" that occur after term. (In this paper I consider term as the first part of the birth process, occurring at the end of pregnancy.) In the first stage of childbirth, the cervix (the opening of the uterus into the vagina) dilates to its fullest to allow for the passage of the baby. In the second stage, the baby moves out of the open cervix, through the vagina, and is born. The third stage is the expulsion of the placenta. The second example of a point at which anomalies arise is in "going into labor," or entering the first stage.

The medical model of labor is best represented by "Friedman's Curve" (Friedman, 1959). To develop this curve, Friedman observed labors and computed averages for each "phase" of labor. He defined a *latent phase* as beginning with the onset of labor, taken as the onset of regular uterine contractions, to the beginnings of an *active phase*, when cervical dilation is most rapid. The onset of regular contractions can only be determined retroactively. *Williams Obstetrics* (Hellman and Pritchard, 1971), the classic obstetric text, says that the first stage of labor (which contains the two "phases") "begins with the first true labor pains and ends with the complete dilation of the cervix" (1971:351). "True labor pains" are distinguished from "false labor pains" by what happens next:

> The only way to distinguish between false and true labor pains, however, is to ascertain their effect on the cervix. The labor pains in the course of a few hours produce a demonstrable degree of effacement (thinning of the cervix) and some dilation of the cervix, whereas the effect of false labor pains on the cervix is minimal (1971:387).

The concept of "false" labor serves as a buffer for the medical model of "true" labor. Labors which display an unusually long "latent phase," or labors which simply stop, can be diagnosed as "false labors" and thus not affect the conceptualization of true labor. Friedman (1959:97) says:

> The latent phase may occasionally be found to be greater than the limit noted, and yet the remaining portion of the labor, the active phase of dilatation, may evolve completely normally. These unusual cases may be explained on the basis of the difficulty of determining the onset of labor. The transition from some forms of false labor into the latent phase of true labor may be completely undetectable and unnoticed. This may indeed be an explanation for the quite wide variation seen among patients of the actual duration of the latent phase.

In creating his model, Friedman obtained average values for each phase of labor, both for women with first pregnancies and for women with previous births. Then he computed the statistical limits and equated statistical normality with physiological normality:

> It is clear that cases where the phase-duration fall outside of these (statistical) limits are probably abnormal in some way. . . . We can see now how, with very little effort, we have been able to define average labor and to describe, with proper degree of certainty, the limits of normal (1959:97).

Once the equation is made between statistical abnormality and physiological abnormality, the door is opened for medical intervention. Thus, statistically abnormal labors are medically treated. The medical treatments are the same as those for induction of labor: rupture of membranes, hormones, and Cesarian section.

"Doing something" is the cornerstone of medical management. Every labor which takes "too long" and which cannot be stimulated by hormones or by breaking the membranes will go on to the next level of medical management, the Cesarian section. Breaking the membranes is an interesting induction technique in this regard: physicians believe that if too many hours pass after the membranes have been ruptured, naturally or artificially, a Cesarian section is necessary in order to prevent infection. Since physicians within the hospital always go on from one intervention to the next, there is no place for feedback; that is, one does not get to see what happens when a woman stays in first stage for a long time without her membranes being ruptured.

Hospital labors are shorter than home-birth labors. A study by Mehl (1977) of 1,046 matched, planned home and hospital births found that the average length of first-stage labor for first births was 14.5 hours in the home and 10.4 hours in the hospital. *Williams Obstetrics* reports the average length of labor for first births was 12.5 hours in 1948 (Hellman and Pritchard, 1971:396). For subsequent births, Mehl found first-stage labor took an average of 7.7 hours in the home and 6.6 hours in the hospital. Hellman and Pritchard reported 7.3 hours for the same stage. Because 1948 hospital births are comparable to contemporary home births, and because contemporary hospital births are shorter, it is probable that there has been an increase in "interventionist obstetrics," as home-birth advocates claim. These data are summarized in Table 1.

The Home-Birth Approach

Home-birth advocates see each labor as unique. While statistical norms may be interesting, they are of no value in managing a particular labor. When the nurse-midwives have a woman at home, or in the out-of-hospital birth-center, both the nurse-midwife and the woman giving birth want to complete birth without disruption. Rather than using arbitrary time limits, nurse-midwives look for progress, defined as continual change in the direction of birthing. A more

Table 1.   Labor Timetables for the First and Second Stages of Birth, for First and Subsequent Births

Birth	Length of First Stage of Labor (hours)		
	Home 1970s	*Hospital 1948*	*Hospital 1970s*
First	14.5	12.5	10.4
Subsequent	7.7/8.5[a]	7.3[b]	6.6/5.9[a]
	Length of Second Stage of Labor (minutes)		
First	94.7	80	63.9
Subsequent	48.7/21.7[a]	30[b]	19/15.9[a]

Note:
a. Second births and third births.
b. Second and all subsequent births.

medically-oriented nurse-midwife expressed her ambivalence this way:

> They don't have to look like a Freidman graph walking around, but I think they sould make some kind of reasonable progress (Personal interview).

Unable to specify times for "reasonable" progress, she nonetheless emphasized the word "reasonable," distinguishing it from "unreasonable" waiting.

A nurse-midwife with more home-birth experience expressed more concern for the laboring woman's subjective experience:

> There is no absolute limit—it would depend on what part of the labor was the longest and how she was handling that. Was she tired? Could she handle that? (Personal interview).

A labor at home can be long but "light," uncomfortable but not painful. A woman at home may spend those long hours going for a walk, napping, listening to music, even gardening or going to a movie. This light labor can go for quite some time. Another nurse-midwife described how she dealt with a long labor:

> Even though she was slow, she kept moving. I have learned to discriminate now, and if it's long I let them do it at home on their own and I try and listen carefully and when I get there it's toward the end of labor. This girl was going all Saturday and all Sunday, so that's 48 hours worth of labor. It wasn't forceful labor, but she was uncomfortable for two days. So if I'd have gone and stayed there the first time, I'd have been there a whole long time, then when you get there you have to do something. (Personal interview).

3. Delivery: Pushing Time Limits

The Hospital Approach

The medical literature defines the second stage of labor, the delivery, as the period from the complete dilatation of the cervix to the birth of the fetus. Hellman and Pritchard (1971) found this second stage took an average of 80 minutes for first births and 30 minutes for all subsequent births in 1948. Mehl (1977) found home births

took an average of 94.7 minutes for first births and, for second and third births, 48.7 to 21.7 minutes. Contemporary medical procedures shorten the second stage in the hospital to 63.9 minutes for first births and 19 to 15.9 minutes for second and third births (Mehl, 1977).

The modern medical management of labor and delivery hastens the delivery process, primarily by the use of forceps and fundal pressure (pressing on the top of the uterus through the abdomen) to pull or push a fetus out. Friedman (1959) found the second stage of birth took an average of 54 minutes for first births and 18 minutes for all subsequent births. He defined the "limits of normal" as 2.5 hours for first births and 48 minutes for subsequent births. Contemporary hospitals usually apply even stricter limits, and allow a maximum of two hours for first births and one hour for second births. Time limits vary somewhat within U.S. hospitals, but physicians and nurse-midwives in training usually do not get to see a three-hour second stage, much less anything longer. "Prolonged" second stages are medically managed to effect immediate delivery.

Mehl (1977) found low forceps were 54 times more common and mid-forceps 21 times more common for prolonged second-stage and/or protracted descent in the hospital than in planned home births. This does not include the elective use of forceps (without "medical" indication), a procedure which was used in none of the home births and 10 percent of the hospital births (four percent low forceps and six percent mid-forceps). Any birth which began at home but was hospitalized for any reason, including protracted descent or prolonged second stage (10 percent of the sample), was included in Mehl's home-birth statistics.

The Home-Birth Approach

Nurse-midwives and their out-of-hospital clients were even more highly motivated to avoid hospitalization for prolonged delivery than for prolonged labor. There is a sense of having come so far, through the most difficult and trying part. Once a mother is fully dilated she may be so close to birth that moving her could result in giving birth on the way to the hospital. Contrary to the popular image, the mother is usually working hard but not in pain during the delivery, and as tired as she may be, is quite reluctant to leave home.

Compare the situation at home with what the nurse-midwives saw in their training. In a hospital birth the mother is moved to a delivery table at or near the end of cervical dilation. She is usually strapped into leg stirrups and heavily draped. The physician is scrubbed and gowned. The anesthetist is at the ready. The pediatric staff is in the room. It is difficult to imagine that situation continuing for three, four, or more hours. The position of the mother alone makes that impossible. In the medical model, second stage begins with complete cervical dilation. Cervical dilation is an "objective" measure, determined by the birth attendant. By defining the end of the first stage, the birth attendant controls the time of formal entry into second stage. One of the ways nurse-midwives quickly learn to "buy time" for their clients is in measuring cervical dilation:

> If she's honestly fully dilated I do count it as second stage. If she has a rim of cervix left, I don't count it because I don't think it's fair. A lot of what I do is to look good on paper (Personal interview).

Looking good on paper is a serious concern. Nurse-midwives expressed their concern about legal liability if they allow the second stage to go on for more than the one- or two-hour hospital limit, and then want to hospitalize the woman. One told of allowing a woman to stay at home in second stage for three hours and then hospitalizing her for lack of progress. The mother, in her confusion and exhaustion, told the hospital staff that she had been in second stage for five hours. The nurse-midwife risked losing the support of the physician who had agreed to provide emergency and other medical services at that hospital. Even when a nurse-midwife's experiences cause her to question the medical model, the constraints under which she works may thus prevent her from acting on new knowledge. Nurse-midwives talked about the problems of charting second stage:

> If I'm doing it for my own use I start counting when the woman begins to push, and push in a directed manner, really bearing down. I have to lie sometimes. I mean I'm prepared to lie if we ever have to go to the

hospital because there might be an hour or so between full dilation and when she begins pushing and I don't see—as long as the heart tones are fine and there is some progress being made—but like I don't think—you'd be very careful to take them to the hospital after five hours of pushing—they [hospital staff] would go crazy (Personal interview).

> All my second stages, I write them down under two hours: by hospital standards two hours is the upper limit of normal, but I don't have two-hour second stages except that one girl that I happened to examine her. If I had not examined her, I probably would not have had more than an hour and a half written down because it was only an hour and a half that she was voluntarily pushing herself (Personal interview).

Not looking for what you do not want to find is a technique used by many of the nurse-midwives early in their transition away from the medical model. They are careful about examining a woman who might be fully dilated for fear of starting up the clock they work under:

> I try to hold off on checking if she doesn't have the urge to push, but if she has the urge to push, then I have to go in and check (Personal interview).

With more home-birth experience, the nurse-midwives reconceptualized the second stage itself. Rather than starting with full dilatation, the "objective" measure, they measured the second stage by the subjective measure of the woman's urge to push. Most women begin to feel a definite urge to push, and begin bearing down, at just about the time of full dilatation. But not all women have this experience. For some, labor contractions ease after they are fully dilated. These are the "second-stage arrests" which medicine treats by the use of forceps or Cesarian section. Some nurse-midwives reconceptualized this from "second-stage arrest" to a naturally occurring rest period at the end of labor, after becoming fully dilated, but before second stage. In the medical model, once labor starts it cannot stop and start again and still be "normal." If it stops, that calls for medical intervention. But a nurse-midwife can reconceptualize "the hour or so between full dilation and when she starts pushing" as other than second stage. This is more than just buying time for clients: this is developing an alternative set of definitions, reconceptualizing the birth process.

Nurse-midwives who did not know each other and who did not work together came to the same conclusions about the inaccuracy of the medical model:

> My second stage measurement is when they show signs of being in second stage. That'd be the pushing or the rectum bulging or stuff like that. . . . I usually have short second stages [laughter]. Y'know, if you let nature do it, there's not a hassle (Personal interview).

> I would not, and this is really a fine point, encourage a mother to start pushing just because she felt fully dilated to me. I think I tend to wait till the mother gets a natural urge to push. . . . the baby's been in there for nine months (Personal interview).

It may be that buying time is the first concern. In looking for ways to avoid starting the clock, nurse-midwives first realize that they can simply not examine the mother. They then have the experience of "not looking" for an hour, and seeing the mother stir herself out of a rest and begin to have a strong urge to push. The first few times that hour provokes anxiety in the nurse-midwives. Most of the nurse-midwives told of their nervousness in breaking timetable norms. The experience of breaking timetable norms and having a successful outcome challenges the medical model; it is a radicalizing experience. This opportunity for feedback does not often exist in the hospital setting, where medicine's stringent control minimizes anomalies. A woman who has an "arrested" second stage will usually not be permitted to sleep, and therefore the diagnosis remains unchallenged. Forceps and/or hormonal stimulants are introduced. The resulting birth injuries are seen as inevitable, as if without the forceps the baby would never have gotten out alive.

4. Expulsion of the Placenta

The Hospital Approach

Third stage is the period between the delivery of the baby and the expulsion of the placenta. In hospitals, third stage takes five minutes or less

(Hellman and Pritchard, 1971; Mehl, 1977). A combination of massage and pressure on the uterus and gentle pulling on the cord are used routinely. Hellman and Pritchard (1971:417) instruct that if the placenta has not separated within about five minutes after birth it should be removed manually. In Mehl's (1977) data, the average length of the third stage for home births was 20 minutes.

The Home-Birth Approach

For the nurse-midwives, the third stage timetable was occasionally a source of problems. Sometimes the placenta does not slip out, even in the somewhat longer time period that many nurse-midwives have learned to accept. Their usual techniques—the mother putting the baby to suckle, squatting, walking—may not have shown immediate results:

> I don't feel so bad if there's no bleeding. Difficult if it doesn't come, and it's even trickier when there's no hemmorhage because if there's a hemmorhage then there's a definite action you can take; but when it's retained and it isn't coming it's a real question— is it just a bell-shaped curve and that kind of thing— in the hospital if it isn't coming right away you just go in and pull it out (Personal interview).

> I talked with my grandmother—she's still alive, she's 90, she did plenty of deliveries—and she says that if the placenta doesn't come out you just let the mother walk around for a day and have her breastfeed and it'll fall out. And I believe her. Here I would have an hour because I am concerned about what appears on the chart (Personal interview).

> If there was no bleeding, and she was doing fine, I think several hours, you know, or more could elapse, no problem (Personal interview).

Why the Rush? The Functions of Timetables

The Hospital Approach

There are both medical and institutional reasons for speeding up the birth. The medical reasons are: (1) A prolonged third stage is believed to cause excessive bleeding. (2) The second stage is kept short in order to spare the mother and the baby, because birth is conceptualized as traumatic for both. (3) The anesthetics which are routinely used create conditions encouraging, if not requiring, the use of forceps. The position of the woman also contributes to the use of forceps because the baby must be pushed upwards.

There are several institutional reasons for speeding up birth. Rosengren and DeVault (1963) discussed the importance of timing and tempo in the hospital management of birth. Tempo relates to the number of deliveries in a given period of time. The tempo of individual births are matched to the space and staffing limitations of the institution. If there are too many births, the anesthetist will slow them down. An unusually prolonged delivery will upset the hospital's tempo, and there is even competition to maintain optimal tempo. One resident said, "Our [the residents'] average length of delivery is about 50 minutes, and the pros' [the private doctors'] is about 40 minutes" (1963: 282). That presumably includes delivery of baby and placenta, and probably any surgical repair as well. Rosengren and DeVault further note:

> This "correct tempo" becomes a matter of status competition, and a measure of professional adeptness. The use of forceps is also a means by which the tempo is maintained in the delivery room, and they are so often used that the procedure is regarded as normal (1963:282).

Rosengren and DeVault, with no out-of-hospital births as a basis for comparison, apparently did not perceive the management of the third stage as serving institutional needs. Once the baby is quickly and efficiently removed, one certainly does not wait 20 minutes or more for the spontaneous expulsion of the placenta.

Hospitals so routinize the various obstetrical interventions that alternative conceptualizations are unthinkable. A woman attached to an intravenous or a machine used to monitor the condition of the fetus cannot very well be told to go out for a walk or to a movie if her contractions are slow and not forceful. A woman strapped to a delivery table cannot take a nap if she does not feel ready to push. She cannot even get up and move around to find a better position for pushing. Once the institutional forces begin,

the process is constructed in a manner appropriate to the institutional model. Once a laboring woman is hospitalized, she will have a medically constructed birth.

Therefore, not only the specific rules, but also the overall perspective of the hospital as an institution, operate to proscribe hospital-birth attendants' reconceptualization of birth. Practitioners may "lose even the ability to think of alternatives or to take known alternatives seriously because the routine is so solidly established and embedded in perceived consensus" (Holtzner, 1968:96).

The Home-Birth Approach

In home births the institutional supports and the motivations for maintaining hospital tempo are not present; birth attendants do not move from one laboring woman to the next. Births do not have to be meshed to form an overriding institutional tempo. Functioning without institutional demands or institutional supports, nurse-midwives are presented with situations which are anomalies in the medical model, such as labors stopping and starting, the second stage not following immediately after the first, and a woman taking four hours to push out a baby without any problems—and feeling good about it. Without obstetrical interventions, medically defined "pathologies" may be seen to right themselves, and so the very conceptualization of pathology and normality is challenged.

In home or out-of-hospital births, the routine and perceived consensus is taken away. Each of the nurse-midwives I interviewed stressed the individuality of each out-of-hospital birth, saying that each birth was so much "a part of each mother and family." They described tightly-knit extended-kin situations, devoutly religious births, party-like births, intimate and sexual births—an infinite variety. The variety of social contexts seemed to overshadow the physiological constants. That is not to say that constraints are absent, but that at home the constraints are very different than they are within hospitals. At home, the mother as patient must coexist or take second place to the mother, wife, daughter, sister, friend, or lover.

Summary and Conclusions

The hospital setting structures the ideology and the practice of hospital-trained nurse-midwives. Home birth, by contrast, provides an ultimately radicalizing experience, in that it challenges the taken-for-granted assumptions of the hospital experience. Timetables provide structure for the hospital experience: structures—statistical constructions, models, or attempts at routinization or standardization—are not necessarily bad in and of themselves. Medical timetables, however, have termed pathological whatever does not conform to statistical norms, which are themselves based on biased samples and distorted by structural restraints imposed in the interests of efficiency. Thus, the range of normal variation does not permeate the model.

One final conclusion to be drawn from this research is a reaffirmation that knowledge, including medical knowledge, is socially situated. Medical reality is a socially constructed reality, and the content of medical knowledge is as legitimate an area of research for medical sociology as are doctor-patient relations, illness behavior, and the other more generally studied areas.

NOTE

The author thanks Maren Lockwood Carden, Leon Chazanow, Sue Fisher, Betty Leyerle, Judith Lorber, Eileen Moran, and the anonymous *Social Problems* reviewers.

REFERENCES

Friedman, Emmanuel
1959 "Graphic analysis of labor." Bulletin of the American College of Nurse-Midwifery 4(3):94–105.
Hellman, Louis, and Jack Pritchard (eds.)
1971 Williams Obstetrics. 14th edition. New York: Appleton-Century-Croft.
Holtzner, Bukart
1968 Reality Construction in Society. Cambridge, MA: Schenkmann.
Kuhn, Thomas S.
1970 The Structure of Scientific Revolutions. Chicago: University of Chicago Press.
Mehl, Lewis
1977 "Research on childbirth alternatives: What can it tell us about hospital practices?" Pp. 171–208 in David Stewart and Lee Stewart (eds.), Twenty-First Century Obstetrics Now. Chapel Hill, N.C.: National Association of Parents and Professionals for Safe Alternatives in Childbirth.
Miller, Rita Seiden
1977 "The social construction and reconstruction of physiological events: Acquiring the pregnant identity." Pp. 87–145 in Norman K. Denzin (ed.), Studies in Symbolic Interaction. Greenwich, CT: JAI Press.
Rindfuss, Ronald R.
1977 "Convenience and the occurrence of births: Induction of labor in the United States and Canada." Paper presented at the 72nd annual meeting of the American Sociological Association, Chicago, August.
Rosengren, William R., and Spencer DeVault
1963 "The sociology of time and space in an obstetric hospital." Pp. 284–285 in Eliot Friedson (ed.), The Hospital in Modern Society. New York: Free Press.
Roth, Julius
1963 Timetables: Structuring the Passage of Time in Hospital Treatment and Other Careers. Indianapolis: Bobbs Merrill.
Rothman, Barbara Katz
1982 In Labor: Women and Power in the Birthplace. New York: Norton.

Part Three

Contemporary Critical Debates

Up until this point we have presented our analysis of health and medical care as if all critical analysts were more or less in agreement. But in health care, as in any social and intellectual enterprise, controversies and debates rage over the source of problems and appropriate solutions. In Part Three we present articles illustrative of contemporary debates on two different but related critical issues in the sociology of health and illness.

Individual Responsibility and Health

With growing recognition of the limitations of medical care and the environmental and behavioral components of much of modern disease, a debate has emerged as to who is responsible for individual health. For many years, the medical model conceptualized disease as one of those things, like earthquakes or tornados, over which humans simply had no control. When critics began to articulate the relationships among society, behavior, and sickness however, it became clear that disease is socially patterned, is connected with the values of society, and, importantly, much of it can be prevented.

A series of articles in *The New York Times* (2/3/80–2/5/80) presented information about ". . . petrochemical companies [which] have quietly tested thousands of American workers to determine if any of the genes they were born with are what industry doctors call 'defective,' making the employees especially vulnerable to certain chemicals in the workplace. The process is called genetic screening." An enormous controversy surrounds genetic screening; some workers, scientists, and union leaders claim that such testing is in fact a "Brave New World nightmare, an Orwellian stew in which the victims of toxic chemicals will be blamed for having faulty genes." These critics ". . . want industry to place the emphasis on cleaning up the workplace, not deciding which workers ought to be removed from conditions that could ultimately be bad for all.

Central to the controversy surrounding genetic screening (and the topic of the articles in this section) is the issue of who is responsible for an individual's health. Specifically, to what extent are we, as individuals, responsible for preventing disease and maintaining our own health? One of the most articulate spokespersons for the argument that individuals are ultimately responsible for their own health is John Knowles, former Director of Massachusetts General Hospital and past President of the Rockefeller Foundation. In "The Responsibility of the Individual" Knowles argues that people are born healthy and made sick by personal "misbehavior" and environmental conditions. While acknowledging the role of the environment in creating disease, his emphasis is on the "bad habits" of individuals, which he sees as the cause of much of our current state of unhealthiness. These bad habits include ". . . over-eating, too much drinking, taking pills, staying up at night, engaging in promiscuous sex, driving too fast, and smoking cigarettes. . . ." According to this view, these behaviors are encouraged because our society has subordinated individual responsibility to "individual rights." Solutions to health problems should by and large focus on changing the behaviors of people, who are themselves simultaneously victims and victimizers, via education, rewards and punishments, etc., thus allowing them to improve their health through their own efforts. Preservation of health should be a public duty. Knowles rejects what he terms the "liberal" ideology which stresses societal responsibility for the ills of humanity, and, in fact, he blames this ideology for eroding individual responsibility in the first place.

Knowles makes a good case for the importance of individual change and self-improvement. There is little doubt that better health could be promoted and much disease prevented if only we could adopt healthier lifestyles and relinquish some of our "bad habits." There are, however, several problems with his argument. Knowles condemns ". . . sloth, gluttony, alcoholic intemperance, reckless driving, sexual frenzy, and smoking . . ." in essentially moralistic terms. He does not address the problem of pain and suffering, which has its roots in flawed institutions and environments over which, at least as individuals, people have little or no control. He ignores the obvious efforts—the spending of huge sums of money for medical help, the hours spent waiting to see physicians, etc.—that people *do* make in an attempt to make or keep themselves healthy. If these efforts are misdirected, then we must ask why people believe in them. Nor does Knowles address the problem of the very limited power people have to effect changes over those social organizations and institutions that produce the toxic chemicals, the noise, the stress, etc. which lead so many to seek relief through such unhealthy means as alcohol, cigarettes, and licit or illicit mood-altering drugs.

Robert Crawford's article "Individual Responsibility and Health Politics" explores the problems of seeing individual responsibility for health in the context of what he sees as a "victim-blaming" ideology. As Crawford notes, focusing attention on the victims of problems (such as environmental pollution or stress-induced alcohol or cigarette addiction) ignores and thereby masks the role of the particular social arrangements that may be disease-producing and the inability of individuals to prevent or cure those diseases themselves. He also argues that the ideology of individual responsibility helps "justify shifting the burden of costs back to users" and legitimate a retrenchment from social responsibility. The moralism of much of the writing of those advocating individual responsibility for health, as Crawford observes, is a moralism that ultimately blames ill health on those with the least power and resources to effect change for the better.

The social scientist must ask who gains and who "pays" in these differing views of the relative responsibility of individuals for their own health—that is, what are the social consequences of each perspective? For those who advocate individual responsibility, the broad social arrangements which exist (the status quo) are not to be challenged. Rather, strategies of *adaptation* should be developed for individuals who, from the "liberal" perspective, are the victims of those very social arrangements to which they're being encouraged to adapt.

No one, of course, claims that the individual has absolutely no power to effect changes in life style that will promote health and well being. It can be argued, however, that these efforts need not be limited to individual adjustment, but can involve collective efforts at community change and social reform, in addition to individual self-help. The balance ultimately struck between the opposing views expressed in the Knowles and Crawford articles is likely to be a crucial determinant of the future course of medical care efforts in the United States.

30

The Responsibility of the Individual

John H. Knowles

....

More than half the reduction in mortality rates over the past three centuries occurred before 1900 and was due in nearly equal measure to improved nutrition and reduced exposure to air- and water-borne infection. The provision of safe water and milk supplies, the improvement in both personal and food hygiene, and the efficient disposal of sewage all helped to reduce the incidence of infectious disease. Vaccination further reduced mortality rates from smallpox in the nineteenth century and from diphtheria, pertussis, tetanus, poliomyelitis, measles, and tuberculosis in the twentieth century, although the contribution of vaccinations to the overall reduction in mortality rates over the past hundred years is small (perhaps as small as 10 percent) as contrasted with that due to improved nutrition and reduction in the transmission of infectious disease.[1] An even smaller contribution has been made by the introduction of medical and surgical therapy, namely antibiotics and the excision of tumors, in the twentieth century.

Over the past 100 years, infanticide has declined in the developed countries as changes in reproductive practice, such as the use of contraceptives, have been introduced to contain family size and reduce national growth rates of population, thus sustaining the improvement in health and standards of living. The population of England and Wales trebled between 1700 and 1850 without any significant importation of food. If the birth rate had been maintained, the population by now would be some 140 million instead of the 46 million it actually is. Changes in reproductive behavior maintained a rough balance between food production and population growth and allowed standards of living to rise. A similarly remarkable change in reproductive behavior occured in Ireland following the potato famines of the eighteen-forties, and birth rates have been sustained voluntarily at a low level to this day in that largely Catholic country.

Improvement in health resulted from changes in personal behavior (hygiene, reproductive practices) and in environmental conditions (food supplies, provision of safe milk and water, and sewage disposal). Cartesian rationalism, Baconian empiricism, and the results of the Industrial Revolution led the medical profession into scientific and technical approaches to disease. The engineering approach to the human machine was strengthened by the germ theory of disease which followed the work of Pasteur and Koch in the late nineteenth century. The idea was simple, unitary, and compelling: one germ—one disease—one therapy. Population factors, personal behavior, and environmental conditions were neglected in such a pure model or paradigm of approach and were picked up by elements less powerful and perceived increasingly as marginal to health, i.e., politicians, state departments, and schools of public health. The medical profession hitched its wagon to the rising stars of science and technology. The results have been spectacular for some individuals in terms of cure, containment of disease, and alleviation of suffering; as spectacular in terms of the horrendous costs compounding now at a rate of 15 percent annually; and even more spectacular to some because allocation of more and more men and women, money, and machines has affected mortality and morbidity rates only marginally. The problem of diminishing returns, if current trends continue, will loom as large and pregnant to the

American people in the future as the mushrooming atomic cloud does today.

I will not berate the medical profession, its practitioners and its professors—they reflect our culture, its values, beliefs, rites, and symbols. Central to the culture is faith in progress through science, technology, and industrial growth; increasingly peripheral to it is the idea, vis-à-vis health, that over 99 percent of us are born healthy and made sick as a result of personal misbehavior and environmental conditions. The solution to the problems of ill health in modern American society involves individual responsibility, in the first instance, and social responsibility through public legislative and private voluntary efforts, in the second instance. Alas, the medical profession isn't interested, because the intellectual, emotional, and financial rewards of the present system are too great and because there is no incentive and very little demand to change. But the problems of rising costs; the allocation of scarce national resources among competing claims for improving life; diminishing returns on health from the system of acute, curative, high-cost, hospital-based medicine; and increasing evidence that personal behavior, food, and the nature of the environment around us are the prime determinants of health and disease will present us with critical choices and will inevitably force change.

Most individuals do not worry about their health until they lose it. Uncertain attempts at healthy living many be thwarted by the temptations of a culture whose economy depends on high production and high consumption. Asceticism is reserved for hair-shirted clerics and constipated cranks, and everytime one of them dies at the age of 50, the hedonist smiles, inhales deeply, and takes another drink. Everyone is a gambler and knows someone who has lived it up and hit 90 years, so bad nurture doesn't necessarily spell doom. For others, a genetic fatalism takes hold: Nature—your parents' genes—will decide your fate no matter what you do. For those who remain undecided, there is alway the reassuring story—and we all know it—ot someone with living parents who has led a temperate, viceless life and died of a heart attack at the age of 45. As for stress, how about Winston Churchill at the age of 90! And he drank brandy, smoked cigars, never

exercised, and was grossly overweight! Facing the insufferable insult of extinction with the years, and knowing how we might improve our health, we still don't do much about it. The reasons for this peculiar behavior may include: (1) a denial of death and disease coupled with the demand for instant gratification and the orientation of most people in most cultures to living day by day; (2) the feeling that nature, including death and disease, can be conquered through scientific and technologic advance or overcome by personal will; (3) the dispiriting conditions of old people leads to a decision by some that they don't want infirmities and unhappiness and would just as soon die early; (4) chronic depression in some individuals to the extent that they wish consciously or unconsciously for death and have no desire to take care of themselves; and (5) the disinterest of the one person to whom we ascribe the ultimate wisdom about health—the physician.

Prevention of disease means forsaking the bad habits which many people enjoy—overeating, too much drinking, taking pills, staying up at night, engaging in promiscuous sex, driving too fast, and smoking cigarettes—or, put another way, it means doing things which require special effort—exercising regularly, going to the dentist, practicing contraception, ensuring harmonious family life, submitting to screening examinations. The idea of individual responsibility flies in the face of American history which has seen a people steadfastly sanctifying individual freedom while progressively narrowing it though the development of the beneficent state. On the one hand, Social Darwinism maintains its hold on the American mind despite the best intentions of the neo-liberals. Those who aren't supine before the Federal Leviathan proclaim the survival of the fittest. On the other, the idea of individual responsibility has been submerged to individual rights—rights, or demands, to be guaranteed by government and delivered by public and private institutions. The cost of sloth, gluttony, alcoholic intemperance, reckless driving, sexual frenzy, and smoking is now a national, and not an individual, responsibility. This is justified as individual freedom—but one man's freedom in health is another man's shackle in taxes and insurance premiums. I believe the idea of a "right" to health should be replaced by the idea of an individual moral obligation to preserve one's own health—a public duty if you will. The individual then has the "right" to expect help with information, accessible services of good quality, and minimal financial barriers. Meanwhile, the people have been led to believe that national health insurance, more doctors, and greater use of high-cost, hospital-based technologies will improve health. Unfortunately none of them will.

More and more the artificer of the possible is "society"—not the individual; he thereby becomes more dependent on things external and less on his own inner resources. The paranoid style of consumer groups demands a fight against something, usually a Big Bureaucracy. In the case of health, it is the hospitals, the doctors, the medical schools, the Medicaid-Medicare combine, the government. Nader's Raiders have yet to allow that the next major advances in the health of the American people will come from the assumption of individual responsibility for one's own health and a necessary change in habits for the majority of Americans. We do spend over $30 billion annually for cigarettes and whiskey.

The behavior of Americans might be changed if there were adequate programs of health education in primary and secondary schools and even colleges—but there aren't. School health programs are abysmal at best, confining themselves to preemptory sick calls and posters on brushing teeth and eating three meals a day; there are no examinations to determine if anything's been learned. Awareness of danger to body and mind isn't acquired until the mid-twenties in our culture, and by then patterns of behavior are set which are hard to change. Children tire of "scrub your teeth," "don't eat that junk," "leave your dingy alone," "go to bed," and "get some exercise." By the time they are sixteen, society says they shall have cars, drink beer, smoke, eat junk at drive-ins, and have a go at fornication. If they demur, they are sissies or queer or both. The pressure of the peer group to do wrong is hardly balanced by the limp protestations of permissive parents, nervously keeping up with the Joneses in suburban ranch houses crammed with snacks and mobile bars.

The barriers to the assumption of individual responsibility for one's own health are lack of knowledge (implicating the inadequacies of formal education, the all-too-powerful force of advertising, and of the informal systems of continuing education), lack of sufficient interest in, and knowledge about, what is preventable and the "cost-to-benefit" ratios of nationwide health programs (thereby implicating all the powerful interests in the heath establishment, which couldn't be less interested, and calling for a much larger investment in fundamental and applied research), and a culture which has progressively eroded the idea of individual responsibility while stressing individual rights, the responsibility of society-at-large, and the steady growth of production and consumption ("We have met the enemy and it is us!"). Changing human behvior involves sustaining and repeating an intelligible message, reinforcing it through peer pressure and approval, and establishing clearly perceived rewards which materialize in as short a time as possible. Advertising agencies know this, but it is easier to sell deodorants, pantyhose, and automobiles than it is health.

What is the problem? During the nineteenth and early twentieth centuries, communicable disease was the major health problem in the United States. In 1900, the average life expectancy at birth was 49.2 years. By 1966, it had increased to 70.1 years, due mainly to marked reduction in infant and child mortality (between birth and age 15). By mid-century, accidents were by far the leading cause of death in youngsters, and the majority of accidents were related to excessive use of alcohol by their parents, by adults generally, and even occasionally by themselves. While 21 years were added to life expectancy at birth, only 2.7 years were added to it at age 65—the remaining life expectancy at age 65 being 11.9 years in 1900 and 14.6 in 1966. The marked increase in life expectancy at birth was due to the control and eradication of infectious disease, directly through improved nutrition and personal hygiene, and environmental changes, namely, the provision for safe water and milk supplies and for sewage disposal.

Today, the major health problems in the United States are the chronic diseases of middle and later age, mainly heart disease, cancer, and strokes. Death and disability in middle age is premature and potentially preventable. For those under 44 years, the leading causes of death are accidents, heart disease, cancer, homicide, and suicide. For those under 25 years, accidents are by far the most common cause of death, with homicide and suicide the next leading causes. Of the roughly 2 million deaths in the United States in 1969, 50 percent were due to heart disease (40%) and strokes (10%); 16 percent to cancer; and 8 percent to accidents (6%), homicide (1%), and suicide (1%). But death statistics tell only a small part of the story. For every successful suicide, an estimated ten others, or 200,000 people, have made the attempt. For every death due to accidents, hundreds of others are injured, and many of those are permanently disabled. Over 17 percent, or 36 million people, have serious disabilities limiting their activities.

Premature death and disability are far too common. For the 178,000 people between the ages of 45 and 64 years who died of heart disease in 1969, 1.2 million (or 3 percent of the 40.5 million people in this age group) were chronically disabled because of heart disease.[2] For the over 30,000 people who died of cirrhosis of the liver in 1969—a disease related directly to excessive ingestion of alcohol together with poor nutrition—as many as 10 million people suffer from alcoholism and varying degrees of malnutrition. Twenty-six million Americans, 11 million of whom receive no federal food assistance, live below the federally defined poverty level, a level which does not support an adequate diet.

The control of communicable disease depended as much (or even more) on broad changes in the environment attendant upon economic development (improved housing and nutrition, sanitary engineering for safe water supplies, and sewage disposal) as it did on the individual's knowledge and behavior (need for immunization, personal hygiene, and cooperation with case finding). However, control of the present major health problems in the United States depends directly on modification of the individual's behavior and habit of living. The need for improved nutrition remains unchanged. The knowledge required to persuade the individual to change his habits is far more complex, far less dramatic in its results, far more difficult to organize and convey—in short, far less appeal-

ing and compelling than the need for immunization, getting rid of sewage, and drinking safe water. Even the problems of immunizing the population in contemporary America are difficult, however—witness the failure to eradicate measles ten years after the technical means became available.

Studies by Breslow and Belloc[3] of nearly 7,000 adults followed for five and one-half years showed that life expectancy and health are significantly related to the following basic health habits:

1) three meals a day at regular times and no snacking;
2) breakfast every day;
3) moderate exercise two or three times a week;
4) adequate sleep (7 or 8 hours a night);
5) no smoking;
6) moderate weight;
7) no alcohol or only in moderation.

A 45-year-old man who practiced 0–3 of these habits has a remaining life expectancy of 21.6 years (to age 67), while one with 6–7 of these habits has a life expectancy of 33.1 years (to age 78). In other words, 11 years could be added to life expectancy by relatively simple changes in habits of living, recalling that only 2.7 years were added to life expectancy at age 65 between 1900 and 1966. Breslow also found that the health status of those who practiced all seven habits was similar to those 30 years younger who observed none.

A large percentage of deaths (estimates up to 80 percent) due to cardiovascular disease and cancer are "premature," that is, occur in relatively young individuals and are related to the individual's bad habits. Heart disease and strokes are related to dietary factors, cigarette smoking, potentially treatable but undetected hypertension, and lack of exercise. Cancer is related to smoking (oral, buccal, lung, and bladder cancer) and probably to diets rich in fat and refined foodstuffs and low in residue (gastrointestinal and perhaps breast and prostatic cancer) and to the ingestion of food additives and certain drugs, or the inhalation of a wide variety of noxious agents. Certain occupational exposures and personal hygienic factors account for a small but important fraction of the total deaths due to cancer. Theoretically, all deaths due to accidents, homicide, and suicide are preventable.

Stress appears to play a critical role in disease. The stress of adjusting to change may generate a wide variety of diseases, and change is the hallmark of modern society. It is know that the death rate for widows and widowers is 10 times higher in the first year of bereavement than it is for others of comparable age; in the year following divorce the divorced persons have 12 times the incidence of disease that married persons have. People living in primitive societies insulated from change have low blood pressures and blood cholesterol levels which do not vary from youth to old age. Blood pressure and cholesterol tend to rise with age in our culture and are thought to be a prime cause of heart attacks and strokes. Studies indicate that up to 80 percent of serious physical illnesses seem to develop at a time when the individual feels helpless or hopeless. Studies on cancer patients have revealed lives marked by chronic anxiety, depression, or hostility and a lack of close emotional ties with parents—significantly greater than in a control group.

Despite the well-known hazards of smoking, per-capita consumption of cigarettes is expected to increase in 1975–76 after having been relatively stable between 1963—when the Surgeon General sounded the warning against smoking—and 1973, at 211 packs annually per person over 18 years. Some 15 percent of boys and girls under 18 years smoke cigarettes. Cigarette production is increasing at about 3.5 percent per year due to population growth and to a marked increase in smoking in teenage girls, which has risen from 8 to 15 percent in the past several years. If cigarette smoking were to be eliminated entirely, a 20 percent reduction in deaths due to cancer would result (based on the assumption that 85 percent of lung cancer is causally related to cigarette smoking). If all contributing environmental factors and personal bad health habits were eliminated, it is possible that cancer could be virtually eliminated as a cause of death. This would increase the average life expectancy at birth by 6 to 7 years, and at age 65 by 1.4 years for men and 2.1 years for women. The use of averages gives an erroneous impression, however, for one out of six people die of cancer. The elimination of cancer would mean that one out of six people would live 10.8 years longer.

Bad nutritional status (of the too-much-fat-intake-resulting-in-obesity type) can predispose the individual to heart attacks, strokes, cancer of the gastrointestinal tract, diabetes, liver and gall-bladder disease, degenerative arthritis of the hips, knees, and ankles, and injuries. It is estimated that 16 percent of Americans under the age of 30 years are obese, while 40 percent of the total population, or 80 million Americans, are 20 or more pounds above the ideal weight for their height, sex, and age. Over 30 percent of all men between 50 and 59 years are 20 percent overweight and 60 percent are at least 10 percent overweight.

Excessive use of alcohol is directly related to accidents and to liver disease (cirrhosis) as well a to a wide variety of other disorders, including vitamin deficiencies, inflammation of the pancreas, esophagus, and stomach, and muscular and neurologic diseases. Alcohol is a strong "risk factor" in cancer of the mouth, pharynx, larynx, and esophagus. More than 50 percent and probably nearer to 75 percent of all deaths and injuries due to automobile accidents are associated with the excessive use of alcohol. Alcoholism in one or both parents is significantly associated with home injuries to children (more than 50 percent in some studies). The prevalence of "heavy-escape" drinkers in the United States has been estimated at 6.5 million people (5.4 percent of total adult population), and the figures for those who use alcohol chronically and excessively range up to 10 million adults. Teenage drinking is now nearly universal. A study of high school students revealed that 36 percent reported getting drunk at least four times a year (remember, 15 percent smoke!). An increased frequency of cancer of the mouth, pharynx, larynx, and esophagus is seen in those who both smoke and drink and is less frequent, but still significantly higher than normal, in those who only smoke or only drink.

Dietary factors play a major role in cardiovascular disease and cancer. The major variable, as deduced from studies of migrant populations, seems to be fat content. For example, cancer of the large bowel as well as that of the breast and prostate is much more common in the United States than in Japan, and seems to be related to the difference in fat intake. The American derives 40 to 45 percent of his calories from fat, whereas the Japanese obtains only 15 to 20 percent of his calories from that source. Japanese descendants living in the United States have an incidence of bowel cancer similar to that seen in native Americans. Although the mechanism has not been established, it would appear that high fat intake (usually with resultant obesity) predisposes the American to both cancer and cardiovascular disease. Data from a long-term study of cardiovascular disease in Framingham, Massachusetts, indicate that each 10 percent reduction in weight in men 35–55 years old would result in a 20 percent decrease in the incidence of coronary disease. A 10 percent increase in weight would result in a 30 percent increase in coronary disease.[4]

The incidence of cancer of the colon and rectum in Americans both white and black is 10 times the incidence estimated for rural Africans. The removal of dietary fiber and a high intake of refined carbohydrates typical of diets in developed countries such as the United States result in a slowed transit time of food through the intestines. This is thought to facilitate the development of cancer, along with such diseases as diverticulitis, appendicitis, and even hemorrhoids. Prudence would dictate a reduction in fat and refined carbohydrates (and therefore increased fiber content) in the American diet. High-carbohydrate diets typical in the American culture also lead to dental caries, and may, over time, increase the risk of acquiring diabetes.

Knowledge of cancer and evidence for its multiple causes have increased to the point where the statement can be made with confidence that over 80 percent of human neoplasms depend either directly or indirectly on environmental factors. The term "environmental factors" includes cancer-provoking substances or carcinogens in the food and the drugs we ingest, the air we breath, the water we drink, the occupations we pursue, and the habits we indulge. There are three major groups at high risk of cancer: (1) those with known host factors such as genetic and other congenital defects and immunologic-deficiency disease; (2) those with exposure to environmental contaminants known to produce cancer; and (3) those

with certain demographic characteristics which reflect as yet unknown carcinogenic factors such as place of residence or migration.[5]

The familial occurrence of cancer is a well-known phenomenon. A significant two to four times excess occurrence in relatives of patients has been noted in cancer of the stomach, breast, large intestine, uterus, and lung. Increased familial incidence has also been noted in leukemia, brain tumors in children, and sarcomas. Individuals with hereditary deficiencies of the immune system of the body develop malignant diseases of the blood vessels and lymphatic system. Acquired immunodeficiency also leads to the development of cancer. When patients with kidney transplants are given drugs over a long time to suppress the immune system in order to prevent rejection of the grafted kidney, cancer of the lymphatic system (lymphoma of the reticulum-cell-sarcoma type), frequently confined to the brain, and cancer of the skin develop in a significant proportion of the patients. Women who have had genital herpes (herpes simplex virus 2) have an increased incidence of cancer of the cervix of the uterus and constitute a high-risk population. People with pernicious anemia with associated gastritis develop cancer of the stomach at five times the rate of the normal population. Cirrhosis is associated with an increased incidence of cancer of the liver. Patients with diabetes have two times the incidence of cancer of the pancreas as normal individuals. The presence of gallstones and kidney stones increases the risk of developing cancer in the respective organs. Single episodes of trauma have been implicated in cancer of the bone, breast, and testicles. Chronic irritation of a skin mole may lead to cancerous degeneration, called malignant melanoma.

Environmental factors include tobacco, alcohol, radiation, occupation, drugs, air pollutants, diet, viruses, and other organisms, and sexual factors. The evidence on cigarette smoking is incontrovertible. It greatly increases the risk of lung cancer as well as cancer of the mouth, pharynx, larynx, esophagus, and urinary bladder. The incidence of cancer in cigarette smokers is higher in urban than rural dwellers, suggesting that air pollutants are additional major causative factors. Occupational exposure to asbestos fibers results in lung cancer, but here again the incidence is higher in those who smoke. Alcohol as a carcinogenic agent in malignancy of the mouth, larynx, esophagus, and liver (in association with cirrhosis) has been noted. A major long-term effect of radiation is cancer. Radiologists are ten times more likely to die of leukemia than are physicians not exposed to x-rays.

The list of drugs known or thought to be carcinogenic also continues to expand. Studies have shown that post-menopausal women given estrogens (so-called "replacement therapy" to diminish menopausal complaints and advertised to "keep women feminine") are five to fourteen times more likely to develop cancer of the uterus (endometrial cancer) than post-menopausal women not given the drug. (Other factors known to be associated with uterine cancer such as obesity, high blood pressure, never having borne a child, and age were not significant variables in these studies.) The risk increased with dosage size and duration of estrogen therapy. Other studies have shown beyond a doubt that the daughters of women given diethylstilbestrol (DES) during pregnancy are at higher risk of developing a rare form of cancer of the vagina. Despite this knowledge, DES is still being given to pregnant women to prevent spontaneous abortion. Most astounding has been the discovery of over 100 cases of liver tumors in women taking oral contraceptive pills. Most of the tumors were benign, but some showed cancerous degeneration and others ruptured with hemorrhage into the abdomen. Many carcinogenic agents incite the disease only many years after the initial exposure (e.g., atomic-bomb radiation) or after prolonged use, so it is not known whether an epidemic of liver tumors will ultimately develop in oral-contraceptive users. (The "pill" also causes a small but significant risk for heart attacks in users.) Long-term epidemiologic research is needed to establish knowledge necessary for control programs, but there is sufficient knowledge now to suggest that we should sharply restrict use of many drugs.

Sexual factors (both hormonal and behavioral) play a role in the causation of cancer of the breast and uterus (cervix and body of the uterus), penis, prostate, and testis. Cancer of the cervix occurs much more frequently in women who have had many sexual partners beginning at an early age, who come from a lower socioeconomic status,

and who have had infection with Herpes simplex virus type 2, which is transmitted venereally. Celibate women are at very low risk, although they are at high risk for cancer of the breast. Cancer of the penis occurs in those who have poor penile hygiene and are uncircumcised in infancy (circumcision after the age of two years does not protect against the disease).

Attempts to prevent disease and improve and maintain health involve multifaceted strategies and expertise from many disciplines. Fundamental to any and all such attempts is sufficient empirical knowledge, i.e., knowledge gained through observation and trial-and-error experimentation that allows the advocate to convey his information with sufficient conviction to change the behavior of his audience. Although a great deal of information is available, the whole field of preventive medicine and health education needs far more fundamental research and long-term field experimentation. The biological and epidemiological effects of a wide variety of pollutants, the cost-benefit ratios of many available screening services, the influence of financial sanctions on changing health behavior, the use of the mass media and their effect on cognition and behavior, the long-term effects of various therapeutic regimens on the morbidity and mortality of individuals with asymptomatic high blood pressure, the long-term effects of marked reduction of fat in the diet on the incidence of cancer and heart disease, the influence of personal income on the development of cancer and coronary disease (the death rate from both lung cancer and coronary disease is significantly lower for the affluent than for the poor) are all examples of problems that need study. These problems demand for their solution the participation and integration of the disciplines of the biological sciences, the behavioral and social sciences (psychology, economics, cultural anthropology, political science), and public health (epidemiology and biostatistics).

It is a sad fact that of a total annual national expenditure on health of $120 billion, only 2 to 2.5 percent is spent on disease prevention and control measures, and only 0.5 percent each for health education and for improving the organization and delivery of health services. The national (federal) outlay for environmental-health research is around 0.25 percent of total health expenditures. These relatively meagre expenditures speak for the lack of interest in fields that rationally demand a much heavier commitment. The support of fundamental biomedical research has also flagged alarmingly in the past several years. The basic biological mechanisms of most of the common diseases are still not well enough known to give clear direction to preventive measures.

Strategies for improving health must include the incorporation of preventive measures into personal health services and into the environment, and individual and mass educational efforts.[6] For example, in dealing with the health problem of heart attacks, preventive measures would include screening for high-risk factors (high blood pressure, elevated blood cholesterol and fat levels, overweight, cigarette smoking, stress, and family history) and making available emergency services and measures for rapid transit to hospital-based coronary-care units; environmental measures would include altering food supply to reduce the intake of fat (i.e., those substances that raise blood cholesterol) and encouraging experiments in reducing work-related stress; and individual and mass educational efforts would include encouraging the use of screening examinations, the cessation of smoking, the maintenance of optimal weight with a balanced, low-fat diet, and obtaining regular exercise. Carrying out such a strategy involves many variables—convincing the doctor to play his pivotal role (and most medical educators and physicians are singularly uninterested in prevention), altering financing mechanisms to provide incentives to use preventive services (and most health insurance is, in fact, "disease insurance" which does not cover health education and preventive measures), and stimulating public as well as private efforts to exercise restraint on advertising and to exert positive sanctions for dissemination of health information through the mass media.

The health catastrophe related to automobile accidents presents a different type of problem. Here, personal-health services include availability of rapid transportation and first aid, emergency medical services, and definitive acute-care services in regional general hospitals; environmental measures would relate to road and highway construction (including lighting, warning signs, speed limits, safety rails), and the design and construction of automobiles for safety; and educational measures would include driver training, relicensing with eye examination, avoidance of alcohol and other drugs before driving, and reduction of speed. Which of these efforts will produce the most benefit at least cost? An interesting answer was provided during the oil-embargo energy crisis which necessitated reductions in speed limits and in the use of vehicles. The result in California was a 40 percent reduction in death rates from automobile accidents during the month of February, 1974, as contrasted with the previous February. Accidents on the New Jersey Turnpike dropped by one-fifth from 1973 to 1974, and fatalities were down by almost one-half, the lowest figure since 1966. Meanwhile, many people won't change their habits and wear seat belts, stop drinking, or reduce speed—and are annoyed with the restrictions on their freedom when someone tries to make them.

Dental health involves the personal services of the dentist and dental hygienist, the environmental measures of fluoridation of water supplies and the dietary restriction of refined carbohydrates, and the educational measures of prudent dietary habits, brushing the teeth, and visiting the dentist regularly. Where is the greatest benefit-cost ratio to be found? There is unequivocal evidence that fluoridation of water supplies will reduce dental caries by as much as 60 percent. It is safe and inexpensive, costing only 20 cents a year per person to prevent dental decay in children. Fluoridation of water supplies began about 1950. By 1967 over 3,000 communities with some 60 million people had adopted fluoridation. But the pace of change has slowed considerably, and the majority of people still lack fluoridated water due to fears of poisoning and resistance to what is perceived as an encroachment on their freedom. This highest benefit-cost dental-health program is still unavailable to the majority of Americans. Personal dental services are unavailable to large segments of our population and qualify as a luxury item.

. . . .

But what is the responsibility of the individual in matters pertaining to health? The United States now spends more on health in absolute terms and as a percentage of the gross national product than any other nation in the world—from $39 billion or 5.9 percent of the GNP in 1965 to $120 billion or 8.3 percent of the GNP in 1975 (over $550 per person per year). No one—but no one—can deny the fact that billions of dollars could be saved directly—and billions more indirectly (in terms of family suffering, time lost, and the erosion of human capital)—if our present knowledge of health and disease could be utilized in programs of primary, secondary, and tertiary prevention. The greatest portion of our national expenditure goes for the caring of the major causes of premature, and therefore preventable, death and/or disability in the United States, i.e., heart disease, cancer, strokes, accidents, bronchitis and emphysema, cirrhosis of the liver, mental illness and retardation, dental caries, suicide and homicide, venereal disease, and other infections. If no one smoked cigarettes or consumed alcohol and everyone exercised regularly, maintained optimal weight on a low fat, low refined-carbohydrate, high fiber-content diet, reduced stress by simplifying their lives, obtained adequate rest and recreation, understood the needs of infants and children for the proper nutrition and nurturing of their intellectual and affective development, had available to them, and would use, genetic counseling and selective abortion, drank fluoridated water, followed the doctor's orders for medications and self-care once disease was detected, used available health services at the appropriate time for screening examinations and health education-preventive medicine programs, the savings to the country would be mammoth in terms of billions of dollars, a vast reduction in human misery, and an attendant marked improvement in the quality of life. Our country would be strengthened immeasurably, and we could divert our energies—human and financial—to other pressing issues of national and international concern.

But so much conspires against this rational ideal: our historic emphasis on rugged individualism, social Darwinism, and unrestricted freedom together with our recent emphasis on individual rights as contrasted with responsibilities; a neo-liberal ideology which has stressed societal responsibility and the obligations of the beneficent state, resulting in an erosion of individual responsibility and initiative; a credit-minded culture which does it now and pays for it later, whether in drinking and eating or in buying cars and houses; an economy which depends on profligate production and consumption regardless of the results to individual health, or to the public health in terms of a wide variety of environmental pollutants; ignorance (and therefore a lack of conviction and commitment) on the part of both producers and consumers as to exact costs and benefits of many preventive and health-education measures, a reflection of the sparse national commitment to research in these areas: the failure, conceptually, to view health holistically, i.e., its interdependence with educational attainment, poverty, the availability of work, housing and the density of populations, degree of environmental pollution (air, water, noise, mass-media offerings), and levels of stress in work, play, and love; and finally, the values and habits of the health establishment itself. One cannot hope to develop a rational health system if the parts of the whole that bear on health are moving in irrational ways.

Within the health system, medical educators and the teaching hospitals display only acute curative, after-the-fact medicine. The rewards—intellectually, financially, and emotionally—for specialist care far outweigh those for the low-status generalist (primary-care physican) or public health worker. The specialty organizations (surgeons, internists, radiologists, for example), the American Medical Association, the Association of American Medical Colleges, the American Hospital Association, the "disease-insurance" companies, as well as governmental insurance programs (Medicare-Medicaid), pay lip service or no service to reordering priorities and sanctions to the needs of the people for prevention and health education. Present plans for national health insurance do not contend with the issues of preventive medicine and health education. Over 65 percent of the 4.5 million workers in the health system are employed in hospitals, and their interests demand more expenditures and an even higher priority for acute, curative, after-the-fact medicine and the care of those with chronic disease. There is one health educator for every 17,000 people, while there is one physician for every 650 and one nurse for every 280 people.

Research priorities stress biological and not

epidemiological, social, and environmental research. Even here, we should be willing to take decisive action when inferential evidence, e.g., the production of cancer in animals by drugs, is available, unacceptable as this may be to scientists. I cannot believe that man was meant to ingest drugs and artificial-food substances, breathe polluted air, or have his ears banged mercilessly by the uproar of industrial society. Those who do work in the field of prevention and health education have too often stressed social control (some have called them "health fascists") rather than social change and have become curiously indifferent to the needs and aspirations of families, communities, and particularly minority groups. Those places where benefit-cost ratios are potentially most favorable for programs of health education and prevention—and where long-range research could be conducted—have been neglected: the schools and universities, places of work, hospitals and clinics, and obviously, doctors' offices. Very little is known about how television functions as a cognitive medium; little sophistication is shown by interested experts in developing sanctions, i.e., financial or other incentives, to modify bad habits of living. Those in the health professions play a minimal role in supporting the needs of minority groups for better housing and jobs, higher income, and improved transportation—not realizing that the fulfillment of these needs will reduce stress and anxiety and therefore improve health by reducing susceptibility to disease or to the disease-provoking habits of smoking and drinking.

If the health establishment isn't interested and the consumers don't want or demand health education and preventive medicine, what is to be done? First of all we should look at a few concrete changes in behavior which, through a variety of mechanisms, have improved health:

1) When the Surgeon General issued his report on the hazards of smoking in 1964, 52 percent of the male population smoked cigarettes. Through massive public educational programs and restrictions on advertising, the percentage was reduced over a 10-year period to roughly 42 percent. (This desirable change has been accompanied, however, by an equally undesirable increase in teen-age smoking, particularly among females, and no change in the 41 percent of 17-to-25-year-olds who smoke.)

2) During World War I, the United Kingdom increased taxes on alcohol, reduced the amount of alcohol available for consumption, and restricted the hours of sale. Consumption of alcohol fell and, with it, deaths from cirrhosis of the liver—from 10.3 per 100,000 people in 1914 to 4.5 in 1920. Following the war, the regulations governing the amount of alcohol allowed for consumption and the hours of its sale were relaxed, but taxes on alcoholic beverages were continually increased. By 1936, the death rate due to cirrhosis was down to 3.1 per 100,000, and it has remained at this level in that country. In the United States, wartime prohibition also reduced the cirrhosis death rate, from 11.8 per 100,000 in 1916 to 7.1 per 100,000 in 1920; it was still 7.2 in 1932, the year before prohibition was ended. But following the repeal of prohibition, the death rate from cirrhosis climbed steadily to an all-time high of 16.0 deaths per 100,000 in 1973, five times the rate in Great Britain. These results suggest a national strategy for the United States of (a) steadily increasing taxes on alcoholic beverages, (b) a massive public education program on the hazards of alcohol plus restrictions on all advertising, (c) aid to farmers and companies to help them shift to other crops and products. Increased tax income should temporarily help to defray the costs of public health education. The same strategy should be applied to cigarettes.

3) The marked reduction in auto fatalities and injuries during the oil crisis suggests that a permanent reduction of speed limits combined with sanctions to limit the use of automobiles would more than justify the cost of enforcing such a program.

4) A program to improve the self-care of patients with diabetes (tertiary prevention) at the University of Southern California resulted in a 50 percent reduction in emergency-ward visits, a decrease in the number of patients with diabetic coma from 300 to 100 over a two-year period, and the avoidance of 2,300 visits for medications. The theme was, "You must take responsibility for your own health." Savings were estimated at $1.7 million. In other studies involving the care and education of diabetics, hemophili-

acs, and others, hospital readmissions decreased by over 50 percent. These efforts resulted in tremendous savings of time and money and reflected vastly improved self-care in cases of chronic disease.

5) A heart-disease-prevention program run by Stanford University similarly demonstrated that an intensive program of health education and preventive medicine—utilizing personal instructions, television spots, and printed material—resulted in a markedly higher level of information about the disease by the community and a marked improvement in dietary habits and in the reduction of smoking among those at high risk.

. . . .

I began by saying that the health of human beings is determined by their behavior, their food, and the nature of their environment. Over 99 percent of us are born healthy and suffer premature death and disability only as a result of personal misbehavior and environmental conditions. The sociocultural effects of urban industrial life are profound in terms of stress, and unnatural sedentary existence, bad habits, and unhealthy environmental influences.[7] The individual has the power—indeed, the moral responsibility—to maintain his own health by the observance of simple, prudent rules of behavior relating to sleep, exercise, diet and weight, alcohol, and smoking. In addition, he should avoid where possible the long-term use of drugs. He should be aware of the dangers of stress and the need for precautionary measures during periods of sudden change, such as bereavement, divorce, or new employment. He should submit to selective medical examination and screening procedures.

These simple rules can be understood and observed by the majority of Americans, namely the white, well-educated, and affluent middle class. But how do individuals in minority groups follow these rules, when their members include disproportionately large numbers of the impoverished and the illiterate, among whom fear, ignorance, desperation, and superstition conspire against even the desire to remain healthy? Here we must rely on social policies *first,* in order to improve education, employment, civil rights, and economic levels, along with efforts to develop accessible health services.

Beyond these measures, the individual is powerless to control disease-provoking environmental contaminants, be they drugs, air and water pollutants, or food additives, except as he becomes knowledgeable enough to participate in public debate and in support of governmental controls. Here, we must depend on the wisdom of experts, the results of research, and the national will to legislate controls for our protection, as damaging as they may be, in the short run, to our national economy.

When all is said and done, let us not forget that he who hates sin, hates humanity. Life is meant to be enjoyed, and each one of us in the end is still able in our own country to steer his vessel to his own port of desire. But the costs of individual irresponsibility in health have now become prohibitive. The choice is individual responsibility or social failure. Responsibility and duty must gain some degree of parity with right and freedom.

REFERENCES

1. T. McKeown, *The Modern Rise of Population* (London, 1976), pp. 152–63.
2. M. Susser, ed., *Prevention and Health Maintenance Revisited (Bulletin of the New York Academy of Medicine.* 51[January, 1975], pp. 5–243), p. 96.
3. N. B. Belloc and L. Breslow, "The Relation of Physical Health Status and Health Practices," *Preventive Medicine,* 1(August, 1972), pp. 409–21; see also "Relationship of Health Practices and Mortality." *Preventive Medicine,* 2(1973), pp. 67–81.
4. F. W. Ashley, Jr., and W. B. Kannel, "Relation of Weight Change to Changes in Atherogenic Traits: The Framingham Study," *Journal of Chronic Diseases,* 27(March, 1974), pp. 103–14.
5. J. F. Fraumeni, ed., *Persons at High Risk of Cancer: An Approach to Cancer Etiology and Control* (New York, 1975), p. 526.
6. L. Breslow, "Research in Strategy for Health Improvement," *International Journal of Health Services.* 3(1973), pp. 7–16.
7. J. H. Knowles, *Health in America. Health Service Prospects: An International Survey* (London, 1973), pp. 307–34.

31

Individual Responsibility and Health Politics

Robert Crawford

· ·

... The contention ... is ... that although health is a complex matter and therefore requires several kinds of efforts, individual responsibility is the key ingredient. In place of admittedly expensive and ineffective medical services, it is said, individual change must be the focus of the nation's efforts to promote and maintain health. People should use the medical system less and instead adopt healthy lifestyles: or, as it was declared by one pundit, "living a long life is essentially a do-it-yourself proposition." These assertions perform the function of *blaming the victim*. They avert any serious discussion of social or environmental factors and instead locate the problem of poor health and its solution in the individual. Further, they imply, sometimes explicitly, that since people's own misbehavior is the heart of the problem of health and illness, people should *demand less* medical care. Rights and entitlements for access to medical services are almost by definition now considered inappropriate. Thus, in becoming a premise for public policy, these pronouncements are providing the material for a new public philosophy by which problems are defined and answers proposed.

Similar ideologies of individual responsibility have always been popular among providers and academics trying to justify inequality in the utilization of medical services. During the period of rapid expansion in the health sector, higher morbidity and mortality rates for the poor and minorities were explained by emphasizing their lifestyle habits, especially their health and utilization behavior. These "culture of poverty" explanations emphasized delay in seeking medical help, resistance to medical authority, and reliance on unprofessional folk healers or advisors. As Catherine Riessman summarizes:

> According to these researchers, the poor have undergone multiple negative experiences with organizational systems, leading to avoidance behavior, lack of trust, and hence a disinclination to seek care and follow medical regimens except in dire need.[1]

Now, in a period of fiscal crisis and cost control, the same higher morbidity rates and demands for more access through comprehensive national health insurance are met with a barrage of statements about the limits of medicine and the lack of appropriate health behavior. Several commentators now link overuse by the poor with their faulty health habits. Again, education is seen as the solution. Previously the poor were blamed for not using medical services enough, for relying too much on their own resources, for undue suspicion of modern medicine. Now they are blamed for relying too much on medical services and not enough on their own resources. In both cases, of course, structural factors are rarely mentioned; but structural factors are behind this ideological shift.

The Crisis of Costs

The cost crisis is transforming the entire political landscape in the health sector. What makes inflation in the health sector so critical in the 1970s is not only its spectacular rate but also its concurrence with wider economic and fiscal crises. We now face a situation in which inflation and expenditures for human services have become the primary targets of a strategy aimed at restoring "optimal conditions" for investment and growth in the corporate sector. The costs of medical services to government have aggravated a fiscal crisis in which the direction of public spending is the issue and raising taxes is considered inimical to corporate priorities. Further, high medical costs have become a direct threat to the corporate sector in two important ways: first, by adding significantly to the costs of production through increases in health benefit settlements with labor; and, second, by diverting consumer expenditures from other corporate products. The fact that large corporations have extensively invested in medical and health-related products does not significantly alter this picture.

The costs of production for corporations are being dramatically affected by increases in benefit settlements. General Motors claims it spent more money with Blue Cross and Blue Shield in 1975 than it did with U.S. Steel, its principal supplier of metal. Standard Oil of Indiana announced that employee health costs for the corporation had tripled over the past seven years.[2] Chrysler estimates that in 1976 it paid $1,500 per employee for medical benefits or a total of $205 million in the United States. "Unlike most other labor costs that can and do vary with the level of production," the corporation complains, "medical costs continue to rise in good times as well as bad."[3] The implications for consumer costs are obvious. General Motors added $175 to the price of every car and truck by passing on its employee medical benefit costs. In a period in which consumption and investment are stalled, while foreign competition adds an additional barrier to raising prices, such figures are startling. Corporate and union leaders are expressing in every possible forum their concern over the impact of rising medical costs upon prices, wages, and profits.

Thus, substantial political pressures are being mobilized to cut the direct costs to corporations and to cut the indirect costs of social programs generally. The politics of growth that dominated the previous period are giving way to the politics of curbing the growth in the present period. Just a few years ago the political emphasis was on increasing utilization. Now it is on reducing utilization. Besides regulatory measures, the strategies being adopted include cutbacks in public programs, especially Medicaid, and public hospitals and a shifting of the burden of costs back to employees, old people, and consumers in general.[4] In addition, corporations, often with the participation of unions, are adopting new internal strategies aimed at curbing costs.[5]

Most important is the growing consensus among corporate and governmental leaders that comprehensive national health insurance is unacceptable at current cost levels. In his campaign for the presidency, Jimmy Carter, aware of its popular appeal and importance to organized labor, committed himself to a comprehensive insurance program; but, in reminding the nation in April 1977 that balancing the budget by 1981 is his paramount domestic goal, Carter warned that the costs of such a program would be prohibitive. Secretary of Health, Education, and Welfare, Joseph Califano, more explicitly argued that cost control is a necessary precondition for national health insurance or "some other system."[6] These and numerous other signs indicate that the prospects for comprehensive insurance are receding behind a shield of rhetoric and a language of gradualism.

Popular Demand for the Extension of Rights and Entitlements

In order to understand the importance of a new ideology that tells people they must rely less on the medical system and more on themselves, the cost crisis must be viewed in the context of the legacy of the preceding period, a time in which popular expectations of medicine and political demands for unhindered access to medical services reached their highest levels. Growth reinforced those expectations, as did years of propaganda by a medical and research establishment strengthened by occasional but spectacular medical successes. Medicine was promoted in almost religious terms, a promise of deliverance from pain and illness even a "death of death."

For years people were conditioned to believe in the value of consuming high levels of medical services and products. At a time when these beliefs became celebrated cultural values, large numbers of people continued to experience difficulty in obtaining regular access to primary care services and faced financial disaster for unusual medical expenses. Access came to be considered an essential component of family and personal security and an integral part of the wage bargain for organized labor. The idea of medical care as a right became widely accepted in a period in which rights were forced onto the political agenda of the nation. By the early 1970s popular pressures for national health insurance began to swell. As benefits shrink in the face of uncontrollable inflation, the sentiment for a comprehensive program continues to build.

Now, however, just at the point when medical care had become broadly viewed as a right and there is a growing demand for the extension of entitlements, people are suddenly being pressured to use the system less. If people are to modify their expectations, if their demands for guaranteed access are to be sidetracked, and if legislators and other policymakers are to be convinced of the necessity for retrenchment, a new ideology must be developed to replace the unquestioned power of medicine and to break the link between the provision of services and popular political demands. People will not relinquish their expectations unless their belief in medicine as a panacea is broken and the value of access is replaced with a new preoccupation with boot-strapping activities aimed at controlling at-risk behaviors. In a political climate of fiscal, energy, and cost crises, self-sacrifice and self-discipline emerge as popular themes. In lieu of rights and entitlements, individual responsibility, self-help and holistic health move to the center of discussion.[7]

The Politics of Retrenchment

The flavor of the ideology is evident in the comments of some of its more explicit proponents. Both direct policy proposals and indirect

policy implications are abundant. With an implied attack on social programs, for example, Victor Fuchs, a noted health economist, writes: "Some future historian, in reviewing mid-twentieth century social reform literature may note . . . a 'resolute refusal' to admit that individuals have any responsibility for their own stress."[8] Robert Whalen, Commissioner of the New York Department of Health, more explicitly makes the tie with high medical costs: "Unless we assume such individual and moral responsibility for our own health, we will soon learn what a cruel and expensive hoax we have worked upon ourselves through our belief that more money spent on health care is the way to better health."[9]

As do many advocates of individual responsibility, Walter McNerney, president of the Blue Cross Association, incorporates elements of both the Illichian and radical critiques of technology-heavy, distorted, and iatrogenic medicine: "We must stop throwing an array of technological processes and systems at lifestyle problems and stop equating more health services with better health. . . . People must have the capability and the will to take greater responsibility for their own health."[10] John Knowles, the late president of the Rockefeller Foundation, spoke more directly to the problem of expectations: "The only thing we've heard about national health insurance from everybody is that it won't solve the problems."[11] Knowles argued that the "primary critical choice" facing the individual is "to change his personal bad habits or stop complaining. He can either remain the problem or become the solution to it: Beneficent Government cannot—indeed, should not—do it for him or to him.[12]

The attack on rights is explicit. Leon Kass, writing in *The Public Interest,* states that "it no more makes sense to claim a right to health than a right to health care.[13] "How can we go talking about a right to health," Robert Morrison asks, "without some balancing talk about an individual's responsibility to keep healthy."[14] Again, Knowles offers a clear articulation:

The idea of individual responsibility has been submerged in individual rights—rights or demands to be guaranteed by Big Brother and delivered by public and private institutions. The cost of sloth, gluttony, alcoholic intemperance, reckless driving, sexual frenzy and smoking have now become a national, not an individual, responsibility, and all justified as individual freedom. But one man's or woman's freedom in health is now another man's shackle in taxes and insurance premiums.[15]

What Knowles is suggesting by national responsibility is public policy aimed at changing individual behavior—and using economic or other sanctions to do it. Economic sanctions on individuals, such as higher taxation on the consumption of cigarettes and alcohol, or higher insurance premiums to those engaging in at-risk behaviors are becoming a popular theme. A guest editorial appeared last year in *The New York Times,* for example, introducing the idea of "Your Fault Insurance."[16] More extreme sanctions are proposed by Leon Kass:

> All the proposals for National Health Insurance embrace, without qualification, the no-fault principle. They therefore choose to ignore, or to treat as irrelevant, the importance of personal responsibility for the state of one's own health. As a result, they pass up an opportunity to build both positive and negative inducements into the insurance payment plan, by measures such as *refusing or reducing benefits for chronic respiratory disease care to persons who continue to smoke* (emphasis added).[17]

These sanctions may be justified under the rubric of "lack of motivation," "unsuitability for treatment," or "inability to profit from therapy."[18] Why waste money, after all, on people whose lifestyle contravenes good therapeutic results, or, as Morrison put it, on a "system which taxes the virtuous to send the improvident to the hospital."[19] In the new system the pariahs of the medical world and larger numbers of people in general could be diagnosed as lifestyle problems, referred to a health counselor, and sent home. At the very least, the victim-blaming ideology will help justify shifting the burden of costs back to users. A person who is responsible for his or her illness should be responsible for the bill as well.[20]

The Social Causation of Disease

If the victim-blaming ideology serves as a legitimization for the retrenchment from rights and entitlements, in relation to the social causation of disease it functions as a colossal masquerade. The complexities of social causation are only beginning to be explored. The ideology of individual responsibility, however, inhibits that understanding and substitutes instead an unrealistic behavioral model. It both ignores what is known about human behavior and minimizes the importance of evidence about the environmental assault on health. It instructs people to be individually responsible at a time when they are becoming less capable as individuals of controlling their total health environment.[21] Although environmental factors are often recognized as "also relevant," the implication is that little can be done about an ineluctable, technological, and industrial society.

A certain portion of illness is, at some level, undoubtedly associated with individual behavior, and if that behavior were altered, it could lead to improved health. Health education efforts aimed at changing individual behavior should be an important part of any health strategy. Offered in a vacuum, however, such efforts will achieve only marginal results. Sociologist John McKinlay has argued convincingly that the frequent failure of health education programs is attributable to the failure to address the social context. He concludes that:

> Certain at-risk behaviors have become so inextricably intertwined with our dominant cultural system (perhaps even symbolic of it) that the routine display of such behavior almost signified membership in this society. . . . To request people to change or alter these behaviors is more or less to request the abandonment of dominant culture.[22]

What must be questioned is both the effectiveness and the political uses of a focus on lifestyles and on changing individual behavior without changing social structure and processes. Just as the Horatio Alger myth was based on the fact that just enough individuals achieve mobility to make the possibility believable, so too significant health gains might be realized by some of those able to resist the incredible array of social forces aligned against healthy behavior. The vast majority, however, will remain unaffected.

The crisis of social causation is characterized

by a growing awareness and politicization of environmental and occupational sources of disease in the face of the failure of medicine to have a significant impact on the modern epidemics, especially cancer. In just the last few years the American people have been inundated with scientific and popular critiques of the environmental and occupational sources of cancer. These revelations have been accompanied by a constant flow of warnings about environmental dangers: air pollution, contamination of drinking supplies, food additive carcinogens, PCB, asbestos, kepone, vinyl chlorides, pesticides, nuclear power plants, saccharine, and even more. The Environmental Protection Agency, the Occupational Safety and Health Administration, and the Food and Drug Administration have been among the most embattled government agencies in recent years.

While there is considerable debate over threshold-limit values, the validity of animal research applications to humans, and specific policy decisions by the above agencies, awareness is growing that the public is being exposed to a multitude of environmental and work place carcinogens. Although many people still cling to the "it won't happen to me" response, the fear of cancer is becoming more widespread. A recent Gallup Poll found that cancer is by far the disease most feared by Americans, almost three times its nearest competitor.[23] The fear is not unwarranted. Cancer is a disease of epidemic proportions. Samuel Epstein, a noted cancer expert, claims that "more than 53 million people in the U.S. (over a quarter of the population) will develop some form of cancer in their lifetimes, and approximately 20 percent will die of it."[24]

Pressure on industrial corporations has been building for years. An occupational health and safety movement from within industry is gaining momentum. Many unions are developing programs and confronting corporate management on health and safety issues. Although suffering from severe setbacks, the environmental movement still poses a serious challenge as environmental consciousness is reinforced by the politicization of public health issues. Government agencies and the courts have never been so assertive, despite the repeated attempts by industry to undermine these efforts. The political

constraints on the growth of the nuclear power industry and governmental pressures on steel are not lost on other industries.

The threat to corporate autonomy is clear. One reads almost daily of the economic blackmail threatened by corporations if regulations are imposed, whether production shutdowns, plant closings, or investment strikes. Corporations move their plants to more tractable communities or countries. Advertising campaigns promoting the image of public-spirited corporate activities attempt to counter the threat that the decision to subordinate people's health to profits will become yet more apparent. In short, the "manufacturers of illness" are on the defensive. They must seek new ways to blunt the efforts of the new health activists and to shift the burden of responsibility for health away from their doorstep.

The Politics of Diversion

Victim-blaming ideology offers a perfect oportunity. "For once we cannot blame the environment as much as we have to blame ourselves," says Ernst Wynder, president of the American Health Foundation. "The problem is now the inability of man to take care of himself."[25] Or as New York Health Commissioner Whalen writes: "Many of our most difficult contemporary health problems, such as cancer, heart disease and accidental injury, have a built-in behavioral component. . . . *If they are to be solved at all*, we must change our style of living" (emphasis added).[26] Alternatively, Leon Kass, fearing the consequences of a focus on social causation, warns of "excessive preoccupations, as when cancer phobia leads to government regulations that unreasonably restrict industrial activity."[27]

One after another, the lifestyle proponents admit to the environmental and occupational factors that affect health, but then go on to assert their pragmatism. Victor Fuchs, for example, while recognizing environmental factors as "also relevant," asserts that "the greatest potential for reducing coronary disease, cancer, and other major killers still lies in altering personal behavior." He philosophizes that "emphasizing social responsibility can increase security, but it may be the security of the 'zoo'—purchased at the expense of freedom."[28] Carlson recognizes that social causation "raises some difficult political problems, because if we find the carcinogens in certain places in our environment, we run into institutional forces which will oppose dealing with them." Thus, "we may have to intervene at other levels here."[29] The practical focus of health efforts, in other words, should not be on the massive, expensive, politically difficult, or even politically dangerous task of overhauling our work and community environments. Instead, the focus must be on changing individuals who live and work within those settings. In the name of pragmatism, efficacy is thus ignored.

There are several other expressions of the ideology that should be noted. The diffusion of a psychological world view often reinforces the masking of social causation. Even though the psychiatric model substitutes social for natural explanations, problems still tend to be seen as amenable to change through personal transformation, with or without therapy. And, with or without therapy, individuals are ultimately held responsible for their own psychological well-being. Usually no one has to blame us for some psychological failure; we blame ourselves. Thus, psychological impairment can be just as effective as moral failing or genetic inferiority in blaming the victims and reinforcing dominant social relations.[30] People are alienated, unhappy, drop-outs, criminals, angry, and activists, after all, because of maladjustment to one or another psychological norm.

The ideology of individual responsibility for health lends itself to this form of psychological obfuscation. Susceptibility to at-risk behaviors, if not a moral failing, is at least a psychological failing. New evidence relating psychological state to resistance or susceptibility to disease and accidents can and will be used to shift more responsibility to the individual. Industrial psychologists have long been employed with the intention that intervention at the individual level is the best way to reduce plant accidents in lieu of costly production changes. The implication is that people make themselves sick, not only mentally but physically. If job satisfaction is important to health, people should seek more rewarding employment. Cancer is a state of mind.

In another vein, many accounts of the current disease structure in the United States link disease with affluence. The affluent society and the lifestyles it has wrought, it is suggested, are the sources of the individual's degeneration and adoption of at-risk behaviors. Michael Halberstam, for example, writes that "most Americans die of excess rather than neglect or poverty."[31] Knowles's warnings about "sloth, gluttony, alcoholic intemperance, reckless driving, sexual frenzy and smoking," and later about "social failure," are reminiscent of a popularized conception of decaying Rome.[32] Thus, even though some may complain about environmental hazards, people are really suffering from overindulgence of the good society; it is overindulgence that must be checked. Further, by pointing to lifestyles, which are usually presented as if they reflect the problems of homogenized, affluent society, this aspect of the ideology tends to obscure the reality of class and the impact of social inequality of health. It is compatible with the conception that people are free agents. Social structure and constraints recede amid the abundance.

Of course, several diseases do stem from the lifestyles of the more affluent. Discretionary income usually allows for excessive consumption of unhealthy products; and, as Joseph Eyer argues, everyone suffers in variable and specific ways from the nature of work and the conditioning of lifestyles in advanced capitalist society.[33] But are the well-established relationships between low income and high infant mortality, diseases related to poor diet and malnutrition, stress, cancer, mental illness, traumas of various kinds, and other pathologies now to be ignored or relegated to a residual factor?[34] While long-term inequality in morbidity and mortality is declining, for almost every disease and for every indicator of morbidity, incidence increases as income falls.[35] In some specific cases the health gap appears to be widening.[36] Nonetheless, health economist Anne Somers reassures that contemporary society is tending in the direction of homogeneity:

If poverty seems so widespread, it is at least partly because our definition of poverty is so much more generous than in the past—a generosity made possible only by the pervasive affluence and the impressive technological base upon which it rests. . . . This point—that the current crisis is the result of progress rather than retrogression or decay—is vitally important not only as a historical fact but as a guide to problem solving in the health field as elsewhere.[37]

Finally, by focusing on the individual, the ideology performs the classical role of individualist ideologies in obscuring the class structure of work and the worker's lack of control over working conditions. The failure to maintain health in the work place is attributed to some personal flaw. The more than 2.5 million people disabled by occupational accidents and diseases each year and the 114,000 killed are not explained by the hazards or pace of work as much as by the lack of sufficient caution by workers, laziness about wearing respirators or other protective equipment, psychological maladjustment, including an inability to minimize stress, and even by the worker's genetic susceptibility. Correspondingly, the overworked, overstressed worker is offered transcendental meditation, biofeedback, psychological counseling, or some other holistic approach to healthy behavior change, leaving intact the structure of employer incentives and sanctions that reward the retention of work place hazards and health-denying behavior.

Moreover, corporate management appears to be integrating victim-blaming themes into personnel policies as health becomes an important rubric for traditional managerial strategies aimed at controlling the work force. Holding individual workers responsible for their susceptibility to illness or for their psychological state is not only a response to growing pressures over occupational hazards but it also complements management attempts to control absenteeism and enhance productivity. Job dissatisfaction and job-induced stress (in both their psychological and physical manifestations), principal sources of absenteeism and low productivity, will more and more become identified as lifestyle problems of the worker. Workers found to be "irresponsible" in maintaining their health or psychological stability, as manifest in attendance and productivity records, will face sanctions, dismissals or early retirement, rationalized as

stemming from employee health problems. Already the attack on sick-day benefits is well underway. The push toward corporate health maintenance organizations will further reinforce managerial use of health criteria for control purposes.

One such control mechanism is pre-employment and periodic health screening, which is now in regular use in large industry. New businesses are selling employee risk evaluations, called by one firm "health hazard appraisals." Among the specific advantages cited for health screening by the Conference Board, a business research organization, is the selection "of those judged to present the least risk of unstable attendance, costly illness, poor productivity, or short tenure."[38] Screening also holds out the possibility of cost savings from reduced insurance rates and compensation claims. It also raises, however, the possibility of a large and growing category of "high-risk" workers who become permanently unemployable—not only because of existing, incapacitating illnesses but because of their *potential* for becoming ill.

In a period in which we have become accustomed to ozone watches in which "vulnerable" people are warned to reduce activity, workers are being screened for susceptibility to job hazards. Even though they alert individuals to their higher risks, these programs do not address the hazardous conditions that to some degree affect all workers. Thus, all workers may be penalized *to the extent* that such programs function to divert attention from causative conditions. To the degree that the causative agent remains, the more susceptible workers are also penalized in that they must shoulder the burden of the hazardous conditions either by looking for another, perhaps nonexistent, job; or, if it is permitted, by taking a risk in remaining. At a United Auto Workers conference on lead, the union's president summed up industry's tactics as "fix the worker, not the workplace." He further criticized the "exclusion of so-called 'sensitive' groups of workers, the use of dangerous chemical agents to artificially lower workers' blood lead levels, the transfer of workers in and out of high lead areas, and the forced use of personal respirators instead of engineering controls to clean the air in the workplace."[39] These struggles to place responsibility are bound to intensify.

. . . .

NOTE

For helpful comments and editorial suggestions, mostly on an earlier draft, thanks to Evan Stark, Susan Reverby, John McKnight, Nancy Hartsock, Sol Levine, Cathy Stepanek, Isaac Balbus, and participants in the East Coast Health Discussion Group. I am especially indebted to Lauren Crawford who provided many hours in discussion and in preparation of this manuscript.

REFERENCES

1. "The Use of Health Services by the Poor," *Social Policy 5,* 1 (1974): 42.
2. *Chicago Sun-Times,* 16 March 1976.
3. "Inflation of Health Care Costs, 1976," hearings before the Sub-Committee on Health of the Committee on Labor and Public Welfare, United States Senate, 94th Congress (Washington, D.C.: U.S. Government Printing Office, 1976), pp. 656–60.
4. Daniel Fox and Robert Crawford, "Health Politics in the United States," in *Handbook of Medical Sociology,* edited by H. E. Freeman, S. Levine, and L. Reeder, (Englewood Cliffs, N.J.: Prentice-Hall 3rd ed., 1979); Ronda Kotelchuck, "Government Cost Control Strategies," *Health-PAC Bulletin,* no. 75, March–April 1977, pp. 1–6.
5. *The Complex Puzzle of Rising Health Costs: Can the Private Sector Fit it Together?* (Washington, D.C.: Council on Wage and Price Stability, December 1976).
6. *New York Times,* 26 April 1977.
7. The ideology of individual responsibility threatens to incorporate and use the self-help movement for its own purposes. Self-help initially developed as a political response to the oppressive character of professional and male domination in medicine. As such, the self-help movement embodies some of the best strands of grassroots, autonomous action, of people attempting at some level to regain control over their lives, and a response to the overmedicalization of American life. However, because the movement has focused on individual behavior and only rarely addressed the social and physical environment, and because it has not built a movement that goes beyond self-care to demanding the medical and environmental prerequisites for maintaining health, it lends itself to the purposes of victim-blaming. Just as the language of helping obscured the unequal power relationships of a growing therapeutic state (in other words, masking political behavior by calling it therapeutic) the language of self-help obscures the power relations underlying the social causation of disease and the dominant interests that now seek to reorder popular expectations of rights and entitlements for access to medical services.
8. Fuchs, *Who Shall Live?* (New York: Basic Books, 1974), p. 27.
9. *New York Times,* 17 April 1977.
10. *Conference on Future Directions in Health Care,* pp. 4–5.
11. Ibid., pp. 28–29.
12. "The Responsibility of the Individual," in *Doing Better and Feeling Worse: Health in the United States,* ed. by John Knowles (New York: Norton and Co., 1977), p. 78.
13. L. Kass "Regarding the End of Medicine and the Pursuit of Health," *Public Interest* 40 (Summer 1975): 38–39.
14. Quoted in ibid., p. 42.
15. *Conference in Future Directions in Health Care,* pp. 2–3.
16. 14 October 1976.
17. Kass, p. 71.
18. William Ryan, *Blaming the Victim* (New York: Vintage Books, 1971).
19. Quoted in Kass, p. 42.
20. These remarks are in no way intended to imply that access to more services, regardless of their utility for improved health status, is a progressive position. Medical services as a means to maintain health have been grossly oversold. As Paul Starr comments "a critic like Illich argues that because medical care has made no difference in health, we should not be particularly concerned about access. He has turned the point around. We will have to be especially concerned about inequalities if we are to make future investments in medical care effective" (p. 52). The argument here is that medical expenditures are presently distorted toward unnecessary and ineffective activities that serve to maximize income for providers and suppliers. Political conditions favoring an effective an just reallocation of expenditures are more likely to develop in the context of a publicly accountable system that must allocate services within statutory contraints and a politically determined budget. In such a system political struggles against special interests, misallocation, or under-

funding will obviously continue, as will efforts to achieve effectiveness and reponsiveness. The concept and definition of need will move to the center of policy discussions. With all the perils and ideological manipulations that process will entail, it is better that such a debate take place in public than be determined by the private market.

Further, viable programs of cost control must be formulated, first as an alternative to the cutback strategy and, second, as the necessary adjunct to establishing effective and relevant services. Technology-intensive and overuse-related sources of inflationary costs are directly related to the problem of ineffectiveness as well as to iatrogenesis.

21. "Special Issue on the Economy, Medicine and Health," ed. by Joseph Eyer, *International Journal of Health Services 7*, 1 (January 1977); "The Social Etiology of Disease, Part I," *HMO-Network for Marxist Studies in Health*, no. 2, January 1977.

22. "A Case for Refocussing Upstream: The Political Economy of Illness" (Boston University, unpublished paper, 1974). Reprinted in this book.

23. *Chicago Sun-Times*, 6 February 1977.

24. "The Political and Economic Basis of Cancer," *Technology Review 78*, 8(1976): 1.

25. *Conference on Future Directions in Health Care*, p. 52.

26. *New York Times*, 17 April 1977.

27. Kass, p. 42

28. Fuchs, pp. 26, 46.

29. *Conference on Future Directions in Health Care*, p. 116.

30. Thomas Szasz, *Ideology and Insanity: Essays on the Psychiatric Dehumanization of Man* (Garden City, N.Y.: Doubleday-Anchor Press, 1970).

31. Quoted in Anne Somers, *Health Care in Transi-tion: Directions for the Future* (Chicago: Hospital Research and Educational Trust, 1971), p. 32.

32. See note 15, above.

33. "Prosperity as a Cause of Disease," *International Journal of Health Services 7*, 9(January 1977) 125–50.

34. R. Hurley, "The Health Crisis of the Poor," in *The Social Organization of Health*, ed. by H. P. Dreitzel (New York: Macmillan, 1971), pp. 83–122; *Infant Mortality Rates: Socioeconomic Factors*, Washington, D.C.: U.S. Public Health Service, series 22, no. 14, 1972; *Selected Vital and Health Statistics in Poverty and Nonpoverty Areas of 19 Large Cities, U.S., 1969–71*, Washington, D.C.: U.S. Public Health Service, series 21, no. 26, 1975; E. Kitagaw and P. Hauser, *Differential Mortality in the U.S.: A Study of Socioeconomic Epidemiology* (Cambridge: Harvard University Press, 1973); Hila Sherer, "Hypertension," *HMO* no. 2, January 1977.

35. *Preventive Medicine USA* (New York: Prodist Press, 1976), pp. 620–21; A. Antonovsky, "Social Class, Life Expectancy and Overall Mortality," *Milbank Memorial Fund Quarterly 5*, 45, no. 2-part 1(1967): 31–73.

36. C. D. Jenkins, "Recent Evidence Supporting Psychologic and Social Risk Factors for Coronary Heart Diseases," *New England Journal of Medicine* 294, 18(1976). 987–94; and 294, 19(1976): 1,003–38, J. Eyer and P. Sterling, "Stress Related Mortality and Social Organization," *Review of Radical Political Economy*, Summer 1977.

37. Somers, p. 77.

38. S. Lusterman, *Industry Roles in Health Care* (New York: National Industrial Conference Board, 1974) p. 31.

39. *Dollars and Sense*, April 1977, p. 15.

The Medicalization of American Society

Only in the twentieth century did medicine become the dominant and prestigious profession we know today. The germ theory of disease, which achieved dominance after about 1870, provided medicine with a powerful explanatory tool and some of its greatest clinical achievements. It proved to be the key that unlocked the mystery of infectious disease and it came to provide the major paradigm by which physicians viewed sickness. The claimed success of medicine in controlling infectious disease, coupled with consolidation and monopolization of medical practice, enabled medicine to achieve a position of social and professional dominance. Medicine, both in direct and indirect ways, was called upon to repeat its "miracles" with other human problems. At the same time, certain segments of the medical profession were intent on expanding medicine's jurisdiction over societal problems.

By mid-century the domain of medicine had enlarged considerably: childbirth, sexuality, death as well as old age, anxiety, obesity, child development, alcoholism, addiction, homosexuality, amongst other human experiences, were being defined and treated as medical problems. Sociologists began to examine the process and consequences of this *medicalization of society* (e.g., Freidson, 1970; Zola, 1972) and most especially the medicalization of deviance (Conrad and Schneider, 1980a). It was clear that the medical model—focusing on individual organic pathology and positing physiological etiologies and biomedical interventions—was being applied to a wide range of human phenomena. Human life, some critics observed, was increasingly seen as a sickness-wellness continuum, with significant (if not obvious) social consequences (Zola, 1972; Conrad, 1975).

Other sociologists, however, argue that although some expansion of medical jurisdiction has occurred, the medicalization problem is overstated. They contend that we recently have witnessed a considerable *de*medicalization. Strong (1979), for instance, points out that there are numerous factors constraining and limiting medicalization, including restrictions on the number of physicians, the cost of medical care, doctor's primary interests in manifestly organic problems, and the bourgeois value of individual liberty.

Recently, Conrad and Schneider (1980b) attempted to clarify the debate by suggesting that medicalization occurs on three levels: (1) the conceptual level, at which a medical vocabulary is used to define a problem; (2) the institutional level, at which medical personnel (usually physicians) are supervisors of treatment organizations or gatekeepers to state benefits; and (3) the interactional level, at which physicians actually treat patients' difficulties as medical problems. While there has been considerable discussion about the types and consequences of medicalization, there has thus far been little research on the actual extent of medicalization and its effects on patients' and other peoples' lives.

In "Medicine as an Institution of Social Control," Irving Kenneth Zola presents the medicalization thesis in terms of the expansion of medicine's social control functions. Renée Fox in "The Medicalization and Demedicalization of American Society" contends that a substantial demedicalization has occurred in American society, and that the concerns of critics of medicalization are overdrawn.

REFERENCES

Conrad, Peter. 1975. "The discovery of hyperkinesis: Notes on the medicalization of deviant behavior." Social Problems 23 (1): 12–21.

Conrad, Peter and Joseph W. Schneider. 1980a. Deviance and Medicalization: From Badness to Sickness. St. Louis: C.V. Mosby.

1980b. "Looking at levels of medicalization: A comment on Strong's critique of the thesis of medical imperialism." Social Science and Medicine 14A (1): 75–79.

Freidson, Eliot. 1970. Profession of Medicine. New York: Dodd, Mead.

Strong, P.M. 1979. "Sociological imperialism and the profession of medicine: A critical examination of the thesis of medical imperialism." Social Science and Medicine 13A (2): 199–215.

Zola, Irving Kenneth. 1972. "Medicine as an institution of social control." Sociological Review 20 (November): 487–504.

32

Medicine as an Institution of Social Control

Irving Kenneth Zola

The theme of this essay is that medicine is becoming a major institution of social control, nudging aside, if not incorporating, the more traditional institutions of religion and law. It is becoming the new repository of truth, the place where absolute and often final judgments are made by supposedly morally neutral and objective experts. And these judgments are made, not in the name of virtue or legitimacy, but in the name of health. Moreover, this is not occurring through the political power physicians hold or can influence, but is largely an insidious and often undramatic phenomenon accomplished by "medicalizing" much of daily living, by making medicine and the labels "healthy" and "ill" *relevant* to an ever increasing part of human existence.

Although many have noted aspects of this process, by confining their concern to the field of psychiatry, these criticisms have been misplaced.[1] For psychiatry has by no means distorted the mandate of medicine, but indeed, though perhaps at a pace faster than other medical specialties, is following instead some of the basic claims and directions of that profession. Nor is this extension into society the result of any professional "imperialism," for this leads us to think of the issue in terms of misguided human efforts or motives. If we search for the "why" of this phenomenon, we will see instead that it is rooted in our increasingly complex technological and bureaucratic system—a system which has led us down the path of the reluctant reliance on the expert.[2]

Quite frankly, what is presented in the following pages is not a definitive argument but rather a case in progress. As such it draws heavily on observations made in the United States, though similar murmurings have long been echoed elsewhere.[3]

An Historical Perspective

The involvement of medicine in the management of society is not new. It did not appear full-blown one day in the mid-twentieth century. As Sigerist[4] has aptly claimed, medicine at base was always not only a social science but an occupation whose very practice was inextricably interwoven into society. This interdependence is perhaps best seen in two branches of medicine which have had a built-in social emphasis from the very start—psychiatry[5] and public health/preventive medicine.[6] Public health was always committed to changing social aspects of life—from sanitary to housing to working conditions—and often used the arm of the state (i.e. through laws and legal power) to gain its ends (e.g. quarantines, vaccinations). Psychiatry's involvement in society is a bit more difficult to trace, but taking the histories of psychiatry as data, then one notes the almost universal reference to one of the early pioneers, a physician named Johan Weyer. His, and thus psychiatry's involvement in social problems lay in the objection that witches ought not to be burned; for they were not possessed by the devil, but rather bedeviled by their problems—namely they were insane. From its early concern with the issue of insanity as a defense in criminal proceedings, psychiatry has grown to become the most dominant

rehabilitative perspective in dealing with society's "legal" deviants. Psychiatry, like public health, has also used the legal powers of the state in the accomplishment of its goals (i.e. the cure of the patient through the legal proceedings of involuntary commitment and its concomitant removal of certain rights and privileges).

This is not to say, however, that the rest of medicine has been "socially" uninvolved. For a rereading of history makes it seem a matter of degree. Medicine has long had both a *de jure* and a *de facto* relation to institutions of social control. The *de jure* relationship is seen in the idea of reportable diseases, wherein, if certain phenomena occur in his practice, the physician is required to report them to the appropriate authorities. While this seems somewhat straightforward and even functional where certain highly contagious diseases are concerned, it is less clear where the possible spread of infection is not the primary issue (e.g. with gunshot wounds, attempted suicide, drug use and what is now called child abuse). The *de facto* relation to social control can be argued through a brief look at the disruptions of the last two or three American Medical Association Conventions. For there the American Medical Association members—and really all ancillary health professions—were accused of practicing social control (the term used by the accusers was genocide) in first, *whom* they have traditionally treated with *what*—giving *better* treatment to more favored clientele; and secondly, *what* they have treated—a more subtle form of discrimination in that, with limited resources, by focusing on some diseases others are neglected. Here the accusation was that medicine has focused on the diseases of the rich and the established—cancer, heart disease, stroke—and ignored the diseases of the poor, such as malnutrition and still high infant mortality.

The Myth of Accountability

Even if we acknowledge such a growing medical involvement, it is easy to regard it as primarily a "good" one—which involves the steady destigmatization of many human and social problems. Thus Barbara Wootton was able to conclude:

Without question . . . in the contemporary attitude toward antisocial behaviour, psychiatry and humanitarianism have marched hand in hand. Just because it is so much in keeping with the mental atmosphere of a scientifically-minded age, the medical treatment of social deviants has been a most powerful, perhaps even the most powerful, reinforcement of humanitarian impulses; for today the prestige of humane proposals is immensely enhanced if these are expressed in the idiom of medical science.[7]

The assumption is thus readily made that such medical involvement in social problems leads to their removal from religious and legal scrutiny and thus from moral and punitive consequences. In turn the problems are placed under medical scientific scrutiny and thus in objective and therapeutic circumstances.

The fact that we cling to such a hope is at least partly due to two cultural-historical blindspots—one regarding our notion of punishment and the other our notion of moral responsibility. Regarding the first, if there is one insight into human behavior that the twentieth century should have firmly implanted, it is that punishment cannot be seen in merely physical terms, nor only from the perspective of the giver. Granted that capital offenses are on the decrease, that whipping and torture seem to be disappearing, as is the use of chains and other physical restraints, yet our ability if not willingness to inflict human anguish on one another does not seem similarly on the wane. The most effective forms of brain-washing deny any physical contact and the concept of relativism tells much about the psychological costs of even relative deprivation of tangible and intangible wants. Thus, when an individual because of his "disease" and its treatment is forbidden to have intercourse with fellow human beings, is confined until cured, is forced to undergo certain medical procedures for his own good, perhaps deprived forever of the right to have sexual relations and/or produce children, *then* it is difficult for the patient *not* to view what is happening to him as punishment. This does not mean that medicine is the latest form of twentieth century torture, but merely that pain and suffering take many forms, and that the removal of a despicable inhumane procedure by current standards does not necessarily mean that its replacement will be all that beneficial. In part, the satisfaction in seeing the chains cast off by Pinel may have allowed us for far too long to neglect examining with what they had been replaced.

It is the second issue, that of responsibility, which requires more elaboration, for it is argued here that the medical model has had its greatest impact in the lifting of moral condemnation from the individual. While some sceptics note that while the individual is no longer condemned his disease still *is,* they do not go far enough. Most analysts have tried to make a distinction between illness and crime on the issue of personal responsibility.[8] The criminal is thought to be responsible and therefore accountable (or punishable) for his act, while the sick person is not. While the distinction does exist, it seems to be more a quantitative one rather than a qualitative one, with moral judgments but a pinprick below the surface. For instance, while it is probably true that individuals are no longer directly condemned for being sick, it does seem that much of this condemnation is merely displaced. Though his immoral character is not demonstrated in his having a disease, it becomes evident in what he does about it. Without seeming ludicrous, if one listed the traits of people who break appointments, fail to follow treatment regimen, or even delay in seeking medical aid, one finds a long list of "personal flaws." Such people seem to be ever ignorant of the consequences of certain diseases, inaccurate as to symptomatology, unable to plan ahead or find time, burdened with shame, guilt, neurotic tendencies, haunted with traumatic medical experiences or members of some lower status minority group—religious, ethnic, racial or socio-economic. In short, they appear to be a sorely troubled if not disreputable group of people.

The argument need not rest at this level of analysis, for it is not clear that the issues of morality and individual responsibility have been fully banished from the etiological scene itself. At the same time as the label "illness" is being used to attribute "diminished responsibility" to a whole host of phenomena, the issue of "personal responsibility" seems to be re-emerging within medicine itself. Regardless of the truth and insights of the concepts of stress and the perspective of psychosomatics, whatever else they do, they bring man, *not* bacteria to the center of the stage and lead thereby to a re-examination of the individual's role in his own demise, disability and even recovery.

The case, however, need not be confined to professional concepts and their degree of acceptance, for we can look at the beliefs of the man in the street. As most surveys have reported, when an individual is asked what caused his diabetes, heart disease, upper respiratory infection, etc., we may be comforted by the scientific terminology if not the accuracy of his answers. Yet if we follow this questioning with the probe: "Why did you get X now?", or "Of all the people in your community, family, etc. who were exposed to X, why did you get . . . ?", then the rational scientific veneer is pierced and the concern with personal and moral responsibility emerges quite strikingly. Indeed the issue "why me?" becomes of great concern and is generally expressed in quite moral terms of what they did wrong. It is possible to argue that here we are seeing a residue and that it will surely be different in the new generation. A recent experiment I conducted should cast some doubt on this. I asked a class of forty undergraduates, mostly aged seventeen, eighteen and nineteen, to recall the last time they were sick, disabled, or hurt and then to record how they did or would have communicated this experience to a child under the age of five. The purpose of the assignment had nothing to do with the issue of responsibility and it is worth noting that there was no difference in the nature of the response between those who had or had not actually encountered children during their "illness." The responses speak for themselves.

The opening words of the sick, injured person to the query of the child were:
   "I feel bad"
   "I feel bad all over"
   "I have a bad leg"
   "I have a bad eye"
   "I have a bad stomach ache"
   "I have a bad pain"
   "I have a bad cold"
The reply of the child was inevitable:
   "What did you do wrong?"
The "ill person" in no case corrected the child's perspective but rather joined it at that level.

On bacteria
   "There are good germs and bad germs and sometimes the bad germs . . ."
On catching a cold
   "Well you know sometimes when your mother says, 'Wrap up or be careful or you'll catch a cold,' well I . . ."
On an eye sore
   "When you use certain kinds of things (mascara) near your eye you must be very careful and I was not . . ."
On a leg injury
   "You've always got to watch where your're going and I . . ."

Finally to the treatment phase:
On how drugs work
   "You take this medicine and it attacks the bad parts . . ."
On how wounds are healed
   "Within our body there are good forces and bad ones and when there is an injury, all the good ones . . ."
On pus
   "That's the way the body gets rid of all its bad things . . ."
On general recovery
   "If you are good and do all the things the doctor and your mother tell you, you will get better."

In short, on nearly every level, from getting sick to recovering, a moral battle raged. This seems more than the mere anthropomorphising of a phenomenon to communicate it more simply to children. Frankly it seems hard to believe that the English language is so poor that a *moral* rhetoric is needed to describe a supposedly amoral phenomenon—illness.

In short, despite hopes to the contrary, the rhetoric of illness by itself seems to provide no absolution from individual responsibility, accountability and moral judgment.

The Medicalizing of Society

Perhaps it is possible that medicine is not devoid of potential for moralizing and social control. The first question becomes: "what means are available to exercise it?" Freidson has stated a major aspect of the process most succinctly:

The medical profession has first claim to jurisdiction over the label of illness and *anything* to which it may be attached, irrespective of its capacity to deal with it effectively.[9]

For illustrative purposes this "attaching" process may be categorized in four concrete ways: first, through the expansion of what in life is deemed relevant to the good practice of medicine; secondly, through the retention of absolute control over certain technical procedures; thirdly, through the retention of near absolute access to certain "taboo" areas; and finally, through the expansion of what in medicine is deemed relevant to the good practice of life.

1. The Expansion of What in Life Is Deemed Relevant to the Good Practice of Medicine

The change of medicine's commitment from a specific etiological model of disease to a multi-causal one and the greater acceptance of the concepts of comprehensive medicine, psychosomatics, etc., have enormously expanded that which is or can be relevant to the understanding, treatment and even prevention of disease. Thus it is no longer necessary for the patient merely to divulge the symptoms of his body, but also the symptoms of daily living, his habits and his worries. Part of this is greatly facilitated in the "age of the computer," for what might be too embarrassing, or take too long, or be inefficient in a face-to-face encounter can now be asked and analyzed impersonally by the machine, and moreover be done before the patient ever sees the physician. With the advent of the computer a certain guarantee of privacy is necessarily lost, for while many physicians might have probed similar issues, the only place where the data were stored was in the mind of the doctor, and only rarely in the medical record. The computer, on the other hand, has a retrievable, transmittable and almost inexhaustible memory.

It is not merely, however, the nature of the data needed to make more accurate diagnoses and treatments, but the perspective which accompanies it—a perspective which pushes the physician far beyond his office and the exercise of technical skills. To rehabilitate or at least alleviate many of the ravages of chronic disease,

it has become increasingly necessary to intervene to change permanently the habits of a patient's lifetime—be it of working, sleeping, playing or eating. In prevention the "extension into life" becomes even deeper, since the very idea of primary prevention means getting there *before* the disease process starts. The physician must not only seek out his clientele but once found must often convince them that they must do something *now* and perhaps at a time when the potential patient feels well or not especially troubled. If this in itself does not get the prevention-oriented physician involved in the workings of society, then the nature of "effective" mechanisms for intervention surely does, as illustrated by the statement of a physician trying to deal with health problems in the ghetto.

> Any effort to improve the health of ghetto residents cannot be separated from equal and simultaneous efforts to remove the multiple social, political and economic restraints currently imposed on inner city residents.[10]

Certain forms of social intervention and control emerge even when medicine comes to grips with some of its more traditional problems like heart disease and cancer. An increasing number of physicians feel that a change in diet may be the most effective deterrent to a number of cardiovascular complications. They are, however, so perplexed as to how to get the general population to follow their recommendations that a leading article in a national magazine was entitled "To Save the Heart: Diet by Decree?"[11] It is obvious that there is an increasing pressure for more explicit sanctions against the tobacco companies and against high users to force both to desist. And what will be the implications of even stronger evidence which links age at parity, frequency of sexual intercourse, or the lack of male circumcision to the incidence of cervical cancer, can be left to our imagination!

2. Through the Retention of Absolute Control over Certain Technical Procedures

In particular this refers to skills which in certain jurisdictions are the very operational and legal definition of the practice of medicine—the right to do surgery and prescribe drugs. Both of these take medicine far beyond concern with ordinary organic disease.

In surgery this is seen in several different sub-specialties. The plastic surgeon has at least participated in, if not helped perpetuate, certain aesthetic standards. What once was a practice confined to restoration has now expanded beyond the correction of certain traumatic or even congenital deformities to the creation of new physical properties, from size of nose to size of breast, as well as dealing with certain phenomena—wrinkles, sagging, etc.—formerly associated with the "natural" process of aging. Alterations in sexual and reproductive functioning have long been a medical concern. Yet today the frequency of hysterectomies seems not so highly correlated as one might think with the presence of organic disease. (What avenues the very possibility of sex change will open is anyone's guess.) Transplantations, despite their still relative infrequency, have had a tremendous effect on our very notions of death and dying. And at the other end of life's continuum, since abortion is still essentially a surgical procedure, it is to the physician-surgeon that society is turning (and the physician-surgeon accepting) for criteria and guidelines.

In the exclusive right to prescribe and thus pronounce on and regulate drugs, the power of the physician is even more awesome. Forgetting for the moment our obsession with youth's "illegal" use of drugs, any observer can see, judging by sales alone, that the greatest increase in drug use over the last ten years has not been in the realm of treating any organic disease but in treating a large number of psychosocial states. Thus we have drugs for nearly every mood:

> to help us sleep or keep us awake
> to enhance our appetite or decrease it
> to tone down our energy level or to increase it
> to relieve our depression or stimulate our interest.

Recently the newspapers and more popular magazines, including some medical and scientific ones, have carried articles about drugs which may be effective peace pills or anti-aggression tablets, enhance our memory, our perception, our intelligence and our vision (spiritually or otherwise). This led to the easy prediction:

> We will see new drugs, more targeted, more specific and more potent than anything we have. . . . And many of these would be for people we would call healthy.[12]

This statement incidentally was made not by a visionary science fiction writer but by a former commissioner of the United States Food and Drug Administration.

3. Through the Retention of Near Absolute Access to Certain "Taboo" Areas

These "taboo" areas refer to medicine's almost exclusive license to examine and treat that most personal of individual possessions—the inner workings of our bodies and minds. My contention is that if anything can be shown in some way to affect the workings of the body and to a lesser extent the mind, then it can be labelled an "illness" itself or jurisdictionally "a medical problem." In a sheer statistical sense the import of this is especially great if we look at only four such problems—aging, drug addiction, alcoholism and pregnancy. The first and last were once regarded as normal natural processes and the middle two as human foibles and weaknesses. Now this has changed and to some extent medical specialties have emerged to meet these new needs. Numerically this expands medicine's involvement not only in a longer span of human existence, but it opens the possibility of medicine's services to millions if not billions of people. In the United States at least, the implication of declaring alcoholism a disease (the possible import of a pending Supreme Court decision as well as laws currently being introduced into several state legislatures) would reduce arrests in many jurisdictions by 10 to 50 percent and transfer such "offenders" when "discovered" directly to a medical facility. It is pregnancy, however, which produces the most illuminating illustration. For, again in the United States, it was barely seventy years ago that virtually all births and the concomitants of birth occurred outside the hospital as well as outside medical supervision. I do not frankly have a documentary history, but as this medical claim was solidified, so too was medicine's claim to a whole host of related processes: not only to birth but to prenatal, postnatal, and pediatric care; not only to conception but to infertility; not only to the process of reproduction but to the process and problems of sexual activity itself; not only when life begins (in the issue of abortion) but whether it should be allowed to begin at all (e.g. in genetic counselling).

Partly through this foothold in the "taboo" areas and partly through the simple reduction of other resources, the physician is increasingly becoming the choice for help for many with personal and social problems. Thus a recent British study reported that within a five year period there had been a notable increase (from 25 to 41 percent) in the proportion of the population willing to consult the physician with a personal problem.[13]

4. Through the Expansion of What in Medicine Is Deemed Relevant to the Good Practice of Life

Though in some ways this is the most powerful of all "the medicalizing of society" processes, the point can be made simply. Here we refer to the use of medical rhetoric and evidence in the arguments to advance any cause. For what Wootton attributed to psychiatry is no less true of medicine. To paraphrase her, today the prestige of *any* proposal is immensely enhanced, if not justified, when it is expressed in the idiom of medical science. To say that many who use such labels are not professionals only begs the issue, for the public is only taking its cues from professionals who increasingly have been extending their expertise into the social sphere or have called for such an extension.[14] In politics one hears of the healthy or unhealthy economy or state. More concretely, the physical and mental health of American presidential candidates has been an issue in the last four elections and a recent book claimed to link faulty political decisions with faulty health.[15] For years we knew that the environment was unattractive, polluted, noisy and in certain ways dying, but now we learn that its death may not be unrelated to our own demise. To end with a rather mundane if depressing example, there has always been a constant battle between school authorities and their charges on the basis of dress and such habits as smoking, but recently the issue was happily resolved for a local school administration when they declared that such restrictions were necessary for reasons of health.

The Potential and Consequences of Medical Control

The list of daily activities to which health can be related is ever growing and with the current operating perspective of medicine it seems infinitely expandable. The reasons are manifold. It is not merely that medicine has extended its jurisdiction to cover new problems,[16] or that doctors are professionally committed to finding disease,[17] nor even that society keeps creating disease.[18] For if none of these obtained today we would still find medicine exerting an enormous influence on society. The most powerful empirical stimulus for this is the realization of how much everyone has or believes he has something organically wrong with him, or put more positively, how much can be done to make one feel, look or function better.

The rates of "clinical entities" found on surveys or by periodic health examinations range upwards from 50 to 80 percent of the population studied.[19] The Peckham study found that only 9 percent of their study group were free from clinical disorder. Moreover, they were even wary of this figure and noted in a footnote that, first, some of these 9 percent had subsequently died of a heart attack, and, secondly, that the majority of those without disorder were under the age of five.[20] We used to rationalize that this high level of prevalence did not, however, translate itself into action since not only are rates of medical utilization not astonishingly high but they also have not gone up appreciably. Some recent studies, however, indicate that we may have been looking in the wrong place for this medical action. It has been noted in the United States and the United Kingdom that within a given twenty-four to thirty-six hour period, from 50 to 80 percent of the adult population have taken one or more "medical" drugs.[21]

The belief in the omnipresence of disorder is further enhanced by a reading of the scientific, pharmacological and medical literature, for there one finds a growing litany of indictments of "unhealthy" life activities. From sex to food, from aspirins to clothes, from driving your car to riding the surf, it seems that under certain conditions, or in combination with certain other substances or activities or if done too much or too little, virtually anything can lead to certain medical problems. In short, I at least have finally been convinced that living is injurious to health. This remark is not meant as facetiously as it may sound. But rather every aspect of our daily life has in it elements of risk to health.

These facts take on particular importance not only when health becomes a paramount value in society, but also a phenomenon whose diagnosis and treatment has been restricted to a certain group. For this means that that group, perhaps unwittingly, is in a position to exercise great control and influence about what we should and should not do to attain that "paramount value."

Freidson in his recent book *Profession of Medicine* has very cogently analyzed why the expert in general and the medical expert in particular should be granted a certain autonomy in his researches, his diagnosis and his recommended treatments.[22] On the other hand, when it comes to constraining or directing human behavior *because* of the data of his researches, diagnosis and treatment, a different situation obtains. For in these kinds of decisions it seems that too often the physician is guided not by his technical knowledge but by his values, or values latent in his very techniques.

Perhaps this issue of values can be clarified by reference to some not so randomly chosen medical problems: drug safety, genetic counselling and automated multiphasic testing.

The issue of drug safety should seem straightforward, but both words in that phrase apparently can have some interesting flexibility—namely what is a drug and what is safe. During Prohibition in the United States alcohol was medically regarded as a drug and was often prescribed as a medicine. Yet in recent years, when the issue of dangerous substances and drugs has come up for discussion in medical circles, alcohol has been officially excluded from the debate. As for safety, many have applauded the A.M.A.'s judicious position in declaring the

need for much more extensive, longitudinal research on marihuana and their unwillingness to back leglization until much more data are in. This applause might be muted if the public read the 1970 Food and Drug Administration's "Blue Ribbon" Committee Report on the safety, quality and efficacy of *all* medical drugs commercially and legally on the market since 1938.[23] Though appalled at the lack and quality of evidence of any sort, few recommendations were made for the withdrawal of drugs from the market. Moreover there are no recorded cases of anyone dying from an overdose or of extensive adverse side effects from marihuana use, but the literature on the adverse effects of a whole host of "medical drugs" on the market today is legion.

It would seem that the value positions of those on both sides of the abortion issue needs little documenting, but let us pause briefly at a field where "harder" scientists are at work—genetics. The issue of genetic counselling, or whether life should be allowed to begin at all, can only be an ever increasing one. As we learn more and more about congenital, inherited disorders or predispositions, and as the population size for whatever reason becomes more limited, then, inevitably, there will follow an attempt to improve the quality of the population which shall be produced. At a conference on the more limited concern of what to do when there is a documented probability of the offspring of certain unions being damaged, a position was taken that it was not necessary to pass laws or bar marriages that might produce such offspring. Recognizing the power and influence of medicine and the doctor, one of those present argued:

> There is no reason why sensible people could not be dissuaded from marrying if they know that one out of four of their children is likely to inherit a disease.[24]

There are in this statement certain values on marriage and what it is or could be that, while they may be popular, are not necessarily shared by all. Thus, in addition to presenting the argument against marriage, it would seem that the doctor should—if he were to engage in the issue at all—present at the same time some of the other alternatives:

Some "parents" could be willing to live with the risk that out of four children, three may turn out fine.

Depending on the diagnostic procedures available they could take the risk and if indications were negative abort.

If this risk were too great but the desire to bear children was there, and depending on the type of problem, artificial insemination might be a possibility.

Barring all these and not wanting to take any risk, they could adopt children.

Finally, there is the option of being married without having any children.

It is perhaps appropriate to end with a seemingly innocuous and technical advance in medicine, automatic multiphasic testing. It has been a procedure hailed as a boon to aid the doctor if not replace him. While some have questioned the validity of all those test-results and still others fear that it will lead to second class medicine for already underprivileged populations, it is apparent that its major use to date and in the future may not be in promoting health or detecting disease but to prevent it. Thus three large institutions are now or are planning to make use of this method, not to treat people, but to "deselect" them. The armed services use it to weed out the physically and mentally unfit, insurance companies to reject "uninsurables" and large industrial firms to point out "high risks." At a recent conference representatives of these same institutions were asked what responsibility they did or would recognize to those whom they have just informed that they have been "rejected" because of some physical or mental anomaly. They calmly and universally stated: none—neither to provide them with any appropriate aid nor even to ensure that they get or be put in touch with any help.

Conclusion

C. S. Lewis warned us more than a quarter of a century ago that "man's power over Nature is really the power of some men over other men, with Nature as their instrument." The same could be said regarding man's power over health and illness, for the labels health and illness are remarkable "depoliticizers" of an issue. By locat-

ing the source and the treatment of problems in an individual, other levels of intervention are effectively closed. By the very acceptance of a specific behavior as an "illness" and the definition of illness as an undesirable state, the issue becomes not whether to deal with a particular problem, but *how* and *when*.[25] Thus the debate over homosexuality, drugs or abortion becomes focused on the degree of sickness attached to the phenomenon in question or the extent of the health risk involved. And the more principled, more perplexing, or even moral issue, of *what* freedom should an individual have over his or her own body is shunted aside.

As stated in the very beginning this "medicalizing of society" is as much a result of medicine's potential as it is of society's wish for medicine to use that potential. Why then has the focus been more on the medical potential than on the social desire? In part it is a function of space, but also of political expediency. For the time rapidly may be approaching when recourse to the populace's wishes may be impossible. Let me illustrate this with the statements of two medical scientists who, if they read this essay, would probably dismiss all my fears as groundless. The first was commenting on the ethical, moral, and legal procedures of the sex change operation:

> Physicians generally consider it unethical to destroy or alter tissue except in the presence of disease or deformity. The interference with a person's natural pro-creative function entails definite moral tenets, by which not only physicians but also the general public are influenced. The administration of physical harm as treatment for mental or behavioral problems—as corporal punishment, lobotomy for unmanageable psychotics and sterilization of criminals—is abhorrent in our society.[26]

Here he states, as almost an absolute condition of human nature, something which is at best a recent phenomenon. He seems to forget that there were laws promulgating just such procedures through much of the twentieth century, that within the past few years at least one Californian jurist ordered the sterilization of an unwed mother as a condition of probation, and that such procedures were done by Nazi scientists and physicians as part of a series of medical experiments. More recently, there is the misguided patriotism of the cancer researchers under contract to the United States Department of Defense who allowed their dying patients to be exposed to massive doses of radiation to analyze the psychological and physical results of simulated nuclear fall-out. True, the experiments were stopped, but not until they had been going on for *eleven* years.

The second statement is by Francis Crick at a conference on the implications of certain genetic findings:

> Some of the wild genetic proposals will never be adopted because the people will simply not stand for them.[27]

Note where his emphasis is: on the people not the scientist. In order, however, for the people to be concerned, to act and to protest, they must first be aware of what is going on. Yet in the very privatized nature of medical practice, plus the continued emphasis that certain expert judgments must be free from public scrutiny, there are certain processes which will prevent the public from ever knowing what has taken place and thus from doing something about it. Let me cite two examples.

> Recently, in a European country, I overheard the following conversation in a kidney dialysis unit. The chief was being questioned about whether or not there were self-help groups among his patients. "No" he almost shouted "that is the last thing we want. Already the patients are sharing too much knowledge while they sit in the waiting room, thus making our task increasingly difficult. We are working now on a procedure to prevent them from even meeting with one another."

The second example removes certain information even further from public view.

> The issue of fluoridation in the U.S. has been for many years a hot political one. It was in the political arena because, in order to fluoridate local water supplies, the decision in many jurisdictions had to be put to a popular referendum. And when it was, it was often defeated. A solution was found and a series of state laws were passed to make fluoridation a public health decision and to be treated, as all other public health decisions, by the medical officers

best qualified to decide questions of such a technical, scientific and medical nature.

Thus the issue at base here is the question of what factors are actually of a solely technical, scientific and medical nature.

To return to our opening caution, this paper is not an attack on medicine so much as on a situation in which we find ourselves in the latter part of the twentieth century; for the medical area is the arena or the example *par excellence* of today's identity crisis—what is or will become of man. It is the battleground, not because there are visible threats and oppressors, but because they are almost invisible; not because the perspective, tools and practitioners of medicine and the other helping professions are evil, but because they are not. It is so frightening because there are elements here of the banality of evil so uncomfortably written about by Hannah Arendt.[28] But here the danger is greater, for not only is the process masked as a technical, scientific, objective one, but one done for our own good. A few years ago a physician speculated on what, based on current knowledge, would be the composite picture of an individual with a low risk of developing atherosclerosis or coronary-artery disease. He would be:

> ... an effeminate municipal worker or embalmer completely lacking in physical or mental alertness and without drive, ambition, or competitive spirit; who has never attempted to meet a deadline of any kind; a man with poor appetite, subsisting on fruits and vegetables laced with corn and whale oil, detesting tobacco, spurning ownership of radio, television, or motorcar, with full head of hair but scrawny and unathletic appearance, yet constantly straining his puny muscles by exercise. Low in income, blood pressure, blood sugar, uric acid and cholesterol, he has been taking nicotinic acid, pyridoxine, and long term antocoagulant therapy ever since his prophylactic castration.[29]

Thus I fear with Freidson:

> A profession and a society which are so concerned with physical and functional wellbeing as to sacrifice civil liberty and moral integrity must inevitably press for a "scientific" environment similar to that provided laying hens on progressive chicken

farms—hens who produce eggs industriously and have no disease or other cares.[30]

Nor does it really matter that if, instead of the above depressing picture, we were guaranteed six more inches in height, thirty more years of life, or drugs to expand our potentialities and potencies; we should still be able to ask: what do six more inches matter, in what kind of environment will the thirty additional years be spent, or who will decide what potentialities and potencies will be expanded and what curbed.

I must confess that given the road down which so much expertise has taken us, I am willing to live with some of the frustrations and even mistakes that will follow when the authority for many decisions becomes shared with those whose lives and activities are involved. For I am convinced that patients have so much to teach to their doctors as do students their professors and children their parents.

NOTE

This paper was written while the author was a consultant in residence at the Netherlands Institute for Preventive Medicine, Leiden. For their general encouragement and the opportunity to pursue this topic I will always be grateful.

It was presented at the Medical Sociology Conference of the British Sociological Association at Weston-Super-Mare in November 1971. My special thanks for their extensive editorial and substantive comments go to Egon Bittner, Mara Sanadi, Alwyn Smith, and Bruce Wheaton.

REFERENCES

1. T. Szasz: *The Myth of Mental Illness*, Harper and Row, New York, 1961; and R. Leifer: *In the Name of Mental Health*, Science House, New York, 1969.
2. E.g. A. Toffler: *Future Shock*, Random House, New York, 1970; and P. E. Slater: *The Pursuit of Loneliness*, Beacon Press, Boston, 1970.
3. Such as B. Wootton: *Social Science and Social Pathology*, Allen and Unwin, London, 1959.
4. H. Sigerist: *Civilization and Disease*, Cornell University Press, New York, 1943.
5. M. Foucault: *Madness and Civilization*, Pantheon, New York, 1965; and Szasz: *op. cit.*
6. G. Rosen: *A History of Public Health*, MD Publications, New York, 1955; and G. Rosen: "The Evolution of Social Medicine", in H. E. Freeman, S. Levine and L. G. Reeder (eds): *Handbook of Medical Sociology*, Prentice-Hall, Englewood Cliffs, N.J., 1963, pp. 17–61.
7. Wootton: *op. cit.*, p. 206.
8. Two excellent discussions are found in V. Aubert and S. Messinger: "The Criminal and the Sick", *Inquiry*, Vol. 1, 1958, pp. 137–160; and E. Freidson: *Profession of Medicine*, Dodd-Mead, New York, 1970, pp. 205–277.
9. Freidson: *op. cit.*, p. 251.
10. J. C. Norman: "Medicine in the Ghetto", *New Engl. J. Med.*, Vol. 281, 1969, p. 1271.
11. "To Save the Heart; Diet by Decree?" *Time Magazine*, 10th January, 1968, p. 42.
12. J. L. Goddard quoted in the *Boston Globe*, August 7th, 1966.
13. K. Dunnell and A. Cartwright: *Medicine Takers, Prescribers and Hoarders*, in press.
14. E.g. S. Alinsky: "The Poor and the Powerful", in *Poverty and Mental Health*, Psychiat. Res. Rep. No. 21 of the Amer. Psychiat. Ass., January 1967; and B. Wedge: "Psychiatry and International Affairs", *Science*, Vol. 157, 1961, pp. 281–285.
15. H. L'Etang: *The Pathology of Leadership*, Hawthorne Books, New York, 1970.
16. Szasz: *op. cit.*, and Leifer: *op. cit.*
17. Freidson: *op. cit.*; and T. Scheff: "Preferred Errors in Diagnoses", *Medical Care*, Vol. 2, 1964, pp. 166–172.
18. R. Dubos: *The Mirage of Health*, Doubleday, Garden City, N.Y., 1959; and R. Dubos: *Man Adapting*, Yale University Press, 1965.
19. E.g. the general summaries of J. W. Meigs: "Occupational Medicine", *New Eng. J. Med.*, Vol. 264, 1961, pp. 861–867; and G. S. Siegel: *Periodic Health Examinations—Abstracts from the Literature*, Publ. Hlth. Serv. Publ. No. 1010, U.S. Government Printing Office, Washington, D.C., 1963.
20. I. H. Pearse and L. H. Crocker: *Biologists in Search of Material*, Faber and Faber, London, 1938; and I. H. Pearse and L. H Crocker: *The Peckham Experiment*, Allen and Unwin, London, 1949.
21. Dunnell and Cartwright: *op. cit.*; and K. White, A. Andjelkovic, R. J. C. Pearson, J. H. Mabry, A. Ross and O. K. Sagan: "International Comparisons of Medical Care Utilization", *New Engl. J. of Med.*, Vol. 277, 167, pp. 516–522.
22. Freidson: *op. cit.*

23. *Drug Efficiency Study—Final Report to the Commissioner of Food and Drugs,* Food and Drug Adm. Med. Nat. Res. Council, Nat. Acad. Sci., Washington, D.C., 1969.
24. Reported in L. Eisenberg: "Genetics and the Survival of the Unfit", *Harper's Magazine,* Vol. 232, 1966, p. 57.
25. This general case is argued more specifically in I. K. Zola: *Medicine, Morality, and Social Problems—Some Implications of the Label Mental Illness,* Paper presented at the Amer. Ortho-Psychiat. Ass., March 20–23, 1968.
26. D. H. Russell: "The Sex Conversion Controversy", *New Engl. J. Med.,* Vol. 279, 1968, p. 536.
27. F. Crick reported in *Time Magazine,* April 19th, 1971.
28. H. Arendt: *Eichmann in Jerusalem—A Report on the Banality of Evil,* Viking Press, New York, 1963.
29. G. S. Myers quoted in L. Losagna: *Life, Death and the Doctor,* Alfred Knopf, New York, 1968, pp. 215–216.
30. Freidson: *op. cit.,* p. 354.

33

The Medicalization and Demedicalization of American Society

Renée C. Fox

. . . .

Along with progressive medicalization, a process of demedicalization seems also to be taking place in the society. To some extent the signs of demedicalization are reactions to what is felt by various individuals and groups to be a state of "*over*-medicalization." One of the most significant manifestations of this counter-trend is the mounting concern over implications that have arisen from the continuously expanding conception of "sickness" in the society. Commentators on this process would not necessarily agree with Peter Sedgwick that it will continue to "the point where everybody has become so luxuriantly ill" that perhaps sickness will no longer be "in" and a "blacklash" will be set in motion;[1] they may not envision such an engulfing state of societally defined illness. But many observers from diverse professional backgrounds have published works in which they express concern about the "coercive" aspects of the "label" illness and the treatment of illness by medical professionals in medical institutions.[2] The admonitory perspectives on the enlarged domain of illness and medicine that these works of social science and social criticism represent appear to have gained the attention of young physicians- and nurses-in-training interested in change, and various consumer and civil-rights groups interested in health care.

This emerging view emphasizes the degree to which what is defined as health and illness, normality and abnormality, sanity and insanity varies from one society, culture, and historical period to another. Thus, it is contended, medical diagnostic categories such as "sick," "abnormal," and "insane" are not universal, objective, or necessarily reliable. Rather, they are culture-, class-, and time-bound, often ethnocentric, and as much artifacts of the preconceptions of socially biased observers as they are valid summaries of the characteristics of the observed. In this view, illness (especially mental illness) is largely a mythical construct, created and enforced by the society. The hospitals to which seriously ill persons are confined are portrayed as "total institutions": segregated, encompassing, depersonalizing organizations, "dominated" by physicians who are disinclined to convey information to patients about their conditions, or to encourage paramedical personnel to do so. These "oppressive" and "counter-therapeutic" attributes of the hospital environment are seen as emanating from the professional ideology of physicians and the kind of hierarchial relationships that they establish with patients and other medical professionals partly as a consequence of this ideology, as well as from the bureaucratic and technological features of the hospital itself. Whatever their source, the argument continues, the characteristics of the hospital and of the doctor-patient relationship increase the "powerlessness" of the sick person, "maintain his uncertainty," and systematically "mortify" and "curtail" the "self" with which he enters the sick role and arrives at the hospital door.

This critical perspective links the labeling of illness, the "imperialist" outlook and capitalist behavior of physicians, the "stigmatizing" and "dehumanizing" experiences of patients, and the problems of the health-care system more generally to imperfections and injustices in the society as a whole. Thus, for example, the various forms of social inequality, prejudice, discrimination, and acquisitive self-interest that persist in capitalistic American society are held responsible for causing illness, as well as for contributing to the undesirable attitudes and actions of physicians and other medical professionals. Casting persons in the sick role is regarded as a powerful, latent way for the society to exact conformity and maintain the status quo. For it allows a semi-approved form of deviance to occur which siphons off potential for insurgent protest and which can be controlled through the supervision or, in some cases, the "enforced therapy" of the medical profession. Thus, however permissive and merciful it may be to expand the category of illness, these observers point out, there is always the danger that the

society will become a "therapeutic state" that excessively restricts the "right to be different" and the right to dissent. They feel that this danger may already have reached serious proportions in this society through its progressive medicalization.

The criticism of medicalization and the advocacy of demedicalization have not been confined to rhetoric. Concrete steps have been taken to declassify certain conditions as illness. Most notable among these is the American Psychiatric Association's decision to remove homosexuality from its official catalogue ("Nomenclature") of mental disorders. In addition, serious efforts have been made to heighten physicians' awareness of the fact because they share certain prejudiced, often unconscious assumptions about women, they tend to over-attribute psychological conditions to their female patients. Thus, for example, distinguished medical publications such as the *New England Journal of Medicine* have featured articles and editorials on the excessive readiness with which medical specialists and textbook authors accept the undocumented belief that dysmenorrhea, nausea of pregnancy, pain in labor, and infantile colic are all psychogenic disorders, caused or aggravated by women's emotional problems. Another related development is feminist protest against what is felt to be a too great tendency to define pregnancy as an illness, and childbirth as a "technologized" medical-surgical event, prevailed over by the obstetrician-gynecologist. These sentiments have contributed to the preference that many middle-class couples have shown for natural childbirth in recent years, and to the revival of midwifery. The last example also illustrates an allied movement, namely a growing tendency to shift some responsibility for medical care and authority over it from the physician, the medical team, and hospital to the patient, the family, and the home.

A number of attempts to "destratify" the doctor's relationships with patients and with other medical professionals and to make them more open and egalitarian have developed. "Patients' rights" are being asserted and codified, and, in some states, drafted into law. Greater emphasis is being placed, for example, on the patient's "right to treatment," right to information (relevant to diagnosis, therapy, prognosis, or to the giving of knowledgeable consent for any procedure), right to privacy and confidentiality, and right to be "allowed to die," rather than being "kept alive by artificial means or heroic measures . . . if the situation should arise in which there is no reasonable expectation of . . . recovery from physical or mental disability."[3]

In some medical milieux (for example, community health centers and health maintenance organizations), and in critical and self-consciously progressive writings about medicine, the term "client" or "consumer" is being substituted for "patient." This change in terminology is intended to underline the importance of preventing illness while stressing the desirability of a non-supine, non-subordinate relationship for those who seek care to those who provide it. The emergence of nurse-practitioners and physician's assistants on the American scene is perhaps the most significant sign that some blurring of the physician's supremacy vis-à-vis other medical professionals may also be taking place. For some of the responsibilities for diagnosis, treatment, and patient management that were formerly prerogatives of physicians have been incorporated into these new, essentially marginal roles.[4]

Enjoinders to patients to care for themselves rather than to rely so heavily on the services of medical professionals and institutions are more frequently heard. Much attention is being given to studies such as the one conducted by Lester Breslow and his colleagues at the University of California at Los Angeles which suggest that good health and longevity are as much related to a self-enforced regimen of sufficient sleep, regular, well-balanced meals, moderate exercise and weight, no smoking, and little or no drinking, as they are to professionally administered medical care. Groups such as those involved in the Women's Liberation Movement are advocating the social and psychic as well as the medical value of knowing, examining, and caring for one's own body. Self-therapy techniques and programs have been developed for conditions as complicated and grave as terminal renal disease and hemophilia A and B. Proponents of such regimens affirm that many aspects of managing even serious chronic illnesses can be handled safely at home by the patient and his family, who

will, in turn, benefit both financially and emotionally. In addition, they claim that in many cases the biomedical results obtained seem superior to those of the traditional physician-administered, health-care-delivery system.

The underlying assumption in these instances is that, if self-care is collectivized and reinforced by mutual aid, not only will persons with a medical problem be freed from some of the exigencies of the sick role, but both personal and public health will thereby improve, all with considerable savings in cost. This point of view is based on the moral supposition that greater autonomy from the medical profession coupled with greater responsibility for self and others in the realm of health and illness is an ethically and societally superior state.

We have the medicine we deserve. We freely choose to live the way we do. We choose to live recklessly, to abuse our bodies with what we consume, to expose ourselves to environmental insults, to rush frantically from place to place, and to sit on our spreading bottoms and watch paid professionals exercise for us. . . . Today few patients have the confidence to care for themselves. The inexorable professionalization of medicine, together with reverence for the scientific method, have invested practitioners with sacrosanct powers, and correspondingly vitiated the responsibility of the rest of us for health. . . . What is tragic is not what has happened to the revered professions, but what has happened to us as a result of professional dominance. In times of inordinate complexity and stress we have been made a profoundly dependent people. Most of us have lost the ability to care for ourselves. . . . I have tried to demonstrate three propositions. First, medical care has less impact on health than is generally assumed. Second, medical care has less impact on health than have social and environmental factors. And third, given the way in which society is evolving and the evolutionary imperatives of the medical care system, medical care in the future will have even less impact on health than it has now. . . . We have not understood what health is. . . . But in the next few decades our understanding will deepen. The pursuit of health and of well-being will then be possible, but only if our environment is made safe for us to live in and our social order is transformed to foster health, rather than suppress joy. If not, we shall remain a sick and dependent people. . . . The end of medicine is not the end of health but the beginning. . . .[5]

The foregoing passage (excerpted from Rick Carlson's book, *The End of Medicine*) touches upon many of the demedicalization themes that have been discussed. It proclaims the desirability of demedicalizing American society, predicting that, if we do so, we can overcome the "harm" that excessive medicalization has brought in its wake and progress beyond the "limits" that it has set. Like most critics of medicalization on the American scene, Carlson inveighs against the way that medical care is currently organized and implemented, but he attaches exceptional importance to the health-illness-medical sector of the society. In common with other commentators, he views health, illness, and medicine as inextricably associated with values and beliefs of American tradition that are both critical and desirable. It is primarily for this reason that in spite of the numerous signs that certain *structural* changes in the delivery of care will have occurred by the time we reach the year 2000, American society is not likely to undergo a significant process of *cultural* demedicalization.

Dissatisfaction with the distribution of professional medical care in the United States, its costs, and its accessibility has become sufficiently acute and generalized to make the enactment of a national health-insurance system in the foreseeable future likely. Exactly what form that system should take still evokes heated debate about free enterprise and socialism, public and private regulation, national and local government, tax rates, deductibles and co-insurance, the right to health care, the equality principle, and the principle of distributive justice. But the institutionalization of a national system that will provide more extensive and equitable health-insurance protection now seems necessary as well as inevitable even to those who do not approve of it.

There is still another change in the health-illness-medicine area of the society that seems to be forthcoming and that, like national health insurance, would alter the structure within which care is delivered. This is the movement toward effecting greater equality, collegiality, and accountability in the relationship of physicians to patients and their families, to other medical professionals, and to the lay public. Attempts to reduce the hierarchical dimension in the physician's role, as well as the increased insistence on patient's rights, self-therapy, mutual medical aid, community medical services and care by non-physician health professionals, and the growth of legislative and judicial participation in health and medicine by both federal and local government are all part of this movement. There is reason to believe that, as a consequence of pressure from both outside and inside the medical profession, the doctor will become less "dominant" and "autonomous," and will be subject to more controls.

This evolution in the direction of greater egalitarianism and regulation notwithstanding, it seems unlikely that all elements of hierarchy and autonomy will, or even can, be eliminated from the physician's role. For that to occur, the medical knowledge, skill, experience, and responsibility of patients and paramedical professionals would have to equal, if not replicate, the physician's. In addition, the social and psychic meaning of health and illness would have to become trivial in order to remove all vestiges of institutionalized charisma from the physician's role. Health, illness, and medicine have never been viewed casually in any society and, as indicated, they seem to be gaining rather than losing importance in American society.

It is significant that often the discussions and developments relevant to the destratification and control of the physician's role and to the enactment of national health insurance are accompanied by reaffirmations of traditional American values: equality, independence, self-reliance, universalism, distributive justice, solidarity, reciprocity, and individual and community responsibility. What seems to be involved here is not so much a change in values as the initiation of action intended to modify certain structural features of American medicine, so that it will more fully realize long-standing societal values.

In contrast, the new emphasis on health as a right, along with the emerging perspective on illness as medically and socially engendered, seems to entail major conceptual rather than structural shifts in the health-illness-medical matrix of the society. These shifts are indicative of a less fatalistic and individualistic attitude toward illness, increased personal and communal espousal of health, and a spreading conviction that health is as much a consequence of the good life and the good society as it is of professional medical care. The strongest impetus for demedicalization comes from this altered point of view. It will probably contribute to the decategorization of certain conditions as illness, greater appreciation and utilization of non-physician medical professionals, the institutionalization of more preventive medicine and personal and public health measures, and, perhaps, to the undertaking of non-medical reforms (such as full employment, improved transportation, or adequate recreation) in the name of the ultimate goal of health.

However, none of these trends implies that what we have called *cultural* demedicalization will take place. The shifts in emphasis from illness to health, from therapeutic to preventive medicine, and from the dominance and autonomy of the doctor to patient's rights and greater control of the medical profession do not alter the fact that health, illness, and medicine are central preoccupations in the society which have diffuse symbolic as well as practical meaning. All signs suggest that they will maintain the social, ethical, and existential significance they have acquired, even though by the year 2000 some structural aspects of the way that medicine and care are organized and delivered may have changed. In fact, if the issues now being considered under the rubric of bioethics are predictive of what lies ahead, we can expect that in the future, health, illness, and medicine will acquire even greater importance as one of the primary symbolic media through which American society will grapple with fundamental questions of value and belief. What social mechanisms we will develop to come to terms with these "collec-

tive conscience" issues, and exactly what role physicians, health professionals, biologists, jurists, politicians, philosophers, theologians, social scientists, and the public at large will play in their resolution remains to be seen. But it is a distinctive characteristic of an advanced modern society like our own that scientific, technical, clinical, social, ethical, and religious concerns should be joined in this way.

REFERENCES

1. Sedgwick, "Illness—Mental and Otherwise," *The Hastings Center Studies*, 1:3(1973), p. 37.
2. In addition to Illich, *Medical Nemesis*, and Kittrie, *The Right To Be Different*, see, for example, Rick J. Carlson, *The End of Medicine* (New York, 1975); Michael Foucault, *Madness and Civilization* (New York, 1967); Eliot Freidson, *Professional Dominance* (Chicago, 1970); Erving Goffman, *Asylums* (New York, 1961); R. D. Laing, *The Politics of Experience* (New York, 1967); Thomas J. Scheff, *Being Mentally Ill* (Chicago, 1966); Thomas S. Szasz, *The Myth of Mental Illness* (New York, 1961); and Howard D. Waitzkin and Barbara Waterman, *The Exploitation of Illness in Capitalist Society* (Indianapolis, 1974).
3. This particular way of requesting that one be allowed to die is excerpted from the "Living Will" (revised April, 1974 version), prepared and promoted by the Euthanasia Educational Council.
4. See the article by David Rogers, "The Challenge of Primary Care," in *Daedalus*, 106, Winter, 1977:81–103.
5. Carlson, *The End of Medicine*, pp. 44, 141, and 203–31.

Part Four

Toward Alternatives in Health Care

As part of a critical sociological examination of American health and medical care, it is important that we explore what can be done to create alternatives to improve health in our society. In so doing, we look beyond the "medical model" and the current organization and delivery of medical services. We can conceptualize these alternatives as Community Initiatives, Comparative Health Policies, and Prevention and Society. In the first section of Part Four we examine several community-based alternatives to existing medical services and discuss their problems and limitations, as well as their potential for improving health care. In the second section we examine alternatives on the broader, societal level by looking at the health care systems of three other countries. In the final section we consider the potential of prevention as an alternative way of reorienting our approach to health problems. We cannot claim to provide *the* answer to our "health crisis" here. However, we believe the answers to our health care problems will ultimately be found by searching in the directions pointed out in this section of the book.

Community Initiatives

Several issues emerge when we examine and evaluate community-level efforts to improve medical care. The first such issue pertains to inherent limitations of such efforts. It is widely argued that the possibilities for change within the existing societal and medical care system are inherently limited. Although some of the most exciting and interesting health innovations have occurred through local efforts on the community level—e.g., women's self-help clinics, neighborhood health centers—these efforts are constantly being shaped and limited by the societal context in which they emerge and in which, often, they must struggle to survive. The realities of the present system (e.g. the professional dominance of physicians, the control of medical payments by the insurance industry and medical care providers, and the limitations imposed by existing medical organizations on access to their services) constitute systemic boundaries to the power of community alternative health care organizations to effect real change. Some critics even contend that these societal-level constraints will, in the very nature of things, always undermine the progressive potential of alternative services: the medical establishment will either coopt their successes or use their unavoidable difficulties as evidence of their failure (Taylor, 1979; Kronenfeld, 1979).

A central issue related to this entire discussion of community alternatives is the idea of medical "self-help." The 1970s saw a widespread and increasing interest in self-help or self-care. Self-help groups and other indigenous initiatives in health care emerged as adjuncts and alternatives to medical care. Self-help and mutual aid have a long history in Western society (Katz and Bender, 1976). While critics like Ivan Illich (1976) see self-help as a panacea for our medical ills, most view it as having a more limited role. Self-help groups can provide assistance, encouragement, and needed services to people with chronic and disabling conditions that involve emotional and social problems not provided for by traditional medical care (Gussow and Tracy, 1976). They can also create alternative services, as in the women's health movement. Equally important, self-help groups can aid in demystifying medicine, build a sense of community among people with similar problems, and provide consumer control of, and low-cost, services.

While the idea of self-help is really not a new notion, it appears on today's medical scene as a somewhat radical departure from the traditional medical notion of a compliant patient and an expert physician. Self-help organizations such as Alcoholics Anonymous (AA) predate the current self-help wave and have apparently successfully demonstrated the possibility of people helping themselves and one another to better health. Often taken as a model for other groups, AA focuses upon behavior, symptoms, and a perception of alcoholism as a chronic and individual problem. It also insists that alcoholics need the continuous social support of other nondrinking alcoholics to maintain their sobriety. A number of analysts (e.g., Kronenfeld, 1979: 263) have noted that AA and other self-help programs modeled on it are somewhat authoritarian in their structure. AA, for example, does not question existing societal and cultural arrangements which may have contributed to the drinking problems of its members.

In part as a response to the recognition of the limitations of modern medicine and in reaction to frustrations with existing medical care options, self-help groups and the ideology of self-help have become increasingly popular, not only among former patients of the existing system, but also among professional critics of American medical care (see for example, Illich, 1976; Levin, Katz and Holst, 1976; Carlson, 1975). There is, however, a tendency in these approaches to focus on individual responsibility for change without stressing simultaneously the difficulties of individual change within existing social arrangements. This has led several critics to note the potential for victim-blaming in recommendations for self-help (Kronenfeld, 1979; Ehrenreich, 1978) and the limitations of self-help approaches for many of the health problems of various, especially non-middle-class populations in the United States.

It is nonetheless clear that the idea of self-help is an exciting prospect and one would certainly not want to see the energy and excitement contained within it diminished. The self-help movement has given rise to a range of important criticisms of existing medical care and to a number of significant discoveries for improved health. Self-help approaches envision the possibility of people taking control over their own lives as well as of demystifying traditional medical care. However, unless self-help incorporates a strategy for community *and* societal change, it is likely to reduce this potential vision to the simplistic contention that people are responsible for their own stresses and diseases. Although providing mutual support and encouraging individuals to alter their "unhealthy" behaviors, self-help programs only rarely confront the real options of what people can do as individuals. What is needed, then, is a linking together of self-help movements with struggles for community and social change—in essence, a politicization of self-help.

The promise and reality of community initiatives are evident in each of the articles in this section. In the first, "Improving the Health Experiences of Low Income Patients," Catherine Kohler Riessman discusses how innovations in medical care for the poor usually locate the target problem either in the "culture of poverty" or, more rarely, in the "culture of medicine." After noting some of the inherent biases and difficulties of the culture of poverty approach, she examines two community-based alternatives—birthing centers and pediatric home care—that attempt to change the organization and culture of medical care. These alternatives are largely initiated by professionals, although not necessarily doctors, and are not self-help projects in any major sense. Yet programs like these, and the hospice for the terminally ill, are significant innovations in medical care. While they leave services in professional control, they create a more cooperative situation between the patient and provider, support more social and family involvement, encourage noninstitutional care, are less expensive, and, in the cases presented here, are real alternatives available for poor patients.

The other two articles focus more directly on self-help, providing quite different examples of people reassessing their own health needs and developing alternative health services through collective, community efforts.

The second article, "Politicizing Health Care" by John McKnight, describes a fascinating and innovative community effort to assess health needs and design local medical care alternatives aimed at improving health in the community. In this project, people discovered a number of important things, including: (1) many "medical" problems had little to do with disease, and could more accurately be termed "social problems"; (2) they could, as a community, take collective action to make real changes in their own health; (3) they could build alternative organizations for meeting their health and social needs and in the process include heretofore ignored groups (e.g., the elderly) as productive contributors to the community's health; and (4) they could develop new "tools" of production which would remain under their own control and which would serve their own particular needs. Despite these marvelous lessons, McKnight acknowledges the limitations of local efforts to change the basic maldistribution of resources and services and notes the need for self-help efforts to come to grips with "external" authorities and structures.

In the last selection, Ann Withorn, in her article "Helping Ourselves," discusses the limits and potentials of self-help. Focusing her discussion in part on two of the most influential health-related self-help movements—the women's health movement and Alcoholics Anonymous—Withorn evaluates the place of self-help in progressive change. For well over a decade the women's health movement has been the most important self-help movement in the health field. It emerged as part of the Women's Liberation Movement and in the context of a growing recognition of the role of medicine in the oppression of women. The women's health movement has established gynecological self-help clinics, educated women about their health and bodies (e.g., books like *Our Bodies, Our Selves*), challenged the use of dangerous medicines and procedures (e.g., DES, the Dalcon Shield, Caesarian rates), organized politically to protect the choice of abortion and reproductive rights, and empowered women to question their medical care. As with other community initiatives, there have been struggles. The women's self-help movement has been faced with conflicts arising from its challenge of medical prerogative and continually has been faced with problems in financing its alternative services, particularly for poor women who must rely on public funds and other third-party payments for their medical services. The women's health movement has sometimes imposed limitations on itself by rejecting much of what traditional medicine has to offer.

But even with these difficulties, the women's health movement manages to connect supportive mutual aid with a struggle for political change and is our best exemplar for seeing the potential of self-help in the larger context of progressive reform.

REFERENCES

Carlson, R.J. 1975. The End of Medicine. New York: John Wiley.

Ehrenreich, John. 1978. "Introduction: The cultural crisis of modern medicine." Pp. 1–35 in John Ehrenreich [ed.] The Cultural Crisis of Modern Medicine. New York: Monthly Review Press.

Gussow, Zachary and George Z. Tracy. 1976. "The role of self-help clubs in the adaptation to chronic illness and disability." Social Science and Medicine 10 (7/8): 407–414.

Illich, Ivan. 1976. Medical Nemesis: The Expropriation of Health. New York: Pantheon Books.

Katz, A.H. and E.I. Bender. 1976. "Self-help groups in Western society." Journal of Applied Behavioral Science 12: 265–282.

Kronenfeld, Jennie J. 1979. "Self care as a panacea for the ills of the health care system: An assessment." Social Science and Medicine 13A: 263–267.

Levin, L., A. Katz and E. Holst. 1976. Self-Care: Lay Initiatives in Health. New York: Prodist.

Taylor, Rosemary C. R. 1979. "Alternative services: The case of free clinics." International Journal of Health Services 9, 2: 227–253.

34

Improving the Health Experiences of Low Income Patients

Catherine Kohler Riessman

Over the last several decades there has been a debate about the relationship between social class and the use of medical care. Historically, the poor used fewer health services than the middle class. More recently, however, low income groups have come to exceed the middle class in service use,[1] leading some to conclude that equality of access has been achieved.

However, analyses based on rates of use are severely misleading, since they fail to take into account the poor health of the economically disadvantaged. In studies which compare individuals with the same level of illness, low income groups have the lowest use of services.[2] In addition, crude comparisons of physician visits obscure important regional, racial, and age differences. For although income differentials in total use have narrowed considerably since the early 1960s, sizable gaps remain for particular groups and for particular health problems.

Children's health visits reveal particularly marked class and racial differentials. Young children from families with incomes less than $5,000 a year are almost twice as likely as children from families with incomes $25,000 or more not to have had a physician visit in the last year. Despite higher rates of disability, poor and minority children have fewer total visits than affluent and white children. The difference in the average number of physician visits by race is especially striking, with white children under seventeen having 4.3 visits per year compared to 2.9 for black children. Class and racial differences in immunization rates are also striking. A recent national survey found that 45 percent of children ages 1–4 who lived in urban poverty areas were immunized against polio, compared to 54 percent of equivalent non-poverty area children. In comparing racial groups the findings were even more marked: 40 percent of non-white children compared to 64 percent of whites.[3]

Cumulatively, these findings suggest that despite improvements since the 1960s, social class and race continue to limit access to medical care. This article will focus primarily on class. As a theoretical context for the later discussion, I will identify the two perspectives which have shaped the analysis of class differences in health behavior, briefly evaluating the evidence for each perspective. Following this, I will describe two programs which represent structural innovations in the delivery of medical care to low income women and children: birth centers and pediatric home care. These programs provide the beginnings of an alternative vision of care, for they depart from customary structures and medical practices in certain key ways.

Two major explanations have been suggested for the relationship between social class and the use of health services. The first argues that the poor are less likely than the middle class to use health services—and particularly preventive services—because of a "culture of poverty." Others argue that the explanation lies in social structural arrangements.

The Culture of Poverty View

The culture of poverty explanation argues that the lack of attention to health is part of a "way of life"—an entrenched culture of values and attitudes which encourages dependency and discourages self reliance.[4] According to this view, the poor are less likely to use medical care because of a constellation of culturally transmitted health beliefs and predispositions.[5] Important among these is a crisis-oriented approach to life which leads the poor to accord greater priority to immediate rewards than to long-term goals. As a consequence, medical care is sought only in emergency situations or in times of severe illness, and often after considerable delay. Poor groups seek immunizations, prenatal care, and asymptomatic checkups less frequently because they lack a "psychological readiness" and future orientation. Low income people use preventive services less and are less knowledgeable about appropriate health behavior because their culture does not place a high value on health. They have negative attitudes toward medical care and do not believe in its efficacy. Experiencing a sense of helplessness and resignation in coping with their environment, the poor do not exhibit the active, individually responsible, and disciplined behavior necessary in seeking appropriate medical care. As Rosenblatt and Suchman state:

> The body can be seen as simply another class of object to be worn out but not repaired. Thus teeth are left without dental care . . . Corrective eye examinations, even for those who wear glasses, are often neglected . . . It is as though . . . blue collar groups think of the body as having a limited span of utility, to be enjoyed in youth and then to suffer with and to endure stoically with age and decrepitude.[6]

This culture is passed from generation to generation, creating a self-propelling cycle of poverty and poor health. Efforts to intervene and change patterns of behavior will be largely fruitless given the values and traditions deeply embedded in the culture. Rosenstock summarizes this perspective:

> The culture of poverty may originally have been based on a history of economic deprivation, but it seems to be a culture exhibiting its own rationale,

and structure, and reflecting a way of life that is transmitted to new generations. It is therefore suggested that while financial costs may serve as barriers to obtaining health services, their removal would probably not have the effect of creating widespread changes in health behavior of the poor, at least not in the foreseeable future.[7]

While the culture of poverty concept has been widely criticized,[8] it remains an influential paradigm within the social sciences. Many health investigators rely implicitly on aspects of this theory when they use personal and cultural deficits to explain class differences in health behavior (e.g. particular health attitudes, individual and subcultural belief systems, and psychological predispositions such as external locus of control).[9] These individual and social characteristics are often examined without taking into account the context of care—the characteristics of the medical systems to which different classes have access. The paradigm is also influential in current national health policy, which emphasizes improving health by changing individual values and behaviors.

The Structural View

The alternative perspective emphasizes the structural constraints which prevent low income people from having genuine access to quality medical care.[10] There are, according to this view, two types of constraint. The first is material. Poor people, by definition, have fewer financial resources with which to purchase care in the medical marketplace, particularly services of a preventive nature. Even with health insurance programs, such as Medicaid, there is evidence that equal access does not exist for all groups. Many low income people are not eligible for these governmental programs and many states provide inadequate coverage because benefits are limited.[11] Thus low utilization may be seen as a realistic adaptation to economic circumstances.

The second set of structural constraints stems from the very organization of medical care services. In our two-class system of care, middle-class people are likely to receive care in private offices whereas poor people are likely to receive care in public clinics, or in out-patient departments and emergency rooms of general hospitals.[12] In these settings, care can often be impersonal and dehumanized. Further compounding the problem is inadequate transportation in poor neighborhoods, as well as inconvenient clinic hours and long waits in the hospitals themselves. Providers in these settings have little control over the nature of their work, for they are responsible typically for seeing large numbers of patients in block appointment systems. Under these conditions, there is little chance for providers to have on-going relationships with particular patients. In addition, the patients in these settings often have to maneuver between many specialty clinics to obtain the services they need, and the services themselves are likely to be disease-oriented (or curative) rather than preventive. Cumulatively, these characteristics of the system have a deterrent effect, discouraging people from seeking care, particularly preventive care.

According to the structural argument, it is this "culture of medicine,"[13] rather than deficits in the culture of the patient, that is responsible for the low utilization rates among some segments of the poor. This medical culture is comprised of the particular habits, customs, and expectations of health professionals as well as the needs of the bureaucratic organizations in which they work. An important part of the medical culture is the emphasis on high technology and sub-specialty care. To low income patients, this culture and its attendant institutions may seem, in Anselm Strauss's words:

> . . . terribly massive and complex, crowded and busy; while the personnel seem often impersonal, brusque, or even insulting . . . physicians go from patient to patient, spending brief moments with most . . . patients may sit for long periods of time waiting to be called . . . Patients see all of this and may simply respond fatalistically to the rush and bustle.[14]

In sum, the structural view assigns primary responsibility for the alienation of low income patients to their material disadvantage and to the systems barriers they face when seeking care. According to this perspective, the poor have had multiple negative experiences with organizational systems, leading to avoidance behavior, lack of trust, and hence a disinclination to seek care and follow medical regimens except in dire need. The assumption is that "good" experiences will result in behavior change. The lack of appropriate utilization of health care by lower socioeconomic groups is not deeply culture bound, according to this view. It can be modified if there are changes in professionals and the organization of medical care.

The Evidence

Ten years ago I reviewed the evidence on the relationship between social class and the use of medical services in an attempt to test the power of the culture of poverty explanation compared to the structural view.[15] I critically examined evaluative research from a series of demonstration programs which were initiated in the 1960s, including neighborhood health centers, family planning and comprehensive care programs. Cumulatively, the data revealed that the health behavior of the poor could be radically altered, and within a relatively short period of time, by introducing structural changes in the way services were offered.

More recent research provides further support for these findings. Although methodological problems remain,[16] the findings confirm the primary importance of characteristics of the medical care system in suppressing or enhancing use among low income groups.[17,18]

Interestingly, there is some recent evidence that attitudes themselves may no longer be a factor at all in determining utilization among the poor. In a study in the Chicago area, blacks and persons with low education, compared to whites and the well-educated, had more symptoms and were *more* likely to endorse the idea of visiting a doctor for symptoms. However, these same groups used public services as their source of care and, consistent with previous research, this type of medical care was associated with fewer visits.[19]

In sum, the evidence reveals that deficits in the system of care rather than individual characteristics of patients are primarily responsible for unequal use. Moreover, it appears that the problem is not economic, at least in a narrow sense. When a variety of factors are examined simultaneously, different levels of financial coverage do not explain why those with lower incomes use medical care less frequently.[20] Rather, the evidence strongly suggests that the problem lies in broader economic arrangements which insure a two-class system of care. Diana Dutton underscores the implications of the results:

> neither improved financial access nor health education efforts alone will eliminate current income differentials in use, unless accompanied by structural improvements in existing delivery systems. Fundamental changes in the organization and distribution of care must occur, if equitable patterns of use are to be more than health policy rhetoric.[21]

The Current Crisis

Increasingly conservative national health care policy has dramatically changed the availability of medical services in the United States. Federal budget cuts have eliminated many medical organizations, most notably neighborhood health centers, that were developed in the 1960s as structural alternatives to traditional medical services. Despite the indisputable evidence of the efficacy of these programs in reducing or eliminating class differences in access and use of preventive medical services, national health policy seems to have rejected a structural approach in favor of a policy of changing individuals.

Paralleling the increasingly conservative changes in national health policy, the past decade has seen a growing scholarship that has reexamined many of the assumptions and claims of medical practice, concluding that much of the "health crisis" is a consequence of medicine itself. These writings locate the cause of a range of problems in the "culture" of medicine, including the beliefs, customs, and behaviors of physicians, as well as the political and economic relationship of medicine to other institutions, including the state. Some have used their critiques to challenge the medical paradigm itself, including its reliance on technology, professional expertise, and curative treatments that result in, among other things, the separation of the sick from potentially supportive networks of friends and family. These critiques are perhaps best exemplified in the statements of the women's health movement.[22]

In light of government retrenchment from structural solutions, as well as the simultaneous recognition of the questionable value of those services that do exist, an analysis of utilization needs to be reconceptualized. The issue is not simply the availability and access of medical services to the poor, but also an assessment of the services themselves.

Are there models in the current period which offer any promise? More specifically, do programs exist which improve the health experiences of low income patients by changing the structure of medical care, so as to provide easier access, greater equality between provider and consumer, and more humane care?

I will describe two programs which are currently operating and which can be evaluated on the basis of these criteria. The two models are birth centers and home care for chronically ill children. These programs represent alternative approaches to meeting the health care needs of women and children. In addition, each program provides a model of care which is potentially corrective of key aspects of the culture of medicine.

Perhaps most interesting, these programs represent innovations which emerged from challenges from within the professional community. The first set of programs—birth centers—is an innovation from nurse-midwifery. This service arose at the same time feminists were challenging traditional medical approaches to women's problems, including birth. The second program—home care for chronically ill children—is an innovation from medicine. It was developed by a Department of Pediatrics of an urban teaching hospital.

Birth Centers

The management of childbirth has undergone dramatic changes in this century. Whereas in 1900 only 5 percent of babies were born in hospitals, by 1979 97.4 percent of all births occurred in hospitals—the vast majority of these attended by physicians. More recently, there is evidence of a trend away from hospital and physician-centered birth. In particular, there has been an increase in planned home births as well as in free standing birth centers. Although precise data are not available on the proportion of total births occurring in these alternative sites,[23] it is suggestive that the number of free standing birth centers increased from three in 1975 to over one hundred in 1982.[24] Primary care in these centers is generally provided by certified nurse-midwives rather than by obstetricians.

The growth of free standing birth centers has been spurred by a number of factors. Most important, the childbirth education movement of the 1960s leveled a pointed critique at childbirth practices, drawing attention to the "cultural warping of childbirth"[25] by American medicine. Birth is defined as a pathological event and treated in ways which remove the woman's control over the experience. As part of this medicalization of birth, drugs and technology are routinely used—to induce labor, to speed it up, to dull the pain, to monitor the fetus, to remove it surgically. The high rate of Caesarian sections is of particular concern—now estimated to be 25 percent of all births. Critics argue that all these procedures carry risks for both mother and infant. In addition, the critique of childbirth challenges the medical practice of separating the woman from family during labor and from the infant after delivery. Although an alienating experience for women in general, research has shown that hospital based birth is particularly dehumanized for low income women.[26]

Out of this critique, an alternative childbirth movement began, as women—particularly middle-class women—began to question their doctors' advice. Frustrated by traditional obstetrical practice, child bearing families searched for alternative ways to handle birth. This social movement occurred simultaneously with the emergence of a general increase in the valuing of the "natural." Some women chose to bypass the medical care system entirely, having their babies at home attended by lay midwives, family, and friends. Others turned o the new specialists within nursing—certified nurse-midwifes— who had been trained in the 1960s and 1970s to provide maternity care to poor women in medically underserved areas.

One response of medicine to these challenges

was to try to make the hospital a more humane place for childbirth. Hospitals made efforts to modify birth, rather than run the risk of loosing it. "Birthing rooms" were established where low risk"* women could deliver in a home-like atmosphere, accompanied by family. Although preferable to the delivery room atmosphere, some argue that these changes involve primarily cosmetic improvements and do not fundamentally alter medical control over the birth process.[27] Moreover, few women (less than 10 percent) ever enter and give birth in these hospital birthing rooms.

In this context, nurse-midwives established free standing birth centers, aided by a small group of progressive obstetricians. The centers are facilities separate from hospitals and provide prenatal, peripartum, and neonatal care for low risk pregnancies. It is estimated that in 45 percent of the centers, the primary care provider is a certified nurse-midwife, who refers to consulting physicians those clients needing medical supervision, hospitalization for pregnancy, labor or delivery. In an additional 29 percent of the centers, both physicians and certified nurse-midwives provide care within the Center.[28] Structured typically as nonprofit corporations, most centers are licensed and meet local health and safety codes. They generally have cooperative agreements with a laboratory, an ambulance service, and a tertiary

---

*The concept of risk appears to be somewhat elastic and therefore subject to considerable ideological use. First, although it has been estimated that roughly 90 percent of births are uncomplicated, estimates appear to be expanding in the medical literature. Now included are social criteria, such as age, marital status, and poverty, as well as more traditional medical criteria, such as diabetes, previous birth history, etc. This may provide further evidence of medicalization. Second, prediction of complications appears to be limited. In the Institute of Medicine review, approximately 20 percent of women evaluated as low risk experienced complications necessitating transfer during labor or delivery. Alternatively, approximately 14 percent of women assessed ineligible for delivery in a low risk setting experienced no complications. Thus "risk" appears to be, in some respects, a retrospective diagnosis; all women are assumed to be "at risk" for complications, thereby legitimating routine hospitalization. Thirdly, in medical discourse, the notion of risk is always considered in the context of alternative birth practices, and never with respect to hospital based birth, the interventions of physicians, or medical technology. These aspects are assumed to be benign, or risk free.

care hospital in case these are needed. The recognized prototype for birth centers is the Maternity Center Association in New York City, which developed and evaluated risk criteria, staffing patterns, and programs of care.

Su Clinica Familiar is one of the oldest birth centers.[29] Unlike others, this birth center is part of a family oriented rural health clinic. Located in the Rio Grande valley of Southern Texas, it services a predominantly Mexican-American population of agricultural workers and their families. Almost half of the families are below the poverty level in the two counties served by the program, and the birth rate is high. One-third of the patients are teenage mothers. As a consequence of economic disadvantage and age, these women are at high risk for delivering low birth weight infants and for other complications. Before the center opened, women did not have easy access to prenatal care. These women delivered either at home, frequently in the temporary shelters erected for migrant farm workers, or in hospitals which were geographically remote. The local hospital refused to admit them because they were uninsured. Maternity services began in 1972, initially provided only by nurse-midwives. These were joined in practice in 1978 by several obstetrician-gynecologists who were funded by the National Health Service Corps. This added staff made care accessible for those patients who previously were referred to hospitals because of high risk, and also allowed for consultation by the midwives regarding complications of labor and delivery. Between 1972 and 1979, over 1,400 babies were born in *Su Clinica Familiar*—93 percent attended by nurse-midwives.

Maternity care in a birth center is distinctive. Typically, a woman is seen for all phases of the birth process in the center—for childbirth education, prenatal care, and for labor and delivery. In order to insure a healthy mother and baby, nutritional counseling is a major emphasis of the prenatal period. Because many of the women at *Su Clinica Familiar* are poor, supplementary foods are provided, if possible, through the Women and Infant Care (WIC) program. Through a sanitary program staff members stress the improvement of environmental conditions and identify deficient condititons such as impure water and housing code violations. These are brought to the attention of local authorities for correction.

The management of the labor and delivery in a birth center is in sharp contrast to customary hospital practice. Family members are encouraged to take turns staying with the woman during labor. Every member of the family is encouraged to visit, including children. A nurse-midwife is also in constant attendance. The woman is encouraged not to lie on her back, but otherwise any position for labor and delivery is acceptable. There are no routine pubic hair shaves or enemas. Nor are fetal monitors and IVs typically used. Women are allowed oral intake of fluids or food. During labor and delivery, pain medication is used minimally. Instead, women are carefully prepared for the birth experience and supported emotionally through it by family and staff. Women are encouraged to deliver in a variety of positions, because it is believed that the customary lithotomy position (on the back) is responsible for a large proportion of episiotomies and other complications, as well as failure to progress in labor.

Immediately upon delivery, the infant is placed on the mother's abdomen. The mother is encouraged to touch the baby while the cord is being clamped and cut. The mother's gown is removed and the nude baby is placed between the mother's breasts. A warmed pad is placed over both. It is routine practice to keep the infant skin to skin with the mother for an extended period after the delivery. For those mothers wishing to breastfeed, the initial feeding occurs shortly after birth.

After the birth, the woman spends twenty-four hours at the center and then returns home. At *Su Clinica*, she is visited by a nurse-midwife on the third and tenth days after delivery.

Although evaluative data are limited, there are several indicators which suggest the maternity program at *Su Clinica Familiar* is effective in improving the health of the infants born there. The first is the prematurity rate. As stated earlier, these women are at greater risk than middle-class women for delivering low birth weight babies. In 1974 the prematurity rate (babies weighing less than 5½ pounds) was 3.5 percent at *Su Clinica*, compared to 7.4 percent for the nation as a whole, 7.6 percent for Texas. Second, evidence is provided by the favorable birth weight distribution for the 760 babies born at the center between 1972 and 1976. Also, Apgar scores for these babies suggest excellent fetal outcome.[30]

Although these descriptive data are impressive, they still leave a number of questions unanswered. The 760 consecutive births on which the evaluation was based represent a selected sample of women who gave birth in the center during the first four years of the program's operation. Not all applicants, however, were accepted to the program and also information is lacking on patients transferred to hospitals because of complications during labor and delivery. Studies in other birth centers have shown that a proportion of cases are found ineligible for service initially, and a significant number are transferred later. For example, at the Childbearing Center of the Maternity Center Association in New York City (which serves a middle-class population and as a prototype has the most restrictive criteria in the U.S.), almost 9 percent were considered ineligible at application, 16 percent were transferred during pregnancy, and an additional 19 percent during labor.[31]

Birth centers offer an alternative for women who want active, involved births, as free as possible from technological intervention and attended by providers who are also women. As such, they can be seen as a response to the critique of the culture of medicine. They also can be evaluated in relation to the structural critique for, as the case of *Su Clinica* shows, this center provides greater access to prenatal care and a safe birth environment for low income migrant women.

Yet there may be a paradox here. While clearly a more humane approach to childbirth for all women, the birth center approach may have particular problems for low income women. These women are more likely than middle-class women to have complicating conditions of pregnancy such as hypertension and diabetes, suggesting greater need for physician input. Birth centers usually refer these patients who need more intensive care. In addition, research suggests that low income women are less overtly critical of technology-intensive, hospital-based childbirth practice. Margaret Nelson found strong class differences in women's attitudes and expectations about the birth experience. Working-class women wanted their births to be fast and easy, whereas middle-class women wanted a pleasurable, natural experience.[32] Further, working-class women do not expect their mates to be involved in the pregnancy and birth, whereas the norms among middle-class couples are for a high degree of involvement by men.

These findings suggest that the expectations and realities of poor women's lives may not be entirely congruent with the birth center approach to childbirth. Of course, poor women might prefer alternative approaches to managing birth once they had experience with them.

In this regard, it is interesting to note that *Su Clinica* has made greater use of forceps and antepartum oxytocin than centers serving more middle-class populations.[33] While strict comparisons are impossible, *Su Clinica* also appears to use medication with greater frequency than the national average in birth centers, although still less than the hospital average. It is not clear whether this is due to a higher rate of complications at *Su Clinica* (as the women are in poorer health) or to the interventions of physicians in the early years of the Center (rather than transferring complicated cases to the hospital physicians came to *Su Clinica* to deal with problems). It is also possible that the women themselves have a difficult orientation to childbirth and the nurse-midwives are responding to that orientation by greater use of medication.

Besides the social class issue, there are a series of other issues confronting birth centers. There has been considerable political controversy, particularly among professional organizations representing different medical interests. On the one hand, the American Public Health Association has endorsed the birth center concept, stating that birth to healthy mothers can occur safely in birth centers outside of acute care hospitals and that these centers have a potential for reducing health costs. This organization developed guidelines for licensing and regulating birth centers.[34] On the other hand, the American College of Obstetrics and Gynecology (A.C.O.G.) remains opposed to birth outside of hospitals. In a position paper, this group stated that "the potential hazards to both mother and fetus . . .

required standards of safety which are provided in the hospital setting."[35]

Another wing of the attack by organized medicine has been against the professional autonomy of certified nurse-midwives—a central feature of the birth center. The A.C.O.G. insists on physician direction of the health care team. At Congressional hearings the organization submitted written testimony which stated that it was:

> unalterably opposed to independent practice (i.e. practice without physician direction) by nurse midwives. . . . The health care team must be responsible for maternal health services, and that team must function *with the direction of a physician.* . . . The A.C.O.G. approves of reimbursement to the health care team for midwifery services *if those services are rendered by a member of a health care team directed by a qualified obstetrician-gynecologist* (emphasis in original).[36]

These Congressional hearings documented that in many parts of the country nurse-midwives are facing stiff resistance from physicians, medical societies, hospital departments of obstetrics and pediatrics, companies which provide malpractice insurance, state boards of health, and not infrequently, resistance by nurses as well. Forms of harassment have included placement of unjustifiable restrictions on practice, difficulty in obtaining a Medicaid provider number, and reimbursement and licensure refusal.[37] A widespread form of harassment by obstetricians has been the refusal to provide the usual medical consultation and referral services available to other health care providers in any given community, such as family practitioners. After hearing extensive testimony on these issues, the committee concluded that certified nurse-midwives are facing restraint of trade and unfair intimidation, which is preventing them from responding to consumer demand for their services.[38]

It is significant that physicians are less concerned about the practice of nurse-midwifery in medically underserved areas, such as the Frontier Nursing Services in Kentucky. Opposition may be related to the middle-class composition of women who are now opting for nurse-midwifery services. Opposition may also be related to the tightening market conditions facing obstetricians nationally. According to a government report,

there is a surplus of obstetrics professionals, due to a declining birth rate and the consolidation of underutilized obstetric services. The ideal solution might be a complementary relationship between physicians and nurse-midwives, with obstetricians and neonatologists managing only the high risk cases. Yet this sort of rational allocation of obstetric resources has not occurred, perhaps because the management of only 10 percent of cases would not insure high incomes. According to one government study, obstetricians may be unwilling to relinquish the low risk mother because she represents the obstetrician's "bread and butter."[39]

Maternity center births managed by nurse-midwives in consultation with obstetrical specialists are clearly more cost effective than traditional hospital and physician centered births. This is due to lower overhead, the absence of expensive technology, and the lower salaries of the professionals providing care (nurse-midwives' incomes on average are one-fifth of the incomes of obstetrician-gynecologists).[40] In a recent survey, the average reported charge for birth center services was $801 with a range of $200 to $1,700. The average comparable hospital care was $1,713, with a range from $550 to $3,750. Thus birth center charges are roughly 48 percent of the hospital charges.[41] Many birth centers have also become eligible for third-party reimbursement.

In light of these economic facts, it is not surprising that the birth industry is looking increasingly attractive to the corporate sector, as well as to physician investors. A recent article in the *Wall Street Journal* described plans for expansion by several proprietary chains into the delivery business.[42] In addition, physicians increasingly have been employing certified nurse-midwives in their private practices. The hope is that women may be more attracted to these practices and less to birth centers. Cumulatively, these trends suggest that physician opposition lessens only when physicians can gain control over nurse-midwives.

In spite of the promise of alternative birth centers, good evaluation research is lacking on these programs. A recent report by the Institute of Medicine of the National Academy of Sciences underscored the need for more rigorous research on all birth settings.[43] Most studies of birth centers have been observational, frequently based on samples from single centers. Only a few studies have compared centers.[44] Although results are encouraging and suggest many beneficial effects, descriptive data need to be augmented by more rigorous evidence if public policy is to be changed. For example, although it is clearly beneficial for children's health that roughly 95 percent of infants born in birth centers are being breastfed upon discharge (compared to 45 percent nationally) and that 60 percent of these births on average were unmedicated,[45] it is not clear to what extent these effects are attributable to the birth setting itself. Selection factors may be responsible, for women who are desirous of a "natural" birth experience may be more likely to select birth centers. A prospective study currently in process is examining a wide array of variables and promises to shed some light on the selection issue. Preliminary findings suggest no difference in pregnancy outcome between births in a birth center and a carefully matched group of women delivering in a hospital.[46]

Pediatric Home Care

Another alternative to traditional medical practice for low income patients is home care for chronically ill children. The program that I will describe serves a predominantly poor and largely black and Hispanic population in New York City. It represents a structural innovation, for it provides access to care for a population of children who have many unmet health care needs.[47] The program also alters the culture of medicine in certain key respects.

During the recent decades, home care programs have developed for the elderly and for home bound adults, but rarely for other groups. In particular, it is assumed that children are portable and therefore can be brought to the doctor for care. Especially if they have major illnesses, it is thought that care should be provided in the hospital or its clinics, where special facilities and technologies are available. There is some research evidence that home care can be as effective as traditional hospital care for children with specific medical problems, but until recently there was little evidence that home care was a viable model for children with a variety of illness conditions.

A movement to establish a home care program for children began among physicians in a hospital in the Bronx in the early 1970s.[48] The impetus for the program was the presence of a number of seriously ill children who spent extended periods of time living in the wards of a large municipal hospital. Many factors had led to the hospital's becoming a "home" for these children. They had serious on-going medical problems, resulting in frequent life-threatening situations and crises. They were on many medications and received complex treatments in an effort to control their symptoms. These realities may have frightened their families and, as a result, some appeared to have virtually turned over the ill child to the hospital. At the same time, there was a lack of alternative facilities for these children, as well as a lack of community supports to assist their families—many of whom were poor. Finally, the bureaucratic institution created its own form of dependency in both the parents and children. Children were less active because the hospital treated them as if they were sick. Families relinquished control because hospital routines allowed for only limited parental participation.

The movement to establish the program also received impetus from the particular intellectual and political climate of the late 1960s. Programs to provide primary care for poor children in the community had been established with seed money from the Office of Economic Opportunity and the Child and Youth Programs. The success of these programs influenced the perceptions of some of the physicians about what might be possible with more seriously ill children. Other physicians—particularly the subspecialists—continued to believe that hospital care was preferable medically for these children. It was only with a promise of a rigorous evaluation that the program gained administrative approval.

In this context, Pediatric Home Care was established at Bronx Municipal Hospital Center, a 950 bed general hospital which is a major clinical affiliate of the Albert Einstein College of Medicine.[49] The program is physically located in an out-patient wing of the hospital. Services are provided to patients throughout the Bronx by a team composed of a pediatrician, a pediatric nurse practitioner, a social worker, a case aide, a technician, a part-time physical therapist, and a consulting psychiatrist. Other specialists from the Department of Pediatrics are available for specific cases.

Care is provided in the home whenever possible. The pediatric nurse practitioner makes frequent home visits, handling much of the routine care in this setting. Because the patient's family is considered a critical part of the health care team, family members are encouraged in these home visits to ask questions and to become involved in understanding the child's illness. Also, family members are taught how to perform essential medical procedures to keep the child out of crisis. For example, parents of children with tracheostomies are trained to do suctioning and provided with the necessary equipment. In order to encourage this self care, the family's problem solving methods and coping patterns are reinforced and supported. By integrating medical and social services in this way, the staff expects that families can assume greater care for their children and children can remain in their homes. If hospitalization is needed, the pediatric home care staff admits the child and continues its involvement throughout the hospitalization, thus ensuring continuity of care.

In 1978, the program was evaluated, using a pre-test–post-test experimental design.[50] A sample of 219 children with a variety of chronic physical conditions was randomly assigned either to the pediatric home care program or to the sources of care traditionally available in the hospital complex (standard care). The children had a wide variety of chronic conditions, with most having multiple conditions.[51] Regarding their social characteristics, the children were predominantly poor and largely black or Hispanic. Thirty-three percent of the families had annual income of less than $5,000, and 55 percent were receiving public assistance. Fifty-six percent of the mothers had less than a high school education. The study compared home care with standard care on a broad spectrum of outcome indicators which might be sensitive to the kinds of interventions described earlier. In particular, the evaluation assessed whether the

program affected both the child's and the mother's psychological adjustment, as well as whether there were differences in levels of satisfaction between the programs. Data on these indicators were obtained by bilingual interviewers in structured household interviews with mothers in both groups at three points in time. A statistical analysis compared home care and standard care at the various follow up points.

After six months in the home care program, children had significantly fewer psychological problems. Their mothers also tended to fare better emotionally. In fact, women whose children did not recieve the home care program became more symptomatic over the first six month period. Not surprisingly, mothers who received home care were significantly more satisfied with their children's medical care. There were no significant differences between home care and standard care on the impact of the illness on the family or the functional status of the child.

These findings suggest some of the beneficial effects that can occur when the structure of care is altered. More specifically, the results show that many of the secondary sequelae of chronic illness in children—behavioral problems, for example— can be reversed by a program of medical care which integrates a psychosocial perspective. In addition, the program has positive effects on the mothers. It is well known that the presence of a severely ill child is a major stressor which creates psychological distress for parents in general and for mothers in particular. Symptomatology in mothers can be ameliorated, the results suggest, by a program of care which emphasizes home visiting and emotional support.

In contrast to the concerns of some of the hospital physicians, the home care program did not lead to a deterioration in the child's health, as measured by functional status. Nor did it lead to a greater burden for the family. In fact, the impact of the child's illness on the family was considerable for both groups but declined in a similar fashion over time.

Unfortunately, data are not available on some other indicators which should be assessed—such as the health status of the child, number of days of hospitalization, frequency of immunizations and other preventive care, as well as cost of service. Admittedly, some of these factors are very difficult to measure, especially with a diagnostically mixed group of children of varying ages. Yet, it is important to state that while satisfaction with care is important and the reduction of secondary sequelae in both mother and child is impressive, these may not be sufficient indicators of a successful health strategy, even for a population as severely ill as this. Nor do the data tell us what particular ingredients in the program of home care were associated with the beneficial effects. Was it the home visiting and support provided by pediatric nurse practitioners? Was it the environmental interventions made by social service staff? Was it the continuity of care assured by a stable group of permanent staff, in contrast to the staff of trainees rotating through various clinics in the standard care model? Future research is needed to answer these questions.

Conclusion

This paper described two medical care programs which can improve the health experiences of low income people by making structural changes in the medical care system, as opposed to changing individual behavior of patients. Birth centers represent an alternative approach for women. Pediatric home care represents an alternative approach for children which, in turn, also benefits women.

The two programs represent strategies for correcting the structural barriers to care for low income people. Both programs are alternatives to traditional hospital or clinic-based care. The birth center I described made care available to a population that previously lacked maternity services. Although systematic data are lacking on various indicators of access, on the face of it the evidence points to an increase in availability of community based services for pregnant women. The pediatric home care program I described also removed structural barriers to care in a most graphic way—by home visits. Using rigorous research methods the program demonstrated its effectiveness.

In addition to structural change, each program can be evaluated in light of a broader critique of medicine. The two programs altered the traditional "culture of medicine" in certain key ways. First, professional roles were modified. In particular, nurses expanded their functions in both programs. Moreover, in the case of certified nurse-midwives, they altered the care giving role, rather than merely assuming the physician's role in birth. These changes in professional roles were not without conflict, as the birth center example particularly shows. Second, the patient-provider relationship was modified. There was greater emphasis on mutual participation and self care in both programs rather than the more usual model of active physician and passive patient.[52] Third, medical knowledge was shared and thus, perhaps, demystified. Information about the birth process and about specific childhood illnesses was communicated and, it appears, in ways that enhanced patients' sense of control over these experiences. Finally, patients in both programs were treated within a kinship context. Both programs encouraged social network members to assist in care, rather than stripping the patient from potentially supportive relationships. In sum, there were improvements in the *terms of care,* as well as in the *availability of care.*

At the same time, however, neither program addresses certain other aspects of the critique of medicine. Neither birth centers nor home care fundamentally challenge the biomedical model. Rather, the human experiences of birth and childhood illness are still seen as medical events—albeit family centered medical events. Care is still entrusted primarily to health professionals—albeit nurses with extended training. There is little overt criticism of medicine's notions of risk, and thus physican control over care in "high risk" situations is often unquestioned. In other words, disease is still understood as residing with the individual body, with treatment entrusted to a hierarchically ordered system of medical practitioners. A broader vision would place illness in a broader ecological context and see its occurrence and treatment as is inextricably linked to broader social arrangements.

As a consequence of the more limited vision of the two programs, it is unlikely that either program by itself would improve the unfavorable health status of low income populations. In spite of model services, the poor are likely to continue to have more disease, disability, and distress than their middle class counterparts. Neither of the medical care programs I described fundamentally addressed the social determinants of disease. Both programs were, in McKinlay's words, "downstream efforts."[53] Neither altered the pathogenic conditions of life which poor people face in this capitalist society: inadequate food and housing, exploitation and occupational hazards at the workplace, and the other constraints imposed by the absence of power. Yet the programs do demonstrate the limited benefits that can be achieved when we simultaneously alter both structures of care and aspects of the culture of medicine.

This analysis suggests a number of broader implications for progressive health policy. First, we now have ample evidence that by removing structural barriers to care and increasing access, we can eradicate class differences in the use of both preventive and curative services. Research findings overwhelmingly support the significance of structural change, as opposed to changing individual attitudes and behaviors—the strategy suggested by the culture of poverty position. At the same time, the argument suggests that increasing access by itself is not enough. In addition, it is necessary to alter the nature of the service itself—or the culture of medicine. More specifically, we need to change how medical care is experienced by low income patients. Both programs I described represent beginning steps in this direction. Finally, if the ultimate goal is to improve health itself, the provision of medical care alone is insufficient, no matter how accessible and humanely offered it may be. Simply put, poor health is the outcome of the circumstances of poor people's lives. Thus if we are to improve health, and not merely access, potent social medicines will be necessary.

REFERENCES

1. National Center for Health Statistics, *Health, United States, 1982.* DHHS Pub. No. (PHS) 83-1232. Public Health Service. Washington: U.S. Government Printing Office, 1982, Table 90.
2. J. Kleinman, M. Gold, and D. Makuc, "Use of Ambulatory Care by the Poor: Another Look at Equity." *Medical Care* 19 (1981): 1011–1029; M. P. LaPlante, "Have the Disadvantaged Really Achieved Equal Access to Medical Care? A Reconsideration." Paper read at Annual Meeting, American Public Health Association, Montreal, 1982.
3. D.B. Dutton, "Children's Health Care: The Myth of Equal Access," in *Better Health for Our Children: A National Strategy,* Volume 4. DHHS (PHS) Pub. No 79-55071. Public Health Service. Washington: U.S. Government Printing Office, 1981. National Center for Health Statistics, *Health, United States 1982,* Table 25.
4. O. Lewis, "The Culture of Poverty," *Scientific American* 215, 4 (1966): 19–25.
5. Classic works in sociology which employ this perspective include E. Suchman, "Social Patterns of Illness and Medical Care," in *Patients, Physicians and Illness,* E.G. Jaco (ed.) (New York: Free Press, 1972), pp. 262–279; S.S. Kegeles et al., "Surveys of Beliefs about Cancer Detection and Taking Papanicolauo Tests, *Public Health Reports* 80 (September 1965): 815–824; E.L. Koos, *The Health of Regionville* (New York: Columbia University Press, 1954).
6. D. Rosenblatt and E. Suchman, "Blue Collar Attitudes and Information Toward Health and Illness, in *Blue Collar World,* Shostak and Gomberg (eds.) (Englewood Cliffs, N.J: Prentice Hall, 1964), pp. 341–349.
7. I.M. Rosenstock, "Prevention of Illness and Maintenance of Health" in *Poverty in Health: A Sociological Analysis,* Kosa, Antonovsky, and Zola (eds.) (Cambridge, Ma.: Harvard Univ. Press, 1975), p. 188.
8. E.B. Leacock (ed.), *The Culture of Poverty: A Critique* (New York: Simon and Schuster, 1971); W. Ryan, *Blaming the Victim* (New York: Pantheon, 1971); C.A. Valentine, *Culture and Poverty: Critique and Counterproposals* (Chicago: Univ. of Chicago Press, 1968); B. Valentine, *Hustling and Other Hard Work* (New York: Free Press, 1978).
9. M.H. Becker, C.A. Nathanson, R.H. Drachman, and J.P. Kirscht, "Mothers' Health Beliefs and Children's Clinic Visits: A Prospective Study," *Journal of Community Health* 3 (1977): 125–35; L.A. Crandall and R. P. Duncan, "Attitudinal and Situational Factors in the Use of Physicians Services by Low Income Persons," *Journal of Health and Social Behavior* 22 (1981): 64–77; M. Seeman and T.E. Seeman, "Health Behavior and Personal Autonomy: A Longitudinal Study of the Sense of Control in Illness," *Journal of Health and Social Behavior* 24 (1983): 144–160.

10. Classic works which employ this perspective include R.S. Duff and A.B. Hollingshead, *Sickness and Society* (New York: Harper and Row, 1968); A. Strauss, "Medical Ghettos" in *Patients, Physicians and Illness,* pp. 381–388.

11. E. Blake, "Medicaid: The Fading of a Dream." *Health PAC Bulletin* 51 (1973): 13–19; K. Davis, "Equal Treatment and Unequal Benefits: The Medicare Program" in *Health, Illness and Medical Care,* G.L. Albrecht and P.C. Higgins (eds.) (Chicago: Rand McNally, 1979), pp. 384–415.

12. National Center for Health Statistics. *Health, United States 1982,* Table 35.

13. S. Levine, N. Scotch, and G. Vlasak, "Unraveling Technology—Culture and Public Health," *American Journal of Public Health* 59 (1969): 237–244.

14. A. Strauss, "Medical Ghettos," p. 152.

15. C.K. Riessman, "The Use of Health Services by the Poor," *Social Policy* 5 (1974): 41–49.

16. D. Mechanic, "Correlates of Physician Utilization: Why Do Major Multivariate Studies of Physician Utilization Find Trivial Psychosocial and Organizational Effects?" *Journal of Health and Social Behavior* 20 (1979): 387–396.

17. D.B. Dutton, "Explaining the Low Use of Health Services by the Poor: Costs, Attitudes, or Delivery Systems," *American Sociological Review* 43 (1978): 348–368; D.B. Dutton, "Patterns of Ambulatory Health Care in Five Different Delivery Systems," *Medical Care* 17 (1979): 221–243.

18. T.G. Rundall and J.R.C. Wheeler, "The Effect of Income on Use of Preventive Care: An Evaluation of Alternative Explanations," *Journal of Health and Social Behavior* 20 (1979): 397–406.

19. K. Sharp, C.E. Ross, and W.C. Cockerham, "Symptoms, Beliefs and the Use of Physicians Services Among the Disadvantaged." *Journal of Health and Social Behavior* 24 (1983): 255–263.

20. D.B. Dutton, "Explaining the Use of Health Services by the Poor ..."; T.G. Rundall and J.R.C. Wheeler, "The Effect of Income on Use of Preventive Care. . . ."

21. D.B. Dutton, "Explaining the Use of Health Services by the Poor ... ," p. 363.

22. See S. Bell, "Political Gynecology," *Science for the People* 11 (Sept./Oct. 1979): 8–29; Boston Women's Health Book Collective, *Our Bodies, Our Selves,* 2nd ed. rev. (New York: Simon and Schuster, 1979); S.B. Ruzek, *The Women's Health Movement* (New York: Praeger, 1979).

23. Current recording methods classify births that take place in free standing birth centers as hospital births. The precise type of provider is also not reliably entered on birth certificates.

24. A.B. Bennetts and E.K.M. Ernst, "Free Standing Birth Centers," in *Research Issues in the Assessment of Birth Settings.* Institute of Medicine Pub. No. IOM-82-04. Washington, D.C.: National Academy Press, 1982.

25. D. Haire, *The Cultural Warping of Childbirth.* (Hillside, N.J.: International Childbirth Education Association, 1972).

26. S. Arms, *Immaculate Deception* (New York: Bantam, 1975); C.K. Riessman "Women and Medicalization: A New Perspective." *Social Policy* 14 (Summer, 1983): 3–18; N.S. Shaw, *Forced Labor* (New York, Pergamon, 1974).

27. B.K. Rothman, *In Labor* (New York: Norton, 1982); R.G. DeVries "The Alternative Birth Center: Option or Cooptation?" *Women and Health* 5 (1980): 47–60.

28. Cooperative Birth Center Network News 1 (Summer, 1983).

29. The material on *Su Clinica* is drawn from A. Murdaugh, "Experiences of a New Migrant Health Clinic," *Women and Health* 1 (1976): 25–29; Annual Report of Su Clinica, 1979; Ten Years of Health Care at Su Clinica Familiar, 1982.

30. A. Murdaugh, "Experiences of a New Migrant Health Clinic."

31. R.W. Lubic, "Evaluation of an Out of Hospital Maternity Center for Low Risk Patients," in *Health Policy and Nursing Practice,* L. Aikin (ed.) (New York: McGraw Hill, 1981), pp. 90–116.

32. M.K. Nelson, "Working Class Women, Middle Class Women, and Models Childbirth," *Social Problems* 30 (1983): 284–297; M.K. Nelson, "The Effect of Childbirth Preparation on Women of Different Social Classes," *Journal of Health and Social Behavior* 23 (1982): 339–352.

33. A.B. Bennetts and E.K.M. Ernst, "Free Standing Birth Centers."

34. American Public Health Association, Guidelines for Licensing and Regulating Birth Centers: Policy Statement 8209 (PP). *American Journal of Public Health* 73 (1983): 331–334.

35. American College of Obstetrics and Gynecology, District II, Position Paper on Out of Hospital Maternity Care, 1976.

36. Letter from E.E. Nichols, M.D., Director of Practice Activities, A.C.O.G. Subcommittee on Oversight and Investigations of the Committee on Interstate and Foreign Commerce, House of Representatives, 96th Congress, December, 1980. (Washington, D.C.: U.S. Government Printing Office, 1981), p. 176.

37. U.S. Federal Trade Commission, "Competition Among Health Practitioners—The Influence of the Medical Profession on the Health Manpower

Market; Case Study: The Childbearing Center." Unpublished report, February, 1981.

38. Senator Albert Gore, Subcommittee on Oversight and Investigations . . . ,1981.

39. U.S. Federal Trade Commission, 1981.

40. Cooperative Birth Center Network News, 1983.

41. Cooperative Birth Center Network News, 1983. Caution is indicated in interpreting these cost data, as the charges for "comparable care" in a hospital are difficult to quantify and likely to be unreliable.

42. *Wall Street Journal* "Special Deliveries." November 29, 1983, p. 60.

43. *Research Issues in the Assessment of Birth Settings,* 1982.

44. A.B. Bennetts and R.W. Lubic, "The Free Standing Birth Center," *The Lancet* (1982): 378–380; Cooperative Birth Center Network News, 1983.

45. A.B. Bennetts and R.W. Lubic, "The Free Standing Birth Center."

46. G.E. Baraffi and W.S. Dellinger, "Alternative Birthing: An Evaluation of Quality of Care." Paper presented at Annual Meeting of the American Public Health Association, Los Angeles, Ca., 1981.

47. R.E.K. Stein, D.J. Jessop, C.K. Riessman, "Health Care Services Received by Children with Chronic Illness," *American Journal of Disabled Children* 137 (1983): 225–230.

48. For a full description of how the Pediatric Home

Care Program came about see D.J. Jessop and R.E.K. Stein, "A Service Delivery Program and its Evaluation: A Case Study in the Sociology of Applied Research," *Evaluation and the Health Professions,* Vol. 6, No. 1 (Sage, 1983), pp. 99–114.

49. For a full description of the program see R.E.K. Stein, "Pediatric Home Care: An Ambulatory Special Care Unit," *Journal of Pediatrics* 92 (1978) 495–499.

50. For a full description of the evaluation see R.E.K. Stein and D.J. Jessop, "The Effects of Pediatric Home Care: Findings from the Pediatric Ambulatory Care Treatment Study," *Pediatrics,* forthcoming.

51. These included asthma, seizure disorders, hemoglobinopathy, congenital heart disease, malignancies, diabetes mellitus, and congenital anomalies such as meninglomyocele/hydrocephaleus and biliary atresia.

52. T. Szasz and M. Hollender, "A Contribution to the Philosophy of Medicine: The Basic Models of the Doctor-Patient Relationship," *Journal of the American Medical Association* 97 (1956): 585–88.

53. John B. McKinlay, "A Case for Refocussing Upstream: The Political Economy of Illness" in *The Sociology of Health and Illness: Critical Perspectives,* P. Conrad and R. Kern (eds.) (New York: St. Martin's Press, 1981), pp. 613–633.

35

Politicizing Health Care

John McKnight

Is it possible that out of the contradictions of medicine one can develop the possibilities of politics? The example I want to describe is not going to create a new social order. It is, however, the beginning of an effort to free people from medical clienthood, so that they can perceive the possibility of being citizens engaged in political action.

The example involves a community of about 60,000 people on the west side of Chicago. The people are poor and Black, and the majority are dependent on welfare payments. They have a voluntary community organization which encompasses an area in which there are two hospitals.

The neighborhood was originally all white. During the 1960s it went through a racial transition and over a period of a few years, it became largely populated with Black people.

The two hospitals continued to serve the white people who had lived in the neighborhood before transition, leaving the Black people struggling to gain access to the hospitals' services.

This became a political struggle and the community organization finally "captured" the two hospitals. The boards of directors of the hospitals then accepted people from the neighborhood, employed Black people on their staffs, and treated members of the neighborhood rather than the previous white clients.

After several years, the community organization felt that it was time to stand back and look at the health status of their community. As a result of their analysis, they found that, although they had "captured" the hospitals, there was no significant evidence that the health of the people had changed since they had gained control of the medical services.

The organization then contacted the Center for Urban Affairs where I work. They asked us to assist in finding out why, if the people controlled the two hospitals, their health was not any better.

It was agreed that the Center would do a study of the hospitals' medical records to see why people were receiving medical care. We took a sample of the emergency room medical records to determine the frequency of the various problems that brought the people into the hospitals.

We found that the seven most common reasons for hospitalization, in order of frequency, were:

1. Automobile accidents.
2. Interpersonal attacks.
3. Accidents (non-auto).
4. Bronchial ailments.
5. Alcoholism.
6. Drug-related problems (medically administered and nonmedically administered).
7. Dog bites.

The people from the organization were startled by these findings. The language of medicine is focused upon disease—yet the problems we identified have very little to do with disease. The medicalization of health had led them to believe that "disease" was the problem which hospitals were addressing, but they discovered instead that the hospitals were dealing with many problems which were not disease. It was an important step in increasing consciousness to recognize that modern medical systems are usually dealing with maladies—social problems—rather than disease. Maladies and social problems are the domain of citizens and their community organizations.

A Strategy For Health

Having seen the list of maladies, the people from the organization considered what they ought to do, or could do, about them. First of all, as good political strategists, they decided to tackle a problem which they felt they could win. They didn't want to start out and immediately lose. So they went down the list and picked dog bites, which caused about four percent of the emergency room visits at an average hosptial cost of $185.

How could this problem best be approached? It interested me to see the people in the organization thinking about that problem. The city government has employees who are paid to be "dog-catchers," but the organization did not choose to contact the city. Instead, they said: "Let us see what we can do ourselves." They decided to take a small part of their money and use it for "dog bounties." Through their block clubs they let it be known that for a period of one month, in an area of about a square mile, they would pay a bounty of five dollars for every stray dog that was brought in to the organization or had its location identified so that they could go and capture it.

There were packs of wild dogs in the neighborhood that had frightened many people. The children of the neighborhood, on the other hand, thought that catching dogs was a wonderful idea—so they helped to identify them. In one month, 160 of these dogs were captured and cases of dog bites brought to the hospitals decreased.

Two things happened as a result of this success. The people began to learn that their action, rather than the hospital, determines their health. They were also building their organization by involving the children as community activists.

The second course of action was to deal with something more difficult—automobile accidents. "How can we do anything if we don't understand where these accidents are taking place?" the people said. They asked us to try to get information which would help to deal with the accident problem, but we found it extremely difficult to find information regarding when, where, and how an accident took place.

We considered going back to the hospitals and looking at the medical records to determine the nature of the accident that brought each injured person to the hospital. If medicine was thought of as a system that was related to the possibilities of community action, it should have been possible. It was not. The medical record did not say, "This person has a malady because she was hit by an automobile at six o'clock in the evening on January 3rd at the corner of Madison and Kedzie." Sometimes the record did not even say that the cause was an automobile accident. Instead, the record simply tells you that the person has a "broken tibia." It is a record system that obscures the community nature of the problem, by focusing on the therapeutic to the exclusion of the primary cause.

We began, therefore, a search of the data systems of macroplanners. Finally we found one macroplanning group that had data regarding the nature of auto accidents in the city. It was data on a complex, computerized system, to be used in macroplanning to facilitate automobile traffic! We persuaded the planners to do a printout that could be used by the neighborhood people for their own action purposes. This had never occurred to them as a use for their information.

The printouts were so complex, however, that the organization could not comprehend them. So we took the numbers and transposed them onto a neighborhood map showing where the accidents took place. Where people were injured, we put a blue X. Where people were people were killed, we put a red X.

We did this for all accidents for a period of three months. There are 60,000 residents living in the neighborhood. In that area, in three months, there were more than 1,000 accidents.

From the map the people could see, for example, that within three months six people had been injured, and one person killed, in an area 60 feet wide. They immediately identified this place as the entrance to a parking lot for a department store. They were then ready to act, rather than be treated, by dealing with the store owner because information had been "liberated" from its medical and macroplanning captivity.

The experience with the map had two consequences. One, it was an opportunity to invent several different ways to deal with a health problem that the community could understand. The community organization could negotiate with the department store owner and force a change in its entrance.

Two, it became very clear that there were accident problems that the community organization could not handle directly. For example, one of the main reasons for many of the accidents was the fact that higher authorities had decided to make several of the streets through the neighborhood major throughways for automobiles going from the heart of the city out to the affluent suburbs. Those who made this trip were a primary cause of injury to the local people. Dealing with this problem is not within the control of people at the neighborhood level—but they understood the necessity of getting other community organizations involved in a similar process, so that together they could assemble enough power to force the authorities to change the policies that serve the interests of those who use the neighborhoods as their freeway.

The third community action activity developed when the people focused on "bronchial problems." They learned that good nutrition was a factor in these problems, and concluded that they did not have enough fresh fruit and vegetables for good nutrition. In the city, particularly in the winter, these foods were too expensive. So could they grow fresh fruit and vegetables themselves? They looked around, but it seemed difficult in the heart of the city. Then several people pointed out that most of their houses were two story apartments with flat roofs. "Supposing we could build a greenhouse on the roof, couldn't we grow our own fruit and vegetables?" So they built a greenhouse on one of the roofs as an experiment. Then, a fascinating thing began to happen.

Originally, the greenhouse was built to deal with a health problem—inadequate nutrition. The greenhouse was a tool, appropriate to the environment, that people could make and use to improve health. Quickly, however, people began to see that the greenhouse was also an economic development tool. It increased their income because they now produced a commodity to use and also to sell.

Then, another use for the greenhouse appeared. In the United States, energy costs are extremely high and a great burden for poor people. One of the main places where people lose (waste) energy is from the rooftops of their houses—so the greenhouse on top of the roof converted the energy loss into an asset. The energy that did escape from the house went into the greenhouse where heat was needed. The greenhouse, therefore, was an energy conservation tool.

Another use for the greenhouse developed by chance. The community organization owned a retirement home for elderly people, and one day one of the elderly people discovered the greenhouse. She went to work there, and told the other old people and they started coming to the greenhouse every day to help care for the plants. The administrator of the old people's home noticed that the attitude of the older people changed. They were excited. They had found a function. The greenhouse became a tool to empower older people—to allow discarded people to be productive.

Multility vs. Unitility

The people began to see something about technology that they had not realized before. Here was a simple tool—a greenhouse. It could be built locally, used locally and among its "outputs" were health, economic development, energy conservation and enabling older people to be productive. A simple tool requiring a minimum "inputs" produced multiple "outputs" with few negative side effects. We called the greenhouse a "multility."

Most tools in a modernized consumer-oriented society are the reverse of the greenhouse. They are systems requiring a complex organization with multiple inputs that produce only a single output. Let me give you an example. If you get bauxite from Jamaica, copper from Chile, rubber from Indonesia, oil from Saudi Arabia, lumber from Canada, and labor from all these countries, and process these resources in an American corporation that uses American labor and professional skills to manufacture a commodity, you can produce an electric toothbrush. This tool is what we call a "unitility." It has multiple inputs and one output. However, if a tool is basically a labor-saving device, then the electric toothbrush is an anti-tool. If you added up all the labor put into producing it, its sum is infinitely more than the labor saved by its use.

The electric toothbrush and the systems for its production are the essence of the technological mistake. The greenhouse is the essence of the technological possibility. The toothbrush (unitility) is a tool that disables capacity and maximizes exploitation. The greenhouse (multility) is a tool that minimizes exploitation and enables community action.

Similarly, the greenhouse is a health tool that creates citizen action and improves health. The hospitalized focus on health disables community capacity by concentrating on therapeutic tools and techniques requiring tremendous inputs, with limited output in terms of standard health measures.

Conclusions

Let me draw several conclusions from the health work of the community organization.

First, out of all this activity, it is most important that the health action process has strengthened a community organization. Health is a political issue. To convert a medical problem into a political issue is central to health improvement. Therefore, as our action has developed the organization's vitality and power, we have begun the critical health development. Health action must lead away from dependence on professional tools and techniques, towards community building and citizen action. Effective health action must convert a professional-technical problem into a political, communal issue.

Second, effective health action identifies what

you can do at the local level with local resources. It must also identify those external authorities and structures that control the limits of the community to act in the interest of its health.

Third, health action develops tools for the people's use, under their own control. To develop these tools may require us to diminish the resources consumed by the medical system. As the community organization's health activity becomes more effective, the swollen balloon of medicine should shrink. For example, after the dogs were captured, the hospital lost clients. Nonetheless, we cannot expect that this action will stop the medical balloon from growing. The medical system will make new claims for resources and power, but our action will intensify the contradictions of medicalized definitions of health. We can now see people saying: "Look, we may have saved $185 in hospital care for many of the 160 dogs that will not now bite people. That's a lot of money! But it still stays with that hospital. We want our $185! We want

to begin to trade in an economy in which you don't exchange our action for more medical service. We need income, not therapy. If we are to act in our health interest, we will need the resources medicine claims for its therapeutic purposes in order to diminish our therapeutic need."

These three principles of community health action suggest that improved health is basically about moving away from being "medical consumers."

The experience I have described suggests that the sickness which we face is the captivity of tools, resources, power, and consciousness by medical "unitilities" that create consumers.

Health is a political question. It requires citizens and communities. The health action process can enable "another health development" by translating medically defined problems and resources into politically actionable community problems.

36

Helping Ourselves

Ann Withorn

Self help has emerged as a widely acclaimed "major thrust" of the eighties. Popular magazines, *The New York Times* and the federal government have all recognized the potential of the "self help movement" to influence human service policies and programs. Hundreds of thousands of self help groups now exist across the country. Some are affiliated with nation-wide organizations while others are more isolated local efforts where people join together to help themselves cope with and cure a wide range of human problems. Ideologically they range from

the conservative piety of an Alcoholics Anonymous to the radical feminism of feminist "self-health" activities.[1]

Is this activity simply an extension of the self-absorption of the seventies? Is it a retreat into individual solutions and a ploy to keep people from demanding what they need from the state? Or does it reflect a growing, healthy skepticism of professionals and the welfare state bureaucracy? Could it be a sign of a potentially important rise in commitment to popular democracy?

These questions are of some importance in the

United States. The simple magnitude of current self help activity, especially among working class people, calls upon us to have, at least, an analysis of its political implications and an understanding of its appeal. Further, the experience of feminist self help suggests that there may be ways to combine selected self help activity with a broader socialist and feminist strategy. At its best, self help may even serve as one way to formulate a progressive politics which is more grounded in the daily experience of working class life and which thereby helps define socialism more broadly than the economistic formulations which so often characterize it. In addition, an understanding of the power of self help as a means for individual change may also go farther in comprehending the fundamental inadequacies of the social service provided by the modern welfare state.

What Is Self Help?

The nature of self help itself gives rise to the contradictory questions raised above. Self help is the effort of people to come together in groups in order to resolve mutual individual needs. Today this activity consists of individuals sharing concerns about personal, emotional, health or family problems. Sometimes community or ethnic groups which organize to improve their neighborhoods or social situations also call themselves self-help groups. The major reasons for defining an activity as self help are that it involves group activity and meetings of the people with the problem, not outside experts or professionals, and that the main means by which difficulties are addressed are mutual sharing, support, advice-giving and the pooling of group resources and information. Members benefit as much from the sharing of their problems and the process of helping others as they do from the advice and resources provided by others. In most cases there is a strong ethic of group solidarity, so that individual members become concerned about the progress of other group members as well as in their own "cure".

Within this broad common definition, however, there is wide variety in focus and emphasis for self help groups. At one end of the spectrum are the politically aware feminist self-help efforts, in health care, rape crisis, battered women shelters and other service areas. Here self help is self-conscious, empowering democratic effort where women help each other and often provide an analysis and an example from which to criticize and make feminist demands on the systyem. At the other end are groups which focus on the specific problem only, like AA, other "anonymous" groups or disease victim groups, with self help used only as a means for coping with a problem, not an alternative model for society or even service delivery. In between are groups which have selected self help as a means to help themselves but which also come to draw from the process ways to suggest broader changes, often in the social services system and sometimes in the whole social system. While all share key aspects of self help and all may teach certain critical lessons about the importance of social networks and group solidarity, their differences are crucial and need to be understood and evaluated as a part of any critique of self help.

Historical Roots of Self Help

Some of the comforts and supports now provided by self-conscious self help groups have always been available. Prior to industrial development village and family networks were the primary means by which people helped each other survive the economic, health and other social difficulties associated with a hard life. As industrial disruption made such supports less accessible early nineteenth century workers began to band together in new forms of "mutual aid" organizations composed of individual craft workers or, in America especially, of groups of ethnically homogeneous workers. These early groups formed to provide for the basic economic and social needs not available from employers, the state, the church or geographic community. Meager resources were pooled to provide burial and family insurance, limited food, clothing and economic support in times of ill health, disability and family crisis. In Britain and the U.S., the emergence of these "burial societies", "workingmen's aid" associations, "friendly societies" and immigrant aid associations reflected constant efforts

by workers to help each other and help themselves to cope with the health and social problems associated with capitalist development. The
remaining records of such groups show a growing sense of collective responsibility within the
groups and the gradual creation of social networks which performed wider social functions
than only the insurance of economic survival.[2]

It is easy to admire these self-consious workers'
efforts, like that of Workmen's Circle, to form "an
organization that could come to their assistance in
terms of need, and especially in case of sickness,
that would provide them and their families with
plots and decent burials in case of death and
extend some measure of help to their surviving
dependents, that would, finally, afford them
congenial fellowships and thereby lessen the
loneliness of their lives in a strange land."[3] It is
important, however, to avoid romanticizing this
early self help activity. Some groups were controlled by the more conservative and established
elements in the craft or community who kept the
groups from gaining a more broad "class" identification. Others served as a base from which to
distrust or ignore, rather than identify with, the
needs of other workers not in the same craft or
ethnic group. And, at best, these early groups
could only provide the most minimal assistance to
their members, still leaving them with major
social disadvantages. All these problems were
pointed out at the time by radicals in the labor and
black movements, especially. But, in times when
public aid was extremely punitive and largely
non-existent even such limited efforts were recognized as crucial to the survival and strength of
workers and their families. But they were also,
perhaps, the only means of survival. Self help was
the only help available. It was not developed as a
better, more humane, alternative means of support; originally it was the only means of support.
This is a crucial difference between early self help
and current efforts.

. . . .

Self Help as a Service Activity

There is an interesting parallel to these such
tensions in the professional developments of the

period. Just as the more conservative trade
unionists and black leadership supported self
help as a means for worker and community
independence, so did the more conservative
doctors, lawyers and social workers who worked
in the private sector. The private health and
welfare establishment saw individual and group
change coming out of self help activities. More
liberal professionals argued that this strategy
abandoned the poor and they, therefore, allied
with progressive people in demanding more
public programs. They argued that it was unrealistic to expect the victims of society to help
themselves and that outside intervention—from
expert professionals funded by the government—
was the only reasonable hope for change. These
liberal social workers and medical experts gained
power in federal and state programs throughout
the 1930s and 40s, so that by the 1950s the
public health and welfare establishment had
become as critical of self help as a service strategy
as leftists were of it as political tactic.

Yet self help came into its own as a service
activity during the 1930s and 40s, in spite (or
perhaps because) of increasing professional hostility. As the private and public insurance and
welfare establishments grew, self help changed
form, moving from group provision of welfare
insurance and burial services to a process of
social supports for dealing with a range of
personal, family and emotional problems. The
process of self help became important not for
itself, as a model and base for democratic
self-support, but as a means to achieve personal
goals for change or to come to terms with
unavoidable difficulties.

The poverty of the Depression gave rise to
many self help service projects. Food, clothing
and housing exchanges developed, European
refugees and internal immigrants organized mutual aid groups. Most important, however, was
the birth of Alcoholics Anonymous (AA) in
1935; it has served as a primary model for self
help service activities since its inception. It was
founded by a pair of mid-western professionals
who found little help in the medical, social work
or psychiatric professionals and who began to
develop a behavior oriented, religiously imbued,
program of group support and pressure for
alcoholics. The model consisted of admitting the

power of one's problem and drawing help from fellow alcoholics, as well as from a "higher power", in order to learn to stop drinking. This was to be done by developing a network of fellow alcoholics, by attending frequent—even daily—meetings where discussions take place about personal experiences with alcohol and where the goal of sobriety is to be achieved "one day at a time". Drawing upon such basic, simple principles AA grew rapidly, reaching 400,000 by 1947 and currently involving more than 700,000 alcoholics a year.

It is easy for socialists and professionals to criticize Alcoholics Anonymous. Its religious pietism is fundamentalist and limiting. Despite its proclaimed organizational refusal to take federal money or political positions, its veterans have increasingly designed and defined alcholism services across the country in harmony with AA principles. These programs often exclude women and those who have not "hit bottom" with their drinking, as well as a range of people less comfortable with the somewhat simplistic "Twelve Steps". Its appeal has been largely limited to whites. Yet AA does appear to have a higher success rate than other forms of professional help with the complex problems associated with alcoholism. It does attract a largely working-class population who have little recourse to private services. It also offers alcoholics the experience of a non-drinking community where they can learn to like themselves better, admit to their problems, trust others and begin to rebuild their lives.

. . . .

Other self help services have formed using the Anonymous model, where the focus is on the problem faced and the process of mutual help and support is valued as an effective means to the end, not as a goal in itself. Gamblers Anonymous, Overeaters Anonymous, Parents Anonymous (for people who have abused their children) are only three of the dozens of groups which are modelled closely on AA and attempt to help people admit that they have a problem and get help from others in the same situation to overcome it. All groups rely on "recovering" victims to help others, a helping role which is

often a major form of continuing improvement for the old time members. Although some groups make greater use of professionals than others, in all peers assume primary roles and outside social networks often grow out of such groups which provide people with a wide range of supports. While there is no hard data, such anonymous groups (most of which, except AA, have been founded since the mid-fifties) seem to attract a largely white working- and middle-class population and create strong loyalities among those helped.

Since the 1940s other services which use self help as a major means of helping people cope with or resolve personal difficulties have emerged. Many drug programs have used self help activities to create "alternative communities" characterized by mutual disclosure, support and pressure. Since the 1940s (and mushrooming in the 1970s) there has been a steady increase in health-oriented self help programs for the families of victims of cancer and other diseases, and for the victims themselves. Stroke victims, cancer victims, heart disease patients, parents of children with Down's Syndrome (to name only a few of thousands) have come together to discuss their feelings, reactions and symptoms and to help each other emotionally. While these programs are often supported by the medical system they frequently come to share vocal and strong criticisms of professionalism and professional care.

The social welfare and medical establishments have reacted to all this increasing self help activity with different types of responses. Sometimes groups have been criticized (often during the initial phases) for "resisting professional treatment" or for avoiding reality. The more critical the groups become of the quality of professional care (a component of almost all self help groups, no matter what their origins) the more they are resisted by doctors and social workers. However, until this happens they are often supported by professionals as another form of service, especially for people with "difficult" problems, i.e. those problems like alcoholism, drug abuse, "incurable" cancer, senility and other afflictions not amenable to conventional intervention. Indeed, the federal government has become enamoured with self help approaches, providing funds for certain efforts and even identifying the existence of a "continuum of care" including self help at one end and full institutional care at the other, all of which will require some form of public support and monitoring.

As with AA, it is easy to criticize. Most of these self help service efforts can be legitimately viewed as methods by which the established medical, mental health and social work professions get people to provide services to themselves which the professionals won't or can't provide. Cheap care and an avoidance of public responsibility may be obvious. Yet progressives working in these fields also have supported self help services, in recognition of the limits of professional care and in order to support the creation of a stronger, less fearful consumer consciousness, among clients or victims of problems as varied as alcoholism, drug abuse, cancer and chronic disease. In addition, many members of such self help service groups find them much more helpful and acceptable forms of care than other, more professional, services. Such groups may provide release and support which come from sharing and comraderie. These results cannot be disregarded, especially for people who felt desperately alone before the experience. A working class veteran of AA, Overeaters Anonomyous and Smoke Enders reflected similarly on what self help meant to her:

> Self help groups really help. They make you feel like you are not alone with yourself or your problem. You share with others and find out you are not the only one who smokes in the shower or bakes two pies for your family and eats one before anyone comes home. I'm not sure how it works, but somehow you feel like trying again.
>
> My sister had, in fact, a daughter that died. She had always laughed at me for my "groups," but after that happened she joined one herself. She just couldn't handle it alone, feeling so guilty and not knowing anyone with the same problem. That's what self help means to me.

Particularly important to many people in self help groups is the opportunity to help others with similar problems. The experience of doing this can be powerful and strengthening, especially for people who have only felt like victims before.

In short, as a form of social service, self help groups have proven themselves to be helpful and empowering to many, despite their potential use as a vehicle for providing cheaper services to unwanted clients. As one aspect of the general social services system, self help services seem a secure and welcome addition. The question remains, however, whether this increased self help activity has any underlying impact for progressive change. For such discussions we must look to recent efforts of the women's movement.

The Importance of Feminist Self Help

If it weren't for the development of feminist self help, especially in health, we might be less interested in the whole question of whether self help can be a serious part of a socialist strategy. Self help would be seen as merely a social service with little broader political impact. But the impressive efforts of women around the country to take self help seriously as a healthy form of relationship between women and to wed this with feminist analysis may suggest a more general model for reuniting self help with political practice.

Self help has been a central part of most feminist service work, which has, in turn, been a major area of the feminist movement. Since the late sixties, when women's liberation groups developed "consciousness-raising", the model of women sharing and helping other women has been a basic feminist strategy. Feminist historians looked back and found self help equivalents throughout the history of women—who have formed strong self helping women's networks within the family, neighborhoods and community as a means for basic survival and emotional support.

Out of this history, and an emerging understanding that "the personal is political," feminists were able to take the process of self help more seriously, to value the experience of working and sharing together in itself, as well as to appreciate the quality of the product of such work. Women were compelled, then, to be more self-conscious in their self help approaches and to proclaim them as central to feminist goals. In

"Jane", an early underground Chicago-based abortion clinic, for example, women developed models of abortion care which included sharing all processes and procedures, discussion of feelings and the trading of mutual experiences among the women abortion-workers and the women seeking abortions. Their approach became standard in many feminist services. *Our Bodies Our Selves,* the classic women's self health care book offered professional information mixed with personal experiences and has been used as a basis for women's health groups across the country. It too has helped to establish the notion of self help—mutual sharing of feelings, information and skills—as a basic tenet of feminist activity.[4]

As feminist services became a major approach of the women's movement—including everything from women's multi-purpose centers, to day care, health and nutrition services, rape and battered women's programs—self help came along as standard feminist practice. The meaning varied, however. In some places it simply meant collective decision-making by staff and a sharing of feelings and information with women who came for service. It was seen as a natural outgrowth of ideas of sisterhood and feminist theory. In the feminist health clinics, however, feminist self help has been most fully defined, has become in Elizabeth Somers words "both a philosophy and a practice through which we become active creators of our destinies."[5]

Feminist clinics insisted on education and group involvement of all who came to the clinics. This was viewed as an important antidote to the standard medical model of doctor as god and patient as grateful recipient of his care. Health care workers forged different relationships with women who came for care and also began to explore and share a growing criticism of the medical "knowledge" about women's bodies. The most self-conscious programs, the Femininst Women's Health Centers, led in developing clear guidelines for self help in health care which included pelvic self examinations, group examinations and discussions. They shared an explicit philosophy that self help is more than, and different from, the traditional "delivery" of service:

Self help is not being simply service oriented . . . we do not want to be middle women between the MD's and the patients. We want to show women how to do it themselves. . . . We do not examine women. We show women how to examine themselves . . . We neither sell nor give away self help . . . we share it. (Detroit Women's Clinic, 1974)

Feminist self help in health care and other service areas developed in conjunction with the broader feminist movement. Knowledge of the inadequacies and brutality of male dominated medicine came along with a heightened awareness of the prevalence of rape and women-battering. The system-supporting aspects of all medical and welfare care forced women into developing new models and into looking to each other for information and support. The early successes of many groups in raising the consciousness of women who came for "service" was heartening and sustaining. Sustained practice meant that feminists have been able to put the principles of self help to the test, to explore the need for structure and specialization within a self help framework, to discover the complexities of many health and emotional problems and to determine when professional help may, indeed, be neccessary.

All this learning and growth has not been without costs, however. Health centers, particularly, have suffered intense bureaucratic harassment from the medical profession which has been anxious to protect its right to control who practices medicine. Most self help programs have suffered from funding problems of a similar sort. The medical and social welfare establishments demand "legitimacy" before they provide money—through third party payments (Medicaid, private insurance) or direct service contracts. They require, at the very least, a professional "cover" for most alternative services and often refuse funding until bureaucratic, hierarchical structures are actually in place. Some battered women's shelters originally received money, in light of favorable publicity, with minimal hassles, but as time passed welfare agencies pressed to fund a "range" of services (i.e., non-feminist programs), with more familiar, professional approaches. In addition, inflation and cut backs have also limited the amount of money available.

The problems have not been all external either. The time and emotional demands of most self help services have made it hard for most groups to sustain staff, much less to do the continual political education neccessary to make the self help offered truly feminist in content. Women with professional aspirations and a lack of feminist values have been drawn to self help efforts. Their pressure can push already overextended feminists to leave rather than fight creeping bureaucracy, "efficiency" and professionalization in their midst. When this happens the mutual aid, democratic and sharing aspects of the service fade as surely as they do when public bureaucracies directly take over.

When such problems are coupled with current general decline in a broad-based feminist movement, they become even more difficult to endure and struggle with. Even in well-functioning self help projects women feel more isolated and less sure of what it all means, as expressed by a women's health worker in 1979:

> After we finally got our license then we had all this paperwork to do all the time. The women's community seemed less interested because we weren't in crisis anymore. The women who wanted to work in the center are more interested in health care than feminism. It just seems to take more effort to be feminist these days, to raise political issues in the groups or work meetings. We're still trying and do OK but I guess it's a lot harder than it used to be.

Feminist services, then, have not totally solved old problems with self help. They have shown that it is possible for participation in self help to be an effective means for political growth and development. Especially the health services have shown us that self help may often be an intrinsically better model of care and may, thereby, offer an immediate and personal way for people to understand what is wrong with public and private health and welfare services. All have shown the natural links between a democratic feminist movement and the process of self help. Women who have participated in such programs talk about themselves as "permanently changed. I don't think I can ever accept without criticism the old authoritarian models again." But over time the pressures to provide services on a large scale, with adequate funding, work against the ability to work in a self help manner. Is it reasonable to assume that we could really provide feminist self help services to all the battered women who need them, for example? And if it is not, we are always stuck with the limits of even the most effective self help efforts—that the harder we work and the better we function, the greater the demand and the more impossible it is to meet.

Problems and Potential of Self Help

Given all this, how should progressive people respond to the likelihood that self help services are likely to continue to grow and re-form in the future? The current momentum and recognition of existing programs seems unstoppable and will probably be even more appealing to administrators wishing to support an image of continued service provision in times of real cut backs. An increasingly popular answer to anyone with a problem will predictably be: "Join, or form, a self help group."

. . . .

As advanced capitalism lurches along, services and the service economy will become more important. Self help services may play an increasingly important role in this. On the hopeful side, self help activity has the potential to become a base from which people can criticize, demand and affect the nature of the service system in a positive way and out of which progressive workers and clients can form meaningful alliances. On the negative side, self help services may help to provide an opportunity for another professional cover-up. See, we have a humane system. We even let people take care of each other, after they are near death or incapacitated by emotional and personal problems.

The problem, assuming these options, becomes one of how to assist self help efforts in achieving their potential as a base for criticism and change rather than providing tacit reaffirmation of professional hegemony and the capitalist welfare state.

In promoting the potential of self help we cannot, however, ignore certain limits which may be built into the activity. First, we cannot deny that the nature of self help, and the enormity of the difficulties which bring people to it, often emphasize only the personal dimensions of people's problems. Even if the social components of problems are admitted, as they are in feminist and some other self help efforts, the stress remains on how the victim can change, rather than on the implications for broader social action. There can even be a new form of victim blaming which takes place in self help: "We are so fucked up only we can help each other." Admittedly this is an aspect of all psychological services, but the self help model, with emphasis on social support and reciprocity, may serve to mask the individualistic approach more. It also may make it harder for people to move on to other activities because the self help group may form the only support system people know (AA has a strong history of this: people become professional alcoholics, still centered in the group and their problem, long after drinking has ceased to define their lives). For self help activity to lead to broader criticism of the social service system or the whole of society, these tendencies must be recognized and alternatives made available, at least to those who can make use of them.

Second, even with self help set in a broader context, the questions of scope and relationship to the state will still affect us. Self help activity is probably only a limited service tactic which, while it can form a base for criticizing and pressuring the larger system, can never fully replace the professional, bureaucratized services, at least under capitalism. This is a more difficult proposition to accept in practice than it sounds in theory. We get sucked in, we want to "save the world" and it is difficult to remember the political analysis which tells us that the problems we face are generated by social forces beyond our immediate control. It is hard, as those involved in self help often admit, to have to push the state to provide services which we know will be inferior to what we can do through self help (but on a limited scale). All this leads to burnout and frustration, especially when broader movements are not active enough to help us keep our activity in perspective.

Finally, there are some philosophical problems associated with self help, which are similar to those surrounding many populist efforts. Many self help groups, especially including

feminist activities, become so skeptical of organization and expertise that they become almost mystical and anti-intellectual. While the social origins of current organizations and expertise may lead to this, as an overall approach it becomes self-defeating. In the process of self help, some people become "experts" in the problem: must they then leave the group? Or groups tend to "reinvent the wheel", perpetually relearning everything about problems from a feminist, working class, consumer or black perspective. While Barbara Ehrenreich's and Deidre English's suggestion that we "take what we want of the technology without buying the ideology" sounds good, the full criticism of all professionalism which is inherent in healthy self help may make this difficult.[6]

Furthermore, we still have to fight rampant specialization in self help groups. Granted, DES daughters have different needs from mastectomy patients and from ex-mental patients, but to be effective, self help concerns will need to be linked together in broader analysis of processes and problems. All this must be accomplished while recognizing that people in immediate pain may resent any deviation from their immediate problems.

These are serious drawbacks, not to be ignored. Yet current circumstances suggest that progressive people should, still, become involved in many facets of self help. We have the accumulated experience of feminist self help to guide us away from some of the worst pitfalls. We have the undeniable broad public interest in self help to provide a responsive climate for our efforts. Finally, and most importantly, we have a national social and economic situation which may make self help once again a necessity for survival. Inflation and creeping recession have already made daily living more tenuous and pressured. The cut backs in social services make professional supports less available, subject to more competition among those deserving service and more bureaucratization and formalities before services can be delivered. Given such a set of factors, it is not unreasonable to support and initiate self help efforts as both a broad base for criticism and change in the social service system as well as favorable settings for people to become exposed to socialist and feminist ideas and practice.

The primary base for our involvement in self help groups can even be personal. Most of us experience problems in our lives as women, men, parents, children, lovers, survivors, drinkers, procrastinators, shy people, fat people, lonely people. Joining or starting a self help group can help us as people, not just as activists with an agenda. This has been a major source of strength within the women's movement. Women have helped each other and been helped themselves with some real personal and political issues in their lives. The sharing and loss of isolation which comes from self help activity are real and can provide us with tangible energy and strength.

. . . .

Finally, then, the impulse which brings people, including ourselves, to seek mutual aid instead of professional care is a healthy one. It embodies the faith in oneself and others that is essential if we are ever to achieve a more equal society. We cannot allow the all-too-real limitations of the current practice of self help to obscure the equally real opportunity.

NOTES

1. There is a very large current literature on self help. The leading figures in this area are Frank Riessmann and Alan Gartner, who have written *Self Help in the Human Services* (Josey Bass, 1977) and sponsor the National Self Help Clearinghouse (CUNY, 33 West 42nd St., Room 1227, New York, NY 10036).
2. For a useful review of this history see Alfred H. Katz and Eugene I. Bender, "Self Help Groups in Western Society: History and Prospects," in *The Journal of Applied Behavioral Science,* XII, no. 3 (1976).
3. Maximillian C. Hurwitz, *The Workers Circle* (New York, 1936).
4. Pauline B. Bart, "Seizing the Means of Reproduction: An Illegal Feminist Abortion Collective—How and Why it Worked," Abraham Lincoln School of Medicine, University of Illinois, Chicago.
5. *Ibid.*
6. Helin I. Marieskind and Barbara Ehrenreich, "Towards Socialist Medicine: The Women's Health Movement," *Social Policy,* September–October, 1975.

Comparative Health Policies

When we seek alternatives to our own medial care organization we do well to look at other societies for comparison and guidance, especially societies that have similar health problems or have developed innovative organizational solutions (see Sidel and Sidel, 1983). While no medical system is without problems and none is completely transferable to the United States, there are lessons to be learned in considering alternative models to our own.

In this section we briefly examine the health policies of Germany, Canada, and Great Britian. Since Germany is now divided into two nations (East and West), we will be able to examine four medical care systems. Three of these countries (East Germany being the exception) are western, industrialized democracies with powerful and advanced medical professions, which makes them generally comparable to the United States. It should be noted that there are, of course, specific ways in which they are not comparable. Nevertheless, by comparing health systems we are better able to see the consequences and potentials of different national policies on the provision of medical services.

The United States remains the only industrialized nation without a national health program. Many such proposals have been introduced in Congress in the past seventy-five years only to have been ultimately defeated. After the passage of Medicare and Medicaid in 1965 many policymakers felt that national health insurance was an idea whose time had come (Margolis, 1981). Dozens of different proposals were introduced during the 1960s and 1970s and many analysts believed that we would have a national health insurance program by 1980. With the advent of the Reagan administration and a general orientation toward reductions in government spending on social programs, there is little discussion today among American policymakers about national health insurance.

It is problematic to reform health policies piecemeal as has occurred in the United States. Fixing one problem creates another; for example, Medicare and Medicaid paid for medical services for the elderly and poor but, lacking cost controls, fueled inflationary medical costs. We believe that some type of comprehensive and universal national health system is necessary in the United State to increase equity, improve access to services, and control costs. Hence we look to other societies for models and guidance. Before proceeding we should make one distinction clear. When we discuss national health policies, we can differentiate between national health *insurance* (NHI) and a national health *service* (NHS). Both assume that adequate health care is a basic right of the population. NHI essentially puts the financing of a medical system under government control, typically by providing some type of health insurance where the premiums are paid by taxes. NHI also pays for medical services, so there is no or minimal direct cost to the patient. Canada and West Germany are examples of such policies. An NHS, on the other hand, reorganizes medical services in addition to having the government pay directly for those services. It "socializes" medicine in that it treats medical care as a public utility and places much more control of the medical system in the hands of the government. Great Britain and East Germany are examples of such policies.

Donald W. Light, in "Comparing Health Care Systems: Lessons from East and West Germany," presents us with four contrasting models of health-care systems. By first looking at these "ideal-typical" models we can see how different political values, social goals, control, costs, and type of administration affect the organization and delivery of medical services. Light then shows how these models vied with one another, culminating with the political division in 1945 when West Germany opted for a largely professional model while East Germany adopted a state model. Adopting different policies gave these health care systems rather distinctive orientations with different consequences.

Canada is a country rather similar to the United States, although with a much smaller population (23 million). Between 1947 and 1971 Canada gradually introduced a national health policy that guaranteed medical care as a right for everyone. The form of NHI that Canada adopted is financed out of a progressive income tax and results in an increased equity of health services and a remarkable control of health costs. The NHI policy, implemented by the Canadian provinces, has been able to control health expenditures at about 7 percent of the GNP while in the United States expenditures have soared to 10 percent. Canada's cost for a health insurance system that covers everyone (as opposed to the fragmented American system which excludes 10 percent of the population) actually costs over $100 per capita *less* than in the United States (Lee, 1982). This results from lowering administrative costs, removing the profitability from selling health insurance, and being able to set a national policy for cost controls. Canada, although implementing a progressive financing system, has still maintained a fee-for-service, private enterprise orientation in the delivery of services. From all indications, the health status of Canadians is equal to or better than that of Americans.

In his article "Canada's Path, America's Choices: Lessons from the Canadian Experience with National Health Insurance," Theodore R. Marmor discusses some of the similarities and differences between the two health systems. He describes the effect of NHI on cost controls, physicians' incomes, and access to care. Marmor notes how one could adapt some of the Canadian innovations to develop an NHI in the United States.

Another model for health service delivery is Britain's National Health Service (NHS). In 1948 Great Britain reorganized its medical system to create a national health service. (See Stevens, 1966, for an account of NHS's formation and early development.) The NHS is a public system of medicine: hospitals, clinics, physicians, and other medical personnel work under the auspices and control of the Ministry of Health of the British Government. The fee-for-service system has all but been eliminated: the NHS is financed by tax revenues (through "progressive taxation"), with essentially no cost to the patient at the time of services, and physicians paid stipulated yearly salaries. This system has reduced the "profit motive" in medicine. For example, it is well know that Great Britain has about half the amount of surgery per capita as does the United States. The incomes of physicians are relatively low by American standards (or, perhaps more correctly, American physicians' incomes are astronomical by international standards). There exist two levels of physicians in the NHS, the community-based GP and the hospital-based consultant. Until recently the higher status and incomes of the hospital consultants were a source of dissatisfaction to GPs. While the rigid two-tier system still exists, some of the inequities have been reduced.

During its thirty-year development, the NHS has managed admirable accomplishments, including: (1) eliminating financial barriers to access; (2) making the system more rational and equitable; (3) providing care on a community level with community-based primary physicians; (4) maintaining a high level of medical-care quality; and (5) controlling costs. This final point deserves elaboration.

The NHS seems to be a more cost efficient method of delivering health care than the largely private American system. Great Britain spends about 6 percent of its gross national product on health, whereas America spends nearly 10 percent. Specifically, the British government spent only about $300 per citizen per year in 1978 for health care, compared to $863 per person for all public and private health care in the United States that same year (Malone, 1979: 22). And by most measures the health status of the populations are roughly equal. Further, there is evidence that the NHS delivers medical care more equitably (Stevens, 1983). The British have controlled costs by "rationing" medical services (Aaron and Schwartz, 1984). While all necessary medical services are more or less readily available, patients who wish elective services must "queue up" for them. There are, in fact, two- and three-year waiting lists for some elective medical care. There is little doubt that we as a nation cannot afford all the medical services we are scientifically capable of providing (Fuchs, 1975), so it is likely we too will have to adopt some type of rationing. It is undoubtedly more humane and just when medical services are rationed on the basis of need rather than on the ability to pay.

The NHS is by no means a medical utopia (Turshen, 1977). As it is a public service, it must compete with other services (e.g., education) for funding and thus by some accounts is perpetually underfinanced. While inequities of services have lessened, they have not disappeared. The high status of the hospital consultant is a continuing problem and reinforces NHS emphasis on "sick care" rather than prevention. In the final analysis, however, the NHS delivers better care to more parts of the population at less cost (and with no discernible difference in "health" status) than is accomplished in the United States and cannot be ignored as a possible alternative model for medical care delivery in American society.

In "A National Health Service: Principles and Practice," Derek Gill comments on the basic principles of the British NHS—universality, equity, and public accountability—and gives a detailed account of how the system operates. He reviews some persistent dilemmas as well as the successes of the NHS. Gill is particularly astute in his presentation of ways to increase the public accountability of medicine and to further protect patients' interests and control rising costs. He argues that central to increasing accountability is a reduction in the functional autonomy of the medical profession and an increase in the public's participation in health-care decisions. He concludes with some thoughts on how the principles of the NHS might some day be applied to the American medical system.

A fundamental emphasis of all four health policies is that they view health care as a right and develop a universal and comprehensive orientation toward the delivery of medical services. As we struggle to achieve a more equitable and reasonable American health system, we will want to look closely at these other systems for ways of reforming our own.

REFERENCES

Aaron, J. Henry, and William B. Schwartz. 1984. The Painful Prescription: Rationing Hospital Care. Washington, D.C.: The Brookings Institution.

Fuchs, Victor. 1975. Who Shall Live? New York: Basic Books.

Lee, Sidney S. 1982. "Health Policy, A Social Contract: A Comparison of the United States and Canada." Journal of Public Health Policy: 293–301.

Malone, Patrick. 1979. "British medicine/American medicine: Leaning closer but still an ocean apart." New Physician 28 (December): 20–24.

Margolis, Richard J. 1981. "National Health Insurance—A Dream Whose Time Has Come?" Pp. 486–501 in Peter Conrad and Rochelle Kern (eds.), The Sociology of Health and Illness: Critical Perspectives. New York: St. Martin's.

Sidel, Victor W., and Ruth Sidel. 1983. A Healthy State. rev. ed. New York: Pantheon.

Stevens, Rosemary. 1966. Medical Practice in Modern England. New Haven: Yale University Press.

Stevens, Rosemary. 1983. "Comparisons in Health Care: Britain as a Contrast to the United States." Pp. 281–304 in David Mechanic (ed.), Handbook of Health, Health Care and the Health Professions. New York: Free Press.

Turshen, Meredith. 1977. The British National Health Services: Its Achievements and Lessons for the United States. Washington D.C.: Health Service Action.

37

Comparing Health Care Systems: Lessons from East and West Germany

Donald W. Light

The United States has a peculiar health care system. It is so unusual that only by comparing it with other systems can those of us who live inside it gain the perspective we need to understand how it works. Moreover, the American system is facing major crises that are leading to the largest social and economic changes of the century. Only the United States among industrialized nations does not provide financial coverage for medical services used by its citizens. Only the United States takes such a punitive approach to care for the poor. While Congress finally provided medical insurance for the poor (Medicaid) decades after most other advanced nations, payments are so low that many physicians will not treat Medicaid patients. In recent years, moreover, eligibility rules have changed so that more and more of the poor no longer "qualify" for Medicaid and have no general coverage at all. On the other hand, for those who have coverage, the United States provides among the best clinical care in the world.

In order to understand the American system, or the German, Canadian, British, Russian, or Chinese systems, we need some models that identify the central differences between these systems. The next few pages outline a set of comparative models showing how different systems work and indicating how the American system acquired its present imbalances. We will then turn to Germany, an extraordinary country in which all of the major models of health care interacted with each other. At the same time, Germany provides the unique opportunity to see what happened when Communism took over one half of a modern health care system.

Comparative Models of Health Care Systems

The challenge to all health care systems is how to meet the health needs of a people in a just, effective, and affordable way. Many systems meet the challenge poorly. They ignore some of the health needs, as the Soviet Union (and to a lesser degree all countries) responds ineffectively to widespread alcoholism. Or they provide effective care in an expensive way that does not justly distribute it to all social classes. A useful way to examine how different countries meet the challenge is the four models presented below. They do not always apply to a whole country but some part of the system, a point to be discussed later. But first, it is important to emphasize that medical care and health services are acts of political philosophy. Political and social values inform the choices made, the institutions formed, and the funds provided or withheld. The numerous studies indicating that medical care, despite its great expense and technical prowess, has only a modest effect on the health status of a people makes this non-medical emphasis all the more plausible (Dubos, 1965; McKeown, 1979; McKinlay and McKinlay, 1977; Benham and Benham, 1976; Auster, Leveson and Sarachek, 1972; Gray, 1982). Seemingly apolitical acts such as removing cancerous tissue, treating hypertension with drugs, medicalizing alcoholism or hyperactive children, or treating patients one by one all involve basic political values (Conrad and Schneider, 1980). The technological thrust of modern medicine is itself highly political in its definition of what problems are important to address and how they are to be defined. Likewise, the decision to eliminate environmental pollutants and social class differences would require almost a political revolution. One can only ban nuclear power, alter polluting industries, and monitor the health behavior of individuals through national policy and programs, not individual action. Thus, seemingly nonpolitical decisions about how to treat a cancer or a case of hypertension are freighted with political values about responsibility and cause.

The term *values* means something broader than "ideology" and narrower than "culture." Ideology connotes a logical consistency and coherence that may not be present, or if present as in some Communist countries, is not sufficient to account for the shape of social welfare institutions such as the health care system. Political culture, on the other hand, has such breadth and contains so many elements that it is not useful for analysis. Thus the four models that follow show how the organization, financing, and power of different health-care systems are united by political values that define their character. Like all models and ideal types, these lose the rich complexity of actual events as they elucidate the basic forces at play. As general models, they allow one to think comparatively about the German experience and other health care systems such as our own.

The Mutual Aid Model

As its name implies, the mutual aid model consists of people organizing themselves in order to help each other and make provisions for their needs. It is found whenever people are discontent with current services (e.g., the women's health movement) or have no services to meet their needs. As applied to health, the mutual aid model has a core value of improving the health of fellow members. From this core derives a sense of individual responsibility and mutual responsibility for each others' needs. This leads to an epidemiological rather than clinical way of thinking about group patterns of illness and collective needs. Social control and behavioral education can result, but it is among colleagues of many years rather than by an outside bureaucracy. The

mutual aid perspective also leads to planning and coordinating services. Generally, all members contribute to a sickness fund, which then contracts for professional services and organizes educational activities. This makes mutual aid groups independent from both the state and the professions. Mutual aid societies, like the nineteenth century worker-initiated sickness funds in Germany and the "friendly societies" in Great Britain and to a lesser degree union-controlled medical services, are forms of self-help organization and foster a consumer-controlled medical care system.

Mutual aid groups are organizationally often small, informal, and have little hierarchy. They assume members are active and informed. In these ways they exemplify the model of collectivist organizations as described by Rothchild-Whitt (1979). Authority rests in the group as a whole. Social control comes from peer pressure and belief in the organization's goals. Social relations are informal and collegial. Specialization is kept to a minimum, as is hierarchy. Nevertheless, there is the danger that leaders will take over the organization. One must not forget that it was from observing socialist labor parties that Robert Michel developed his Iron Law of Oligarchy.

The State Model

One of the most common approaches to health care is the state model as is found in Great Britain (a democratic example) or the People's Republic of China (an autocratic example). As Table 2 indicates, its core goal is to strengthen the state by fostering a healthy, vigorous population. In one sense, this parallels the core goal of mutual aid groups at a more impersonal, macro level. As a consequence, both take an epidemiological approach to health care, and both want to minimize costs. Both lead to emphasizing primary care, prevention, and health promotion. The fundamental differences center around power and the image of the individuals in the system. The state takes a more paternalistic and controlling role, leading perhaps to compulsory programs and forms of indoctrination. Planning and coordination of services is done centrally. From this centralization follow decisions about

Table 1.   The Mutual Aid Model of a Health Care System

Inherent Values and Goals	*To improve the health of fellow members.* To promote ties and mutual support among members. To promote democratic decision making, shared responsibility. To educate and prevent diseases. To make each member provider of care for self and others. To minimize health care costs. To be sure no major outside force (state, profession) controls the health system.
Organization	A loose federation of member groups. Administratively collegial. Egalitarian services. Emphasis on low-tech, primary care and preventive programs. Strong ties to community programs (educational, occupational, social service). Organized around epidemiological patterns of illness.
Key Institutions	Mutual Benefit associations.
Power	Local control within common rules. State and profession relatively weak; facilitative role.
Finance and Cost	Members contribute to an insurance fund which contracts with physicians and facilities for service. Cost about half the % GNP of the professional model. Doctors' share of all costs less than professional model.
Image of the Individual	Active, self-responsible, informed member of the group.
Division of Labor	Egalitarian. More teams and delegation. Fewer physicians and specialists.
Medical Education	Favor cooperative, egalitarian training of health care teams.

labor, the nature of professional education, the proportion of specialists, their distribution, and the proportion of non-physicians. The state model regards health as a source of power and freedom. By maintaining health and restoring the ill, citizens become freer and more productive (King, 1973; Heidenheimer, 1973; Lockart, 1981). The state emphasizes that health care is a cooperative venture between the state and individual citizens; for without active participation, success will be limited.

There are two variants of the state model, the democratic and autocratic approach. In the democratic model, such as found in Great Britain, power is decentralized to regional and district councils. In the autocratic model, such as found in the Soviet Union, China, and East Germany, power is concentrated in a Ministry of Health and in the central party. Professional societies play a smaller role or no role at all, and the system is used to pursue larger political goals of indoctrination and loyalty.

Under the state model, physicians and the other providers are likely to be employees on salary, or providers on a capitation payment system. The state usually runs hospitals and clinics by means of an elaborate bureaucracy. Patients are typically assigned to or choose a

Table 2.   The State Model of a Health Care System

Inherent Values and Goals	*To strengthen the state via a healthy, vigorous population.* To minimize illness via preventive medicine, public health, and patient education. To control the health care system. To minimize the cost of health care to the state. To provide good, accessible care to all sectors of the population. * To indoctrinate, through health care; and enhance loyalty to the state. * To increase the power of the state.
Organization	A national, integrated system. Administratively decentralized * (or hierarchical). Egalitarian services and recruitment patterns. Organized around primary care units. Strong ties with health programs in other social institutions. Organized around epidemiological patterns of illness.
Key Institutions	The Ministry of Health. Regional/district councils (or regional/district health officers).
Power	* State the sole power. * Professor associations prohibited. OR Tiers of representative councils. Active partnership with medical associations.
Finance and Cost	All care free, from taxes. Doctors' share of costs less.
Image of the Individual	A member of society. Thus the responsibility of the state, but also responsible to stay healthy.
Division of Labor	Proportionately fewer physicians and more nurses, etc. Fewer specialists. More middle-level providers (nurse-clinicians); more delegation; more teamwork.
Medical Education	A state system for all providers and extensive continuing education.

* features of the autocratic state model.

primary-care physician with whom they normally stay. These physicians manage their care and call in specialists when they think it necessary. The medical profession is weak, and in the pure case, the medical association is crushed or outlawed. Matters of licensure, regulation, and quality assurance are usually carried out by state officials. On the other hand, those physicians who run the system have a degree of power unknown in any other model. By the same token they and other officials of the state or party are likely to receive a special class of care. Despite these secondary effects, the system tends to be relatively inexpensive and succeeds in keeping the health of its people at a high level. All these characteristics are correlates but not necessary features of the state model that reflect its underlying values.

The Professional Model

Although we naturally think that medicine belongs to the medical profession, a coherent profession attempting to run a health care system is a twentieth century phenomenon. As Brian Abel-Smith (1976) notes, the medical profession in many other countries coalesced under the pressure of health care being organized by workers and their unions as industrialization brought larger numbers of them together. Mutual aid societies proliferated with industrialization through Austria, Switzerland, Scandinavia, and Great Britain and more sporatically elsewhere. In Great Britain there were seven million members of "friendly societies" by 1900 who received cash benefits, the services of a physician, and prescribed drugs. "Thus in these countries the consumers of medical care came to be organized before the doctors were effectively organized, and they were in a position to dictate the terms of service of the doctors whom they engaged to provide services. From being master, doctors found themselves servants of the funds" (Abel-Smith, 1976:9). The societies selected some doctors, thereby excluding others. Lay committees often handled disciplinary matters, and the societies determined renumeration. Physicians found these terms so intolerable that an international movement arose for a "free profession." A similar series of events occurred in many Latin American and European countries. Thus the professional model developed not very long ago in response to the mutual benefit model and was highly political.

The core value of the professional model is to enhance the power and effectiveness of the medical profession. From this value comes an emphasis on physician control and high quality. Economically, the professional model emphasizes fee-for-service and professional autonomy. Unlike the other two models, the professional approach focuses on the individual patient and organizes itself to be as effective and powerful as it can in responding to individual cases.

In the professional model, health is an individual responsibility and medical care is a professional responsibility. State intervention into either is considered a pernicious form of "creeping socialism." This leads to clinical thinking and case-by-case planning to address the individual treatment needs of one's patients. Thus, explicitly using medicine for social control or introducing Big Brother health indoctrination is repugnant to the values of the professional model; for it values above all the special relationship that arises when an individual patient chooses an individual physician and pays him individually. This means that health services appear in a relatively unplanned way in response to demand. The United States is the only country where, until recently, professional values had a rather free hand in shaping the organization and delivery of services.

The professional model holds that only the medical profession is qualified to educate, license, and monitor medical practice. State laws merely serve to facilitate and enforce this principle. Health care is not to get entangled in other areas such as housing, food, welfare, or employment, and ideally it should not depend on any state financing; for the hand that feeds soon controls. Thus physicians should remain free agents, taking neither salaries nor capitation payments because both of these weaken the doctor-patient relationship.

Like other professions, the medical profession values expertise. It bestows prestige and often income on the specialist and the subspecialist. Thus an entire system of institutions, financing, and politics arises to promote professional expertise. At the heart of this system are medical schools and their medical centers. Since expertise is a matter of technique and knowledge, the professional model is driven by a heavy focus on technical breakthroughs and research. These usually have a negligible or only marginal effect on the health status of a population, because they focus on esoteric problems or advanced stages of disease. Consequently, the professional model leads to expensive, hospital-based care of high quality. This focus on specialized clinical skills also means that the professional model gives public health little support. The budgets of public health departments are usually the poor stepchild of budgets for hospitals where the victims of poor public health are later treated at great expense. Medical schools under this model and the physicians they produce focus little on nutrition, pollution, preventive medicine, or oc-

Table 3.   The Professional Model of a Health Care System

Inherent Values and Goals	*To provide the best possible clinical care to every sick patient.* To develop scientific medicine to its highest level. To protect the autonomy of physicians and keep the state or others from controlling the health care system. To increase the power and wealth of the profession. To generate enthusiasm and admiration for the medical profession.
Organization	A loose federation. Administratively collegial and decentralized. Services and recuitment follow the stratification of the society. Emphasis on acute, hi-tech intervention and specialty care. Organized around hospitals and private offices. Weak ties with other social institutions. Organized around clinical cases and doctors' preferences.
Key Institutions	Physicians' associations. Autonomous physicians and hospitals.
Power	Profession the sole power. Uses state powers to enhance its own. Protests state interferences. Protests, boycotts all competing models of care.
Finance and Cost	Private payments, by individual or through private insurance plans. Doctors' share of costs more.
Image of the Individual	A private individual. Chooses how to live and when to use the medical system.
Division of Labor	Proportionately more physicians. More specialists. More individual clinical work by the physician; less delegation.
Medical Education	A private and/or autonomous system of schools with tuition. Disparate, loosely coupled continuing education.

cupational health and instead value specialized, technological interventions and hospital care.

A closer examination of the special doctor-patient relationship reveals a high value placed on individual freedom for the physician at the expense of patient autonomy. The professional model does not favor sharing information with patients, so that the relationship is highly asymmetrical and makes the patient dependent on the doctor's decisions. These decisions, in turn, produce income so that the fee system contains an inherent conflict of interest between the patient's health and the physician's income. Brian Abel-Smith (1976), in a magisterial overview of health care systems, identifies the systemic effects of fee-for-service, especially when

accompanied by coverage from health insurance. First, if physicians can charge for any fee in the book, true specialization gets watered down; for various specialists take on general patients and cases outside their area as a source of income. This pattern is widespread now in the United States and is growing rapidly (Aiken et al., 1979). Second, the quality of care declines insofar as physicians treat patients beyond or beneath their specialty training; for the best care is given by those working on problems near the peak of their abilities. In general ambulatory care, this peak is rather low because most cases are not technically complex. Third, the fee system tends to focus on specific tests and procedures, because they are easily identified for reimbursement, and it discourages listening, talking, counseling, and coordinating care. Fourth, the fee system exacerbates geographic maldistribution because a physician can come into an oversupplied area and generate new business. Finally, the fee system encourages costs to be run up at every point in the system.

The dependency fostered by the doctor-patient relationship has tended to belittle patient initiative. The political value on dependency, on technical and cultural power over the patient, has been a major source of power for the profession. Its price has been lower "compliance" with doctor's orders and therefore less effective medicine. In more recent times it has also blinded the profession from adjusting to the need for active, knowledgeable patients in managing chronic disorders and from recognizing basic cultural shifts towards self-help as reflected in the women's health movement, the gay health movement, or workers' health collectives. These the followers of the professional model have persistently opposed.

The Corporatist Model

The principle goal of the corporatist model is to counterbalance the conflicting priorities and value of consumers (mutual-aid), government (state), and providers (profession) so that the organization and financing of care can be equitably negotiated. Found in Canada, West Germany, Italy, and other countries, it binds these groups together in bargaining units that make key decisions about the health care system. The article by Theodore Marmor that follows this article provides rich detail of how a corporate approach works in Canada to control health-care costs.

In many corporatist models, as in the West German model, the government sets the rules and then umpires. It lays down rules about what decisions have to be made, what information each party must provide, and what the balance of power in the corporate body should be. Then the government steps aside and watches. When one group or another (usually the medical profession) gets too dominant, the government may step in and alter the rules to reestablish the counterbalance of powers. This approach has the advantage

of getting the government out of the business of running health care services. The corporatist model leaves that to the providers and consumers.

In order for the corporatist model to work, each of the major parties must be organized. The medical profession is already organized in professional associations, but it may have to be reorganized for the task of negotiating the system. In Germany, for example, physicians were organized into sickness fund (i.e., health insurance) associations. More important, consumers have to be organized into a coherent body. After all, they are the ones who ultimately pay the bill. Unions can play a major role in representing workers who pay premiums. Sometimes the policy holders of health insurance funds are the voice of the consumer, as if in the United States we had Blue Cross–Blue Shield Policy Holders Associations. Employers also pay premiums in most countries, and they also need to have an organized voice such as the Chamber of Commerce in the United States. Finally, the state is interested in meeting the health needs of the nation at a reasonable price, and the state can express its viewpoint by imposing budget ceilings and by laying down requirements about who must be served for what range of problems. This prevents the other groups from ignoring or short-changing the poor, the elderly, or minorities.

Given that the mutual-aid model has been used less and less in the twentieth century and lacks power against the state and professional models, given that in a number of countries like the United States people do not want a state-run system, and given that the professional model leads to very expensive care that overlooks important health needs, it is not surprising that a number of countries have turned to some variant of the corporatist model. It provides countervailing forces to the medical profession without the state taking over. It provides a legal framework for managing vested interests in the health care industry.

German Health Care: A Synthesis of Models

While it is easiest to characterize whole countries with one model or another, these models often interact within one country or have their own

Table 4. The Corporatist Model of a Health Care System

Inherent Values and Goals	*To join together employees, employers, and physicians in administering the health care system.* To minimize conflict between those served, those who provide and those who pay. To balance costs against provider.
Organization	Numerous funds by occupation and geography with administrative and negotiating boards of employees' and employers' representatives. Citizens must join a fund. Physicians and health facilities are autonomous and bargained with for services. Thus, see the Professional Model. (Other original features subject to negotiation.)
Key Institutions	Sickness fund boards and sickness fund physicians' associations. State as setter of rules and referee.
Power	Countervailing power structure subject to imbalance by one party or another. Statutory power to determine financing, mix and range of services. State as setter of rules and referee.
Finance and Cost	Employers and employees contribute premiums. Costs depend on balance of interests in negotiations. Have tended to be high due to professional dominance. Doctors' share has tended to be high because they run services and dominate negotiations, but not inherent in model.
Image of the Individual	A private individual. Chooses how to live and when to use the medical system.
Division of Labor	Physician dominated, because services run by physicians.
Medical Education	Has not been a point of focus, though model allows for it to be.

niches. In the United States, for example, the system of veterans' hospitals and the health care system for federal employees are state models even though they are islands in a larger system that follows the professional model. Likewise, some of the early health maintenance organizations (HMOs) such as Kaiser-Permanente on the West Coast are mutual-aid models. In Germany we can see these different systems in dynamic tension from the opening gun in 1883 when the German health care insurance system was formed. Bismarck initiated a series of social insurance programs to quell socialist sentiments among the burgeoning ranks of workers pouring into the factories when the industrial revolution came to Germany. It was a political response to a

sociological reality. Away from their families and villages where relatives and neighbors helped out in times of sickness, these workers were unprotected by their corporate employers when accidents and illness struck. Bismarck's goal was to establish a health care system run by the government so that workers would depend on and appreciate the state for their welfare and thus be less attached to trade unions. Although Germany had only become a nation-state as recently as 1870, Bismarck's initiative built on a Prussian tradition of state responsibility for citizens' health. Compulsory health insurance began in the eighteenth century for civil servants. By the early nineteenth century, Prussia had laws regulating provisions for health care for miners and domestic servants as well. After 1848, the state passed laws allowing municipalities to require that workers join mutual welfare funds and that employers contribute to them. "The feudal obligation of the employer to his work-people was given legislative force in a society developing national markets where the employer without an obligation to pay to a sick fund might undercut the employer who has such an obligation" (Abel-Smith, 1976:14). Two important motives were to reduce poor relief and to undermine socialist activity, but the choice of tactics is itself revealing.

For a long time, Germans have valued a strong state. Hegel took the state model to its logical end-point by arguing that individual identity and reality only come through the state. "The state is the true embodiment of mind and spirit, and only as its member does the individual share in truth, real existence and ethical status" (in Kohn, 1946:111). This view is echoed by many German writers and philosophers, and so one is not surprised to learn that Bismarck was regarded as the personification of the state (Craig, 1978, ch. 5). He seems to have assented to this opinion, which meant that serious opposition was not to be tolerated. One might say that serious opposition was a contradiction in terms. Thus he launched an attack on the Social Democratic Party and passed a law which "gave local police authorities the right to forbid the existence of clubs and organizations of any kind, including cooperative funds and publications that supported social democratic, socialist, or communist activities designed to subvert the existing political and social order" (Craig, 1978:145–146). The results were devastating. Forty-five of the forty-seven party newspapers were suppressed immediately, and all trade unions were crushed. Berlin, the seat of both socialism and the largest concentration of Jews in Europe, was put into a minor state of seige. Hatred of socialism and Jews fused in the minds of many as they would again fifty years later.

Bismarck did not succeed, because of an equally strong tradition of mutual aid. The old tradition of workers banding together and providing protection when a member was struck down by illness or accident asserted itself. Workers' sickness funds dated back to coalmine workers in the thirteenth century and spread to the guilds over the next 250 years. By the eighteenth century, they were well established and used by a numbers of labor groups (Abel-Smith, 1976, ch. 1). As Germany and other nations industrialized, this guild-like tradition was adapted by unions and sometimes employers of factory workers to suit their circumstances. Thus, in the debates over Bismarck's program for a state-run system, the distaste of both workers and employers for governmental administration combined with the vested interest of existing sickness funds to produce a national plan for health care run by the sickness funds. Employers and employees would manage the funds and negotiate with physicians for services. Preexisting funds were joined by new ones organized by locality and by occupation. Financing came from premiums; the funds have never received government subsidies. Thus Bismarck succeeded in tying workers to employers and preventing unions from taking over health care, but he failed in having the state run the system.

At first the national health insurance program grew slowly. Membership was compulsory for only manual laborers. But over the years, new legislation enlarged the circle of workers to which it applied. More important, employees paid two-thirds of the premiums and held two-thirds of the seats on the sickness fund boards. Because employers showed relatively little interest in these funds, they became worker managed. With the help of sympathetic physicians interested in workers' health and social medicine, the funds pioneered a number of efficient delivery systems, including a prototype of the ambulatory health maintenance organization (HMO) in which physicians would be hired to provide services for preestablished salaries or fees. They also created a type of preferred provider organization (PPO) in which funds would contract with a closed panel of community physicians for services. Some of the larger funds contracted with hospitals for inpatient care and even published pamphlets about health care for their members. They also used non-physician providers to hold costs down. Thus many of the programs designed to hold costs down in the United States today were pioneered by worker-run health insurance funds over sixty years ago in Germany.

As these funds matured and expanded, the German medical profession became increasingly concerned. First, the widening circle of eligible workers was beginning to cut into the patient panels of private practitioners. Second, the funds drove a hard bargain for contracted services so that physicians who worked for them received less money per case in return for guaranteed business. Third, some physicians were offended by having worker-managers administrate their services and review quality of care. It was considered unprofessional. It more deeply offended social sensibilities to have people of "low breeding" and little education overseeing educated gentlemen (Stone, 1980, ch. 3).

It is important to note that during the nineteenth century, physicians in Germany were not recognized as a profession and did not have strong organizations. They had tried many times to attain legal recognition as a profession, which under German law would guarantee them a monopoly over health care, but they had failed and were legally considered a business. Thus the medical profession had not even been mentioned in the law for health insurance, and sickness funds could hire any kind of providers they wished. Indeed they did retain a variety of non-physician providers. Gradually, one German state after another changed physicians' status from a business to a profession over the period of 1887 to 1926, but the national government did not (Stone, 1980, ch. 3). Thus, physicians found themselves the weakest party to the new sickness funds.

Around 1900, resentment against the sickness funds and the feeling that their income was declining from physician surplus and competitive contracts led physicians to create an organization more forceful than the existing medical associations. They were also disturbed that the Social Democrats were active again and calling for the nationalization of physicians into a system of free medical care. Moreover, some of the workers' funds became interested in a new system of care that would reduce the number of referrals, hospitalizations, and prescriptions by limiting them to the average of the previous three years. Other features of the system included providing on-call service outside of regular clinic hours and being on duty having a rotation system for handling weekend emergencies. In short, the system was not too different from contemporary cost-containing, case management systems being developed in the United States today. Trying out this system led to the first doctors' strike, which ended by the government intervening on the physicians' behalf. Soon thereafter, a militant doctors' union, the *Leipziger Verband* (LV) was formed and began to use strong-arm tactics. Combining doctors' strikes with boycotts to prevent workers' funds from bringing in scabs, the LV won ninety percent of its conflicts, which numbered about *two hundred doctors' strikes a year*. Within four years, half of all German physicians had joined the LV, and by its tenth anniversary over seventy percent were members. The LV also created strike funds, a job placement agency, a credit union, a widows' fund, a pension fund, and a burial fund.

Within a few short years the balance of power had shifted, and indeed one could say that physicians finally coalesced as a profession around opposition to self-managed, workers' sickness funds. Relations with the funds remained strained, and the government finally intervened in 1913 to create committees on admitting physicians to funds, writing contracts, and arbitrating conflicts which had equal representatives of physicians and funds. Subsequent conflicts and strikes led to a series of decrees in the 1920s and early 1930s which further strengthened the medical profession by creating regional associations of insurance doctors with statutory power to bargain for medical services and virtual monopoly over ambulatory care. This also meant that sickness funds could no longer bargain with individual providers, thus eliminating a major source of competition and flexibility that still plagues the health care system today. In essence, the LV had become part of the government, invested with public authority to represent all insurance physicians. Its strong, pro-physician presence is still felt in its power to place members on the executive committees of these associations (Stone, 1980, ch. 3).

Despite growing concessions to their demands, German physicians still remained discontent. The government decrees during the 1920s and early 1930s which had given them statutory powers had also strengthened the sickness funds by giving them new authority to monitor physicians' performance and by creating a capitation system. This meant that physicians were paid a fixed sum per year for all care for each patient. It put physicians at risk if they exceeded the year's budget. Moreover, some sickness funds continued to run clinics, HMOs, PPOs, and other systems of care which compromised the profession's control over ambulatory care. Medical associations took the funds to court, but the courts largely ruled in favor of the funds. It was not until the National Socialists came to power under Hitler that the profession was finally able to crush worker-run sick funds. Within a short time, physicians joined the Nazi Party in greater numbers than any other profession and charged those working with the funds of being Jewish, socialist, or communist. Hitler's emergency decrees against communists and socialists (again, perceived as never far from Jews) in 1933 read like Bismarck's Socialism Law of 1878 and had an even more devastating effect. Members of local medical societies prosecuted sickness fund physicians with such reckless zeal that many of those charged as socialist or Jewish had their cases reversed by Hitler's Minister of Labor for lack of evidence. It was a witch hunt, a moment of revenge by the majority of private physicians against the worker-run sick funds and physicians sympathetic to them. The mutual aid model was crushed by the state and the profession. By 1936, workers' programs in health care had been destroyed, physicians involved had been forbidden from practicing, and the self-management of sickness funds had been replaced by appointed administrators as part of Hitler's effort to enhance loyalty to the state through health and welfare programs (deWitt, 1978). New laws further strengthened the power of physicians, first by finally recognizing them nationally as a profession and outlawing other clinicians from practicing medicine, and second by strengthening their hand as a national bargaining unit against the various and regional sickness funds. Thus the medical profession had risen from the weakest to the strongest party within the corporate model, shaping the sick funds and their delivery system. As Deborah Stone concluded, "it seems clear from this history that the idea that the medical profession's political strength derives entirely from its special status as a profession or from its monopoly on technical expertise must be dismissed" (1980:53).

The Division of Germany After 1945

After 1945 in the Soviet occupied zone, both East German Communists and Russian advisors saw the opportunity to create a comprehensive system of social medicine that would build on the work of Johann Peter Frank, Alfred Grotjahn, and other German socialists who had had a wide influence on state models of social medicine in other countries, notably in Central and Eastern Europe (Rosen, 1979:36). The emphasis of these German pioneers on public health and preventive medicine through an integrated system of care had influenced Lenin when he created the Soviet health care system (Rosen, 1979; Kohn, 1946; Durant and Durant, 1965, 1967; Riasanovsky, 1967). The Soviets inherited a centralized state system which under the tsars had controlled medical education, the medical profession, and most hospitals for a long time; but it lacked an emphasis on public health. Faced with mass starvation and epidemics, Lenin kept central control but refocused the system towards prevention and primary care. Speaking of the typhus epidemic, Lenin said, "Comrades all attention to this problem! Either socialism conquers the lice, or the lice will conquer socialism." The Soviets set out to establish local health stations throughout the country and then coordinate them through a central health organization. At the same time they dissolved the two leading medical associations because of their resistance to socialist medicine. At the Fifth All-Russian Congress of Soviets in 1918, six principles of health care policy were laid down.

1. Health care is a responsibility of the state.
2. Health care should be available to all citizens at no direct cost to the user.
3. The proletariat occupies a preferential position in Soviet society, including its health care delivery system.
4. There should be centralized and unified administration of health care policy.
5. "Public" health depends upon active citizen involvement.

6. The primary substantive emphasis in Soviet health care is on prophylactic or preventive medicine (Leichter, 1979:211).

The Soviets moved rapidly to create a network of territorial and occupational polyclinics that provided preventive, public health, curative, and rehabilitative services. These were financed by a social insurance scheme based on the German model that initially covered workers and the poor but not peasants or the self-employed. This preference for the proletariat was also reflected in medical school admissions as part of a design to create a Marxist-oriented medical profession.

Thus the Soviets arrived in Germany fresh from the experience of developing their own health care system based to a considerable degree on German ideas. They and prominent German socialist physicians significantly altered the German health care system by integrating ambulatory and hospital care, providing free care to all, establishing regional systems of care under a central administration, developing a network of rural and urban clinics, instituting a comprehensive system of preventive care, and creating a government-run system of occupational medicine. More than East Germans would like to admit, their health care system echoes the state model which Bismarck and later Hitler tried to manifest, a direct descendent of the German political tradition that values a strong paternalistic state which looks after the welfare of its citizens and uses welfare services to bind citizens to the state.

West Germany: Professional Dominance

It is commonly observed that in the postwar period, the West German system continued the corporatist model that had developed before. While this is true, it overlooks the changing balance of countervailing powers in the corporatist model. The Allied forces were reluctant to impose any particular system on West Germany during reconstruction, but the German medical profession was not so reticent. Although West Germans were in general intent on de-Nazifying their society, the medical profession quickly mobilized to secure the gains it had won during the Nazi period and to secure laws that discouraged or prevented workers' sickness funds from governing themselves or running medical services for their members. They succeeded in prohibiting industrial physicians or public health physicians from treating patients and securing a monopoly over ambulatory care by office-based physicians. Other rules discouraged physicians from using physician extenders or creating clinics. By the 1960s, capitation had been replaced by fee-for-service, and costs escalated until the state intervened during the late 1970s to put caps on health budgets. In other ways as well, the medical profession took over the corporatist model. Specialization among physicians grew rapidly, fees focused and reinforced technical procedures, and hospitals gained an increasing proportion of the health budget.

What distinguishes the West German system from more classic cases of the professional model, such as the United States, is that all this happened within a powerful legal framework that allows imbalances to be checked. In the corporatist model, the state serves as umpire and rule-marker; so when imbalances become too great, the state intervenes or changes the rules. As professional priorities for hospital care, specialization, and fees that encourage expensive services have driven prices up, new cost containment laws have been passed to put caps on health budgets.

Comparing Differences Between East and West Germany

What difference does it make that the Communist state took over the East German system and the medical profession gained dominance over the West German system? First is a profound difference in the relation between the individual and the health care system. In West Germany, especially after the rule of Hitler, great emphasis was placed on individual rights and noninterference by the state. If people want to abuse their bodies, get sick with noncontagious diseases and not seek treatment, that is their business. The health care system is there to be used when *patients* decide to use it. In East Germany, the government believes that people's health is its responsibility and that, conversely, citizens have an obligation to the state to stay healthy. This echoes an historic view that the health of a people is a major economic resource, a view not unique to Communist societies. Great Britain, Sweden, and other democratic state systems take the same view. At a smaller level, so do a growing number of U.S. corporations such as Ford and John Deere, which act like little societies as they establish health-promotion programs and elaborate gymnasiums for their employees at the same time they develop cost-effective medical services that emphasize preventive and primary care (VanBell, 1984; Fox and Spies, 1984).

East and West Germany also differ in their concepts of illness and health care. East Germany takes an epidemiological approach while West Germany takes an individual approach. East German officials focus on the illness patterns of a community or a factory, while West Germans focus on the illnesses of an individual. This means that the West German system cannot plan or allocate resources where they are needed as easily as the East German system—a price of democracy. The concept of health is also different. The East German system defines health functionally: if you can work and take care of your affairs, you are healthy. In West Germany, as in the United States, there is an emphasis on the psychological sense of well-being: people worry about whether they are *feeling* good. Fashion magazines and soft-drink ads go further to suggest that something is wrong if you don't feel *great*. One result of this difference is that mental problems are not given much attention in East Germany. This is somewhat shared by West Germans because of shared cultural heritage that de-emphasizes mental illness. Thus, insurance coverage for psychotherapy in West Germany was recently cut to reduce health costs.

A third difference, of course, is the role of the medical profession in the two countries. In West Germany, physicians are relatively autonomous and powerful individuals, especially in ambulatory care. We have already described their growing collective power during the early twentieth century and after World War II. In East Germany, the medical profession as an autonomous association was eliminated, and physicians work for the state. Those in high office have extraordinary power, but the others serve as clinical technicians in a delivery system not shaped by professional values.

This difference leads to a fourth, the division of labor and organization of services. In East Germany, more clinical care is delegated to non-physicians, particularly nurses. There is not the strong feeling that every case must be treated by a physician for competent care to take place. The East Germans also integrated ambulatory and hospital care, and they designed a system of hospitals and clinics that has small ones at the local level, larger and more sophisticated ones at the regional level, and a few outstanding facilities for the most difficult cases. The West Germans continued the separation of ambulatory from hospital care—community physicians cannot admit patients to hospitals and do not have appointments on hospital staffs. This is as the medical societies wanted it: the community physician as gatekeeper to hospitals without competition from them. This division of turf was once proposed in the United States but turned down. Thus specialists and the outpatient departments of hospitals in the United States directly compete with general practitioners and family doctors. In West Germany, neither ambulatory care nor hospitals are particularly organized into a hierarchy of medical sophistication. Rather, as in the United States, everyone wants the "best" care when that is not possible by definition. Thus the West German system is relatively unplanned and unintegrated compared to the East German system.

A fifth important difference is prevention. The East German system is designed to prevent illness or treat it in the early stages. Thus, the East Germans have instituted a system of industrial medicine, which featured physicians inspecting factory conditions who were employed by the government rather than by the factories, medical stations for primary care located where many employees worked, and a national program to minimize illness among workers. The East Germans, again out of their ideology which emphasizes a healthy society of workers, pioneered a comprehensive program of health care for pregnant women and mothers of young children. The program includes an extensive leave of absence with full pay and a guarantee that the mother's job will be there when she returns several months after her baby is born; systematic prenatal check-ups; a regular schedule of well-baby visits for nutrition, immunizations, and medical care; and a nationwide network of infant-care facilities often located at offices and factories where the mothers work. The East Germans consider this program an excellent investment both in the mothers as part of the labor force and in the children as the next generation's healthy workers. This is one program where the West Germans have competed with and largely matched the East Germans; but in occupational health they are far behind. The East German programs in prevention also reach farther into public schools as well as into workplaces than do West German programs.

Finally, the East German system costs about half as much as the West German system as measured by the percent of GNP spent on health care, yet the measures of health are comparable. Thus, the East German system is far more efficient in keeping the nation healthy, though citizens prefer the ammenities of West German health care. This reminds one of discussions in the United States about the British health care system. It is far cheaper and more efficient than ours in getting the job done, but who would prefer it?

In conclusion, while none of these differences necessarily stem from Communist ideology, they do emanate from basically different values that guide the policies and organization of health care systems.

NOTE

This article is based on *The Impact of Political Values on Health Care: The German Experience,* by Professor Light, Alexander Schuller and others, published by the M.I.T. Press, 1985.

REFERENCES

Abel-Smith, B. 1976. *Value for Money in Health Services: A Comparative Study.* New York: St. Martin's Press.

Aiken, L. 1979. "The Contributions of Specialists to the Delivery of Primary Care: A New Perspective," *New England Journal of Medicine,* 300(24):1363–1370.

Auster, R., I. Leveson, and D. Sarachek. 1972. "The Production of Health: An Exploratory Study." Pp. 135–158 in V. Fuchs (ed.), *Essays in the Economics of Health and Medical Care.* New York: National Bureau of Economic Research.

Benham, L., and A. Benham. 1976. "The Impact of Incremental Medical Services on Health Status, 1963–1970." Pp. 217–228 in R. Andersen, J. Dravits, and O. W. Anderson (eds.), *Equity and Health Services.* Cambridge, MA: Ballinger.

Conrad, P., and J. W. Schneider. 1980. *Deviance and Medicalization: From Badness to Sickness.* St. Louis: Mosby.

Craig, G. 1978. *Germany: 1860–1945.* New York: Oxford University Press.

deWitt, T. E. J. 1978. "The Economics and Politics of Welfare in the Third Reich," *Central European History,* 11(3):256–278.

Dubos, R. 1965. *Man Adapting.* New Haven: Yale University Press.

Durant, W., and A. Durant. 1965. *The Age of Voltaire.* New York: Simon & Schuster.

Durant, W., and A. Durant. 1967. *Rousseau and Revolution.* New York: Simon & Schuster.

Eberstadt, N. 1981. "The Health Crisis in the USSR," *New York Review of Books.* (February 19):23–30.

Eckstein, H. 1960. *Pressure Group Politics: The Case of the British Medical Association.* Stanford University Press.

Fox, P. D., and J. J. Spies. 1984. "Weighing Alternative Systems." *Business and Health.* 1(3), January: 5–10.

Gray, A. M. 1982. "Inequalities and Health. The Black Report: A Summary and Comment." *International Journal of Health Services,* 12(3):349–380.

Heidenheimer, A. J. 1973. "The Politics of Public Education, Health, and Welfare in the USA and Western Europe: How Growth and Reform Potentials have Differed." *British Journal of Political Science,* 3:315–340.

King, A. 1973. "Ideas, Institutions, and the Policies of Governments: A Comparative Analysis: Parts I, II, & III." *British Journal of Political Science,* 3.

Kohn, H. 1946. *Profits and Peoples.* New York: Collier Books.

Leichter, H. N. 1979. *A Comparative Analysis to Policy Analysis: Health Care Policy and Four Nations.* New York: Cambridge University Press.

Light, D. W. 1982. "Lay Medicine and the Medical Profession: An International Perspective." Pp. 94–109 in Herder-Dorneich, P. and A. Schuller. *Spontanitat oder Ordmung: Laienmedizin gegen professionelle Systeme.* Stuttgart, Germany: Kohlhammer.

Lockhart, C. 1981. "Values and Policy Conceptions of Health Policy Elites in the United States, United Kingdom, and the Federal Republic of Germany."

Journal of Health Politics, Policy and Law, 6(1):96–119.

Marmor, T., and D. Thomas. 1971. "The Politics of Paying Physicians: The Determinants of Government Payment Methods in England, Sweden, and the United States," *International Journal of Health Services,* 71–78.

Marmor, T., and D. Thomas. 1972. "Doctors, Politics and Pay Disputes: 'Pressure Group Politics' Revisited," *British Journal of Political Science,* 2:412–442.

McKinlay, J. E., and S. B. McKinlay. 1977. "The Questionable Contribution of Medical Measures to the Decline of Mortality in the United States in the Twentieth Century," *Milbank Memorial Fund Quarterly,* 53.

McKeown, T. 1979. *The Role of Medicine: Dream, Mirage, or Nemesis?* Princeton, NJ: Princeton University Press.

Naisbett, J. 1982. *Megatrends: Ten New Directions Transforming our Lives.* New York: Warner.

Riasanovsky, N. 1967. *Nicholas I: An Official Na-tionality in Russia, 1825–1855.* Berkeley: University of California Press.

Rimlinger, G. V. 1971. *Welfare Policy and Industrialization in Europe, America, and Russia.* New York: John Wiley & Sons.

Rosen, G. 1979. "The Evolution of Social Medicine." Pp. 23–50 in H. E. Freeman, S. Lavine, and L. G. Reeder (eds.) *Handbook of Medical Sociology.* Englewood Cliffs, NJ: Prentice Hall.

Rothchild-Witt, J. 1979. "The Collectivist Organization: An Alternative to Rational-Bureaucratic Models." *American Sociological Review,* 44:509–527.

Starr, P. 1982. *The Transformation of American Medicine.* New York: Basic.

Stevens, R. 1971. *American Medicine and the Public Interest.* New Haven, CT: Yale University Press.

Stone, Deborah. 1980. The Limits of Professional Power: National Health Care in the Federal Republic of Germany. Chicago: University of Chicago Press.

VanBell, R. J. 1984. "The 'selling' of an HMO." *Business and Health.* 1(3), January: 18–20.

38

Canada's Path, America's Choices: Lessons from the Canadian Experience with National Health Insurance

Theodore R. Marmor

Medical care and national health insurance are major issues in contemporary American politics. The public is uneasy about the costs of illness and the reliability of access to medical services. Congressmen, public officials, and health pressure groups have proposed competing national health-insurance plans and have tried to estimate their effects on cost, quality, and access. An informed understanding of other national experiences with governmental health insurance would aid our policy discussion and choice. In particular, Canada's national health-insurance program, which resembles some American proposals of the last decade, can tell us much about both the impact of a new national health-insurance plan on medical care and the reactions of national policymakers and the public to this impact.

The primary purpose of Canadian national

health insurance is the elimination of financial barriers to health care. Although there has been universal government medical-hospital insurance in Canada only since 1971, a federal hospital-insurance program was enacted in the late 1950s, and a federal medical-insurance program covering physicians and related services was enacted in the mid-1960s. The provinces sequentially adopted programs meeting standards of universality, coverage, and administration, becoming eligible for federal cost sharing (roughly 50 percent) between 1966 and 1972.

Administered by the provinces with heavy federal subsidy, the Canadian system initially lacked both the appropriate means and powerful incentives to control inflation. Because of the federal subsidy, the provinces lacked sufficient incentives, particularly in the early years; because of provincial administration, the federal government lacked the means. In 1977 the federal government established upper limits on the percentage increases of hospital- and medical-care insurance costs that it would share, leaving each province the responsibility of paying costs beyond the federal subsidy. This action has apparently provided sufficient incentive for the provinces to take measures to contain costs.

Under the national insurance system, hospitals are financed on the basis of annually negotiated prospective budgets. Physicians are reimbursed on a fee-for-service basis, but these fees are determined by provincewide, negotiated uniform fee schedules. Private insurance companies are allowed to offer coverage only for various forms of additional services, such as private-room accommodation in hospitals.

Similarities and Differences

The Canadian national health-insurance experience is especially applicable when reviewing American proposals, because both Canadian society and its health-care concerns are strikingly similar to our own. The United States is closer to Canada than to any other nation in that Canadian political authority is decentralized and its tradition of dispute over federal power in some ways resembles our own. A major difference between the American and Canadian experiences, however, often put forward as problem-atic for using Canada as a "most similar system," is the greater constitutional and political independence of the Canadian provincial governments, compared to the American states. Canadian health insurance *had* to be decentralized; both the form and content of Canadian health-care legislation rest on a constitutional division of powers between the provinces and the federal government that generally reserves health care to provincial jurisdiction. If the United States chooses a centralized insurance program, on the other hand, it may have to rely more on European experience. But the greater the role the United States assigns to decentralized units, the more it can learn from the Canadian programs.

Public officials of both countries worry about the proportion of national resources going to medical care and wonder what marginal health improvement it brings. They also want to assure equal access—financially, geographically, and socially. A vocal minority in each country wants major reorganization of care, sometimes including stricter regulation of medical-care providers. After many years of expansion, both Canadians and Americans began in the 1970s to try to reduce the use of expensive hospital services and to stabilize the number of hospital beds and, to a lesser extent, physicians.

The structure of the health industry and the history of voluntary health insurance in Canada and the United States are strikingly similar. American and Canadian hospitals are largely "voluntary" and not government owned, and physicians in both are still typically paid under a fee-for-service system. The two countries adjusted similarly to the growth of health insurance, largely private at first, but increasingly more public in the postwar period.

A second major difference between the two countries lies in the divergent routes they have taken to national health insurance. Canadian national insurance began with hospital coverage, followed a decade later by full-scale coverage of physicians' charges. In contrast, the United States has been extending protection gradually to additional segments of the population, first the aged, then the poor, and perhaps in the end to everyone.[1] These historical differences should not, however, deter health-care planners from useful comparison.

Whatever the differences, Canada and the

United States, having converged at extensive insurance coverage, have faced and still do face similar choices in health care and public policy. But Canada does not constitute a laboratory for the full range of possible health-insurance programs. Two potentially important program elements have been tried less extensively in Canada than in the United States: substantial co-insurance, or deductibles, and prepaid group practice. It should thus be kept in mind that Canadian experience bears most directly on those proposals in the United States that would follow Canadian example.

Co-payment and Cost Control

Canadian and American cost curves were strikingly parallel until 1971. The trends of prices, utilization, and expenditures were similar, and the proportions of national resources spent on health were almost identical until 1971 (see Figures 1 and 2). Since 1971 medical-care expenditures have escalated more rapidly in the United States than in Canada (see Figure 3).

Some suggest that requiring patients to pay deductibles, or co-insurance, as is more common in the United States, makes them more cost-conscious. Canadian analysts are skeptical. Some modest point-of-service charges to raise revenue or discourage unnecessary use are permitted by the Canadian system, but they have proved unpopular. For most Canadians, national health insurance contains no cost sharing up to the federally mandated standards, except for drug bills in ambulatory care. To go beyond the standards of the public program (especially the ward accommodation standard for hospitalization), many Canadians purchase supplementary-coverage insurance.

Some modest co-payment was tried under Canadian Medicare—in Saskatchewan from 1968 to 1972—but its effect on total expenditures is unknown. It did, however, reduce utilization by the poor and the old. There is little evidence in Canada that co-payment reduced the "least medically necessary" care. It also inhibits initial visits more than it does those initiated by physicians. Certain commentators hold that the patient, after initial consultation, depends on the physician's judgments on treatment which are not influenced by co-payment. But co-payment

does, as the Canadian economist R. G. Evans has pointedly said, "involve perverse wealth transfers—from the ill to the healthy and, to the extent that the poor . . . are less healthy than the rich, from low-to-high-income classes."[2] Although co-payments are politically unpopular in Canada, recommendation that they be instituted still periodically pops up.

Co-payment is clearly not a dead issue in the United States. Indeed, many major national health-insurance proposals rely on co-payment for family health expenditures. American co-payment plans differ from Canadian models in two ways. First, some vary the amounts of co-payment with family income to reduce the regressive effects of fixed dollar co-payments. The major effect of co-payment under those plans would be to reduce government-program costs. But the likely supplementation of national health-insurance proposals would reduce the out-of-pocket expenditures of the middle- and upper-income groups buying supplementary insurance. The distribution of actual cost sharing with almost certain supplementation by private insurance would be sharply different from that of the formal proposals.

Second, some American national health plans use substantial patient cost sharing to limit federal program costs. Political figures are reluctant to advocate "new" federal expenditures, even if they have to mislabel mandated nongovernmental expenditures as "private health spending."

Inflation in Hospital and Physician Costs

Beginning in 1948, the Canadian National Health Grant Program financed nationwide hospital expansion. Unlike the construction program advanced in the United States under the Hill-Burton Act, the Canadian plan was specifically intended to prepare the way for national hospital insurance. Canada and the United States proceeded in the postwar period from somewhat different starting points in regard to number and costs of hospital beds; nevertheless, they experienced very similar trends through the early 1970s. In 1971 Canada had more hospital beds per capita and higher rates of hospital admissions, patient days of care, and expenditures per capita (see Figure 4).

Canada experienced a rapid increase not in hospital *use,* but in *expenditures* for hospital

Figure 1. *Expenditures on Personal Health Care in the United States and Canada,*
1953–1973 (As a percent of personal income)

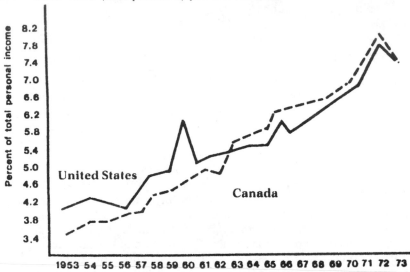

SOURCES: United States 1953–71. Uwe Reinhardt and William Branson, "Preliminary Tabulation
of Selected Comparative Statistics on the Canadian and U.S. Health Care Systems" (August
1974), mimeo; 1972–73, Minister of National Health and Welfare (Canada), *National Health
Expenditures in Canada, 1960–1973* (Ottawa, April 1975), Table 6, p. 16, Canada: 1953–71,
R. G. Evans, "Beyond the Medical Marketplace: Expenditure, Utilization and Pricing of Insured
Health Care in Canada," in *National Health Insurance: Can We Learn from Canada?* ed.
Spyros Andreopoulos (New York: John Wiley & Sons, 1975), Table 3, p. 140; 1972–73, same
as for U.S.

services. As in the United States, most of this
resulted from higher expenses per patient day,
not from increased per capita use. From 1953 to
1971, Canadian hospital expenditures per capita
(in constant dollars) increased 259 percent while
hospital patient days per capita grew by only 29
percent.[3] In turn, most of these higher costs
reflected mounting wage bills.

Evans suggested that hospital admission is not
very sensitive to price; the reduction in point-of-
service costs of care did not lead to a large
increase in utilization. If this is so, co-payment
requirements for patients will restrain neither use
nor costs and will redistribute costs only to the
hospitalized ill. Cost-sharing provisions in a
number of current U.S. national health-insurance
proposals seem questionable on this issue.

Canadian experiences becloud other cost-con-
trol methods proposed in the United States;
detailed budget-review and incentive-reimbursement schemes with global (as opposed to line)
budgeting. Canada has employed detailed budget

review since the mid-1960s, and although it is
apparently a good instrument for detecting fraud,
it fails to check expenditures alone. Some provinces have partially replaced it with global
budgets and reimbursement policies. Certain
American authorities, like Judy and Lester Lave in
their book *The Hospital Construction Act*, advocate reform of reimbursement such that hospitals
are no longer guaranteed that revenues will equal
costs regardless of their productivity. The Laves
recommend an incentive-reimbursement system
on a case basis using a formula that assures the
hospital of operating and capital costs. Deficits
would force inefficient hospitals to improve their
management, change the nature of their operations, or shut down.[4]

Our Canadian interpreters provide evidence
that such a system, however appealing theoretically, is difficult to implement. For political
reasons, poorly managed hospitals are rarely
allowed to fail: capital funds are supplied separately from operating budgets, case-mix adjust-

Figure 2. *Comparison of Trends in Hospital Sector in United States and Canada, 1961–1971*

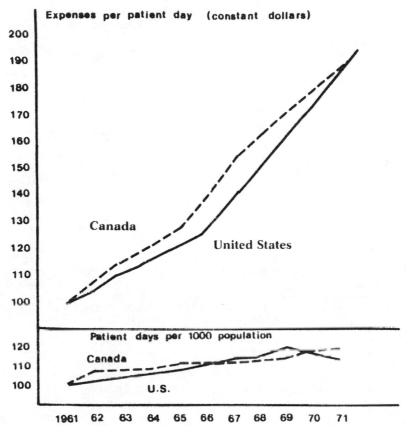

SOURCES: Unadjusted data: Uwe Reinhardt and William Branson, "Preliminary Tabulation of Selected Comparative Statistics on the Canadian and U.S. Health Care Systems" (August 1974), mimeo; U.S. price deflator (Consumer Price Index): Bureau of Labor Statistics, *Monthly Labor Review* 1961–1971. Canadian price deflator (Consumer Price Index): Statistics Canada, *Canada's Yearbook.*

ments are not well worked out, and hospital managers do not seek "profits" as strongly as they do improved services—and thereby larger budgets. However, for all of its implementation difficulties, regulation through the global budget works in a way our mode of regulation does not.

The most recent analysis of the Canadian experience indicates that through slow adjustment of a combination of management incentives and *supply* constraints, significant control of service *volume* has been achieved, and this

compensates for less success in controlling the costs of hospital services.[5] The mechanisms employed include steps to reduce the number of beds and the rate of increase in the number of physicians, a fee structure that does not favor specialists, and encouragement of performance of procedures in hospitals, where frequency controls are greater. The results are that acute hospital utilization and bed-population ratios are down, and rates of hospital manpower use per patient day are almost static.

Figure 3. *Health Expenditures as a Percent of the Gross National Product, United States and Canada*

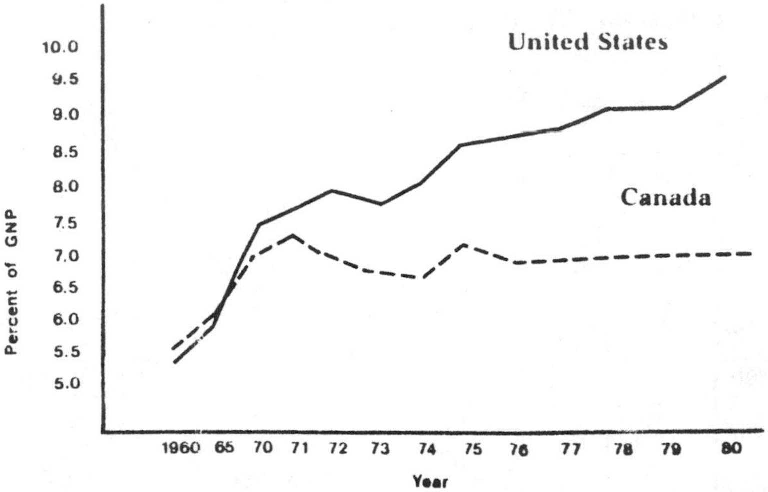

SOURCES: Department of National Health and Welfare (Canada). *National Health Expenditures in Canada, 1960–1975,* Information Systems Branch (Ottawa, January 1979); Department of National Health and Welfare (Canada), "National Health Expenditures in Canada, 1970–1978" (unpublished, provisional), Health Information Division (Ottawa, August 1980): Department of Health, Education and Welfare (United States), *Health United States, 1979,* DHEW Pub. (PHS) 80–1232 (Washington, D.C.: U.S. Government Printing Office, 1979).

National Health Insurance and Physicians' Income

Canadian experience with medical insurance is strikingly relevant to the American health-care debate in regard to important complaints about physicians' fees and incomes, about the inflationary impact of their practices, and about their maldistribution by location and speciality. One strategy that has been advanced in the United States—and embodied in several national health-insurance bills—is detailed specification of fees and peer review of the appropriateness of both the pattern and the price of care.

Canadian data on the fees and incomes of physicians raise issues of interest to the United States. Figure 5 shows that about the time medical insurance was introduced, Canadian physicians' fees started to decline sharply relative to other prices. Figure 6 illustrates, for the same period, that the real income of Canadian physicians increased. This is somewhat obscured in

Figure 6 because of the various dates when different provinces entered the Medicare (physicians' services) program. By comparing each province's first year in the program, Table 1 shows how large the impact of national health insurance really was on physician income. The average increase in net physician income (deflated by the Canadian Consumer Price Index) was more than twice as great during the transition to national health insurance as it was in the immediately previous period.

Studies in Quebec show absolutely no increase in the number of physician visits per capita after Medicare. Although comparable data are not available for other provinces, there is no reason to expect substantial differences. Thus it does not appear that the increase in physician income can be attributed to increased work loads.

Under national health insurance, Canadian fee-for-service reimbursement raised physician incomes in two main ways. The first, and the simpler, result was the reduction of bad debts

Figure 4. *Hospital Utilization—Canada and the United States, 1960–1971*

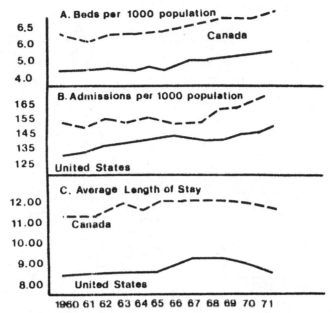

SOURCE: Uwe Reinhardt and William Branson. "Preliminary Tabulation of Selected Comparative Statistics on the Canadian and U.S. Health Care Systems" (August 1974), mimeo.

and collection expenses. The second result was the leveling up of fees, which physicians have traditionally varied somewhat according to patients' income and insurance coverage. Canada provided reimbursement at some 90 percent of established fees. Under national health insurance, physicians tried to establish their highest rates as "customary," even though those rates were not necessarily the average fee received or even the fee most frequently asked. If national health insurance reimburses at the highest rate, net earnings will increase and, just as with bad-debt reduction, will not show up as official fee increases.

There is some evidence that negotiations about fee structures and reimbursement policies are now yielding some protection from physician prerogatives to increase their income. From an all-time high in 1970, physicians' relative incomes fell steadily until 1978.[6] But this protection does not come cheap. Bitter controversies in British Columbia, Ontario, Quebec, and other provinces suggest that physician incomes will be a continuous public issue, not simply a dispute

between the profession and the government. All American discussants are prepared for controversy over the level of fees in a national health-insurance program and over variations in fees by education or location—but not over how fees should be adjusted when a government program removes the issue of bad debts and "reduced" fees completely.

Professional review of the pattern of service—"peer review"—is a heated issue among American physicians; Canadian concern about patterns of costly services that do not show up in excessive billing but do show up in extra servicing is parallel. Canadian experience suggests that claims review can weed our egregious cases of excessive and inappropriate claims, but cannot control the fee-for-service system's tendency toward increased units of care. Paradoxically, insistence on fee-for-service payment in societies like Canada and the United States actually threatens professional independence, because it implies governmental review. As Brian Abel-Smith observed, there is a paradox underlying attempts to preserve the free and independent

Figure 5. *Ratio of Physician Fees Index to the Consumer Price Index in the United States and Canada, 1957–1972 (1957=100)*

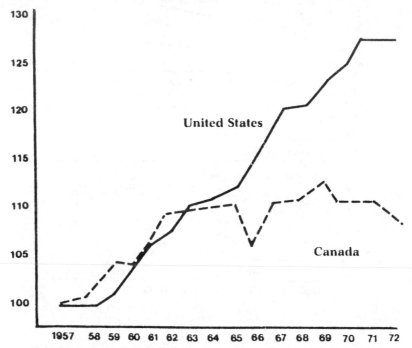

SOURCES: United States: unadjusted data, U.S. Department of Commerce, Bureau of the Census, *Statistical Abstract of the United States* (various issues); price deflator (Consumer Price Index), Bureau of Labor Statistics, *Monthly Labor Review,* (1959–1971). Canada: unadjusted data, R. G. Evans, "Beyond the Medical Marketplace: Expenditure, Utilization and Pricing of Insured Health Care in Canada," in *National Health Insurance: Can We Learn from Canada?* ed. Spyros Andreopoulos (New York: John Wiley & Sons, 1975), p. 70.

practice of medicine in that fee-for-service payment enables private free-market medicine to be combined readily with health insurance. But because there are such considerable incentives for abuse, it is not long before the insurance program's interference with medical practice becomes much greater than occurs or needs to occur when physicians are salaried employees in government service.[7]

Nevertheless, Canadian experience suggests for the United States that this mode of payment will predominate in the post-national-health-insurance world. A less punitive, more equitable form of fee-for-service regulation, not a shift to salary or capitation, is our own realistic need.

Access to Care

Some Americans still believe in training more physicians to improve their geographical distribution and to increase fee competition. What would seem to be the common sense view—that increasing the supply of physicians will either significantly improve their distribution or lower their price—is challenged by a number of Canadian commentators, and the national government fears that a saturation point for certain specialities is near or has been reached in some provinces. More physicians are practicing in underdoctored areas, but dramatic increases in the number of physicians apparently do not keep fees down. Competitive forces had been weak-

Figure 6. *Ratio of Physician Net Income to Consumer Price Index, United States and Canada, 1959–1971 (1959=100)*

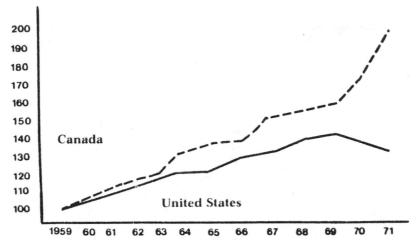

SOURCE: Uwe Reinhardt and William Branson. "Preliminary Tabulation of Selected Comparative Statistics on the Canadian and U.S. Health Care Systems" (August 1974), mimeo.

ened even before national health insurance by patients' inability to question the price or quality of services provided and their coverage by widespread private insurance.

Americans hope that the lowering of financial barriers will distribute access to care much more fairly than our present arrangements do, promoting more nearly equal medical attention to those of different races, incomes, locations, ages, and connections with physicians. The Canadian experience offers mixed results.

First, on the basis of Canada's experience, we should expect relatively modest changes in the overall utilization of hospitals and physicians. The fears that "cheap" care will foster runaway utilization thus appear unrealistic; they ignore the impact of preexistent health insurance, the barriers to care that financing will not change, and the rationing that doctors will impose. The Canadian experiment contradicts projections of sharply increased use (or crowded offices) based on estimates of the elasticity of demand for medical care in the United States.

Canadian success in redistributing access depends very much on initial expectations. The evidence suggests that national health insurance redistributed access moderately from "rich" to "poor." The R. G. Beck study of Saskatche-

wan, measuring access by the proportion of nonusers of medical care services by income class, found that nonuse by the lowest income class declined substantially, and nonuse by other income classes remained stable.[8] The study of P. E. Enterline and associates in Quebec showed not only an increase in the use of physician care by income groups under $5,000, but a decline in physician visits for income groups above $9,000 (Table 2).[9]

A 1979 report on the distributional and redistributional aspects of the Canadian health-insurance program confirmed these earlier conclusions; it concluded that after appropriate adjustment for family size and demographic factors, low-income people receive more hospital and medical care than upper-income people.[10]

More medical-care personnel are now available in poorer regions. Maurice LeClair reported that in Newfoundland the supply of medical practitioners in relation to population increased between 20 and 30 percent in the first three years of the Medicare program.[11] But there is no evidence that such redistribution took place everywhere.

Redistribution of care to the less advantaged is still a salient issue in the United States. Karen Davis has argued that equal entitlement to

Table 1. The Effect of National Health Insurance on Net Physician Earnings (Divided by the Consumer Price Index) (Percentage Change Over Two-Year Periods)

First Full Year of Participation in a Program Covering Physician Services		Period Ending with First Full Year of Province's Participation		Immediately Previous Period	
Province					
Saskatchewan	1963[a]	32.5%	(1961–63)	2.7%	(1959–61)
British Columbia	1969	5.3	(1967–69)	16.5	(1965–67)
Newfoundland	1970	26.2	(1968–70)	21.4	(1966–68)
Nova Scotia	1970	34.4	(1968–70)	21.1	(1966–68)
Ontario	1970	12.5	(1968–70)	17.0	(1966–68)
Manitoba	1970	37.1	(1968–70)	12.3	(1966–68)
Alberta	1970	10.6	(1968–70)	26.5	(1966–68)
Quebec	1971	42.1	(1969–71)	8.2	(1967–69)
Prince Edward Island	1971	60.5	(1969–71)	1.0	(1967–69)
New Brunswick	1971	26.6	(1969–71)	10.6	(1967–69)
Average		28.8%		13.7%	

SOURCE: Nominal data, from Spyros Andreopoulos, ed., *National Health Insurance: Can We Learn from Canada?* (New York: John Wiley and Sons, 1975). Price deflator (Consumer Price Index), from Statistics Canada, *Canada's Yearbook, 1972.*
[a]Saskatchewan adopted a provincial health-insurance plan before national health insurance.

Table 2. Redistributive Effects of Medicare Measured by Average Annual Visits to a Physician by Income Group Before and After Medicare, 1962–72 (in Montreal Metro Area) (Percentage Change as Increase or Decrease Over Approximately a Two-Year Period)

Income in Dollars	Average Number of Visits	Change in Visits
$0–$3,000	7.8%	18% gain
$3,000–$5,000	6.0%	9% gain
$5,000–$9,000	4.7%	no change
$9,000–$15,000	4.9%	4% loss
$15,000 and over	4.8%	9% loss
All income groups	5.0%	no change

SOURCE: Modified from Claude Castonguay, "The Quebec Experience: Effects on Accessibility," *National Health Insurance: Can We Learn from Canada?* ed. Spyros Andreopoulos (New York: John Wiley and Sons, 1975).

Medicare-program benefits has unequal results, with greater benefits for the higher-income aged, and that income-conditioned programs like Medicaid only partially redress the balance. The significant cost sharing of Medicare in the United States is probably responsible for this pattern, the implications of which Davis does not sufficiently take into account. America's better-off aged, less deterred by cost sharing, use more expensive services and buy more supplementary insurance for deductibles and co-insurance. If that is the case, and if Medicaid reduces those out-of-pocket expenditures for the poorest, one should expect that the poorest and the richest would use disproportionately larger shares of the Medicare budget. But Canadian national health insurance suggests that where out-of-pocket costs are trivial, equal benefits are associated with increasing access for the disadvantaged.

The issue of access leads to another distinction now recognized worldwide—that between health and use of medical services. The 1974 Canadian government book *A New Perspective on the Health of Canadians* emphasized that Canadians cannot expect more medical care to make them much healthier. The report has had a worldwide impact on health-care policy analysis. In the United States this argument against more medical care is raised against national health insurance itself. In Canada it arises from the removal of much inequity and anxiety by national health insurance and does not remove the rationale for insurance. The arguments for Canadian national health insurance are more financial and ethical than strictly medical. Once the fear of destitution due to illness is abolished in the United States, and the noneconomic features of access are recognized, American leaders too may well turn more enthusiastically to environmental factors for what a group of Canadian leaders recognized as the "key to better national health and reduced rates of increases in health costs."

NOTES

This chapter is adapted from T. R. Marmor and Edward Tenner, "National Health Insurance: Canada's Path, America's Choices," *Challenge* 2 (May–June 1977): 13–21. The author wishes to thank Julie Greenberg, who ably assisted at every stage of this adaptation.

1. For further discussion on the establishment of Medicare, refer to T. R. Marmor, *The Politics of Medicare* (Chicago: Aldine, 1973). Medicare as well as Medicaid and other programs are treated in T. R. Marmor and J. Morone, "Health Programs of the Kennedy-Johnson Years: An Overview," in *Toward New Human Rights: The Social Policies of the Kennedy and Johnson Administration,* ed. David Warner, (Austin, Tex.: LBJ School of Public Affairs, University of Texas, 1977), pp. 157–82. The history of Medicaid is reviewed in T. R. Marmor, "Welfare Medicare: How Success

can be a Failure," *The Yale Law Journal,* July 1976, 85:1149. National health insurance alternatives are evaluated in J. Feder, J. Holohan, and T. R. Marmor, eds., *National Health Insurance: Conflicting Goals and Policy Choices,* (Washington, D.C.: The Urban Institute, 1980).

2. M. L. McBarer, R. G. Evans, and G. L. Stoddart, *Controlling Health Care Costs by Direct Charges to Patients: Snare or Delusion?* Occasional Paper 10 (Toronto: Ontario Economic Council, 1979), p. 111.

3. The nominal data are from R. G. Evans, "Beyond the Medical Marketplace: Expenditure, Utilization and Pricing of Insured Health Care in Canada," in *National Health Insurance: Can We Learn from Canada?* ed. Spyros Andreopoulos (New York: John Wiley and Sons, 1975), pp. 138–42. The price deflator is the Canadian Consumer Price Index from Statistics Canada, *Canada's Yearbook,* 1972.

4. Judy Lave and Lester Lave, *The Hospital Construction Act* (Washington, D.C.: The American Enterprise Institute, 1974).

5. R. G. Evans, "Is Health Care Better in Canada than in the U.S.?" Paper presented at the University Consortium for Research on North America Seminar, Cambridge, Mass., Dec. 2, 1980, p. 26.

6. Ibid., p. 19.

7. Brian Abel-Smith, "Value for Money in Health Services," *Social Security Bulletin,* July 1974, 37:22.

8. R. G. Beck, "Economic Class and Access to Physician Services Under Medical Care Insurance," *International Journal of Health Services,* 1973, 3:341–55.

9. P. E. Enterline, et al., *New England Journal of Medicine,* Nov. 28, 1973, p. 289.

10. J. A. Boulet and D. W. Henderson, *Distributional and Redistributional Aspects of Government Health Insurance Programs in Canada,* Discussion Paper #146 (Ottawa: Economic Council of Canada, 1979).

11. Maurice LeClair, "The Canadian Health Care System," in Andreopoulos, *National Health Insurance,* p. 75.

39

A National Health Service: Principles and Practice

Derek Gill

It seems reasonable to assume that some restructuring of the American health care delivery system is likely in the not too distant future.[1] This is not the place to discuss the history of attempts to change the American health care system, but it is perhaps worth noting that as early as the decade preceding World War I, suggestions were emerging in American society for the introduction of the principle of health insurance established earlier by Bismarck in Germany and subsequently in Great Britain in 1911. In the Depression some political and social pressure developed to consider national health insurance for American health care delivery, but the movement had little impact. During World War II, many unions were able to bargain effectively for fringe benefits which included a variety of schemes to provide health insurance for the work force, particularly in the automobile industry. Subsequent to World War II, pressure slowly began to build up to reduce the plight of the poor and the elderly by doing something to remove the financial barrier between the poor and the elderly and medical care services. Hence, in 1965 Medicare and Medicaid were introduced to deal with the glaringly obvious problems that medical care costs presented to the elderly, the deprived, and the underprivileged.

Since 1965, there has been a growing public and political awareness of the need to alter the American medical care delivery system in order to protect the population from the often financially disastrous consequences of illness and disease. In 1973, what was basically the first form of catastrophic health insurance was introduced on a national basis. In that year the United States government made itself responsible for assuming, in large part, fiscal immunity for the cost of treatment to sufferers of end-stage renal disease. The two basic treatments for end-stage renal disease, hemodialysis and kidney transplantation, are both horrendously expensive. Persons suffering from these conditions might have to meet medical bills of up to $30,000 in any one financial year. Such enormous costs dramatically demonstrated the need for government involvement in the care of citizens suffering from this particular illness.

Although other medical treatments are comparatively less expensive, the fifteen years since the introduction of Medicare and Medicaid have been accompanied by vast increases in the cost of medical services in general. Although figures on medical costs are difficult to generate, it seems reasonable to suppose that the current average cost of an uncomplicated delivery is somewhere between $1,000 and $1,500. Hence, for example, the birth of a baby could absorb approximately 10 percent of the annual income of an American average wage earner without health insurance. It is, therefore, not surprising that both Republican and Democratic administrations have recently accepted the need to sponsor measures to ameliorate the financial burden placed on the American public by the increasing costs of medical care services.

While general agreement exists on the need for such measures, the mode of financing medical and related services generates considerable dispute. The range of solutions proposed is considerable, with most Republican legislators, and the American Medical Association, recommending an expansion of private health insurance schemes, under systems which would leave the basic structure of medical service provision in this country relatively intact. Liberal Democrats, on the other hand, including Senator Edward Kennedy and his supporters, have advocated the development of what might be described as a full-fledged national health service. Kennedy, for example, has expressed admiration for the British National Health Service. But, of course, the British system is the product of a long process of socio-historical development which reflects ideological developments and social change more or less peculiar to the British Isles and is thus not directly or wholly exportable.

Principles of a National Health Service

The concept of a *national* health service clearly implies the ideal of delivery of medical and health care services uniformly to all members of society. The concept of a national health service also implies that the quality of medical care available should be uniform across the nation. This second implication of a national health service relates to the principle of equity and further implies that medical care services should be provided in such a way that no one is barred from access to them. In general, this means the delivery of services at zero cost at point of delivery. If medical services are not "free" at point of delivery, those least able or unable to bear the cost of such services are denied equity. These principles of uniform distribution of uniform quality medical services can become truly viable only under the overarching principle of public accountability. The principle that distinguishes a national health service from all other forms of medical and health care delivery is that it is a delivery system accountable, through the body politic, to the population it serves. In practice, the degree of public accountability of a national health service may be limited, as indeed is the case in Great Britain, in relation to the profession of medicine. Nevertheless, once the principles underlying a national health service have been accepted, the functional and professional autonomy of the medical-care industry is limited, to a greater or lesser degree, by the government.

The principles of health-service universality, equity, and accountability are in a sense sequels to a political principle developed very much further in British and Continental political systems than has been the case in the United States: greater emphasis upon collectivism than upon individualism. The nations of Europe have seen the emergence of powerful collectivist Communist and socialist political parties which have had an obvious impact upon the political ideologies and social realities of European society. The establishments, the power elites in these societies, have had to respond to collectivist pressures stemming from left-wing ideologies and to come to terms with a shift towards a collectivist ethic and away from the historically dominant individualistic ideologies of the eighteenth and nineteenth centuries. The development of national health services and other reformist medical care delivery systems are the natural consequence of the gradual development of a collectivist ideology. Of course, collectivist principles do not have to predominate to influence change. Once significant components of the social, educational, economic, and political infrastructure of the social system provide at least partial support for a collectivist social philosophy, the introduction of a medical care delivery system based on the principles of universality, equity, and public accountability is more or less inevitable. The British National Health Service is only one example of this more or less "national" phenomenon. It is also evidence in Scandinavia, the East Europen Bloc countries, and to a lesser extent, in the medical care systems of the Low Countries, France and Germany.

The British National Health Service in Principle and in Practice

In countries characterized by the Western liberal-democratic tradition of representative democracy, the simplest way to achieve health-care public accountability, universality, and equity is to place in public ownership all forms of medical service provision. Once medical resources are publicly owned, they become open to public control. Given the predominance of the hospital in modern Western medical care, it is particularly important that the hospital sector be nationalized, and this is what the British government did in 1948.

Nevertheless, medicine is a powerful profession and highly effective as a political pressure group, so the extent of public control and public accountability, although theoretically absolute once medical care resources have been nationalized, is limited by the extent to which the profession and other groups and interests in the medical care industry are able to influence the body politic. Thus, although the British hospital sector was nationalized in 1948, the elite of British medicine (hospital consultants and surgeons) were permitted a limited degree of private practice. Senior hospital physicians could elect full- or part-time commitment to the National Health Service and continue taking care of private patients, and, indeed, they were permitted to utilize some beds within the National Health Service to accommodate private patients. In this sense, a private sector still persists within the British National Health Service (NHS) and insurance companies have sprung up, notably the British United Provident Association, to provide financial coverage for those who choose to pay premiums and receive part of their medical care within the private sector. The major advantage to the patient of the private sector in Britain seems to be the opportunity "to jump the queue." In parts of the country where waiting lists for elective surgery may be very long, the private patient can enter hospital for surgical care at times convenient to the consumer rather than wait upon the convenience of the system. As one might expect, the private sector in the United Kingdom is relatively small, affecting perhaps five to seven million people, but, nevertheless, it breaches the principle of equity. Those who can afford private care can be treated at their convenience and are thus able to sidestep one of the most unpleasant characteristics of the system, waiting time. Moreover, senior hospital staff have continued to do comparatively well in terms

of salary and service conditions compared with physicians in the local authority health services and general practitioners.[2]

Nevertheless the state has been able to impose a measure of control upon the medical profession. Studies of the Emergency Medical Service established during World War II revealed that many hospitals up and down the country were desperately short of consultant staffs and surgeons. The National Health Service was able to redistribute senior hospital staff by preventing the teaching hospitals and other highly prestigious secondary and tertiary care institutions from recruiting additional staff and by restricting senior appointments to hospitals in those parts of the country which had a shortage of consultant obstetricians/gynecologists, surgeons, internal medicine specialists, and so on. Some degree of control was also imposed upon the primary care sector by steps taken to influence the distribution of new recruits to general practice. The distribution of general practitioners in the National Health Service was gradually affected by a negative (as opposed to a positive) system of control. Physicians were never directed to where they might practice (positive control). Rather variations in general practitioner/population ratios in different parts of the country were assessed in such a way as to provide at least some positive incentives for general practitioners who were prepared to set up practice in under-doctored areas, as well as to limit or, indeed, even to eliminate employment possibilities in areas of the country considered adequately served or over-doctored. This latter scheme had some degree of success in improving the overall general practitioner/population ratios across the country, but its effectiveness was limited by the fact that most of the increase in the output from medical schools that occurred during the first twenty-five years of the NHS was absorbed into the shortage areas in the *hospital* sector. Hence there were fewer general practitioners available to be affected by the system of negative control in the primary care sector (1,2).

When Britain's National Health Service was first introduced, it was assumed that, while initially the expense of the service would increase, expenditure would eventually level off as the backlog of hitherto untreated disabilities was gradually eradicated. Expenditure on health care, it was felt, would soon peak, and perhaps in the long term decline as the population became more healthy. The removal of the financial barrier between doctor and patient did lead to an increase in the utilization of health services and, presumably, to higher standards of health in the population, but the costs of the NHS continued to accelerate. Today most authorities believe that the demand for health care services is virtually insatiable. Indeed the pressure of rising demand upon health care resources is becoming so great, both in terms of the increasing proportion of the gross national product allocated to the health industry and the increasing manpower demands to meet the increased use of health care services, that many national health care systems are now not only attempting to improve the efficiency of health care delivery, but also to ration the supply.

Any attempt to assess the impact of the National Health Service upon the health status of the British population is necessarily fraught with difficulty. The major improvements in the health status of the British population in the period 1850 through the early part of the twentieth century were almost certainly the consequence of improved standards of living and improved hygienic conditions stemming from public health measures of the nineteenth century, rather than the result of improvement in the medical treatment of illness and disease. In more recent years, however, biomedical knowledge and the management and treatment of a whole range of illness and disease conditions have improved dramatically. The question necessarily becomes: Has the National Health Service, whose basic systemic change was the removal of the financial barrier between the doctor and patient, been successful in enabling the general population to derive benefit from these advances in medical knowledge and technique?

The death rate per 1,000 of population in England and Wales shows very little variation between 1949 and 1971–1973, although the expectation of life for males at birth was increased from 66.3 years for the period 1948–1950 to 69.2 years for the period 1971–1973 and for females from 71.0 to 75.2 years respectively (data from Department of Health and Social Security, 1974). The mortality statistics related to reproduction show a fairly significant

decline. This decline has been accompanied by an increasing proportion of hospital confinements, until, today, virtually all women who choose to do so can be delivered in a hospital. There is no doubt that declines in perinatal and maternal mortality are due in part to the better supervision and management of pregnancy and parturition made possible because well over 90 percent of maternity cases are now delivered in the hospital. On the other hand, one cannot ignore the possibility that part of the improvement is due to a rise in the "biological efficiency" consequent upon continuing improvements in standards of living of the generations of women born during or after World War II.

There is no doubt that the standard of eye care has improved tremendously since the inception of the National Health Service. When spectacles first became available on the NHS, demand completely outstripped supply. Many people, previously unable to afford eye testing and prescriptions for spectacles, were able to receive diagnosis and treatment through the NHS.

Cartwright's representative sampling of the population indicated that the British people are very satisfied with the treatment and the care they receive in hospitals and with the services provided by their general practitioners (3,4). It is notoriously difficult, however, to interpret patients' expression of satisfaction with the services they receive since, in most instances, when they present themselves for treatment they are often under considerable stress and fearful, and alleviation of this stress and fear is itself like to generate high levels of satisfaction. Moreover, as Stimson and Webb (5) have shown, when patients are encouraged to talk about their experiences in general practice outside the surgery setting, either in groups or individually with the research workers, they are more forthcoming with critical comments. The "stories" the patients present to the research workers often depict the doctor/patient interaction in such a way as to cast a more favorable light on the patient in terms of his or her involvement in the interaction. In a sense, the patients "rewrite" the consultation episode, depicting themselves in a more active role than was actually the case, thus compensating, perhaps, for what they perceived as an imbalance of power in the doctor/patient relationship. Nevertheless, the general popularity and sense of satisfaction with the NHS are such that neither political party has attempted either to abolish or even significantly alter the basic structure of the system, and any attempt to do so would probably mean political suicide for the party involved.

In general the NHS has turned out to be a fairly successful mechanism for the provision of health care services to the British population at zero cost at point of delivery. No one in Britain need be without medical care because of financial barriers; no one has to face complete financial disaster as a result of an illness. While sickness benefits and disability pensions do not provide for a standard of living commensurate with that most fully employed people enjoy from wages or salaries, they nevertheless afford a considerable cushion against extreme impoverishment as a result of illness.

The NHS absorbs less than 6 percent of the gross national product. This is much less than either America or Canada spends on health care and is below the level of expenditure in most European countries as well. The relatively low cost of the British National Health Service is partly due to a continued maldistribution of health care resources across the country and, therefore, an inequitable inconsistency of medical care standards. Moreover, certain forms of elective surgical intervention are rationed by means of the waiting list. Even the most prestigious and powerful element of the medical profession, the hospital doctors, have had to get used to operating with limited financial resources. Even though the hospital sector absorbs the vast majority of financial resources devoted to health care, this sum is still much less than the specialists and consultants would prefer to have available. Yet, despite the apparent power and political influence of the elite of the medical profession, the state's intervention in the health care sector has continued to limit the overall cost of health care provision against the constant clamor of the leaders of the profession for more and more resources to be devoted to health care in general and to the hospital sector in particular.

This is not to say that the community and primary care services have received an adequate or even an appropriate portion of health care expenditure. These less prestigious and powerful sections of the profession have consistently been underfinanced because the state has used funds that might have been available to them to appease the leaders of the profession. Indeed, all sections of the health care professions, general practitioners, junior hospital doctors, senior consultants and surgeons, nursing staff, and support workers, from orderlies to secretaries and janitors, have complained bitterly about the rationing of financial resources to the health care sector. That a covert system of rationing of health care expenditure should have been introduced and maintained despite constant pressure from these various health care interest groups is in itself surprising.

The state's intervention into health care has in various ways limited the functional autonomy of the profession of medicine. This state of affairs owes much to the emergence of the reformist tradition in British politics in the nineteenth century, the gradual institutionalization of radicalism in the latter part of the nineteenth century and the early part of the twentieth century, and the emergence of the Labour Party as a powerful force on the British political scene. Socialism has as one of its central tenets the need to distribute scarce resources equitably and with due regard to competing social and humanitarian priorities. Medicine, therefore, has had to accept, albeit most reluctantly, the fact of competition from other forms of social expenditure aimed at improving the quality of life for the less privileged and to acknowledge that the state has the right and the duty to monitor the allocation of resources to education, welfare, transport and communication, housing—to all forms of public expenditure aimed at improving the standard of living of the population.

In recent years the financial problems of the NHS have been exacerbated by the need to pay higher salaries and wages to nursing staff, hospital ancillary workers, and junior hospital doctors. In the past, nurses were subjected to a high degree of social control both during training and subsequently. Trainees were expected to live in and were paid hardly enough to provide them with pocket money. Even after completing training, nurses were expected to live frugal lives dedicated only to duty. Hospital ancillary workers, while not subjected to similarly rigid social controls, were also poorly paid. Semi-skilled and unskilled manual workers, particularly in service industries where the units of production are relatively small (in this case hospitals), tended to lag behind in the development of an effective trade union structure, thus placing themselves in a poor bargaining position during wage negotiations with employers. However, nurses and hospital ancillary workers have, in recent years, organized much more effectively, and this has led to the generation of substantial wage and salary increases. (Junior hospital doctors have been similarly successful in extracting considerable salary increases from the NHS. Nurses and junior hospital doctors have, in short, discovered the advantages to be gained by injecting an element of traditional "trade unionism" into their professional organizations.)

These wage and salary increases have had to be paid for in overall economic circumstances in which the resources allocated to the medical sectors of society have risen only very slowly or remained static. The impact of such increases can be quite dramatic. East Anglia, for example, has been poorly provided with medical resources for many years. In 1976–1977 the region was awarded an increased annual budget in the form of development funds to improve service provision. A large portion of the funds—in the Cambridgeshire area over 50 percent—was absorbed by an increase in salaries to junior hospital doctors (6).

Recent changes in the allocation of funds across regional and area health authorities have created considerable anxiety in the ranks of the medical profession, particularly those who work in the better-endowed sectors. The elite of the profession, the senior staff of the university teaching hospitals, had become accustomed to annual budget increases. Generally speaking, funds were previously allocated on the previous year's budget, plus a little extra, depending upon the government's overall generosity towards the NHS. Consequently, the richer regions tended to maintain or even increase their share of the financial cake while the poorer regions, in real terms, had to make do with minimal-growth budgets. The Resource Allocation Working Party has now begun to change this situation. Rich regions will receive no or very limited budget increases, whereas the poorer regions will receive slightly more generous allocations. However, the pace of these changes has been very slow and is likely to remain slow in the foreseeable future.

Under these circumstances, it is not surprising that the medical profession should look to alternative sources of income for the NHS. The British Medical Association (BMA) in its evidence to the Royal Commission on the NHS (7) has advocated the reintroduction of a fee-for-service system of payment for medical services. Patients would pay physicians directly and subsequently be reimbursed by the NHS. The BMA also advocated the introduction of "hotel" charges for hospitalized patients and substantial increases in prescription charges. The assumption of the BMA is that revenues available to the NHS would be substantially increased by these proposals. However, as the Radical Statistics Health Group (8) makes clear, and as the Labour Party argues in its document, "The Right to Health" (9), these mechanisms would be administratively wasteful as well as socially expensive. If precedent is any guide and the principle of at least minimal social justice is to be preserved, exceptions would have to be introduced for the elderly, the chronically sick, children, nursing mothers, the unemployed, physically and mentally handicapped persons, etc. The administrative costs of such a scheme would clearly absorb a large proportion of the revenue so generated. Moreover, the scheme would have to be buttressed by the hateful apparatus of the means test.[3] Ample evidence already exists of the low rate of take-up of benefits and/or exemptions when both medical and social services are provided under means tests. The end result of such proposals, critics aver, would simply be to penalize the poor for their underprivileged position in society.

Where fee-for-service payment mechanisms are the predominant mode for remunerating medical doctors, the medical marketplace tends to be characterized by high physician income, especially for surgeons. In West Germany and the United States, for example, physicians' incomes may exceed the average industrial wage by a factor of six or seven (10). Some United States physicians enjoy incomes as high as $150,000 per year or higher. There is also increasing evidence from the United States that rates of surgical interventions are increased by fee-for-service payments (11).

Large increases in the NHS budget are unlikely to occur now or in the forseeable future. Public money will continue to be in short supply while the United Kingdom's economy continues to suffer from balance-of-payments problems. Increasing revenue by increasing charges to patients, if appropriate safeguards were introduced to protect the less well-off, would generate very little additional income. In the immediate future the best mechanism for increasing the resources available to the NHS is probably increased efficiency within the service, which might make available some monies for both current and capital expenditure. Attempts to improve the efficiency of the NHS will, however, almost certainly impinge upon the profession's functional autonomy, so jealously guarded by the medical establishment, if not by all physicians.

Our discussion thus far leads to the inescapable conclusion that public accountability of the profession of medicine in Britain both will and ought to increase in the future. Leading commentators such as Rudolph Klein and Margaret Stacey have been severely critical of the complaint procedures available to patients in the British National Health Service. They both feel that mechanisms for increasing the public accountability of the profession of medicine are necessary if patients' concerns over treatment and their sense of satisfaction or dissatisfaction with the health service are to be taken seriously. Klein proposes the establishment of a Council of Professions, which would operate in a manner similar to that of the Press Council. Stacey considers the possibility of establishing a government inspectorate to oversee the operation of the NHS (but assumes that this would be totally unacceptable to the profession).

The major problem, however (characteristic of the complaints procedures in both the hospital and primary care sectors), is that the persons who hear and pass judgment on complaints are not independent of the branch of the service which employs them. (This is not the case with the Health Service Commissioner, but he is specifically excluded from hearing complaints which may occur in the practice of medicine.) It

seems reasonable to suggest that the public should have the right to expose errors to independent arbitrators, if for no other reason than to ensure that the same mistake is not made again. Marx long ago and Dahrendorf (12) more recently, demonstrated that conflict, either open or institutionalized, is endemic in industrialized capitalist social systems. This being so, the wisest course would seem to be to simply recognize potential conflict situations in the NHS and introduce truly effective mechanisms to handle such disagreements—regardless of whether or not these mechanisms are seen by the medical profession as threats to its autonomy.

When a conflict does emerge between a doctor and a patient, the imbalance of power in the doctor/patient relationship places the patient at a disadvantage. A complaints procedure, if it is to be equitable, must address this problem. Community health councils may help reduce this imbalance of power by providing the patient with a knowledgeable advocate to help the patient make his complaint.

To whom should the complaint be addressed? The Health Service Commissioner (HSC), as noted above, is independent of the NHS, and a simple extension of his jurisdiction to complaints arising from clinical practice might, at first sight, seem attractive. However, the HSC and his staff are relatively remote from everyday medical practice. His staff would have to travel to the complaint area, collect evidence, hear the complaint, and make recommendations. A more efficient alternative might be to appoint tribunals in each region, chaired by a senior lawyer and including lay persons as well as physicians, but not physicians from the area in which the complaint originated. The tribunals would, of course, be independent of the NHS structure and thus ensure for both doctor and patient a fair hearing. This system would have the additional merit of being relatively familiar to the British public, since tribunals of a very similar kind exist to deal with, for example, complaints concerning allocations made by the public officials who supervise welfare supplementary benefits.

One further change needs to be introduced at the primary care level if the patients' interests are to be protected. At present, general practitioners can remove patients from their lists without having to give reason for such action. A patient who wishes to make a complaint against his doctor may be hesitant to do so if he is aware of this proviso. It seems reasonable to suggest that a general practitioner should not be allowed to remove a patient from his list without demonstrating just cause. The arbitrator in such cases might, again, be the tribunals described above.

While the changes suggested above may improve the procedures for handling complaints, they are unlikely to prove beneficial in the area of cost. On the contrary, in the short term the implementation of such a system would undoubtedly impose an additional drain on NHS funds. In the long term, however, economies of scale might be generated if experience shows that one tribunal could deal with complaints concerning both hospital and general practitioner's services. At present, two separate mechanisms are in place to deal with such complaints.

Although Stacey is pessimistic concerning her suggestion that a government inspectorate might be established for the NHS, the rudiments of a medical inspection system are to be found in the monitoring of prescription charges to which general practitioners are subjected. Tricker's proposal for improving the efficiency and capability of the Prescription Pricing Authority (PPA) by computerizing its day-to-day operation could make this monitoring system even more effective: more accurate and up-to-date information could be provided on general practitioners' prescribing habits, the rate of utilization of new drugs, etc. If these objectives were realized, then the PPA might be capable of undertaking a wider set of responsibilities.

Such additional responsibilities might introduce a higher degree of rationality into prescribing patterns by expanding even further the data base of the PPA. The lists of medicines commonly prescribed by general practitioners could be extracted from the PPA files and submitted to a panel of experts, as was done in the Sainsbury Committee's inquiry into the pharmaceutical industry and the NHS (13). The panel could be asked to identify those drugs for which there was no evidence of therapeutic effectiveness, to define minimum effective dosages, etc. This information could then be passed on to general practitioners, together with a computerized breakdown of their

own prescribing habits. GPs who persisted in irrational prescribing behavior might then have remuneration withheld for that part of their medical practice. Alternatively, a restricted list of medicines available from prescriptions by GPs might be developed, and drugs prescribed that were not on this list might be made available only when the GP stated his reasons in writing. The PPA might also be required to provide GPs with a list of generic rather than brand names commonly prescribed drugs. The local pharmacist could then fill the prescription utilizing the cheapest available generic drug in his stock. If the GP felt that a particular brand-name drug was necessary for a particular patient, he or she could so indicate on the prescription form. Experiments on the lines suggested above could be introduced for large numbers of GPs and the results analyzed by the computerized PPA system, the data assessed, and the procedure made routine for all primary care practitioners if the results were successful.

An even greater cost saving might be introduced if the rate of admissions to hospital medical wards for adverse drug reactions could be reduced from its present level of 5 percent. The feasibility of computer based information systems providing guidance on drug-drug interactions, contraindications for particular drugs used in combination, and other serious side effects has already been demonstrated, although physicians may be reluctant to utilize such systems if the procedures to be followed at the computer terminal are complicated or involve much waiting time (14). The cost of introducing computer terminals into every GP's office would probably be prohibitive, but developments in the field of mini-computers and micro-processors may eventually overcome this economic problem. A centrally located drug information system might be established, the responsibility of which would be to update on a monthly basis information derived from the pharmaceutical manufacturers, the medical journals, etc., on drug characteristics, dosages, adverse reactions, etc. If such a system were linked to a restricted list of available medications, this information could be mailed to general practitioners initially perhaps in the form of printed sheets, but ultimately in an electronic form which the GP would insert into his desk micro-processor. This suggestion may seem rather fanciful at this stage, but the rate of development in the electronics industry is so fast that such a process may soon be economically feasible.

In the large hospitals, a computer-based drug information system would be both effective and economical. Both patients and staff are concentrated in a relatively small area, and access to suitably placed terminals should not present a problem. The staff of the pharmacy could also be charged with the responsibility of making random spot checks on the medications of patients, and this information could be fed back into the computer or sent directly to the patient's physician. Physicians would then have, routinely, advice from pharmacologists about side effects, drug interactions, etc., available to them in addition to the information supplied by the computer system. Such a system might also enable hospitals to economize on drug expenses on a large scale. Recently, a California hospital experimented with such a system and reported a 10 percent drop in medication costs over a three month period (however, this report still awaits validation).

Apart from the public health movement, the practice of medicine has generally been a matter of doctor/patient interaction in a relatively isolated situation. Other parties may be present during the interaction—the son or daughter of an aged parent, the mother of a child, a husband, a wife, etc.—but the attending physician alone is responsible for the medical decisions made about the patient, even if another physician is called in as a consultant. When the body of knowledge concerning illness and disease available to the profession was limited, the fact that most medical decisions were made in relative isolation probably did not matter very much. Today the circumstances are very different. There has been a vast expansion in medico-scientific knowledge in this century, particularly since World War II. In these circumstances, physicians are less able to make informed clinical decisions based on their own isolated clinical experience and selective recall of previous cases. Currently the half-life of medical knowledge is said to be about seven years. Most modern medical care systems are beginning to introduce continuing education programs for physicians, and some countries are even beginning to establish compulsory relicensure examinations.

If the medical profession continues to insist upon individual functional autonomy—the right of each physician to exercise clinical judgment without referring to his or her peers and without making use of institutionalized mechanisms for updating his or her data base—the interests of patients will not be adequately protected. If necessary, a shift from an individualistic to a collectivist orientation must be imposed upon the medical profession.

The British General Medical Act of 1858 assured the profession a virtual monopoly in the treatment of illness and disease. Only today are the full implications of this decision being recognized. The terms of the Act of 1858 also gave responsibility to the profession for monitoring the training, licensure, and conduct of its members. Few safeguards were incorporated to protect the interests of patients. (George Bernard Shaw, reflecting on the potential misuse of the power of professional groups, suggested in the 1890s that "all professions are a conspiracy against the laity.") The intervention of the state in the British medical care system has, it has been argued, done something to redress the imbalance of power characteristic of physician/patient relationships. This is perhaps true, but it is clear that the state must continue to accept responsibility for monitoring the procedures and practices of medical doctors in order to protect the interest of patients.

While the state may be able to act indirectly as the protector of patients' rights and interests, the NHS structure provides few opportunities for the general public to have its say. For example, induction of labor has recently become a routine delivery procedure in certain parts of the country. Induction of labor attracted severe condemnation from various consumer groups and supporters of women's rights. Mrs. Jean Robinson, the chairperson of the Patients' Association, an independent pressure group funded on a shoestring, was almost alone in officially representing the concerns of women who were worried about encouraging further expansion of deliveries by induction. At least, however, certain categories of pregnant women had an advocate prepared to argue their case knowledgeably and forcefully.

In general, the mechanisms available to assist patients or patients' representatives to plead their case are relatively primitive and underdeveloped. The Community Health Councils, particularly through publication of their annual reports, may be able to expose to wider scrutiny new medical practices and procedures as they emerge. Nevertheless, direct representation of the public interest in the structure of organization of the NHS is limited. Involved in this issue are the difficult problems associated with representative v. participatory democracy and the relationship between national and local government.

The NHS has only been moderately successful in equitably redistributing medical resources across the nation. Allocation of scarce resources to the medical system, a responsibility of the central government, must be balanced against the demands of other components of the welfare state—housing, education, social services, etc. In Britain, the political system is reasonably sophisticated, and more or less centrist, with forms of socialism and conservatism competing for votes in national elections. The Parliaments that emerge out of the British political system are, however, recognizably, if marginally, different in their approach to NHS. The Conservatives generally favor the retention of concepts such as self-help, some competition, restriction of public expenditures, retention of private beds, etc. The Labour Party generally favors collective responsibility, cooperation rather than competition with the economic sector, continuing or expanding public expenditure, and the elimination of private beds. In the 1979 General Election, had the Labour Party been reelected, phase-out of private beds would probably have continued, with appropriate directions emanating from the Department of Health and Social Security (D.H.S.S.) being given to the district management teams via the various regional and local health authorities. However, the Conservatives were returned to power, and it is probable that the elimination of private beds from the NHS will be discontinued, and just possible that even more assistance will be made available to the private sector. Thus the different ideological perspectives of the two major political parties in Britain influence the day-to-day operational procedures of the NHS. Policy guidelines are devised in Parliament,

operationalized by the DHSS, and transmitted downwards through the hierarchical administrative structure for implementation at the area and district levels. These administrative procedures clearly follow the principles of representative democracy and of centralized direction and control typical of a nationally organized medical care system.

What of the principles of participatory democracy? Since the Reorganization Act of 1973, some administrative directives have been introduced which increase the participation of hospital ancillary workers in the committee structure at area and regional levels (see Figure 1). Porters, domestics, and technologists are, therefore, slightly better represented than previously. Such changes are clearly appropriate but they do little to increase general public participation in the NHS. Britain is currently grappling with proposals for devolution of political and administrative power and the NHS is unlikely to remain isolated from the growing demand for more direct participation in matters which directly affect local and regional circumstances. Consideration needs to be given to the relationships between local government and the NHS. At all three levels, regional, area, and district, it might be sensible to introduce directly elected committees to which NHS management would be answerable. The DHSS would continue to formulate policy, which would, of course, reflect national politics. In this way, the professionals and the administrators of the NHSS would be answerable to regional and local elected bodies for the way in which they interpret and implement national guidelines. Such proposals would introduce an additional level of representative democracy into the NHS, but because the catchment areas would relate to the administrative units of the regional and local health authorities, a sense of closer public involvement in the operation of the NHS might be engendered.

At the district level, further public involvement could be induced by introducing arrangements which would enable the public to be represented in the neighborhood health centers. As more and more health and social work professionals practice out of health centers, some direct public participation on their boards of management would increase the degree of participation of patients and public representatives. Such arrangement could also be gradually extended to group practices.

Public representation in NHS and accountability of the medical care system to the social system could be further improved by greater recognization of the potential benefits to be derived by the institutionalization of other groups with monitoring responsibilities. The community health councils, for example, are comprised of an interesting mixture of local-authority representatives, members of voluntary organizations, and state appointees. These councils might develop a degree of quasi-professional expertise sufficient to generate a different perspective on medical services than that held by health care professionals and the managers. Measures designed to encourage the development of differing perspectives on the role of medicine and the medical care

system in society can only serve to better protect the interests of patients and the public.

Arrangements to increase the public accountability of the profession of medicine and the medical care system take on particular significance when one considers the socio-historical origins and present development of the British health care system. In the late nineteenth and early twentieth centuries, both the political and industrial wings of the working class movement were in their early formative stages. Much more socio-historical research needs to be undertaken before these early stages can be completely understood, but it seems reasonable to hypothesize that the early phases of the development of the socialist movement tended to generate a much more radical political and social atmosphere than that which prevails in Britain today. The early socialists, and also to some degree the

Figure 1. *The Reorganized National Health Service*

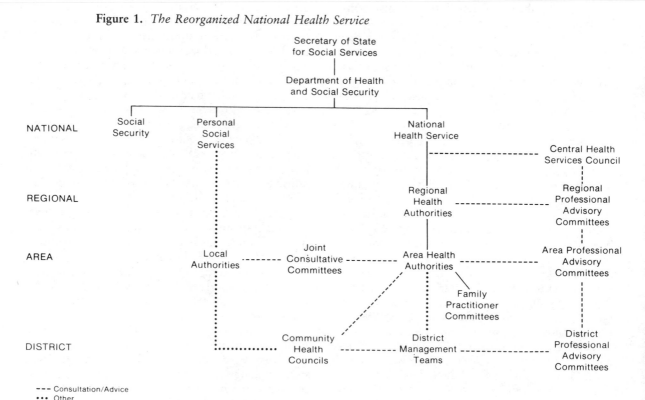

Source: Management Arrangements for the Reorganised National Health Service, HMSO, 1972.

early trade unionists, tended in their writings and public statements to challenge more directly the irrationality and exploitative nature of the capitalist infrastructure. The Labour Party today, as Dingwall (15) has suggested, tends to adopt a "social democratic" position in which basic challenges to the capitalist infrastructure of a mixed economy are underplayed. Only industries and services which cannot survive in a mixed economy are nationalized. The profitable private sector is left relatively free and uncontrolled. (As Chamberlain once remarked, "Whoever is in power in Parliament, it is the Conservatives who run the country.") Only the industrial wing of the labor movement occasionally emerges to challenge the dominant ideologies of the establishment. A recent example of this phenomenon is the National Union of Public Employees' campaign against private beds in the NHS. It is to be hoped that the trade union movement will continue to represent the interests of the working class and to continue to challenge the establishment whenever the opportunity arises. Mechanisms which generate the information upon which such challenges can be erected can help ensure that the public interest in the NHS (and elsewhere in the social fabric of British society) is protected.

But the health status of populations is affected by the general social and economic conditions which prevail in a society, even more than it is by devolution of its medical care system. Moreover, it was a professor of medical history (16) who established this fact in the British context, not a clinical specialist. This finding was dependent upon the work of epidemiologists, medical historians, and, to a lesser extent, social scientists. In the light of this new awareness of the importance of social and economic conditions, the responsibility placed upon the new specialty of community medicine which emerged out of the 1974 reorganization is truly awesome. If this specialty is to maintain the investigative tradition of epidemiologists and medical historians it must continue to take into account aspects of the social structure which impinge upon the health status of the population. Improvements in economic conditions and dietary standards might, for example, be the best method for reducing rates of infant mortality. Community medicine

under the 1973 Act is responsible for "determining the health care needs of communities and assessing the extent to which current service provision does or does not meet those needs." Poor-Law medical officers in the nineteenth century found themselves simply prescribing "medical necessities"—decent food and drink—for the sick poor. Community medicine specialties in the last quarter of the twentieth century must monitor the socio-economic conditions which determine the health status of the population—work, patterns, of leisure, diet, housing, etc. As Virchow stated long ago, "Medicine is a social science."

Application of National Health Service Principles to Medical Care in the United States

The key element in a national health service is the public ownership of medical care resources, particularly the hospital sector. This objective may seem to be a practical and political impossibility in the United States, but certain characteristics of the current United States medical system make nationalization of the hospital sector not quite so impossible as it might at first glance seem.[4] The Veterans Administration Hospital System operates rather like a small-scale national health service. Each hospital is publicly owned and staffed by public employees. Patients are treated without regard to their ability to pay.

Other similarities exist between the American and the British medical care systems. Departmental regions and the regional officers and the Health Systems Agencies (HSAs) resemble the Regional and Area Health Authorities of the English system. These administrative units are charged with the planning, development, integration, and coordination of medical services. Moreover, the parallelism may become even greater in the future. The English system of centralization, previously dominated by a strong central government authority passing on its directives to the regions, areas, and districts, was modified somewhat by the 1974 reorganization, but central control is still being attacked as too constraining. In addition, the establishment of community health councils was an attempt, however rudimentary, to involve the local public more closely in the affairs of the NHS. The looser federal structure of American government already ensures delegation of authority at the local level. Indeed this would appear to be one of the basic principles underpinning present HSA legislation. All that is required in the United States system is the strengthening of policy making at the central level, which would then set the limits within which the HSAs could adjust medical service provision to reflect the specific circumstances of their constituent communities. In this respect, the situation in America today is more advantageous than that which faced the English in 1948.

Medicare and Medicaid are somewhat reminiscent of Lloyd George's Health Insurance Act of 1911. Both introduced a degree of fiscal protection for the medically indigent, if one accepts that the elderly, because they usually live on fixed incomes and have a high rate of utilization of medical services, are actually or potentially indigent. Actually, the 1911 Act was vastly inferior to Medicare and Medicaid in that only lower-paid members of the gainfully employed were covered by Lloyd George's scheme. Medicaid and Medicare cover much wider segments of the population. Medicare and Medicaid also represent a strengthening of the collectivist ethic on the American scene, as did the introduction of what amounted to catastrophic health insurance for the sufferers of end-stage renal disease in 1973. The collectivist ethic is, as noted above, essential to the establishment and development of a national health service.

Nevertheless, it would be unrealistic to end this short essay on too optimistic a note so far as a United States national health service is concerned. The emergence of the National Health Service in Britain owed much to the development of socialist principles in the British political spectrum. While one would not want to argue that socialism and the Labour Party were solely responsible for the introduction of the present British medical care system, the gradual (but occasionally violent) development of working-class movement involving a radical shift towards a collectivist morality undoubtedly played an important part in the genesis of the NHS. Most observers would agree that America has yet to produce a viable working-class movement, let alone an effective socialist political party. Per-

haps radical reform of the American medical care industry will be impossible until the country's political system can present real ideological alternatives, real choices between left and right, to the electorate.

NOTES

1. The medical sociology seminar series of the Departments of Sociology and Family and Community Medicine at the University of Missouri-Columbia provide an opportunity for medical sociologists at the institution to present their work to graduate students and colleagues for critical review. I gratefully acknowledge the comments and suggestions of Sylvester Alubo, Ed Brent, Jim Campbell, Lisbeth Claus, Tim Diamond, Robert Hagemen, Stan Ingman, Phyllis Kultgen, Hans Mauksch, Andrew Twaddle, and Cheryl Tyree on an earlier draft of this essay. Grateful thanks are also due to Peter Conrad for editorial comments and suggestions. Most of the material presented here was originally presented in D. G. Gill, "The British Health Service: A Sociologist's Perspective," United States Department of Health, Education and Welfare, 1980.
2. In Britain, the separation of general practice and consultant (hospital sector) practice has historically been strict. Consultants have long enjoyed a higher status than practitioners, who have often been refused access to a hospital.
3. In the means test, an individual's income is closely examined by an investigator from the NHS, and specified exemption from charges is made if the income falls below a specified minimum amount.
4. I am grateful to my wife, Lucille Salarno Gill, for suggesting this line of analysis.

REFERENCES

1. Gill, D. G. *The British National Health Service: A Sociologist's Perspective*. The Fogarty International Center, U.S. Department of Health and Welfare, September, 1980.
2. Butler, J. R. *Family Doctors and Public Policy*. London: Routledge & Kegan Paul, 1973.
3. Cartwright, A. *Human Relations and Hospital Care*. London: Routledge & Kegan Paul, 1964.
4. Cartwright, A. *Patients and Their Doctors*. London: Routledge & Kegan Paul, 1967.
5. Stimson, G. and Webb, B. *Going to See the*

Doctor: The Consultation Process in General Practice. London: Routledge & Kegan Paul, 1975.

6. Heller, T. *Restructuring the Health Service.* Croom Helm, London, 1978.

7. British Medical Association. Evidence to the Royal Commission on the National Health Service. Chapter VII. Finance. *Brit. Med. J.* 7, 1977.

8. Radical Statistics Health Groups. In Defense of the N.H.S. 9, Poland St., London, 1977.

9. The Labour Party. The Right to Health. Transport House, London, 1977.

10. Reinhardt, V. Health Costs and Expenditures in West Germany and the U.S. Chapter X in *International Health Costs and Expenditures.* Ed., Teh-Wei Hu, John F. Fogarty International Center, D.H.E.W. No. (NIH) 76–1067, 1976.

11. Stroman, D. F. *The Quick Knife: Unnecessary Surgery U.S.A.* Kennikat Press, New York and London, 1979.

12. Dahrendorf, R. *Class and Class Conflict in an Industrial Society.* Routledge & Kegan Paul, London, 1949.

13. H.M.SO. Report of the Committee of Inquiry into the Relationship of the Pharmaceutical Industry with the National Health Service 1965–67. (Sainsbury Committee) Cmnd. 3410, London, 1967.

14. Mullins, P.; Laning, L.; Leonard, M.; Doll, J.; Hadidi, R.; and Raffel, G. Drug Information Services/Systems: An Historical Overview, Current Status, Need for Evaluation and Proposed Evaluation Methodology. Health Services Research Center/Health Care Technology Center, University of Missouri-Columbia, U.S.A. 1978.

15. Dingwall, R. Inequality and the National Health Service. In *Essays on the N.H.S.* Eds., Atkinson, P.; Dingwall, R.; and Mucott, A. Croom Helm, London, 1979.

16. McKeown, T. *The Role of Medicare: Dream, Mirage, or Nemesis.* The Nuffield Provincial Hospital Trust. London, 1976.

Prevention and Society

Prevention is a watchword for health in the 1980s. A number of factors contribute to the renewed interest in prevention. While a few fresh concepts have emerged (e.g., focus on "lifestyle's" effect on health) and a few new discoveries have been made (e.g., relating hypertension to heart disease), the current attention paid to prevention has not been spurred by scientific break-throughs. Rather it is primarily a response to the situations described in this book: the dominant sick care orientation of the medical profession; the increase in chronic illness; the continuing uncontrolled escalation of costs; and the influence of third-party payers. And prevention efforts are going beyond the medical profession. Insurance companies give rate reductions to individuals with healthy lifestyles (e.g., nonsmokers) and numerous major corporations are introducing worksite "wellness" and health promotion programs. This new prevention orientation is occurring in a cultural environment that has become sensitized to various forms of health promotion including health foods, health clubs, jogging and exercise.

There is little doubt that if we are serious about reorienting our approach to health from "cure" to prevention of illness, medicine must become more of a "social science." Illness and disease are socially as well as biophysiologically produced. For over a century, under the reign of the germ-theory "medical model," medical research searched for specific etiologies (e.g., germs or viruses) of specific diseases. With the present predominance of chronic disease in American society, the limitations of this viewpoint are becoming apparent. If we push our etiological analysis far enough, as often as not we come to sociological factors as primary causes. We must investigate environments, lifestyles, and social structures in our search for etiological factors of disease with the same commitment and zeal we investigate bodily systems and begin to conceptualize preventive measures on the societal level as well as the biophysical. This is not to say that we should ignore or jettison established biomedical knowledge; rather, we need to focus on the production of disease in the interaction of social environments and human physiology.

The Surgeon General's report on disease prevention and health promotion titled *Healthy People* (1979) took steps in this direction. The report recognizes the "limitations of modern medicine" and highlights the importance of behavioral and social factors for health. It de-emphasizes the role of physicians in controlling health activities and argues persuasively for the need to turn from "sick care" to prevention. Most significantly, the report officially legitimatizes the centrality of social and behavioral factors in caring for our health. It argues that people must take responsibility for changing disease-producing conditions and take positive steps toward good health. In some circles, *Healthy People* was deemed a revolutionary report, more significant even than the 1964 Surgeon General's report on smoking. The fact, however, that most people have not yet heard about this 1979 report, much less are familiar with what it says, raises some questions about its potential impact on health behavior.

Yet from a sociological perspective the report is also something of a disappointment. While social and behavioral factors are depicted as central in causation and prevention of ill health, a close reading shows that most of these factors are little more than "healthy habits." The report exhorts people to adopt better diets, with more whole grains and less red meat, sugar, and salt; to stop smoking; to exercise regularly; to keep weight down; to seek proper prenatal and postnatal care; and so forth. While these things are surely important to prevention of illness, we must today conceptualize prevention more broadly and as involving at least three levels; medical, behavioral, and structural (see Table 1). Simply, medical prevention is directed at the individual's body; behavioral prevention is directed at changing people's behavior; and structural prevention is directed at changing the society or environments in which people work and live.

Healthy People urges us to prevent disease on a behavioral level. While this is undoubtedly a useful level of prevention, some problems remain. For example, social scientists have very little knowledge about *how* to change people's (healthy or unhealthy) habits. The report encourages patient and health education as a solution, but clearly this is not sufficient. Most people are aware of the health risks of smoking or not wearing seat belts, yet roughly 30 percent of Americans smoke and 80 percent don't regularly use their seat belts. Sometimes individual habits are responses to complex social situations, such as smoking as a coping response to stressful and alienating work environments. Behavioral approaches focus on the individual and place the entire burden of change on the individual. Individuals who do not or

Table 1. Conceptualization of Prevention

Level of Prevention	Type of Intervention	Place of Intervention	Examples of Intervention
Medical	Biophysiological	Individual's body	Vaccinations; early diagnosis; medical intervention.
Behavioral	Psychological (and Social Psychological)	Individual's behavior and lifestyle	Change habits or behavior (e.g., eat better, stop smoking, exercise, wear seat belts); learn appropriate coping mechanisms (e.g., meditation).
Structural	Sociological (social and political)	Social structure, systems, environments	Legislate controls on nutritional values of food; change work environment; reduce pollution; floridate water supplies.

cannot change their unhealthy habits are often seen merely as "at risk" or noncompliant patients, another form of the blame-the-victim response to health problems. *Healthy People* rarely discusses the structural level of causation and intervention. It hardly touches on significant social structural variables such as gender, race, and class and is strangely silent about the corporate aspects of prevention (Conrad and Schlesinger, 1980).

In "The Politics of Prevention," Rosemary C. R. Taylor examines the social origins of the current lifestyle or behavioral ideology of prevention (recall the Fuchs and the Knowles articles in this volume). She analyzes how a consensus is forged supporting individual rather than social forms of prevention and how this is related to rising medical costs. Clearly promotion of these alternative prevention policies will focus intervention and affect outcomes differently. While Taylor does not specifically promote a form of prevention, she outlines the limitations of a strategy that is widely hailed as an important alternative.

John McKinlay, in our final article, "A Case for Refocussing Upstream: The Political Economy of Illness," argues that we need to change the way we think about prevention and start to "refocus upstream," beyond healthy habits to the structure of society. He suggests we should concentrate on and investigate political-economic aspects of disease causation and prevention, and in particular "the manufacturers of illness." McKinlay singles out the food industry as a major manufacturer of illness. However, the major contribution of his article is to go beyond the conventional view of prevention as a biomedical or lifestyle problem to a conceptualization of prevention as a socio-economic issue.

Prevention can be a key alternative to our health care dilemma when it focuses at least as directly on the structural as on the behavioral level of intervention.

REFERENCES

Conrad, Peter and Lynn Schlesinger. 1980. "Beyond healthy habits: Society and the pursuit of health." Unpublished manuscript.

U.S. Department of Health, Education and Welfare. 1979. Healthy People: The Surgeon General's Report on Health Promotion and Disease Prevention. Washington D.C.: U.S. Government Printing Office.

40

The Politics of Prevention

Rosemary C. R. Taylor

Prevention is the new catchword in American health care policy. What it will mean in practice in the long run, however, is the subject of an important political struggle. Increasingly, preventive strategies are being shaped by an ideology that attributes to individuals the responsibility for their own health and well-being. It is an ideology that has captured the American imagination in the last five years even though the activities it generates—jogging and exercise programs, anti-smoking campaigns and changes in diet—may be largely confined to the middle class. This article analyzes the emergence in the late seventies of the prevailing consensus about the appropriate content of a prevention policy in the United States. This policy has been constructed, in part, by a particular heterogeneous social coalition, which I shall describe. The material interests of certain historical actors do not fully explain why the assumptions about the etiology of disease that inform current preventive policy have come to constitute the dominant interpretation of social reality for Americans. Elsewhere, I explore more thoroughly the relationship between policy developments and popular beliefs (Taylor, 1981). I argue that the ideology of prevention currently adopted by the state is so widely accepted because it is congruent with changes in other cultural ideals, because it is promoted by the organization of American medical care, and because it effectively translates, for many people, their subjective experience of the relationship between their health and aspects of their everyday life. Here, I concentrate on the question of how one version of prevention has come to shape the state's health-related funding decisions and policy initiatives.

First it must be explained how any version of prevention could have assumed such importance in political debate. After all, it was not so long ago that most critics bemoaned the fact that high-technology medicine received the lion's share of resources for health care, while preventing disease was a strategy ritualistically alluded to but rarely funded to any substantial degree. To many, the roots of the new enthusiasm for prevention seem self-evident: it has been demonstrated beyond doubt that medicine is a relatively minor influence on health. The best estimates are that the medical system (doctors, drugs, hospitals) affects about 10 percent of the usual indices for measuring health.... The remaining 90 percent are determined by factors over which doctors have little or no control, from individual life-style (smoking, exercise, worry), to social conditions (income, eating habits, physiological inheritance), to the physical environment (air and water quality). (Wildavsky, 1977)

If medical care has such little effect, adherents of this argument imply, we should be spending money and energy on the things that do affect our health—namely, preventive measures.

When the relationship between health and health care was questioned in this way, it fueled concern about the cost of the latter. Avoidable sickness, it was argued, was costing the nation too much and contributing to an alarming inflation rate and a shaky economy. In 1950, funding of health expenditures accounted for 4 percent of total federal expenditures. This ratio increased to 8.6 percent in 1970, 10.4 percent in 1975, and 12 percent in 1979 (Freeland and Schendler, 1981). The high cost of hospitalization—the major contributor to spiraling expenditures—has not been absorbed by insurance, and so the social cost has been increased and the poor distribution of resources exacerbated. Low-income groups have not been the only ones to protest. Large corporations turn a jaundiced eye toward medical costs, as the size of the fringe benefits they have to pay to unionized workers assumes an even greater proportion of their wage bill. Prevention, in this view, is a necessity to hold the medical cost crisis in check.

A variety of solutions has been proposed to deal with the dual problem of a health care system that is both too expensive and no longer markedly effective in promoting improvements in health levels. For rising costs, regulation of different degrees of sophistication was the favorite remedy of the late seventies. President Carter tried and failed to impose a ceiling on hospital expenditure. Other measures attempted to curtail the prerogatives of doctors. President Reagan introduced competition as the panacea of the eighties. Cutting back all social services has become a politically viable strategy and is activated in the health care system by denying Medicaid to former recipients and by closing municipal hospitals. Consumers, too, come in for their share of the blame, and it is on the question of consumer attitudes that the critics of both cost and efficacy can join forces. Consumers should become more cost-conscious, say the policy makers who are concerned about the self-indulgence of the worried well. Patients should take action themselves before they are forced to turn to ineffective health care services that may prove positively harmful to them in the long run, say the critics of modern medicine. Both propositions fall under the umbrella remedy of prevention, but there agreement ends.

While most critics agree that prevention is a good thing, they interpret the term in different ways. Disagreements are inevitable because they stem from two underlying theories about the causes of illness in contemporary society that are incompatible. For some, modern disease can be largely attributed to the stress of life and the nature of work under capitalism (Eyer and

Sterling, 1977), and to more specific environmental threats such as air pollution, carcinogenic chemicals, food additives, and industrial accidents. Prevention, then, entails far-reaching social reforms. The etiological theories that convince others focus on individual behavior. The diseases of civilization—cancer, heart disease, and stroke—are diseases of affluence, according to this view. People eat too much, drink too much, don't take exercise, and kill themselves by driving recklessly. Prevention in these terms means persuading individuals, through education or sanctions, to change their self-destructive habits.

The meaning of a prevention policy has thus been a matter of contention in the political arena. Historically, each theoretical orientation toward disease and prevention (let us call them social and individualist) has been predominant during different periods in the United States. But recently the emphasis on individual behavior has garnered more political support than efforts to tackle the social determinants of disease. Under the Reagan Administration, pressure by food manufacturers has all but killed congressional efforts to require the industry to include sodium content on food labels, the Clean Air and Clean Water Acts have been attacked, and both the Occupational Safety and Health Act/Administration (OSHA) and the Environmental Protection Agency (EPA) have been seriously weakened by cuts. Meanwhile, the office for Disease Prevention and Health Promotion, which is one of the few health-related agencies to escape the Reagan cuts this year, concentrates exclusively on life-style issues.

How can one explain the success of the individualist appeal? I shall consider three explanations, two of which are widely accepted as fact in different political circles. According to the first, scientific research has demonstrated beyond reasonable doubt that damaging life-styles are behind the modern epidemics of cancer, heart disease, and stroke. "The recognition that adult chronic disease risk factors can be easily identified in childhood, and that they are largely the result of life-style habits (i.e., cigarette smoking, poor eating habits, and lack of exercise) acquired early in life, has led many to the conclusion that the primary prevention of chronic disease must begin with children," argues an article in the

Journal of Chronic Diseases (Williams et al. 1979). In the course of a more polemical argument, Whelan claims that "the parts of the cancer causation puzzle now assembled point directly to the harmful aspects of our individual habits, particularly cigarette smoking and dietary excesses" (Whelan, 1979). When it is acknowledged that environmental or occupational factors may be responsible for a certain percentage of deaths, pragmatism is cited as the reason to concentrate on life-styles: social reconstruction is unrealistic and expensive.

Advocates of the second explanation (for example, Salmon and Berliner, 1979) argue that particular actors—usually industry and government—stand to benefit, both ideologically and financially, from such measures as cost-sharing insurance plans that emphasize the necessity of changing personal habits. They stand to lose a great deal from analyses indicating the importance of social factors that might encourage political efforts to impose new restrictions on capital. The national emphasis on individual restraint and self-help, according to this interpretation, has been publicized, if not actually generated, by corporations under attack for the occupational and environmental hazards they promote. These corporations, says Crawford, "must seek new ways to blunt the efforts of the new health activists and to shift the burden of responsibility for health away from their doorstep" (Crawford, 1979).

Finally, Renaud has argued in a provocative paper that state intervention in the field of health care will inevitably ignore social influences on health. There are "structural constraints which preselect the issues to which the state in capitalist societies is capable of responding" (Renaud, 1975). The first and easiest option for the state will be to blame individuals for their own bad health. But one must not look to the "Machiavellian wills of some powerful individuals or groups under the control of some medical empire" (Renaud, 1975) to explain the limits to state action. It is, rather, the result of the "deeply embedded and camouflaged logic of the capitalist social order in health."

None of these explanations provide a satisfactory account of changes in health care policies concerning prevention. Research findings about the connection between life-style factors and the chronic diseases are far from conclusive. "The base of information for prevention is still imperfect," argues a recent article in *The Lancet:*

> To give a specific example, there is a well-established relation between a high incidence of coronary artery disease and a life-style which includes heavy smoking and drinking, lack of exercise, overeating, and (much more dubiously) "stress," whatever that means. But within that package, we know little of the relative importance of the various factors, and possibly no single one of them is as important as a family history of coronary artery disease (about which nothing can be done). . . . (Black, 1982)

Smoking is widely acknowledged as a significant cause of lung cancer, although adherents of the social approach argue that focusing on smokers' self-destructive behavior downplays the political and economic obstacles to antismoking campaigns such as the revenues to federal, state, and local governments from tobacco taxes. The relationship between other life-style factors and cancer causation is contested (Epstein and Swartz, 1981). Moreover, the argument that the empirical findings of science accumulate and gradually yield a body of data that persuades policy makers of the necessity for individual-focused preventive measures ignores what we know of their social construction. Much of the data now being heralded as conclusive proof of the self-destructiveness of human habits is not new. What we need to account for is the "discovery" of this knowledge and the way it has been used.

Blaming corporate pressure for the individualist approach is also unsatisfactory. Theoretically this argument is based on a view of the state as a simple instrument of capital, and of ideas as the direct reflection of capital's interests. It is also not clear that costs could be controlled or that corporations would gain substantially from preventive measures of this kind. Holtzman has argued, for example, that in times like the present when unemployment is high,

> it might even be argued that with labor in plentiful supply, there is little incentive to improve the health of potential workers. As the demand for skilled labor diminishes, it may not cost too much to train a

replacement for a worker who dies prematurely or who becomes disabled. Companies could even save money by premature deaths; long disability and retirement payments would be reduced. (Holtzman, 1979)

Politically such an explanation is also problematic, because it essentially dismisses many of the "preventive" alternatives in the health care field—self-help groups, holistic health advocates and practitioners—as the peddlers of reformism and the victims of co-optation. It overlooks the genuinely progressive movements of the 1960s and 1970s within health care to demystify medicine and encourage patients to rely on their own resources.

While Renaud is careful not to allocate blame for restrictive state intervention and preventive policies to specific individuals or groups, he does not cast much light on the politics of policy development. Politics, in fact, almost disappears from his account. His emphasis on the overall tendency of capitalism to turn health needs into a commodity leads him to omit the details of that process. While he does admit the possibility of the emergence of class struggle and thus partial reform—"timid efforts . . . to partially implement a new, more preventive and more community-oriented medicine" (Renaud, 1975) under particular historical conditions—it remains for others to spell out those political and economic circumstances.

I suggest that the prevailing ideology of prevention must be understood within a broader framework than perspectives stressing the autonomy of science, the exclusive influence of industry, or the logic of capitalism will allow. Policy decisions take place within a shared cognitive understanding of a problem and its causes. We need to understand how a consensus was forged at the level of national policy on the advisability of the individualist approach. To disentangle the theoretical and intuitive bases of the viewpoints espoused by legislators, physicians, and corporate managers among others, we must examine the social relations and the economic constraints that make those theories plausible to the various actors. Medicine, for example, is a system of relationships involving, at the minimum, client and physician. Preventive strategies used in practice must therefore stem to some extent from

the contemporary requirements of the doctor/patient relationship (Rosenberg, 1979). Having clarified what it is about the social situations of different groups that leads them to adopt different theories about the etiology of chronic diseases, I argue that the apparent consensus about the appropriateness of individual-focused preventive measures emerges from a political struggle. Advocates for the social approach exist, but they currently have little influence on policy decisions.

Costs and Benefits: Capital and Labor

Bernard Kramer, in a 1977 *American Journal of Public Health* editorial, reflects on the reasons for the antagonism directed at antismoking campaigns (and many other attempts at public intervention on behalf of the public's health). He concludes that in a time of austerity people may have become increasingly responsive to "corporate foot-dragging with respect to public-health measures" (Kramer, 1977). I suggest that although capital in the United States may be opposed to certain preventive measures, it has seized on others with enthusiasm.

Large American corporations with a highly unionized work force are worried that their health care costs have become a significant business expense: "Second only to energy costs, their expenditures for health care are rising more rapidly than any other factor in the cost of industrial products" (Gifford and Anlyan, 1979). Physicians, according to *Forbes,* don't recognize "the depths of concern on the part of those paying the bills—and that is business" ("Physician Heal Thyself" 1977). But health care, asserts General Motors, is an expensive proposition not just for the corporations directly affected: such costs added $175 to the cost of every car and truck built by GM in 1976 (Burns, 1977). By 1980, spurred on by information from the President's Council of Physical Fitness that premature deaths cost American industry more than $25 billion and 132 million workdays of lost production annually, Xerox, Exxon, Pepsico, General Foods, and North American Rockwell have developed extensive physical fitness programs for employees (Lowery, 1980).

At first glance, it would seem that industry should try anything and everything currently being marketed as "prevention." If illnesses were to be prevented, detected earlier, and treated wisely when they proved to be chronic conditions, surely less would be paid out in employee health benefits, and so group health insurance premiums for companies would go down. It turns out, however, that prevention may be the new watchword in corporate benefit plans, although corporations are more interested in certain kinds of health hazards and certain kinds of sick workers than others. The bulk of corporate advertising regarding ill health and destructive lifestyles has concentrated on executives and their vulnerability to heart attacks. A personnel director interviewed by *Harvard Business Review* makes clear why. "Our experience indicates that the cost of a heart attack or heart failure ranges from a minimum of three times an executive's annual salary to millions, depending on the severity of the illness and his role in the corporate structure." "Think of the cost," the article urges, "hospital and physician's fees, disability compensation, work loss, life insurance, and other rehabilitation costs or replacement costs" (White, 1978).

Recent work, however, suggests that the image of the driven executive—miserable in spite of his power, money, and prestige, overstressed, and unable to relax—is largely a myth. Several studies have shown that executives actually have fewer heart attacks than blue-collar workers and that their mortality rate ranges from 30 percent to 10 percent lower than that of the general population. A survey of the working and living habits of 2,000 executives in the New York City area concludes, "The great bulk of executives—87 percent—cope well with their jobs, have better than average health habits, are not dismayed by the pressures of business" (Boroson, 1978). Why then does the myth persist that executives run a special risk from the pressures of an increasingly stressful work life, and why are companies so willing to subsidize preventive measures for a reasonably healthy group among their workers? One answer is certainly that they see executives as more valuable workers who need to be nurtured with more care. "There is no provision in the federal income-tax law," asserts

one analyst advocating the benefits of a tax-deductible medical reimbursement plan, "which prevents the corporate employer from discriminating in favor of, and limiting the health and medical care benefits to, the officers, executives, supervisors, and other highly paid employees" (Bartz, 1977).

There is also a second answer to the paradox. By focusing on heart disease as the real threat to workers' health and by promoting the relatively low-cost strategies required to foster preventive care in this area, companies direct attention away from those diseases that claim as many lives but that affect "less valuable" workers and are potentially more expensive to alleviate. An estimated 100,000 workers die each year, according to OSHA, and three or four times that number are disabled, as a result of occupational disease (illnesses attributable to new chemicals being introduced into industrial products and processes, as opposed to workplace accidents, which occur at a rate of 2,000 a month). But corporations rarely mention the threat of industrial accidents or cancer in their new-found zeal for prevention. In fact, they are currently engaged in disputing the figures and the measures of federal agencies like EPA, OSHA, the Consumer Product Safety Commission (CPSC), and the United States Department of Agriculture (USDA), which are promulgating regulations to protect workers and consumers from these hazards.

Recent political developments have woven a new strand in corporate ideology. The techniques employed in the ongoing battle with government regulatory agencies have definitively shaped the emerging industry-wide imagery about disease patterns and their etiology. The core of these techniques is cost-benefit analysis, which, as David Noble (1980) has documented, lies at the heart of the petrochemical industry's efforts to fight the recent health and environmental challenge to its activities. Its demand that regulating agencies pay greater attention to the economic costs of regulation and that they adopt formal quantitative procedures for estimating and comparing the costs and benefits of alternative actions has been successful. Noble reports that regulatory agencies are now "clogged with reports, studies, consultants, and procedural motions," regulators have been hamstrung by "mathematical gymnastics" and the basic policy questions have been obscured. Above all, the appeal of the chemical industry to risk-accounting methods has generated a new political rhetoric: life is inescapably risky, and the acknowledged risk of cancer from some of its products is to be put "in perspective," compared with other risks and balanced against product benefits. The net result is to trivialize concern with carcinogens in the workplace.

Unions continue to pressure management over a wide range of occupational health issues. Petrochemical workers have pressed for investigations into the high incidence of brain cancer among them; miners have fought efforts to reduce fines for mine safety violations. But in a period of economic recession, when many unions are more concerned with the threat of widespread layoffs and plant closings, occupational health and safety problems must often take second place. In this context it becomes plausible for companies to focus on the vulnerability of a few executives to heart attacks, to indict unhealthy life-styles, and to place the burden of health squarely on workers and consumers.

Corporate profits, however, are affected by more than the growth of the social wage and the threat of stiffer pollution and safety standards. Perhaps the most chronic worry for many American corporations in the seventies has been productivity, which, they believe, has been adversely affected by absenteeism. In accounting for their absence from work, American workers reported that illness and injury kept them off the job twice as often as personal and civic reasons. From 1973 to 1976, illness and injury accounted for about three-fourths of all hours lost in manufacturing (Hedges, 1977). Absenteeism statistics probably do not accurately reflect social and medical reality. Employees stay away from work on occasion because it is boring. Nevertheless, many corporations are coming to agree with the president of Blue Cross in Wisconsin who worked with Kimberley-Clark to set up a health maintenance program for its salaried employees, the entire cost of which was paid by the firm. "Preventive medicine has enormous potential dividends of greater health and happiness, lower medical costs, and increased productivity," he declared, and the proposition is increasingly reflected in business publications ("Kimberley-

Clark," *Paper Trade Journal*, 1977). Healthy workers, they assert, are happier, more efficient workers. Preventive programs can reduce turnover, sick leave, and workers' compensation payments, improve productivity, and prevent unionization (Fields, 1978; Wright, 1978; Pritchett, 1977).

The insurance industry has concurred with and encouraged this trend, which has become even more attractive with the current recession. "Until the recent financial squeeze, insurers of health had little to worry about other than competition between companies and regulation by government," argues an insurance publication. But now, "squeezed financially and facing a crisis of credibility, the providers of health care are no longer considered infallible, the doctor is no longer God, and we, the insurers, are on the spot" (Melcher, 1981). Efforts to restrain costs have focused on the wrong things—"the supply side of the health economics equation." The solution is to focus on the demand side, a demand generated by a growing and aging population. Insurance recognizes that higher costs won't reduce demand because "that demand is driven by mortal fear" (Maher, 1981). Prevention is the logical way to break the cycle of spiraling costs: "The next step is ours, not the government's. We must find a way to package, market, sell, and make money on wellness" (Melcher, 1981). And wellness, as Blue Cross and Blue Shield have advertised for some time, comes from helping yourself since "you, the individual, are in control of the major risk factors" for most chronic diseases.

The preventive strategies of individual companies will doubtless vary, conditioned by the status of the economy, the character of their work force, and the particular brand of risk accounting that they adopt in making their calculations. However, from the character of the programs that now exist, one can predict that they will all be inspired by a restrictive individualist version of prevention. Perhaps the most persuasive evidence for this claim comes from the proceedings of the National Conference on Health Promotion Programs in Occupational Settings sponsored by the Department of Health, Education, and Welfare in 1979. Representatives from industry, unions, insurance companies, and the scientific community discussed ideal approaches to health promotion programs in the workplace. All the "risk reduction components" dealt with factors that individuals could be motivated to change in some way. Most striking is the discussion of "stress management," the component most likely to indicate the part played by larger environmental and occupational hazards in illness. While acknowledging that "studies have suggested an association between environmental stress and disease . . . it must be recognized," continues the report,

> that it is a combination of factors within and outside the work situation that interact and contribute to disease. . . . Certain personality, cognitive, and behavior characteristics of an employee interact with characteristics of the environment and influence this association. . . . An occupationally based stress reduction program could cause people to *change their life-styles* for the sake of their health and at the same time reduce absenteeism, enhance productivity, and decrease insurance and medical costs. (McGill, 1979; emphasis added)

The concrete procedures advocated to help people change their life-styles are assertiveness training and "coping" procedures such as the relaxation response. Changing the workplace is not at issue. This orientation was strengthened by the overturning in court of citations issued by OSHA against a chemical plant that excluded women of child-bearing potential from working in the lead pigment department because exposure to lead levels might harm fetuses or affect fertility. The director of health and safety of the union involved summed up the pervasive company ideology: "Alter the worker, don't alter the workplace" ("Pigment Plant. . .," The New York *Times,* 1980; Shabecoff, 1980).

Medical Practice and Social Decision Rules

Within the medical profession there is a vigorous debate about the meaning and scope of preventive *medicine*. The field is conventionally divided into three categories: tertiary prevention (the containment, amelioration, or cure of clinical disease), secondary prevention (the detection and

diagnosis of disease, often through screening procedures), and primary prevention (the removal of the underlying cause of disease through immunization, controlling environmental factors, or modifying personal behavior) (White, 1975). Physicians would agree that historically tertiary prevention has been their proper domain. The debate is joined over the proper form of primary prevention. Results from behavior modification will be trifling, argues Leon Eisenberg, compared with "the potential from state and federal action against environmental pollution, adulteration of food and water, and occupational hazards. Much more is known than is being put to use because of the political difficulties and the economic dislocation that would be involved" (Eisenberg, 1977). By contrast, an editorial in *Preventive Medicine* asserts:

> In the past it was possible to prevent major mortality and morbidity by relatively simple governmental or public health action on water, nutrition, and housing. But the underlying causes of today's "top five" disease categories are quite different. Most of the conditions in question are linked to aspects of personal behavior. . . . It is time preventive medicine came to terms with current patterns of disease and tried to modify the personal behavior of those at particular risk rather than attempt to change the behavior of whole communities. (Holland, 1975)

The medical profession seems, at first sight, to be afflicted with the same disagreements that divide the public.

In practice, however, physicians tend to focus on treatment to the detriment of prevention of any kind. Therapeutics, as Charles Rosenberg has argued, have to be understood within the configuration of ideas and relationships that constitute medicine. A doctor's therapeutic tools condition how he understands health and disease. Modern surgery, drugs, and technology lead him to interpret disease in terms of the classical biomedical model, which claims that most diseases are caused by specific identifiable agents and that basic medical research, if adequately funded, will yield the answer. Eisenberg (1977) argues that the vaccine model of prevention dominates physician understanding of today's health problems.

Physicians will evaluate preventive measures in light of the requirements of the contemporary doctor/patient relationship. "We don't know the causal mechanisms of most chronic diseases," claims one physician, "but our patients think we do and many of us pretend we do too. Everyone, including doctors, wants an explanation for the occurrence of disease, so we provide it" (Spencer, 1978). Patients may want some tangible action from their doctor while prevention, more often than not, means that the doctor does nothing. The patient seeks short-term relief rather than the long-term solutions and regimens that primary prevention dictates. Physicians too may be deprived of some of the satisfaction of their profession by preventive measures. "Doctors get their pleasure from making people feel better, and it's hard to make an asymptomatic patient feel better" (Smith, 1976), argues a candid physician. The medical profession will often advise patients to change their behavior only if that strategy does not interfere with the emotional and personal relationships both doctors and patients expect from medicine.

To be accepted, primary prevention strategies would have to be in accord with a physician's conception of scientific medical practice. Do they confirm his experience with prognosis and the natural history of certain diseases? When preventive medicine was used as a justification for the development of Health Maintenance Organizations (HMOs), the American Medical Association (AMA) disputed it first on the grounds of cost. "The maintenance function—examinations and preventive care—will have the benefit of identifying some previously undiagnosed illness," argued John R. Kernodel, spokesman for the AMA, during hearings before the Subcommittee on Health of the Senate Labor and Public Welfare Committee in November, 1971. "But the process of examination itself may be disproportionately high, resulting in higher overall costs rather than savings. We just do not know the cost-benefit ratio" (Brown, 1976). Furthermore, said Kernodel, prevention wasn't like medicine, it was tricky stuff.

But can HMOs discover a magic so far unrevealed to the rest of us? A magic that will somehow motivate people to drive more carefully, exercise more frequently, eat more sensibly, smoke less, and worry less? Can the HMOs discover an educational magic, so far unavailable to the Public Health Service, which will reduce the incidence of the single most common communicable disease—gonorrhea? (Brown, 1976)

True, the medical profession hadn't been able to cope with these problems, but, AMA representatives were arguing, neither had anyone else. They were primarily opposed to HMOs because they would undermine traditional modes of practice, but Kernodel's remarks reflect the belief of many physicians that perhaps trying to change individuals' behavior was a lost cause and it certainly wasn't scientific.

But prevention is an idea supported by constituencies that the medical profession cannot afford to ignore. When they acknowledge its importance, physicians' discourse is increasingly shaped by the individualist version. It is an ideology that derives its power from changes not only in the character of modern medicine but also in the social situation of the medical profession.

Challenges to the authority of the latter in the last decade have not been without effect. The attack on the medical profession in the sixties differed from earlier criticism: it focused on the nature of social relationships in medicine and the scope of physicians' jurisdiction. Too many social and personal problems were being defined as merely or primarily medical problems, it was argued, granting the profession a dangerous degree of power (Illich, 1976). There are some indications that physicians do not altogether welcome the wide-ranging responsibility they have acquired, or at least not in all areas. Power over decisions about when to turn off life-sustaining machinery is a mixed blessing. Physicians are also frustrated by the intractable problems posed by patients suffering from alcoholism, mental illness, obesity, and drug addiction. In these circumstances the ideology of individual responsibility is seductive. Typical of its articulation is the conclusion to an article on the philosophy of preventive medicine: "This theme of 'Feeling Good,' a nationally televised weekly series on health, puts the responsibility for health where it should be, on the individual rather than on the physician" (Smith, 1976). These ideas are echoed in the editorials and the correspondence of the major medical journals over the last five years (Cimmino, 1978; Baker, 1978).

Social theories about the etiology of the chronic diseases would require physicians to step outside the traditional purview of scientific medicine and dabble in politics, or at least involve themselves with the larger social world of their patients. Acknowledging the importance of patients' life-styles, on the other hand, does not necessarily mean embroiling themselves in the dangerous, uncharted waters of behavior change. Patients will have to do most of the work themselves, but "if the patient has become aware of his personal risks and has resolved to make changes, the physician then assumes leadership in guiding the patient's own actions to improve his health" (Fowinkle, 1977). Paramedical personnel can then tend to the minimal services patients may require from the medical world, but "we need physicians to determine what should be done in the first place by paramedical personnel, we need physicians to evaluate the outcome of such services, and certainly a physician is needed initially to help determine the *content* of any health educational program" (Carter, 1976).

Confronted by the surge of public interest in holistic medicine, self-help techniques, and other preventive measures, the profession has moved to assert its authority in the field. It has not been a pioneer by any means, preferring to refine and adapt the area of curative medicine, but it does not wish to watch a new health-related area of activity grow and develop outside the domain of medicine. So, while it will not itself leap to experiment with new techniques, it will draw under the wing of "preventive medicine" individualist innovations that garner critical public support.

Legitimacy and Politics

Under both the Carter and Reagan Administrations, prevention has become a central plank in the federal government's health care policy. As the eighties began, Health and Human Services Secretary Richard S. Schweiker left no doubt that prevention was to be defined in individualist terms: "Across the spectrum of health care policy, we will turn to the self-healing power of consumer choice and patient awareness" (Fisher, 1981).

Concern over health care costs is one major impetus for the state's embrace of the life-style approach to preventive measures. Until World War II the state was not really involved in the direct financing of health care. After the war the state's involvement deepened: first through the Hill-Burton program that provided federal money for the construction of hospitals, then through the establishment of the National Institutes of Health with congressionally backed increases in biomedical research, and finally with the introduction of the Medicare and Medicaid programs in the mid-sixties. The United States spent an estimated $247 billion for health care in 1980, an amount equal to 9.4 percent of the Gross National Product, which was viewed as a serious contribution to inflation. Of that expenditure 42.2 percent came from public funds (Gibson and Waldo, 1981). In its role as provider of medical assistance to eligible old and poor people, the state is now in the business of paying for direct services. In addition, it is a large employer, with responsibility for financing a significant part of the health-insurance premiums of its 10 million employees and annuitants and their family members (Iglehart, 1981). Rising medical care costs, therefore, pose a series of problems for the state; competition and prevention have been adopted as the solutions.

Yet the implementation of cutbacks and the appeal to self-restraint have met growing political opposition. Health care is a particularly important realm symbolically. The events of the sixties raised expectations and created a sense of entitlement to good medical care. The legitimacy of the welfare state is closely tied to developments in health care, and the notion that health means more and better services dies hard. The choice for the state between a prevention based on life-style changes versus a prevention of social reform may take second place to the choice between the status quo of high-technology curative medicine and prevention of any kind. In 1978, summarizing the state's priorities in health care, President Carter observed that "prevention is both cheaper and simpler than cure," yet he acknowledged:

> We have stressed the latter and have ignored to an increasing degree the former. In recent years we have spent 40 cents out of every health dollar on hospitalization. In effect we've made the hospital the first line of defense instead of the last. By contrast we've spent only three cents on disease prevention and control, less than half a cent on health education, and one quarter of a cent on environmental health research. (Venkateson, 1978)

The Carter Administration tried to expand both social and individualist preventive measures. Several state agencies, pressured by the environmental movement, moved to curb the power of industry to pollute the air and water and adulterate the nation's food. While capital sought to focus attention solely on heart disease, the state also emphasized the economic loss and the suffering caused by cancer. Many of the sanctions brought to bear by OSHA on industry hardly constituted severe penalties, but EPA took a tougher line with a greater degree of success. U.S. Steel, for example, whose steel mills situated in heavily industrialized areas are among the worst industrial polluters, agreed to comply with antipollution laws on a fixed schedule (Shabecoff, 1979). The government went so far as to admit liability itself in certain cases of occupational disease, notably asbestosis, where it recognized both the failure of Public Health Service doctors to warn asbestos workers of hazardous conditions in plants and the right to a safe workplace under federal law of workers on defense contracts—a move that, according to a senior corporate official in one of the nation's largest chemical companies, could encourage further suits against industry and "become a powerful monkey wrench" in dealing with occupational-health problems (Burnham, 1977).

At the same time, the agencies within the health care bureaucracy attacked destructive life-styles with a vengeance. The Office of Health Promotion focused on antismoking campaigns. In 1979, smoking was listed in HEW publications as a major, if not *the* major, risk factor in every significant cause of death in the United States, illustrating what one entrepreneur (the then Secretary of HEW Joseph Califano) with a particular theory about the relationship between individual habits and health can do. In the introduction to the Surgeon General's report, *Healthy People,* he expanded his criticism of self-indulgent behavior:

> Indeed, a wealth of scientific research reveals that the key to whether a person will be healthy or sick, live a long life or die prematurely, can be found in several simple personal habits: one's habits with regard to smoking and drinking; one's habits of diet, sleep, and exercise; whether one obeys the speed laws and wears seat belts; and a few other simple measures (U.S. Department of Health, Education and Welfare, 1979)

President Reagan was inaugurated in 1981 and faced growing budget deficits, a deepening fiscal crisis, and an outcry on the part of capital against regulatory controls. In the area of prevention the life-style emphasis flourished, consistent with the political ideology of republicanism, which "emphasizes voluntarism, decentralization, and education to empower people to advance their own interests" (Allegrante and Green, 1981). The state continued its attack on cancer, but through different means because its etiology was redefined. "The public is growing increasingly aware of the link between cancer and their lifestyles," said Schweiker. "With our help they are becoming prevention-oriented" ("Cancer Prevention Cited," *The Blue Sheet,* 1982). He lauded the National Cancer Institute's new chemo-prevention program for "focusing more on how we can interfere in the later stages of carcinogenesis [with synthetic vitamin A] to prevent cancer, instead of concentrating exclusively on substances which initiate the cancer process." Social approaches to prevention, however, were abruptly curtailed: the hazardous waste program was cut for fiscal 1982 from $141.4 million to $107.2 million; the 1983 air research budget will be 42 percent lower in actual purchasing power than in 1981; the Centers for Disease Control are being systematically stripped of their scientists and researchers, to mention but a few of the cuts ("Supplement," *The Nation's Health,* 1982).

There is nothing inevitable about the shift in

health policy toward an individualist definition of prevention (and toward competition rather than regulation to control costs). A particular social coalition espouses it, albeit for somewhat different reasons. Yet even within that coalition there are tensions over the content and direction of the prevention/competition strategy. In the seventies, Califano's promotion of antismoking campaigns as Secretary of HEW finally led him to question tax subsidies for tobacco companies. As President Carter's popularity declined in the polls, his assurances to the tobacco industry increased. This issue was central in Califano's departure from the Administration. Schweiker's promise to put preventive medicine "at the very top of the department's health agenda" was greeted with a stony silence at the annual meeting of the AMA in 1981 (Reinhold, 1981). The Administration's proposals to reduce levels of coverage or change the content of the Federal Employees Health Benefits Program have led to a battle between the Office of Personnel Management, which administers the program, health insurers who provide the coverage, and several federal-employee unions (Iglehart, 1981).

Although health clubs and exercise salons are enjoying an unprecedented boom, acceptance of the individualist version of prevention is not total. A Harris poll at the beginning of 1982 found that the public seems to oppose many of the cutbacks in social preventive measures: "People are scared to death over toxic waste spills and carcinogens in drinking water, such that a 94 percent majority wants the Clean Water Act kept as it is or made tougher" ("Reagan Health Policy," *The Blue Sheet*, 1982). Union leaders in the Northeast are trying to start a national movement to resist union concessions on wages, benefits, work rules, and health and safety issues (Serrin, 1982).

The battle over prevention brings into conflict not only the interests of capital, labor, the environmental movement, the insurance companies, and the medical profession, but those of state agencies such as EPA, the Office of Management and Budget, and the Department of Health and Human Services (DHHS). When, for example, a bill was proposed by Waxman, the House Energy and Commerce Health Subcommittee chairman, advocating the "mandatory

creation" of assistant directors for prevention in NIH, it was opposed by the DHHS Assistant Secretary for Health who claimed that "NIH and its institutes have already acted, or are taking actions, to accomplish the subcommittee's goals" ("HHS Opposes," *The Blue Sheet*, 1982). One of those actions turned out to be the adoption of a revised definition of prevention research, which allowed the percentage of its activities that qualified as prevention-related to rise from 16.9 percent to 70 percent. Waxman questioned the move, arguing that:

> public health people . . . feel that what may be happening is that the prevention professionals are not being consulted or brought in to look at how prevention in a more traditional sense could be carried out at NIH, and what we have is a redefining of what could fit into the category called prevention without rethinking strategies to direct research toward it.

These kinds of conflicts produce contradictions in state policy: DHHS vigorously pursues health education while the Medicare provisions do not permit reimbursement of preventive services. Internal conflict is exacerbated because many health-related activities do not fall under the jurisdiction of the official "health" agencies. Although organized labor and environmental groups have won some important victories in the last 20 years—the formation of EPA, OSHA, and the Toxic Substances Control Act are notable examples—they have been promoted by agencies other than the Department of Health and Human Services. They are not, therefore, always included in discussions of the nation's health care policy. Especially when they fall under the jurisdiction of the Department of Labor, a conservative Administration can justify reduction of funding and minimal implementation in the name of reducing constraints on the productivity of industry. The state, as neo-Marxists emphasize, should not be conceptualized as a monolithic entity governed by a self-conscious, united group of managers. The different strands of opinion resulting from the clash between the objectives of labor and capital are reflected in the positions of different agencies within the state. Certain agencies—the Food and Drug Administration (FDA), for example—while acting within the confines of a capitalist state, will be more open to pressure from different class factions. The exact form that the conflict within the state takes will be shaped by the state's structure. What kind of access is guaranteed for representatives of labor to OSHA? What relationships are structurally possible between the scientific community and the FDA?

Conclusion

Prevention has become a battle cry to deal with a variety of issues, but its content and its underlying strategy are contested. It grows out of the intersection of different sets of problems and different sets of solutions that do not always neatly correspond. For capital and the state the critical problems are costs, productivity, and credibility; for the medical profession they are public hostility, new corporate interests in health care whose power parallels their own, and a state intent on controlling physicians; for the public they are a decrease in medical services, a declining economy, and the fear that everyday life is becoming less amenable to control. Sometimes some of these forces can join together under one banner to attack their respective demons: prevention is the answer to all problems.

Consensus is lacking, however, on the specific programs that should constitute a strategy of prevention. Two etiological theories dictate two very different directions: a theory that blames self-destructive habits and a theory that points to social factors. The advocates of neither theory can agree on all the practical implications of their theoretical orientation. Part of the resultant confusion is undoubtedly due to the state of medical knowledge in the field. There is no tried body of practice on which to base predictions about which techniques of behavior change will work and which will not. The debates drag on, for example, over the relative contribution of smoking and air pollution to cancer and then over what techniques will actually disuade people from smoking, drinking, or worrying. Studies of behavior change require long time periods to yield convincing results, and critics emphasize that there is no clear cost-benefit calculation that one can make about their payoff.

But policy makers choose selectively among available research to justify the decisions they make about the strategies they choose to label preventive. Conclusive data on the etiology of chronic disease would not dramatically change the character of the contemporary debate over prevention. Corporations will continue to argue for the control of heart disease, hoping to preserve their executives and decrease the size of the social wage; the state seeks to cut back on the services it can no longer afford in favor of exhortations to its citizens to live better lives; parts of the labor movement will fight for improved safety and health at work. Self-destructive habits will probably continue to be the focus of attack at the level of national policy in the immediate future, but Renaud's predictions about the inexorable logic of capitalism and the inevitable indifference of the state to social influences on health are too absolute. The relative power of "scientific" arguments will depend on how they are translated by the medical community, and how they resonate with more intuitive popular images of health and medicine. The individualist version of prevention makes sense to Americans in a period marked by antagonism to state intervention and the celebration of individual self-reliance. But as the attack on their standard of living becomes more severe, they are likely to find less plausible the claim that health, like everything else, is simply a matter of willpower.

REFERENCES

Allegrante, J.P. and Green, L.W. "Sounding Board—When Health Policy Becomes Victim Blaming." *New England Journal of Medicine* 305 (December, 1981), pp. 1528–1529.

Baker, H. "Let's Try More Prevention," correspondence. *Canadian Medical Association Journal* 118 (May, 1978), pp. 1034–1036.

Bartz, Dan. "Received Business Deduction for Personal Medical Expenses." *Supermarketing* 32 (April, 1977), p. 46.

Black, D. "The Aims of a Health Service." *Lancet* 1 (Apr. 24, 1982), pp. 952–954.

Boroson, Warren. "The Myth of the Unhealthy Executive." *Across the Board* 15 (February, 1978), pp. 10–16.

Brown, Lawrence D. "The Story of HMO." Case

prepared for Executive Programs in Health Policy and Management, Harvard School of Public Health (1976).

Burnham, David. "Asbestos Workers' Illness—and Their Suit—May Change Health Standards." The New York *Times* (Dec. 20, 1977), p. 30.

Burns, John E. "Spiraling Hospital Costs and the 41st Annual IMS Clinic," editorial. *Industrial Management* 19 (May/June, 1977), editorial page.

"Cancer Prevention Cited as Alternative to Environmental Emphasis." *The Blue Sheet,* vol. 25, no. 2 (June 2, 1982), pp. 8–9.

Carter, Earl T. "Preventive Medicine," correspondence. *Minnesota Medicine* 59 (June 1976), pp. 399–401.

Cimmino, Christian V. "Preventive Medicine: Applause and Argument," correspondence. *Virginia Medical* 105 (August, 1978), p. 549.

Crawford, Robert. "Individual Responsibility and Health Politics in the 1970s," in Susan Reverby and David Rosner (eds.), *Health Care in America* (Philadelphia: Temple University Press, 1979), pp. 247–268.

Eisenberg, Leon. "The Perils of Prevention: A Cautionary Note," editorial. *New England Journal of Medicine* 297 (December, 1977), pp. 1230–1232.

Epstein, S. and Swartz, Joel B. "Fallacies of Lifestyle Cancer Theories." *Nature* 289 (Jan. 15, 1981), pp. 126–130.

Eyer, Joseph and Sterling, Peter. "Stress-Related Mortality and Social Organization." *The Review of Radical Political Economics* 9 (Spring, 1977), pp. 1–44.

Fields, Gregg. "Occupational Health Becomes a Specialty for More Physicians: Workers, Government Insist on Preventive Medicine; Companies Expect Savings." *Wall Street Journal* (Oct. 24, 1978), p. 18.

Fisher, M.J. "Competition, Prevention Keys to Reagan Health Strategy." *National Underwriter* 85 (June 26, 1981), p. 43.

Fowinkle, Eugene W. "New Directions in Preventive Medicine." *Journal of the Tennessee Medical Association* 70 (December, 1977), pp. 894–896.

Freeland, M.S. and Schendler, C.E. "National Health Expenditures: Short-Term Outlook and Long-Term Projections." *Health Care Financing Review* 2 (Winter, 1981), pp. 97–126.

Gibson, R.M. and Waldo, D.R. "National Health Expenditures, 1980." *Health Care Financing Review* 2 (September, 1981), pp. 1–54.

Gifford, James F. and William G. Anlyan. "Sounding Board—The Role of the Private Sector in an Economy of Limited Health-Care Resources." *New England Journal of Medicine* 300 (April, 1979), pp. 790–793.

Hedges, Janice Neipert. "Absence from Work—Measuring the Hours Lost." *U.S. Bureau of Labor Statistics, Monthly Labor Review* 100 (October, 1977), pp. 16–23.

"HHS Opposes 'Mandatory' NIH Prevention Plan; Definition Shift Questioned." *The Blue Sheet* (Apr. 28, 1982), p. 5.

Holland, Walter W. "Prevention: The Only Cure," editorial. *Preventive Medicine* 4 (1975), pp. 387–389.

Holtzman, Neil A. "Prevention: Rhetoric and Reality." *International Journal of Health Service* 9 (1979), pp. 25–39.

Iglehart, J.K. "Health Policy Report: The Administration Responds to the Cost Spiral." *New England Journal of Medicine* 305 (November, 1981), pp. 1359–1364.

Illich, Ivan. *Medical Nemesis: The Expropriation of Health* (New York: Random House, 1976).

"Kimberly-Clark is Spending Millions To Insure Employees' Health Well-Being." *Paper Trade Journal* 161 (December, 1977), p. 40.

Kramer, Bernard M. "Behavioral Change and Public Attitudes towards Public Health," editorial. *American Journal of Public Health* 67 (October, 1977), pp. 911–913.

Lowery, Donald. "In Andover, an Ex-coach Fits Right In." *The Boston Globe* (Aug. 15, 1980), p. 56.

Maher, T.M. "THAA Urges Disease Prevention Programs." *National Underwriter* 85 (Aug. 22, 1981), pp. 1, 25.

McGill, Alice M. (ed.). Proceedings of the National Conference on Health Promotion Programs in Occupational Settings. (Washington, D.C.: U.S. Department of Health, Education, and Welfare, 1979).

Melcher, G.W., Jr. "A New Challenge for Health Insurers." *National Underwriter* 85 (May 2, 1981), pp. 11, 14, 16, 17.

Noble, David. "Cost-Benefit Analysis." *Health/Pac Bulletin,* vol. 11, no. 6 (July/August, 1980), pp. 1–2, 7–12, 27–40.

Pamphlets in *Design for Life* series. Blue Cross, Blue Shield, Connecticut.

"Physician, Heal Thyself . . . Or Else!" *Forbes* (Oct. 1, 1977), pp. 40–46.

"Pigment Plant Wins Fertility-Risk Case: Government's Challenge Rejected on Policy Excluding Women from a 'Hazardous' Area." The New York *Times* (Sept. 8, 1980), p. A14.

Pritchett, S. Travis. "Can Employee Benefits Also Be Employer Benefits?" *American Society of Chartered Life Underwriters—CLU Journal* 31 (April, 1977), pp. 40–45.

"Reagan Health Policy Opposed by Most of Public." *The Blue Sheet* (June 9, 1982), pp. 13–14.

Reinhold, Robert. "Medical Leaders Growing Wary over Reagan Health-Care Plans." The New York *Times* (Feb. 16, 1981), p. A12.

Renaud, Marc. "On the Structural Constraints to State Intervention in Health." *International Journal of Health Services,* vol. 5, no. 4 (1975), pp. 559–570.

Rosenberg, Charles F. "The Therapeutic Revolution: Medicine, Meaning, and Social Change in Nineteenth-Century America," in Charles F. Rosenberg and Morris J. Vogel (eds.), *The Therapeutic Revolution, Essays in the Social History of American Medicine* (Philadelphia: University of Pennsylvania Press, 1979), pp. 3–25.

Salmon, J. Warren and Berliner, Howard S. "Can the Holistic Health Movement Turn Left?" Paper presented to the Annual Meeting of the American Public Health Association, New York, November 7, 1979.

Serrin, William. "Labor is Resisting More Concessions." The New York *Times* (June 13, 1982), p. 29.

Shabecoff, Philip. "E.P.A. Reported Near an Accord with U.S. Steel." The New York *Times* (May 22, 1979). p. A1.

Shabecoff, Philip. "U.S. Appeals Ruling on Women in Hazardous Jobs." The New York *Times* (Sept. 9, 1980), p. B9.

Smith, John E. "The Philosophy of Preventive Medicine." *Minnesota Medicine* 59 (March, 1976), pp. 196–199.

Spencer, F.J. "The Great Preventive Life-Style Cop-Out," editorial. *Virginia Medical* 105 (April, 1978), p. 327.

"Supplement: The President's Budget Proposal." *The Nation's Health* (March, 1982).

Taylor, R.C.R. "The Transformation of Collective Demands." Paper presented to the Conference on the Crisis in the Welfare State, Trieste, Italy, June, 1981.

U.S. Department of Health, Education, and Welfare. Public Health Service. *Healthy People: The Surgeon General's Report on Health Promotion and Disease Prevention* (Washington, D.C.: USGPO, 1979).

Venkateson, M. "Preventive Health Care and Marketing: Positive Aspects," in Philip D. Cooper, William J. Kehoe, and Patrick E. Murphy (eds.), *Marketing and Preventive Health Care: Interdisciplinary and Interorganizational Perspectives* (Chicago: American Marketing Association, 1978), pp. 12–25.

Whelan, Elizabeth. "The Politics of Cancer." *Policy Review* 10 (Fall, 1979), pp. 33–46.

White, James R. and Steinbach, Gary. "Motivating Executives To Keep Physically Fit." *Harvard Business Review* 56 (March/April 1978), pp. 16, 184, 186.

White, Kerr L. "Prevention as a National Health Goal," editorial. *Preventive Medicine* 4 (1975), pp. 247–251.

Wildavsky, Aaron. "Doing Better and Feeling Worse: The Political Pathology of Health Policy." *Daedalus* (Writer, 1977), pp. 105–123.

Williams, C.L., et al. "Chronic Disease Risk Factors Among Children. The 'Know Your Body' Study." *Journal of Chronic Diseases* 32 (1979), pp. 505–513.

Wright, H. Beric. "Why Keep Fit?" *Accountant* 16 (March, 1978), pp. 350–352.

41

A Case for Refocussing Upstream: The Political Economy of Illness

John B. McKinlay

My friend, Irving Zola, relates the story of a physician trying to explain the dilemmas of the modern practice of medicine:

"You know," he said, "sometimes it feels like this. There I am standing by the shore of a swiftly flowing river and I hear the cry of a drowning man.

So I jump into the river, put my arms around him, pull him to shore and apply artificial respiration. Just when he begins to breathe, there is another cry for help. So I jump into the river, reach him, pull him to shore, apply artificial respiration, and then just as he begins to breathe, another cry for help. So back in the river again, reaching, pulling, applying, breathing and then another yell. Again and again, without end, goes the sequence. You know, I am so busy jumping in, pulling them to shore, applying artificial respiration, that I have *no* time to see who the hell is upstream pushing them all in."[1]

I believe this simple story illustrates two important points. *First,* it highlights the fact that a clear majority of our resources and activities in the health field are devoted to what I term "downstream endeavors" in the form of superficial, categorical tinkering in response to almost perennial shifts from one health issue to the next, without really solving anything. I am, of course, not suggesting that such efforts are entirely futile, or that a considerable amount of short-term good is not being accomplished. Clearly, people and groups have important immediate needs which must be recognized and attended to. Nevertheless, one must be wary of the *short-term nature* and *ultimate futility* of such downstream endeavors.

Second, the story indicates that we should somehow cease our preoccupation with this short-term, problem-specific tinkering and begin focussing our attention upstream, where the real problems lie. Such a reorientation would minimally involve an analysis of the means by which various individuals, interest groups, and large-scale, profit-oriented corporations are "pushing people in," and how they subsequently erect, at some point downstream, a health care structure to service the needs which they have had a hand in creating, and for which moral responsibility ought to be assumed.

In this paper two related themes will be developed. *First,* I wish to highlight the activities of the "manufacturers of illness"—those individuals, interest groups, and organizations which, in addition to producing material goods and services, also produce, as an inevitable by-product, widespread morbidity and mortality. Arising out of this, and *second,* I will develop a case for refocussing our attention away from those individuals and groups who are mistakenly held to be responsible for their condition, toward a range of broader upstream political and economic forces.

The task assigned to me for this conference was to review some of the broad social structural factors influencing the onset of heart disease and/or at-risk behavior. Since the issues covered by this request are so varied, I have, of necessity, had to make some decisions concerning both emphasis and scope. These decisions and the reasoning behind them should perhaps be explained at this point. With regard to what can be covered by the term "social structure," it is possible to isolate at least three separate levels of abstraction. One could, for example, focus on such subsystems as the family, and its associated social networks, and how these may be importantly linked to different levels of health status and the utilization of services.[2] On a second level, one could consider how particular organizations and broader social institutions, such as neighborhood and community structures, also affect the social distribution of pathology and at-risk behavior.[3] Third, attention could center on the broader political-economic spectrum, and how these admittedly more remote forces may be etiologically involved in the onset of disease. . . .

. . . [In this paper] I will argue, for example, that the frequent failure of many health intervention programs can be largely attributed to the inadequate recognition we give to aspects of social context. . . . The most important factor in deciding on the subject area of this paper, however, is the fact that, while there appears to be a newly emerging interest in the political economy of health care, social scientists have, as yet, paid little attention to the *political economy of illness.*[4] It is my intention in this paper to begin to develop a case for the serious consideration of this particular area.

A political-economic analysis of health care suggests that the entire structure of institutions in the United States is such as to preclude the adequate provision of services.[5] Increasingly, it seems, the provision of care is being tied to the priorities of profit-making institutions. For a long time, criticism of U.S. health care focussed on the activities of the American Medical Association and the fee for service system of physician payment.[6] Lately, however, attention appears to be refocussing on the relationship between health care arrangements and the structure of big business.[7] It has, for example, been suggested that:

> ... with the new and apparently permanent involvement of major corporations in health, it is becoming increasingly improbable that the United States can redirect its health priorities without, at the same time, changing the ways in which American industry is organized and the ways in which monopoly capitalism works.[8]

It is my impression that many of the political-economic arguments concerning developments in the organization of health care also have considerable relevance for a holistic understanding of the etiology and distribution of morbidity, mortality, and at-risk behavior. In the following sections I will present some important aspects of these arguments in the hope of contributing to a better understanding of aspects of the political economy of illness.

An Unequal Battle

The downstream efforts of health researchers and practitioners against the upstream efforts of the manufacturers of illness have the appearance of an unequal war, *with a resounding victory assured for those on the side of illness* and the creation of disease-inducing behaviors. The battle between health workers and the manufacturers of illness is unequal on at least two grounds. In the *first* place, we always seem to arrive on the scene and begin to work after the real damage has already been done. By the time health workers intervene, people have already filled the artificial needs created for them by the manufacturers of illness and are habituated to various at-risk behaviors. In the area of smoking behavior, for example, we have an illustration not only of the lateness of health workers' arrival on the scene, and the enormity of the task confronting them, but also, judging by recent evidence, of the resounding defeat being sustained in this area.[9] To push the river analogy

even further, the task becomes one of furiously swimming against the flow and finally being swept away when exhausted by the effort or through disillusionment with a lack of progress. So long as we continue to fight the battle downstream, and in such an ineffective manner, we are doomed to frustration, repeated failure, and perhaps ultimately to a sicker society.

Second, the promoters of disease-inducing behavior are manifestly more effective in their use of behavioral science knowledge than are those of us who are concerned with the eradication of such behavior. Indeed, it is somewhat paradoxical that we should be meeting here to consider how behavioral science knowledge and techniques can be effectively employed to reduce or prevent at-risk behavior, when that same body of knowledge *has already* been used to create the at-risk behavior we seek to eliminate. How embarrassingly ineffective are our mass media efforts in the health field (e.g., alcoholism, obesity, drug abuse, safe driving, pollution, etc.) when compared with many of the tax exempt promotional efforts on behalf of the illness generating activities of large-scale corporations.[10] It is a fact that we are demonstrably more effective in persuading people to purchase items they never dreamt they would need, or to pursue at-risk courses of action, than we are in preventing or halting such behavior. Many advertisements are so ingenious in their appeal that they have entertainment value in their own right and become embodied in our national folk humor. By way of contrast, many health advertisements lack any comparable widespread appeal, often appear boring, avuncular, and largely misdirected.

I would argue that one major problem lies in the fact that we are overly concerned with the war itself, and with how we can more effectively participate in it. In the health field we have unquestioningly accepted the assumptions presented by the manufacturers of illness and, as a consequence, have confined our efforts to only downstream offensives. A little reflection would, I believe, convince anyone that those on the side of health are in fact losing. . . . But rather than merely trying to win the way, we need to step back and question the premises, legitimacy and utility of the war itself.

The Binding of At-Riskness to Culture

It seems that the appeals to at-risk behavior that are engineered by the manufacturers of illness are particularly successful because they are constructed in such a way as to be inextricably bound with essential elements of our existing dominant culture. This is accomplished in a number of ways: (a) Exhortations to at-risk behavior are often piggybacked on those legitimized values, beliefs, and norms which are widely recognized and adhered to in the dominant culture. The idea here is that if a person *would only do X,* then they would also be doing Y and Z. (b) Appeals are also advanced which claim or imply that certain courses of at-risk action are subscribed to or endorsed by most of the culture heroes in society (e.g., people in the entertainment industry), or by those with technical competence in that particular field (e.g., "doctors" recommend it). The idea here is that if a person *would only do X,* then he/she would be doing pretty much the same as is done or recommended by such prestigious people as A and B. (c) Artificial needs are manufactured, the fulfilling of which becomes absolutely essential if one is to be a meaningful and useful member of society. The idea here is that if a person *does not do X, or will not do X,* then they are either deficient in some important respect, or they are some kind of liability for the social system.

Variations on these and other kinds of appeal strategies have, of course, been employed for a long time now by the promoters of at-risk behavior. The manufacturers of illness are, for example, fostering the belief that if you want to be an attractive, masculine man, or a "cool," "natural" woman, you will smoke cigarettes; that you can only be a "good parent" if you habituate your children to candy, cookies, etc.; and that if you are a truly loving wife, you will feed your husband foods that are high in cholesterol. All of these appeals have isolated some basic goals to which most people subscribe (e.g., people want to be masculine or feminine, good parents, loving spouses, etc.) and make claim, or imply, that their realization is only possible through the exclusive use of their product or the regular display of a specific type of at-risk behavior. Indeed, one can argue that

certain at-risk behaviors have become so inextricably intertwined with our dominant cultural system (perhaps even symbolic of it) that the routine public display of such behavior almost signifies membership in this society.

Such tactics for the habituation of people to at-risk behavior are, perhaps paradoxically, also employed to elicit what I term *"quasi-health behavior."* Here again, an artificially constructed conception of a person in some fanciful state of physiological and emotional equilibrium is presented as the ideal state to strive for, if one is to meaningfully participate in the wider social system. To assist in the attainment of such a state, we are advised to consume a range of quite worthless vitamin pills, mineral supplements, mouthwashes, hair shampoos, laxatives, pain killers, etc. Clearly, one cannot exude radiance and success if one is not taking this vitamin, or that mineral. The achievement of daily regularity is a prerequisite for an effective social existence. One can only compete and win after a good night's sleep, and this can only be ensured by taking such and such. An entrepreneurial pharmaceutical industry appears devoted to the task of making people overly conscious of these quasi-health concerns, and to engendering a dependency on products which have been repeatedly found to be ineffective, and even potentially harmful.[11]

There are no clear signs that such activity is being or will be regulated in any effective way, and the promoters of this quasi-health behavior appear free to range over the entire body in their never-ending search for new areas and issues to be linked to the fanciful equilibrium that they have already engineered in the mind of the consumer. By binding the display of at-risk and quasi-health behavior so inextricably to elements of our dominant culture, a situation is even created whereby to request people to change or alter these behaviors is more or less to request abandonment of dominant culture.

The term "culture" is employed here to denote that integrated system of values, norms, beliefs and patterns of behavior which, for groups and social categories in specific situations, facilitate the solution of social structural problems.[12] This definition lays stress on two features commonly associated with the concept of culture. The *first* is the interrelatedness and interdependence of the various elements (values, norms, beliefs, overt life styles) that apparently comprise culture. The *second* is the view that a cultural system is, in some part, a response to social structural problems, and that it can be regarded as some kind of resolution of them. Of course, these social structural problems, in partial response to which a cultural pattern emerges, may themselves have been engineered in the interests of creating certain beliefs, norms, life styles, etc. If one assumes that culture can be regarded as some kind of reaction formation, then one must be mindful of the unanticipated social consequences of inviting some alteration in behavior which is a part of a dominant cultural pattern. The request from health workers for alterations in certain at-risk behaviors may result in either awkward dislocations of the interrelated elements of the cultural pattern, or the destruction of a system of values and norms, etc., which have emerged over time in response to situational problems. From this perspective, and with regard to the utilization of medical care, I have already argued elsewhere that, for certain groups of the population, underutilization may be "healthy" behavior, and the advocacy of increased utilization an "unhealthy" request for the abandonment of essential features of culture.[13]

The Case of Food

Perhaps it would be useful at this point to illustrate in some detail, from one pertinent area, the style and magnitude of operation engaged in by the manufacturers of illness. Illustrations are, of course, readily available from a variety of different areas, such as: the requirements of existing occupational structure, emerging leisure patterns, smoking and drinking behavior, and automobile usage.[14] Because of current interest, I have decided to consider only one area which is importantly related to a range of largely chronic diseases—namely, the 161 billion dollar industry involved in the production and distribution of food and beverages.[15] The present situation, with regard to food, was recently described as follows:

The sad history of our food supply resembles the energy crisis, and not just because food nourishes our bodies while petroleum fuels the society. We long ago surrendered control of food, a vital resource, to private corporations, just as we surrendered control of energy. The food corporations have shaped the kinds of food we eat for their greater profits, just as the energy companies have dictated the kinds of fuel we use.[16]

From all the independent evidence available, and despite claims to the contrary by the food industry, a widespread decline has occurred during the past three decades in American dietary standards. Some forty percent of U.S. adults are overweight or downright fat.[17] The prevalence of excess weight in the American population as a whole is high—so high, in fact, that in some segments it has reached epidemic proportions.[18] There is evidence that the food industry is manipulating our image of "food" away from basic staples toward synthetic and highly processed items. It has been estimated that we eat between 21 and 25 percent fewer dairy products, vegetables, and fruits than we did twenty years ago, and from 70 to 80 percent more sugary snacks and soft drinks. Apparently, most people now eat more processed and synthetic foods than the real thing. There are even suggestions that a federal, nationwide survey would have revealed how serious our dietary situation really is, if the Nixon Administration had not cancelled it after reviewing some embarrassing preliminary results.[19] The survey apparently confirmed the trend toward deteriorating diets first detected in an earlier household food consumption survey in the years 1955–1965, undertaken by the Department of Agriculture.[20]

Of course, for the food industry, this trend toward deficient synthetics and highly processed items makes good economic sense. Generally speaking, it is much cheaper to make things look and taste like the real thing, than to actually provide the real thing. But the kind of foods that result from the predominance of economic interests clearly do not contain adequate nutrition. It is common knowledge that food manufacturers destroy important nutrients which foods naturally contain, when they transform them into "convenience" high profit items. To give one simple example: a wheat grain's outer layers are apparently very nutritious, but they are also an obstacle to making tasteless, bleached, white flour. Consequently, baking corporations "refine" fourteen nutrients out of the natural flour and then, when it is financially convenient, replace some of them with a synthetic substitute. In the jargon of the food industry, this flour is now "enriched." Clearly, the food industry employs this term in much the same way that coal corporations ravage mountainsides into mud flats, replant them with some soil and seedlings, and then proclaim their moral accomplishment in "rehabilitating" the land. While certain types of food processing may make good economic sense, it may also result in a deficient end product, and perhaps even promote certain diseases. The bleaching and refining of wheat products, for example, largely eliminates fiber or roughage from our diets, and some authorities have suggested that fiber-poor diets can be blamed for some of our major intestinal diseases.[21]

A vast chemical additive technology has enabled manufacturers to accquire enormous control over the food and beverage market and to foster phenomenal profitability. It is estimated that drug companies alone make something like $500 million a year through chemical additives for food. I have already suggested that what is done to food, in the way of processing and artificial additives, may actually be injurious to health. Yet, it is clear that, despite such well-known risks, profitability makes such activity well worthwhile. For example, additives, like preservatives, enable food that might perish in a short period of time to endure unchanged for months or even years. Food manufacturers and distributors can saturate supermarket shelves across the country with their products because there is little chance that they will spoil. Moreover, manufacturers can purchase vast quantities of raw ingredients when they are cheap, produce and stockpile the processed result, and then withhold the product from the market for long periods, hoping for the inevitable rise in prices and the consequent windfall.

The most widely used food additive (although it is seldom described as an additive) is "refined" sugar. Food manufacturers saturate our diets with the substance from the day we are born

until the day we die. Children are fed breakfast cereals which consist of 50 percent sugar.[22] The average American adult consumes 126 pounds of sugar each year—and children, of course, eat much more. For the candy industry alone, this amounts to around $3 billion each year. The American sugar mania, which appears to have been deliberately engineered, is a major contributor to such "diseases of civilization" as diabetes, coronary heart disease, gall bladder illness, and cancer—all the insidious, degenerative conditions which most often afflict people in advanced capitalist societies, but which "underdeveloped," nonsugar eaters never get. One witness at a recent meeting of a U.S. Senate Committee, said that if the food industry were proposing sugar today as a new food additive, its "metabolic behavior would undoubtedly lead to its being banned."[23]

In sum, therefore, it seems that the American food industry is mobilizing phenomenal resources to advance and bind us to its own conception of food. We are bombarded from childhood with $2 billion worth of deliberately manipulative advertisements each year, most of them urging us to consume, among other things, as much sugar as possible. To highlight the magnitude of the resources involved, one can point to the activity of one well-known beverage company, Coca-Cola, which alone spent $71 million in 1971 to advertise its artificially flavored, sugar-saturated product. Fully recognizing the enormity of the problem regarding food in the United States, Zwerdling offers the following advice:

> Breaking through the food industry will require government action—banning or sharply limiting use of dangerous additives like artificial colors and flavors, and sugar, and requiring wheat products to contain fiber-rich wheat germ, to give just two examples. Food, if it is to become safe, will have to become part of politics.[24]

The Ascription of Responsibility and Moral Entrepreneurship

So far, I have considered, in some detail, the ways in which industry, through its manufacture and distribution of a variety of products, generates at-risk behavior and disease. Let us now focus on the activities of health workers further down the river and consider their efforts in a social context, which has already been largely shaped by the manufacturers upstream.

Not only should we be mindful of the culturally disruptive and largely unanticipated consequences of health intervention efforts mentioned earlier, but also of the underlying ideology on which so much of this activity rests. Such intervention appears based on an assumption of the *culpability of individuals* or groups who either manifest illness, or display various at-risk behaviors.

From the assumption that individuals and groups with certain illnesses or displaying at-risk behavior are responsible for their state, it is a relatively easy step to advocating some changes in behavior on the part of those involved. By ascribing culpability to some group or social category (usually ethnic minorities and those in lower socio-economic categories) and having this ascription legitimated by health professionals and accepted by other segments of society, it is possible to mobilize resources to change the offending behavior. Certain people are responsible for not approximating, through their activities, some conception of what *ought* to be appropriate behavior on their part. When measured against the artificial conception of what ought to be, certain individuals and groups are found to be deficient in several important respects. They are *either* doing something that they ought not to be doing, *or* they are not doing something that they ought to be doing. If only they would recognize their individual culpability and alter their behavior in some appropriate fashion, they would improve their health status or the likelihood of not developing certain pathologies. On the basis of this line of reasoning, resources are being mobilized to bring those who depart from the desired conception into conformity with what is thought to be appropriate behavior. To use the upstream-downstream analogy, one could argue that people are blamed (and, in a sense, even punished) for not being able to swim after they, perhaps even against their own volition, have been pushed into the river by the manufacturers of illness.

Clearly, this ascription of culpability is not limited only to the area of health. According to popular conception, people in poverty are largely to blame for their social situation, although recent evidence suggests that a social welfare system which prevents them from avoiding this state is at least partly responsible.[25] Again, in the field of education, we often hold "dropouts" responsible for their behavior, when evidence suggests that the school system itself is rigged for failure.[26] Similar examples are readily available from the fields of penology, psychiatry, and race relations.[27]

Perhaps it would be useful to briefly outline, at this point, what I regard as a bizarre relationship between the activities of the manufacturers of illness, the ascription of culpability, and health intervention endeavors. *First,* important segments of our social system appear to be controlled and operated in such a way that people must inevitably fail. The fact is that there is often no choice over whether one can find employment, whether or not to drop out of college, involve oneself in untoward behavior, or become sick. *Second,* even though individuals and groups lack such choice, they are still blamed for not approximating the artificially contrived norm and are treated as if responsibility for their state lay entirely with them. For example, some illness conditions may be the result of particular behavior and/or involvement in certain occupational role relationships over which those affected have little or no control.[28] *Third,* after recognizing that certain individuals and groups have "failed," we establish, at a point downstream, a substructure of services which are regarded as evidence of progressive beneficence on the part of the system. Yet, it is this very system which had a primary role in manufacturing the problems and need for these services in the first place.

It is around certain aspects of life style that most health intervention endeavors appear to revolve and this probably results from the observability of most at-risk behavior. The modification of at-risk behavior can take several different forms, and the intervention appeals that are employed probably vary as a function of which type of change is desired. People can *either* be encouraged to stop doing what they are doing which appears to be endangering their survival (e.g., smoking, drinking, eating certain types of food, working in particular ways); *or* they can be encouraged to adopt certain new patterns of behavior which seemingly enhance their health status (e.g., diet, exercise, rest, eat certain foods, etc.). I have already discussed how the presence or absence of certain life styles in some groups may be a part of some wider cultural pattern which emerges as a response to social structural problems. I have also noted the potentially disruptive consequences to these cultural patterns of intervention programs. Underlying all these aspects is the issue of behavior control and the attempt to enforce a particular type of behavioral conformity. It is more than coincidental that the at-risk life styles, which we are all admonished to avoid, are frequently the type of behaviors which depart from and, in a sense, jeopardize the prevailing puritanical, middle-class ethic of what ought to be. According to this ethic, activities as pleasurable as drinking, smoking, overeating, and sexual intercourse must be harmful and ought to be eradicated.

The important point here is which segments of society and whose interests are health workers serving, and what are the ideological consequences of their actions.[29] Are we advocating the modification of behavior for the *exclusive* purpose of improving health status, or are we using the question of health as a means of obtaining some kind of moral uniformity through the abolition of disapproved behaviors? To what extent, if at all, are health workers actively involved in some wider pattern of social regulation?[30]

Such questions also arise in relation to the burgeoning literature that links more covert personality characteristics to certain illnesses and at-risk behaviors. Capturing a great deal of attention in this regard are the recent studies which associate heart disease with what is termed a Type A personality. The Type A personality consists of a complex of traits which produces: excessive competitive drive, aggressiveness, impatience, and a harrying sense of time urgency. Individuals displaying this pattern seem to be engaged in a chronic, ceaseless and often fruitless struggle with themselves, with others, with circumstances, with time, sometimes with life itself. They also frequently exhibit a free-floating, but well-rationalized form of hostility, and almost always a deep-seated insecurity.

Efforts to change Type A traits appear to be based on some ideal conception of a relaxed, non-competitive, phlegmatic individual to which people are encouraged to conform. Again, one can question how realistic such a conception is in a system which daily rewards behavior resulting from Type A traits. One can clearly question the ascription of near exclusive culpability to those displaying Type A behavior when the context within which such behavior is manifest is structured in such a way as to guarantee its production. From a cursory reading of job advertisements in any newspaper, we can see that employers actively seek to recruit individuals manifesting Type A characteristics, extolling them as positive virtues.[33]

My earlier point concerning the potentially disruptive consequences of requiring alterations in life style applies equally well in this area of personality and disease. If health workers manage to effect some changes away from Type A behavior in a system which requires and rewards it, then we must be aware of the possible consequences of such change in terms of future failure. Even though the evidence linking Type A traits to heart disease appears quite conclusive, how can health workers ever hope to combat and alter it when such characteristics are so positively and regularly reinforced in this society?

The various points raised in this section have some important moral and practical implications for those involved in health related endeavors. *First*, I have argued that our prevailing ideology involves the ascription of culpability to particular individuals and groups for the manifestation of either disease or at-risk behavior. *Second*, it can be argued that so-called "health professionals" have acquired a mandate to determine the morality of different types of behavior and have access to a body of knowledge and resources which they can "legitimately" deploy for its removal or alteration. (A detailed discussion of the means by which this mandate has been acquired is expanded in a separate paper.) *Third*, [it] is possible to argue that a great deal of health intervention is, perhaps unwittingly, part of a wide pattern of social regulation. We must be clear both as to whose interests we are serving, and the wider implications and consequences of the activities we support through the application of our expertise. *Finally,* it is evident from arguments I have presented that much of our health intervention fails to take adequate account of the social contexts which foster and reinforce the behaviors we seek to alter. The literature of preventive medicine is replete with illustrations of the failure of contextless health intervention programs.

The Notion of a Need Hierarchy

At this point in the discussion I shall digress slightly to consider the relationship between the utilization of preventive health services and the concept of need as manifest in this society. We know from available evidence that upper socio-economic groups are generally more responsive to health intervention activities than are those of lower socio-economic status. To partially account for this phenomenon, I have found it useful to introduce the notion of a *need hierarchy.* By this I refer to the fact that some needs (e.g., food, clothing, shelter) are probably universally recognized as related to sheer survival and take precedence, while other needs, for particular social groups, may be perceived as less immediately important (e.g., dental care, exercise, balanced diet). In other words, I conceive of a *hierarchy of needs,* ranging from what could be termed "primary needs" (which relate more or less to the universally recognized immediate needs for survival) through to "secondary needs" (which are not always recognized as important and which may be artificially engineered by the manufacturers of illness). Somewhere between the high priority, primary needs and the less important, secondary needs are likely to fall the kinds of need invoked by preventive health workers. Where one is located at any point in time on the need hierarchy (i.e., which particular needs are engaging one's attention and resources) is largely a function of the shape of the existing social structure and aspects of socio-economic status.

This notion of a hierarchy of needs enables us to distinguish between the health and illness behavior of the affluent and the poor. Much of the social life of the wealthy clearly concerns secondary needs, which are generally perceived as lower than most health related needs on the need hierarchy. If some pathology presents itself, or some at-risk behavior is recognized, then they naturally assume a priority position, which eclipses most other needs for action. In contrast, much of the social life of the poor centers on needs which are understandably regarded as being of greater priority than most health concerns on the need hierarchy (e.g., homelessness, unemployment). Should some illness event present itself, or should health workers alert people and groups in poverty to possible further health needs, then these needs inevitably assume a position of relative low priority and are eclipsed, perhaps indefinitely, by more pressing primary needs for sheer existence.

From such a perspective, I think it is possible to understand why so much of our health intervention fails in those very groups, at highest risk to morbidity, whom we hope to reach and influence. The appeals that we make in alerting them to possible future needs simply miss the mark by giving inadequate recognition to those primary needs which daily preoccupy their attention. Not only does the notion of a need hierarchy emphasize the difficulty of contextless intervention programs, but it also enables us to view the rejection as a non-compliance with health programs, as, in a sense, rational behavior.

How Preventive Is Prevention?

With regard to some of the arguments I have presented, concerning the ultimate futility of downstream endeavors, one may respond that effective preventive medicine does, in fact, take account of this problem. Indeed, many preventive health workers are openly skeptical of a predominantly curative perspective in health care. I have argued, however, that even our best preventive endeavors are misplaced in their almost total ascription of responsibility for illness to the afflicted individuals and groups, and through the types of programs which result. While useful in a limited way, the preventive orientation is itself largely a downstream endeavor through its preoccupation with the avoidance of at-risk behavior in the individual and with its general neglect of the activities of the manufacturers of illness with foster such behavior.

Figure 1 is a crude diagrammatic representation of an overall process starting with (1) the activities of the manufacturers of illness, which (2) foster and habituate people to certain at-risk behaviors, which (3) ultimately result in the onset of certain types of morbidity and mortality. The predominant curative orientation in modern medicine deals almost exclusively with the observable patterns of morbidity and mortality, which are the *end points* in the process. The much heralded preventive orientation focuses on those behaviors which are known to be associated with particular illnesses and which can be viewed as the *midpoint* in the overall process. Still left largely untouched are the entrepreneurial activities of the manufacturers of illness, who, through largely unregulated activities, foster the at-risk behavior we aim to prevent. This *beginning point* in the process remains unaffected by most preventive endeavors, even though it is at this point that the greatest potential for change, and perhaps even ultimate victory, lies.

It is clear that this paper raises many questions and issues at a general level—more in fact than it is possible to resolve. Since most of the discussion has been at such an abstract level and concerned with broad political and economic forces, any ensuing recommendations for change must be broad enough to cover the various topics discussed. Hopefully, the preceding argument will also stimulate discussion toward additional recommendations and possible solutions. Given the scope and direction of this paper and the analogy I have employed to convey its content, the task becomes of the order of constructing fences upstream *and* restraining those who, in the interest of corporate profitability, continue to push people in. In this concluding section I will confine my remarks to three selected areas of recommendations.

Recommended Action

a. Legislative Intervention. It is probably true that one stroke of effective health legislation is equal to many separate health intervention endeavors and the cumulative efforts of innumerable health workers over long periods of time. In

Figure 1.

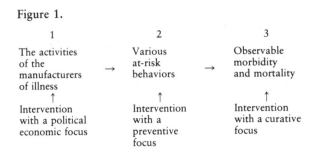

terms of winning the war which was described earlier, greater changes will result from the continued politicization of illness than from the modification of specific individual behaviors. There are many opportunities for a legislative reduction of at-riskness, and we ought to seize them. Let me give one suggestion which relates to earlier points in this paper. Widespread public advertising is importantly related to the growth and survival of large corporations. If it were not so demonstrably effective, then such vast sums of money and resources would not be devoted to this activity. Moreover, as things stand at present, a great deal of advertising is encouraged through granting it tax exempt status on some vague grounds of public education.[35] To place more stringent, enforceable restrictions on advertising would be to severely curtail the morally abhorrent pushing in activities of the manufacturers of illness. It is true that large corporations are ingenious in their efforts to avoid the consequences of most of the current legislative restrictions on advertising which only prohibit certain kinds of appeals.

As a possible solution to this and in recognition of the moral culpability of those who are actively manufacturing disease, I conceive of a ratio of advertising to health tax or a ratio of risk to benefit tax (RRBT). The idea here is to, in some way, match advertising expenditures to health expenditures. The precise weighting of the ratio could be determined by independently ascertaining the severity of the health effects produced by the manufacture and distribution of the product by the corporation. For example, it is clear that smoking is injurious to health and has no redeeming benefit. Therefore, for this product, the ratio could be determined as say, 3 to 1, where, for example, a company which spends a non-tax deductible $1 million to advertise its cigarettes would be required to devote a non-tax deductible $3 million to the area of health. In the area of quasi-health activities, where the product, although largely useless, may not be so injurious (e.g., nasals sprays, pain killers, mineral supplements, etc.), the ratio could be on, say, a 1 to 1 basis.

Of course, the manufacturers of illness, at the present time, do "donate" large sums of money for the purpose of research, with an obvious understanding that their gift should be reciprocated. In a recent article, Nuehring and Markle touch on the nature of this reciprocity:

> One of the most ironic pro-cigarette forces has been the American Medical Association. This powerful health organization took a position in 1965 clearly favorable to the tobacco interests. . . . In addition, the A.M.A. was, until 1971, conspicuously absent from the membership of the National Interagency Council on Smoking and Health, a coalition of government agencies and virtually all the national health organizations, formed in 1964. The A.M.A.'s largely pro-tobacco behavior has been linked with the acceptance of large research subsidies from the tobacco industy—amounting, according to the industry, to some 18 million dollars.[36]

Given such reciprocity, it would be necessary for this health money from the RRBT to be handled by a supposedly independent government agency, like the FDA or the FTC, for distribution to regular research institutions as well as to consumer organizations in the health field, which are currently so unequally pitted against the upstream manufacturers of illness. Such legislation would, I believe, severely curtail corporate "pushing in" activity and publicly demonstrate our commitment to effectively regulating the source of many health problems.

b. The Question of Lobbying. Unfortunately, due to present arrangements, it is difficult to discern the nature and scope of health lobbying activities. If only we could locate (a) who is lobbying for what, (b) who they are lobbying with, (c) what tactics are being employed, and (d) with what consequences for health legislation. Because these activities are likely to jeopardize the myths that have been so carefully engineered and fed to a gullible public by both the manufac-

turers of illness *and* various health organizations, they are clothed in secrecy. Judging from recent newspaper reports, concerning multimillion dollar gift-giving by the pharmaceutical industry to physicians, the occasional revelation of lobbying and political exchange remains largely unknown and highly newsworthy. It is frequently argued that lobbying on behalf of specific legislation is an essential avenue for public input in the process of enacting laws. Nevertheless, the evidence suggests that it is often, by being closely linked to the distribution of wealth, a very one-sided process. As it presently occurs, many legitimate interests on a range of health related issues do not have lobbying input in proportion to their numerical strength and may actually be structurally precluded from effective participation. While recognizing the importance of lobbying activity and yet feeling that for certain interests its scope ought to be severely curtailed (perhaps in the same way as the proposed regulation and publication of political campaign contributions), I am, to be honest, at a loss as to what should be specifically recommended. . . . The question is: quite apart from the specific issue of changing individual behavior, *in what ways could we possibly regulate the disproportionately influential lobbying activities of certain interest groups in the health field?*

c. Public Education. In the past, it has been common to advocate the education of the public as a means of achieving an alteration in the behavior of groups at risk to illness. Such downstream educational efforts rest on "blaming the victim" assumptions and seek to *either* stop people doing what we feel they "ought not" to be doing, *or* encourage them to do things they "ought" to be doing, but are not. Seldom do we educate people (especially schoolchildren) about the activities of the manufacturers of illness and about how they are involved in many activities unrelated to their professed area of concern. How many of us know, for example, that for any 'average' Thanksgiving dinner, the turkey may be produced by the Greyhound Corporation, the Smithfield Ham by ITT, the lettuce by Dow Chemical, the potatoes by Boeing, the fruits and vegetables by Tenneco or the Bank of America?[38] I would reiterate that I am not opposed to the education of people who are at risk to illness, with a view to altering their behavior to enhance life chances (if this can be done successfully). However, I would add the proviso that if we remain committed to the education of people, we must ensure that they are being told the whole story. And, in my view, immediate priority ought to be given to the sensitization of vast numbers of people to the upstream activities of the manufacturers of illness, some of which have been outlined in this paper. Such a program, actively supported by the federal government (perhaps through revenue derived from the RRBT), may foster a groundswell of consumer interest which, in turn, may go some way toward checking the disproportionately influential lobbying of the large corporations and interest groups.

NOTES AND REFERENCES

1. I.K. Zola, "Helping—Does It Matter: The Problems and Prospects of Mutual Aid Groups." Addressed to the United Ostomy Association, 1970.
2. See, for example, M.W. Susser and W. Watson, *Sociology in Medicine,* New York: Oxford University Press, 1971. Edith Chen, et al., "Family Structure in Relation to Health and Disease." *Journal of Chronic Diseases,* Vol. 12 (1960), p. 554–567; and R. Keelner, *Family III Health: An Investigation in General Practice,* Charles C. Thomas, 1963. There is, of course, voluminous literature which relates family structure to mental illness. Few studies move to the level of considering the broader social forces which promote the family structures which are conducive to the onset of particular illnesses. With regard to utilization behavior, see J.B. McKinlay, "Social Networks, Lay Consultation and Help-Seeking Behavior," *Social Forces,* Vol. 51, No. 3 (March, 1973), pp. 275–292.
3. A rich source for a variety of materials included in this second level is H.E. Freeman, S. Levine, and L.G. Reeder (Eds.), *Handbook of Medical Sociology,* New Jersey: Prentice-Hall, 1972. I would also include here studies of the health implications of different housing patterns. Recent evidence suggests that housing—even when highly dense— may not be directly related to illness.
4. There have, of course, been many studies, mainly by epidemiologists, relating disease patterns to certain occupations and industries. Seldom, however, have social scientists pursued the conse-

quences of these findings in terms of broader political economy of illness. One exception to this statement can be found in studies and writings on the social causes and consequences of environmental pollution. For a recent elementary treatment of some important issues in this general area, see H. Waitzkin and B. Waterman, *The Exploitation of Illness in Capitalist Society,* New York: Bobbs-Merrill Co., 1974.
5. Some useful introductory readings appear in D.M. Gordon (Ed.), *Problems in Political Economy: An Urban Perspective,* Lexington: D.C. Heath & Co., 1971, and R. C. Edwards; M. Reich and T. E. Weisskopf (Eds.), *The Capitalist System,* New Jersey: Prentice-Hall, 1972. Also, T. Christoffel; D. Finkelhor and D. Gilbarg (Eds.), *Up Against the American Myth,* New York: Holt, Rinehart and Winston. 1970. M. Mankoff (Ed.), *The Poverty of Progress: The Political Economy of American Social Problems,* New York: Holt, Rinehart and Winston, 1972. For more sophisticated treatment see the collection edited by D. Mermelstein, *Economics: Mainstream Readings and Radical Critiques,* New York: Random House, 1970. Additionally useful papers appear in J. B. McKinlay (Ed.), *Politics and Law in Health Care Policy.* New York: Prodist, 1973, and J. B. McKinlay (Ed.), *Economic Aspects of Health Care,* New York: Prodist, 1973. For a highly readable and influential treatment of what is termed "the medical industrial complex," see B. and J. Ehrenreich, *The American Health Empire: Power, Profits and Politics,* New York: Vintage Books, 1971. Also relevant are T. R. Marmor, *The Politics of Medicare,* Chicago: Aldine Publishing Co., 1973, and R. Alford, "The Political Economy of Health Care: Dynamics Without Change," *Politics and Society,* 2 (1972), pp. 127–164.
6. E. Cray, *In Failing Health: The Medical Crisis and the AMA,* Indianapolis: Bobbs-Merrill, 1970. J.S. Burrow, AMA—*Voice of American Medicine,* Baltimore: Johns Hopkins Press, 1963. R. Harris, *A Sacred Trust,* New York: New American Library, 1966. R. Carter, *The Doctor Business,* Garden City, New York: Dolphin Books, 1961. "The American Medical Association: Power, Purpose and Politics in Organized Medicine," *Yale Law Journal,* Vol. 63, No. 7 (May, 1954), pp. 938–1021.
7. See references under footnote 5, especially B. and J. Ehrenreich's *The American Health Empire,* Chapter VII, pp. 95–123.
8. D.M. Gordon (Ed.), *Problems in Political Economy: An Urban Perspective,* Lexington: D.C. Heath & Co., 1971, p. 318.

9. See, for example, D. A. Bernstein, "The Modification of Smoking Behavior: An Evaluative Review," *Psychological Bulletin,* Vol. 71 (June, 1969), pp. 418–440; S. Ford and F. Ederer, "Breaking the Cigarette Habit," *Journal of American Medical Association,* 194 (October, 1965), pp. 139–142; C. S. Keutzer, et al., "Modification of Smoking Behavior: A Review," *Psychological Bulletin,* Vol. 70 (December, 1968), pp. 520–533. Mettlin considers evidence concerning the following techniques for modifying smoking behavior: (1) behavioral conditioning, (2) group discussion, (3) counselling, (4) hypnosis, (5) interpersonal communication, (6) self-analysis. He concludes that:

> Each of these approaches suggests that smoking behavior is the result of some finite set of social and psychological variables, yet none has either demonstrated any significant powers in predicting the smoking behaviors of an individual or led to techniques of smoking control that considered alone, have significant long-term effects.

In C. Mettlin, "Smoking as Behavior: Applying a Social Psychological Theory," *Journal of Health and Social Behavior,* 14 (June, 1973), p. 144.

10. It appears that a considerable proportion of advertising by large corporations is tax exempt through being granted the status of "public education." In particular, the enormous media campaign, which was recently waged by major oil companies in an attempt to preserve the public myths they had so carefully constructed concerning their activities, was almost entirely non-taxable.

11. Reports of the harmfulness and ineffectiveness of certain products appear almost weekly in the press. As I have been writing this paper, I have come across reports of the low quality of milk, the uselessness of cold remedies, the health dangers in frankfurters, the linking of the use of the aerosol propellant, vinyl chloride, to liver cancer. That the Food and Drug Administration (F.D.A.) is unable to effectively regulate the manufacturers of illness is evident and illustrated in their inept handling of the withdrawal of the drug, betahistine hydrochloride, which supposedly offered symptomatic relief of Meniere's Syndrome (an affliction of the inner ear). There is every reason to think that this case is not atypical. For additionally disquieting evidence of how the Cigarette Labeling and Advertising Act of 1965 actually curtailed the power of the F.T.C. and other federal agencies from regulating cigarette advertising and nullified all such state and local regulatory efforts, see L. Fritschier, *Smoking and Politics: Policymaking and the Federal Bureaucracy,* New York: Meredith, 1969, and T. Whiteside, *Selling Death: Cigarette Advertising and Public Health,* New York: Liveright, 1970. Also relevant are Congressional Quarterly, 27 (1969) 666, 1026; and U.S. Department of Agriculture, Economic Research Service, *Tobacco Situation,* Washington: Government Printing Office, 1969.

12. The term "culture" is used to refer to a number of other characteristics as well. However, these two appear to be commonly associated with the concept. See J. B. McKinlay, "Some Observations on the Concept of a Subculture." (1970).

13. This has been argued in J. B. McKinlay, "Some Approaches and Problems in the Study of the Use of Services," *Journal of Health and Social Behavior,* Vol. 13 (July, 1972), pp. 115–152; and J. B. McKinlay and D. Dutton, "Social Psychological Factors Affecting Health Service Utilization," chapter in *Consumer Incentives for Health Care,* New York: Prodist Press, 1974.

14. Reliable sources covering these areas are available in many professional journals in the fields of epidemiology, medical sociology, preventive medicine, industrial and occupational medicine and public health. Useful references covering these and related areas appear in J. N. Morris, *Uses of Epidemiology,* London: E. and S. Livingstone Ltd., 1967; and M. W. Susser and W. Watson, *Sociology in Medicine,* New York: Oxford University Press, 1971.

15. D. Zwerling, "Death for Dinner," *The New York Review of Books,* Vol. 21, No. 2 (February 21, 1974), p. 22.

16. D. Zwerling, "Death for Dinner." See footnote 15 above.

17. This figure was quoted by several witnesses at the *Hearings Before the Select Committee on Nutrition and Human Needs,* U.S. Government Printing Office, 1973.

18. The magnitude of this problem is discussed in P. Wyden, *The Overweight: Causes, Costs and Control,* Englewood Cliffs: Prentice-Hall, 1968; National Center for Health Statistics, *Weight by Age and Height of Adults: 1960–62.* Washington: *Vital and Health Statistics,* Public Health Service Publication #1000, Series 11, #14, Government Printing Office, 1966; U.S. Public Health Service, Center for Chronic Disease Control, *Obesity and Health,* Washington: Government Printing Office, 1966.

19. This aborted study is discussed in M. Jacobson, *Nutrition Scoreboard: Your Guide to Better Eating,* Center for Science in the Public Interest.

20. M.S. Hathaway and E. D. Foard, *Heights and Weights for Adults in the United States,* Washington: Home Economics Research Report 10, Agricultural Research Service, U.S. Department of Agriculture, Government Printing Office, 1960.

21. This is discussed by D. Zwerling. See footnote 16.

22. See *Hearings Before the Select Committee on Nutrition and Human Needs,* Parts 3 and 4, "T.V. Advertising of Food to Children," March 5, 1973 and March 6, 1973.

23. Dr. John Udkin, Department of Nutrition, Queen Elizabeth College, London University. See p. 225, *Senate Hearings,* footnote 22 above.

24. D. Zwerling, "Death for Dinner." See footnote 16 above, page 24.

25. This is well argued in F. Piven and R. A. Cloward, *Regulating the Poor: The Functions of Social Welfare,* New York: Vintage, 1971; L. Goodwin, *Do the Poor Want to Work?,* Washington: Brookings, 1972; H. J. Gans, "The Positive Functions of Poverty," *American Journal of Sociology,* Vol. 78, No. 2 (September, 1972), pp. 275–289; R. P. Roby (Ed.), *The Poverty Establishment,* New Jersey: Prentice-Hall, 1974.

26. See, for example, Jules Henry, "American Schoolrooms: Learning the Nightmare," *Columbia University Forum,* (Spring, 1963), pp. 24–30. See also the paper by F. Howe and P. Lanter, "How the School System is Rigged for Failure," *New York Review of Books,* (June 18, 1970).

27. With regard to penology, for example, see the critical work of R. Quinney in *Criminal Justice in America,* Boston: Little Brown, 1974, and *Critique of Legal Order,* Boston: Little Brown, 1974.

28. See, for example, S. M. Sales, "Organizational Role as a Risk Factor in Coronary Disease," *Administrative Science Quarterly,* Vol. 14, No. 3 (September, 1969), pp. 325–336. The literature in this particular area is enormous. For several good reviews, see L.E. Hinkle, "Some Social and Biological Correlates of Coronary Heart Disease," *Social Science and Medicine,* Vol. 1 (1967), pp. 129–139; F. H. Epstein, "The Epidemiology of Coronary Heart Disease: A Review," *Journal of Chronic Diseases,* 18 (August, 1965), pp. 735–774.

29. Some interesting ideas in this regard are in E. Nuehring and G. E. Markle, "Nicotine and Norms: The Reemergence of a Deviant Behavior" *Social Problems,* Vol. 21, No. 4 (April, 1974), pp. 513–526. Also, J.R. Gusfield, *Symbolic Crusade: Status Politics and the American Temperance Movement,* Urbana, Illinois: University of Illinois Press, 1963.

30. For a study of the ways in which physicians, clergymen, the police, welfare officers, psychiatrists and social workers act as agents of social control, see E. Cumming, *Systems of Social Regulation,* New York: Atherton Press, 1968.

31. R. H. Rosenman and M. Friedman, "The Role of a Specific Overt Behavior Pattern in the Occurrence of Ischemic Heart Disease," *Cardiologia Practica,* 13 (1962), pp. 42–53; M. Friedman and R. H. Rosenman, *Type A Behavior and Your Heart,* Knopf, 1973. Also, S. J. Zyzanski and C. D. Jenkins, "Basic Dimensions Within the Coronary-Prone Behavior Pattern," *Journal of Chronic Diseases,* 22 (1970), pp. 781–795. There are, of course, many other illnesses which have also been related in one way or another to certain personality characteristics. Having found this new turf, behavioral scientists will most likely continue to play it for everything it is worth and then, in the interests of their own survival, will "discover" that something else indeed accounts for what they were trying to explain and will eventually move off there to find renewed fame and fortune. Furthermore, serious methodological doubts have been raised concerning the studies of the relationship between personality and at-risk behavior. See, in this regard, G. M. Hochbaum, "A Critique of Psychological Research on Smoking," paper presented to the American Psychological Association, Los Angeles, 1964. Also B. Lebovits and A. Ostfeld, "Smoking and Personality: A Methodologic Analysis," *Journal of Chronic Diseases* (1971).

32. M. Friedman and R.H. Rosenman. See footnote 31.

33. In the *New York Times* of Sunday, May 26, 1974, there were job advertisements seeking "aggressive self-starters," "people who stand real challenges," "those who like to compete," "career oriented specialists," "those with a spark of determination to someday run their own show," "people with the success drive," and "take charge individuals."

34. Aspects of this process are discussed in J. B. McKinlay, "On the Professional Regulation of Change," in *The Professions and Social Change,* P. Halmos (Ed.), Keele: Sociological Review Monograph, No. 20, 1973, and in "Clients and Organizations," chapter in J.B. McKinlay (Ed.), *Processing People—Studies in Organizational Behavior,* London: Holt, Rinehart, and Winston, 1974.

35. There have been a number of reports recently concerning this activity. Questions have arisen about the conduct of major oil corporations during the so-called "energy crisis." See footnote 10. Equally questionable may be the public

spirited advertisements sponsored by various professional organizations which, while claiming to be solely in the interests of the public, actually serve to enhance business in various ways. Furthermore, by granting special status to activities of professional groups, government agencies and large corporations may effectively gag them through some expectation of reciprocity. For example, most health groups, notably the American Cancer Society, did not support the F.C.C.'s action against smoking commercials because they were fearful of alienating the networks from whom they receive free announcements for their fund drives. Both the American Cancer Society and the American Heart Association have been criticized for their reluctance to engage in direct organizational conflict with pro-cigarette forces, particularly before the alliance between the television broadcasters and the tobacco industry broke down. Rather, they have directed their efforts to the downstream reform of the smoker. See E. Nuehring and G. E. Markle, footnote 29, page 522.

36. E. Nuehring and G. E. Markle, footnote 29 above, page 524.

37. The ways in which large-scale organizations engineer and disseminate these myths concerning their manifest activities, while avoiding any mention of their underlying latent activities, are discussed in more detail in the two references cited in footnote 34 above.

38. For a popularly written and effective treatment of the relationship between giant corporations and food production and consumption, see W. Robbins, *The American Food Scandal,* New York: William Morrow and Co., 1974.

Richard W. and Dorothy C. Wertz, "Notes on the Decline of Midwives and the Rise of Medical Obstetricians." Reprinted with permission of Macmillan Publishing Co., from *Lying In: A History of Childbirth in America* by Richard W. and Dorothy C. Wertz. Copyright © 1977 by Richard W. and Dorothy C. Wertz

Eliot Freidson, "Professional Dominance and the Ordering of Health Services: Some Consequences." Reprinted from *Professional Dominance: The Social Structure of Medical Care* by Eliot Freidson. Copyright © 1970 by Atherton Press, Inc. Reprinted with permission from Aldine Publishing Company, New York.

Dorothy Pawluch, "Transitions in Pediatrics: A Segmental Analysis." Reprinted by permission of the Society for Study of Social Problems and the author. 1983.

Victor W. Sidel and Ruth Sidel, "Health Care and Medical Care in the United States." From A HEALTHY STATE by Victor W. Sidel and Ruth Sidel. Reprinted by permission of Pantheon books, a Division of Random House, Inc.

Susan Reverby, "Re-forming the Hospital Nurse: The Management of American Nursing." An earlier version appeared in *Health/Pac Bulletin* 66 (Sept./Oct.) 1975:7–16. Reprinted with permission of Health/Pac and Human Sciences Press.

Nancy Aries and Louanne Kennedy, "The Health Labor Force: The Effects of Change," was written for this volume.

Arnold S. Relman, M.D., "The New Medical-Industrial Complex." Reprinted by permission of *The New England Journal of Medicine*. Vol 303, pp. 963–970, 1980.

Howard Waitzkin, "A Marxian Interpretation of the Growth and Development of Coronary Care Technology." Reprinted by permission of *The American Journal of Public Health* 69 (12): 1260–1268; December, 1979.

Sylvia A. Law, "Blue Cross—What Went Wrong?" Reprinted with permission of Yale University Press from *Blue Cross—What Went Wrong? by Sylvia A. Law and published by Yale University Press.*

Paul Starr, "The Commercial Edge and The Accommodation of Insurance," from *The Social Transformation of American Medicine*, pp. 327–334, Reprinted by permission of Basic Books, Inc. Publishers, Copyright © 1982.

Karen Davis and Diane Rowland, 1983, "Uninsured and Underserved: Inequities in Health Care in the United States," *Milbank Memorial Fund Quarterly/Health and Society* 61(2):149–176. © 1983 Milbank Memorial Fund and Massachusetts Institute of Technology. Reprinted by permission.

Wornie L. Reed, "Suffer the Children: Some Effects of Racism on the Health of Black Infants," was written for the first edition of this book, Copyright © 1981 by St. Martin's Press, Inc.

Barbara Ehrenreich and Deirdre English, "The Sexual Politics of Sickness." Extracts from "The Sexual Politics of Sickness" in *For Her Own Good* by Barbara Ehrenreich and Deirdre English. Copyright © 1978 by Barbara Ehrenreich and Deirdre English. Reprinted by permission of Doubleday & Company, Inc.

Frances B. McCrea, "The Politics of Menopause: The 'Discovery' of a Deficiency Disease." Reprinted by permission of the Society for Study of Social Problems and the author. 1983.

Sandra Klein Danziger, "The Uses of Expertise in Doctor-Patient Encounters During Pregnancy." Reprinted with permission from *Social Science and Medicine,* vol. 12. Copyright 1978, Pergamon Press, Ltd.

Julius A. Roth, "Some Contingencies of the Moral Evaluation and Control of Clientele: The Case of the Hospital Emergency Service." Reprinted from the American Journal of Sociology 77 (1972): 839–856 by permission of the University of Chicago Press. © 1977, The University of Chicago Press.

Marcia Millman, "Medical Mortality Review: A Cordial Affair." Reprinted with permission of William Morrow & Company from *The Unkindest Cut* by Marcia Millman. Copyright ©1976 by Marcia Millman.

Barbara Katz Rothman, "Midwives in Transition: The Structure of a Clinical Revolution." Reprinted by permission of the Society for Study of Social Problems and the author. 1983.

John H. Knowles, "The Responsibility of the Individual." Reprinted by permission of *Daedalus,* Journal of the American Academy of Arts and Sciences, Boston, Massachusetts, Winter, 1977, *Doing Better and Feeling Worse: Health in the United States.*

Robert Crawford, "Individual Responsibility and Health Politics." Reprinted from S. Reverby and D. Rosner (Eds.), *Health Care in America: Essays in Social History* (Philadelphia: Temple University Press, 1979) with the permission of Temple University Press and the author.

Irving Kenneth Zola, "Medicine as an Institution of Social Control." Reprinted with permission from *Sociological Review,* vol. 20, pp. 487–504.

Renée C. Fox, "The Medicalization and Demedicalization of American Society." Excerpted and reprinted by permission of *Daedalus,* Journal of the American Academy of Arts and Sciences, Cambridge, Massachusetts, Winter 1977, *Doing Better and Feeling Worse: Health in the United States.*

Catherine Kohler Riessman, "Improving Health Experiences of Low Income Patients," was written for this volume.

John McKnight, "Politicizing Health Care." Reprinted with permission of the Dag Hammarskjöld Foundation from *Development Dialogue,* 1978, no. 1 Upsala, Sweden.

Ann Withorn, "Helping Ourselves: The Limits and Potential of Self-help." Reprinted by permission of Ann Withorn. From *Radical America,* May–June, 1980: pp. 25–59, as edited by author.

Donald W. Light, "Comparing Health Care Systems: Lessons from East and West Germany," was written for this volume.

Theodore R. Marmor, "Canada's Path, America's Choices: Lessons from the Canadian Experience with National Health Insurance," pp. 77–96. Taken from Ronald L. Numbers, *Compulsory Health Insurance: The Continuing American Debate.* Reprinted by permission of Greenwood Press, Westport, CT, 1982.

Derek Gill, "A National Health Service: Principles and Practice," was written for the first edition of this book, Copyright © 1981 by St. Martin's Press, Inc.

Taylor, Rosemary C. R., "The Politics of Prevention." Reprinted by permission of *Social Policy* published by Social Policy Corporation, New York, New York, © 1982 by Social Policy Corporation.

John B. McKinlay, "A Case for Refocussing Upstream: The Political Economy of Illness." Copyright © 1974 by the American Heart Association. Reprinted with permission.

Index